Armed Batavians

USE AND SIGNIFICANCE OF WEAPONRY AND HORSE GEAR
FROM NON-MILITARY CONTEXTS IN THE RHINE DELTA
(50 BC TO AD 450)

JOHAN NICOLAY

AMSTERDAM UNIVERSITY PRESS

This publication was funded by the Netherlands Organisation for Scientific Research (NWO).

 This book meets the requirements of ISO 9706: 1994, Information and documentation – Paper for documents – Requirements for permanence.

English translated by Annette Visser, Wellington, New Zealand

Cover illustration: Masked helmet from the Waal at Nijmegen. Photo Museum het Valkhof, Nijmegen
Cover design: Kok Korpershoek, Amsterdam
Lay-out: Bert Brouwenstijn, ACVU Amsterdam
Maps and figures: Johan Nicolay and Bert Brouwenstijn, ACVU Amsterdam

ISBN 978 90 5356 253 6
NUR 682
© Amsterdam University Press, Amsterdam 2007

All rights reserved. Without limiting the rights under copyright reserved above, no part of this book may be reproduced, stored in or introduced into a retrieval system, or transmitted, in any form or by any means (electronic, mechanical, photocopying, recording, or otherwise), without the written permission of both the copyright owner and the author of this book.

Armed Batavians

Amsterdam Archaeological Studies 11

Editorial board:
Prof. dr. E.M. Moormann
Prof. dr. W. Roebroeks
Prof. dr. N. Roymans
Prof. dr. F. Theuws

Other titles in the series:

N. Roymans (ed.): *From the Sword to the Plough*
Three Studies on the Earliest Romanisation of Northern Gaul
ISBN 90 5356 237 0

T. Derks: *Gods, Temples and Ritual Practices*
The Transformation of Religious Ideas and Values in Roman Gaul
ISBN 90 5356 254 0

A. Verhoeven: *Middeleeuws gebruiksaardewerk in Nederland (8e – 13e eeuw)*
ISBN 90 5356 267 2

F. Theuws / N. Roymans (eds): *Land and Ancestors*
Cultural Dynamics in the Urnfield Period and the Middle Ages in the Southern Netherlands
ISBN 90 5356 278 8

J. Bazelmans: *By Weapons made Worthy*
Lords, Retainers and Their Relationship in Beowulf
ISBN 90 5356 325 3

R. Corbey / W. Roebroeks (eds): *Studying Human Origins*
Disciplinary History and Epistemology
ISBN 90 5356 464 0

M. Diepeveen-Jansen: *People, Ideas and Goods*
New Perspectives on 'Celtic barbarians' in Western and Central Europe (500-250 BC)
ISBN 90 5356 481 0

G.J. van Wijngaarden: *Use and Appreciation of Mycenean Pottery in the Levant, Cyprus and Italy (ca. 1600-1200 BC)*
The Significance of Context
ISBN 90 5356 482 9

F.A. Gerritsen: *Local Identities*
Landscape and community in the late prehistoric Meuse-Demer-Scheldt region
ISBN 90 5356 588 4

N. Roymans: *Ethnic Identity and Imperial Power*
The Batavians in the Early Roman Empire
ISBN 90 5356 705 4

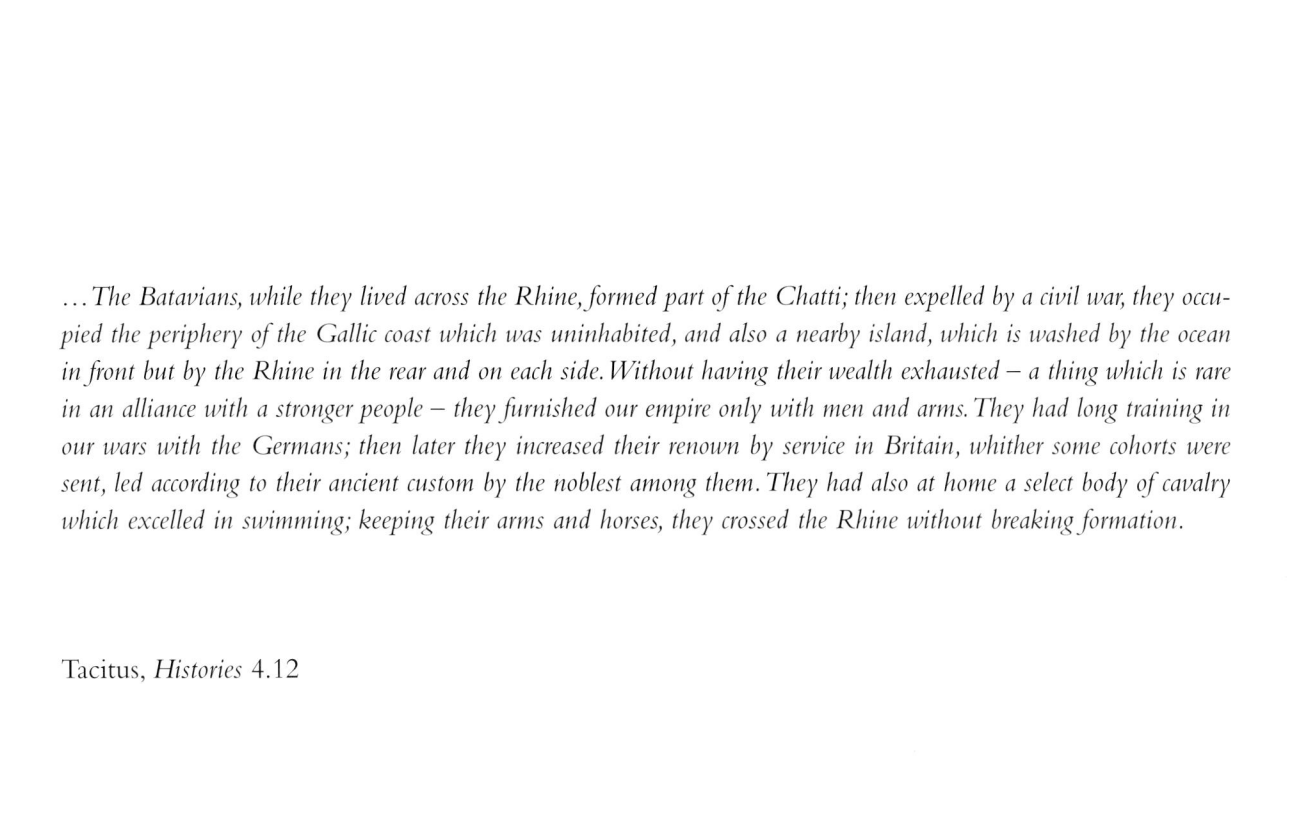

…The Batavians, while they lived across the Rhine, formed part of the Chatti; then expelled by a civil war, they occupied the periphery of the Gallic coast which was uninhabited, and also a nearby island, which is washed by the ocean in front but by the Rhine in the rear and on each side. Without having their wealth exhausted – a thing which is rare in an alliance with a stronger people – they furnished our empire only with men and arms. They had long training in our wars with the Germans; then later they increased their renown by service in Britain, whither some cohorts were sent, led according to their ancient custom by the noblest among them. They had also at home a select body of cavalry which excelled in swimming; keeping their arms and horses, they crossed the Rhine without breaking formation.

Tacitus, *Histories* 4.12

Horse gear pendant, 1st century AD. Recent metal detector find from Tiel-'Passewaaijse Hogeweg' (scale 1:1)

CONTENTS

PREFACE

1	INTRODUCTION	1
1.1	Background, objectives and development of the research	1
1.2	Geographical context and specific characteristics of the research region	3
1.3	'Military' and 'civilian' during the Roman period	10
2	MILITARY EQUIPMENT AND HORSE GEAR: A SURVEY	13
2.1	Military equipment	13
	2.1.1 Defensive weaponry	13
	2.1.2 Offensive weaponry	25
	2.1.3 Belts, aprons and baldrics	34
	2.1.4 Signalling instruments and military distinctions	41
2.2	Horse gear	44
	2.2.1 Bridle	45
	2.2.2 Saddle	47
	2.2.3 Girths	48
2.3	Phasing and historical context	60
3	AN ANALYSIS OF THE FINDS AT THE REGIONAL AND SITE LEVEL	65
3.1	Chronological analysis	65
	3.1.1 Archaeological visibility	66
	3.1.2 Chronological patterns in the finds	68
	3.1.3 Chronological analysis per type of find context	69
3.2	Geographical analysis	72
	3.2.1 Collection method and representativity	74
	3.2.2 Geographical distribution of the finds	81
	3.2.3 The research region in a northwest European context	85
3.3	Composition and spatial distribution at the site level	90
	3.3.1 Rural settlements and cemeteries	91
	3.3.2 The urban centres at Nijmegen	115
	3.3.3 Cult places	120
	3.3.4 Rivers	124
3.4	Conclusion	128
4	PRODUCTION AND SYMBOLIC IMAGERY	129
4.1	The production of weaponry and horse gear	129
	4.1.1 Mediterranean imports	130
	4.1.2 Self-sufficient army units: production in military *fabricae*	131
	4.1.3 The rise of private workshops	134
	4.1.4 Centralised production in state workshops	137
4.2	Decoration and symbolism	138
	4.2.1 Political propaganda: the glorification of the imperial family	138
	4.2.2 The invincibility of Rome	145
	4.2.3 Appeals for divine protection	149

	4.3	Conclusion	155
5		MILITARY EQUIPMENT AND THE LIFE CYCLE OF A ROMAN SOLDIER	157
5.1		The life cycle of a Roman soldier	157
	5.1.1	Enlistment, military service and honourable discharge: *probatus, signatus, miles* and *veteranus*	158
	5.1.2	Veteran's work and place of residence after their *missio honesta*	161
	5.1.3	The origin of veterans who settled in the eastern Rhine delta	164
5.2		Use of weaponry and horse gear during the life of a soldier	166
	5.2.1	The acquisition of military equipment and the question of ownership	166
	5.2.2	Military use: functional objects and symbols of rank, wealth and status	171
	5.2.3	'Social use' after completing military service: personal memorabilia	173
5.3		Types of social use in the different non-military contexts	177
	5.3.1	Ritual deposition at cult places	177
	5.3.2	River finds: deliberate depositions, lost items and washout material	181
	5.3.3	Urban centres: lost objects, deliberate depositions and kept object	189
	5.3.4	Rural settlements: ritual depositions and discarded items	193
	5.3.5	Graves: gifts for the dead	199
5.4		Conclusion	206
6		NON-MILITARY USE OF WEAPONRY AND HORSE GEAR IN URBAN AND RURAL SETTLEMENTS	207
6.1		The bearing of arms by non-soldiers	207
	6.1.1	The *Corpus Juris Civilis*: a ban on weapons possession by civilians?	207
	6.1.2	Lances, spears, arrows and sling shot: hunting weapons	208
	6.1.3	Swords and daggers: weapons for civilian self-defence	211
6.2		Military-civilian use of the *cingulum* and baldric	215
6.3		Non-military uses of horse gear	217
	6.3.1	Local horse breeding to supply the Roman army	217
	6.3.2	Finds of the Gallo-Roman double yoke and the role of horses as draught animals	220
	6.3.3	Protective symbols for civilian mounts	225
6.4		Conclusion	235
7		WARRIORS, SOLDIERS AND CIVILIANS. USE AND SIGNIFICANCE OF WEAPONRY AND HORSE GEAR IN A CHANGING SOCIO-POLITICAL CONTEXT	237
7.1		The pre-Roman situation: the importance of warriorship	237
7.2		Consequences of the Roman takeover: continuity and discontinuity of late Iron Age traditions	244
7.3		A 'civilian' lifestyle at the imperial frontier	251
7.4		'Germanic' newcomers and a revival of martial values?	254
7.5		Conclusion	258

Abbreviations	259
Bibliography	260
Appendices 1-4	287
About the plates and the catalogue	311
Plates 1-96	312

PREFACE

It is with pleasure that I look back on several special years devoted to research in Amsterdam. After I had completed a Master's thesis at the University of Groningen on early medieval gold finds from the Northern Netherlands, the Archaeological Centre of the Vrije Universiteit (ACVU) offered me an opportunity to conduct the PhD research presented in this volume. This was a chance not just to acquaint myself with a period unfamiliar to me and with an entirely new research area, but also to enjoy the stimulus of a new academic environment.

Of central importance to the articulation of the findings presented here is the fact that my doctoral study was part of the research project 'The Batavians: ethnic identity in a frontier situation', funded by the Netherlands Organisation for Scientific Research (NWO). I owe my rapid introduction to Roman archaeology above all to the monthly 'Batavian sessions' in which I discussed my draft chapters with other researchers from the project. These discussions were also instrumental in helping me develop my ideas about the use and significance of weaponry and horse gear in the context of the Batavian frontier.

In addition to Jan Slofstra, Joris Aarts and Henk Hiddink, I would like to acknowledge three people in particular. First and foremost, Nico Roymans, my supervisor, whose knowledge of the Batavian region and of the specific subject matter of my PhD dissertation made him ideal for this role. In addition to his input on matters of substance, I have very much appreciated both the encouragement he gave me to go my own way and his more intensive involvement when and where I needed it.

No less important was Ton Derks. His scholarly enthusiasm and critical but constructive approach have encouraged me throughout my work and have made me a better researcher. Also, his extensive knowledge of historical sources and of military archaeology have kept me from many a pitfall when writing up my research.

Finally, special mention should go to Ivo Vossen. I could not have wished for a better fellow PhD candidate, and academic peer and companion. The time that we spent together was as enjoyable as it was productive. I have particularly fond memories of the conferences both at home and abroad that we attended. Ivo also played an indispensable role in designing my database, producing many distribution maps, and much more.

Carol Van Driel-Murray (UvA) was my chief supervisor and sounding board outside the research team at the Vrije Universiteit. She read several early draft chapters of my dissertation and provided me with helpful feedback. Together we attended the *Roman Military Equipment Conference* in Windisch-Vindonissa (2001), which dealt with my research topic. The discussions that took place there and the positive responses were an important indicator for me that I was on the right track.

A substantial part of my research consisted of compiling inventories of the more than 2,700 weaponry and horse gear finds from the Batavian region. The presentation of the extensive database underpinning this dissertation (www.acvu.nl/nicolay) would not have been possible without the kind cooperation of the staff at museums and archaeological companies. I particularly enjoyed the many visits to amateur detectorists whose collections contain finds from the research region. Not only did they agree to show me their finds, they were almost without exception willing to share with me the full details of the find sites and to lend me items for identification and drawing.

When studying material from various museum collections, I was helped by Marianne Stouthamer (Rijksmuseum van Oudheden, Leiden), Louis Swinkels (Museum het Valkhof, Nijmegen), Lisette LeBlanc (Museum Dorestad, Wijk bij Duurstede), Ruud Borman (Historisch Museum Arnhem), Jan de Hond (Noordbrabants Museum, 's-Hertogenbosch), Bart van den Hurk (Oudheidkundig Museum, St.-Michielsgestel) and Mr Thijssen (Museum Buren en Oranje, Buren).

The following people granted me access to mainly recent, as yet unpublished excavation data: Erik Verhelst, Robert Sep and Stijn Heeren (HBS: excavations at Tiel, Est, Geldermalsen and Elst), Henk Hiddink (HBS: excavation at Groesbeek), Pim Verwers, Jan van Doesburg and Juan van der Roest (ROB and Grontmij: excavations at Wijk bij Duurstede), Wouter Vos, Jan Willem-Beesdman and Frederique van der Chys (ADC: excavations at Kesteren, Houten and Beneden-Leeuwen), Eddy Nijhof (GD'sH: excavation at Empel), Peter van den Broeke (GNBA: excavations at Oosterhout and Lent), Harry van Enckevort and Jan Thijssen (GNBA: excavations at Nijmegen, Wijchen and Elst), Anjolein Zwart (GNBA: excavation at Beuningen), Harry Fokkens and Dieke Wesselingh (IPL and Ministry of Education, Culture and Science: excavations at Oss), and Mieke Smit and Paul Beekhuizen (Gemeente Arnhem: excavations at Arnhem).

When inspecting and selecting metal detection finds from private collections, I spent many absorbing evenings with Fredo van Berkel (Ammerzoden), Arie Bogerd (Schoonrewoerd), Wouter van den Brandhof (Hemmen), Ton van den Brandt (St.-Michielsgestel), Arnold Chambon (Empel), Ben Elberse (Bunnik), Laurens Flokstra (Wijchen), Tom Jansen (Wijchen), Joy de Jong (Molenhoek), Wil Kuijpers (Babberich), Hans Murray (Medel), Dirk Oomen (Arnhem), Danny van de Pol (Soest), Freek and Hugo van Renswoude (Oud Zuilen), Harry Sanders (Elst), Jan Schippers (Den Bosch), Ardwi Schoenmaker (Driebergen), Leo Stolzenbach (St.-Michielsgestel), Ardan Troost (Huis ter Heide), Dick van Veelen (Oosterbeek), Albert Veenhof (ADC), Bas and Natasja Vergburgh (Amersfoort), Anton Verhagen (Empel), Piet Verwey (Hemmen), Henk Vroon (Maurik), Justin Wakker (Beesd), Cees van Wiggelinkhuizen (Geldermalsen) and Roel van Zeelst (Ammerzoden). In addition, Erik Verhelst (HBS) and Thijs Oomen (Ophemert) allowed me to include the BATO collection in my study.

As well as compiling an inventory, drawing and photographing a substantial part of the finds was a major task. For the drawings, I was assisted by Bert Brouwenstijn (ACVU), who devoted many hours to digitally processing my hand-drawn efforts. The photographs were taken by Fred Schuurhof of the Audiovisual Centre at the Vrije Universiteit.

The role played by my family and friends in helping me complete the research and write up the dissertation should not be underestimated. And for simply showing an interest and offering me support and encouragement during the research period of five years, I would like to thank my parents and parents-in-law, my sister and of course my wife Josje.

Finally, I would like to express my special gratitude to Annette Visser in Wellington, New Zealand for the tremendous job she has done of translating my dissertation into English. And thanks is also due of course to the NWO for funding the translation.

Johan Nicolay
Heerenveen, April 2007

1 Introduction

Finds of Roman weaponry and horse gear in rural and especially urban settlements have long been associated with the presence of military guard posts or fortifications.[1] In recent years, however, objects of a military nature have been found in these and other non-military contexts in large numbers, thus opening the way for alternative interpretations. The Roman Military Equipment Conference in Windisch-Vindonissa (2001) was entirely taken up with the subject of Roman soldiers and militaria in the civilian domain.[2] The conference proceedings present an interesting picture of the current state of research. What stands out is the focus on finds from urban centres, with finds from other non-military contexts generally not taken into consideration.[3] Moreover, interpretation tends to confine itself to listing possible explanations, rather than further analysing finds at a site or regional level.[4] The present study seeks to fill this gap by examining the weaponry and horse gear from the eastern Rhine delta – the territory of the Batavians – for the entire Roman period. Underpinning the research is an extensive inventory of about 2,700 'military' items from urban centres, as well as rural settlements, cult places, rivers and graves.

1.1 BACKGROUND, OBJECTIVES AND DEVELOPMENT OF THE RESEARCH

Since the late 1990s, the annual Roman Military Equipment Conference has sparked a growing interest in the study of such equipment.[5] This particular branch of research has long been part of a broader field of study that could be called 'Roman military studies'. In a recent article, James sketches the development of this research tradition in recent decades.[6] His main conclusion is that Roman military studies, already increasingly isolated within current Roman archaeology, risks further erosion of its long-held pre-eminent position unless drastic changes are made. This situation has developed for the following reasons:

1. Military archaeologists have remained quite aloof from the theoretical debate.[7] Their research has built on subjects with a traditional focus: the structure of the Roman army, career paths for officers and the military infrastructure of the frontier provinces.[8]
2. Archaeological research findings are used only to illustrate information from historical and epigraphic sources, with no attention being paid to the (symbolic) meaning that objects have for soldiers.
3. The army is viewed solely as a machine and an institution (the Roman army) rather than as a social organisation (a body of soldiers).[9] With the exception of their careers, there has been no focus on the lives of individual soldiers.

---

[1] See Bishop 1991, 25-26; 2002b, 10-11 (English towns); Lenz 2000, 77-79; 2001, 588-590 (Xanten).
[2] The conference proceedings are published in *Jahresbericht* 2001 of the *Gesellschaft Pro Vindonissa* (2002).
[3] Deschler-Erb/Deschler-Erb 2002 (Augst); Voirol 2002 (Avenches); Buora 2002 (Aquileia); Lenz 2002 (Xanten); Luik 2002 (Iberian towns).
[4] Fischer (2002) is the only one who elaborates on the various possible explanations.
[5] The research findings appear in the conference publication *Journal of Roman Military Equipment Studies*.
[6] James 2002.
[7] In contrast, for instance, to the theoretical debate about 'romanisation' (for a survey, see Derks 1998, 2-9).
[8] See E. Birley 1988; M.P. Speidel 1984a; 1992a.
[9] Peddie 1994 and James 2001 respectively.

4. The army is seen as an isolated entity that operates and has meaning within its own world, rather than in a broader, civilian context.[10] Almost no consideration is given to the position and functioning of soldiers in the military-civilian context of the frontier.

In James' view, in order to break out of this pattern of research, we must on the one hand opt for a more contextualised approach, which examines the interrelationship between the army and the larger geographical and social world in which it operates: "I believe the field of Roman military studies needs to be defined in the broadest terms, to include examination not just of the Roman armies and military installations of the state, but also the context of these within Roman society, culture and politics, and their interrelations – in peace as well as war – with societies beyond the frontiers."[11] On the other hand, our research should not focus on the army as a military institution, but should include individual soldiers and their experiences. Especially artefact studies, in combination with historical data, has a contribution to make to the "…nature of life and experience in military communities."[12]

The present study seeks to take up James' suggestions, and – in keeping with a long, Dutch tradition – to adopt his proposed contextual and social approach as its starting point.[13] This study of weaponry and horse gear from the eastern Rhine delta concentrates not so much on the functional use of these objects within the Roman army, but on their use and significance in both the military and civilian contexts of the frontier. I have used a 'life cycle model' to gain an understanding of specific forms of use and significance in the different contexts where weaponry and horse gear are found (army camps, settlements, cult places, rivers and graves).[14] For the different stages in the life of a soldier, this model helps to establish how soldiers dealt with their equipment, together with the archaeological contexts in which this may have been expressed. A key feature of the model is that it enables us to study soldiers and their archaeologically traceable equipment, not just in the context of the army, but also in the wider, social world in which they operated during and after their military service.

The present study can be seen as a continuation of Roymans' research into late La Tène and early Roman swords and helmets from northern Gaul.[15] Roymans' analysis revealed that militaria from the La Tène period occurred almost exclusively in what we can regard as ritual contexts, namely cult places, rivers and graves (fig. 7.1). The weapons are fairly evenly distributed throughout the research region and are associated with an all-embracing, martial ideology and with various rites of passage in the life of tribal warriors. The military items may have been offered up in rivers and cult places following a military victory or when a man's active life as a warrior came to an end. In addition, it was customary – particularly in the Trier region – to inter warriors and former warriors with part of their weaponry when they died.

Although there is evidence of continuity in the occurrence of swords and helmets in predominantly ritual contexts in the 1st century AD, we see a marked change in the distribution of finds. They are now concentrated in the Rhineland and no longer – or only rarely – in the Gallic interior (fig. 3.12). Roymans sees a connection with the heavy recruitment of manpower for the Roman army in this zone, which led to continuing and probably even stronger martial traditions in native societies. Ritual dealings with weapons are once again explained by a link to transition rituals, this time in the lives of professional soldiers. One such moment would be when veterans returned to the civilian world after 25 years of service. Also, the people in the Treveri territory retained the custom of expressing a deceased warrior's military career – now as a Roman soldier – in the burial ritual.

---

[10] See also James 1999; 2001.

[11] James 2002, 3, and especially 27 ff.

[12] James 2002, 33.

[13] For a contextual and social approach to Dutch military archaeology, see in particular Bloemers 1978; Willems 1981; 1984; Roymans 1996.

[14] See chapter 5.

[15] Roymans 1996, 13 ff. See also chapter 7.

To test Roymans' ideas, this study focuses on one specific region in the frontier zone of northern Gaul, namely the eastern Rhine delta, the presumed territory of the *civitas Batavorum*. The research time frame has been extended to cover the entire Roman period (c. 50 BC – AD 400/450). A key advantage of doing so is that it offers a long-term perspective in the observation and interpretation of changes in the use and significance of objects.[16] Further, the study looks at the full range of military equipment, including – in addition to swords and helmets – other weapon types, belts and *baltei*, as well as cavalry harness. This allows us to both observe patterns in the material over the research period and compare the different categories of finds. I have been able to expand on Roymans' research thanks to the use of metal detectors during excavations and by amateur detectorists, which has led in recent decades to substantial finds in the Nijmegen urban centres and rural settlements. Detector finds are an important addition to the items that may have been ritually deposited in cult places, rivers and graves, enabling us to study not only deposition patterns, but also kinds of use.

The primary objective of the research is as follows: *To gain an understanding, through a socio-cultural analysis of weaponry and horse gear from non-military contexts in the eastern Rhine delta, of the different kinds of use, and of the symbolic significance that these objects had for their owners.*
This analysis comprises the following three parts:

1. A comparative analysis of the material from the different archaeological contexts and periods, with a view to gaining an understanding of the 'circulation' of weaponry and horse gear in the research region during the Roman period (chapter 3). This is preceded by a description of the typology of finds from the Batavian territory and a chronological ordering of the material (chapter 2).
2. An interpretation of the observed patterns to determine the extent to which soldiers, ex-soldiers or non-soldiers used weaponry and horse gear in non-military contexts, and what functional and possible symbolic significance these objects may have had for their owners (chapters 5-6). In the case of soldiers and ex-soldiers, I explore a possible connection with specific stages in their lives and the transition rituals associated with them. Assuming that forms of use and types of meaning are closely linked to the organisation of production, and to the symbolism of the decorations, these aspects are discussed in chapter 4.
3. A long-term analysis to shed light on the continuity or discontinuity of the use and significance of weaponry and horse gear, taking as its starting point the situation in the Late Iron Age (chapter 7).

1.2 GEOGRAPHICAL CONTEXT AND SPECIFIC CHARACTERISTICS OF THE RESEARCH REGION

The geographical area that is the subject of the present study is the presumed territory of the *civitas Batavorum* (fig. 1.1). With the exception of the northern Rhine frontier, we do not know its precise boundaries. However, by using Thiessen polygons, based on the location of the central places of the *civitas*, we can gain a rough idea of its dimensions. In addition to the eastern Rhine delta, the Batavian territory may have included part of the sandy soil region of the Southern Netherlands (fig. 1.2). The western

---

[16] To date there have been almost no regional studies examining the composition of Roman weaponry and horse gear over a longer period. An exception is the work of Feugère and Poux (2002), who have made an inventory of 'military' objects from non-military contexts in three Gallic regions. However, their analysis combines finds from the 1st to the 3rd centuries AD, making it impossible to distinguish any developments in the composition of the material over that period.

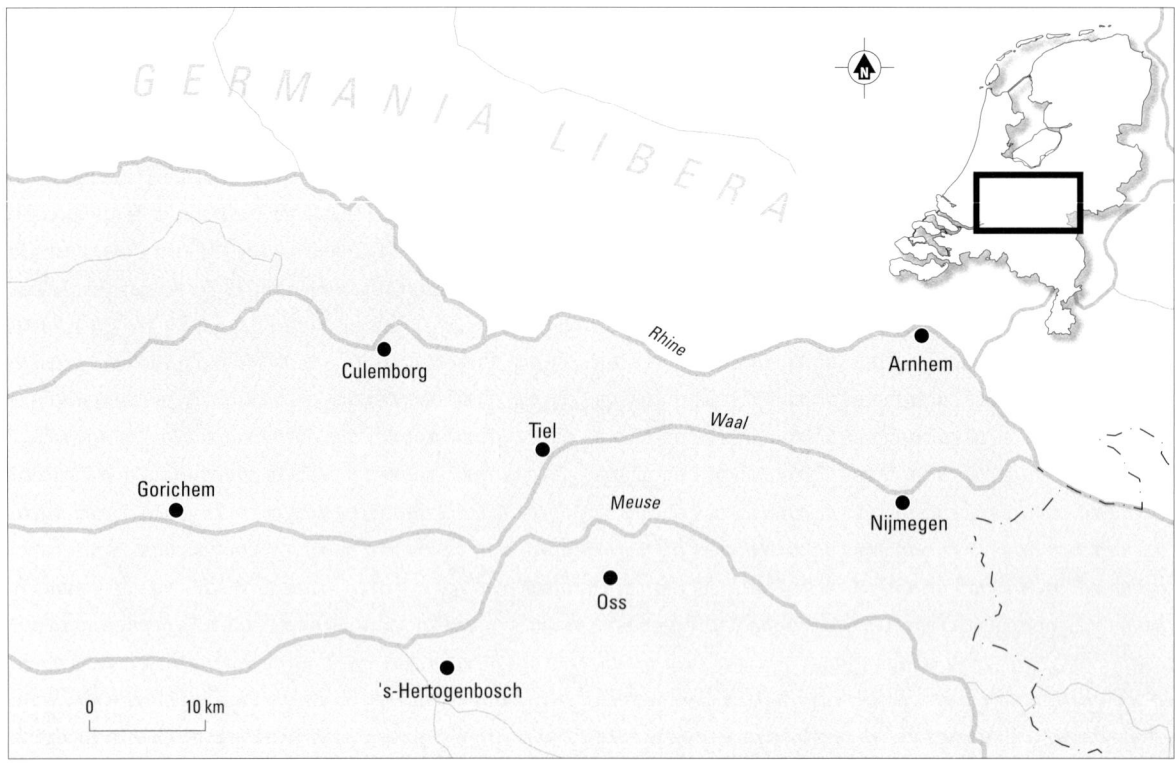

Fig. 1.1. Boundaries of the research region, comprising the assumed territory of the *civitas Batavorum* (dark grey).

and eastern polygon boundary, formed by the Woerden-Gorinchem line and the Dutch-German border respectively, appear to be confirmed by archaeological finds.[17] Interesting here is the distribution pattern of silver or copper 'rainbow cups' or *triquetrum* coins, for the most part 'Batavian' emissions that show a marked clustering in the eastern Rhine/Meuse delta and the bordering sandy soil region.[18] No coins have been found to the west of Woerden, and relatively few to date in the German Rhineland.[19] Our assumption is that the southern border lies further north than the Thiessen polygons indicate.[20] This would mean drawing a straight line, as Vossen does, a little to the south of Cuijck.[21] Estimates put the number of settlements in the research region at about 1,250, suggesting a population of over 50,000 people.[22]

[17] Bloemers (1978) also uses the Woerden-Gorinchem line as the boundary between the Batavian and Cananefatian *civitas*.

[18] Roymans 2004, 67 ff.

[19] It should be noted here that the representativity of the finds from the western Rhine delta and German area is uncertain (see below, aspect 5).

[20] See Willems 1984, 236; Slofstra 1991, note 99. The number of *triquetrum* coin finds from the province of North Brabant is certainly not representative. What does stand out, however, is that finds from this region originate almost exclusively from the presumed territory of the *civitas Batavorum*.

[21] Vossen 2003, note 5. Finds of weaponry and/or horse gear from several more southerly sites are included in the inventory for the sake of completeness. The material in question comes from Esch-'De Kollenberg' (site nr. 87), Gennep-'De Maaskemp' (site nr. 102) and Halder (site nr. 106).

[22] Willems 1984, 235 ff.; Vossen 2003. This number includes the estimated number of still-unknown sites.

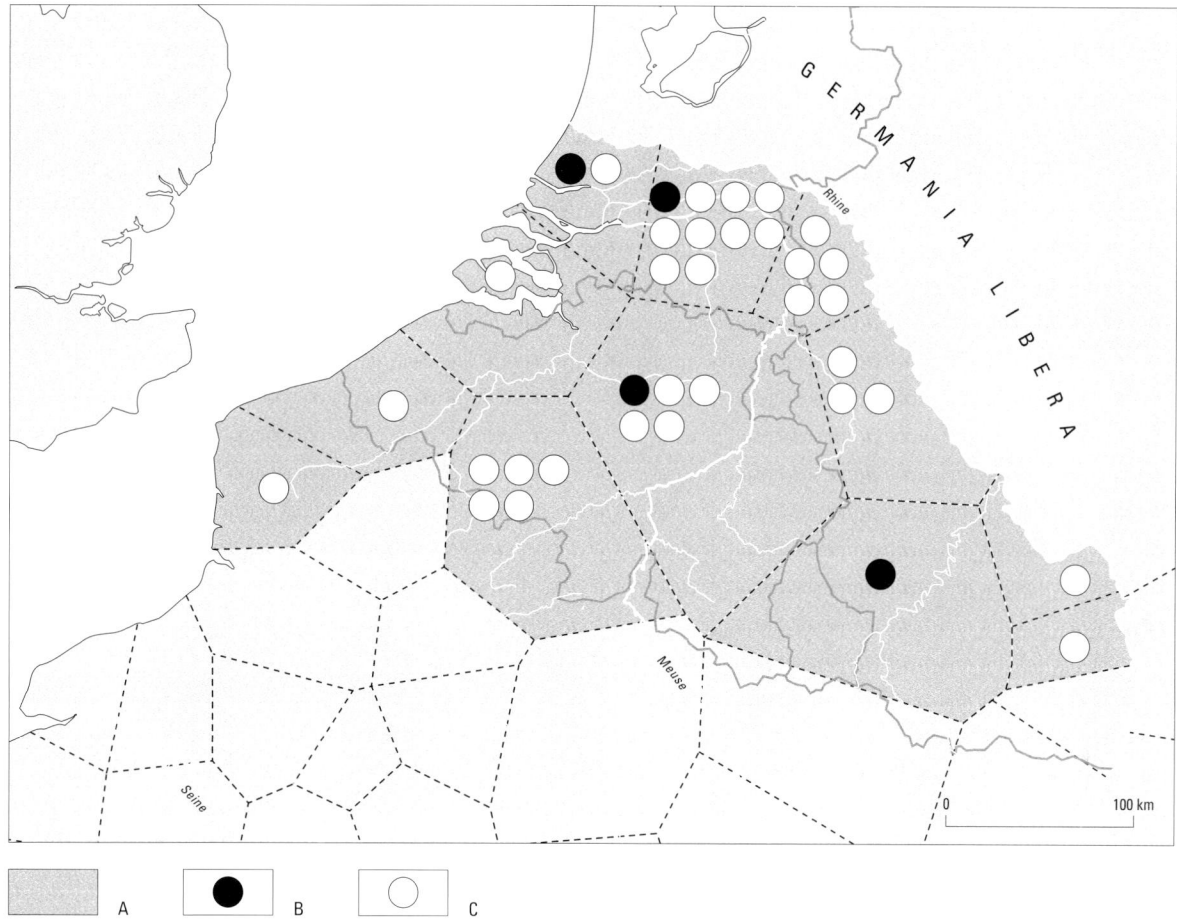

Fig. 1.2. The number of pre-Flavian, 'national' or 'ethnic' auxiliary units per *civitas* in Gallia Belgica. After Roymans 1996, fig. 4.
A recruitment area; B *ala*; C *cohors*.

With its geographical situation, cultural-historical background and wealth of archaeological data, the *civitas Batavorum* – and in particular the core area between the Rhine and Meuse rivers – occupied a special place in the Roman empire.[23] I briefly outline below the factors that are relevant for the analysis and interpretation of finds from this region:

1. The location in the militarised frontier zone of the Roman empire
Immediately south of the Rhine, the *civitas Batavorum* occupied a central position in the Lower Rhine frontier zone. From the time of Roman occupation, there was a constant military presence here, initially in temporary auxiliary camps and later in permanent camps along the Rhine.[24] There was also a legionary fortress on the 'Hunerberg' near Nijmegen, which was manned for some time during the Augustan period and after the Batavian revolt. We can use Kunow's calculations to gain an idea of the number of soldiers stationed in the Rhineland during the Roman period. He puts it at between 35,000 and 42,000 in Lower Germany during the 1st century AD.[25] Despite a reduction in the 2nd and 3rd centuries, this still

[23] See also Derks/Roymans 2003, 99; 2006.
[24] For the military structure of the Lower Rhine region, see especially Bechert/Willems 1995.
[25] Kunow 1987, fig. 32.

left a substantial force of over 20,000 men. The many army camps known from the eastern Rhine delta suggest that a considerable proportion of these men were stationed in the research region, which makes it difficult to overestimate the impact that the army had on the day-to-day life of the Batavians.

2. The situation outside the provincialised core area before the formation of Germania Inferior

Gallia Comata, which had been conquered by Caesar, was divided into provinces under Augustus (27 BC) and into formal *civitates* a short time later (16-13 BC). Thanks to this political and administrative reorganisation, the Rhineland occupied a unique position, forming a military district that was administered from Gallia Belgica. The intention was to make this region part of a large 'German' province (Germania Magna), together with the Germanic territory that was to be annexed as far as the Elbe.

The fact that the Romans regarded the Rhineland as 'German' can be explained in the light of the tribal migrations in the period between Caesar's departure from Gaul (51 BC) and the start of Drusus' campaigns in Germania (12 BC).[26] Some groups from beyond the Rhine, considered trustworthy by the Romans, were transferred to the west bank, in part to fill the vacuum created by Caesar's annihilation of the Eburones. According to Tacitus, the inhabitants of the research region were a splinter group of the Chatti who merged with the remnants of the Eburones living in the Rhine delta to form a new tribal association.[27] This new group bore the name 'Batavians'.

The Varus disaster in AD 9 brought an abrupt halt to Rome's ambitions for Germania. Several years later, after Germanicus had recovered some of the lost legionary standards, plans for a large German province were abandoned once and for all. The shift to a more defensive strategy did not mean, however, that the south and west bank of the Rhine was quickly divided into provinces. This did not happen until the time of emperor Domitianus, when Germania Inferior and Germania Superior were created in about AD 84.

It is unclear to what extent Rhineland frontier societies in the preceding period were administered in terms of the Roman *civitas* model. Roymans suggests that, although less systematically than in the Gallic interior, the Rhineland also underwent political and administrative reform, with the urbanisation that this entailed.[28] With regard to the research region, the founding of the *oppidum Batavorum* in the late-Augustan period would have gone hand in hand with the creation of a formal *civitas* structure. The report of a *summus magistratus* of the *civitas Batavorum* on a c. mid-1st century votive stone from Ruimel shows that the new system initially allowed room for divergent elements.[29] Instead of the usual, two-headed magistrature, there was a monocratic structure, perhaps derived from an older, native form.

Slofstra suggests that up until the Batavian revolt the political restructuring was less sweeping in nature.[30] It was confined to the appointment of *praefecti*, some of whom were members of the native elite, and whose job it was to control the frontier societies, collect taxes and oversee the recruitment of manpower for the *auxilia*. For the rest, the pre-Roman administrative structure was left more or less intact. Slofstra gives the term 'frontier' to the zone controlled by prefects, where no formal *civitates* yet existed.[31] He includes in this frontier the buffer zone of 'Germanic' tribes outside the empire.[32]

---

[26] Responsibility for this probably lay with Agrippa during his first (38 BC) or second governorship of Gaul (19 BC). See Derks 1998, 37-38.

[27] Tacitus, *Hist.* 4.12; for the ethnogenesis of the Batavians, see Roymans 2004, 55 ff.

[28] Roymans 2004, 195 ff.

[29] See also Bogaers 1960/1961, 268-271; Roymans 1990, 22-23, 36; 2004, 201.

[30] Slofstra 2002, 26-28.

[31] However, the term 'frontier' is used more generally in this study to refer to the frontier zone of the Roman empire.

[32] According to Slofstra (2002, 24 ff.), there was a shifting frontier which incorporated Gallia Comata after Caesar's conquests, the later Germanic provinces and the neighbouring 'Germanic' area after Augustus' reforms, and the east-bank tribes 'controlled' by means of diplomatic relations after the Batavian revolt.

3. The large-scale recruitment of manpower for the Roman army
The number of historically and epigraphically documented 'national' or 'ethnic' units, as they are called, gives us an idea of the regional recruitment of men for the *auxilia* (fig. 1.2). The societies in the frontier zone of the empire played a key role here, with the Batavians as the principal supplier in Northern Gaul: in addition to an *ala Batavorum*, there were eight *cohortes Batavorum*.[33] A significant proportion of the emperor's personal bodyguard was also made up of Batavians and we know of Batavian oarsmen in the Rhine fleet. The large-scale supply of troops occurred in the context of a special treaty (*antiqua societas*) which the Batavians, according to Tacitus, maintained with Rome.[34] At the heart of this alliance was exemption from taxation, in return for which the Batavians had to supply soldiers for deployment in defence of the empire:

"…they still retain an honourable privilege in token of their ancient alliance with us. They are not subjected to the indignity of tribute or ground down by the tax-gatherer. Free from imposts and special levies, and reserved for employment in battle, they are like weapons and armour – 'only to be used in war'."[35]

Given the units mentioned above, it is likely that a total of 5,000 to 5,500 Batavian men served in the Roman army at any one time during the pre-Flavian period. In order to maintain this number of troops, estimates suggest that on average every Batavian family must have had at least one son in the army.[36] The fact that the treaty with Rome was restored following the revolt in AD 70 means that this situation would probably have continued largely unchanged until the 2nd century.[37] Clearly, such a supply of manpower must have had an enormous impact on the local population and its social and cultural development, with the military and civilian spheres probably being strongly interlinked.

4. The location in a 'non-villa landscape'
The Batavian countryside was characterised by a specific settlement structure. Almost all of the approximately 1,250 settlements consisted of simple farms, ranging from scattered farmsteads (*Einzelhöfe*) to larger settlements with five or six contemporaneous farms.[38] The houses were of a traditional byre-house type, with people and animals living under one roof, a building tradition linked to an agrarian system whose primary focus was cattle breeding, though always in combination with arable farming.

In contrast to the southern loess soils, villas were the exception in the Batavian countryside.[39] A traditional method of building and settlement structure was closely adhered to, with the occasional addition of *villa*-type elements: a fully or partly tiled roof, a wooden *porticus*, a stone cellar or stone bathhouse.[40] This combination of traditional and new, Roman elements is evident in Druten-'Klepperhei' (fig. 1.3).[41] In the latter half of the 1st century AD a settlement developed here whose layout matches that of Gallo-Roman villa complexes. The settlement had a regular arrangement of a central main building with out-

---

[33] For an overview, see Roymans 1996, table 1; more recently Vossen 2003, 418-420.

[34] For the possible Caesarean origin of this treaty, see Roymans 2004, 55-61. A clue to the Batavians' special status is the Julian citizenship of the most important members of the Batavian elite (Roymans 1996, 24-28).

[35] Tacitus, *Germ.* 29; for the special treaty with Rome, see also *Hist.* 4.12.

[36] Willems 1984, 235; the calculations are based on Bloemers (1978, chapter 5). It should be noted that some of these men would probably have been supplied by client tribes during the pre-Flavian period (Roymans 2004, 205-208; see also Vossen 2003, 422-424).

[37] Tacitus, *Germ.* 29.

[38] General, see Vossen 2003, 424-425.

[39] According to Roymans' terminology (1996, 42 ff.), the eastern Rhine delta forms part of the 'non-villa landscapes'; see also Derks 1998, 55-66.

[40] For a survey, see Slofstra 1991, 159 ff.; Roymans 1996, 72 ff.

[41] Hulst 1978.

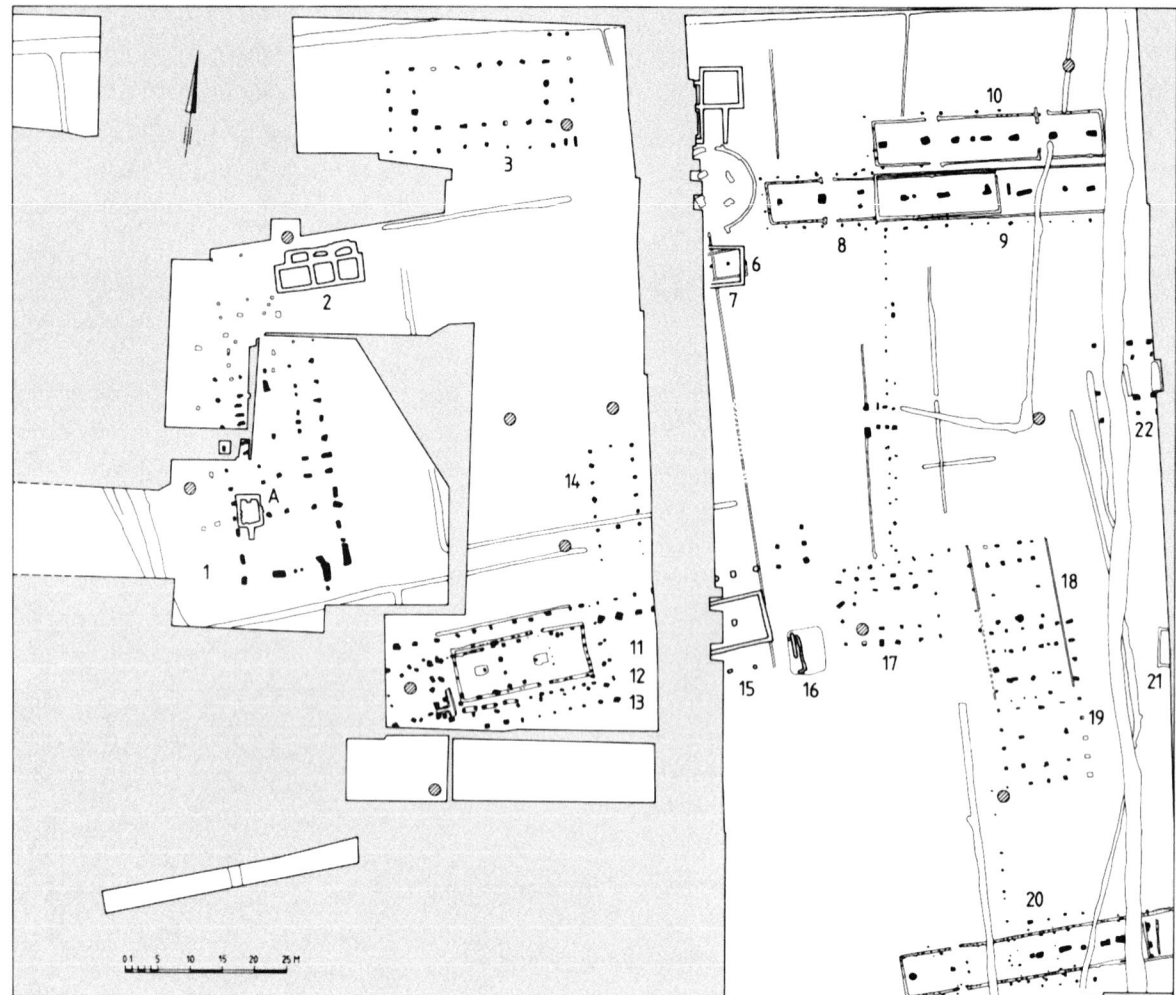

Fig. 1.3. Overview of the 'proto-villa' at Druten-'Klepperhei'. After Slofstra 2002, fig. 4.

buildings grouped into two wings.[42] Although the main building had a stone cellar, mural decorations and a separate bathing area, the house – in keeping with native tradition – was constructed entirely of wood and divided into a living and a stable area.

The development of these settlements, called 'proto-villas', is traditionally explained from an ecological and socio-economic perspective: because of the lack of a flourishing market-oriented, agrarian mode of production, the local elite could not afford 'real' villas.[43] Roymans believes that ideology also played a role, and points to the deeply-rooted tradition of the byre house, which in his view reflects the high cultural value placed on cattle.[44] A 'pastoral ideology' prevailed, which consciously clung to the native tradition of building.

Slofstra recently argued that the landscape of the Rhine delta, dominated by simple rural settlements, should be included in the villa system.[45] Although the customary stone or half-timbered buildings and

[42] Hulst (1978, 148) roughly distinguishes two habitation stages: stage 1 (second half of the 1st century AD), buildings 1-2, 8-10, 16, 20); and stage 2 (2nd century), buildings 1-4, 12-15, 17-19, 22. Not all buildings from the two periods were inhabited contemporaneously and building 21 cannot be dated more precisely than to the Roman period.

[43] See Slofstra 1991, 184; Wesselingh 2000, 223-224.

[44] Roymans 1996, 51-58; see also Derks 1998, 55 ff.

[45] Slofstra 2002, 36-38.

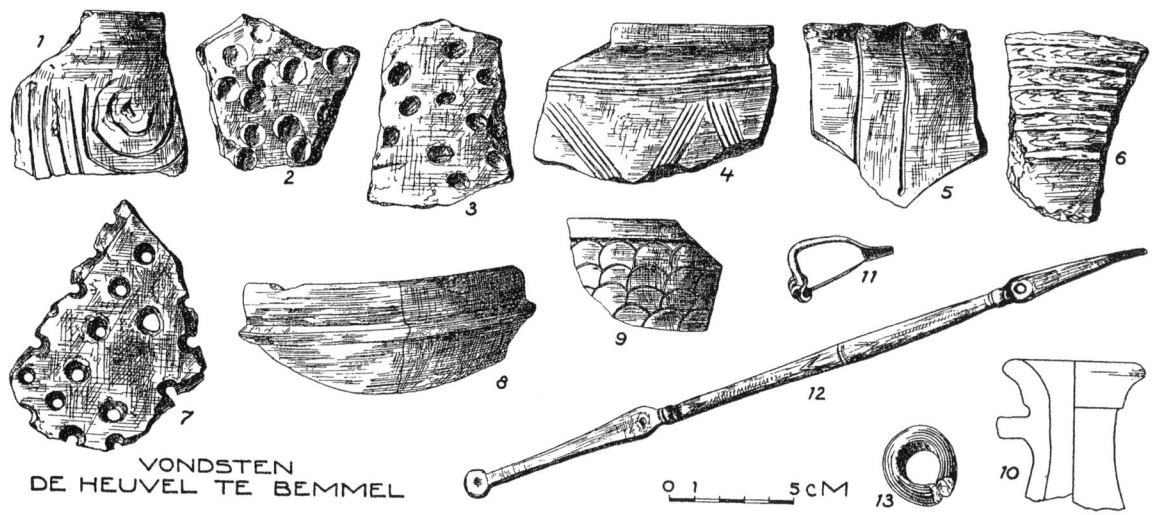

Fig. 1.4. Pottery, a fibula and a shield grip of the 'Germanic' type (nr. 12: 24.1) from the rural settlement of Bemmel-'De Heuvel', found during a small excavation in 1942. The grip is one of the few items of weaponry found in the period before metal detectors were introduced. After Braat 1949, fig. 11.

regular settlement layout are largely absent, he points out that a 'villa mode of production', characterised by a system of dependent labour and the production of surplus for a market, is very much in evidence. However, the Lower Rhine villas did not specialise in arable farming, but in cattle breeding, with the Nijmegen urban centre and above all the army camps as their major markets.

5. The impact of intensive metal detecting on the quantity of finds

In the area of material culture too, the Lower Rhine region – and in particular the core area of the Batavians – occupied a unique position thanks to the relative wealth of metal objects known from this area, rather than the kinds of objects found. Illustrative of the role of intensive metal detecting is the increase in the number of known *triquetrum* coins since the metal detector was introduced in about 1980. Prior to that, only 31 coins from nine sites were documented in the eastern Rhine delta. After 1980, the number increased exponentially, with over 600 coins from 129 sites in the Netherlands now documented.[46] We observe a comparable development in the finds that are the subject of this study. With the exception of river finds, 'military' objects from non-military contexts were a rarity until recently (fig. 1.4). This picture changed completely in the 'detector era'. Systematic use of metal detectors during excavations at the settlement of Wijk bij Duurstede-'De Horden' (1977-1986) and the cult place of Empel-'De Werf' (1991-1993) have brought to light a large volume of metal finds, including weaponry and horse gear.[47] The inventory presented here of almost 2,700 finds from over 300 sites demonstrates that these were not exceptional circumstances. The majority of finds were discovered during excavations using metal detectors (39%) or by amateurs conducting surface surveys (44%).

The wealth of metal finds from the *civitas Batavorum* is also due to a combination of factors quite unique to this region.[48] Firstly, the eastern Rhine delta was especially heavily populated during the

---

[46] Roymans 2004, 67-68.

[47] Van der Roest 1994; Van Driel-Murray 1994. The finds from Wijk bij Duurstede and Empel are published in their entirety for the first time in chapter 3.3.

[48] A somewhat similar situation occurs in the Northern Netherlands terp region (Bazelmans/Gerrets/Pol 2002).

Roman period, resulting in many sites containing Roman material. Secondly, the settlements were situated on fluvial, largely sandy clay or clayey deposits, in which metal is relatively well preserved. In some cases the settlement was covered by a layer of river sediment, which further aids preservation. Thirdly, the settlements in the eastern river delta were located quite close to the surface, thus greatly increasing the chance that ploughing would bring settlement material into the topsoil. This factor is crucial, as metal detectors do not generally penetrate deeper than this top layer. Finally, the Netherlands has a flourishing metal-detecting culture, with the eastern Rhine delta being very intensively worked over by amateur detectorists. Relevant here are the good relations between amateur archaeologists, who are in possession of a significant share of our Roman heritage, and professional archaeologists, who wish to use this information source for research purposes.

The exceptional circumstances in the core area of the *civitas Batavorum* are most apparent if we look at the surrounding areas. In the southern sandy soils, fewer settlements are known, metal is poorly preserved and many settlements lie under thick, artificially-raised *essen* layers. The use of ammonia-rich pig and chicken manure has led to the rapid degeneration of metal objects brought up into the topsoil through deep ploughing. Metal finds are also scarce in the western Rhine delta, despite the fact that metal is well preserved there. This can be explained by the smaller number of settlements, but above all by the location of the sites under a thick layer of river sediment and/or peat and their inaccessibility under large numbers of glass houses. Outside the Netherlands, metal-detecting policy is primarily responsible for the meagre density of finds. Because it is illegal to use metal detectors in Germany and France, fewer people do so and any finds that are made are usually not available for research.

Despite the favourable detecting climate in the research region, it is not improbable that the large number of militaria from the *civitas Batavorum* is more or less representative of the Roman situation. We can assume that there is a link with the historically documented role of the Batavians as the chief Rhineland suppliers of manpower for the *auxilia* and imperial bodyguard.[49]

1.3 'MILITARY' AND 'CIVILIAN' DURING THE ROMAN PERIOD

'Military' and 'civilian' are key terms in the present study, denoting the distinction between settlements, people and objects in the context of the Roman army on the one hand and in a non-military context on the other. Although each refers to clearly distinct concepts in modern, western culture, this distinction did not always hold true in Roman times. A complicating factor in the study of weaponry and horse gear is that, including the period when there was a clearly definable professional army, pieces of 'military equipment' could be used in a civilian context, rendering a specifically military association uncertain. I will briefly outline below the extent to which the military and civilian spheres were separated in northern Gallic societies during the research period and the extent to which weaponry and horse gear can be regarded as military or military-civilian items.

Caesar's conquest of Gaul brought Rome into contact with a tribal world whose military and civilian spheres were strongly intertwined.[50] Political leaders, who were at the same time military leaders, headed retinues of warriors that could be deployed as military units for looting or in times of war. These units were temporary in nature, which meant that men who were farmers in everyday life lent their leaders military assistance for a short period during wartime. Nor is the weaponry and horse gear from this period unequivocally military or civilian. It comprises objects that warriors received from their leader or

---

[49] The use of their military equipment by Batavian veterans is particularly relevant here (see chapter 5).

[50] See chapter 7.1.

father and which expressed their social status and position. At the same time, however, they were military objects that had a function in the context of looting or war.

The auxiliary units deployed by Caesar at the time of the Gallic war still had an irregular, temporary character. This situation probably changed under Augustus, who transformed the existing *auxilia* into regular *cohortes* and *alae*, making them a permanent part of the Roman professional army.[51] Semi-military warriors were replaced by professional soldiers, who served for longer periods.[52] The soldiers had a clearly defined status which distinguished them in a legal sense too from non-soldiers. The same was true of veterans, who make their first appearance in the Gallic world during the Roman period. Unlike the warrior retinues of the preceding period, there are now clearly distinguishable functions for non-soldiers, soldiers and ex-soldiers. For some time, Roman soldiers are also archaeologically recognisable from their equipment. They received weaponry and horse gear from the army, which symbolised their status as soldier or ex-soldier.[53]

Although the principle of a professional army was preserved throughout the Roman period, we see a gradual blurring of the line separating military and civilian in the material culture.[54] Belts and horse gear appear to have been acquired to an increasing degree by civilians during the 1st century. Perhaps as early as the Augustan period, swords belonged to more vulnerable groups such as traders and travellers. With the exception of helmets, armour and shields, especially after the Flavian period, there no longer appear to be strictly military objects, but rather objects with a military-civilian use.

When the *limes* yielded under pressure from 'German' incursions in the 3rd century, we also observe a change in the status of army camps and soldiers. The role of the army camps was taken over by fortified towns and *burgi* on villa terrains. Alongside regular units who found new accommodation in the towns, veterans and civilians – some in private militias – seem to have become involved in defending the frontier provinces.[55] Once again, it is not possible to attribute military objects to soldiers or to armed civilians in this period.

The dividing line between military and civilian became even more blurred during the late-Roman period. From the early 4th century, army camps were almost entirely replaced by fortified, semi-military 'towns', while irregular units in the form of *foederati* again became part of the Roman army.[56] This overlap is also reflected in the use of the belt characteristic of this period: the belt initially symbolised the status of military and civilian officials, soon replaced by a more general, military-civilian use.[57]

When the imperial borders finally gave way to the 'Germans' in the 5th century, we can no longer speak of a separation between military and civilian. The vacuum created by the loss of Roman rule was filled by native leaders, who began maintaining groups of warrior bands. Professional soldiers were supplanted by temporary warriors, who once more were given military equipment by their leaders or fathers.[58]

In any event, we may conclude that the terms 'military' and 'civilian' cannot be satisfactorily applied during the earliest and latest phases of the Roman period. Although a clearly definable standing army existed in the intervening period, it would be true to say that horse gear and specific types of weaponry can only be regarded as exclusively military in the pre-Flavian era. In the other periods, 'military' objects cannot be unequivocally attributed to either soldiers or civilians and should therefore be referred to as 'military-civilian objects'. In other words, we should not label stray finds from these periods as specifically military or civilian. This would require an analysis of larger assemblages, such as the data set presented in this study.

---

[51] See chapter 2.3.
[52] Although irregular units were still formed in times of crisis, such as the Batavian revolt (for examples, Roymans 1996, 27, note 60).
[53] See chapter 5.
[54] See chapter 6.
[55] MacMullen 1967; see also chapter 6.1.3.
[56] See Nicasie 1997.
[57] See chapter 6.2.
[58] See Bazelmans 1999.

2 Military equipment and horse gear: a survey

Finds of military equipment and horse gear from the period between Caesar's conquests (c. 50 BC) and the fall of the empire's northern frontier (early 5th century AD) lie at the heart of the research presented here. The purpose of this chapter is to introduce a functional and chronological classification into both categories of finds so that the material can be analysed further. Firstly, the finds are divided into functional categories (appendix 2).[1] Within each category, they are then arranged typochronologically and – where possible – attributed to *legionarii* or *auxiliarii*.[2] Finally, within each category I identify the finds that are known from non-military contexts in the eastern Rhine delta. In general, the find data consists of stray, often fragmentarily preserved components of weaponry or horse gear. In order to give some idea of the equipment to which these fragments originally belonged, this chapter describes the different types of weaponry and horse gear in considerable detail. The catalogue numbers in the text comprise the site number (which refers to appendix 1) and one or more serial numbers for each site.

2.1 MILITARY EQUIPMENT

The military equipment of a Roman soldier (fig. 2.1) consists first and foremost of weaponry, which can be divided into defensive and offensive weapons (2.1.1-2). In addition, a belt – with its decorative apron – and baldric were used for suspending the sword and dagger (2.1.3). Finally, we can regard signalling instruments and *dona militaria* as indirect components of military equipment (2.1.4).

2.1.1 DEFENSIVE WEAPONRY

Defensive weapons are those items of equipment worn to protect the body. Images on monumental reliefs and gravestones show that helmets, armour and shields were part of the standard equipment of both legionary and auxiliary soldiers.

Helmets
Helmets were standard issue for all Roman soldiers. The addition of crests, tinning and other decorative features demonstrates that, as well as offering protection, a helmet served to express status and to impress opponents. Robinson and Klumbach published general surveys of Roman helmets at much the same time and, like Couissin, arranged them typologically.[3] Although different names are given to the helmet types, both scholars adopt a similar classification. The typology I use here is based on that of Klumbach, which was further elaborated by Schaaff and Waurick (fig. 2.2).[4]

---

[1] The division into categories corresponds to the organisation of the catalogue, with the numbering of the finds from non-military contexts in the research region referring to this catalogue.

[2] The dating of the material and attribution to legionary or auxiliary soldiers is based on references in historical sources, images on monumental reliefs and gravestones, as well as archaeological finds. For a survey of the available sources, see Bishop/Coulston 1993, 19 ff.

[3] Couissin 1926; Klumbach 1974; Robinson 1975.

[4] Schaaff 1988a; 1988b; Waurick 1988.

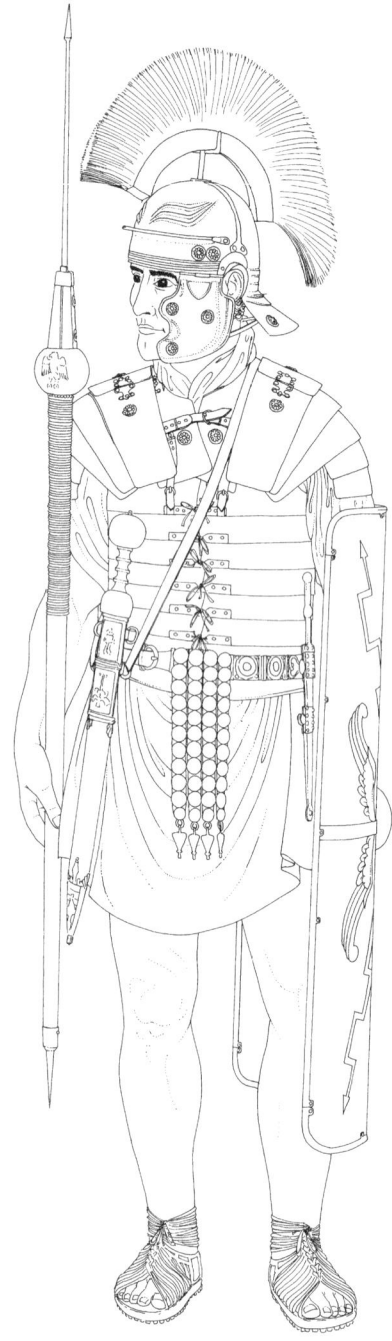

Fig. 2.1. Reconstruction of the military equipment of a Roman infantryman from the 1st century AD. After Deschler-Erb 1999a, fig. 25.

The earliest Roman helmets were of the *Buggenum type* (type A). These bronze, generally tinned helmets have a simple hemispherical shape with a short, flattish neckplate. The top of the helmet terminates in a pointed, generally conical crest knob. There are one or two holes on each side for attaching the cheekpieces, or a strap that could be tied around the chin.[5] Helmets of this type, which date from the second half of the 1st century BC, were worn by legionaries.

Auxiliary troops at that time probably wore native *Port type* helmets made of iron (type B). These comprise a hemispherical bowl, to which a separate neckguard is riveted. The forehead features a decorative stud with stylised, chased eye and eyebrow designs on either side. This helmet type, which has large cheekpieces with deep, round cusps at the front, can be roughly dated to the 1st century BC.

The Buggenum type helmets were supplanted at the beginning of the first millennium by examples of the *Hagenau type* (type C). This bronze helmet, with its longer neckguard and crest knob attached separately, represents a later evolutionary type. A characteristic feature is the semicircular reinforcement band at brow level. Adjacent to the crest knob and behind the browband, the helmets often have holders for a crest and feathers. Helmets of this type can also feature tinned decoration. On each side of the helmet are large cheekpieces with deep, semicircular cusps. Probably worn by legionary infantrymen, these helmets were used until the beginning of the Flavian period.

Coinciding with the Hagenau type were the predominantly iron helmets of the *Weisenau type* (type D) These helmets derived their shape from the Port type and are characterised by a lengthened nape with a wide neckplate, a cutout for the ears and a browband, again with a stylised eyebrow design (variant D1). The crest knob has been replaced by a U-shaped crossbar, to which a crest can be attached. The cheekpieces are narrower at the top to allow room for the ears. Both the helmet and cheekpieces are usually decorated with bronze fittings, which may be tinned. From the reign of Emperor Hadrian, the helmets had a broad, sloping neckplate with ribbing at the nape (variant D2).[6] These marked a transitional form to the later Niederbieber type. Although Weisenau type helmets were initially the exclusive preserve of auxiliary foot soldiers, ownership inscriptions show that legionary soldiers

---

[5] No cheekpieces from this type of helmet have been found to date.

[6] Waurick 1988, 337.

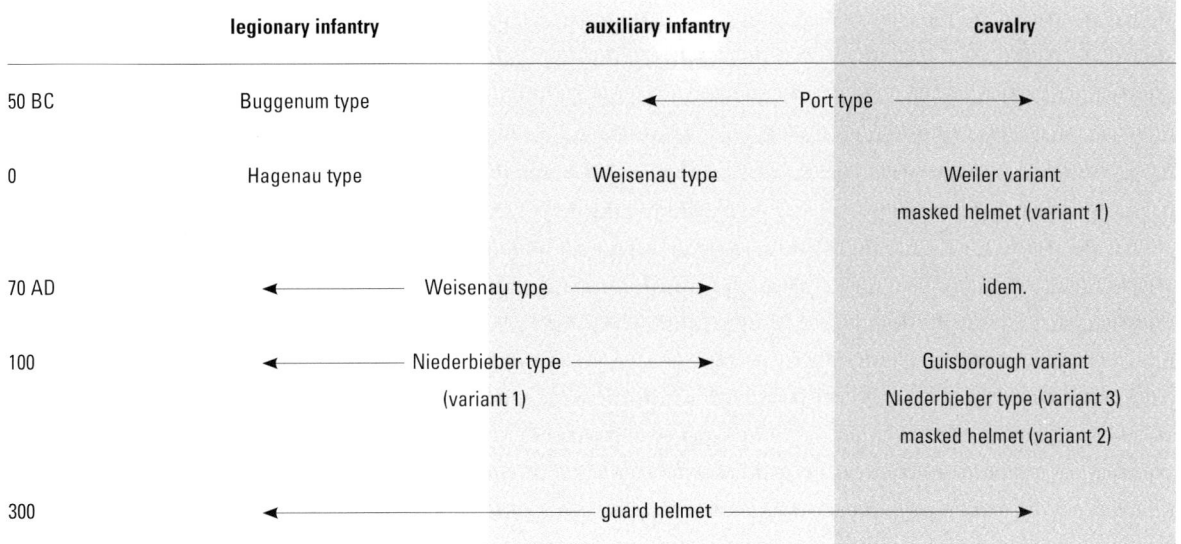

Fig. 2.2. Chronological overview of the helmet types used by the different army units during the Roman era.

were issued with such helmets after 70 AD, when the Hagenau type fell into disuse.[7] Weisenau type helmets occurred until the first quarter of the 2nd century.

A fourth kind of helmet, the *Weiler/Guisborough type* (type E), made its appearance in the first half of the 1st century AD.[8] Helmets in this group, with their longer nape and narrow, sloping neckplate, can be further divided into Weiler and Guisborough variants. The first (variant E1) comprises iron helmets that are completely clad in sheet bronze, which is often chased to resemble hair. In addition to the helmet bowl, the cheekpieces are decorated in bronze. As with later, bronze examples, the cheekpieces may feature a stylised ear. The second variant (E2) is made entirely of fine sheet bronze and is richly ornamented with repoussé human and animal figures. While helmets of the Hagenau and Weisenau types can be attributed to the infantry, ownership inscriptions show that Weiler/Guisborough type helmets were worn primarily by the cavalry.[9] Initially, cavalry helmets were predominantly iron examples of the Weiler variant. In the 2nd century, only bronze helmets of the second variant occurred. Their protective power was more limited and it appears they were no longer worn into battle.

Masks in the form of a stylised, classical face were attached to helmets of the previous type to form *masked helmets* (type F).[10] There are two variants within this group. With the 1st-century variant (F1), an iron mask, the façade of which was often covered with (tinned) sheet bronze, is attached to Weiler type helmets. Finds from the 'Kops Plateau' at Nijmegen reveal that the helmet bowl may have had a covering of fur, or human or animal hair.[11] In the 2nd century, the face was executed in a different style, with bronze examples attached to helmets of the Guisborough type (F2). Thanks to Arrian's manual on cavalry tactics, written in AD 136, the masked helmet is mainly associated with cavalry parade equipment.[12] In contrast to the vulnerable, bronze masked helmets, the heavier, iron examples could also be used in battle.

[7] Waurick 1988, 356; see Klumbach 1974, 12-13.
[8] See also Künzl 1999.
[9] Waurick 1988, 343; compare, however, a grave relief from Saintes, depicting legionary soldiers wearing this type of helmet (Künzl 1999, 151-152, fig. 3).
[10] For a discussion on the origin of masked helmets, see Junkelmann 1996, 22-26.
[11] Van Enckevort/Willems 1994, 127-128, figs. 5-6; see Künzl 1999, 155, fig. 8.
[12] Arrian, *Taktik* 34.2-34.5; see also Garbsch 1978; Junkelmann 1996.

At the beginning of the 2nd century, helmets of the Weisenau and Weiler/Guisborough types were replaced by iron examples of the *Niederbieber type* (type G). These have a long, steep nape, a broad, sloping neckplate and large curved cheekpieces that protected the chin as well as the cheeks. We can distinguish three variants. In the first (variant G1), the bowl has two crossbars, and a broad, often multi-peaked browguard. In the second (variant G2), the crossbar reinforcements have been replaced by decorative strips, making the helmet less robust. The third variant (G3) is a 'decorative helmet' clad in sheet bronze in imitation of the Weiler/Guisborough type helmets. A characteristic feature is the broad bronze strip with embossed hair design attached above the eyebrows. Although Niederbieber type helmets were initially viewed as cavalry helmets, it is most likely that they were worn by both infantry and cavalry.[13] The helmets with crossbars probably belonged to the infantry (G1), while the cavalry was equipped with more ornate helmets (G3). The attribution of the second variant is still unclear. Niederbieber type helmets occurred throughout the 2nd and 3rd centuries.

The 4th century saw the introduction of a completely new kind of helmet, the *guard helmet* (type H).[14] The bowl consists of two parts riveted together with the aid of a central comb. The neckplate and cheekpieces are also separate elements that are fastened with rivets or leather straps. A distinctive feature of these iron helmets is their cladding in sheet silver, which was sometimes gilded, and imitation glass gems. We can distinguish two variants. The first (H1) is characterised by wide cheekpieces covering much of the face and, like the nose guard, attached to the bowl by means of an intermediary piece. The cheekpieces of the second variant (H2) only covered the cheeks and, together with the nose guard, were attached directly to the helmet. Coin portraits of Constantine the Great show a third variant, in which the helmet comb bears a monogram of Christ (H3).[15] Given the inscription on the helmet from Deurne ('*Stablesia VI*') and its association with a spur and two horse bells, the first variant will have been a cavalry helmet, while the second may have been worn by infantrymen.[16] The representation of Constantine as a cavalryman suggests that the third variant was also a cavalry helmet. The different variants are dated to after about 315 and seem to have continued in use during the 4th century. Klumbach assumes that the helmets were derived from an imperial example and were associated with soldiers from the imperial guard or with high-ranking officers.[17] Simple soldiers may have worn less elaborate versions of these variants.[18]

A final, special type of helmet is the *gladiator helmet* (type I). Pflug distinguishes two bronze variants, one succeeding the other chronologically.[19] The first (variant I1) occurred from the late 1st century BC and consists of a hemispherical bowl with a rather flat brim. The helmet had large cheekpieces that protected the entire face and was often decorated with chasework scenes of people and animals. In the 2nd century there appeared an elongated helmet with a separate face shield (variant I2), without relief decoration. No finds of gladiator helmets are known from the 3rd and 4th centuries.

A total of 44 helmets or helmet components are documented from non-military contexts in the research region. The earliest examples are the Buggenum and Port types. In addition to two complete legionary helmets from the River Waal at Millingen (199.1, fig. 2.3) and Pannerden (239.1, fig. 2.3), a stray crest

---

[13] Waurick 1988, 357-361; for the interpretation as cavalry helmets, see Robinson 1975, 89 ff.

[14] Klumbach 1973a.

[15] See A. Alföldi 1932; Migotti 1999; Prins 2000. Migotti (1999) incorrectly interprets the stray appliqué finds bearing the Christ monogram as 'liturgical brooches'. To date, no complete helmets of this variant have been recovered.

[16] Coulston 1990, 146-147; Klumbach 1973a, 9 (guard helmets with horse gear components); specifically for Deurne, see Braat et al. 1973.

[17] Klumbach 1973a, 10-11; 1974, 15. Helmets clad in gold leaf and inlaid with genuine precious stones were probably reserved for the emperor himself.

[18] See for example, Lyne 1994.

[19] Pflug 1988.

knob is known from Ommerenveld (219.1, pl. 7). As with later examples, the helmet from Pannerden has a conical crest knob mounted on to the bowl. The same applies to the crest knob from Ommerenveld, which is attached to a round base that formed part of the bowl. Both examples can be regarded as a transitional form towards the Hagenau type. The only Lower Rhine helmet of the Port type comes from Kessel-Lith (164.1, pl. 6); this is a stray bowl with moulded eyes and eyebrows.

The 1st century AD is particularly well represented in the finds. Six complete helmets and two stray crest knobs from the Hagenau type are documented.[20] In view of its spherical bowl and short neckplate, we can place a helmet from the River Waal at Nijmegen (211.5, fig. 2.3) in the early 1st century. A helmet from Alem (8.1, fig. 2.3), with its longer nape, marks a transitional form towards the Niederbieber type. The Weisenau type helmet also occurs regularly in the eastern Rhine delta. The finds from non-military contexts are made up of five helmets and two cheekpieces. In addition, three ribbed decorative mounts, which were probably fitted to the brow of helmets of this type (variant 1), are known from Oosterhout (222.2-3, pl. 7) and Tiel (240.1, pl. 7).[21] An exception is the red enamel and brass decoration on a complete helmet from the Meuse at Hedel (115.1, pl. 6). As enamel was a common decoration during the late La Tène period, this points to an early dating for this helmet.[22] The characteristic, ribbed nape suggests that two helmets from the Lower Rhine at Rijswijk (254.2-3, fig. 5.12) and a third from Amerongen (12.1) belong to the late variant, while the peaked browband (see the Niederbieber type) also places a third Weisenau type helmet from Rijswijk (254.1, fig. 5.12) in the late 1st century.

For the 1st-century cavalry helmet of the Weiler variant, a complete helmet, two browbands and three cheekpieces are documented. The browband of a helmet from the River Waal at Nijmegen (211.8, fig. 4.8) consists of a laurel wreath which, like a stray band from the same site (211.10), is executed in high relief. Various busts are incorporated into the laurel wreaths. The helmet's cheekpiece, which is clad in sheet bronze, depicts a figure on horseback. A rectangular browband from the Rhine at Amerongen (11.1, fig. 4.7) features a repoussé laurel wreath, with three busts in high relief. The bronze sheeting on stray cheekpieces from IJzendoorn-'De Waard' (139.1, fig. 4.15) and the River Waal at Nijmegen (211.9) and at Tiel (265.1) incorporate an ear decoration and on two occasions a chased image of Mars. A probable helmet comb from the settlement Tiel-'Passewaaije Hogeweg' (242.4, pl. 6) has an uncertain attribution. The tinning suggests a 1st-century date but, although it may be part of a Weiler type cavalry helmet, there are no direct parallels for helmets with such a comb.

For the 1st-century variant of the masked helmet, a helmet with a face shield (211.13, fig. 4.9) and a separate mask (211.12, fig. 2.3) are known from the River Waal at Nijmegen.[23] In the first example, the ornate mask clad in tinned sheet bronze is attached to a browband adorned with busts.

Dating from the 2nd and 3rd centuries are four complete examples, a browband with earguard and two matching cheekpieces of the Niederbieber type. With the exception of a complete helmet from the cult place at Empel (82.25, fig. 5.9) and the Rhine at Amerongen (11.2, fig. 2.3), all finds come from the River Waal at Nijmegen. The bronze helmet from Amerongen, which features crossbars, can be attributed to the infantry. The remaining helmet finds are decorative helmets or a part thereof belonging to cavalry equipment. The iron helmets are decorated with bronze, and in one case have dotted line decorations and partial tinning (211.15, fig. 2.3). Like the stray browband (211.16, fig. 2.3), the browband of a helmet from Nijmegen (211.17) is decorated with wavy locks of hair. The cheekpieces are plain in design and show traces of tinning (211.14).

---

[20] The attribution is uncertain in the case of the crest knob from Gellicum-'Boutenstein' (101.1).

[21] See Robinson 1975, fig. 82; Lenz 2000, Taf. 14.

[22] Ypey 1982, 103; see also M.J. Klein 2003a, Abb. 13.

[23] Although the helmet from the River Waal featured two cheekpieces of the Niederbieber type, it is typologically no later than the early 2nd century AD (Klumbach 1974, 49, 62).

Fig. 2.3. Helmets from non-military contexts in the Batavian region. The numbering refers to the database. Not to scale. After Klumbach 1974, Taf. 7-8, 21-24, 31, 36, 38, 47, 54.

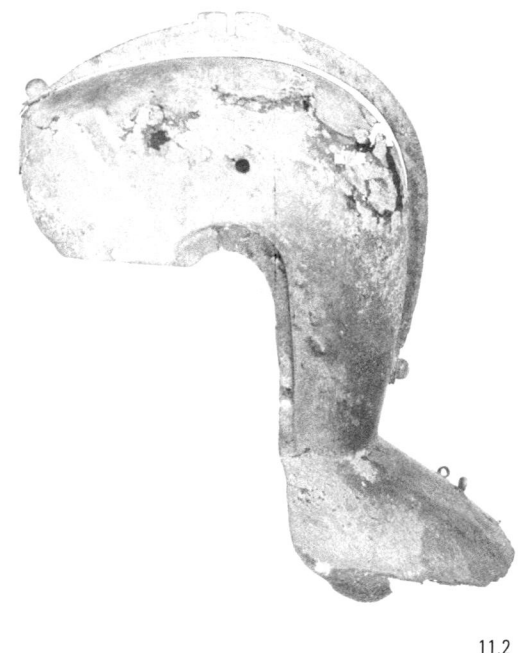

11.2

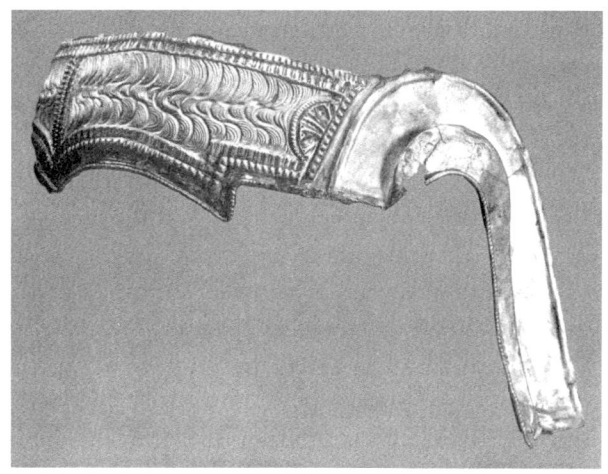

211.16

211.12

211.15

211.19

The few finds of the 2nd and 3rd century cavalry helmet (variant Guisborough) are an undecorated, bronze browband from the River Waal at Nijmegen (211.11) and probably a bronze, moulded cheekpiece from a settlement at Opijnen (233.1). Dating from the same period is a bronze helmet-bowl fragment of a masked helmet from Nijmegen (209.10), which is decorated with locks of hair in repoussé.

The late Roman guard helmet only occurs in small numbers in the finds. The first example is a gilded, helmet comb, possibly of the H2 type (211.18), from the River Waal at Nijmegen. A gilded, bronze helmet fitting has been found at the settlement of IJzendoorn-'Het Hof' (138.3, pl. 7). Towards the top of the rectangular fitting is a wider roundel, bearing a Chri-Rho monogram. Thanks to a recent find in a rural settlement at Lienden, we can now add another gilded bronze helmet fitting with a Chi-Rho monogram, this time executed in relief (174.6, pl. 7).[24] The rectangular fitting has a bronze and a silver pin for fastening.

An exceptional find is that of a gladiator helmet, decorated with chasework animal figures, from the River Waal at Nijmegen (211.19, fig. 2.3). An ownership inscription places this helmet in the second half of the 1st century AD.[25]

Armour

Roman soldiers wore armour to protect their upper body and shoulders. We can distinguish three types of armour: chain mail (*lorica hamata*), scale armour (*lorica squamata*) and plate armour (*lorica segmenta*).[26]

Chain mail (type A) is made up of rows of iron or bronze rings that are linked together. Republican chain mail comprised a sleeveless shirt that provided dual protection at the shoulders by means of additional shoulder pieces. Short chain mail with wide shoulder pieces extending down to the upper arm appeared in the Augustan period. The shoulder pieces of both types were now fastened at the front with two bronze hooks.[27] The hooks take the form of stylised snakes, and the horns that feature on some of the snake heads point to the 'Celtic' origin of this type of armour. Shoulder pieces and armour hooks disappeared towards the end of the 1st century, making way for short-sleeved chain mail.[28] In the late 3rd century, this type of armour was lengthened to well below the waist, while the sleeves reached down to the elbows. Chain mail was probably worn by all military units and occurred up until the late Middle Ages.[29] The diameter of the rings, which gradually increased during the Roman era, is relevant for the dating of stray fragments.[30]

The second type of armour is *scale armour* (type B), which is made up of small overlapping iron or bronze scales. The scales are rectangular in shape, and pointed or rounded at the base. Around the perimeter are tiny holes so that the scales could be tied together and sewn on to a leather or fabric backing. During the 1st century AD, this armour could be reinforced with shoulder pieces fastened with armour hooks.[31] Scale armour was part of Roman equipment from the Republican period onward, with the shape of the scales remaining more or less unchanged until the late Roman period. Although scale armour occurred less frequently than the two other types, it was probably used by all army units.[32]

---

[24] Flokstra 2004.

[25] Klumbach 1974, 15, 68-69.

[26] For a survey of the different types of armour, see Robinson 1975, 145 ff.; Junkelmann 1986, 162 ff.; specifically for plate armour, Bishop 2002a.

[27] For a typological classification of armour hooks, see Deschler-Erb 1991, 20, Abb. 7.

[28] According to Deschler-Erb (1991, 20) armour hooks no longer occurred from the Flavian period onward.

[29] Bishop/Coulston 1993, 85. Ownership inscriptions on two armour hooks from Kalkriese (Franzius 1993, 119, Abb. 7) demonstrate that chain mail was also worn by legionary soldiers. For the dating, see Van der Sanden 1993, 4, table 1.

[30] Lenz 2000, 26-27.

[31] Deschler-Erb 1991, 21, note 97; see also Robinson 1975, pl. 446, 450-451.

[32] Junkelmann 1986, 169; Bishop/Coulston 1993, 85.

A bronze breastplate formed part of both scale armour and chain mail from the mid-2nd century AD onward.[33] The breastplate usually consisted of two rectangular pieces with a semicircular indentation at the neck. The plates could be closed in the middle with the help of distinctive, rectangular hooks with a T-shaped end.[34] The thin sheet bronze and rich chasing show that breastplates had a protective as well as a decorative function. The breastplate probably formed part of cavalry parade equipment, remaining in use until the mid-3rd century.[35]

Characteristic of *plate armour* (type C) was the iron plate construction. The plates were linked together on the inside by leather bindings and on the outside by bronze fasteners. The most common type was the 1st-century *Corbridge type* (C2), in which the girdle plates and backplates were fastened together with loop-shaped tie-hooks and to the shoulder plates with simple buckles (fig. 2.1). The four largest shoulder plates are made up of different parts linked together with lobate, hinged fittings. The shoulder pieces were sometimes decorated with round, rosette fittings. Typical of the pre-Flavian period was the addition of circular grooves around the rivets on the buckles, hinges and tie-hooks.[36]

Recent finds from the battlefield at present-day Kalkriese (D) reveal that the Corbridge type was preceded by similar armour of the *Kalkriese type* (C1). Characteristic of this early armour are buckles and hinges with specific plates. These are wide and rectangular, with a double row of rivets on the one hand (variant C1-A), and narrow, with a single rivet or single row of rivets on the other (variant C1-B).[37] Elongated examples of variant B can be decorated with ridges and scalloped edges. Bishop dates the Kalkriese type from the early Augustan to the early Claudian period, after which it was superseded by the Corbridge type.[38]

The more recent armour gave way to the *Newstead type* (C3) at the beginning of the 2nd century. Although the basic principle remained the same, the method of fastening the iron plates changed. The girdle plates and backplates were now closed with simple loops and suspended from the shoulder plates by means of elongated hooks. Only the lobate shoulder fittings continued to be used, albeit in modified form. An innovation was the round lie loops used to close the girdle plates and backplates.[39] Plate armour continued as part of military equipment until shortly after the mid-3rd century, after which it appeared only in the form of armguards and greaves.[40]

It has long been assumed that plate armour was the preserve of legionary soldiers, or of some specialist parts of the legions. However, substantial finds in auxiliary camps in the northwestern frontier provinces suggest that auxiliary troops were also equipped with armour of this type.[41] There are no indications that the cavalry used plate armour; it was probably too inflexible for their purposes.

There is little evidence of the use of chain mail and scale armour in the Batavian territory. S-shaped hooks have been found in the Nijmegen-'Hees' cemetery (204.1, pl. 7) and the settlement of Houten-'Veerwagenweg' (137.1, pl. 7). Fragments of the actual armour for chain mail have been recovered from the cult place at Empel (82.1, pl. 7) and the settlement of Houten-'Binnenweg' (123.2, pl. 7). The oblong fragment from Empel is three rows wide, with the rings in the middle row closed with rivets, a pattern which is also discernible in the chain mail from Houten. Its diameter (7 mm) places the Empel fragment

---

[33] Robinson 1975, 160-161; Garbsch 1978, 7-8; Junkelmann 1996, 67-75; see also Borhy 1990.

[34] For a reconstruction of the fasteners, see Garbsch 1978, Abb. 1-3.

[35] Garbsch 1978; Junkelmann 1996, 70-71.

[36] Lenz 2000, 25.

[37] See also Deschler-Erb 1999b, 236-237; Lenz 2000, 24, note 165.

[38] Bishop 2002a, 23, fig. 10.1.

[39] Bishop 2002a, 57-58, figs. 6.7, 6.12; see also Jütting 1995, Abb. 3, types 1-4.

[40] Bishop 2002a, 91.

[41] For the discussion, see Deschler-Erb 1991, 19, note 79; Bishop and Coulston (1993, 206-209), however, continue to view plate armour as part of legionary equipment.

Fig. 2.4. Stray bronze *lorica squamata* scales from Nijmegen-*oppidum Batavorum* (from left to right 208.2-4). Scale 1:1. Photos: Gemeente Nijmegen, Bureau Archeologie.

in the 2nd century.[42] The rings from Houten, with a diameter of 16 mm, are clearly larger than the known late Roman examples, suggesting a different type. Various scales from *lorica squamata* have been found in the urban centres at Nijmegen (208.2-4, 209.1, pl. 7, fig. 2.4) and Halder (106.1-4, pl. 7), and a stray plate is known from Maurik-'De Woerd' (183.1) and Tiel-'Passewaaijse Hogeweg' (242.1, pl. 7). Although the often highly ornate breastplates are undocumented in the research region, two T-shaped closures from Arnhem-'De Laar' (15.1, pl. 7) and Hedel-'De Appert' (111.1, pl. 7) show that 2nd- and 3rd-century parade armour also occurred in the eastern Rhine delta.

In contrast to the few finds of the above armour types, a remarkably large number of plate armour components have been recovered. Belonging to the earliest type of armour are four wide, hinged fittings (variant C1-A) from Empel-'De Werf' (82.3-4, 10, 14, pl. 8). Contemporaneous to these are simple, short fittings (variant C1-B) from the settlement of Hedel-'Adelseweg' (110.1, pl. 8) and the River Waal at Nijmegen (211.1, pl. 8). The majority of finds can be classed as the more recent Corbridge type. There are 37 rectangular fittings in total, including 10 with a buckle (pl. 8-9). In addition, 16 loop-shaped tie-hooks and 14 lobate shoulder fittings belong to this armour type (pl. 9-10). Fragments of iron plate were found in association at the cult place at Empel (82.19, 23, fig. 2.5). Based on the shape of two bronze fittings, included in this assemblage, we can attribute the items to an armour set of the Corbridge type. Given the presence of concentric grooves, some of the 1st-century armour components (21x) can be placed in the pre-Flavian period. The more recent Newstead type plate armour is poorly represented in the research region, with only a round tie loop from the vicinity of Zoelen (304.1, pl. 10). A rectangular fitting from Empel-'De Werf' (82.24, pl. 10) has no direct parallels. Given the closure mechanism, this may be a component of plate armour that was worn contemporaneously with the Newstead type.

Shields

Whereas helmets and armour were worn directly on the body to protect the head and upper torso, an additional means of defence was the shield, which was carried separately. It was designed to deflect sword blows and loose projectiles and to protect exposed parts of the body. Reliefs on Trajan's column show that the different units had their own symbol painted on the shields. The decoration may also have reflected the rank of the individual soldier or officer.[43]

Up until the beginning of the 2nd century AD, the legionaries and auxiliaries each carried their own type of shields. Legionary shields were oval to rectangular in shape with curved sides (type A).[44] They were constructed of layers of wood, which were covered in leather.[45] The rim was reinforced with bronze.

---

[42] See Lenz 2000, 26-27.

[43] Junkelmann 1986, 178.

[44] For the typological development, see Junkelmann 1986, 174-175; Bishop/Coulston 1993, 58-59, 81-82; Van Driel-Murray 1986, 139-140; 1988; 1999a, 181-182; 1999b.

[45] An almost completely preserved legionary shield comes from Egypt (Kimmig 1940).

Fig. 2.5. Iron plates and two bronze fittings from plate armour, found at the cult place of Empel-'De Werf' (82.19, 23). Not to scale.

In the centre was a spherical bronze or iron shield boss (*umbo*), with a handgrip on the inside. The legionary shield evolved from an oval shape in the Republican period to a flattened oval in the Augustan era. Elongated *umbones* with pointed ends belong to the oval examples.[46] These were superseded in the 1st century AD by bosses with a rectangular or round base and a central dome.[47] The shield acquired a more rectangular shape from the mid-1st century, but oval shields remained in use.[48]

Although made of the same components, the auxiliary shield differed markedly in shape to that of the legions. It had a less pronounced curve, and was smaller and most commonly oval in shape (type B).[49] The shield bosses were round, with examples with a raised cone predominating up until the Claudian period.[50] These were gradually replaced by bosses with a hemispherical dome. Each type occurs in both iron and bronze. We have insufficient information to assign them to either the infantry or cavalry. One possible clue is the leather finds from Valkenburg, which enabled Groenman-Van Waateringe to reconstruct two shield types. They differ in shape and size, possibly because one type was used by the infantry and the other by the cavalry.[51]

Oval and round shields predominated from the 2nd century (type C), and it is no longer possible to distinguish the shield types of the different units.[52] The shields were covered with leather or linen and, instead of a rim, they featured a strip of leather around the perimeter. Many bosses from this type of shield have been recovered from the Thorsberg peat bog.[53] The round bosses still retained their dome shape and were made of thin bronze. Also characteristic of the 2nd and 3rd centuries are richly ornamented

---

[46] Bockius 1989.

[47] See Klumbach 1966.

[48] Van Driel-Murray (1988, 58) suspects that the oval shield may already have been in widespread use among legionaries in the 1st century.

[49] Groenman-Van Waateringe 1967, 52 ff.; Van Driel-Murray 1999a, 181-182.

[50] Schumacher 1989a, 260; Lenz 2000, 28-29. In contrast to La Tène shield bosses, the Roman examples are characterised by the sharp angle between the conical part and the straight sides.

[51] Groenman-Van Waateringe 1967, 69-71, figs. 16-17. For the allocation of shield bosses based on ownership inscriptions, see Haalebos 1977, 86-87.

[52] Bishop/Coulston 1993, 149-151; see also Oldenstein 1997, 141-143.

[53] Raddatz 1987, Taf. 22-28.

examples featuring repoussé animal and human figures, which we can regard as part of parade shields.[54] Although the oval and round shields remained in use into the 5th century, the shield bosses were replaced at the end of the 3rd century by bronze and iron, generally conical examples, some of which were clad in (gilded) sheet silver.[55]

The shield finds listed in the inventory are made up of shield bosses, handgrips and edgings.[56] Two conical *umbones* from Kessel-Lith (164.4-5, pl. 11, fig. 2.6) can be associated with the 1st-century auxiliary. The same probably applies to two shield grips with wider, rounded ends that were attached to the shield (81.1 and 163.1, pl. 13).[57] Three relatively heavy bronze bosses with a hemispherical dome from the Lower Rhine at Doorwerth (55.1, fig. 2.6), the River Waal at Nijmegen (211.20) and the Waal between Kekerdom and Millingen (144.1) may have belonged to early shields of both the legionary and auxiliary. The first two examples are characterised by a vulvate rib and the third by a hollow edge under the dome. Attributing the edging to a specific type of shield is particularly difficult as it is possible to reconstruct the original shape of the shield in only a few instances. For example, the corner fitting of a rectangular shield from Empel-'De Werf' (82.31, pl. 14) probably belonged to a legionary soldier, while pieces of edging from oval shields from Kessel-Lith (164.3, pl. 14) and Angeren (13.4, pl. 14) may have belonged to auxiliary soldiers. For the remaining 22 edging fragments, it is not possible to identify the shield type (pl. 15).[58]

A shield boss made of thin sheet bronze from the River Waal at Nijmegen (212.1) dates from the 2nd/3rd century. The domed central part is decorated with concentric grooves. A tinned, bronze shield boss of a comparable type is known from a late 1st-century grave at Nijmegen (207.1, fig. 5.20). The early dating of this boss is evident from the associated grip that was common to type-B shields. Unusually, there are no attachment holes in the flat flange of the boss. The same is true of a small shield boss from the River Waal at Nijmegen (211.21, pl. 12): it has decorative openings along the bottom edge of the dome, but no attachment holes. Given its shape and the fact that it is made of thin sheet bronze, we can attribute a small boss from Empel (82.32, pl. 12) to the same type of shield.

Two shield components found at the cult place at Empel differ from documented Roman examples and can be regarded as 'German' (type D). The first is a shield boss tapering to a point with a conical knob at the front (82.33, pl. 12). Such examples are known almost exclusively from Poland and can be dated to the second half of the 2nd century.[59] The second is a shield grip with incised line and circle decorations (82.34, pl. 13) which closely resembles 1st- and 2nd-century examples from North German cemeteries.[60] A more elongated grip decorated with V-shaped grooves comes from Bemmel (24.1, pl. 13). In view of its shape, the end of a handgrip from Dodewaard (53.1, pl. 13) can be assigned to the same type. Two analogous examples come from the vicinity of Xanten.[61] One bears the inscription *c(enturio) Albani*, indicating that this 'German' weaponry was also used in Roman service.

---

[54] Garbsch 1978, 12-13.

[55] Böhme 1974, 111-114.

[56] For two shield bosses from Plasmolen-'Mokerplas' (245.1-2), the type is unknown.

[57] Compare Curle 1911, pl. 34 (nrs. 1, 12); Buckland 1978, fig. 7; Lenz 2000, Taf. 21 (nrs. 158-162).

[58] Examples with no attachment loop might also have been the edging of a sword scabbard; this applies to 11 of the 22 fragments from the research region.

[59] Zieling 1989, type B2b; Van Driel-Murray 1994, 104.

[60] Zieling 1989, type F5; Van Driel-Murray 1994, 104; compare Deschler-Erb 1992.

[61] Schalles 1994b.

2.1.2 OFFENSIVE WEAPONRY

Alongside defensive weaponry, Roman soldiers were equipped with weapons of attack. These can be further divided into weapons designed for hand-to-hand combat and those deployed as projectiles at a greater distance from the enemy. The first group comprises the sword and dagger, and the second the *pilum* and *plumbata*, the lance and spear, the bow and arrow, and artillery.

Swords
Swords can be broken down into three groups: *gladii*, *spathae* and *semispathae* (fig. 2.7). From the early Augustan period, Roman infantrymen used a short sword of the *Mainz type* (type A2), which was derived from the *gladius Hispaniensis* (type A1).[62] Characteristic of this sword is the long, pointed tip of the blade. The bone or wooden hilt is made up of a flat guard, a ridged grip and a round, flattened pommel. The sword scabbard consists of two wooden plates with a leather casing. The perimeter is reinforced with bronze strips, while two or three scabbard bands hold the whole thing together. The upper two bands have a loop on each side so that the scabbard can be suspended from a belt. The upper section and the tip of the scabbard may be decorated with openwork fittings.[63] The scabbard chape terminates in a round or conical knob with a characteristic, ribbed neck.

Fig. 2.6. Bronze shield bosses from Kessel/Lith-'Kesselsche Waarden' (above, 164.4) and the Lower Rhine at Doorwerth (below, 55.1). Not to scale. Bottom figure after Stuart 1986, fig. 149.

Although *gladii* of the Mainz type were used into the Claudio-Neronian period, from the mid-1st century they were replaced by a similar short sword of the *Pompeii type* (type A3).[64] In contrast to their predecessors, these *gladii* have a short, squat tip. The guard is conical, while the pommels are usually spherical. The top of the scabbard is held together by an oblong plate and two bands. The scabbard plate is usually tinned, and decorated with openwork and incised human and animal motifs.[65] The bronze edging is confined to the tip of the scabbard. It terminates at the top in palmette motifs and meets at the base in a plain, round knob. A second fitting may be used to fill the triangular space at the bottom of the scabbard. This type of *gladius* remained in service until the beginning of the 2nd century.

Alongside the standard *gladii* of the Mainz and Pompeii types, 1st-century weapon graves have yielded different kinds of swords that appear to have been worn by auxiliary soldiers (type A4).[66] In terms of

---

[62] Type A1: Connolly 1997, 49-56; types A2-A3: Ulbert 1969b, 120; Junkelmann 1986, 180-184; Deschler-Erb 1999a, 22-28; see also M.J. Klein 2003b.

[63] Von Gonzenbach 1966b; Künzl 1998, 189 ff.

[64] For the dating, see Lenz 2000, 16; Ulbert (1969b, 118-119) and Deschler-Erb (1999a, 23, 28) assume, however, that this type of *gladius* occurred into the Flavian period.

[65] Künzl 1998, 426 ff.; Haalebos et al. 1998, 52-58; see also Mackensen 2000.

[66] Breeze/Close-Brooks/Ritchie 1976, 86-88; Schumacher 1989b, 271-274; compare Watt 1994, 309-315.

	legionary infantry	auxiliary infantry	cavalry
50 BC	gladius Hispaniensis	←——— gladius (-like sword) ———→	
		native spatha	
0	←——— gladius - Mainz type ———→		spatha - Newstead type
		gladius-like sword	
50 AD	←——— gladius - Pompeii type ———→		spatha - Newstead type
		gladius-like sword	
120	←——————— spatha - Straubing/Nydam type ———————→		
300	←——————— spatha - Straubing/Nydam type ———————→		
	←——— semispatha - type C ———→		

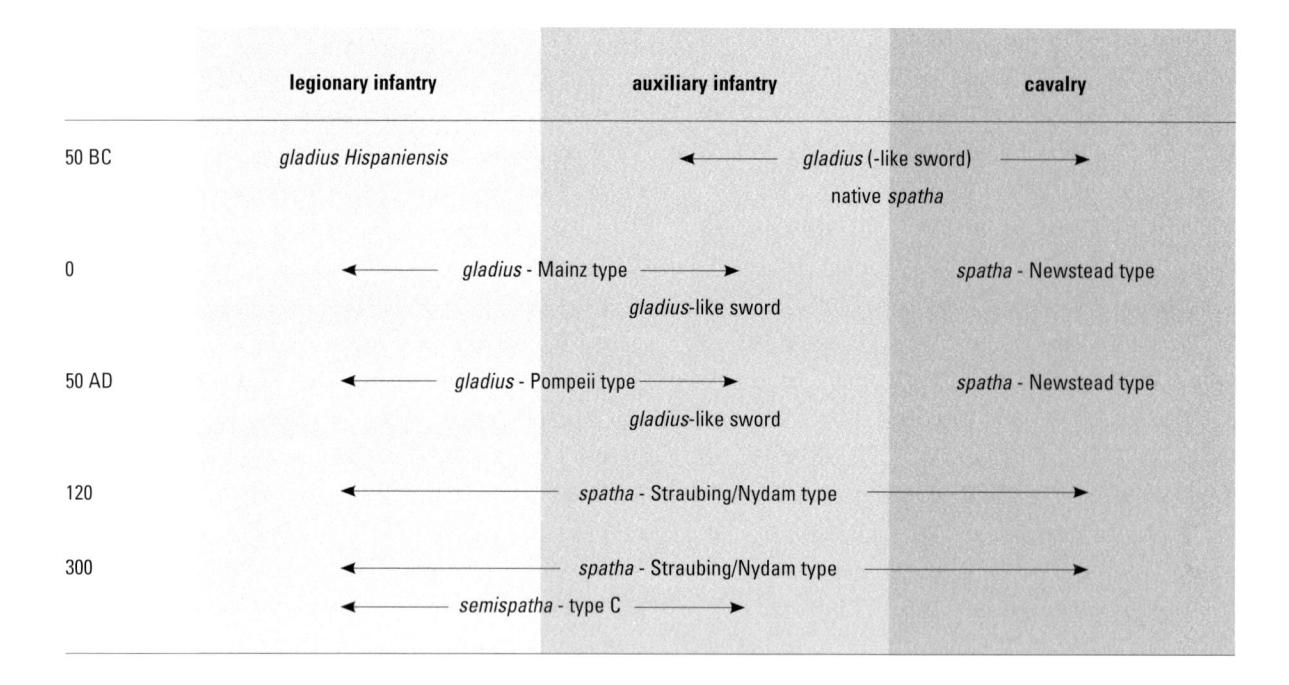

Fig. 2.7. Chronological survey of the types of sword used by the different military units during the Roman period.

length and shape, these swords derived from Roman *gladii*, although they also display non-Roman influences. Examples are known from an Augustan grave at Mehrum and a late 1st-century grave at Camelon.[67] The sword from Mehrum is equal in length to the *gladius* and the scabbard is reinforced with typical Roman scabbard bands. However, the sword tip is short and angular. Further, the scabbard chape comprises a semicircular edging rather than a knob. The example from Camelon is also the same length as a *gladius*, but the arched top of the sword blade is characteristic of late La Tène swords. Some finds from Roman camps show that these 'native' *gladius* imitations were used in a military context.[68]

For the cavalry, the long *spatha* (type B) was a more useful sword than the *gladius*. Although cavalry units probably made partial use of native swords in the Caesarean and early Augustan period, a Roman type developed in the 1st century AD which clearly resembles the Pompeii type *gladius*. We can regard this *Newstead type* sword (type B1) as a combination of the Roman *gladius* and the late La Tène sword.[69] Although the blade length is reminiscent of native *spathae*, the sword has a short point like the Pompeii type *gladius*. The hilt has also been adopted from the *gladius*, but the guard shows La Tène influences. The design of the scabbard is not known.

In the early 2nd century, the *gladius* and *gladius*-like *spatha* were replaced by a new type of sword (the *Straubing-Nydam type*), issued to both infantry and cavalry (type B2).[70] The sword hilt generally has a flattened pommel with a small, bronze knob at the top. The guard is hemispherical. Once again, the sword scabbard is made up of two wooden plates held together by a leather covering. The decorative

---

[67] Gechter/Kunow 1983; Breeze/Close-Brooks/Ritchie 1976.

[68] See Breeze/Close-Brooks/Ritchie 1976, 83-84.

[69] Breeze/Close-Brooks/Ritchie 1976, 84 ('Celtic' sword); Manning 1985, 149-152 ('native' sword); Kemkes/Scheuerbrandt 1997, 35; Lenz 2000, 17; Thomas/Feugère/Dieudonné-Glad 2001; for a reconstruction, see Deschler-Erb 1999a, Abb. 17.

[70] Künzl 1993b, 75 ff.; Oldenstein 1997, 138-139; Lenz 2000, 38-40; see also Raddatz 1987. For the development of the *spatha* in the late Roman period, see Böhme 1974, 97-100; Bishop/Coulston 1993, 162-165.

fittings, the suspension rings and the scabbard knob have disappeared and are now replaced by a new kind of chape and a scabbard slide (fig. 2.14).

From the 2nd century onwards, the chapes consisted of covers that were fitted over the end of the scabbard. They can be divided into three types, depending on their shape and material:[71]
1. Bronze, peltate chapes.
2. Round, iron discs, usually inlaid with niello.
3. Rectangular, bone examples with cut-out bean-shaped openings.

In the late Roman era, the terminal knobs gave way to U-shaped fittings mounted on the front of the scabbard as a decorative element.[72] Flat, oval chapes with three decorative knobs also occur; these were attached to the base of the scabbard, giving it a rectangular shape.[73]

The scabbard was also fitted with a slide for suspension from a baldric (fig. 2.14). The scabbard slide was fastened by leather bindings to the front of the scabbard, with two knobs at the back to prevent the scabbard from shifting. Scabbard slides can be divided into three types:[74]
1. Bronze examples with a trapezoidal central section and a decorative knob at top and bottom.
2. Simple iron examples terminating at the bottom in a rectangular knob and sometimes inlaid with niello.
3. Rectangular, bone examples with an indentation on the reverse for the baldric.

These scabbard slides were replaced in the late 3rd century by large bone or bronze models with concave sides, which continued into the 5th century.[75]

In addition to the *spathae*, the late 3rd century saw the return of a shorter sword, probably the *semispatha* (type C) reported by Vegetius.[76] A significant find has been the 3rd-century assemblage from Künzing, consisting of 14 swords of this type.[77] The swords are remarkably varied in terms of both length and shape. They have either a long, pointed or a short, blunt tip, which suggests that they could be used for either stabbing or slashing. As short swords were highly impractical for mounted combat, the *semispatha* appears to have been primarily an infantry weapon.

In addition to various well-preserved blades and scabbards, sword finds from the research region include bronze scabbard components. A total of 21 finds can be assigned to Mainz type *gladii* (pl. 16, 21-22). For two swords from the River Meuse at Pannerden (239.2) and the River Waal at Millingen (199.2, fig. 2.8), the accompanying scabbard with its characteristic, openwork fitting is still in situ. An unusual scabbard fitting (176.2, pl. 16) featuring Mars astride a chariot has been preserved from a sword found at Lobith-'De Bijland'. Mars is also the central figure on a bronze, partially gilded and tinned scabbard plate from the same site (176.9, pl. 22). The scabbard's wooden front and back plates are still present. Two sword blades from Oosterhout-'Van Boetzelaerstraat' (222.9, pl. 17) and the 'Immerlooplas' at Arnhem (18.1, pl. 17) belong to the Pompeii type, as do a sword and part of the accompanying scabbard from the Lower Rhine at Oosterbeek (220.1, pl. 17, fig. 2.8). A tinned, rectangular fitting, depicting Mars, Victoria and war booty, is preserved on the top of the scabbard. A fourth find is a palmette-shaped edging from Empel-'De Werf' (82.66, pl. 22). The type of *gladius* cannot be established in the case of three swords and ten scabbard bands (pl. 18, 23). Two cruciform bands from the cult place at Empel (82.61-62, pl. 23) belonged to an exclusive sword scabbard.

Five sword blades have been classified on the basis of their length (70-90 cm) as 1st-century cavalry *spathae* (pl. 19). Two narrow sword-blade fragments from Empel-'De Werf' (82.54-55, pl. 19) probably

---

[71] Oldenstein 1976, 110-120; for round, iron chapes, see also Hundt 1953; 1955.
[72] Böhme 1974, 99.
[73] Werner 1966; Böhme 1974, 99.
[74] Oldenstein 1976, 95 ff.
[75] Bishop/Boulston 1993, 164.
[76] Vegetius, *ERM* 2.15.
[77] Herrmann 1969, 129, Abb. 2.

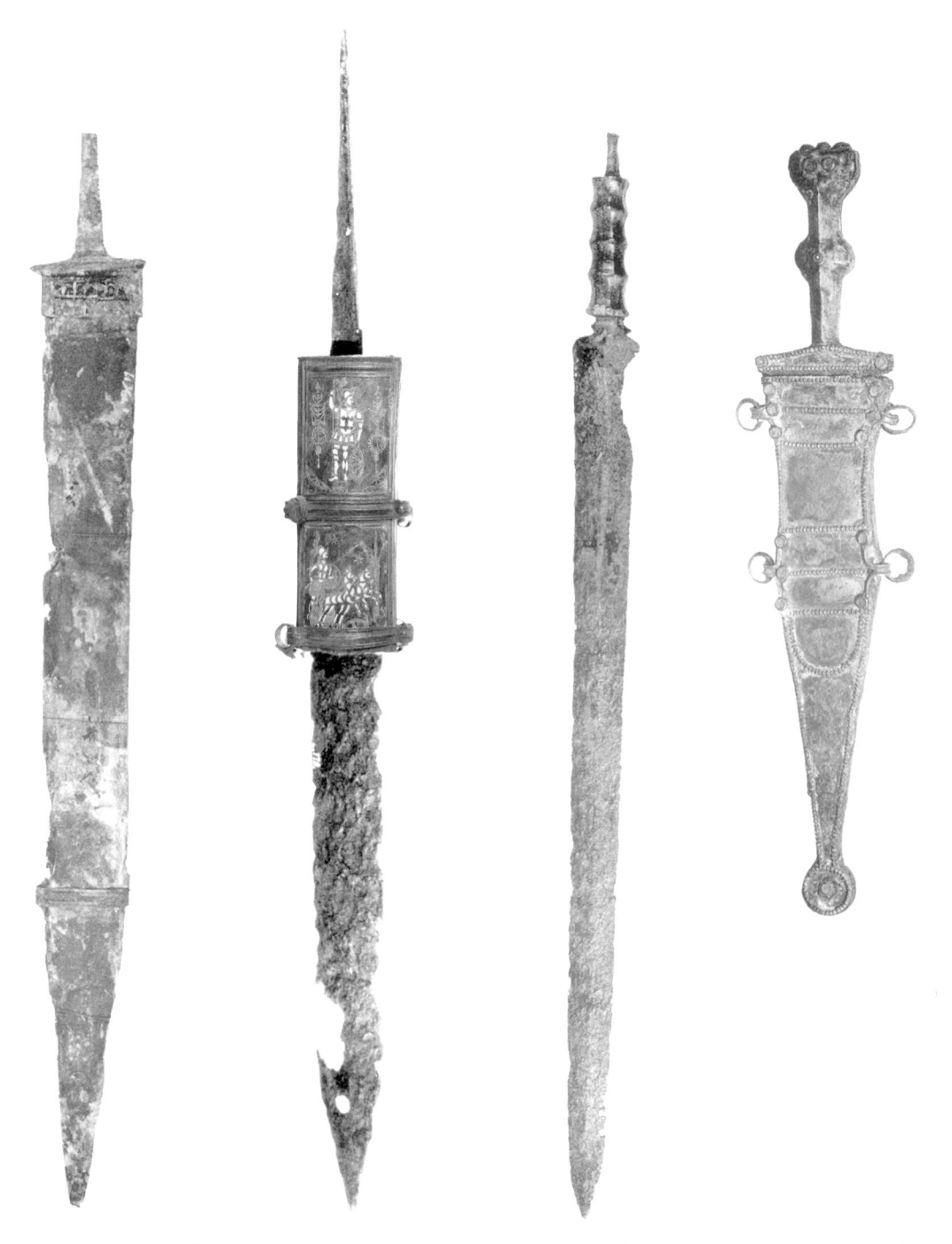

Fig. 2.8. Three swords and a dagger from rivers and a dredge pit in the research region (from left to right 199.2, 220.1, 8.2, 31.2). Not to scale. After Braat 1967, pl. II (nrs. 3-4), V (nr. 2); Willems 1984, fig. 85.

also belonged to this type of sword. The same applies to an almond-shaped fitting with a rectangular opening from Lent-'Steltsestraat' (170.1, pl. 19), which may have been mounted on the base of the guard of a narrow sword.

Two complete sword blades from Alem-'Marensche Waarden' (8.2, pl. 20, fig. 2.8) and Lobith-'De Bijland' (176.4, pl. 20) come from 2nd- and 3rd-century *spathae*. The bone hilt of the first sword is characteristic of the 1st century, pointing to the early date of this example. In addition to an ivory hilt from the River Waal at Rossum (255.2, pl. 21) and probably a second from Lobith-'De Bijland' (176.8), a bone pommel from Empel-'De Werf' (82.56, pl. 21) also belongs to the *spathae* of the 2nd and 3rd centuries.

The remaining sword finds from this period consist of scabbard components. Eleven chapes have been recovered, with the peltate variant predominating (pl. 24). A pointed example from the River Waal at Nijmegen (211.27, pl. 24) has an unusual shape. In three cases, perhaps late examples, the pelta is C-shaped (pl. 24). The remaining variants occur only incidentally with a round, iron chape from Angeren-'Loowaard/Kandia' (13.7, pl. 24) and a rectangular, bone example from Nijmegen (209.14). Also part of the scabbard are 17 slides, which are predominantly trapezoidal (pl. 25). A fine example is a dolphin-shaped slide from Nijmegen (209.12, pl. 25). Iron and bone examples are unknown from the research region; the only rectangular scabbard slide is made of bronze (224.3, pl. 25).

The only late Roman sword is a probable *semispatha* from Druten-'Klepperhei' (58.1, pl. 20).[78] The short blade terminates in a long, pointed tip and, at a total length of 34.5 cm, it is shorter than that of the swords documented from Künzing and London (c. 37-55 cm).[79]

Daggers

Daggers, like swords, were designed for close combat. However, Junkelmann suspects that the 1st-century dagger, which often had a richly ornamented sheath, played a secondary role in battle and should be viewed chiefly as a prestige object.[80] In the 2nd and 3rd centuries too, the dagger was probably only a reserve weapon. Like the *gladius*, it was carried by foot soldiers from both the legions and the auxiliary.

Derived from the late Republican type (type A), the 1st-century dagger has a short blade with a pointed tip and usually a pronounced midrib (type B).[81] The daggers and accompanying sheaths can be broken down into two types, dating from the first and second half of the 1st century AD respectively. With the *Mainz type* (type B1), the dagger blade is broad and squat, and the wooden core is covered front and back with an iron plate. The front plate is usually divided into four decorative zones and may be inlaid with brass, silver, niello and enamel. The *Vindonissa type* (type B2) has a slimline blade and only the front plate of the sheath is made of iron. This plate is for the most part ornamented with silver and red enamel. Attached to the top of the blade in both types is a bone hilt, whose front and back plates are clad in iron and may be richly inlaid. Suspension loops are attached to the edge of the sheath. Both dagger types were in use until the beginning of the 2nd century.

Because daggers rarely feature in 2nd- and 3rd-century monumental images, it was long assumed that their disappearance coincided with that of the *gladius*. However, the discovery of various daggers in a 3rd-century assemblage from Künzing shows that they continued as part of military equipment after the 1st century.[82] Although the basic shape remained unchanged, some innovations were introduced (type C).[83] The blade became longer and wider, and the sheath simpler in design. The wooden sheath was covered with leather and bore a bronze plate on the front. The front plate comprised two hollow strips of bronze that ran along the edge of the sheath and were joined on the front by horizontal bands. The chape sported a small, conical knob. Type-C daggers fell out of favour in the course of the 3rd century, marking the end of military-style daggers.

Non-military contexts in the eastern Rhine delta have yielded few dagger finds. Two well-preserved daggers with iron sheaths from the River Waal at Boven-Leeuwen (31.1, pl. 26) and the 'Lobberdensche

---

[78] The gilded scabbard mount from Tiel-'Bergakker' belongs to a *spatha* of the Krefeld type that was common in the second half of the 5th century and therefore falls outside the period of this study (Bosman/Looijenga 1996; Theuws/Alkemade 2000, 437-438, note 82).

[79] Breeze/Close-Brooks/Ritchie 1976, table 1; Manning 1985, 152.

[80] Junkelmann 1986, 191.

[81] Type A: Connolly 1997, 56-57; type B: Scott 1985a; Obmann 2000, 6-10; see also Exner 1940; M.J. Klein 2003c.

[82] Baatz 1963/1964, 83, Abb. 19.

[83] Oldenstein 1997, 140; Reuter 1999.

Waard' at Pannerden (238.1, pl. 26) are 1st-century examples. The sheath from Leeuwen retains part of the wooden lining, while the one from Pannerden has remnants of leather. Both sheaths are of the B1 type, with the decoration on the front divided into four zones. The sheath from Leeuwen is inlaid with brass, red niello and enamel; niello occurs on the hilt of the accompanying dagger. The inlay of the Pannerden sheath consists of red and green enamel and copper. The iron blade of a third dagger of this type has been recovered from a cemetery at Hatert-'Hulzen' (109.1, pl. 26). The hilt has not been preserved. A sheath plate of a B2-type dagger comes from Angeren-'Loowaard/Kandia' (13.6, pl. 26). The decoration is subdivided in the customary way, and consists of a layer of openwork silver. A 1st-century dagger from Boven-Leeuwen (31.2, fig. 2.8) differs from the usual types in that both the hilt and front sheath plate are made of bronze instead of iron, decorated with chased beading. Traces of soldering on the backward-curving edges of the sheath plate indicate that the reverse was also clad in bronze.

There are no documented finds from the research region of 2nd- and 3rd-century daggers like those from Künzing. However, three peltate chapes will have belonged to dagger sheaths from this period as they are too narrow for *spathae* (type D: 15.2, 54.1, 242.5, pl. 26). No information is available about the further design of dagger sheaths with such chapes.

Pila and plumbata

The *pilum* was a heavy throwing spear with a long, thin shank and a lozenge-shaped tip (fig. 2.1). It was designed to disable armour-clad opponents who carried a shield. With its solid head, great weight and long shank, it was capable not only of penetrating both shield and armour but also of wounding the man behind them. At the base of the wooden shaft was a butt spike, a metal spike which protected the shaft and which – in emergencies – could be used as a weapon. Tacitus describes the *pilum* as a legionary weapon, while auxiliaries were armed with a spear and lance.[84] However, numerous finds from auxiliary camps reveal that auxiliary soldiers also carried *pila*.[85] These weapons have also been recovered from various graves that can be associated with auxiliary soldiers.[86]

We can distinguish two types of *pila*, depending on how the iron shank was mounted on the wooden shaft.[87] In the first (type A), the bottom of the head widens to a flat tongue shape, which is pushed into the wooden shaft and secured with two rivets and an iron collet. The second type (type B) has a round or square socketed head, into which the wooden shaft is inserted and secured by a rivet. The round socket is characteristic of the Republican period (B1), while square-socketed javelins began to appear in the Augustan period (B2). Both types co-existed until the late 1st century AD, after which the first fell into disuse.

When the second type of *pilum* was also discarded in the course of the 3rd century, its place was taken by the *plumbata* (type C).[88] The *plumbata* had a long shaft with a harpoon- or leaf-shaped head. The shaft was weighted with lead to add penetration power. This weapon was probably used into the 5th century.

Various *pila* heads are known from the research region. In addition to one complete example, there are two shafts and eight broken, lozenge-shaped heads (pl. 27). The complete *pilum* head comes from Lobith-'De Bijland' (176.3, pl. 27) and has an elongated shaft decorated with ridged bands and a square socket at the base. Two shafts from Empel-'De Werf' (82.42, pl. 27) and the River Waal at Nijmegen (212.2) have a round and a square socket respectively. The broken *pila* heads can be divided into heavier and lighter examples. An irregularly-shaped head from Wijk bij Duurstede-'De Horden' (291.9, pl. 27) is probably a local imitation.

[84] Tacitus, *Ann.* 12.35; see also Vegetius, *ERM* 2.15.
[85] Haalebos 1977, 82-83; Deschler-Erb 1999a, 19.
[86] Waurick 1994, 14-23.
[87] Junkelmann 1986, 186-189; Deschler-Erb 1999a, 19-20; for developments during the Republican period, see Connolly 1997.
[88] Bennet 1991.

Five elongated heads can probably also be classified as belonging to *pila* (pl. 28). Three have the usual square cross-section and a fourth a triangular one. Part of the wooden shaft, with a bronze socket at the top, has been preserved in a find from Empel-'De Werf' (82.44, pl. 28). As this piece was probably too heavy to be thrown by hand, it may have been used as an artillery projectile. The same applies to a heavy example from Geldermalsen (99.1, pl. 28). Late Roman *plumbatae* are unknown from the research region.

Spears and lances
Spears and lances were weapons of the auxiliary, and more particularly the cavalry, with both weapon types frequently depicted on 1st-century cavalry gravestones. While the deceased cavalryman is portrayed raising a lance, his servant is shown running behind the horse and carrying one or two similar weapons, whose smaller size suggests that they were throwing spears. A writing tablet from the military post at Carlisle (AD 103/5) has been critical for identifying these weapons as spears or lances.[89] The document, which concerns a cavalry unit's spears and lances lost in battle, distinguishes between *lancia pugnatoria* and the smaller *lancia subarmales duas*. Tomlin assumes that the former are lances, and the latter throwing spears.[90] Interestingly, the number of spears and lances referred to matches images on gravestones, which show the cavalry armed with one lance and two spears. We do not know how many spears and/or lances an auxiliary foot soldier carried.

Made up of the same components, spears and lances consisted of a wooden shaft with an often leaf-shaped head at the top and a pointed tip, or spike, at the butt-end. Spears and lances occurred throughout the Roman era but the absence of a typological evolution means that we cannot date them more precisely. The same applies to the butt spike, which is similarly shaped to that of *pila*.

Despite the wide variation in shape and size, we can distinguish several principal types within the category of spear- and lanceheads. The most common are leaf-shaped examples (type A), which can be broken down further into two groups based on length and width, possibly corresponding to spears on the one hand and lances on the other.[91] Characteristic of spears is a relatively short, slimline head, with the blade generally widest in the middle (type A1). Lances have a longer, wider blade that is broadest at the base (type A2). Lanceheads with a very pronounced midrib, going back directly to La Tène examples, occurred during the 1st century AD.[92]

Also in use from the 2nd century onward were long, slimline heads with a triangular or square cross-section (type B).[93] Their most plausible function was as a throwing spear.

Bronze examples featuring a short head with a triangular, square or multi-faceted cross-section (type C) are known from the Danube provinces, in particular Dacia.[94] Although they bear a resemblance to iron artillery heads, different examples have been found in combination with the butt spikes known from spears, lances and *pila*. Moreover, this category of finds is best known from auxiliary camps, although the assumption has been that only legionary camps had mechanical artillery.[95] It is therefore likely that these objects, which date from between 170 and 260/270, were spearheads.

Spear- and lanceheads make up a significant proportion of the weapons of attack recovered in the research region (pl. 29-33, fig. 2.9). Of the leaf-shaped heads, 37 may have belonged to a spear and

[89] Tomlin 1999.
[90] Tomlin 1999, 135-137.
[91] Manning 1985, 162, fig. 33; see also Kemkes/Scheuerbrandt 1997, 37-38. The narrow heads from Manning's groups I-III belong to type A1, while the wider examples from groups III and IV can be classified as type A2. Compare, however, Deschler-Erb (1991, 13-14) and Bishop/Coulston (1993, 69), who are of the view that such a distinction is not possible.
[92] Deschler-Erb 1991, 14.
[93] Bishop/Coulston 1993, 126.
[94] Petculescu 1991c.
[95] Petculescu 1991c, 40; for the use of artillery, see 'mechanical artillery and slings' below.

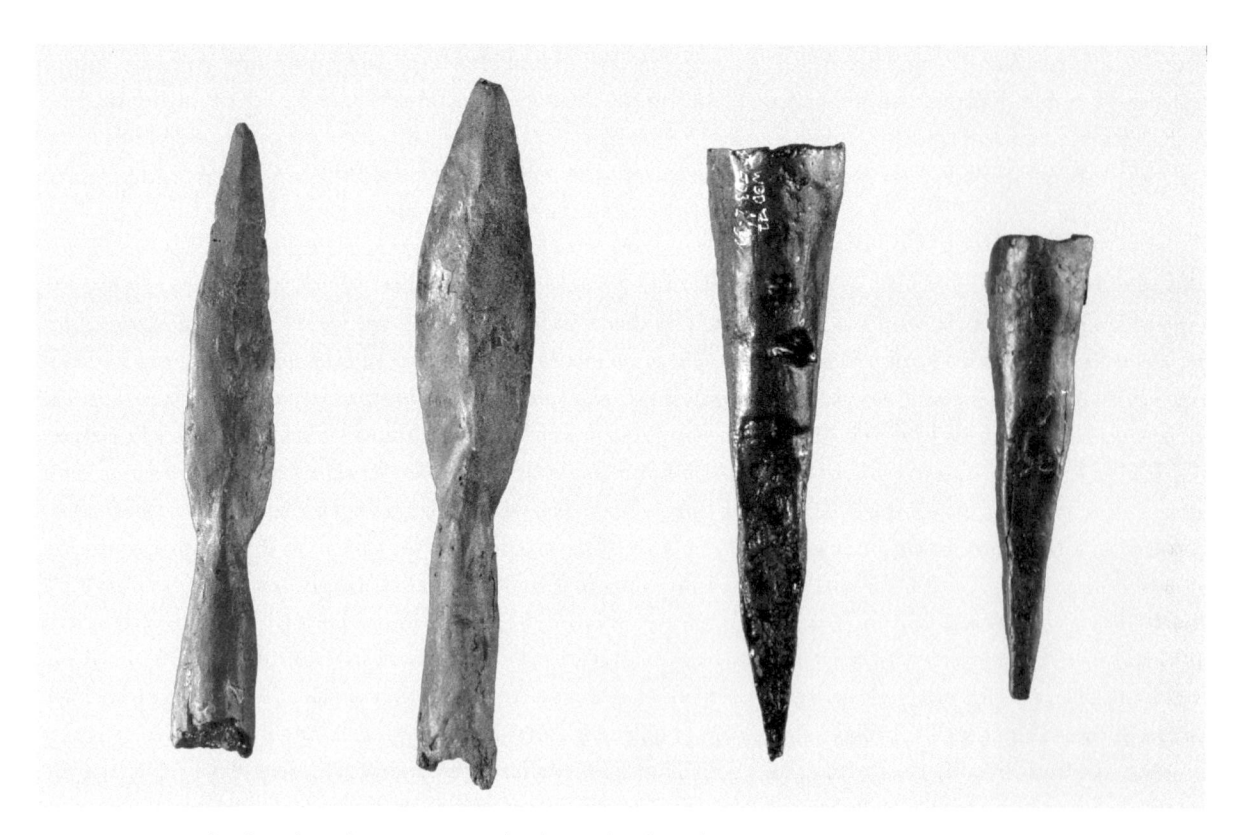

Fig. 2.9. Two spearheads and two lance, spear, or *pilum* butt spikes from the rural settlement of Wijk bij Duurstede-'De Horden' (from left to right 291.19, 22, 17-18). Not to scale.

15 to a lance. For eight examples, there is no data on the specific shape of the blade. A small number of 'spearheads' with an exceptionally long shaft (up to 53 cm) demonstrate the difficulties involved in identifying objects as originating from either spears or lances; these would appear to be most suitable for a lance. Five spearheads and one lancehead have a V-shaped opening on the reverse of the shaft. An unusual example is a spearhead from the River Waal at Nijmegen (211.22). Here the shaft terminates on each side in two pointed 'wings', with a broadening at the transition from the shaft to the blade. It may have been part of a standard or banner.[96] One example from the River Lex near Hagestein (105.1, pl. 32), which has a pyramidal, multi-faceted head and a long, hollow shaft, is of the type characteristic of the Danube provinces.[97] Unlike the examples known to date, this item is made of iron. One category of finds which we cannot ascribe specifically to spears or lances and which also occurs among *pila* is the butt spike, with 11 examples (pl. 34, fig. 2.9). Three are pointed with a V-shaped notch at the back; two examples from Kesteren (166.11-12, pl. 34) terminate in a round knob.

Bows and arrows
The Roman army deployed specialist units (*sagittarii*) that fought solely with bow and arrow.[98] In addition, we can assume that every legionary or auxiliary unit contained a number of soldiers who were armed in this way.[99] Although we regularly encounter bow components, most of the finds are iron heads that were mounted on the tip of the arrow. From the Republican period onward, arrowheads were trilobate (type

[96] See Kemkes/Scheuerbrandt 1997, 45-48.
[97] A similar example made of bronze comes from the Binnen-Maas at Mijnsherenland (Burgers 1968, 130-132).
[98] See J.L. Davies 1977, 261-262; Zanier 1988, 9-10; Junkelmann 1986, 194.
[99] Deschler-Erb 1999a, 22.

A), while solid examples with a pointed, round tip (type B) also occurred during the 1st century AD.[100] Both types were mounted onto the wooden shaft by means of a pointed tang. The type-B arrowheads were replaced in the late 3rd century by ones with a pyramidal point and a pointed or hollow shaft (type C). Leaf-shaped heads with a generally hollow shaft (type D) were in use at the same time.[101]

Only nine arrowheads are known from the research region. One with a round cross-section from Ophemert-'Keizershof' (224.1) can probably be dated to the 1st century AD. A similar example from Wijk bij Duurstede-'De Horden' (291.3, pl. 35) has a hollow shaft, indicating a relatively late dating. An arrowhead from Kesteren-'De Woerd' (166.4, pl. 35) with a rounded-off, square cross-section and a pointed shaft is probably late Roman, as are two leaf-shaped heads with hollow shafts (163.9, pl. 35 and 273.1). Two arrowheads from Kesteren-'De Woerd' (166.3, pl. 35) and Oosterhout-'Van Boetzelaerstraat' (222.4, pl. 35) are of the trilobate type, which occurred throughout the Roman period.

Mechanical artillery and slings
In addition to *pila*, spears, and lances, the Roman army used artillery for the mechanical launching of projectiles. We can distinguish between the *ballista* and the *catapulta*; the former was an engine for firing spherical stone shot, while the latter propelled short, spear-shaped projectiles. According to Vegetius, each legion was equipped with 10 heavy *ballistae* and no less than 55 mobile *catapultae*.[102] For neither artillery type is there any evidence to suggest that they were used by the auxiliary.[103]

Apart from components of the artillery itself, a large number of iron boltheads have been recovered from army camps.[104] These have a solid, pyramidal (type A) or round point (type B) and a long, hollow or pointed shaft. The shape of the point shows that, like the javelin, these projectiles were designed to penetrate shields and armour. In typological terms, boltheads cannot be dated more precisely than to the Roman period.

Clay and lead sling shot are projectiles that do not require mechanical artillery but can simply be fired with a sling. As stray finds of baked-clay sling shot cannot be attributed specifically to either the Iron Age or the Roman era, they have been excluded from this study.[105] We can distinguish five variants of the lead shot characteristic of the Roman period, with almond-shaped examples (type A), used from the Republican period until the 2nd century, being the most prevalent.[106]

All artillery finds from the research region consist of iron boltheads (pl. 35), the majority from Kesteren-'De Woerd' (166.5-8, pl. 35). In addition to one example with a pyramidal head, three damaged heads with a round cross-section have been recovered. Other sites have yielded one bolthead with a round and five with a square cross-section. A different example from Empel-'De Werf', with a long shaft and a leaf-shaped point, probably also belongs to this weapon type (82.41, pl. 35).

Alongside boltheads, various examples of leaden sling shot are represented in the finds (pl. 36). All are almond-shaped with a round cross-section. In addition to six examples from Wijk bij Duurstede-'De

---

[100] For an overview, see Bishop/Coulston 1993, 55, 79, 139 (types A-C); for the trilobate arrowheads, see also Erdmann 1976; J.L. Davies 1977; Zanier 1988.

[101] See Pfahl/Reuter 1996, cat.nr. 68, Abb. 8 (nrs. 12-13); Lenz 2000, 48, Taf. 89 (nrs. 912-913).

[102] Vegetius, *ERM* 2.25.

[103] Baatz 1966; however, see also Campbell (1986), who claims that they may well have had smaller mechanical artillery.

[104] See Bishop/Coulston 1993, 55-56, 81, 115, 139-140. Round, stone sling shot has not been taken into consideration here.

[105] Verwers 1972, 114-117; Van den Broeke 1987, 38.

[106] Morel/Groenman-Van Waateringe 1993, 52, fig. 4.9, Bishop/Coulston 1993, 55, 115; see also Bosman 1995b, fig. 1 (the classification is based on finds from Velsen).

Horden' (291.10-14), stray examples are known from eight sites. Interestingly, all the sling shot shows traces of damage; in one instance, the original shape can barely be recognised.

2.1.3 BELTS, APRONS AND BALDRICS

Parts of a soldier's equipment that cannot be regarded as direct military components, but which were vital for suspending the sword and dagger, are the waist belt and shoulder strap, or baldric. Infantrymen wore an apron attached to the front of the belt.

Belts
There were different ways of wearing the belt and baldric in the 1st century AD.[107] In the first half of the century, two belts were worn crosswise, with the sword suspended from one belt and the dagger from the other. Roughly coinciding with the introduction of the Pompeii type *gladius*, one belt was discarded and both sword and dagger were attached to the remaining belt. Junkelmann points out that this system was confined to rank-and-file soldiers and to low-ranking officers, with officers suspending their sword from a baldric.[108]

First-century belts were narrow, made of leather, and featured a peltate bronze buckle and one or more rectangular bronze belt plates (type A). The buckle, made up of a loop and a tongue, was attached by a hinge to a belt plate. There are five variants of the buckle, based on shape and decoration.[109] The first has a simple, peltate loop, with a rectangular, closed or open widening at the transition to the hinge. In the second, the ends of the pelta are scrolled and the narrow widening terminates in two volutes. The simple buckles of the third variant are rather crudely made and may be inlaid with enamel. The rectangular widening disappears in the fourth variant, and enamel may once again be used. Finally, there are semicircular, openwork buckles in the form of a pelta. Unlike the previous variants, the hinge loops are positioned together in the centre rather than set apart. In general, the first three variants have lily-shaped tongues, with in some cases a stylised animal head. The last examples have a simple, straight tongue. The first two variants were in use from the late Augustan period and were superseded in the Flavian period by the latter three, which occurred until the early 2nd century.

Two tear- or heart-shaped buckles also feature among the pre-Flavian belts.[110] The narrow, forward curving end of the buckle loops terminates in a domed knob or a round, flat disc. A complete belt set found in Velsen shows that these were frogs from which to suspend the dagger.[111]

Rectangular or square belt plates could be added to the belt as decoration. There are four variants, depending on the type of decoration.[112] The first are simple and frequently tinned, while the second are both tinned and inlaid with niello. The third variant consists of thin examples, with chased anthropoid, plant and geometrical motifs, and the final variant is characterised by incised or cast, concentric grooves. The last two variants may feature a decorative hinge on each side. Examples of the first variant were in use from the early Augustan era, with the three other types appearing under Tiberius. A technical innovation in the Tiberian period was to attach the rivets at the back so that they were no longer visible on the front. Niello-inlay examples are known above all from the Claudian period. The different variants

---

[107] Deschler-Erb 1999a, 40; Junkelmann 1986, 161.
[108] Junkelmann 1986, 183. There are no components of the 1st-century baldric in the archaeological record.
[109] Deschler-Erb 1999a, 40-42 (variant 1-3); Oldenstein 1976, 211-212 (variant 4-5); see also Grew/Griffiths 1991.
[110] Grew/Griffiths 1991, 50, figs. 15-16; for the dating, see Lenz 2000, 31.
[111] Bosman 1997, fig. 5.4-5, with reconstruction.
[112] Deschler-Erb 1999a, 43-45; see also Grew/Griffiths 1991; Deschler-Erb 2000, 389; Lenz 2000, 31-32.

Fig. 2.10. Methods of fastening belt buckles, typical of the 2nd and 3rd centuries AD. Redrawn from Oldenstein 1976, Abb. 2, 7.

fell into disuse in the Flavian period. Although 1st-century gravestones show both cavalry and infantry wearing a belt, probably only infantrymen adorned their belts with the belt plates described here.[113]

Like the sword and dagger, the belt also underwent changes in the 2nd century. Although the peltate buckle remained in use, the hinge was replaced by a rectangular loop (type B).[114] The buckle was now attached to the plate by means of a long metal tongue (fig. 2.10), which curved around the belt and was fastened at the back. Oldenstein dates this buckle type to the period from the mid-2nd to the mid-3rd centuries.

Images on grave monuments show that bronze rings also functioned as buckles on wider belts (type C).[115] The belt was fastened by pulling both ends through the ring, folding them back and securing them with two bronze studs (fig. 2.10). The predominantly simple ring buckles are difficult to identify as stray objects among the finds. As a result, finds of this belt type are largely made up of the studs used to fasten the belt. These are either round or square double-headed studs, with a head and foot of equal size.

As in the previous period, decorative fittings could also be added to the 2nd- and 3rd-century belt. These were rectangular in shape, usually openwork or inlaid with enamel.[116] The fittings appear to have adorned only narrow belts fastened with a peltate buckle. Judging by depictions on grave reliefs, ring-buckle belts were wider than those with a peltate buckle and were not fitted with bronze plates.[117]

Both the narrow and broad belts of this period could be embellished with hanging terminals. These display considerable variation, the predominant types having a ribbed terminal or a tear-shaped pendant.[118] In the ribbed examples, the strap could be attached in a notch at the top, while the tear-shaped pendants were attached to the leather by means of an additional fitting.

Belts became broader in the 4th century and an additional narrow belt, also worn around the waist, appears to have been used for suspending a sword. Only the 'real' belt can be traced archaeologically. We

[113] Deschler-Erb 1999a, 45.
[114] Oldenstein 1976, 214-216, Abb. 7, Taf. 75-76; see also Allason-Jones/Miket 1984, cat.nrs. 3.616-622.
[115] Oldenstein 1976, 218-219; 1997, 140; see also Noelke 1986; Von Schnurbein 1995. The ring may be replaced by a square 'buckle'.
[116] Oldenstein 1976, 193-198.
[117] Although Oldenstein (1976, 220-222) ascribed rectangular, openwork fittings with pelta motifs to the wide belt, they are in fact baldric fittings (see 'balteus' below).
[118] Oldenstein 1976, 144-146.

Fig. 2.11. Buckle, decorative fitting and dagger frog from a 1st-century *cingulum* recovered from the rural settlement of Wijk bij Duurstede-'De Horden' (from left to right 291.36, 39, 38). Not to scale.

are able to distinguish four belt types on the basis of grave finds.[119] The first features a large, two-part belt plate around a C-shaped buckle decorated with stylised animal heads (type D). The other end of the belt has a rectangular plate with triangular fittings on each side. Attached at the back is a narrow strap which is drawn through the buckle to fasten the belt. The decorative elements include elongated fittings with crescent-shaped ends, rosette fittings along the bottom edge for the attachment of tweezers or a knife and a tear-shaped terminal. Specific to this type of belt is the *Kerbschnitt*, or chip-carved, decoration on the bronze work. Böhme dates this belt to between about 390 and 430, while Swift adheres to a dating of about 365 to 410.[120]

In the second type, the large belt plates have been replaced by a narrow bronze strip with a ribbed casing (type E). The belt is decorated with rectangular and 'propeller-shaped' belt fittings, while either rosette, round or rectangular fittings may be added along the bottom edge. A characteristic feature of the bronze elements on this belt type is the decoration with beading, incised lines and circles, as well as notched edges. To a lesser extent, chip-carved decoration may still occur. Böhme places the belt in about 430-465.[121]

Two types of belt were still in use during the late Roman period.[122] The first featured a buckle in the form of two dolphins (type F), attached to an openwork belt plate. The belt may be decorated with heavy, 'propeller' mounts. The second type had a semicircular buckle terminating on the reverse in a triangular plate (type G).

---

[119] Böhme 1974, 53 ff.; 1986; Swift 2000, 185 ff.; see also Werner 1958 (type E); Bullinger 1968 (type E); Ypey 1969 (types D-E); Fernández 1999 (types D, F-G).

[120] Böhme 1989, 770; Swift 2000, 201; Böhme (1974, 79-90) initially dated this type of belt to between c. 350 and 400.

[121] Böhme 1989; Böhme (1974, 79-90) initially adhered to a broader dating of between c. 380 and 450.

[122] Böhme 1986, 480-487.

Fig. 2.12. Belt set with remains of the leather belt from a late Roman grave at Wijchen (285.2). Not to scale.

Although little data is available regarding its use by infantrymen or cavalrymen from the 2nd century onward, we can assume that the belt, like the baldric, was in widespread use among Roman soldiers.

Over 250 belt components are documented from non-military contexts in the eastern Rhine delta. A total of 60 items can be assigned to 1st-century belts (pl. 37-39, fig. 2.11). Most buckles are of the first variant (16x), with a single fragmentary buckle from Wijk bij Duurstede (291.34, pl. 37) featuring the volutes characteristic of the second variant. Variant 4, an enamel-inlaid example from Oosterhout (222.12, pl. 37), is also represented by a single buckle. With the exception of the latter, the finds date from the pre-Flavian period. Different again in shape are five C-shaped and two rectangular buckles. A crudely made, C-shaped example from Kessel-Lith (163.10, pl. 38) is the only find made of bone. Only five buckle tongues have been found, three of them lily-shaped (pl. 38). Some of the decorative mounts of belt-type A bear a hinge for attaching the buckle. Eleven fittings belong to the undecorated, pre-Flavian variant, while three examples from Empel-'De Werf' (82.81, 134, 174, pl. 39), with flat studs visible on the front, are Augustan. Of the remaining fittings, four are inlaid with niello (variant 2), three made of chased sheet bronze (variant 3) and four decorated with concentric grooves (variant 4). One exceptional example of variant 3 depicts lotus leaves (291.38, pl. 39, fig. 2.11).[123] We should regard a poorly-made example of variant 4 as a local product (128.4, pl. 39). Finally, six components will have functioned as frogs for suspending the dagger (pl. 38). A heart-shaped example from Wijk bij Duurstede (291.39, pl. 38, fig. 2.11) is composed of two outward-scrolling vines.

The 2nd- and 3rd-century belt is represented by 64 components. Various buckles and decorative fittings come from narrow belts (pl. 40). Four buckles, each of a different shape, have a rectangular loop. Two C-shaped examples with pointed knobs on each side belong to a narrow belt from the same period.[124]

---

[123] Compare Deschler-Erb 1999a, 43, Abb. 21 (nr. 342).

[124] Oldenstein 1976, 216-217. The buckles may also have been horse gear components.

Fig. 2.13. Chip-carved belt fittings from Lent-'Steltsestraat' (170.3-4). The items probably come from a disturbed grave. Scale 1:1. Photos: Gemeente Nijmegen, Bureau Archeologie.

Eleven rectangular fittings are decorative in character, mainly openwork. One of the few exceptions is a solid example from the River Meuse at Heerewaarden (165.1, pl. 40), which has relief motifs. Two mounts from Nijmegen (209.16, 18, pl. 40), composed of vine motifs, have an unusual form. An undecorated example from the Lower Rhine at Wijk bij Duurstede (293.1, pl. 40) has a mushroom-shaped stud at the front, which suggests a different closure mechanism.[125]

The contemporaneous ring-buckle belt also features among the finds (pl. 41). Those belt components that are archaeologically identifiable consist solely of round and square studs for fastening the belt (39x). The studs are of plain design, with a single example of decoration in the form of concentric grooves.

Eight fittings that hung from the ends of the belt could have belonged to both belt types from the 2nd and 3rd centuries (pl. 41). Six are elongated and ribbed at the bottom. Only the tear-shaped pendant of a second variant is preserved (209.21, pl. 41). One terminal has an unusual, conical shape (209.20, pl. 41).

We can regard a buckle from Wijchen (284.4, pl. 40) as a transitional type. Its peltate buckle loop places it among the fourth variant of 1st-century buckles, but instead of hinge loops on the reverse, it has the rectangular opening characteristic of the following period. Given the width of the buckle, it belonged to a wide variant of the type-B belt.

In addition to five complete or partially preserved belt sets from graves (figs. 2.12-13, 7.9), late Roman belt finds comprise 130 stray buckles, fittings (both plain and decorative), edgings and associated tweezers (pl. 42-46). Only a rectangular belt plate from Teeffelen (264.1, pl. 44) can be classed as part of belt-type D. The remaining finds either come from the later type-E belt or are not specific to types D or E. One interesting item comes from Wijchen (284.7, pl. 44). The belt plate of a type-D belt has a plate from the later E-type attached as a repair. Finds of type-F belts are rare and comprise a 'propeller' mount from Arnhem (14.10, pl. 44) and a rectangular, openwork example from Wijchen (284.12). The last belt type (type G) is unknown from non-military contexts in the research region.

Aprons

The apron was a characteristic feature of the 1st-century belt.[126] In imitation of late La Tène examples, the apron originally consisted of a number of leather straps cut from the end of the belt that is drawn through the buckle. The late Augustan period saw the appearance of a separate apron attached to the front of the belt (fig. 2.1). Although often regarded as an extension of the armour, Bishop points out that the leather straps had a decorative rather than a protective function.[127] Images on gravestones show that the apron was worn by legionary and auxiliary foot soldiers. It formed part of the equipment of Roman

---

[125] See Oldenstein 1976, 196, Abb. 5.

[126] Bishop 1992; see also Junkelmann 1986, 161; Fernández 1998.

[127] Bishop 1992, 101; see also Junkelmann 1986, 161.

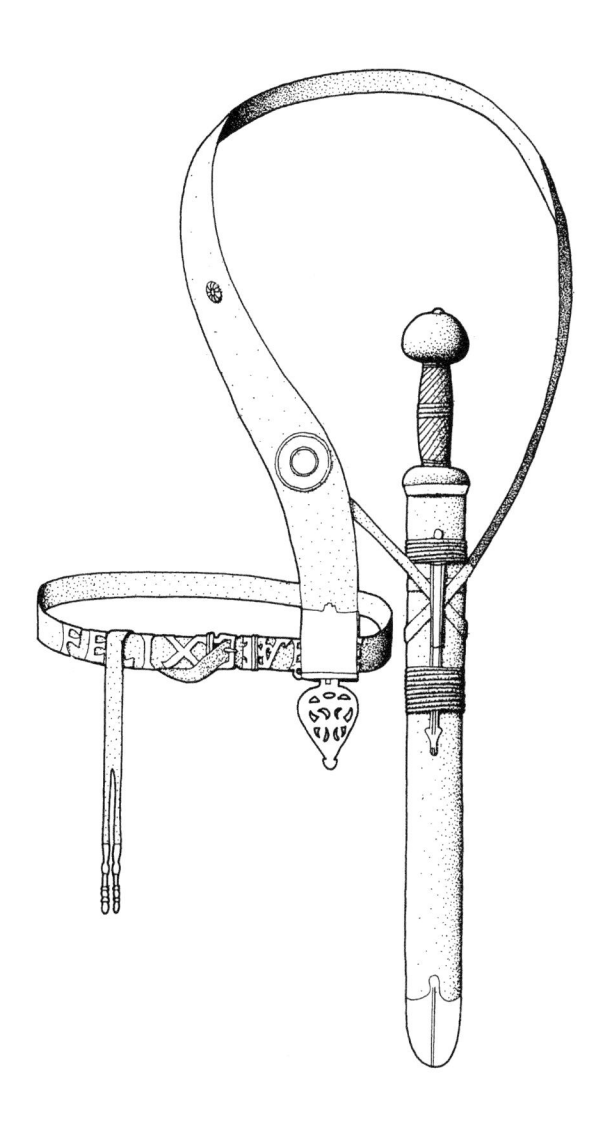

Fig. 2.14. Reconstruction of a belt and baldric, based on the inventory of a weapon grave at Lyon. After Bishop/Coulston 1993, fig. 92.

soldiers from the mid-1st century BC, falling out of favour in the early 2nd century AD.

The entire length of the apron straps could be covered with decorative fittings, with a terminal and then a pendant at the bottom. Grave reliefs show that the fittings were round, square or rectangular. Because similar fittings were also used in horse gear, attribution to the apron is often problematical.[128] Nevertheless, we can with some certainty ascribe the following types to the apron: round examples with repoussé busts and small, rectangular or square undecorated examples.[129] The undecorated fittings were in use from the Augustan period onward, while chased examples occurred primarily in the Flavian period.

Apron terminals are easier to identify because they differ from those used on contemporary horse gear. Rectangular in shape, the terminals were attached by one or two rivets to the end of the leather strap. At the base was a loop for a peltate, tear- or heart-shaped pendant. Of these pendants, only the peltate examples decorated with dotted lines can be attributed with certainty to the apron; the remaining pendants also occur among horse gear. Finally, the terminal may feature a rectangular casing that is only known from aprons.[130]

Some of the finds from the research region are 1st-century apron components (pl. 47).[131] Firstly, there are 14 rectangular or square decorative fittings. Four rectangular casings can also be ascribed to the military apron. Characteristic of the Lower Rhine examples are several domes on the front. The only pendant from the research region comes from Empel-'De Werf' (82.69, pl. 47). This peltate example is tinned and decorated on the front with foliate motifs. A second, tear-shaped pendant is suspended in the hollow of the pelta.

---

[128] Although Bishop (1992, 96) employs a diameter or width of 14 to 20 mm as the criterion for attribution to the apron, fittings of such dimensions also occur among horse gear.

[129] Feugère 1985; Deschler-Erb 1999a, 47-48; Lenz 2000, 32-33.

[130] Deschler-Erb 1999a, 48.

[131] Some of the decorative fittings and pendants classed here as horse gear might also have belonged to the apron.

39

Fig. 2.15. Gilded decorative repoussé eagle, probably from *baltei*, found at two rural settlements at Eimeren (left 74.14, right 75.2). Not to scale.

Baldrics

At the same time as the ring buckle, the baldric appeared, which was used into the 3rd century by both the infantry and cavalry for suspending the *spatha* (fig. 2.14).[132] The baldric, or *balteus*, was a broad leather band tapering at one end into a narrow strip. A *phalera*, with a characteristic, semicircular loop on the reverse, was attached to the broad end of the band that hung in front of the body. The other end of the baldric hung over the soldier's back, with the narrow part wrapped around the sword at the scabbard slide and then attached to the *phalera* loop. The front of the baldric featured, in addition to the *phalera*, a rectangular terminal, from which was suspended a heart- or tear-shaped pendant.[133]

A total of eight objects from the Batavian territory can be ascribed to the *balteus* (pl. 48). These include a complete, tinned *phalera* from Wijk bij Duurstede (288.3, pl. 48) and the broken, semicircular loop of a second example from Ophemert (228.2, pl. 48). A *phalera* from Tiel (142.12, pl. 48) is smaller than the known examples, making attribution to a baldric uncertain. Two fragments of rectangular fittings with simple openwork peltas were attached to the end of the baldric (13.11 and 232.1, pl. 48). The same probably applies to an undecorated example with a central pendant loop from Nijmegen (209.23, pl. 48). Of special interest are a pendant (230.1, pl. 48) and two fragments of rectangular terminals (80.1, 209.15, pl. 48) bearing openwork letters. They come from similar sets which, when complete, together make up the text *Optime Maxime con(serva) numerum omnium militantium* ('Jupiter, protect all warriors') (fig. 4.17, nrs. 1-3).[134] A hitherto unknown group of finds comprises five round, gilded fittings with a repoussé eagle (pl. 48, fig. 2.15). Judging by similar images on two *phalerae* from Vimose (fig. 4.18), we can assume that these too are baldric components. This is further substantiated by the presence of an eagle surrounded by the openwork letters of the *phalerae*.

[132] Stjernquist 1954; Oldenstein 1976, 226-234.

[133] Bishop/Coulston 1993, 135, fig. 91-92; see also Oldenstein 1976, 127-136, 220-222, 223-226.

[134] See Bishop/Coulston 1993, 130-135; Petculescu 1991a. See also chapter 4.2.3.

2.1.4 SIGNALLING INSTRUMENTS AND MILITARY DISTINCTIONS

Signalling instruments and military distinctions are two quite rare categories of finds that form indirect components of the equipment of Roman troops. Signalling instruments were carried by specially-appointed soldiers, while the badges of honour could be earned through courage on the battlefield.[135]

Signalling instruments
Musical instruments such as the *tuba*, *lituus*, *cornu* and *bucina* played a vital role in the Roman army for relaying signals and commands.[136] The *tuba*, used by all units, was a straight tube that gradually tapered at the base into a conical bell (type A). The *lituus* had the same basic shape except that it was curved at the transition to the bell (type B). The auxiliary, and in particular its cavalry units, were probably equipped with this instrument. The third instrument, the *cornu* (type C), is associated with the infantry. It had a long, round tube gradually terminating in a broad bell. A wooden crossbar was attached as reinforcement on the inside of the curve. The final instrument is the *bucina* (type D), whose shape appears to correspond to that of the *tuba*. This instrument, which was used by the different army units, probably served to announce the changing of the guard. The dating of the different types of wind instruments is unknown.

Fig. 2.16. Mouthpiece of a (military) wind instrument, found in the vicinity of Wijk bij Duurstede-'De Horden' (291.41). Not to scale. After Verwers 1978, fig. 2.

Three wind-instrument mouthpieces are known from non-military contexts in the research region. The best preserved example was dredged from the Rhine at Maurik (190.1, pl. 36). The mouthpiece consists of an elongated, somewhat conical tube with a semicircular bell. The tube and bell are decorated with ridges. The second example, from Wijk bij Duurstede-'De Horden' (291.41, pl. 36, fig. 2.16), has a straight tube with a similar bell, but with a broader rim. The third example was recovered at Kesteren-'Hoogeveld' (168.2, pl. 36); the mouthpiece has a straight tube with a conical bell. The shaft narrows on the transition to the bell. Mouthpieces that match the example from Maurik appear to have belonged to a *cornu*.[137] Given the straight tube and the shape of the bell, the two other examples are in all probability *tuba* or *bucina* components.

Military distinctions
Besides their customary wages, Roman soldiers could gain additional rewards in the form of military distinctions, or *dona militaria*.[138] Originally this occurred through the distribution of booty, but standard

---

[135] Standards and banners have not been considered. The only object in the inventory that might have been a banner or standard component is discussed under 'spears and lances' (see above).

[136] Klar 1971; M.P. Speidel 1976, 123 ff.; Junkelmann 1986, 216-218; Deschler-Erb 1999a, 71-73.

[137] A similar mouthpiece comes from a probable military *vicus* at Kesteren (Hulst 1986); see fig. 5.4.

[138] Büttner 1957; Neumann 1976; Maxfield 1981.

Fig. 2.17. Front and back of a *phalera* awarded as a military distinction, from a grave at Nijmegen-'Heuvellust' (205.1). Scale 2:3. After Bogaers 1970/1971, figs. 1-2.

Fig. 2.18. *Phalera* awarded as a military distinction from the rural settlement of Ressen-'Kerkenhof' (251.1). Scale unknown (original object lost). Photo: Museum het Valkhof, Nijmegen.

distinctions were introduced in the Republic period. These were given not just to individual soldiers or officers, but to entire units in recognition of valour in battle.[139] While the type of distinction initially depended on the deed in question, from Augustus onward it was the soldier's rank that determined the type of reward he received. This practice persisted into the 3rd century, after which it appears to have been discontinued.[140] References to military distinctions in literary sources include wreaths (*coronae*), standards (*vexilla*), spears (*hastae*), arm and neck rings (*armillae* and torques) and two types of decorative disc (*phalerae*). Here I will discuss only the armbands, neck rings and decorative discs that are common in the archaeological record.

Distinctions frequently depicted on gravestones are the originally 'Celtic' arm and neck rings (types A-B). Traditionally the spoils of war, they were awarded from the Augustan period onward as badges of honour to centurions or lower-ranking soldiers.[141] Although the armbands were worn in the traditional way around the wrist, the torques were fastened to both shoulders in a new fashion. Various examples of torques, executed in bronze, occur in the archaeological record. Each end of the torque typically featured an ornament in the shape of a lion's head.

From the Augustan period, both infantrymen and cavalrymen received the same reward when an opponent was killed and his equipment seized: a series of nine *phalerae*, which gravestone reliefs show were worn on leather straps on the upper torso (type C). Once again, these decorations were intended for soldiers up to the rank of centurion.[142] In addition to bronze examples in high relief, discs inset with a blue glass medallion occurred into the Claudian period.[143] A Medusa head was a frequently-used decorative motif in the bronze examples, while the glass medallions often portrayed members of the imperial house.

Horse gear from the Claudio-Flavian period includes elaborate *phalerae* and pendants, tinned and richly inlaid with niello, which are also generally interpreted as *dona militaria* (type D).[144] As with the decorative discs worn on the chest, some of the *phalerae* bear a bust of a member of the imperial house.

Armbands and torques bearing the characteristic lion's head are unknown from the eastern Rhine delta. Three decorative discs are of the kind of military distinction that infantrymen and cavalrymen wore on their chests.[145] The first example was recovered at Nijmegen, probably from a grave from the last quarter of the 1st or early 2nd century (205.1, fig. 2.17).[146] It is a bronze *phalera* depicting a winged Amor or Eros. A crudely manufactured *phalera* with a Medusa head came from the River Waal at Nijmegen (211.30). Both feature on the reverse a rectangular looped strap mount and a T-shaped loop for attachment to a leather strap. An example from Ressen-'Kerkenhof' (251.1, fig. 2.18) also features a Medusa head, with a rivet hole beside and below the head. The eyes of Medusa are probably inlaid with silver.

Several elaborate horse gear *phalerae* and accompanying pendants can probably also be classed as military distinctions.[147] The best examples, from an assemblage dredged from the Lower Rhine at Doorwerth (55.2-173, fig. 5.11), are four or five sets of parade equipment that belong together.[148] The centres of

---

[139] In the last instance, they may also have been *donativa* (see chapter 5.2.1).

[140] Maxfield 1981, 248.

[141] Maxfield 1981, 60-61, 86-91; for archaeological examples, see Garbsch 1986a.

[142] Maxfield 1981, 92-95.

[143] For distinctions containing glass medallions, see Boschung 1987.

[144] See Neumann 1976; Brouwer 1982, 155-157. Although the term '*phalera*' refers specifically to items awarded as military distinctions, decorative horse gear discs are generally referred to as *phalerae* in the archaeological literature.

[145] A fourth example, featuring a Medusa head, comes from a settlement situated immediately north of the Rhine at Remmerden (249.1).

[146] Bogaers 1970/1971.

[147] For the discussion of horse gear *phalerae*, see 'strap junctions' and 'looped strap mounts' below.

[148] Holwerda 1931; Brouwer 1982.

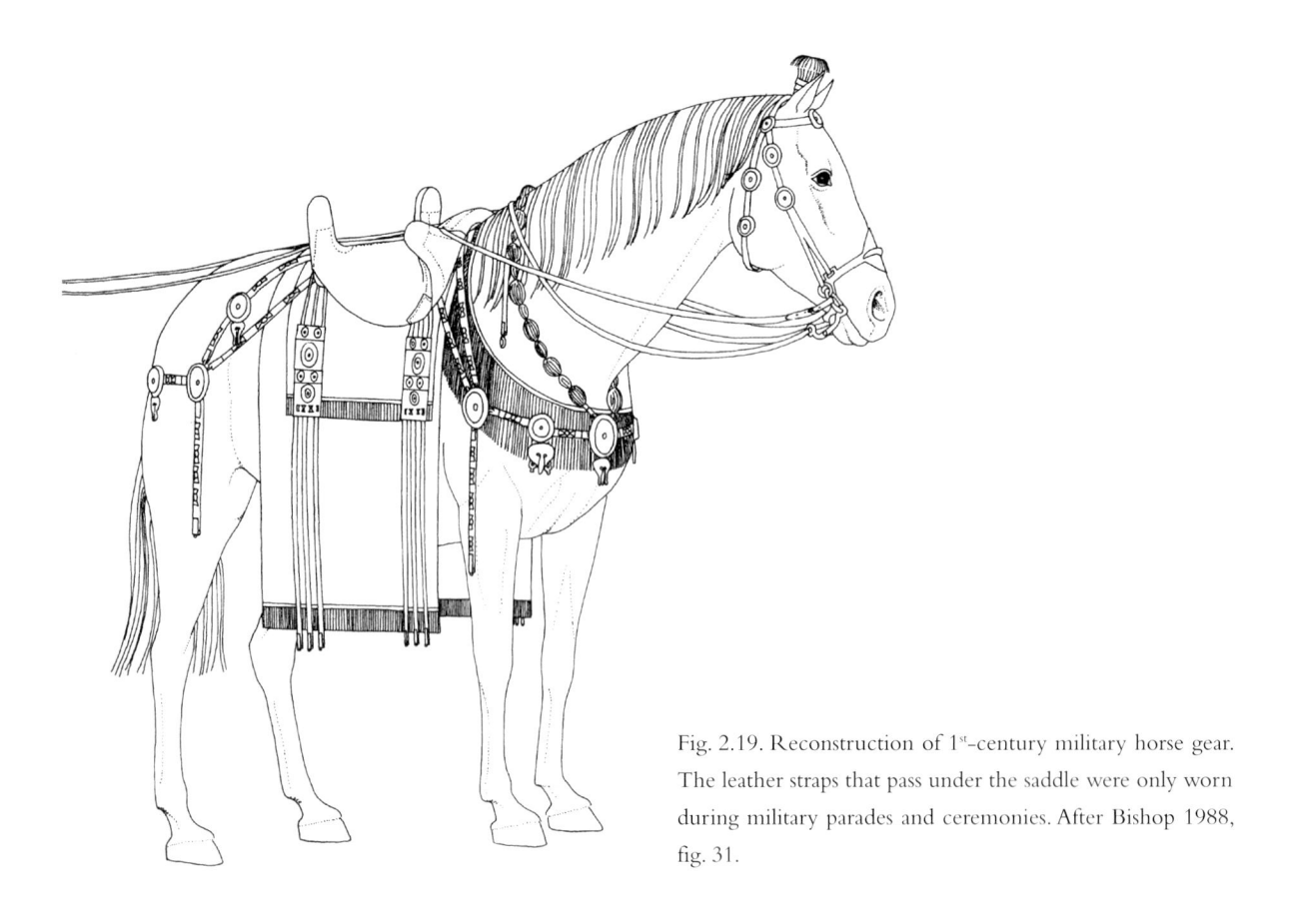

Fig. 2.19. Reconstruction of 1st-century military horse gear. The leather straps that pass under the saddle were only worn during military parades and ceremonies. After Bishop 1988, fig. 31.

two *phalerae* feature a silver medallion with a bust of Victoria (55.34-35, fig. 4.14). The central Victoria medallion is no longer present in a third *phalera* from the same assemblage (55.77). Medallions of this kind, similar to the glass medallions on decorative discs of the previous type, seem to be characteristic of *dona militaria*. A *phalera* with the same silver medallion of Victoria is known from the River Waal at Nijmegen (211.63). Two silver medallions from Nijmegen (208.8-9, fig. 5.14) were probably also part of exclusive *phalerae*. The busts show a male figure in military attire, probably a member of the imperial house.[149] Although difficult to confirm for individual pieces, some of the remaining tinned and niello-inlay horse gear items may also have been part of military distinctions.

2.2 HORSE GEAR

The rich embellishment of military horse gear with bronze elements (fig. 2.19) is a feature of the Roman period. Horse gear can be subdivided into the bridle (2.2.1), saddle (2.2.2) and girths (2.2.3). Although horse gear was also used in civilian contexts, my concern here is with components used by the cavalry, which is attested to by their occurrence in military posts, their representation on monumental reliefs and/or the presence of ownership inscriptions.[150]

---

[149] For an interpretation of such busts, see chapter 4.2.1.

[150] For the non-military use of horse gear, see chapter 6.3.

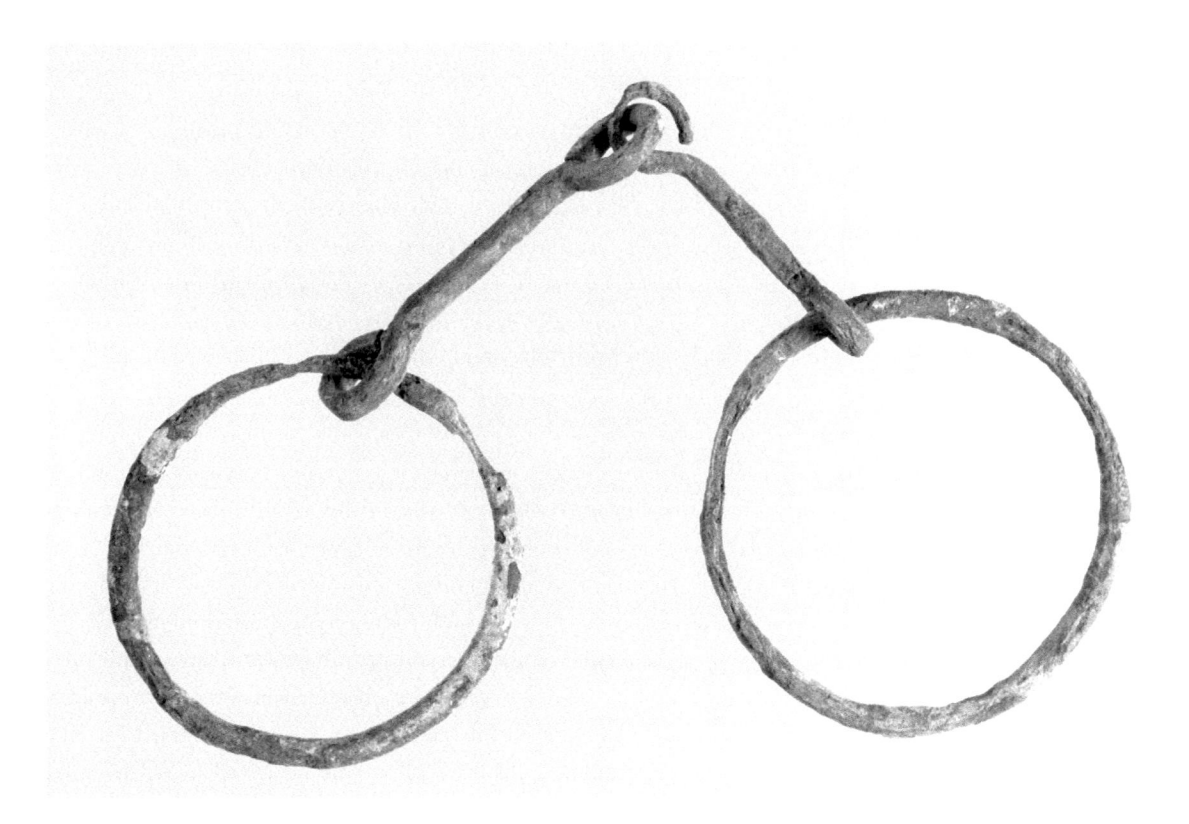

Fig. 2.20. Iron ring bit, dredged from the Dreumelsche Waard at Dreumel (56.2). Not to scale.

2.2.1 BRIDLE

A cavalryman was able to control his horse by means of reins attached to the bridle. In Roman times, the bridle comprised two components: the hackamore, which slid over the horse's nose, and the bit, which went into the horse's mouth. The more exclusive harness worn during parades could include a chamfron fastened to the horse's forehead.

Hackamores
The hackamore was an iron or bronze halter to which the reins and the bit were attached.[151] It was used from the first half of the 1st to the mid-3rd century AD. Hackamores can be subdivided into several more or less regional types according to the shape of the noseband. Characteristic of the Rhineland are examples with a rhomboid widening of the noseband, usually decorated with horizontal ridges (type A). Hackamores in which this wider part terminates top and bottom in a pointed tip with a round knob occurred primarily in Pannonia and Italy (type B). Another Rhineland type with a less specific geographical distribution has a plain, straight noseband (type C1), to which a round or rosette appliqué may be fitted (type C2).

Ten hackamores are documented from non-military contexts in the research region (pl. 49-50). Insofar as we can establish, these are examples of the Rhineland type with the rhomboid noseband. An exceptional example is a complete hackamore from the Rhine at Maurik (190.2, pl. 49), which is richly decorated with niello foliate motifs. A similar decoration is known from a hackamore from Xanten.[152]

[151] Taylor 1975; Lawson 1978, 140-143; Deschler-Erb 1999a, 64-65; for the manner in which they were worn, see Schwinden 1987.
[152] Taylor 1975, 120 (nr. 3), 124, Taf. 56.

Fig. 2.21. Leather chamfron from Newstead (left) and bronze eyeguard from Megen-'De Gouden Ham' (right, 193.1). Not to scale. After Curle 1911, pl. XXI; Stuart 1986, fig. 163.

Bits

The bit is a metal bar placed in the horse's mouth and attached by various means to the hackamore and reins. The Roman bit can be subdivided into four types.[153] The first is a simple iron ring bit (type A), composed of two jointed bars attached directly to the reins by large rings. Dating back to the late Iron Age, it remained in use throughout the Roman period. Specific to the 2nd and 3rd centuries are examples in which the rings were openwork discs.[154]

The second type, a curb bit (or *Hebelstangentrense* in German), had an iron or bronze bit that functioned like a lever (type B). It comprised two long shanks that were linked in the middle and at one end by a bar placed at right angles. We can distinguish two variants. In the first (B1), the front bar is straight and the shanks terminate in loops on the reverse; in the second (B2), the bar features an omega-shaped loop, while the ends of the shanks have round loops. To make the bit more effective, the mouthpiece had spines or discs that pricked into the roof of the horse's mouth when the reins were pulled. Both types occurred from the Republican period onward, with type B1 falling out of favour in the course of the 1st century AD. Type B2 was probably used into the 3rd century.

Contemporaneous examples of the third type (type C) derived from both type-B variants. These too are characterised by either a straight (variant C1) or a loop-shaped bar (variant C2). Attached by rings to this was a simple, curved shank which ran under the horse's muzzle. Characteristic of variant C2 are links with a round and a rectangular loop for attaching the bit to the reins.

The fourth type, which was only used during the first half of the 1st century AD (type D), was of Roman origin.[155] Here the bits consist of a solid bar which, like the previous type, was attached to a semicircular shank. A characteristic feature is the way in which the bar and shank were linked: by means

[153] Lawson 1978, 154-157, Abb. 10; see also Hyland 1992.
[154] Garbsch 1986b.
[155] Lawson 1978, 157, Abb. 10.7; see Pirling 1986, Abb. 2.

46

of a central ring, usually with a round and rectangular loop on the outside. The straight bar went into the central hole, while the curved shank was attached to one of the rectangular or round loops. The remaining loops were for the reins.

With the exception of the curb bit, all types occur in the research region (pl. 50-52). There are two iron ring bits from Empel (82.88-89, pl. 50-51), a third from Dreumel (56.2, fig. 2.20) and a fourth, with bronze rings, from Wijchen (284.13, pl. 50). A bronze mouthpiece from Empel (82.90, pl. 51) probably comes from the same type of bit. A completely preserved iron example from a *tumulus* grave at Esch (87.2, pl. 51) can be ascribed to the 1st-century C1 type. An iron link with a rectangular and a round loop belonged to the less easily dated bit of the second variant (82.91, pl. 52), as probably did two bronze links in the shape of a figure eight (232.2, 296.2, pl. 52). Three round links with loops on the outside are characteristic of type D. An example from Wijk bij Duurstede (291.44, pl. 52) is decorated with concentric grooves and V-shaped indentations. A less easily identified end of a semicircular shank from the same site (291.42, pl. 51) may have been part of a type-C bit.

Chamfrons
During ceremonies and parades, the horse's head could be adorned with a leather chamfron (fig. 2.21).[156] At the eyes were round openings for bronze eyeguards, which were convex and fully openwork to enable the horse to see (type A). Another form of eye protection had a different, pointed shape (type B). The eyeguards of the second type were not part of the leather chamfron but were directly attached to the straps of the headgear. Both types were in use during the 1st and early 2nd century AD.

The subsequent period saw the introduction of a new type of chamfron (type C).[157] Although eyeguards were still used, from the 2nd century onward they were part of a chamfron constructed entirely of bronze. This chamfron comprised three hinged parts. The central piece passed over the horse's nose and was usually richly decorated with chasework images. On each side was a bronze plate covering the side of the head and featuring an openwork eyeguard. Chamfrons of this type persisted into the 3rd century.

Within the research region, a single bronze eyeguard of the first type has been recovered from the 'De Gouden Ham' dredge pit at Megen (193.1, fig. 2.21). The convex eyeguard features geometrical openwork motifs, with holes around the flat perimeter flange for attachment to a leather chamfron. The inventory does not include any parts of bronze chamfrons.

2.2.2 SADDLE

Connolly has used the archaeological record and images on grave reliefs to reconstruct the Roman saddle.[158] The saddle consisted of a leather-covered, wooden core with characteristic bronze 'horns' at each corner, designed to keep the rider in the saddle during battle, as stirrups were not yet known (fig. 2.19). The horned saddle was first used in the Republican period and remained in use throughout the Roman era.

Saddle fittings
Cavalry gravestones that portray the toga-clad deceased reclining on a couch (fig. 7.8) frequently include a second scene showing the cavalryman's horse. In contrast to depictions of triumphant cavalrymen, we

---

[156] Robinson 1975, 190-194; Junkelmann 1996, 79-84; see also Haalebos 1995, 92-93. Officers' horses could also be fitted with a chamfron.

[157] Especially Garbsch 1978, 13-14.

[158] Connolly 1986; see also Connolly/Van Driel-Murray 1991; for saddle horns, see Van Enkevort 1998/1999.

now see a long cloth under the saddle, draped with leather bands that are decorated with fittings. As with the chamfron, these decorative saddle elements were probably parade equipment.[159] Bishop distinguishes two types of saddle fitting – openwork fittings (type A) and those decorated with raised circles (type B).[160] The openwork fittings were used from the Augustan era until the beginning of the Flavian period.[161] Type-B fittings also occurred during the Claudio-Flavian period.

Over 60 decorative fittings come from the Rhine at Doorwerth.[162] In view of their size and their similarity to those depicted on grave reliefs, they will have been attached to saddle straps (55.114-173). The rectangular fittings are tinned on the front and decorated with chased circles. Several are openwork at the bottom to permit the attachment of leaf-shaped appliqués. Narrow, undecorated fittings with two or three large rivets occur in combination with these examples. Two rectangular, tinned and niello-inlay fittings can be ascribed to an as yet unknown type (type C). One narrow fitting was recovered at Houten (127.4, pl. 52), and a wider example at Halder (106.17, pl. 52).

2.2.3 GIRTHS

The girths are the leather constructions designed to keep the saddle in place. The various straps were joined together by buckles and strap junctions. In addition, decorative fittings, pendants and bells were added for decoration, while the hanging straps were reinforced with both functional and decorative terminals. Although the leatherwork is seldom preserved, it is usually possible to identify the function and dating of stray girth components from depictions on cavalry gravestones and several assemblages with more complete sets of horse gear.[163]

Fasteners
Various kinds of fasteners were used during the 1st century AD to make it easy to saddle the horse.[164] In the first type, a simple C-shaped buckle was attached to the plate (type A), while the second type featured a T-shaped hook (type B1), which could be fastened in a keyhole-shaped loop (type B2). A round, projecting knob served to fasten a third type (C). Although the fasteners show little variation, the plates of the different types can be broken down into five variants according to shape.[165] These are simple rectangular fittings (variant 1), waisted rectangular fittings (variant 2), single and double figure-eight fittings (variants 3-4) and ridged fittings (variant 5). The plates of the first two variants are usually tinned and inlaid with niello. In types B1 and C, the plate may be replaced by a round or triangular loop. Types B and C are known from the Augustan period, while type A occurred primarily in the second half of the 1st century.

A wide range of fasteners were also used in the 2nd and 3rd centuries.[166] Firstly, some of the smaller (ring) buckles may have been used for this purpose (type D). Also occurring are heart-shaped fittings terminating in a rectangular loop (type E). These were attached by an almond-shaped stud to one strap,

---

[159] Bishop 1988, 108-109.
[160] Bishop 1988, figs. 37-38.
[161] Deschler-Erb 1991, 35 (type A); Brouwer 1982, 163-164 (type B).
[162] Holwerda 1931; Brouwer 1982.
[163] See Bishop 1988, 68 ff. (monumental reliefs); Palágyi 1981; 1990; 1995; 1997 (grave assemblages). The chronology of the different girth components is based on securely dated items from army camps. For a survey of the available assemblages and their dating, see Lenz 2000, 11-12.
[164] See Brouwer 1982, Taf. 10 (type A-B); Bishop 1988, figs. 54-55 (type B); Wild 1970 (type C).
[165] See Bishop 1988, figs. 54-55.
[166] For types D and F, see Oldenstein 1976, Taf. 75-79; Palágyi 1990, Abb. 15-16; 1995, Abb. 3; 1997, figs. 6.70-71.

while a second strap was pulled through the rectangular opening and fastened with another stud. Finally, fasteners with a rectangular and a semicircular loop were used to link two straps (type F). This time, the straps were pulled through both loops and then fastened with studs. Characteristic of the type-F fasteners are the oblique edges.

Thirteen fittings with a hinge of a type-A buckle are documented in the research region (pl. 52-54). In a few instances, the C-shaped buckle is still present. Fourteen fittings can be classed as type B1 on the basis of the T-shaped hook, and six fittings and two stray loops as type B2. A simple hook from Tiel (242.3, pl. 53) is probably a variant of type B1. There are eight examples of fasteners with a round knob (type C). The fasteners generally have a rectangular plate, in some cases narrowing into a waisted shape. The T-shaped fastener from Lobith-'De Bijland' (176.10, pl. 53) has twisted silver wire inlaid around the perimeter of the rectangular plate. Also of exclusive design is a rectangular fitting with a hinge of a type-A buckle from Nijmegen (209.37, pl. 52). The front is tinned and decorated with dotted lines. For types B1 and C, the plate has been replaced four and five times respectively by a round, rectangular or triangular loop (pl. 53-54).

The grave finds from Esch (c. AD 150-200) show that buckles continued to be used in horse gear in the subsequent period.[167] The interred horse gear included a C-shaped buckle (87.3) and several decorative fittings. Heart-shaped fasteners with a rectangular loop are represented by six examples. In an ornate example from Wijk bij Duurstede-'De Geer' (288.46, pl. 54), the heart-shaped motif has been replaced by a pelta. Finally, three fasteners with a rectangular and semicircular loop functioned as strap fasteners. An example with two rectangular loops from Millingen aan de Rijn (198.1) can be assigned to the same type of fastener.

Strap junctions

A strap junction links the straps securing the saddle at front and back. The junctions found in the archaeological record can be broken down into three types. The first are 'ring junctions', comprising a solid bronze ring to which are attached three or four straps (type A).[168] Linking the ring and the straps is a bronze plate with a thickened loop terminating on the reverse in a narrow backplate. In general, the fittings have the same shapes as the fasteners (variants 1-5).[169] The only one that does not occur in the previous category of finds is the acorn shape (variant 6). Fittings of this variant are usually tinned and inlaid with niello. Only the rectangular and figure-eight plates already occurred in the Augustan period, with a wide and relatively short plate being typical of early examples of variant 1. The other variants were used as strap-junction components from the Claudian period onward.

The second type of strap junction is the '*phalera*', a decorative disc with a characteristic depressed centre and raised perimeter (type B). On the reverse are three or four rectangular fixing bars and/or round loops. Straps were passed through the bars, but were attached to the round loops in a similar fashion as with ring junctions. Characteristic of the strap fitting was the lack of a thickened loop. The front of the discs was tinned and sometimes decorated with niello-inlay vines, vine leaves, and bunches of grapes. In some cases a pendant was attached to the *phalera* (see below). *Phalera* junctions are characteristic of the Claudio-Neronian period.[170]

At the beginning of the 2nd century, the ring and *phalera* junctions were superseded by a new type of strap junction incorporating elements of the two previous types.[171] Although finds from the 2nd and 3rd

---

[167] Van den Hurk 1973, burial II.

[168] An example from Xanten shows that exclusive 'rings' also occur (Lenz 2000, Taf. 40, 384).

[169] See Bishop 1988, figs. 50-51.

[170] Brouwer 1982, 163-164; Deschler-Erb 2000, 385-386.

[171] See Oldenstein 1976, 234; compare Lehner 1923, Taf. IIIb (nr. 15); Massart 2000, figs. 7-8. This type appears to be derived from a combined ring and *phalera* junction (see Curle 1911, pl. LXXIV-6).

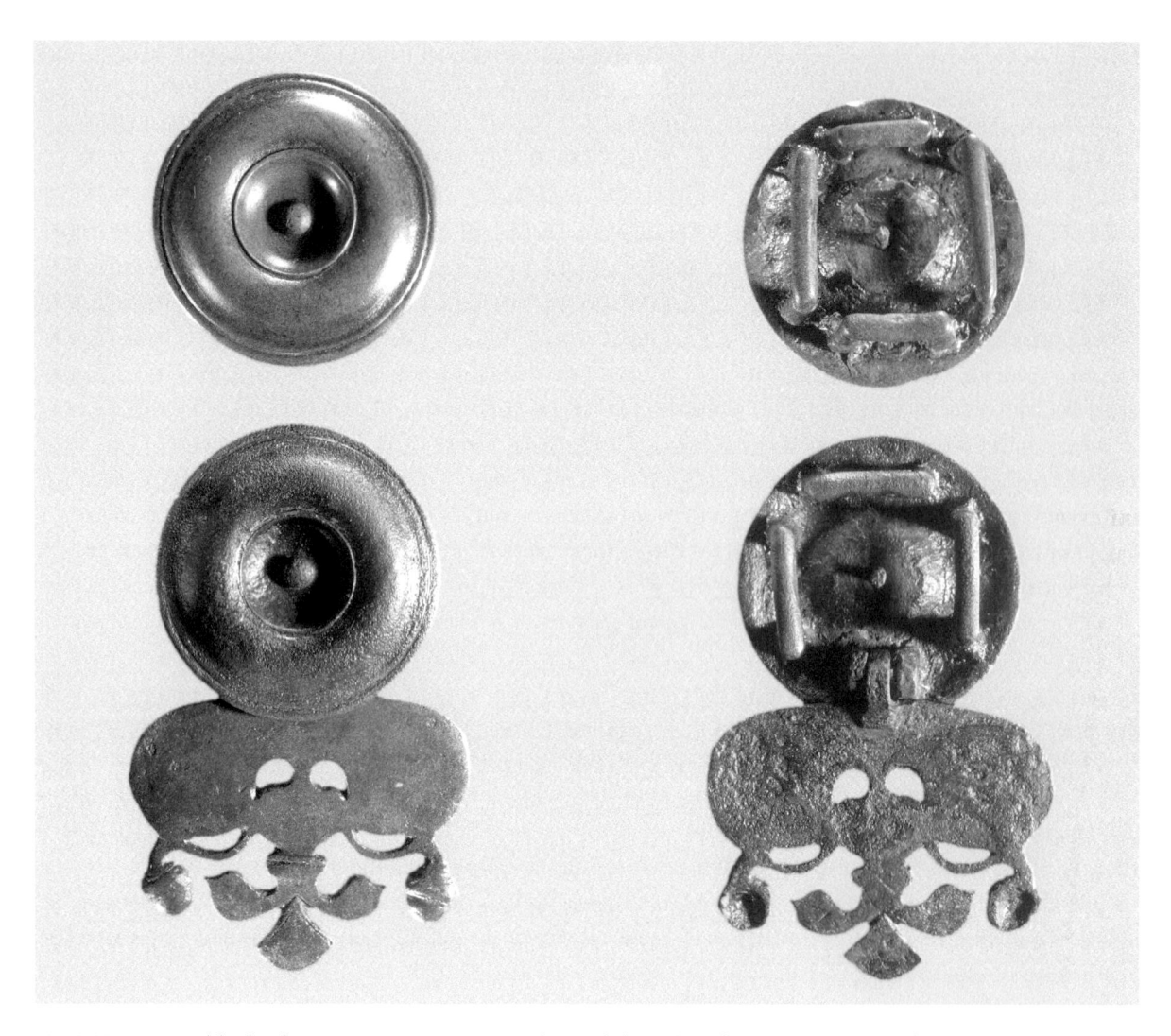

Fig. 2.22. Front and back of two strap junctions, one with a trefoil pendant, from the cult place of Empel-'De Werf' (above 82.127, below 82.128). Not to scale.

centuries are scarce, different examples show that the junction consisted of a round, generally openwork disc, with rectangular or round loops on the outside (type C). The harness straps were passed directly through these rectangular loops and fastened with studs. In the absence of loops, the straps were attached to the perimeter of the openwork ring.

Appearing at the same time were round examples, with four rectangular openings between the front and back plate to hold crossed straps (type D).[172] The simple junctions were undecorated. Types C and D fell into disuse at the end of the 3rd century, at which point strap junctions disappear from the finds.

A large number of ring junctions are known from the eastern Rhine delta. Together with five complete examples, these comprise 81 stray strap fittings (pl. 55-58).[173] Although all types are represented in the

[172] See Palágyi 1997, figs. 6.70, 6.73.
[173] This is the *minimum* number because only fittings with a distinct loop are assigned to this category; some of the fragmentary decorative fittings (see below) will also have belonged to strap junctions. Because bronze rings could be used for different purposes, stray rings have not been included in the study.

finds, figure-eight examples (variant 3: 40x) predominate, and to a lesser extent rectangular ones (variant 1: 19x). There are no distinctively Augustan pieces. Six fittings have a different shape, and in one instance a disc replaces the bronze ring (48.3, pl. 58). A figure-eight example from Houten (128.6, pl. 57) has no central ring; the plates are linked directly to one another. A total of 26 *phalera* junctions feature among the finds (pl. 59), most of them from the assemblage dredged up at Doorwerth (55.73-87, fig. 5.11). In addition to pendants, some *phalerae* have a T-shaped fastener attached. Less exclusive in design are two matching *phalera* junctions from Empel-'De Werf' (82.127-128, pl. 59, fig. 2.22), in one instance with a trefoil pendant. The *phalera* has been replaced by a convex front plate in an example from Wijk bij Duurstede (291.71, pl. 59).

The strap junctions from the 2nd and 3rd centuries are less well-represented (pl. 60). Five round junctions with pelta, vulva and other openwork motifs belong to type C. Only one junction from IJzendoorn (138.17, pl. 60) features loops on the outside, to which the strap fittings are still attached. One variant of this type is an openwork, peltate example with three rectangular loops from Elst (79.17, pl. 60), as is an example from Nijmegen (208.21, pl. 60), which is made up of one triangular and two round loops. Finally, two strap junctions can be ascribed to type D. A gilded example from Ophemert (226.6, pl. 60) consists of round front and back plates joined by four rivets. In a cruciform example from Waardenburg (269.8), the corners are not joined by plates, but by means of cross brackets.

Strap terminals
Strap terminals are a third component of the harness straps. A strap was often left dangling as a decorative element at the junction of two or three straps. A bronze terminal would be attached at the bottom to prevent the strap from curling. It comprised a plate terminating at the base in a round or ridged knob (type A), with a tongue on the reverse that could be curved around the strap. The different variants and their dating are similar to that of the strap-junction fittings (variants 1-6).[174]

Although loops at the bottom of strap junctions point to the presence of hanging straps in the 2nd and 3rd centuries, few strap terminals are known from this period. Openwork examples (type B) once again became characteristic.[175]

Strap terminals, like the other harness components, are a common category of finds in non-military contexts in the research region. Of the examples in the inventory, 40 can be ascribed to the 1st-century type (pl. 61-62). Once again, we find the different types represented, with rectangular examples (variant 1: 19x) now predominant. The presence of a short strap terminal from Oosterhout (222.118, pl. 61), with a wider section at the base, means that the Augustan period is also represented in the finds.[176] Two figure-eight examples from the River Waal at Nijmegen (211.72-73, pl. 61) terminate in a heart and rosette motif; together with two ring junctions (211.60-61, pl. 56) and a decorative fitting (211.64, pl. 64), these were part of the same, exclusive set of horse gear. The same applies to six identical strap terminals from the Rhine at Doorwerth (55.108-113), to which a *phalera*-shaped disc is attached. The strap terminals and *phalerae* are tinned and inlaid with niello.

An openwork, peltate example (306.1, pl. 62) from an unknown site in the research region belongs to the following period. Its basic shape is almost identical to that of the strap junction from Elst (79.17, pl. 60). An openwork example with a trumpet-shaped motifs from Est (89.1, pl. 62) can be placed in the same period.

---

[174] For a survey of types, see Bishop 1988, table 8, figs. 52-53.
[175] See Lehner 1923, Taf. IIIb (nr. 14).
[176] Compare Franzius 1995, Abb. 8 (nr. 8).

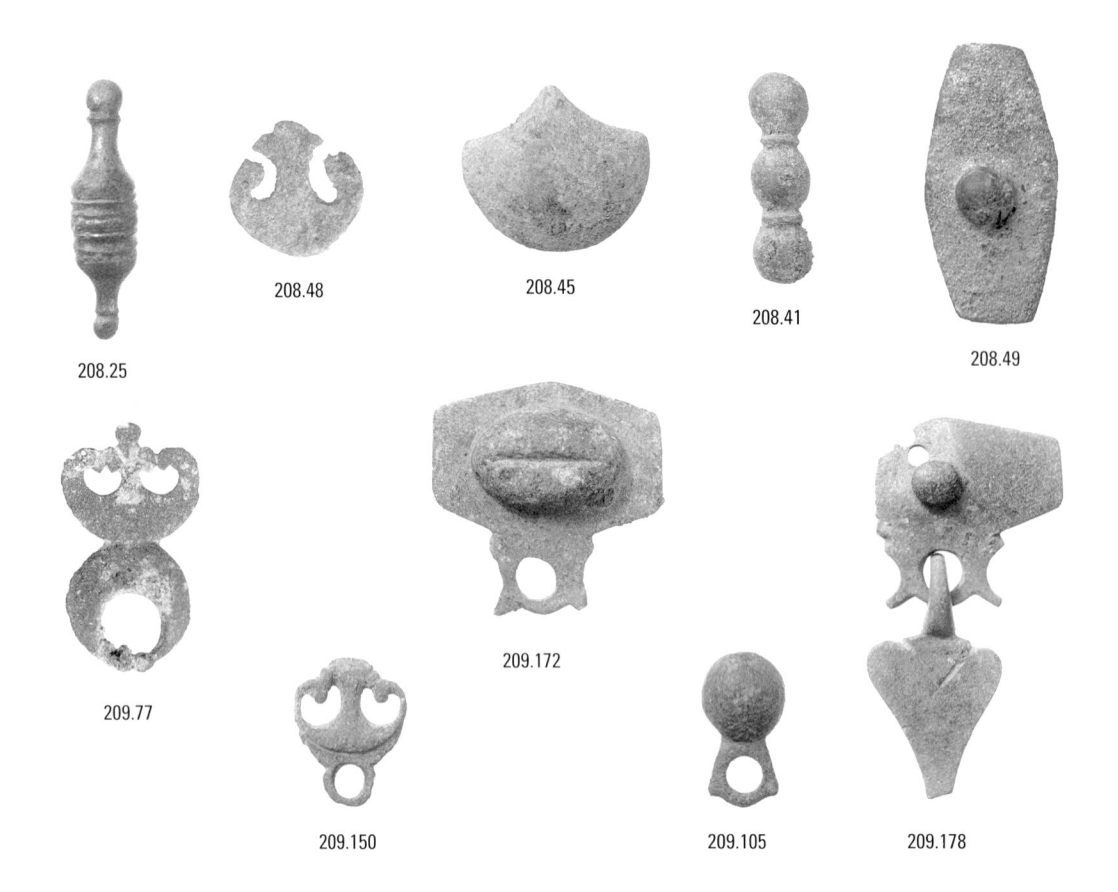

Fig. 2.23. Decorative harness fittings from the urban centres of *oppidum Batavorum* (site nr. 208) and Ulpia Noviomagus Batavorum (site nr. 209) at Nijmegen. The numbering refers to the database. Scale 1:1. Photos: Gemeente Nijmegen, Bureau Archeologie.

Decorative fittings

This category of finds comprises fittings whose primary function was decorative. In the 2nd and 3rd centuries, they may also have been used to attach straps to fasteners (types E-F) or strap junctions (type C). These fittings, which occur in a wide variety of shapes, can be broken down into two chronologically distinct groups, based on the method of fastening.[177]

The first group comprises fittings with one or more simple fixing prongs at the back (type A). To attach the fitting, the prongs were pushed through the leather and fastened on the reverse with washers or narrow backplates. This aspect is of chronological significance because washers and backplates occurred only from the 1st to the early 2nd century.[178] The repertoire of plate types corresponds in part to that of the contemporaneous fasteners, strap junctions and strap terminals (variants 1-6). The acorn-shaped, figure-eight and rectangular fittings could now also be made up of dual, mirrored elements. A further shape that we encounter among other harness components is the tinned *phalera* (variant 7), which is usually decorated with niello. Some of the decorative mounts are executed in other shapes, with the following customary variants:[179]

8. Lozenge-shaped fittings with an undecorated, flat front plate.
9. Round fittings, usually with tinning and niello inlay. The front may feature a phallic appliqué.

---

[177] Fittings designed for wood, characterised by rivets with a square cross-section, are not considered here.

[178] Fittings for buckles, strap junctions and terminals from this period were fastened with similar fixing prongs.

[179] Based partly on Bishop 1988, table 11, fig. 56; Deschler-Erb 1999a, 62-63.

10. Round fittings with four round knobs around the outside. A suspended *lunula*, a round loop or a hinge may replace one of the knobs.
11. Peltate fittings with half-moon or bean-shaped openings. The front may be inlaid with comb-shaped niello strips.
12. Rectangular fittings with round knobs at each end, some featuring a lunula on one of the long sides. The fittings may be inlaid with niello, the lunula with niello or enamel.
13. Male genitalia fittings with an erect phallus.
14. Elongated, oval or almond-shaped fittings with rosette knobs. The oval fittings may be characterised by a central rib and the almond-shaped examples by a multi-faceted dome.
15. Rectangular fittings with a hinge on one of the long sides. Niello may be added.
16. Heart-shaped fittings.
17. Lunate fittings.

Variants 1, 3, 8 and 9 were used by the Roman cavalry from the Augustan period onward, while the remaining fittings appeared in the late Augustan/Tiberian (variants 2 and 13) or Claudio-Flavian period (the remainder). *Phalera*-shaped examples and decoration with niello were particularly prevalent in the Claudio-Neronian period.

Characteristic of the second group are fixing prongs with a fixed, mushroom-shaped stud (type B). As with modern buttons, fastening occurred by pushing the stud through a slit in the leather. According to Oldenstein, decorative fittings with this type of fastener occurred from the mid-2nd to the mid-3rd centuries, while Gschwind demonstrates that they continued in use until well into the 3rd century.[180] In general, it is not possible to date the fittings from this period more precisely. Those with one or more studs can be divided into the following variants:[181]

1. Round and oval fittings, the larger examples of which may be openwork.
2. Round and oval fittings inlaid with enamel.
3. Round, rosette fittings.
4. Mushroom-shaped fittings with a central dome and a flat or slightly curved flange, often decorated with an incised line.
5. Shell-shaped fittings, some of them ridged. A loop for a pendant may be present.
6. Rectangular or square fittings that may be decorated with ridges or enamel. Some of the square fittings feature a pyramidal centre.
7. Lozenge-shaped fittings, some inlaid with enamel.
8. 'Shield fittings' with concave long sides and usually oblique edges. The front may be decorated with enamel.
9. Peltate fittings, simpler in design than variant A11. The plate may comprise various pelta motifs and be inlaid with enamel. In some cases, the pelta is made up of two stylised dolphins. Round fittings, comprising two mirrored peltas, also belong to this variant.
10. Almond-shaped fittings, some of them vulvate owing to the presence of a central rib.
11. Almond-shaped fittings with oblate ends, some with ridged ends.
12. Elongated, rectangular fittings with ribbed, semicircular or flat ends. One of the long sides or ends may feature a loop for a pendant.
13. Elongated, ridged fittings. These occur in a wide range of forms.
14. Winged fittings, narrow at the waist and widening to a rosette or V-shape at each end.
15. Decorative fittings made up of trumpet-shaped motifs. These occur in a wide range of forms.
16. Lunate fittings with spherical arms terminating at the bottom in two round knobs.
17. Vulvate fittings with a hexagonal base and a central, coffee-bean-shaped dome. This vulva motif

---

[180] Oldenstein 1976, 165 ff.; Gschwind 1998.   [181] Based partly on Oldenstein 1976, 136-142, 165 ff.

may be replaced by a central dome, and one of the long or short sides may feature a loop for a pendant.
18. Phallic fittings, similar to examples from the previous period.
19. Flat, heart-shaped fittings with a characteristic almond-shaped or hexagonal stud.
20. Domed tear-shaped fittings.

Decorative fittings are a find category frequently found in the research region. A total of 396 such fittings come from the 1st century (pl. 63-69, fig. 2.23), with the most common variants being rectangular (variant 1-2: 102x), figure-eight (variant 3: 53x), *phalera*-shaped (variant 7: 45x) and round fittings (variant 9: 74x) (fig. 6.8). Unusual variants include a large example shaped like a vine leaf (152.2, pl. 69) and a hexagonal one bearing a panther's head in high relief (181.5, pl. 69). Some fittings have no rivets on the reverse, but were fastened to the girth straps by a separate rivet. A leaf-shaped mount from Nijmegen (209.85, pl. 69) has an alternative method of fastening, namely with split pins. Distinctly early pieces are absent from the material. In view of their form and niello decoration (variant 7), some of the finds can be placed specifically in the Claudio-Neronian period (55x).

Decorative fittings from the subsequent period are represented by no less than 739 finds (pl. 70-80, fig. 2.23). In addition to round and oval examples, some of which are inlaid with enamel (variants 1-2: 227x), other frequently occurring mounts feature pelta (variant 9: 99x), almond-shaped (variant 10: 61x), trumpet-shaped (variant 15: 30x), and vulva motifs (variant 17: 85x) (fig. 6.8). Some fittings cannot be ascribed to a specific variant. These include those in the shape of a swastika (222.116, pl. 80 and 284.41), a human face (228.16, pl. 80), a lion's head (269.33, pl. 80) and a Mediterranean cicada (19.2 and 100.39, pl. 80).

Looped strap mounts
A looped strap mount is a decorative element with one or two rectangular fixing bars on the reverse through which a leather strap can simply be inserted. This horse gear component can be divided into two main groups. The first consists of *phalerae* which, given the presence of only one or two fixing bars, had a decorative function (type AA).[182] These Claudio-Neronian decorative discs are often tinned and inlaid with niello. As with the *phalera* strap junctions, a pendant may be attached to the *phalera*. The presence of a central rivet shows that this type of looped strap mount may have adorned both horizontal and vertical straps.

The second group comprises looped strap mounts whose front plates display considerable variation. The absence of a central rivet to keep the fitting in place suggests that these decorative elements were generally mounted on horizontal straps. To some extent, the same variants occur as with the contemporaneous decorative fittings, permitting us to retain a corresponding division and dating (types A and B, with variants). In contrast to decorative fittings, we are unable to distinguish between the two types on the basis of method of fastening. We therefore cannot attribute with certainty to the 1st or 2nd/3rd centuries any types that do not occur among the decorative fittings.

The majority of *phalerae* from the assemblage of Doorwerth can be classified as belonging to the group of looped strap mounts (55.7-66, fig. 5.11). The reverse features one or two loops, while the front is tinned and inlaid with niello. In addition to four examples from Empel-'De Werf' (82.106, 108-110, pl. 81) and two from Nijmegen (209.41-42), 12 single stray finds are known (pl. 81). Four *phalerae* have a hinge at the back for a pendant.

---

[182] Bishop 1988, fig. 41, types 1-2e.

A total of 62 type-A and type-B looped strap mounts have been recovered (pl. 82-84). Judging by their shape, 19 can be dated to the 1st century AD. The largest group is made up of round strap mounts decorated with knobs (variant A 10: 8x). A different kind, which was suspended from a strap, has a semi-almond shape, (4.1, pl. 82). Forty-four strap mounts belong to the subsequent period, including a relatively large number of ridged examples (variant 13: 12x). Identical strap mounts from Grave (103.1) and Wijchen (284.16, pl. 84) are fashioned into a bearded face. An exceptional example is a solid strap mount, consisting of a vine leaf with a wild boar's head in high relief (5.3, pl. 84). Given the position of the loop, we can deduce that an example with a stylised lion's head once embellished a hanging strap (269.10, pl. 83). The fronts of some strap mounts feature a solid, round loop, whose function is unknown. For 19 strap mounts, we are unable to determine on typological grounds whether they belong to type A or B. This applies mainly to the simple, round examples.

Pendants

In addition to strap fittings and loops, pendants were often used to adorn horse gear. Like the decorative fittings, the pendants can be divided into two chronological groups based on form, method of suspension and decoration. The dating of the first group corresponds roughly to the 1st century AD, while the second group can be placed in the 2nd and 3rd centuries. Some pendants from the first group (type A) were attached with a small, round loop to the hinge of a *phalera* (variants 1-2). Also occurring are pendants with a simple, loop-shaped loop that is turned either forwards or backwards (variant 3-8, 10). These pendants could be attached directly to the leather by a simple fitting.[183] The phallic pendants (variant 9) are a different group again. They feature a large, round loop and were probably fastened with a narrow leather thong.

We can distinguish the following variants among the type-A pendants:[184]

1. Trefoil pendants, consisting of a central leaf with an outward-curving leaf on each side. The central leaf is thicker in the finer examples. Niello work is a common form of decoration.
2. Winged pendants with a basic oval shape, terminating at the base in a rosette knob. Decorative motifs may be added in the form of dotted lines.
3. Winged pendants with a loop-shaped loop terminating at the front in a stylised duck or goose head
4. Oval pendants, often with an openwork pelta or rosette motif at the base.
5. Single-leaf pendants. The front may be decorated with dotted lines. These occur in a wide range of forms.
6. Peltate pendants consisting of a tear- or heart-shaped body with two openings along the upper edge.
7. Round, oval or tear-shaped pendants, some of which are decorated with concentric ridges and grooves.
8. Lunate pendants with flat, suspended arms that may terminate in round knobs. A small, tear-shaped pendant is usually attached inside the lunula.
9. Phallic pendants, with the ends of the phallus pointing either up or down. The larger examples may feature tear-shaped pendants.
10. Lancet- and lozenge-shaped pendants, terminating in a round or biconical knob.

Only the lunate and phallic pendants were in use during the Augustan period.[185] The late Augustan/Tiberian period also saw the appearance of variants 1-3 and 8, with the first three predominating in the

---

[183] See Deschler-Erb 1999a, 58, Taf. 32 (nrs. 626-638).

[184] Based partly on Bishop 1988, table 6, figs. 43-49; Deschler-Erb 1999a, 49-58.

[185] For a survey of the datings, see Deschler-Erb 1999a, 49-58.

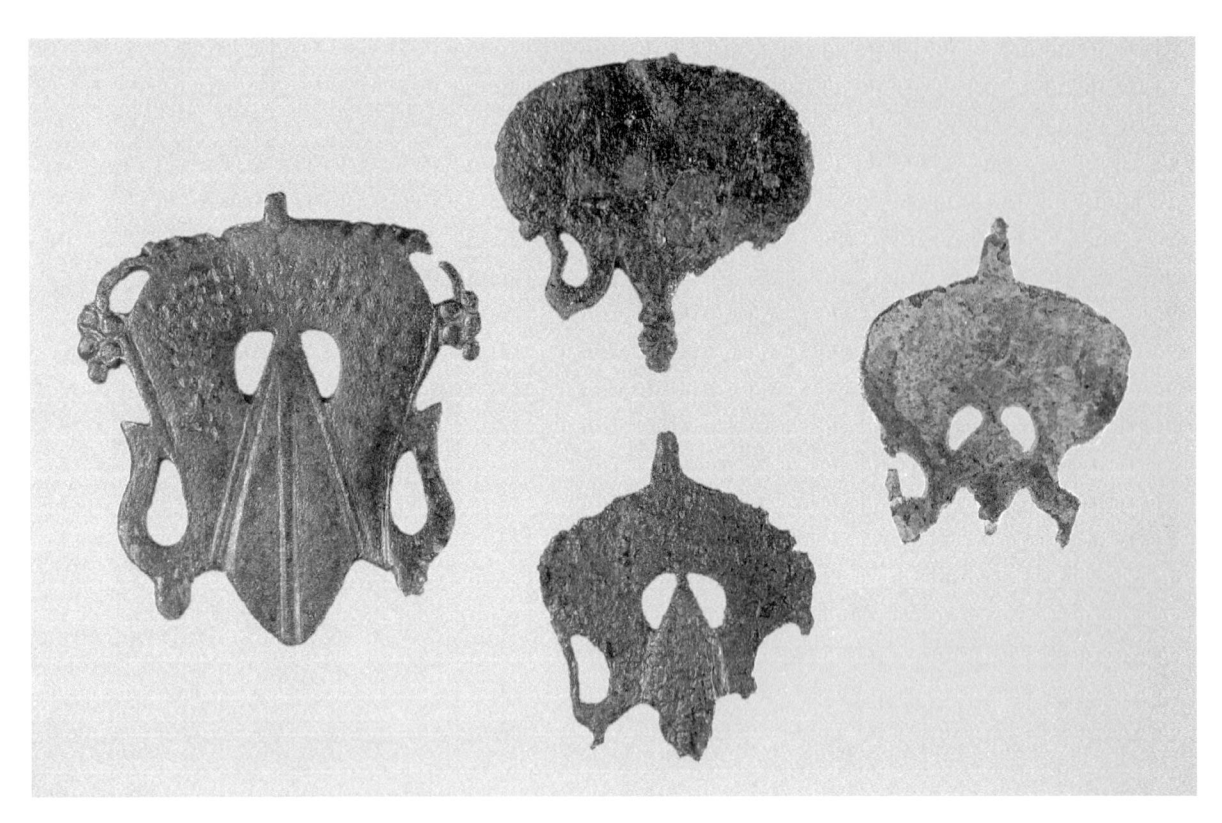

Fig. 2.24. Four trefoil harness pendants from the rural settlement of Wijk bij Duurstede-'De Horden' (left 291.53, bottom 291.54, right 291.59, top 291.60). Not to scale.

Claudio-Neronian period. The Claudian period is the earliest date for the remaining variants, which superseded the late Augustan/Tiberian pendants during the Flavian period at the latest. These more recent pendants disappeared from use at the beginning of the 2nd century. Only the peltate, lunate and phallic pendants continued in a modified form as a component of Roman horse gear.

Although loop-shaped loops still occurred regularly, pendants from the second group (type B) generally had closed, round loops. As with the decorative fittings, it is not possible in typological terms to date pendants from this period more precisely than to the 2nd and 3rd centuries. The decorative elements can be broken down into the following variants on the basis of their form:[186]
1. Round, oval and tear-shaped pendants.
2. Heart-shaped pendants with a peltate openwork upper part.
3. Heart-shaped pendants, terminating at the base in a phallic motif.
4. Phallic pendants with a large, round loop. For some of the pendants, a hole in the wider central part replaces the loop. Some are testicular pendants with a forward-pointing phallus, often also featuring a human head and shoulders.
5. Lunate pendants, with the arms of the lunula turned inward and terminating in round knobs.
6. Solid, acorn-shaped pendants.
7. Openwork peltate, drop- and heart-shaped pendants, usually with a round or rosette terminal knob.

[186] Based partly on Oldenstein 1976, 124-139, 158-164.

Fig. 2.25. Three bronze horse bells from the rural settlement of Rumpt-'De Worden' (from left to right 257.5, 4, 6). Not to scale.

A total of 101 pendants can be assigned to type A (pl. 85-90). Most are tinned trefoil pendants, usually inlaid with niello (38x), including eight exclusive items that may have been awarded as *dona militaria* (fig. 2.24). Two pendants of this variant from Arnhem (15.10, pl. 86) and Tiel (242.30, pl. 86) differ from the usual shape and are executed in openwork scrolls. A pendant from Ewijk bears the ownership inscription of a cavalryman from the *legio Hispana* (93.13, pl. 85). The remaining variants are also represented in the finds. Apart from round, oval and tear-shaped pendants (variant 7: 16x), these are primarily phallic (variant 9: 12x), leaf-shaped (variant 5: 9x) and lunate examples (variant 8: 8x) (fig. 6.10). Exceptions are a winged pendant of a hitherto unknown large size (158.1, pl. 87), a richly ornamented lunate pendant terminating in two eagle's heads (83.1, pl. 89) and a phallic pendant with a central bull's head, with a glass eye still in situ (211.54, pl. 89). Two pendants fall outside the usual variants, while four finds are too fragmentary to be ascribed to any one specific variant.

From the subsequent period, 95 pendants are documented (pl. 90-93), with the phallus (variant 4: 26x), heart-phallus (variant 3: 19x) and lunula (variant 5: 17x) being the most frequent motifs (fig. 6.10). A large, hanging phallus from Rumpt (257.10, pl. 92) is the only one made of lead. A damaged pendant from the River Waal at Nijmegen (211.58, pl. 93) is an unknown variant.

Bronze bells
Various finds from auxiliary camps, particularly the large numbers from a cavalry camp on the 'Kops Plateau' at Nijmegen, tell us that bronze bells were also part of the trappings for a horse.[187] The following types of bell were used by the cavalry during the Roman period:

---

[187] Van Enkevort/Zee 1996, 37.

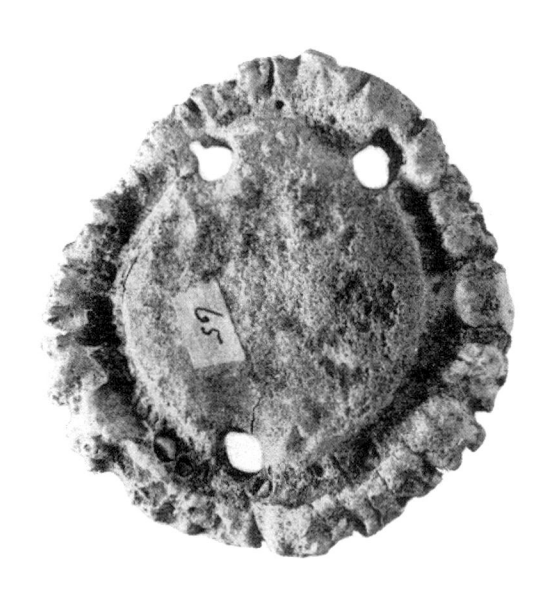

Fig. 2.26. Bone 'amulet' from the Waal at Nijmegen (211.75). Scale 1:1. After Hottentot/Van Lith 1990, Abb. 10 (nr. 21).

A. Tall bells with an oval cross-section, a concave central part and a rectangular loop.
B. Hemispherical bells with a round cross-section and a lozenge-shaped loop. The outside is usually tinned, and the shoulder and body may feature two or more grooves.
C. Tall, conical bells with a rounded, square cross-section and a lozenge-shaped loop. The corners on the bottom rim are thicker or feature tear-shaped knobs. The exterior may be tinned.
D. Conical bells with a rectangular cross-section and a rounded, lozenge-shaped loop. The bottom rim may feature a slight dome at the corners.
E. Conical bells with a faceted shoulder and a round loop.

The types of bell described above can be divided into two chronological groups based on dateable finds from military posts. Types A-B and C are known from the Augustan and late Augustan/Tiberian period onwards respectively, while the other two types can be dated to the 2nd and 3rd centuries. Only type B, without grooves, continues to occur for some time in combination with the later types. As with the other categories of horse gear, no new types are known from the 4th and 5th centuries. However, the assemblage containing the late Roman guard helmet from Deurne shows that bronze bells, which belong typologically in the 2nd and 3rd centuries, may have remained in use for some time.[188]

Seventy-nine bronze bells are documented from non-military contexts in the research region (pl. 94-95, fig. 2.25). Some are well preserved, with the iron clapper still in place. The majority of bells date from the 1st century (58x). Type B is particularly well-represented, with 37 examples. Of types A and B, 14 and 7 bells respectively have been recovered. A fragmentary bell could have belonged to either type. The loop of a large type-A bell from the River Waal at Nijmegen (212.6, pl. 94) bears the number *IV*. Significantly fewer bells – just 17 examples – come from the subsequent period, with nine belonging to type D and eight to type E.

Bone 'amulets'
Bone 'amulets' are a find category that is frequently associated with horse gear. The name 'amulet' is linked to the protective function attributed to these objects.[189] We can distinguish two types: those made of antler and those made of wild boar's teeth.

The first type consists of round discs cut from the base of a red-deer antler (type A) (fig. 6.9).[190] The bone discs can be broken down into four variants, depending on the ornamentation: examples depicting a phallus (variant 1), a V-shaped vulva motif (variant 2), a burnished dome (variant 3) and a smooth, undecorated front (variant 4). Problematical in the interpretation of these objects is the fact that several

---

[188] Braat et al. 1973, 62, Taf. 22, nrs. 1, 3 (type-D bells).
[189] See chapter 6.3.3.
[190] Hottentot/Van Lith 1990; Greep 1994.

examples show remains of iron and bronze rivets, while the presence of lime residue on an example from London indicates that it had been affixed to a wall.[191] Depictions on cavalry gravestones suggest, however, that some will have been horse gear components (fig. 6.13). These decorative discs, which were probably worn on the horse's chest, continued in use during the Roman period.[192]

In addition to round examples, there are lunate 'amulets', with two boar's teeth forming the arms of the lunula (type B).[193] The teeth are mounted in a bronze holder with two suspension loops. Like the round examples, these pendants were probably worn on the horse's chest. This type occurred until the 3rd century, but is known above all from the 1st century AD.

The only bone 'amulet' from a non-military context in the research region is of the first type. It is an undecorated antler disc with three holes around the perimeter, from the River Waal at Nijmegen (211.75, fig. 2.26).

Spurs

Although not strictly speaking belonging to horse gear, spurs are nevertheless directly related to horse riding. The spurs consisted of a U-shaped or semicircular shank that could be attached by a leather strap to the back of each shoe. In the centre of the curve was a prick for spurring the horse on. Roman spurs can be divided into three chronologically distinct types on the basis of the method of fastening.

Type-A spurs were rather narrow and U-shaped, encircling the entire heel and terminating in rectangular, out-turned loops.[194] This type is known from the Augustan period onward and was still being used in the 1st century AD.

The 2nd and 3rd centuries saw the introduction of semicircular spurs in which the rectangular loops were replaced by out-turned, mushroom-shaped (type B1) and T-shaped knobs (type B2). In addition, the ends could simply be curved outwards (type B3). The spurs had a largish, domed prick. Often, however, the actual spur was replaced by a short fitting attached by studs to a leather strap (type C).[195]

Spurs which once again fully encircled the heel are characteristic of the late Roman period (type C).[196] The shanks were of unequal length and terminated in round rivet plates. A third arm with a round rivet plate or a projecting loop is attached at the prick on the top. We can distinguish two variants within this group. In the oldest variant, in use from about 300, the round or semicircular rivet plate was roughly as wide as the shank (D1). This variant was supplanted in about the mid-4th century by a similar version whose rivet plates were twice as wide as the shank (D2). This variant occurred until the end of the 4th century.

The 1st-century type includes a complete spur from Wijk bij Duurstede (291.115, pl. 96) and the fragment of a second example from Buren (40.3, pl. 96). In both cases the U-shaped shank terminates in narrow, rectangular loops. A crudely made spur from Houten (133.2, pl. 69), decorated with grooves, probably belongs to the same period. Three fittings made up of circles date from the 2nd and 3rd centuries. The examples from Kerk-Avezaath (156.1, pl. 96) and Tiel (242.106, pl. 96) were attached by rivets and studs, while the plate from Empel (82.205, pl. 96) has a round loop to hook it to the iron shanks. Belonging to the same period are two stray spur pricks, one with a large, round foot and the other with a square foot (2.5, 11.10, pl. 96). A semicircular spur from the Lek at Hagestein may be a late Roman example (105.11, pl. 96). Although the shanks are not of unequal length, the round rivet plates are characteristic of this period. It is probably an example of type C2.

---

[191] Hottentot/Van Lith 1990, 188; see also Haalebos 1994c, 705.
[192] Deschler-Erb 1991, 32; Greep (1994, 86) places these objects in the 1st and 2nd centuries AD.
[193] Kemkes/Scheuerbrandt 1997, 44, fig. 48.
[194] See Deschler-Erb 1999a, 66.
[195] For types B and C, see Jahn 1921, especially Taf. I.
[196] Keller 1969; Giesler 1978.

2.3 PHASING AND HISTORICAL CONTEXT

The different weapon types and horse gear components can be grouped on typological grounds into four periods, each characterised by a standard set of weaponry and horse gear of more or less uniform design.[197] Given that changes to military equipment – weaponry, the belt and baldric, as well as horse gear – appear to have been systematically introduced at specific times in the Roman era, we can assume a link to different stages of Roman military history that are evident in Germania Inferior and elsewhere. For each period I will outline the historical context, the characteristic equipment and the extent to which we can identify the different military units (the legions versus the auxiliary, infantrymen versus cavalry) on the basis of their equipment.

Period 1 (c. 50-12 BC): Caesar's conquests
When Caesar subjected Gaul between 57 and 50 BC, his army was largely made up of auxiliary troops, in addition to the legions. The supply of native warriors for the auxiliary arose out of treaties with tribes that had been conquered by Rome or were allied to Rome.[198] The earliest auxiliary troops were probably akin to local warrior groups, comprising noble leaders and their *Gefolgschaft*, who will have joined the Roman army as temporary detachments.[199]

The distinction between the regular legions and these irregular auxiliary units was also reflected in their armaments. Because legionary soldiers were supplied with weapons by the army, we see a high degree of standardisation.[200] Legionaries wore Buggenum type helmets, chain mail or scale armour and carried a large, oval shield, together with a *gladius Hispaniensis*, a dagger and a *pilum*.

Little is known about the arms of the earliest auxiliaries. Given their irregular, temporary nature, it seems likely that they were largely responsible for their own weaponry. Interesting here are the weapon finds from cut-off loops of the Rhine at Xanten-'Wardt' and the River Meuse at Kessel-Lith. In both cases, in addition to weapons from the late La Tène period, Roman equipment from the 1st century AD has been recovered. In Xanten-'Wardt', these older finds comprise swords and spearheads, and in Kessel-Lith, a helmet appliqué (164.2, pl. 3), swords and accompanying scabbards (163.3-7, 164.17-21, pl. 1-2), spearheads (163.8, 164.26-28, pl. 3) and horse gear components (164.36, 40, pl. 4).[201] Some of the swords from Kessel-Lith are of the Lower-Rhine Kessel type and can be specifically dated to La Tène D2 (c. 50-15 BC), the period of the earliest auxiliaries.[202] Given the dating, and assuming that these non-Roman weapons were associated with native warriors, we can probably identify them as the weaponry of the earliest, as yet irregular, auxiliary units.[203] What we do know for certain is that almost no Roman equipment occurred in the first period.

Period 2 (c. 12 BC – AD 120): reorganisation of the army under Augustus
The early 1st century AD saw far-reaching changes in military equipment, most likely associated with Augustus' (27 BC – AD 14) sweeping reforms aimed primarily at the auxiliary troops. These were trans-

---

[197] Compare Bishop/Coulston 1993; in my view, the further subdivision proposed by Lenz (2000, 14) is unrealistic as the dating of the different groups of finds is not precise enough for this purpose.

[198] For the history of the auxiliary troops, see Wolters 1990, 109 ff.; Roymans 1996, 20-22.

[199] See chapter 7.1.

[200] For the acquisition of weapons by Roman soldiers, see chapter 5.2.1.

[201] Xanten: Schalles/Schreiter 1993, cat.nrs. Mil 22-26, 34-35, 39, 43-45; Kessel-Lith: see chapter 3.3.4.

[202] Verwers/Ypey 1975; Roymans 2004, 108-112. See also chapter 7.1.

[203] For the interpretation of late La Tène weapons as the possession of native warriors, see chapter 7.1.

formed into regular units – the *cohortes peditata* and *equitata alae* – which thereafter became a standard feature of the Roman army.[204]

One consequence of the remodelling of these former occasional groupings into regular *auxilia* is that they were then equipped with some of the same weapons as the legions. The chief evidence for this is the weapon finds in early Roman graves, from the Middle Rhine region in particular, which – given the native origin of this tradition – compel us to link them with auxiliary soldiers (table 2.1).[205] Although the precise dating of most graves is problematical, the Mainz type *gladius* from the Augustan weapon grave at Someren attests in any case to the use of Roman weaponry by auxiliary troops from the early 1st century onward.[206] This picture is confirmed by numerous finds in 1st-century auxiliary camps of weapons traditionally regarded as characteristic of the legions. These are Kalkriese type plate armour, Mainz type *gladii* and *pila*.[207]

At the same time, however, the equipment of legionary and auxiliary foot soldiers continued to display distinct differences. Whereas legionaries wore helmets of the Hagenau type and carried the characteristic, oval or rectangular legionary shield, the auxiliaries were fitted with Weisenau type helmets and a smaller, predominantly oval shield. In addition, grave finds of non-Roman weaponry show that, on an incidental basis, auxiliaries continued to be equipped with some of their own weapons until the mid-1st century AD.[208]

Like the infantry, the cavalry was probably outfitted quite rapidly with 'Roman' equipment in the 1st century. They carried a long sword that combined elements of the native *spatha* and the Roman *gladius*,

site	weapon type	dating
Someren	Mainz type *gladius*	Augustan
Conflance (F)	masked helmet	first half 1st century
Neeritter	Mainz type *gladius*	pre-Flavian
Wederath (B)	Mainz type *gladius* (2x)	mid-1st century
Septfontaines (L)	*gladius*	mid-1st century
Weiler (B)	Weiler type helmet	mid-1st century
Hellingen (L)	masked helmet	mid-1st century
Maasbree	*gladius*	1st century
Haldern (G)	*gladius*	1st century
Köln-Marienburg (G)	*gladius*	1st century
Temse (B)	*gladius*	1st century
Koblenz-Bubenheim (G)	Weiler type helmet	second half 1st century

Table. 2.1. Sword and helmet finds from 1st-century weapon graves in Germania Inferior and Northern Gaul (after Roymans 1996, appendices 1-2)

[204] For a discussion on the regular/irregular nature of 1st-century auxiliary troops, see Kraft 1951, 35 ff.; Alföldy 1968, 87; Holder 1980, 5-13; Wolters 1990, 109 ff.; Waurick 1994, 23. In view of their name and function in frontier defence, it is highly unlikely that there continued to be temporary *Gefolgschaft*-like units following the Augustan reorganisation. Compare Aarts (2003), who associates the frequent occurrence of Augustan and later Roman coins in rural settlements in the northern frontier zone with payments to regular auxiliary soldiers.

[205] Waurick (1994) mentions several examples. For the attribution of grave inventories to deceased auxiliary soldiers, see chapter 5.3.5.

[206] Roymans/Kortlang 1993, 32-36.

[207] For the attribution of these weapons to legionaries, see for example Bishop/Coulston 1993, 206-209.

[208] See the examples mentioned by Waurick (1994).

a lance and several throwing spears. Their defensive weapons consisted of a Weiler type helmet, a smallish shield, and chain mail and scale armour for the purpose of mobility.

Not only the cavalryman's weaponry underwent change; so too did the trappings of his horse. Despite the native origin of 1st-century horse gear, it was stylistically distinct from the original. Characteristic components are the hackamore and decorative elements which were made of bronze, usually tinned and – in the Claudio-Neronian period – inlaid with niello. Alongside battle equipment was parade gear for processions and tournaments, when richly ornamented straps would be attached to the saddle, and the horse's head adorned with a leather chamfron sporting bronze eyeguards. On such occasions the cavalryman wore a special helmet decorated with human and animal hair (Weiler type), to which a silvered or silver-clad iron mask was attached.

During the 1st century, several innovations in weaponry and horse gear can be linked to three historical events.[209] Firstly, in the transition from the Augustan to the Tiberian era, plate armour was replaced by Corbridge type armour and new decorative elements appeared on the belt and horse gear. Deschler-Erb sees a connection here with the Varus disaster of 9 AD, which had resulted in the major loss of both men and material.[210] It seems that the need to rapidly furnish a mass of new recruits with new equipment was seized as an opportunity to introduce these modifications.

Secondly, the organisation of the Rhine *limes* under Claudius (41-54) was accompanied by various changes. The chief of these was the replacement of the Mainz type *gladius* by a similar Pompeii type short sword in the mid-1st century. Narrower daggers of the Vindonissa type appeared at the same time. We also observe changes in the shape and decoration of harness fittings. Elaborate, niello-inlay items are characteristic of the Claudio-Neronian period, with *phalerae* being key diagnostic artefacts for this period.

Finally, the reorganisation of the troops after the Batavian revolt in 69 AD occasioned a change of equipment in a single area: the Hagenau type infantry helmet was replaced by the already existing Weisenau type. Compared to the reforms under Augustus, the changes introduced at the time of Tiberius, Claudius and Vespasian were only minor. Various opportunities were taken to add new elements to the existing repertoire and to take out of production items that had proven less suitable.

Period 3 (c. AD 120-250/300): investing in the frontier defences under Hadrian
In the early 2nd century, new types of weapons appeared, the sword was worn in a different way and changes were made to the design of horse gear. These innovations appear to have coincided with the period in which Emperor Hadrian (117-138) was preoccupied with frontier defences, resulting – for the first time since Claudius – in army reinforcements and major restoration work on the *limes*.[211] The *terminus post quem* of period 3 is associated with the transition to the late Roman period. Given that most settlements in the Lower Rhine region were abandoned in the second half of the 3rd century, the finds from the research region can predominantly be dated to between c. 120 and 250.[212]

A typical feature of army equipment in the 2nd and 3rd centuries was the growing resemblance between the different units, particularly the infantry. Whereas the 1st-century legions and auxiliary troops wore different types of helmets, these were replaced by Niederbieber type helmets in the 2nd century. The more homogeneous picture that emerges is also reflected in other parts of the equipment. For example, the 1st-century *gladius* and *gladius*-like *spatha* were replaced by a new type of sword worn by both cavalry and infantry. The same applies to the way in which the sword was suspended, with both cavalry and foot soldiers now using a baldric. However, some differences in equipment remained, particularly between

---

[209] See also Lenz 2000, 55.
[210] Deschler-Erb 1999b, 237.
[211] For Germania Inferior, see Kunow 1987, 72-74, Abb. 32; Hessing 1999.
[212] For the history of habitation in the Lower Rhine region, see Willems 1984, 271-272.

the infantry and cavalry. We can regard the *pilum*, the new type of dagger and the belt as characteristic of the infantry, while the cavalry wore a slightly different helmet and was armed with throwing spears and lances. Unlike the previous period, however, there appears to have been a less conscious emphasis on differences between the units, with function apparently being the deciding factor.

Changes are also evident in early 2nd-century horse gear. Although the horned saddle and hackamore continued in unmodified form, the harness components were subject to change. For example, decorative fittings were attached to the leather with fixed, mushroom-shaped studs instead of with rivets and separate washers or backplates. We see a similar change in the spurs, which were also fitted with studs. At the same time, there emerged a new decorative repertoire for horse gear. Tinning and niello inlay gave way to enamel decoration, and we witness a 'Celtic renaissance', characterised by openwork, pelta, heart- and trumpet-shaped motifs.[213] The innovations introduced under Hadrian also left their mark on parade gear. The saddle straps that were richly adorned with plates fell out of favour, and the leather chamfron was supplanted by one made entirely of bronze. Although the masked helmet was retained, it too was now constructed entirely of bronze.

Period 4 (c. AD 300-450): restoring the Rhine limes under Diocletian
After the Roman *limes* succumbed in the third quarter of the 3rd century following invasions from Frankish and other 'Germanic' groups, in about 300 Diocletian (285-305) succeeded to a certain extent in restoring the former situation.[214] The northern provinces once again became part of the Roman empire, and some of the former military posts along the Rhine were put back into service. An additional zone of army camps was established in the hinterland. Although we cannot precisely date the innovations in finds from the late Roman period, it appears most likely that they were associated with this phase of restoring the frontier defences.

Characteristic of the 4th-century units was the appearance of a new type of helmet and a wide belt decorated with large plates. The *plumbata* replaced the *pilum*, and a new, short sword – probably the *semipatha* – emerged alongside the *spatha*. Plate armour was no longer worn, with chain mail and scale armour now becoming the customary types of armour. Although cavalry made up a significant part of the auxiliary troops, we find no horse gear characteristic of this period. We do know of decorative horse gear elements from late Roman contexts, but these belong typologically to the previous period, suggesting that the cavalry continued to use horse gear components characteristic of period 3 well into the 4th century.[215] Only the spurs, in their modified form, can be placed typologically in this period.

[213] See Junkelmann 1996, 86.
[214] For an overview, see Nicasie 1997.
[215] Gschwind 1998.

3 An analysis of the finds at the regional and site level

Although finds of weapons, belts/baldrics and horse gear are generally viewed as characteristic of military sites, the material from the eastern Rhine delta shows that these categories of finds also occur frequently outside army camps and guard posts. The majority of the c. 2,700 objects in the inventory come from rural settlements, ranging from simple hamlets to larger settlements with villa-like structures (fig. 3.1, appendix 1). In addition, a sizeable quantity of material is documented from rivers, the urban centres in Nijmegen and cult places. Only occasionally do objects occur in graves. Thanks to the extensive data set from the research region, we are able to carry out analyses to give us an idea of the use and significance of weaponry and horse gear from different non-military contexts. These analyses are designed to identify patterns in the material that will be elaborated further in subsequent chapters.

This chapter, which looks at the material at different levels of scale, consists of two parts. The first contains chronological and geographical analyses of the material from the region as a whole.[1] The chronological analysis presents the material in various bar charts to give an idea of developments in composition. The geographical analysis focuses on the distribution pattern of the different categories of finds in the eastern Rhine delta, paying special attention to the archaeological context in which the material was found. The research region will be placed in a broader, northwest European context in order to establish whether the patterns observed also apply to material from neighbouring areas.

The second part examines the finds at the site level. In recent decades, various excavations of rural and urban settlements, their associated cemeteries, and cult places in the *civitas Batavorum* have yielded weaponry and horse gear finds. I will firstly examine the excavated sites in terms of the composition and spatial distribution of the finds before giving an overview of the specific archaeological context of the individual objects. Given the lack of context data, I will only examine the composition of some of the larger river assemblages.

3.1 CHRONOLOGICAL ANALYSIS

The previous chapter classified the Roman-era military equipment and horse gear according to function and typochronology. Soldiers in the Roman army were equipped with a standardised set of weaponry and horse gear, which we can subdivide into four chronological groups on typological grounds:

1. c. 50-12 BC[2]
2. c. 12 BC-AD 120
3. c. AD 120-250/300
4. c. AD 300-450

---

[1] Although finds from neighbouring trans-Rhenish Germania have been omitted from the chronological and geographical analyses, they are included in the overview maps of the Batavian region in the interests of completeness (figs. 3.6-3.11).

[2] The possible auxiliary swords of type Kessel are also assigned to the weaponry from this period (see chapter 2.3).

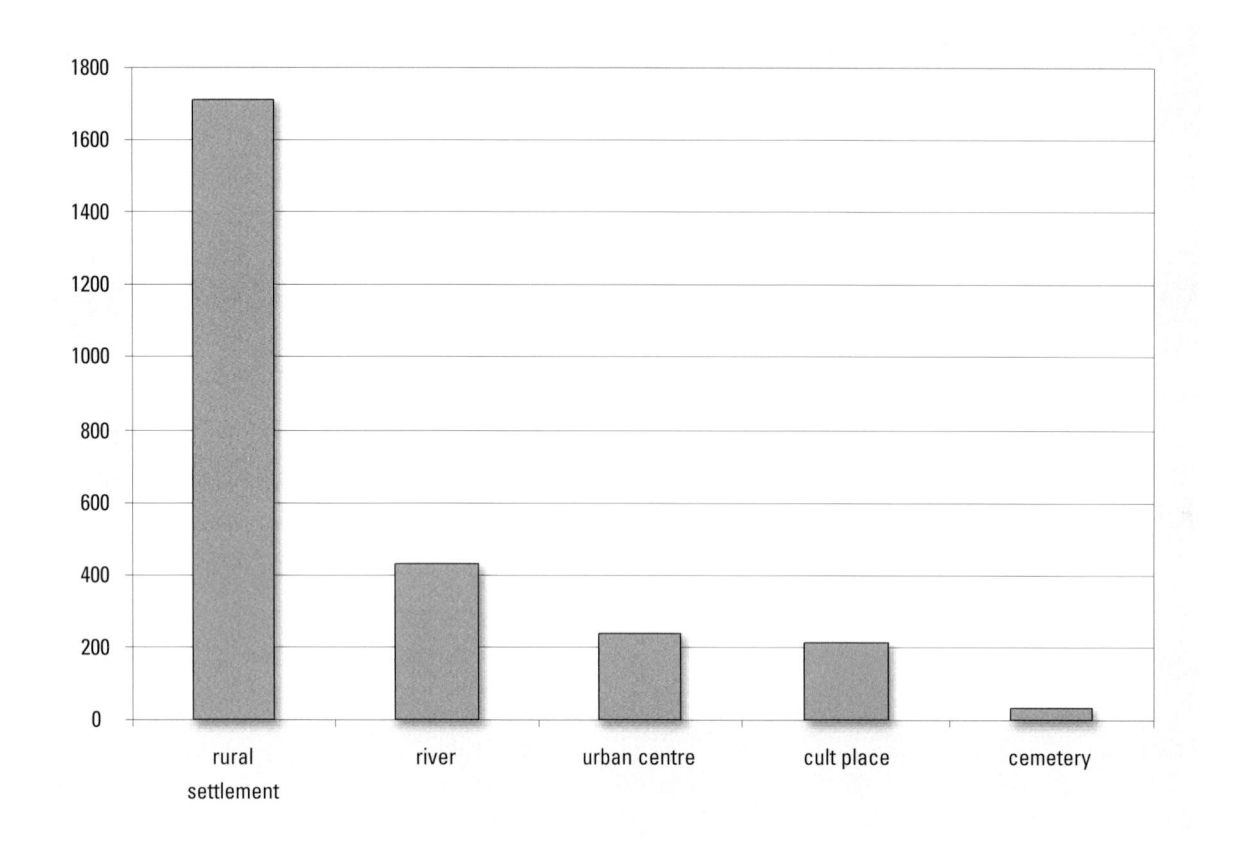

Fig. 3.1. Absolute number of weaponry and horse gear finds from the different non-military contexts in the eastern Rhine delta.

This grouping into phases of a fairly homogenous nature allows us to compare the material from the different periods. The chronological analysis examines the material from the study area in its entirety, and then for each functional find category and type of find context.[3] But first, I will discuss the archaeological visibility of the different categories in order to gain an idea of the representativity of the patterns observed.

3.1.1 ARCHAEOLOGICAL VISIBILITY

The variable number of components that make up an item and the materials used mean that there are distinct differences in archaeological visibility for weaponry and horse gear. In order to establish the implications for chronological patterns in the finds, I will briefly discuss the archaeological visibility of each category. This involves looking at the metal components used for each object in the different periods and the extent to which we are able to identify fragmentary objects. It is also important to establish the extent to which the quantitative composition of the finds may be distorted by fragmentation. This applies in particular to items of equipment that are made up of many elements, such as plate armour.

[3] The analyses only examine finds that can be attributed to one specific period. Less securely dated find categories, such as spear-, lance-, *pila*- and boltheads, are omitted. The matching sets of weaponry and horse gear from Beuningen-'Molenstraat', Empel-'De Werf' and the Lower Rhine at Doorwerth are counted as a single object.

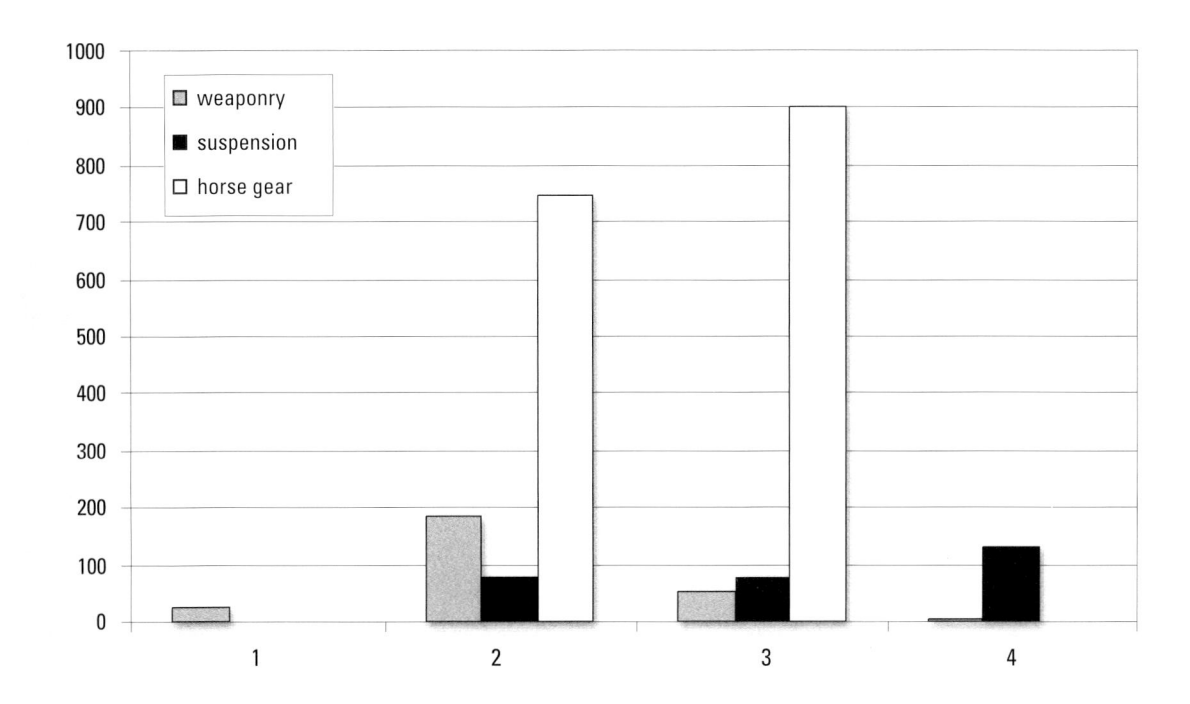

Fig. 3.2. Absolute numbers of weaponry, suspension and horse gear finds from the different non-military contexts in the eastern Rhine delta for each period.

Both chronologically and in relation to one other, defensive weapons display considerable variation in archaeological visibility. Iron and bronze helmets consist of a helmet bowl, cheekpieces and various reinforcing or decorative elements. Almost all the helmets in the archaeological record, which have generally been dredged from rivers, are more or less complete examples. Fragmentary helmet components are difficult to identify, however. For this reason, the number of helmet finds does not appear to be representative, especially in settlements, where finds tend to be of a fragmentary nature. For chain mail made of iron rings, only the bronze tie-hooks are preserved in most instances. At the beginning of the 2nd century, when these hooks were no longer used, the bronze breastplates of parade equipment became the most easily identifiable components (period 3). Scale armour also has limited archaeological visibility as finds usually consist of stray, fragmentary scales. Plate armour, on the other hand, consists of a large number of bronze, readily identifiable closures and hinges. Because various stray components may have belonged to one and the same set of armour, we can assume a general overrepresentation of this category. Compared to helmet finds, armour components therefore occur relatively often in the cult place at Empel and in settlements. The small components of the different types of armour, on the other hand, are seldom identified during dredging operations. Roman-era shields featured an iron or bronze shield boss and grip, and the shield's perimeter was also reinforced with bronze during period 2. Most of the relatively large shield bosses and grips come from rivers. Given that these components are usually difficult to identify in a fragmentary condition, rural sites have yielded almost no finds.[4] The situation is different for 1st-century shield edging, which is often easy to recognise even as a fragment. However, the frequent incidence of this fitting may distort the number of shield finds from period 2.

---

[4] I should point out that not just complete items, but also larger metal fragments that enable us to identify a shield boss or grip, are uncommon in rural settlements; these have probably been melted down.

Swords and daggers also show variation in terms of archaeological visibility. In addition to iron sword blades with a bone or wooden hilt, sword finds frequently consist of bronze scabbard components. In the first two periods, the wooden and leather scabbards featured two or three scabbard bands, a solid terminal knob and decorative fittings. In most cases only the chape and scabbard slide are preserved from *spathae* from period 3. Because these are easier to recognise in fragmentary form than scabbard components from the previous period, swords will probably not be underrepresented in period 3. The situation is different for the late Roman sword, with bronze scabbard components scarcely documented. Both daggers and scabbards were made of iron in period 2, after which the scabbard was partially executed in bronze. However, the bronze components are not distinctive enough to be identified in a fragmentary state. An exception is the peltate chapes of a less common type of dagger (type D). Military daggers cease to occur in period 4. More complete sword and dagger finds come almost exclusively from rivers, whereas the bronze components of sword scabbards and dagger sheaths come primarily from rural sites. In the latter case, sword finds from period 4 and daggers will generally be underrepresented.

In period 2 belts featured a bronze buckle, dagger frogs and decorative plates. The apron was also part of the belt and was adorned with belt plates and pendants. The unadorned belt with a ring buckle was the most frequently occurring type in the subsequent period. Thanks to the presence of bronze closure studs, the belt continues to be easily identifiable among the finds. A baldric also occurs in period 3, with decorative fittings and pendants executed in bronze. The 4th century saw the appearance, alongside the narrow belt, of a broad belt, with a bronze buckle and bronze fittings. Characteristic of period 4 is the occurrence of complete belt sets in graves. The fact that the belt components also tend to be easily identified in a fragmentary state explains the many settlement finds. However, these items are often too small to be detected during dredging. Various stray finds from a single site may have belonged to the same belt set, which could distort the number of belt finds in relation to other categories.

Horse gear components are only known from periods 2 and 3. The majority comprise bronze fasteners, strap junctions and decorative elements that are easily identified in archaeological terms. It is not possible to make a simple comparison of the material from the two periods. For example, more complete sets from rivers and graves show that there was considerable variation in the number of bronze elements making up the harness in periods 2 and 3.[5] The often small harness components, also readily identified in fragmentary form, are documented from rural sites in particular. Because part of the harness components from the same site will have belonged to a set, finds of horse gear will often be overrepresented.

We may conclude that there are major differences in the archaeological visibility of Roman weaponry and horse gear. The difference between items made of iron and entirely or partly of bronze is particularly significant here. The former will be overrepresented, especially in wet contexts, and the latter at rural sites. For this reason, a key question in the chronological analysis concerns the extent to which the patterns observed in the finds are caused by differences in representativity.

3.1.2 CHRONOLOGICAL PATTERNS IN THE FINDS

Figure 3.2 combines the weaponry, suspension components (belt, apron and baldric) and horse gear from the different non-military contexts. Finds from the first period are confined to two helmets and various Kessel type swords. In the subsequent period, finds of weaponry and in particular horse gear show a marked increase. Suspension components are also represented in quite large numbers. In period 3 we observe a decline in weaponry but a peak in horse gear, with the number of belt components

---

[5] See Lehner 1923; Palágyi 1981; 1990; 1995; Brouwer 1982; Jenkins 1985; Massart 2000.

remaining roughly the same. Although weapons virtually disappear from the material in period 4, and horse gear does so completely, belt components continue to occur frequently, with the number even exceeding that of the two previous periods.

In order to test the representativity of this pattern, I will conduct a similar analysis for the specific equipment components, as well as for horse gear. This involves exploring the extent to which chronological trends in the individual find categories match the general pattern. If we present the securely dated offensive and defensive weapons (helmet, armour, shield, sword and dagger) in a bar chart, we do see a correspondence for the different weapon types (fig. 3.3). Firstly, the helmet finds show a marked increase in period 2, after which numbers drop sharply in periods 3 and 4. A similar picture emerges for armour and shields, which are documented mainly in period 2. Although shields and especially armour are over-represented, the finds appear to tie in with the trend for helmets. The same applies to swords, which peak in period 2 and decline in the following periods. It is conspicuous, however, that this is the only type of weapon that continues to occur in relatively large numbers in period 3. The small number of dagger finds also corresponds to the general pattern, with most daggers belonging in period 2.

Belt numbers increased slightly from period 2 to 3, peaking in period 4 (fig. 3.3). These numbers may be distorted by the presence at the same site of various belt components, originally part of the same set. This seems to be especially true of period 4, but can also be observed for periods 2 and 3 (fig. 3.10). Although the apron (period 2) and baldric (period 3) were worn in combination with the belt, their numbers do not match the trend for belts. In both cases, however, the numbers are too small to lead to a major distortion in the general pattern.

With regard to horse gear, we observe interesting differences in composition when we compare finds from periods 2 and 3 (fig. 3.3). There appears to have been a shift from functional and decorative horse gear to primarily decorative gear, with decorative fittings making up a greater share of the material. The extent to which this shift affected the comparability of the finds cannot be immediately established. The greater number of finds from period 3 documented from individual sites suggests that the increase in decorative elements may have led to an overrepresentation of horse gear in this period (fig. 3.11). However, the difference between the number of fittings from periods 2 and 3 is too great to be fully explained by changing harness design.

Although the different categories of objects cannot always be properly compared, in general the chronological patterns in the material appear to present a representative picture. We see this most clearly in the weaponry, but can assume that it applies equally to suspension components and horse gear.

3.1.3 CHRONOLOGICAL ANALYSIS PER TYPE OF FIND CONTEXT

If we assume that the chronological patterns in the material are fundamentally representative, it is interesting to compare the material from the different context types. This involves examining whether finds from rural settlements, the urban centre in Nijmegen, the cult place of Empel-'De Werf' and rivers reveal a specific pattern or tie in with the general one. In view of the scant amount of material from cemeteries, we can eliminate this context from the analysis. Offensive and defensive weapons are presented separately to give a clear picture of the occurrence of weaponry in the different types of context.

Finds from rural settlements are presented in figure 3.4. In terms of chronological distribution, the composition of the material corresponds in part to the general pattern. For example, most of the weapon finds date from period 2, with horse gear peaking in period 3. Despite the few offensive and defensive weapons, both categories reveal an interesting trend. Whereas defensive weaponry shows a distinctive peak in period 2, more offensive weapons are documented from period 3. We see the same for horse gear, which also peaked in period 3. With regard to belt components, the picture matches the general pattern: periods 2 and 3 yielded similar numbers of finds, whereas period 4 saw an increase.

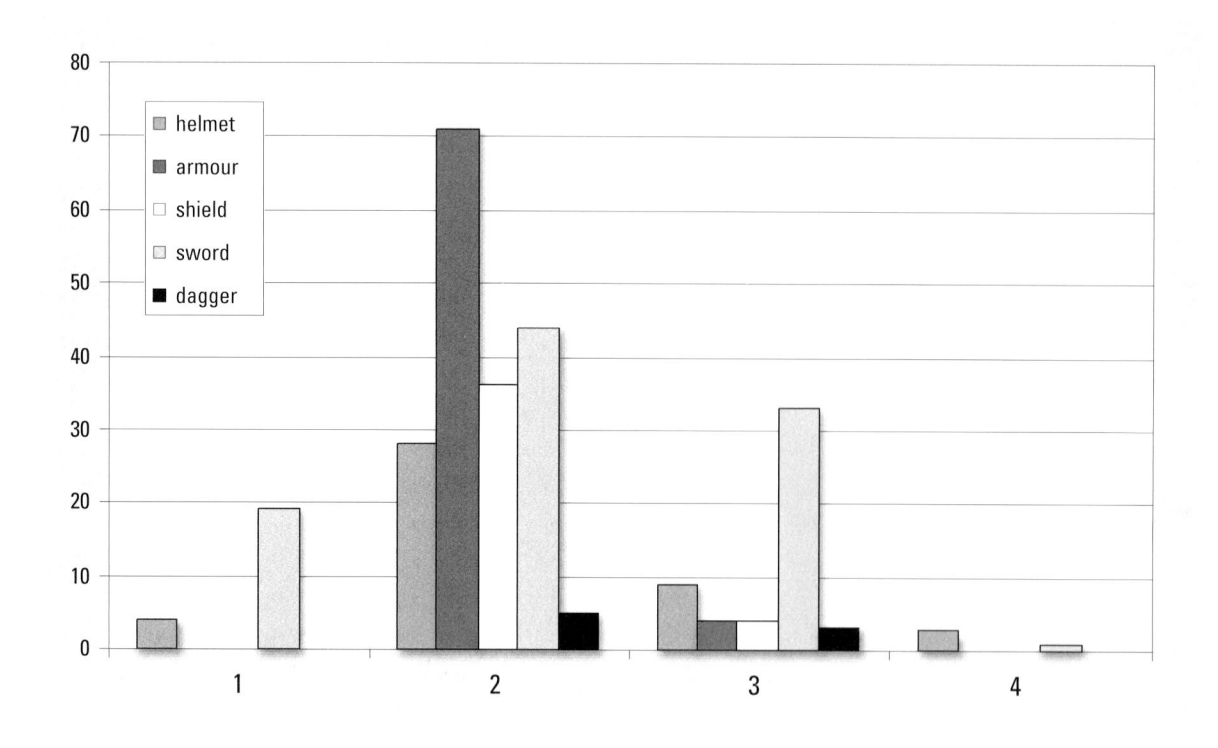

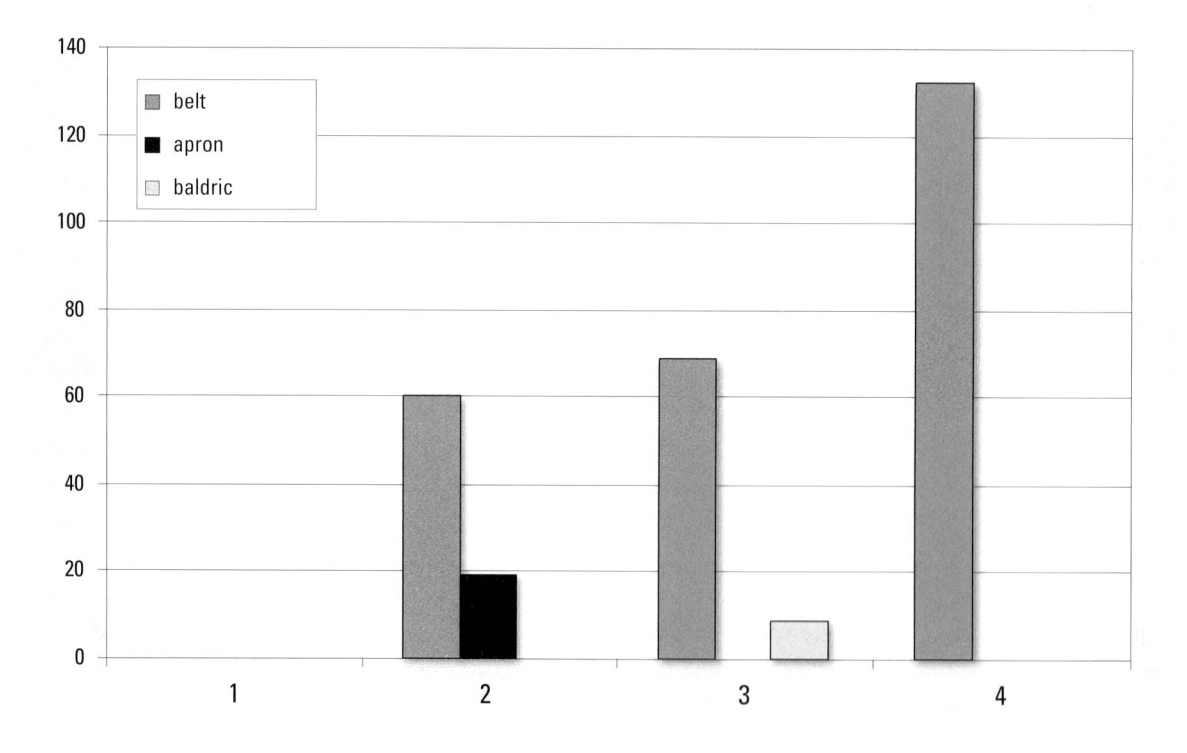

Fig. 3.3 Composition of weaponry (above), suspension (below) and horse gear finds (next page) from the different non-military contexts in the eastern Rhine delta for each period. No horse gear finds are documented from periods 1 and 4.

For the urban centres, the material from *oppidum Batavorum* and Ulpia Noviomagus has been combined since the former was replaced by the latter after the Batavian revolt. Despite the small number of weaponry and suspension components, the finds reveal a pattern largely corresponding to the material

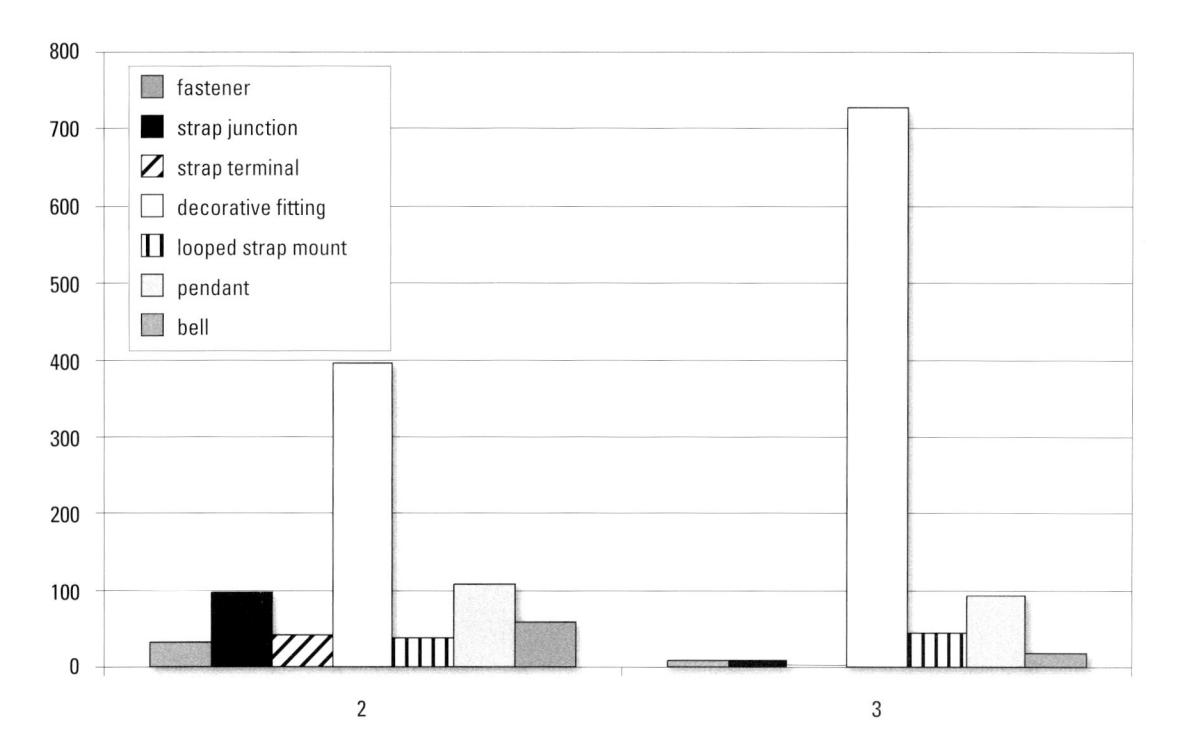

Fig. 3.3. Continued.

from rural settlements (fig. 3.4). Horse gear exhibits the usual peak in period 3, whereas defensive weapons can be dated primarily to period 2 and offensive weaponry exclusively to period 3. What is different is the small number of belt components from period 2. The lack of finds from period 4 is explained by the abandonment of Ulpia Noviomagus in the 3rd century.

As far as cult places are concerned, only Empel-'De Werf' has yielded sufficient material for a chronological analysis (fig. 3.5). Weapon finds match the general pattern, with both offensive and defensive weaponry showing a distinct rise in period 2, followed by a drop in period 3. The pattern is different for horse gear, with most finds dating to period 2. The same picture emerges for belts. As the cult place was abandoned in the 3rd century, the finds from period 4 relate to later, probably non-religious, activities.

The specific collection method means that the river finds are chiefly made up of well-preserved offensive and defensive weapons, whereas the less easily identifiable suspension and horse gear components are represented by relatively few examples (fig. 3.5). In terms of chronological distribution, the finds tie in remarkably well with the pattern for Empel-'De Werf'. The bulk of the weaponry and horse gear dates from period 2, after which both categories show a decline. The lack of belt components from period 2 appears to relate to the fairly non-representative nature of this group.

On the basis of the chronological distribution of weaponry and horse gear, we are able to distinguish between rural and urban settlements on the one hand and cult places and rivers on the other. In settlements, defensive weaponry typically shows a marked decline in the period for which most offensive weapons and especially horse gear are documented. The situation is less clear for suspension components. The material from rural settlements is presumably most representative, which means we can assume comparable numbers of finds from periods 2 and 3. Finds from cult places and rivers reveal a different picture. There is not only a drop in defensive weaponry in period 3, but also in offensive weapons and horse gear. Finds from Empel-'De Werf' reveal that the same is true for suspension components.

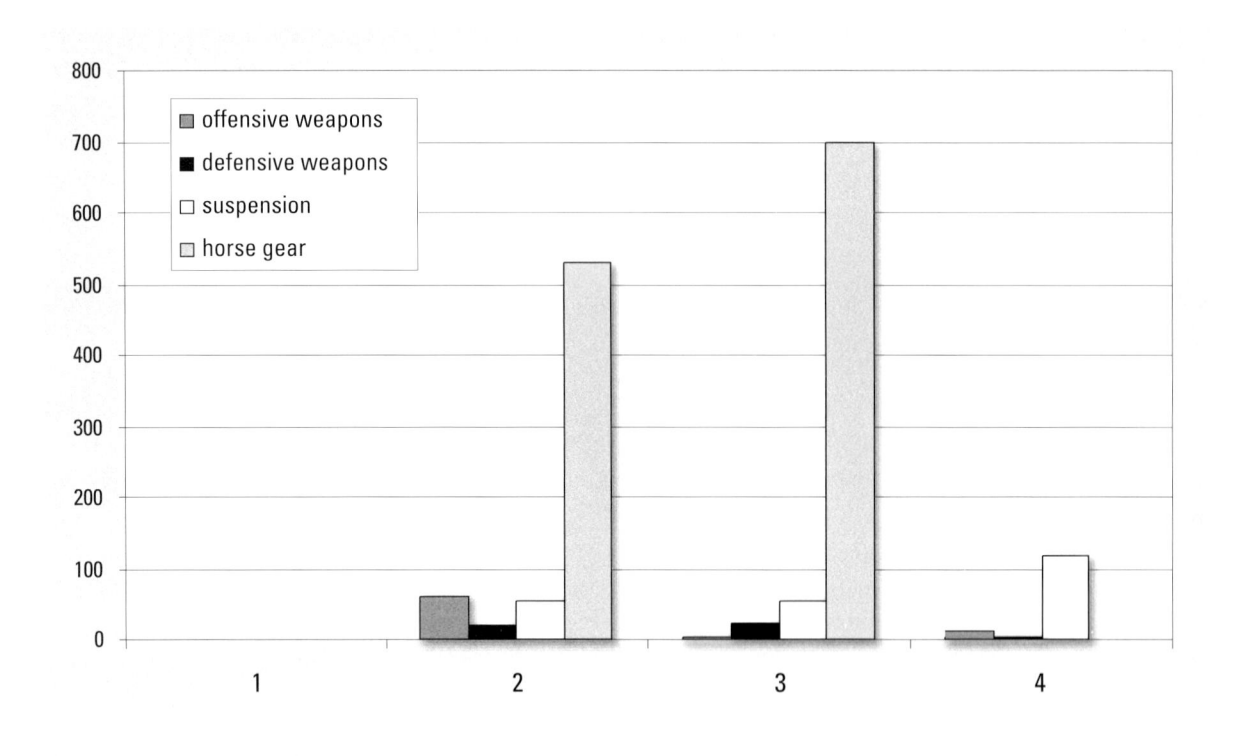

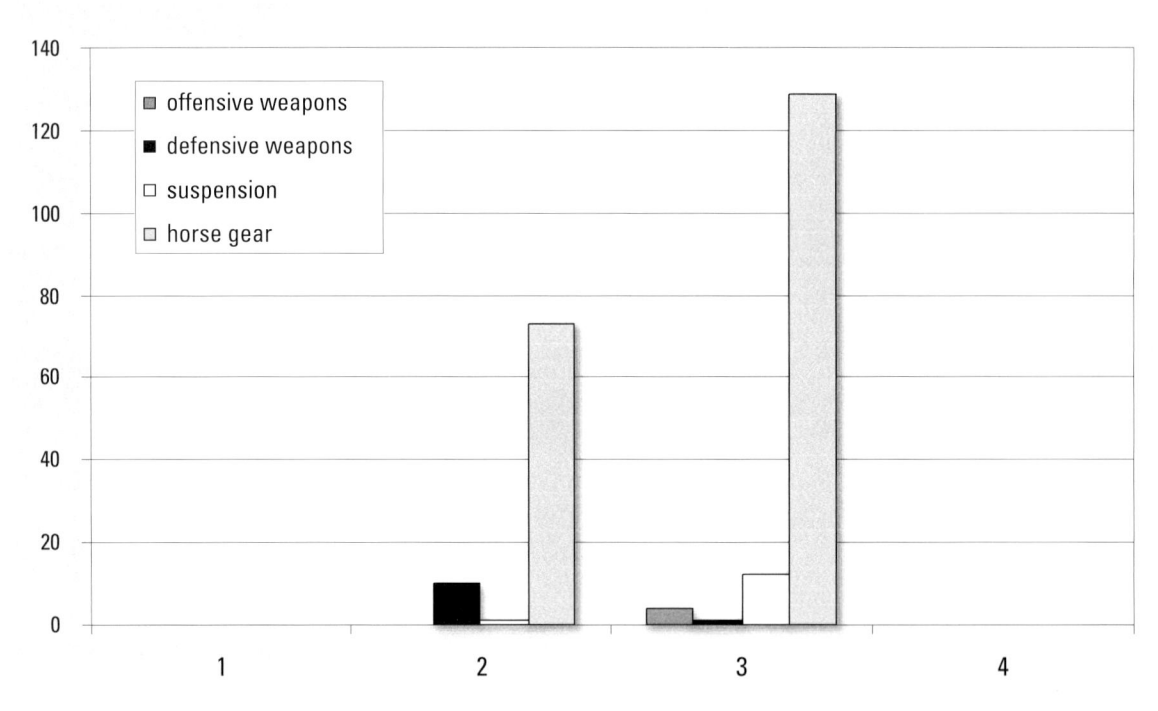

Fig. 3.4. Composition of the militaria from rural settlements in the eastern Rhine delta (above) and the Nijmegen centres *oppidum Batavorum* and Ulpia Noviomagus Batavorum (below) for each period.

3.2 GEOGRAPHICAL ANALYSIS

Together with changes in the composition of the material, geographical distribution patterns for the different functional categories can also provide insights into the use of weaponry and horse gear during the Roman period. This section will look at chronological developments, not only in the geographical

72

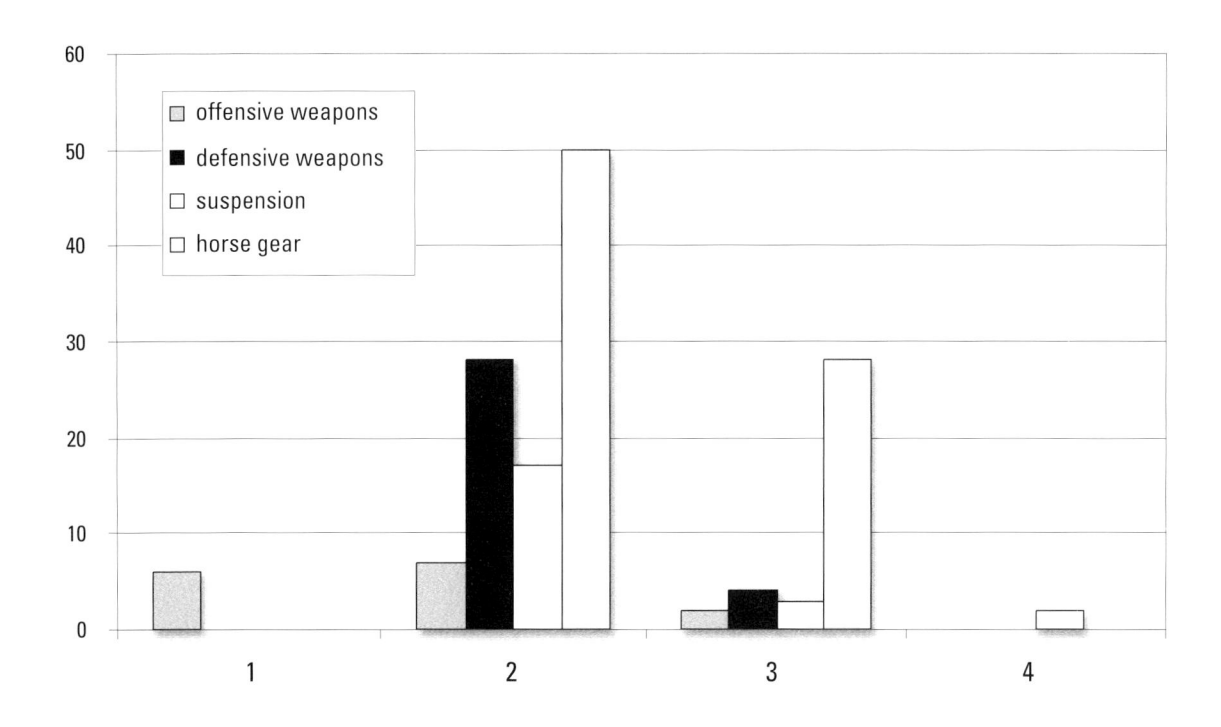

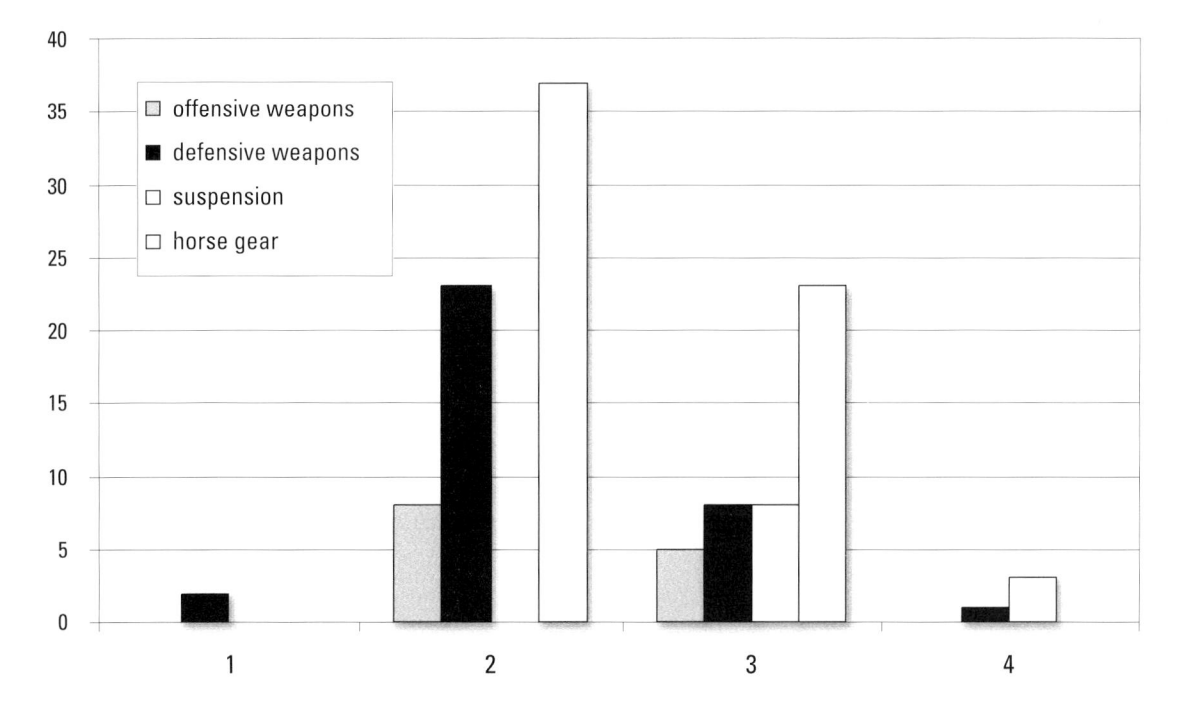

Fig. 3.5. Composition of the militaria from the cult place of Empel-'De Werf' (above) and from river sites in the eastern Rhine delta (below) for each period.

distribution of the material, but also with regard to the occurrence of the different find groups in specific types of context. I will then place the research region within a broader context, comparing the observed patterns with the situation as we know it for northwest Europe. In order to explain how the presented data set came about, I will first briefly outline the collection method and look at the representativity of the data.

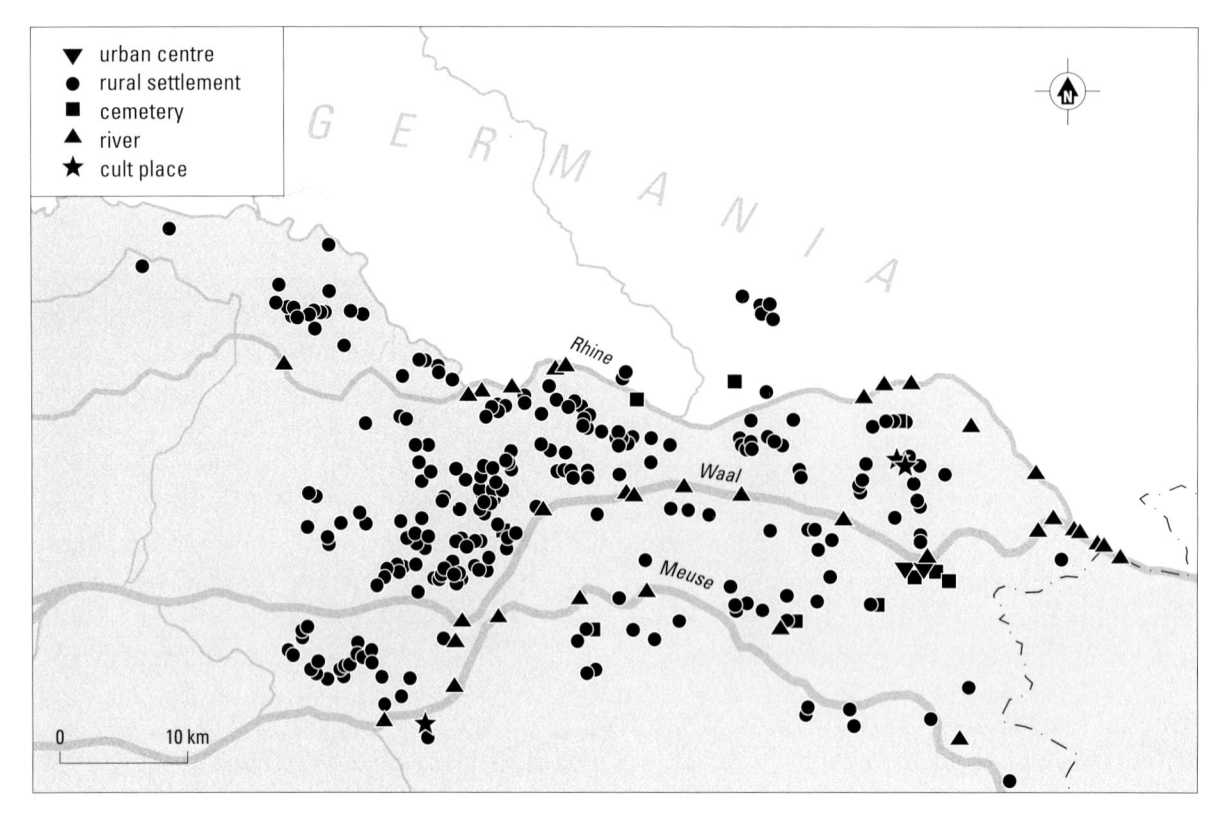

Fig. 3.6. Geographical distribution and types of site in the inventory containing militaria from the eastern Rhine delta.

3.2.1 COLLECTION METHOD AND REPRESENTATIVITY

An overview of sites of Roman weaponry and horse gear documented within the research region reveals that the material occurs across the entire eastern Rhine delta (fig. 3.6). Although we see a clustering of sites in certain parts of the study region, other zones have yielded almost no sites or none at all. To explain how this picture has emerged, I will first outline how the material was collected and then test the representativity of the distribution pattern by comparing it with the distribution of all currently known sites from the Roman period.

The majority of the finds in the inventory were found by amateur archaeologists using metal detectors. This material, generally found in the vicinity of the finder's home, is held in private collections. The survey of collections examined for this study reveals that they occur across the research region (fig. 3.7).[6] Only in the central zone between the Rhine and Waal rivers has no material been documented. We also observe a fairly regular pattern if we look at the size of the collections. With the exception of a collection containing almost 300 objects, belonging to a detectorist in Maurik, collections with about 50-70 weaponry and horse gear finds occur in both the western and eastern part of the research region. The smaller amateur collections from the province of Utrecht are linked to the settlement cluster around Houten, which means that they could in fact be replaced by a single larger dot in this part of the research region. When compiling the inventory of various collections in the vicinity of 's Hertogenbosch, an attempt has been made to map as fully as possible the material from the exceptional sites of Empel-'De Werf' and

[6] Only a portion of the amateur collections containing material from the Batavian region has been examined in the inventory; as a result, the total number of finds from the research region will be considerably larger than the data set compiled for this study.

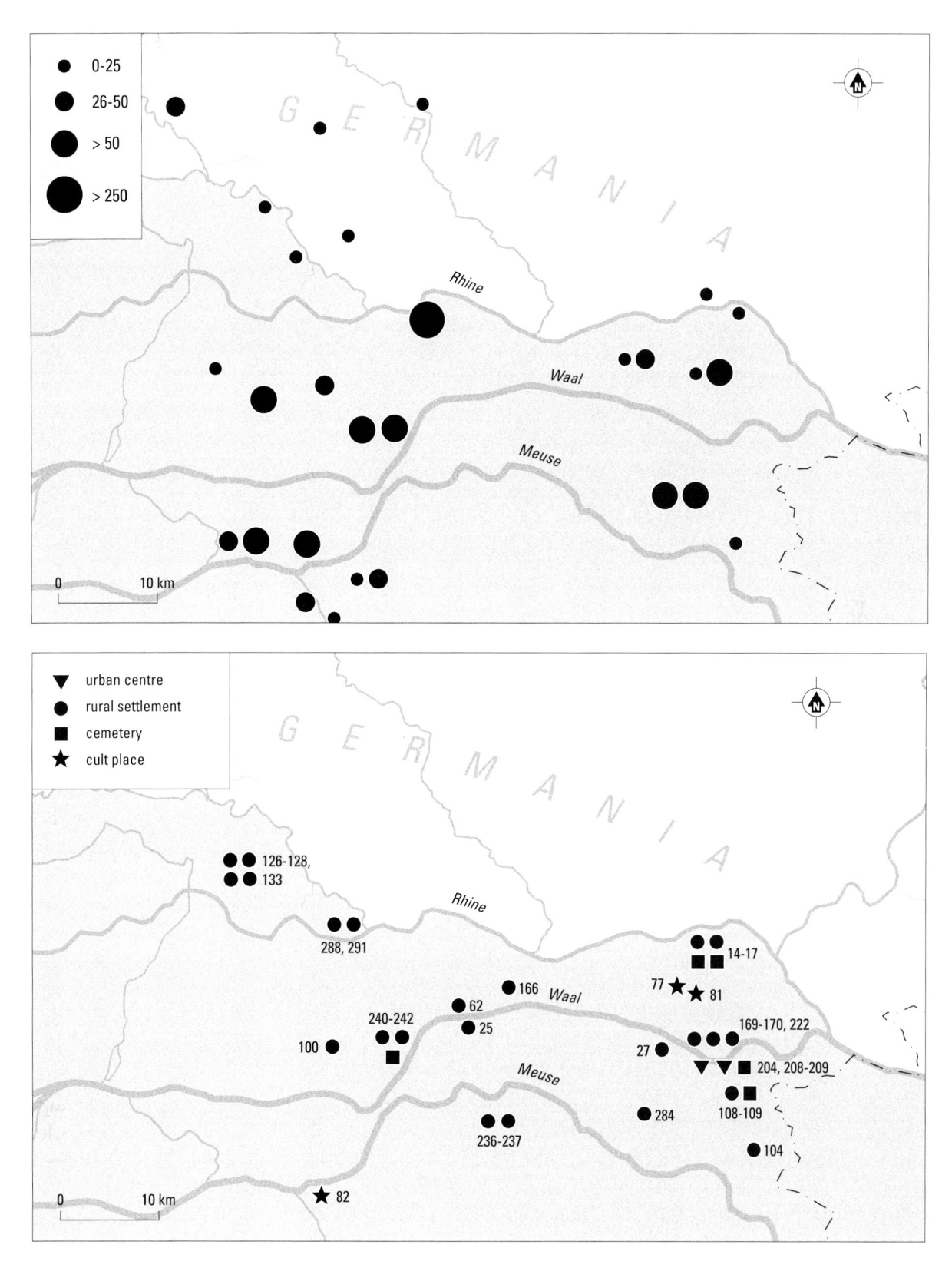

Fig. 3.7. Distribution of the material compiled for this study from amateur collections (above), excavations (below) and rivers or dredge pits (next page). The numbers of the find sites refer to appendix 1.

75

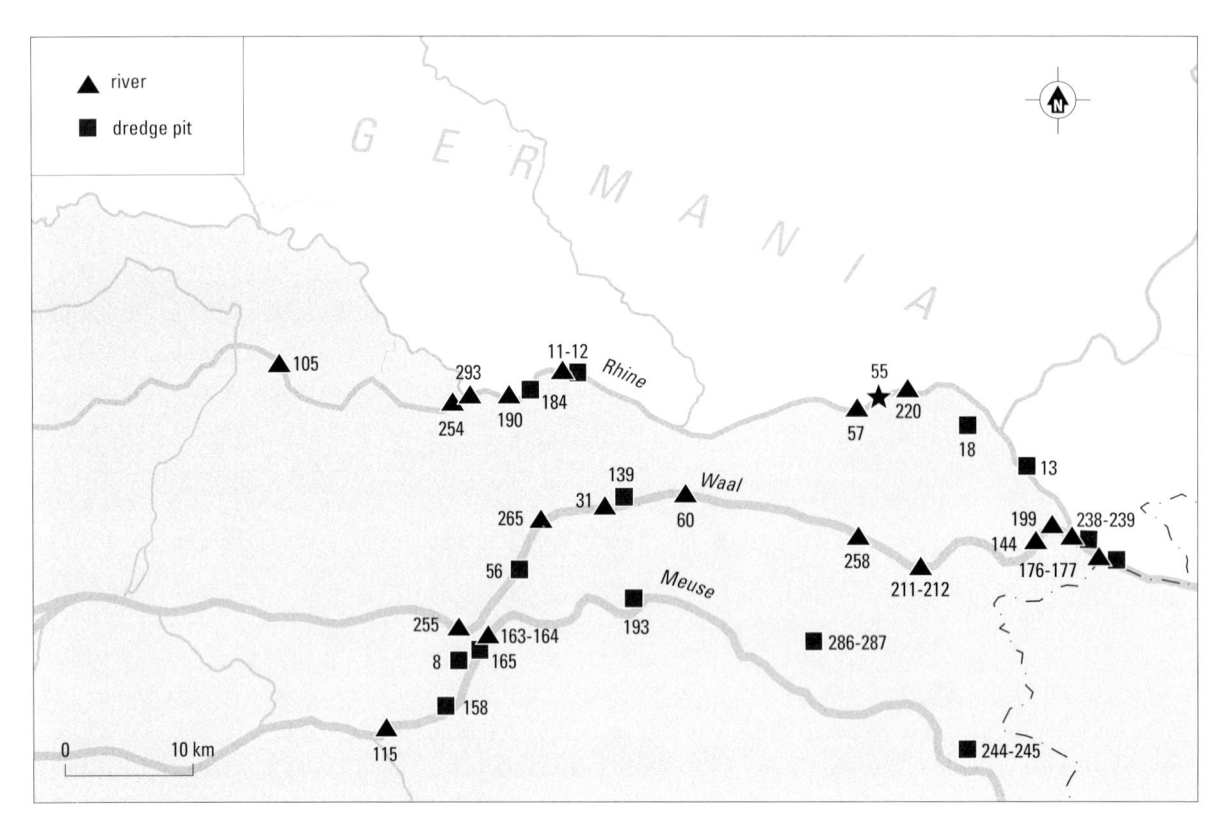

Fig. 3.7. Continued.

Kessel-Lith. The material from private collections is primarily composed of stray finds. If there is nothing to indicate the special nature of a site, these sites are interpreted as rural settlements, the most common type of site in the eastern Rhine delta. Given that cult places are often difficult to identify on the basis of stray finds, ritual assemblages may in some cases have been incorrectly ascribed to rural settlements.

Material from different excavations has been included in the study in order to better understand the composition of finds from individual sites (fig. 3.7). This material originates primarily from rural settlements and their associated cemeteries excavated in recent decades. These excavations, carried out across the study region, have usually involved metal detectors. However, because this was not always done systematically, there are major discrepancies in the number of finds per site. The excavation finds are nevertheless very valuable when it comes to interpreting detector finds that lack a specific context. For example, archaeological research has revealed that weaponry and horse gear from the Batavian countryside are concentrated in inhabited areas and occur only in small numbers in cemeteries. Armed with this knowledge, we can safely conclude that finds made by amateurs at rural sites are generally connected with farmyards. Within the study region, archaeological research has also been conducted in parts of both Nijmegen centres, which means that material from an urban context is well represented. The picture is less representative for cult places. Of these, only the excavation at Empel-'De Werf' resulted in a substantial number of finds. No more than a few stray finds are documented from the cult places at the centre of Elst and Elst-'Westeraam'.[7]

---

[7] For the militaria from Elst-'Westeraam', see Zee 2005; Van Enckevort, in press. The finds from the temple complex at the centre of Elst are not yet published.

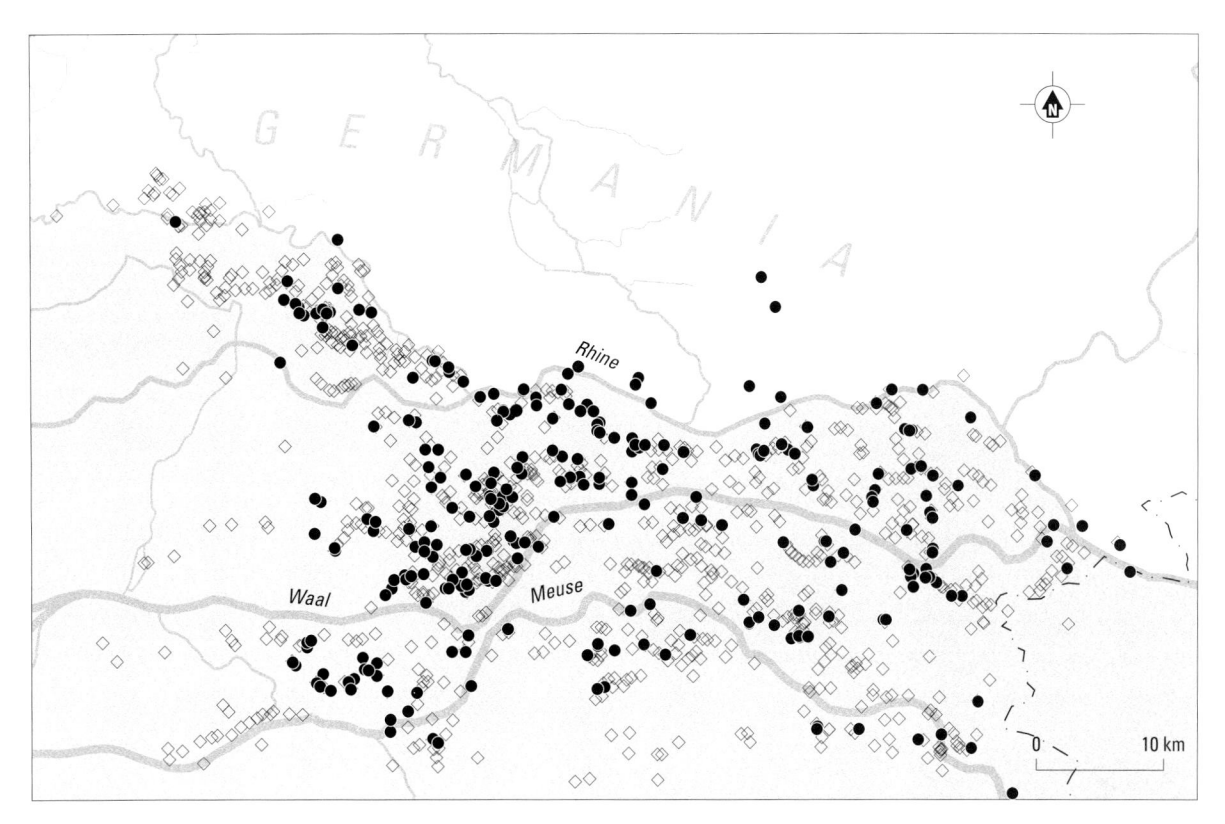

Fig. 3.8. The geographical distribution of weaponry and horse gear from non-military contexts (circles) compared with the currently known Roman find sites in the eastern Rhine delta (squares). Based partly on Vossen, in prep.

Lastly, many sites consist of wet contexts, where Roman finds have been recovered during the course of dredging operations. Here we can make a distinction between finds from active rivers and material from cut-off loops. Although the river sites occur across the (Lower) Rhine, Waal and Meuse, we observe a striking lack of finds in certain parts of these rivers (fig. 3.7). This is partly because the distribution of river sites depends largely on dredging operations in a specific region. No less important is the involvement of dredgers and enthusiasts who identify and collect Roman material.

In order to establish whether or not the overview maps presented here are in fact representative, we need to compare them with the distribution of currently known Roman sites. Vossen's overview map corresponds largely with the distribution of weaponry and horse gear finds (fig. 3.8).[8] In both cases the sites are clustered in the western part of the research region, to the west of Tiel in particular. In the central and eastern part of the region, the sites are more regularly distributed, with the small number of find sites in the central zone between the Rhine and Meuse seemingly associated with the way in which the inventory has been compiled.[9] The western-most part of the study region deviates from this picture, with almost no documented finds. The sandy soils south of the Meuse have also yielded relatively little material. The lack of sites in the western zone appears to be linked to natural conditions. As the result of peat growth, the find sites there are located deeper in the subsoil, making them less noticeable and less accessible to metal detectors. The small number of finds from the sandy soils south of the Meuse is also linked to natural factors. Excavations at Oss have shown that metalwork is poorly preserved in this part of the research region, and often only in deeper features like wells.[10]

[8] Vossen, in prep.

[9] The similar distribution of coins and seal boxes may indicate that the picture is representative (Aarts 2000, map 3.1; Derks/Roymans 2003, fig. 7.6).

[10] See chapter 3.3.1.

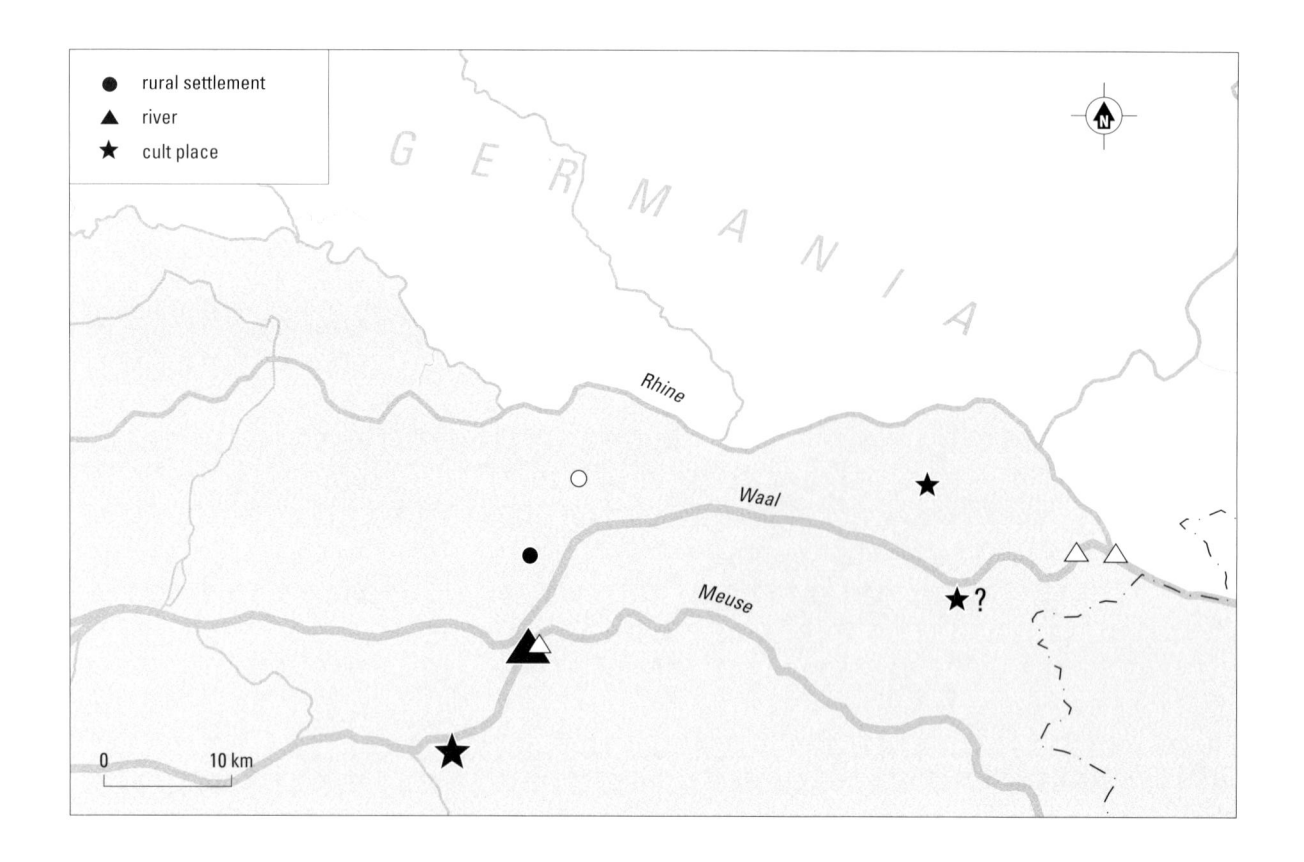

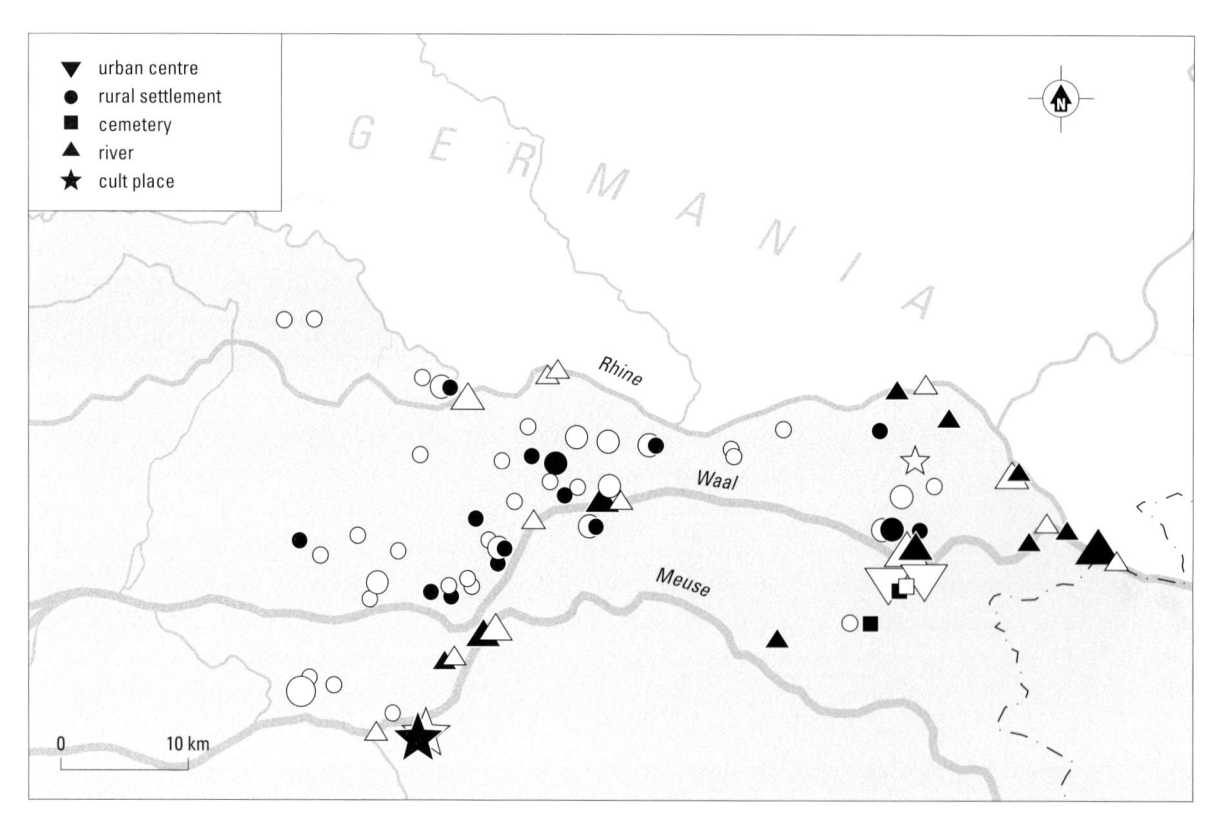

Fig. 3.9. The geographical distribution of offensive (black) and defensive weaponry (white) from the research region (1, 2-5 or more than 5 objects). Above: period 1; below: period 2; next page above: period 3; next page below: period 4.

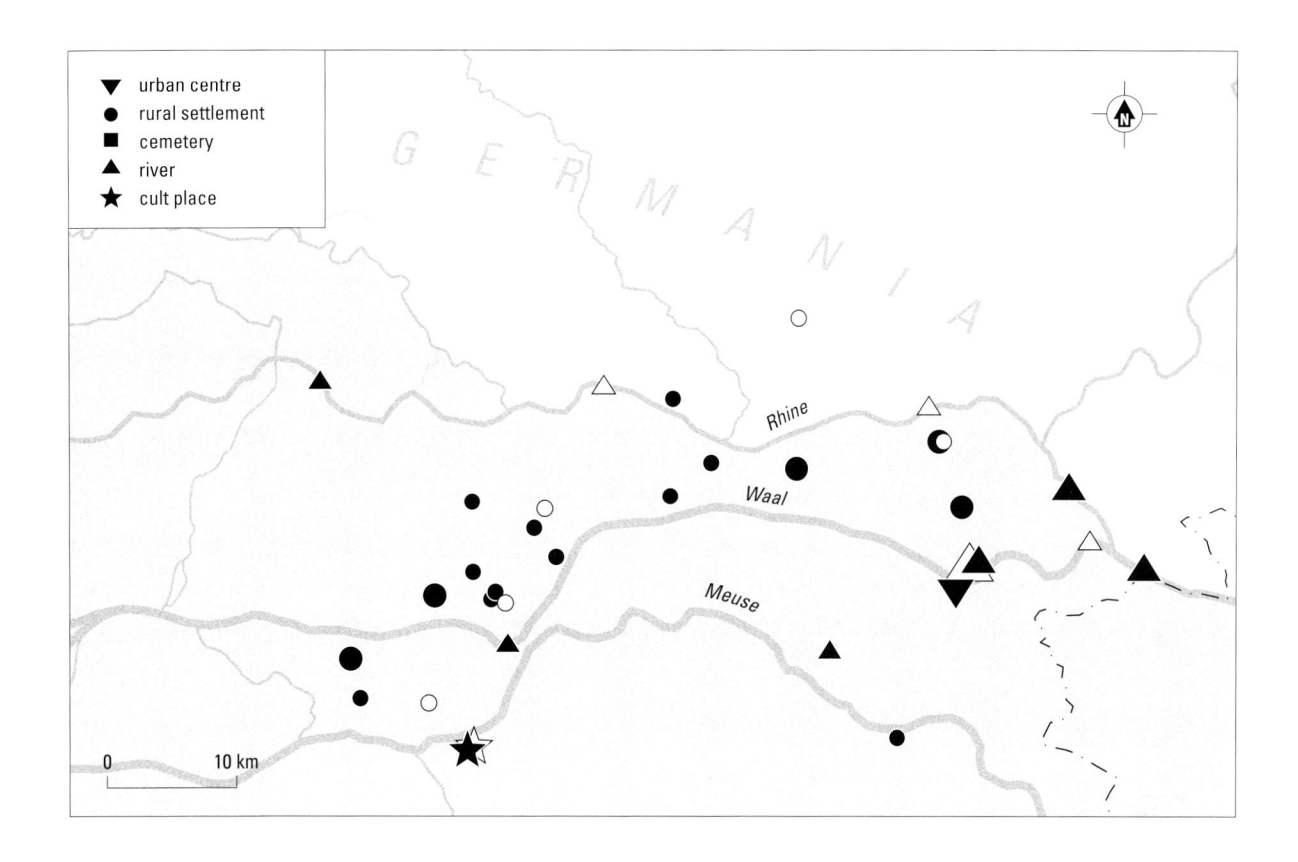

Fig. 3.9. Continued.

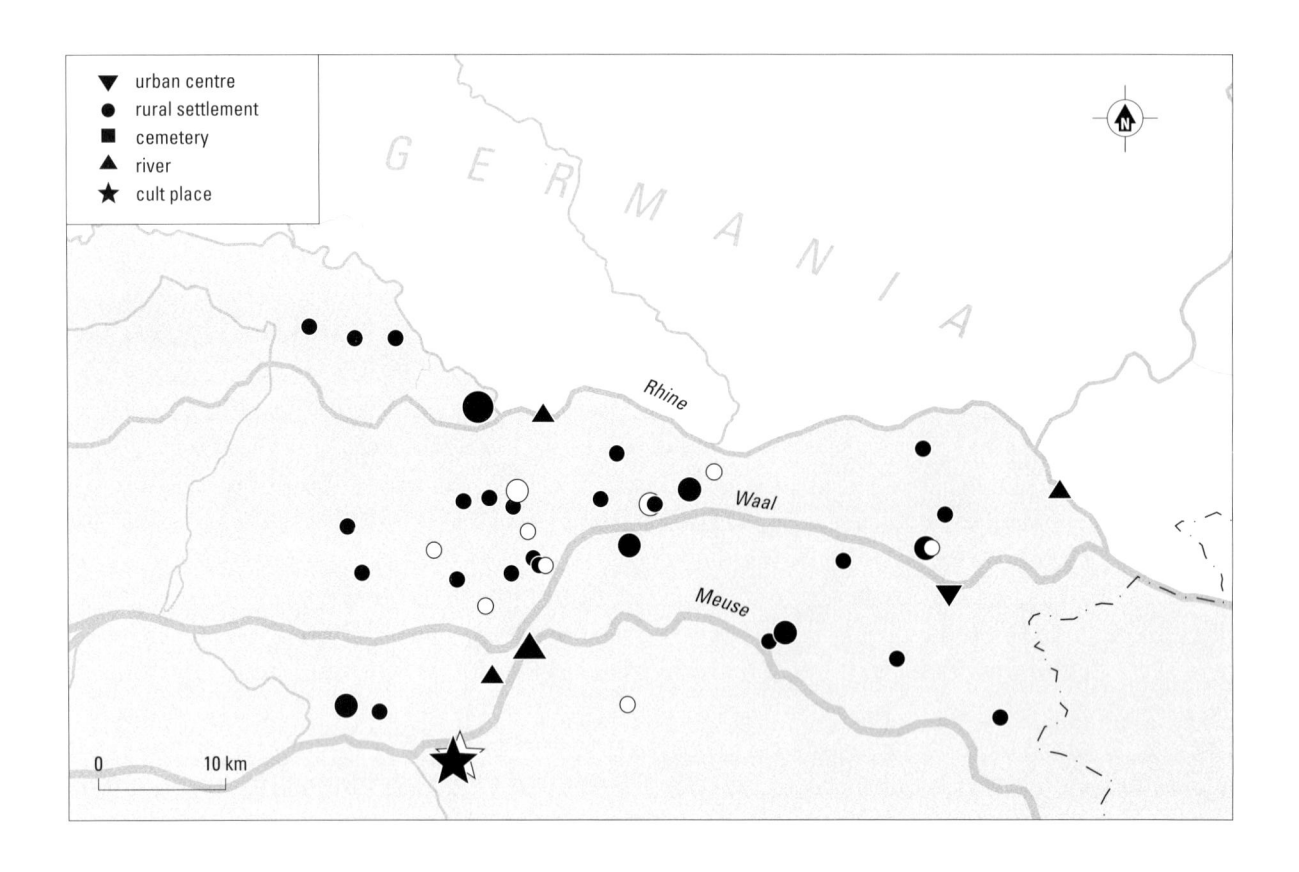

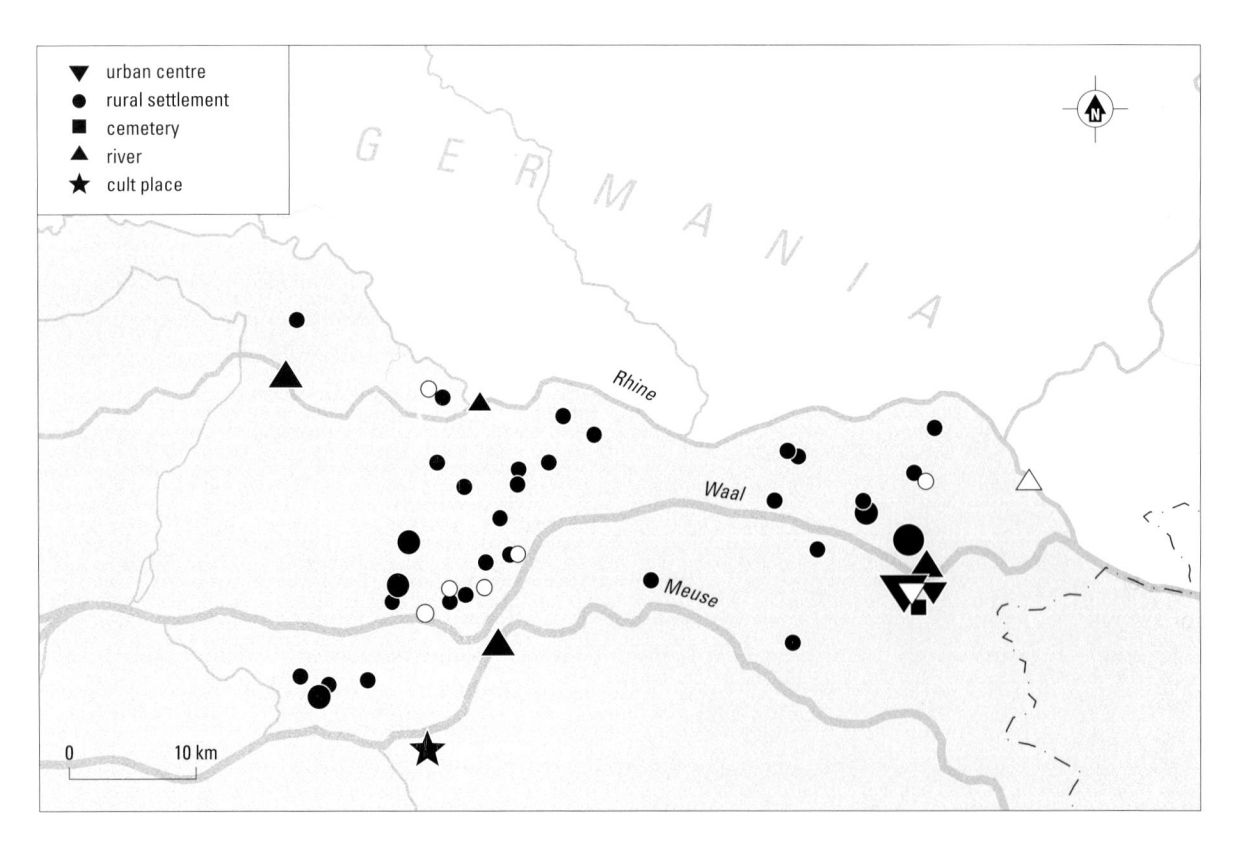

Fig. 3.10. The geographical distribution of belt components (black), as well as apron and baldric components (white) from the research area (1, 2-5 or more than 5 objects). Above: period 2 (belt and apron); below: period 3 (belt and baldric); next page: period 4 (belt).

80

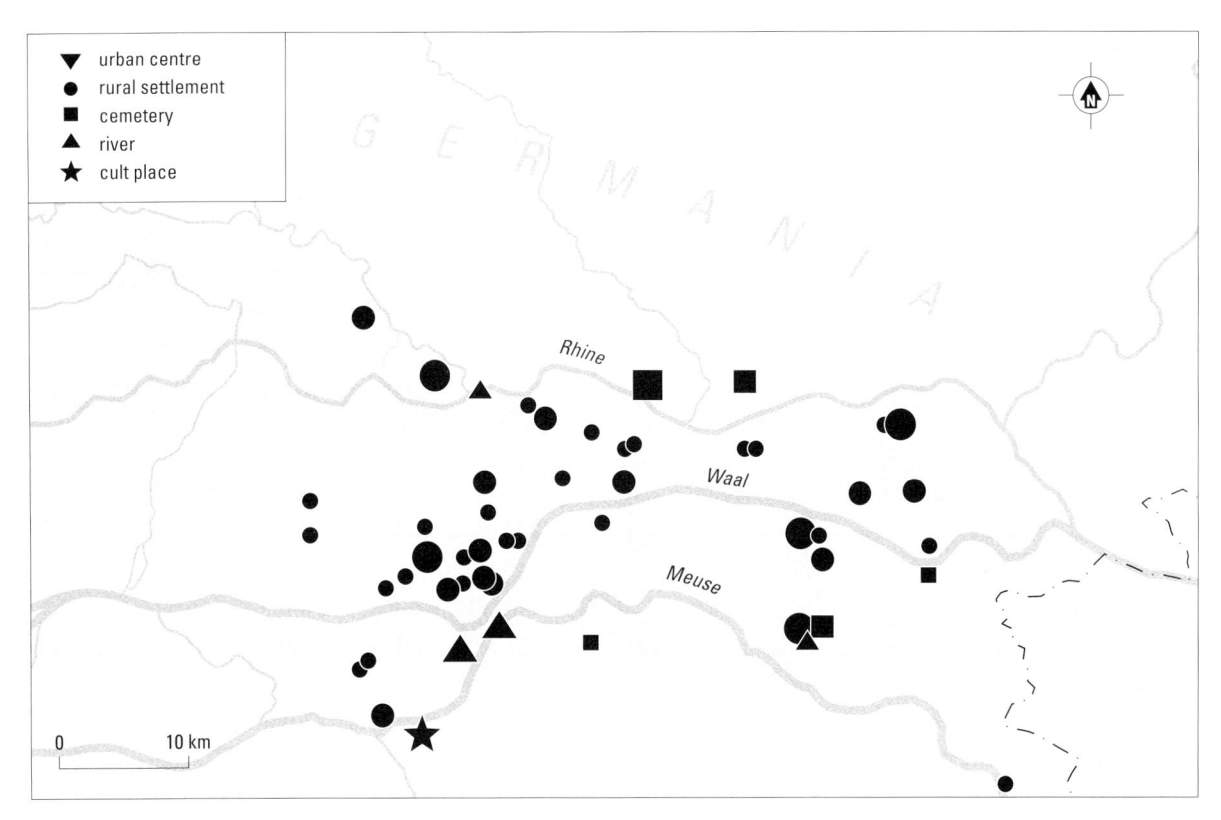

Fig. 3.10. Continued.

Clearly, the distribution of weaponry and horse gear finds is not fully representative of the original, Roman situation. Due to natural conditions or the way in which the inventory was compiled, find numbers in the western and southern peripheral zone as well as in the central part of the research region are probably underrepresented.

3.2.2 GEOGRAPHICAL DISTRIBUTION OF THE FINDS

The finds in the inventory are presented on distribution maps for each period in order to obtain a detailed picture of the geographical distribution of material from the eastern Rhine delta. The number of sites yielding weaponry from period 1 is extremely small (fig. 3.9); alongside several helmets of the Buggenum and Port types from rivers, this is a crest knob from a Buggenum type helmet from a rural settlement at Ommerensche Veld (219.1). The Kessel type swords, which come primarily from Kessel-Lith (12x) and Empel (5x), are of native origin and were possibly worn by soldiers of the earliest auxiliary units. A sword of the same type from the vicinity of Nijmegen (210.1) probably comes from a cult place or settlement. Lastly, bronze components from a Kessel type sword hilt are documented from the rural settlement of Tiel-'Oude Tielseweg' (240.3) and from the temple site in Elst (77.1). In terms of distribution, we can only say that the objects occur in both the western and eastern parts of the Batavian territory.

In period 2 we note a marked increase in the number of sites with weaponry (fig. 3.9), mainly rural settlements. The finds are concentrated in the western part of the research region and consist primarily of bronze *gladii* and plate armour components. The cult place at Empel, the richest site for 1st-century weaponry in the research region, is also part of the western concentration. Weapon components from rivers reveal a more easterly distribution, with the Waal at Nijmegen as the key site. The urban centres of *oppidum Batavorum* and Ulpia Noviomagus have yielded various armour components. Offensive weapons

81

are notably absent from both urban centres. Lastly, we occasionally find weapons as grave goods (a chain mail or scale armour hook, a *spatha* and a dagger). These weapon graves are only documented in the vicinity of Nijmegen.

Despite the decline in the number of find sites, weaponry continues to be distributed across the research region in period 3 (fig. 3.9). In most cases the material comes from rural settlements, with several sword components also occurring in Ulpia Noviomagus and a small number of finds from rivers. Although fewer than in the previous period, the bulk of the finds are documented from the Waal at Nijmegen. With regard to cult places, the same is true of Empel-'De Werf'. Weapon graves are completely unknown from this period. Whereas defensive weapons occur fairly frequently in the previous period, the number of sites with helmets and plate armour components has fallen sharply. The material consists overwhelmingly of offensive weaponry, mainly scabbard slides and chapes. In addition, several peltate dagger chapes have been found from this period.

In period 4 we observe a further decline in the number of find sites containing weapons (fig. 3.9). The defensive weaponry comprises components of exclusive guard helmets from the Waal at Nijmegen (211.18), IJzendoorn (138.3) and Lienden (174.6). The only offensive weapon is the sword blade of a probable *semispatha* from Druten (58.1).

Belt or baldric components are absent from period 1. The distribution of finds from the following period closely parallels that of contemporary weaponry (fig. 3.10). The belt components occur across the entire research region and are concentrated in the western zone. Decorative fittings and an apron pendant have also been found at various sites. The association between the belt and the apron can be seen most clearly in Empel-'De Werf', which yielded – alongside belt components – decorative fittings and a lunate pendant from a military apron. The number of sites with apron finds is probably underrepresented, given that the round decorative fittings, which are difficult to identify, are assigned here to horse gear.

Similar numbers of sites with belt components are documented for the subsequent period (fig. 3.10). The distribution of finds also reveals a similar pattern, with a clustering in the western part of the research region. In addition, various finds have been recovered from Nijmegen and its environs. The belt still occurs on a smaller scale in the cult place at Empel and is also found at various river sites. In addition to belt components, *phalerae*, decorative fittings and pendants of baldrics are known from a few sites. It is conspicuous that the baldric occurs exclusively in settlement contexts and is altogether absent from sites of a ritual nature.

A sizeable number of components of the characteristic wide belt and a few finds of the contemporaneous narrow belt are documented for period 4 (fig. 3.10). With the exception of the concentration of finds from the region west of Tiel, these are distributed fairly evenly across the study region. In addition to several belt sets from graves, the finds consist of one or more stray items from rural settlements. As in the previous period, there are few belt components from rivers. Because the temple at Empel was abandoned in the 3rd century, the few finds from the temple site do not appear to be linked to ritual transactions.

Horse gear makes up the final find category, and can be broken down into material from periods 2 and 3. Finds from period 2 are documented in almost every rural settlement in the eastern Rhine delta where metal detector searches have been conducted (fig. 3.11). Sites yielding more than 10 objects occur across the research region, the richest being Wijk bij Duurstede-'De Horden', Tiel-'Passewaaijse Hogeweg' and Oosterhout-'Van Boetzelaerstraat', each with about 40 finds. A similar number of finds is documented from the urban centres in Nijmegen, and about 100 finds are known from Empel-'De Werf'. In addition, several items of horse gear from this period have been found on the temple sites in and near Elst. The river assemblages show a fairly regular distribution across the research region, with the most important sites once again located in the eastern part. These include the hoard from the Rhine at Doorwerth, consisting of almost 200 components of exclusive parade horse gear.

In period 3 horse gear is found at a similar number of rural settlements (fig. 3.11). The number of objects found per settlement has risen in comparison to the previous period. Once again Tiel (51x)

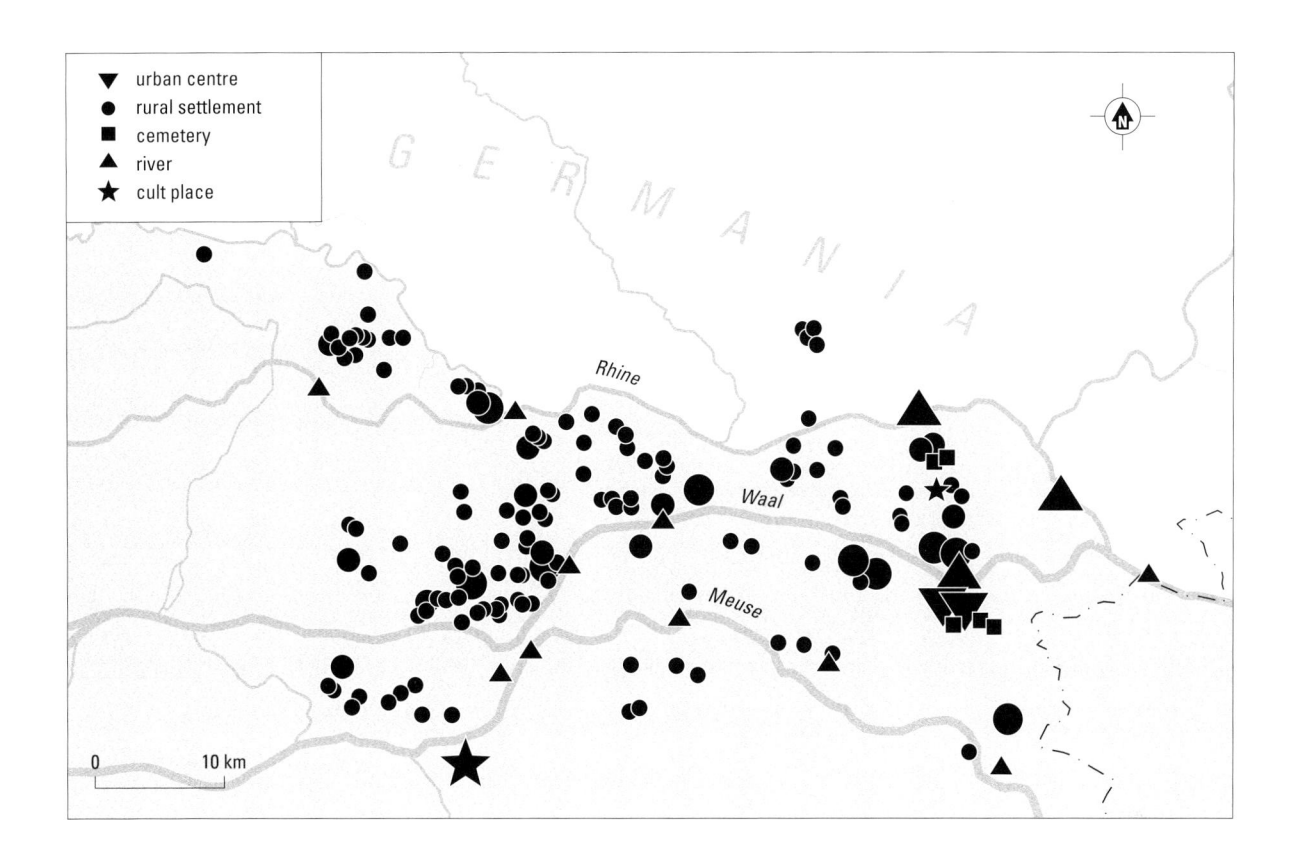

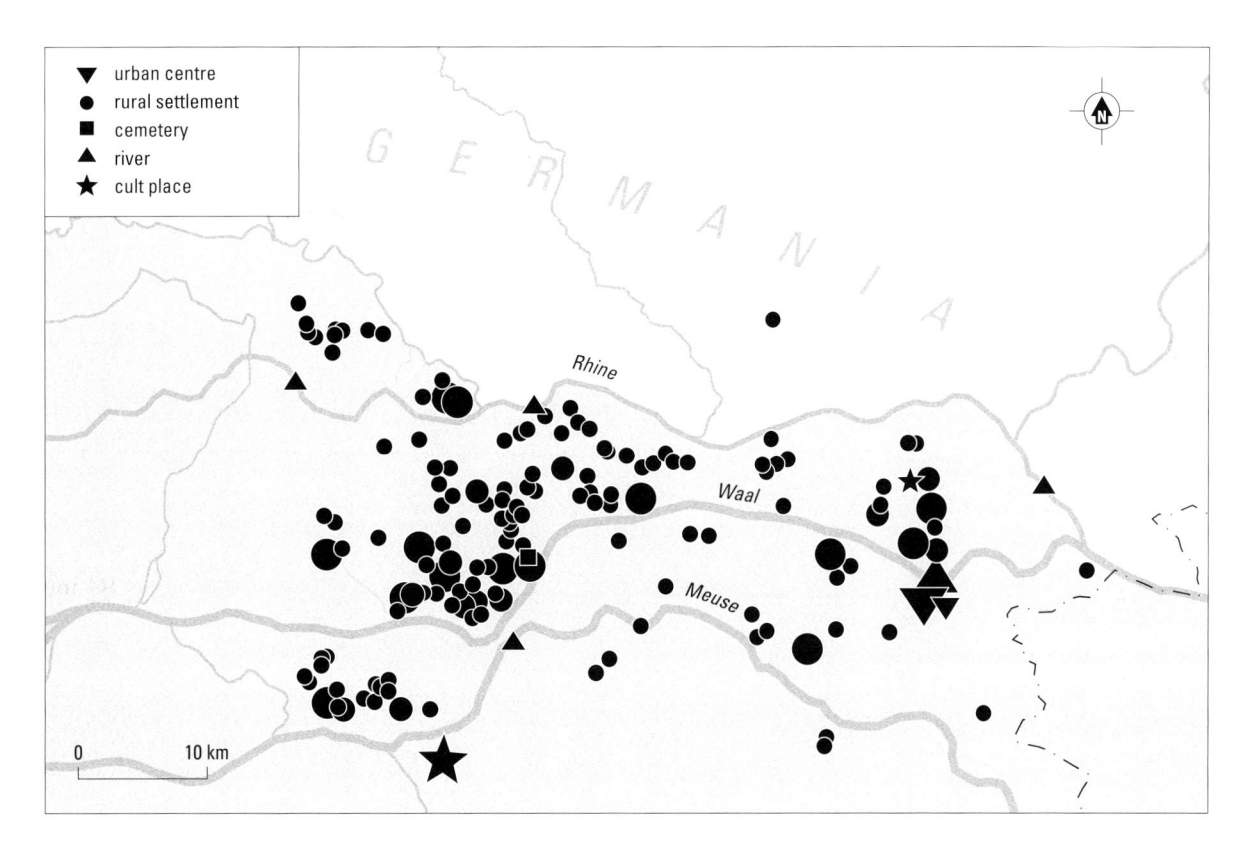

Fig. 3.11. The geographical distribution of horse gear from the research area (1, 2-5 or more than 5 objects). Above: period 2; below: period 3.

83

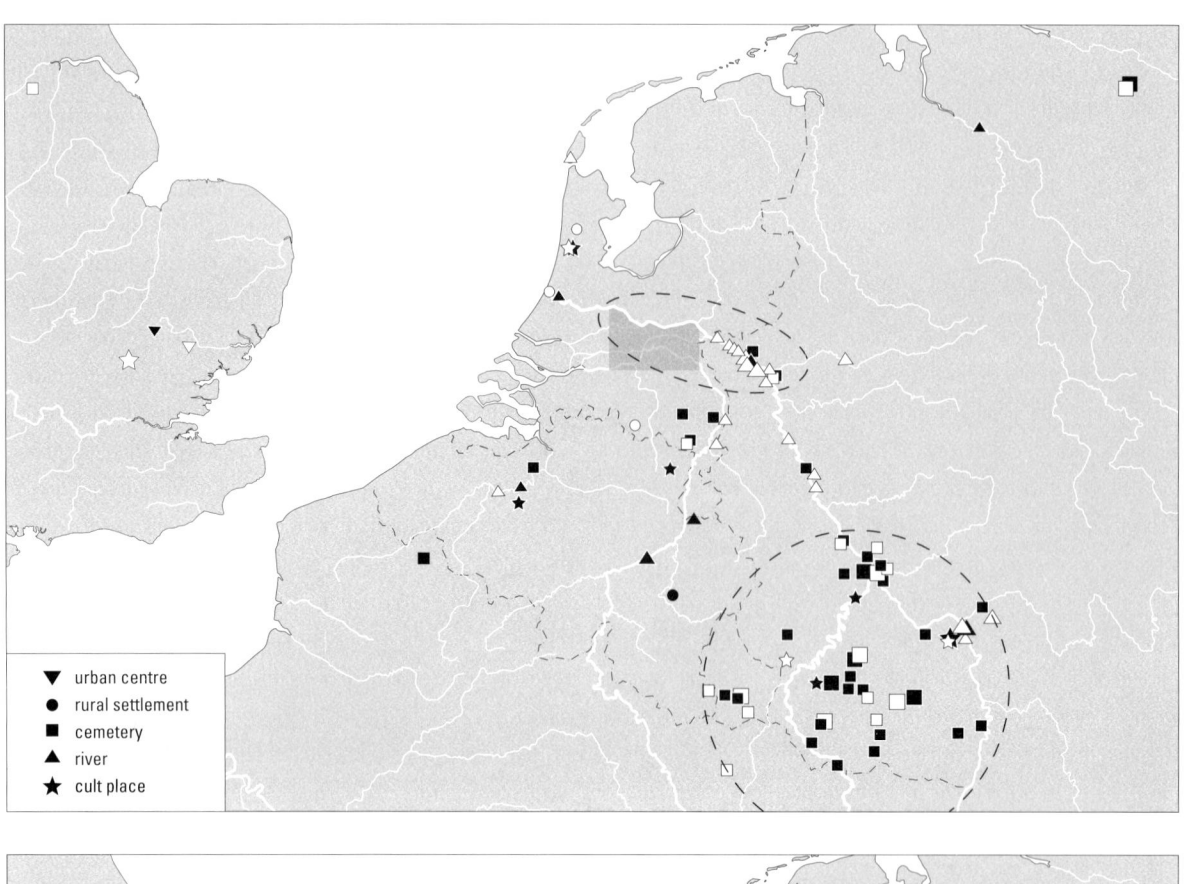

Fig. 3.12. The geographical distribution of offensive (black) and defensive weaponry (white) in northern Gaul, trans-Rhenish Germania and Britannia (large symbols: 2 or more objects). The research region is shown in dark grey. Above: periods 1-2; below: period 3; next page: period 4. After appendix 3.1-2; Böhme 1974, *Fundliste* 19 (supplemented by Braat et al. 1973; Klumbach 1973c).

84

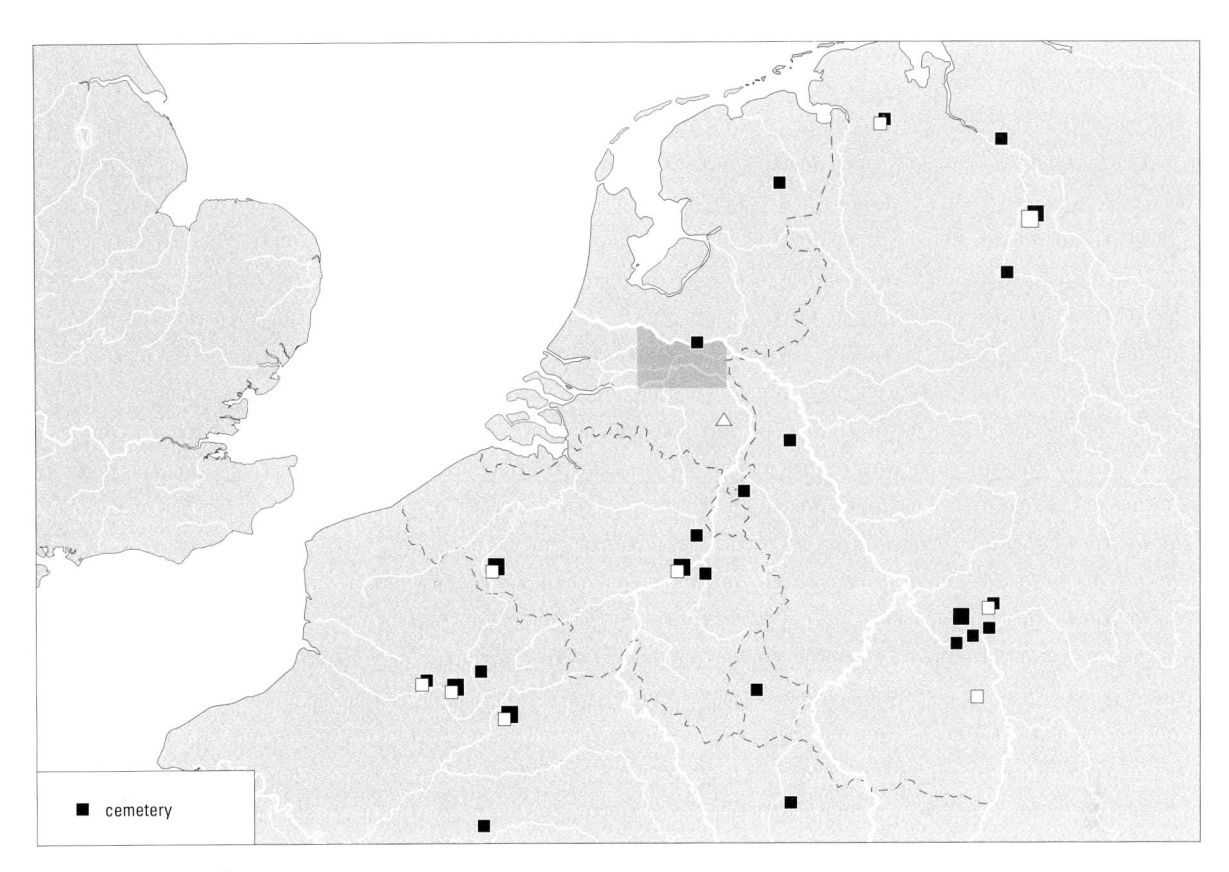

Fig. 3.12. Continued.

and Oosterhout (59x) are among the richer find sites from this period. In addition, over 100 horse gear components are documented from Ulpia Noviomagus. A small number of finds occurs in rivers from this period. The only larger assemblage comes from the Waal at Nijmegen, although here too find numbers show a decline. We see a similar picture in Empel-'De Werf'.

Patterns in the geographical distribution of the material appear to tie in with the results of the chronological analysis. In comparison to the previous period, period 2 shows a marked increase in the number of sites with weapons, suspension components and horse gear. In addition to finds from rural settlements and the urban centre in Nijmegen, a significant portion of the material originates from rivers and cult places. With regard to the transition to period 3, we see striking changes above all in the weaponry. Whereas defensive weapons are documented from relatively many sites in period 2, this category occurs only to a limited extent in the following period. Sword finds, which continue to occur frequently in period 3, are an exception to this. Another difference from the previous period is that we encounter both defensive and offensive weaponry to a lesser extent in rivers and cult places. Suspension and horse gear components from period 3 are documented from a similar number of find sites to the preceding period. Although the trend is less marked than with weaponry, these find categories also occur to a lesser extent in rivers and cult places. Period 4 is characterised not only by the exceptional composition of the finds, but also by the specific use of belts in a funerary context.

3.2.3 THE RESEARCH REGION IN A NORTHWEST EUROPEAN CONTEXT

In order to establish whether or not the situation in the study region is exceptional, I will place the region in a broader, northwest European context. For the overview maps, I make use of already pub-

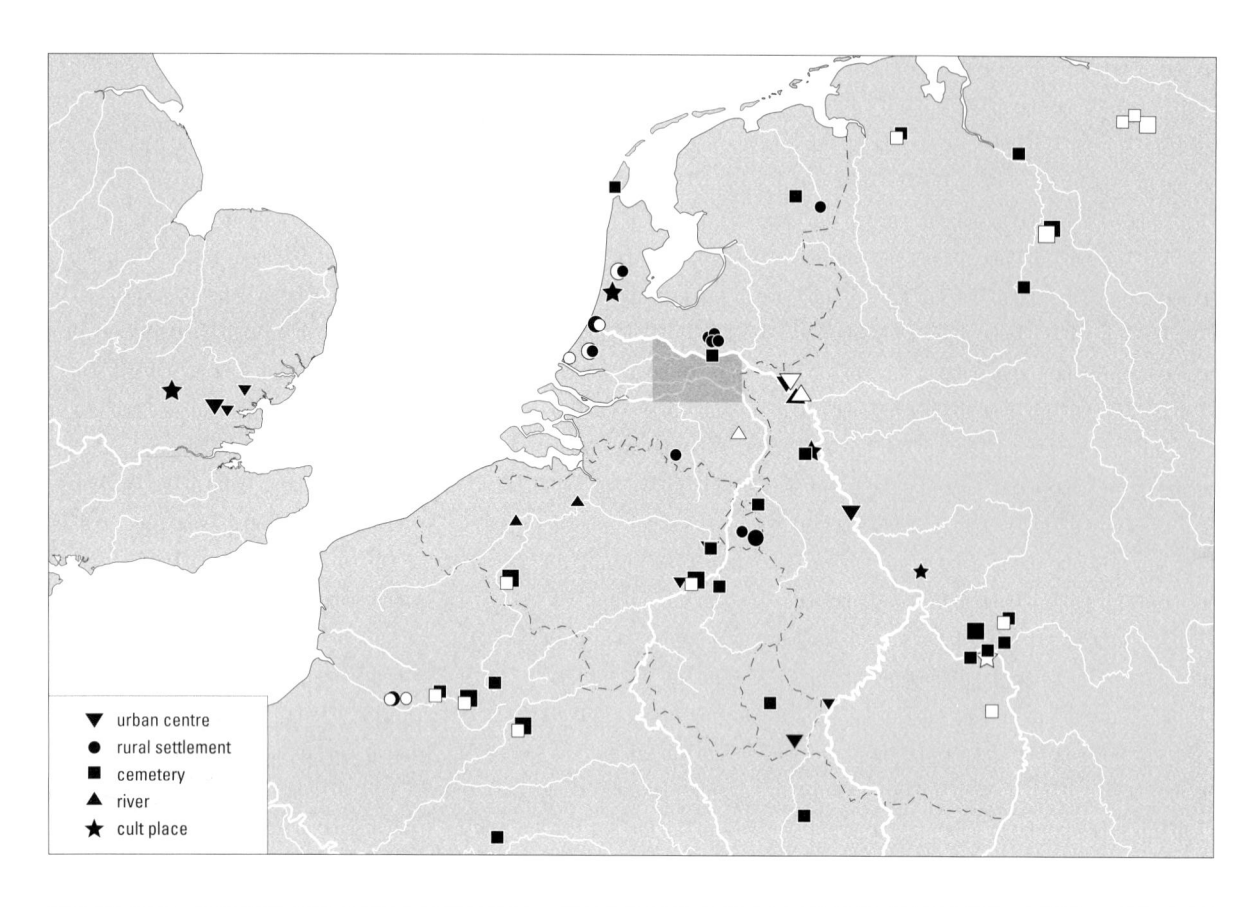

Fig. 3.13. The geographical distribution of suspension (white) and horse gear components (black) in northern Gaul, trans-Rhenish Germania and Britannia (large symbols: 2 or more objects). The research region is shown in dark grey. Above: period 2; below: period 3; next page: period 4. After appendix 3.3-4; Böhme 1974, *Fundliste* 11-12.

86

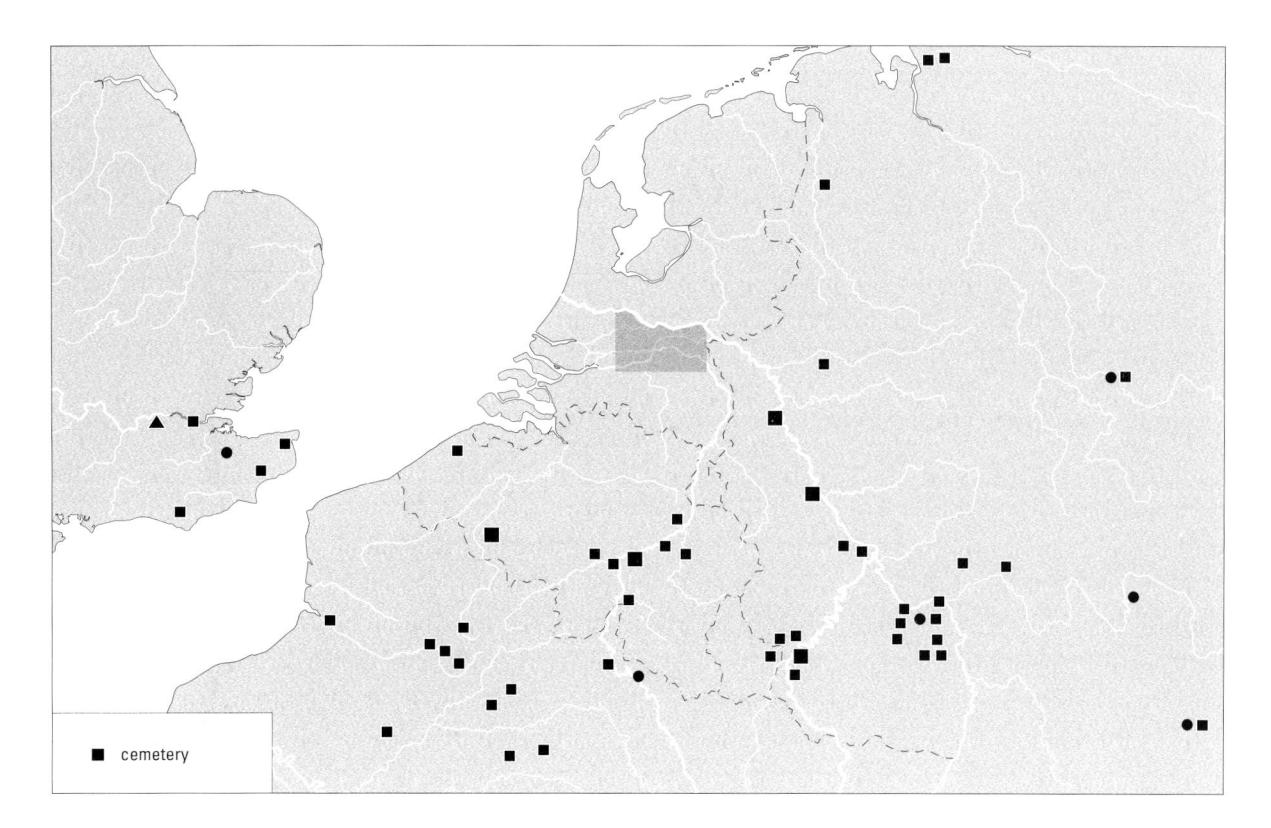

Fig. 3.13. Continued.

lished material which, in almost all cases, has been found during excavations or dredging operations. As a consequence, regional inventories may lead to a distortion of the distribution picture.[11] In addition, the finds from the eastern Rhine delta reveal the importance of metal detector finds. Because there are almost no published amateur collections from surrounding areas, it is hardly possible to make a reliable comparison with other regions. Further, metal detector finds are conspicuously absent from the German Rhineland, where a ban on metal detectors has led to very few finds being reported. We see a similar picture in northern France. For this reason, the discussion of the distribution maps will focus on the more general patterns. The central question is the extent to which the chronological trend corresponds to the situation in the study region.

Roymans has already pointed out that the 1st-century weapon finds are characteristic of the frontier zone of the Roman empire.[12] This picture still holds if new data is added to that considered by Roymans (fig. 3.12). Equipment from periods 1 and 2 that could have been used by the Roman army has been combined here.[13] We observe distinct regional patterns within the frontier zone. For example, the territory of the Treveri is characterised by the deposition of swords and shields in graves. The Batavian territory, on the other hand, is part of a narrow zone that extends as far as present-day Xanten, where weapons have mainly been recovered from rivers. In contrast to graves and rivers, the finds from cult places are not clustered in a specific region. The cult places that have yielded militaria are regularly distributed across the imperial frontier zone. The limited number of weapon finds from rural settlements is most noticeable.

---

[11] Examples are the inventory of 1st-century weapon graves from the territory of the Treveri (Schumachter 1989a; 1989b) and the overview of weapon finds in Belgium (Vanden Berghe 1996).

[12] Roymans 1996, 28 ff.

[13] With regard to period 1, these are Buggenum and Port type helmets and Kessel type swords.

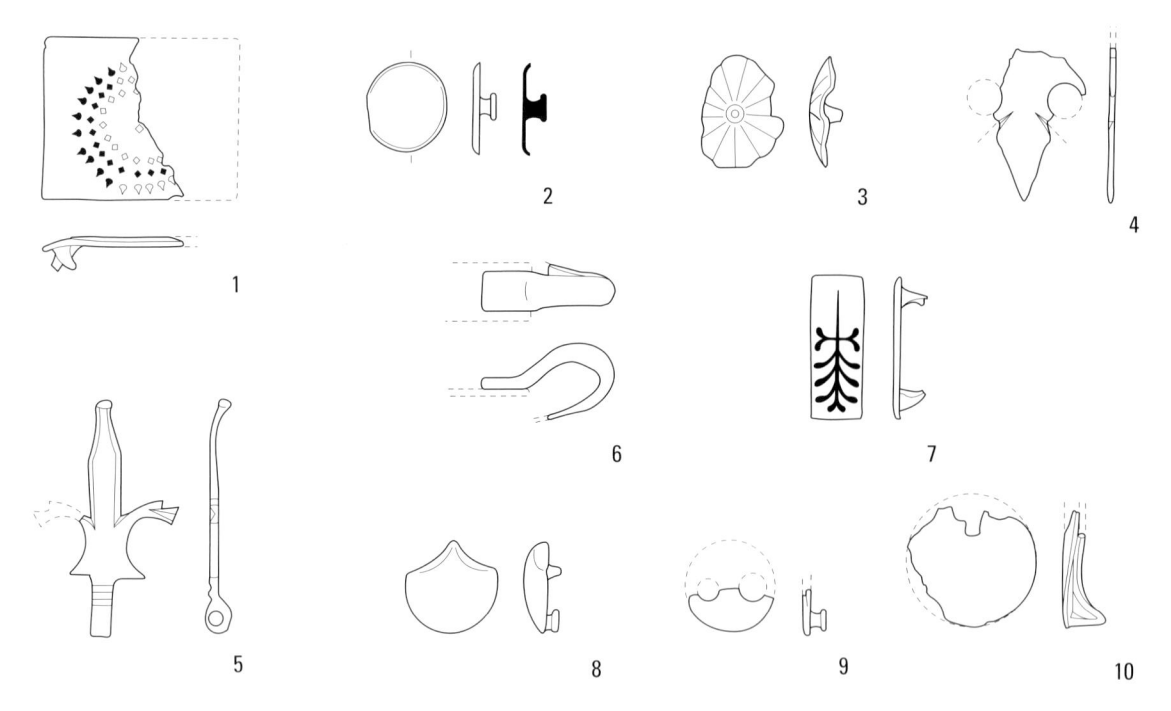

Fig. 3.14. Belt and horse gear components, found by Dutch amateur detectorists at two villa sites at Amiens in France (nrs. 1-4 and 5-10). Scale 2:3.
1 *cingulum* fitting, period 2; 2-4 decorative fittings and horse pendant fragment, period 3; 5 *cingulum* buckle tongue, period 2; 6-7 strap junction loop and decorative horse gear fitting, period 2; 8-10 decorative horse gear fittings and looped strap mount, period 3.

In view of the situation in the study region, this can at least partly be explained by the fact that hardly any metal detector finds in the northern Gallic region have as yet been published. Erdrich's inventory shows that weapons also occur to some extent far into Germania Magna.[14] In addition to finds from an open-air sanctuary at Velsen and from a few rivers, this material comes from rural settlements. The Gallic interior on the other hand is noticeably empty of finds. It is not entirely clear just how much this is due to the inaccessibility of data.[15] What we do know is that military material from graves, cult places and rivers is unknown in this region.[16]

In the following period, weapon finds also show a concentration in the frontier zone (fig. 3.12). In addition, weapons are documented in quite large numbers in trans-Rhenish Germania. A key difference from the previous period is the type of context in which objects are found. Whereas weapons from period 2 originate primarily from cult places, rivers and graves, a greater number of finds for period 3 come from urban and rural settlements. As in the research region, weapon finds from this period are primarily offensive weapons (swords).

For the first time, we also encounter weapons scattered across the Gallic interior in period 4 (fig. 3.12). Strikingly, the finds come almost exclusively from graves. This applies to the Gallic interior, the imperial frontier region and Germania Magna. Weapons from rivers are scarce in this period and material from cult places is altogether absent. It is conspicuous that no finds occur in urban and rural settlements outside the eastern Rhine delta, a picture that presumably ties in with the lack of published data from these context types.

[14] Erdrich 1994; 2001a; 2002.
[15] See the recent publication by Feugère and Poux (2002).
[16] In contrast to late La Tène material (Roymans 1996, figs. 1-2).

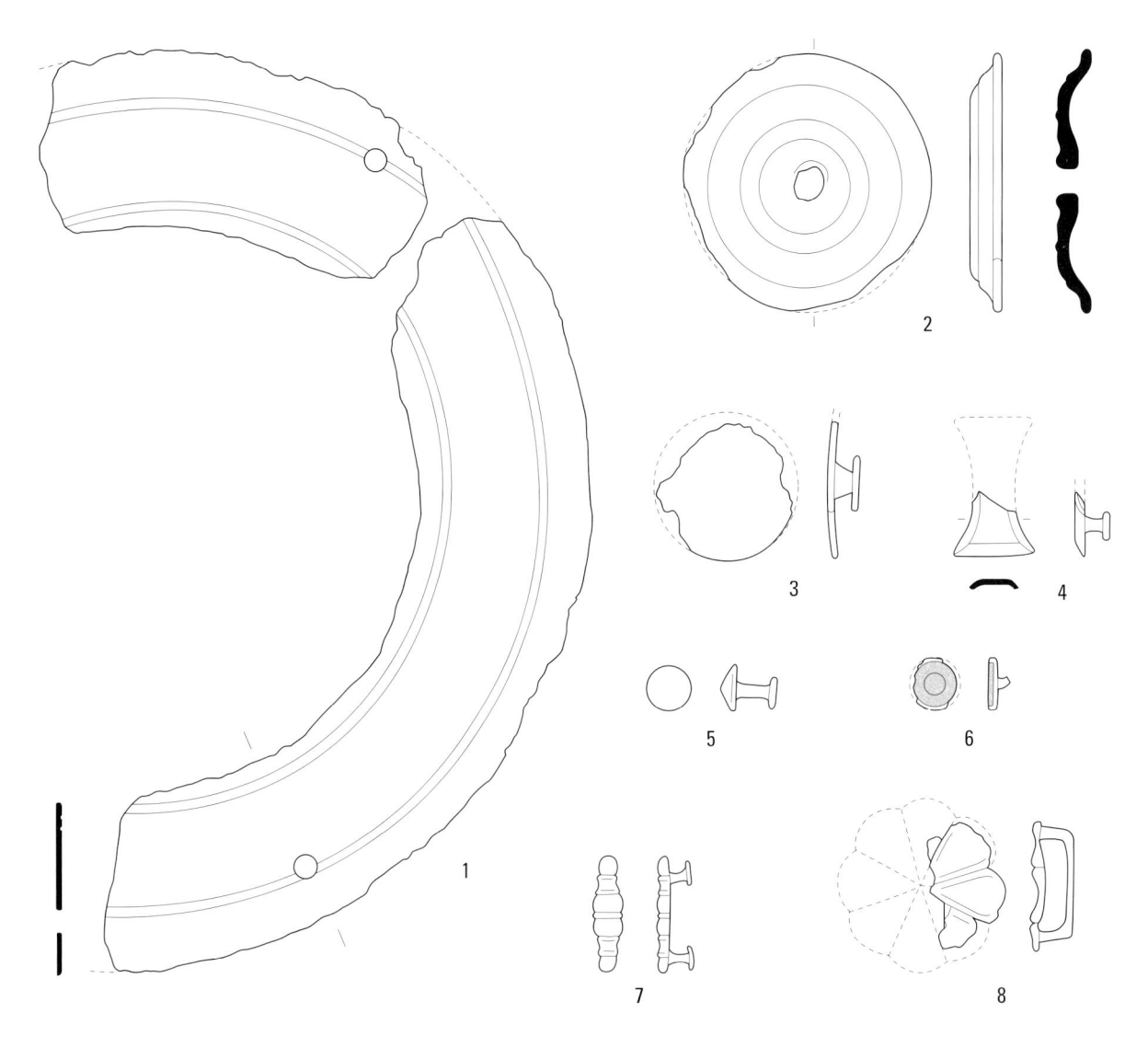

Fig. 3.15. Weaponry and horse gear from the villa site of Hoogeloon-'Kerkakkers'. Scale 2:3.
1 *umbo* flange, period 3; 2 horse gear *phalera*, period 2; 3-8 decorative horse gear fittings and looped strap mount, period 3.

As there are only few finds of belts and horse gear, these categories are presented together. From period 2, too few finds are documented to be able to detect any obvious distribution patterns (fig. 3.13). All that we can say is that this material also appears to occur above all in the imperial frontier zone. Finds from villas in the vicinity of Amiens show that the almost complete absence of finds in the Gallic interior may be a distorted picture (fig. 3.14). Unlike the weaponry in contemporaneous use, suspension components and horse gear have been found quite regularly in urban and rural settlements.

Like weaponry, suspension and horse gear components also occur frequently outside the Roman empire in period 3 (fig. 3.13). In addition, finds from Britannia and the above-mentioned villas near Amiens point to a more general use within the imperial borders (fig. 3.14). Of interest are the many finds from the northern Netherlands *terp* region, demonstrating that Roman horse gear was in general use beyond the imperial borders. The best example is Wijnaldum-'Tjitsma', where a total of 10 decorative fittings and a pendant from this period were found.[17] Both inside and outside the empire, the finds come

---

[17] Erdrich 1994, 207; 1999, 176.

almost exclusively from rural and urban settlements. Illustrative here are the finds from the villa site of Hoogeloon-'Kerkakkers': as well as a fragmentary shield boss, a looped strap fitting and five decorative horse gear items can be placed in period 3 (fig. 3.15).[18]

In addition to weaponry, belt finds occur frequently in the Gallic interior during period 4 (fig. 3.13). The overview map relates to buckles and fittings with chip-carved decoration (type D) dating from the late 4th to the first three decades of the 5th century. Inside the imperial borders, with the exception of the study region, belts are almost exclusively known from graves. Rural settlements in trans-Rhenish Germania have yielded several finds, although here too grave finds predominate.

The overview maps show that the trends observed for the research region fit quite well within a wider, northwest European framework. A large number of offensive and defensive weapons from period 2 are documented outside the *civitas Batavorum*. These have often been found in cult places and rivers, as well as in graves in the territory of the Treveri. Belts and horse gear on the other hand occur more frequently in settlements. In the following period, the bulk of the finds come from urban and rural settlements, with the weaponry consisting mainly of swords. Characteristic of period 4 is the high incidence of swords and belts in the funerary ritual. Notably few finds from this period are documented from other contexts.

3.3 COMPOSITION AND SPATIAL DISTRIBUTION AT THE SITE LEVEL

In addition to the many stray finds by amateur archaeologists using metal detectors, various excavations have yielded weaponry and horse gear – once again, especially when detectors have been employed. This material comes from rural settlements, urban centres, cult places and in some cases graves as well. Unlike stray material collected by amateur archaeologists, these excavation finds have a significant additional value:

1. The nature of the find site can often be pinpointed with certainty.
2. In the case of systematic metal detection, excavation finds present a good picture of the range of objects occurring in a specific context during a specific period.
3. The spatial distribution of the material across the site can be studied and linked to the excavated structures.[19]
4. Data is sometimes available on the specific archaeological context of individual objects.
5. Context datings can inform us about the duration of use of objects.

More than 300 sites have yielded weapons, suspension components and horse gear. I will describe below individual excavated sites per type of context. For each site, I present a brief overview of the structures uncovered and the composition of the weaponry and horse gear finds. I also discuss the spatial distribution of the finds and possible connections with these structures.[20] Finally, I examine the specific archaeological context of the finds, where possible comparing the typological and context datings in order to establish duration of use.

---

[18] However, the horse gear from period 3 is generally not found in association with specifically military items like shield bosses (see above).

[19] This also applies to stray finds from the topsoil, provided these have been properly measured.

[20] Where possible, the exact find location of the objects has been retained on the distribution maps. In the absence of specific find data, the object is placed in the centre of an excavation pit.

3.3.1 RURAL SETTLEMENTS AND CEMETERIES

The introduction of the metal detector has highlighted just how frequently weapons, suspension components and horse gear occur in rural sites. Militaria, ranging from one or a few items to over one hundred finds per site, are documented in virtually every settlement where metal detector searches have been conducted. Generally, the sites are simple farm hamlets with a few byre houses. Finds are also documented from larger settlement complexes with a villa or a villa-like building. Because notably few finds come from the associated cemeteries, these will be discussed together with the settlement finds.

Wijk bij Duurstede-'De Horden' and Wijk bij Duurstede-'De Geer'
A Roman-era rural settlement was fully excavated between 1977 and 1986 at the 'De Horden' site west of Wijk bij Duurstede (fig. 3.16). Habitation, which started here around the beginning of the first millennium and continued into the 3rd century, can be divided into five stages.[21] In the first, pre-Claudian stage, the inhabited area was split into two zones by a ditch running on a northeast-southwest axis. One or two farms in contemporaneous use stood on either side of this ditch. In the two subsequent stages (c. 50-100 AD), the buildings in the western and eastern sections of the site were successively enclosed by rectangular ditch systems. A single farmhouse was located inside the small, western enclosure, whereas the large, eastern quadrant contained two or three houses. The settlement reached its greatest expanse during stages 4 and 5 (c. 100-225 AD). In addition to the house inside the western enclosure, four or five farmhouses were probably in contemporaneous use on the eastern site. The cemetery located east of the settlement was laid out at the same time. The site was abandoned in the early 3rd century, possibly as a result of flooding. Finds of bronze coins show that the site must have been visited at least occasionally in the 4th and the early 5th centuries.[22]

With regard to the social structure inside the settlement complex, Van Es points out that we can distinguish a 'dominant' and several subordinate houses.[23] During the 1st century, the social heart of the settlement seems to have been located in the western part, where the oldest enclosed area is situated and where habitation was confined to a single farmhouse. In addition, early Roman imports have been found primarily in the western part.[24] Although the supposed central building was replaced by a wooden house with a *porticus* in the 2nd century, there are signs that the settlement's focal point shifted eastwards during the 1st century. For example, most coins from the second habitation stage come from the eastern site, whereas a wooden building with a *porticus* – perhaps now the principal building – was built here in the 2nd century.[25] Vos, however, believes that there were two 'dominant' dwellings, one inside the western and one inside the eastern ditched enclosure.[26]

'De Horden' is the first settlement where metal detectors have been used systematically, resulting in substantial numbers of metal finds. In addition to 270 fibulae and almost 240 coins, close to 120 objects can be identified as weaponry, suspension and horse gear components (291.1-117).[27] A layer of river clay covering the find site explains the generally good state of preservation of the material.

The earliest militaria are made up of 47 objects from period 2. The weaponry includes a *gladius* scabbard band and two fittings of type Corbridge plate armour. The *cingulum* too is represented by four

---

[21] Vos 2002, 63 ff.; Van Es (in: Van Es/Hessing 1994, 27-33, 40-45, 58-61, 70-71) assumes four stages; in general, see also Hessing/Steenbeek 1990.
[22] Hessing/Steenbeek 1990, 22; Aarts 1994, fig. 114.
[23] Van Es/Hessing 1994, 42-44, 58-60; Vos 2002, 79 ff.
[24] For the coins, see Aarts 1994, 138-140.
[25] Van Es 1984a, 23; Aarts 1994, 140-141. For an interpretation as a cult building, see Van Es/Hessing 1994, 60.
[26] Vos 2002, 81-83 (buildings H9 and H25).
[27] Van der Roest 1988 (fibulae); Aarts 1994 (coins). With regard to weaponry and horse gear, it should be noted that not all metal finds from 'De Horden' were available for identification.

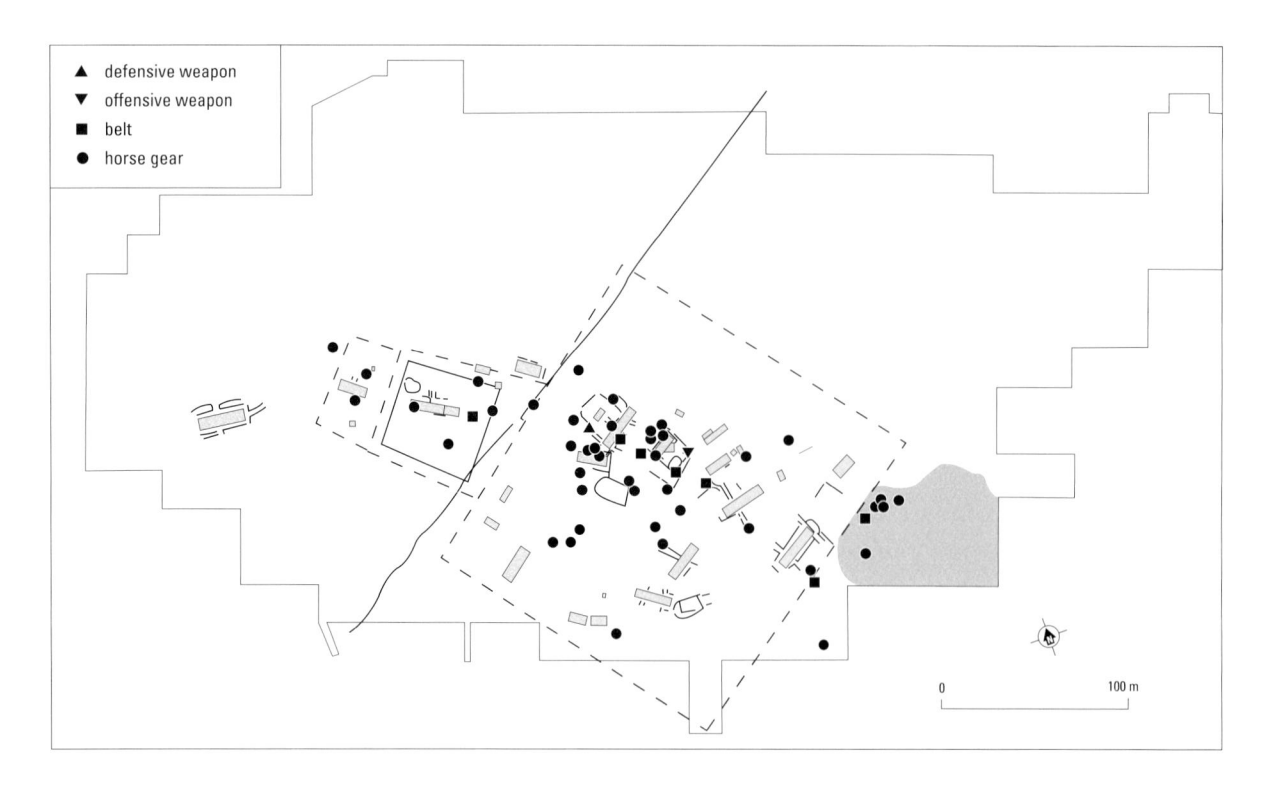

Fig. 3.16. Spatial distribution of militaria from the rural settlement of Wijk bij Duurstede-'De Horden'. Extensions to the ditch system in settlement stages 3 and 4 are indicated by dotted lines. Above: period 2 (stages 1-3); below: period 3 (stages 4-5); next page: non-securely-dated offensive weapons (all stages). Based partly on Van Es/Hessing 1994, figs. 17, 26-27, 42; Vos 2002, figs. 28-33.

▼ offensive weapon

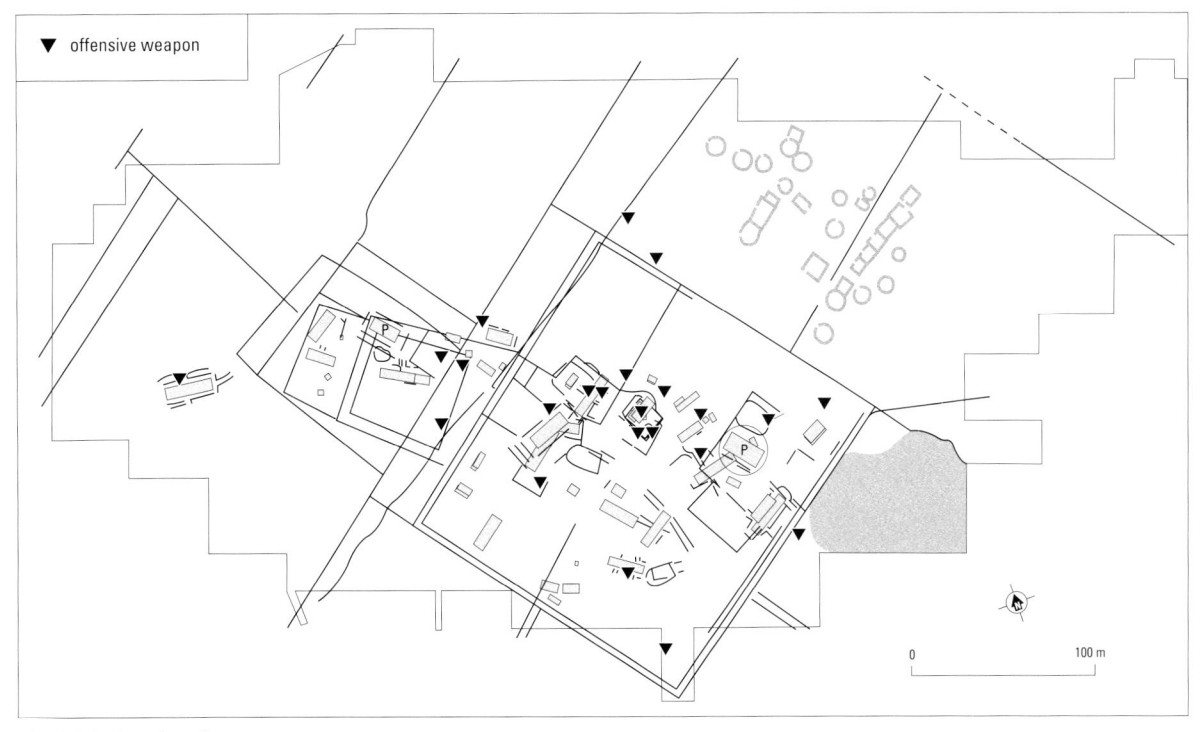

Fig. 3.16. Continued.

peltate buckles, a dagger frog and four belt fittings (fig. 2.11). Most finds consist of horse gear. Alongside 23 decorative fittings, these are one fastener, 10 pendants, five ring junction fittings, two looped strap fittings, two bells and one strap terminal. Eight pendants are of the trefoil type, including two large, exclusive examples that may have been part of *dona militaria* (291.53, 56, fig. 2.24). Two round rings with a round and a rectangular loop belong to the bit. Lastly, we can place a semi-circular spur in this period.

Twenty-nine finds are documented from period 3. There is no weaponry, and the only belt component is a ring buckle stud. The remaining finds consist of horse gear, namely two fasteners, 20 decorative fittings, four pendants and a bell. The abandonment of 'De Horden' quite early in the 3rd century explains the fewer finds from period 3, as well as the lack of late Roman material.

Various iron weapon components are difficult to date: four *pila* heads, two boltheads, an arrowhead and 11 spear- or lanceheads (fig. 2.9). The same applies to three pointed butt spikes from spears, lances or *pila*, six pieces of lead slingshot and the bronze mouthpiece of a military wind instrument, possibly a *tuba* or *bucina* (fig. 2.16). A *pilum* head with an irregular shape was probably produced locally. Lastly, an almond-shaped looped strap fitting and the bronze shank of a bit cannot be attributed specifically to period 2 or 3.

Figure 3.16 presents the finds from 'De Horden' on distribution maps. The majority of the objects from period 2 come from the eastern part of the settlement, with the finds concentrated around the central and western farmyards. A small number of objects have been found inside the western ditches, where the finds also occur around the houses. The only objects from outside the ditched enclosure were found in a natural depression directly east of the settlement. Strikingly few finds come from the settlement ditches.

In period 3 the objects are once again concentrated in the inhabited area, with no finds at all from the cemetery laid out during this period. The material occurs primarily inside the large, square enclosure. In addition to a concentration of finds around the houses in the western part of this area, several items have been found in the vicinity of the wooden *porticus* building on the eastern side. Once again, finds are documented from the natural depression east of the settlement. Various objects come from a small part of the eastern settlement ditch in the immediate vicinity of this depression.

site	object	period	find context	context dating	cat.nr.
'De Horden'	strap fitting hg	3	house wall trench	100-225	291.93
	lancehead	-	house drainage ditch	1-70	291.25
	strap fitting hg	3	house drainage ditch	70-150	291.103
	strap fitting hg	2	house drainage ditch	100-150?	291.91
	spur	3	house drainage ditch	150-225	291.116
	strap fitting hg	2	farmyard ditch	50-100	291.79
	pendant hg	2	farmyard ditch	50-100	291.59
	strap fitting hg	2	farmyard ditch	70-100	291.89
	gladius scabbard	2	farmyard ditch	70-150	291.30
	catapult bolt*	-	farmyard ditch	70-150	291.4
	strap terminal hg	2	farmyard ditch	100-150	291.114
	strap fitting hg *	2	farmyard ditch	100-150	291.113
	bell hg.	2	farmyard ditch	100-150	291.117
	pilum head	-	farmyard ditch	100-225	291.7
	fastener hg*	2	farmyard ditch	100-225	291.47
	strap fitting hg	2	farmyard ditch	100-225	291.83
	strap fitting hg	2	farmyard ditch	100-225	291.87
	pendant hg*	2	ditch path	70-225	291.53
	strap junction hg	2	settlement ditch	70-225	291.68
	ring buckle fastener	3	settlement ditch	70-225	291.40
	strap fitting hg	3	settlement ditch	70-225	291.110
	strap fitting hg	3	settlement ditch	70-225	291.99
	strap fitting hg *	3	settlement ditch	70-225	291.97
	catapult	-	settlement ditch	100-225	291.5
	strap fitting hg	2	settlement ditch	100-225	291.85
	strap junction hg	2	pit	100-150?	291.67
	cingulum fitting	2	pit	100-225	291.38
	butt spike	-	pit	100-225	291.17
	spearhead	-	pit	-	291.21
	bit	2	pit	-	291.44
	arrowhead	2-3	pit	-	291.3
	pendant hg	2	well	70-150	291.62
	lancehead*	-	well	100-225	291.24
'De Geer'	strap fitting hg	3	posthole	300-450	288.37
	fastener hg	3	well	-	288.29

Table 3.1. Overview of the militaria from Wijk bij Duurstede-'De Horden' and Wijk bij Duurstede-'De Geer' with known find contexts and context datings (AD) (hg: horse gear). The 'De Horden' datings are based on Vos' phasing (2002). Objects from the soil immediately above a feature are marked with an asterisk.

If we look at the distribution of less easily dated offensive weapons, including the lead slingshot, we observe a more regular distribution across the settlement site (fig. 3.16). Several finds have also been recovered from outside the rectangular settlement ditch, including the wind instrument that comes from a ditch in one of the surrounding fields.[28] Although the pattern is less clear than for material from periods

2 and 3, once again we see a concentration of finds in the western part of the large ditched enclosure. A clue to the specific dating of the iron weaponry is a lancehead from the drainage ditch of a farmhouse in the earliest settlement stage, located west of the small ditched enclosure (table 3.1). The majority of the objects have a later context dating and can be placed in the 2nd century and the first quarter of the 3rd.

It is conspicuous that the distribution pattern emerging from the finds bears no relationship to the social differentiation suggested by the settlement layout and the distribution of coins and imported items. A small number of objects from period 2 were found inside the western ditched enclosure, whereas in the following period the finds are not concentrated around the supposed principal buildings with a *porticus*. In both periods, finds were concentrated around the farmhouses in the western part of the large ditched enclosure, a picture that is confirmed by the less securely dated weaponry.

With regard to the specific archaeological context of the material, I have already pointed out that almost no objects occur in the larger ditch structures that border the settlement site. Inside the settlement, a sizeable portion of the material comes from smaller ditches (table 3.1). The remaining finds come from pits, wells and the natural depression.

In all cases the context datings overlap wholly or in part with the production period. A decorative fitting (291.79) and a trefoil pendant (291.59), which were manufactured in the Claudio-Neronian period and which ended up in the same farmyard ditch between AD 50 and 100, show a duration of use of a few decades at most.

Part of a second settlement from the Roman era ('De Geer') was excavated 500 metres north of 'De Horden' between 1989 and 1994 (fig. 3.17).[29] A major structural element within the settlement is a rectangular ditch system running at right angles to an old river bed, which silted up at about the beginning of the first millennium, forming a swampy depression during the Roman period. In the centre of the inhabited area, a number of curved ditches were unearthed that can be associated with one or more centrally located buildings (stage 1). Immediately east of these house ditches are several ring ditches, which have largely been ploughed. The actual grave has been preserved within one of the ditches. Judging by the earthenware discovered, it can be dated to the end of the 2nd century.[30] The ditch system appears to have fallen into disuse in the late Roman period (stage 2). A large, two-aisled farmhouse was constructed over the southern ditches, and a small farmhouse with an outbuilding was found inside the northern part of the ditched enclosure. A third, possibly contemporaneous farmhouse is located on the site of the depression. East of the large farmhouse is a late Roman cemetery with several Merovingian graves. The cemetery has largely been disturbed; the excavation yielded only a few grave goods.[31]

Although there is no comprehensive overview of metal finds from 'De Geer', more than 50 objects may have been of a military nature (288.1-54). No more than eight objects date from period 2. These are a plate armour shoulder hinge, as well as a strap junction, four decorative fittings, a strap terminal and a bell of horse gear. The following period is represented by a complete, tinned *phalera* from a baldric and 21 horse gear components. In addition to two fasteners and three pendants, the horse gear consists of decorative fittings. No less than 24 belt components come from period 4. The finds chiefly comprise round and rectangular fittings that were attached to the bottom edge of wide belts. Three tweezers also come from this type of belt. Lastly, a spearhead cannot be dated more precisely than to the Roman period.

The distribution of finds across the settlement area shows how few objects from the different periods were found around the houses (fig. 3.17). This is because cultivation, and presumably levelling, have lowered the site by at least half a metre.[32] The finds from periods 2 and 3 are concentrated in the natural depression,

[28] Verwers 1978.
[29] Van Es 1994; see also the ROB Annual Reports, 1989-1994.
[30] Van Es et al. 1995, 159.
[31] Van Es/Lutter/Van Dockum 1990, 48; Van Es/Van Dockum 1991, 51.
[32] Van Es/Van Dockum 1992, 43.

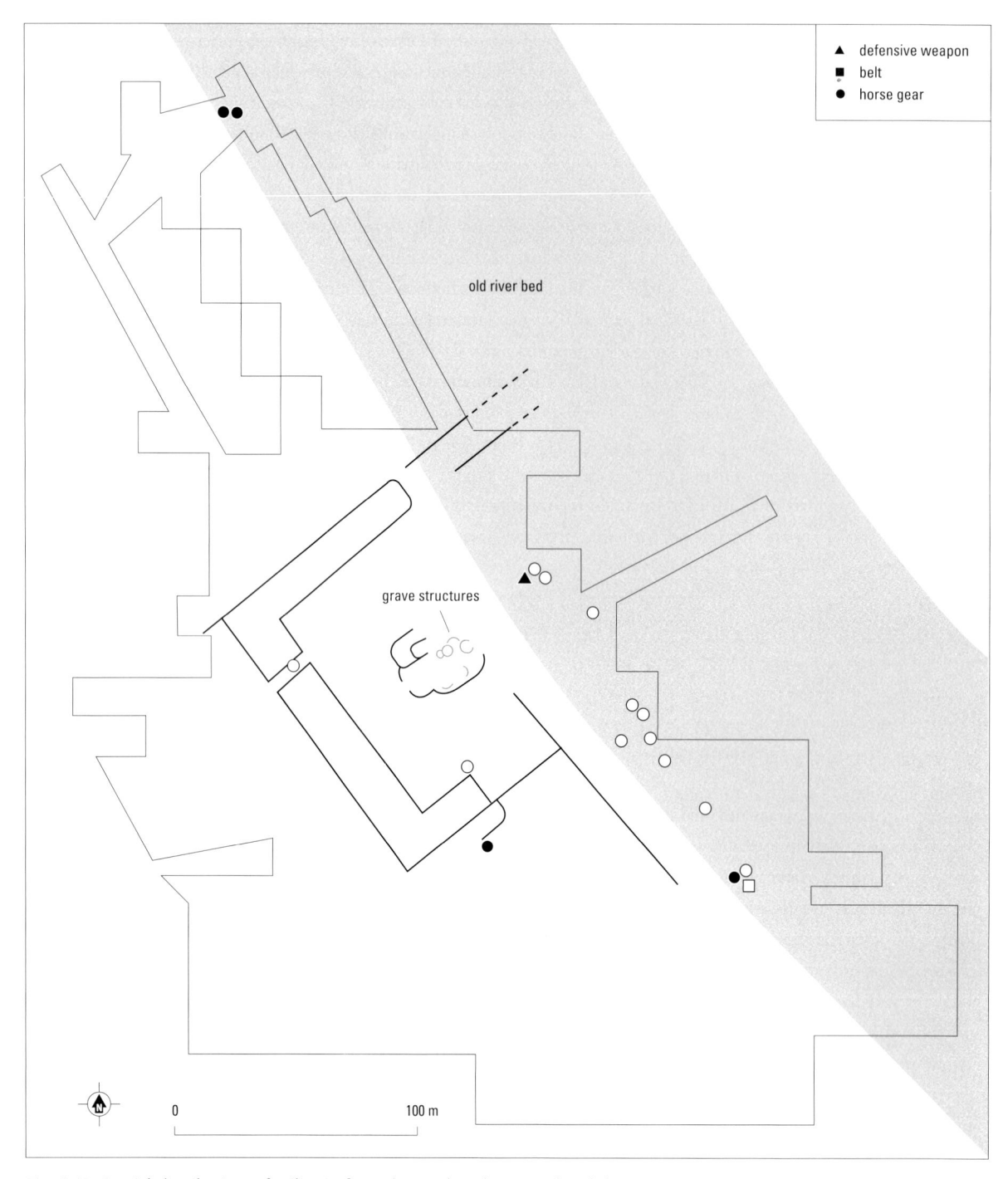

Fig. 3.17. Spatial distribution of militaria from the rural settlement of Wijk bij Duurstede-'De Geer'. Above: periods 2 (black) and 3 (white) (settlement stage 1); next page: period 4 (stage 2). Based partly on Van Es 1994, fig. 195.

with the remaining objects found in the immediate vicinity of the ditch complex. None of the objects were located near the central house. In period 4 too, there is no clear connection between the find distribution and the houses (fig. 3.17), with objects scattered across the inhabited area. Although late Roman belt components are usually known from funerary contexts, for the material from 'De Geer' we see no clustering at the site of the disturbed cemetery.

The precise find context is known for only a few objects found outside the natural depression (table 3.1). A decorative horse gear fitting from period 3 was found in a well and a second, contemporaneous

96

Fig. 3.17. Continued.

example in a posthole. The dating of the well is unknown and the posthole is part of a farmhouse from the late Roman period.

Oss-'Westerveld'
Some settlements and a cemetery, all part of a larger settlement cluster, have been excavated in recent decades on the sandy soils at Oss.[33] At the centre of the cluster is Oss-'Westerveld', a large settlement with

[33] Van der Sanden/Van den Broeke 1987; Van der Sanden 1988; Fokkens 1998; Wesselingh 2000.

Fig. 3.18. Spatial distribution of militaria (period 2) from the rural settlement of Oss-'Westerveld' (settlement stages 1-4). Wells are indicated by grey circles (P: Wooden building with a *porticus*). Based partly on Wesselingh 2000, figs. 187-190.

a rectangular enclosing ditch. South of 'Westerveld' is an extensive cemetery, and there are traces of about a dozen smaller settlements around 'Westerveld'. Possible military finds have only been documented from Oss-'Westerveld' and the smaller Oss-'Vijver'.

The settlement on the Westerveld site was largely excavated between 1980 and 1984 (fig. 3.18).[34] The site appears to have been inhabited uninterruptedly, with six distinctive stages, from the late Iron Age up until the first half of the 3rd century. Around the beginning of the first millennium, the settlement consisted of three or four houses surrounded by a rectangular double ditch (stage 1). The settlement shows a marked growth from AD 25 to 125, with the number of contemporaneous house sites rising to eight or nine (stages 2-4/5). In around AD 100 the farmhouses in the southwest corner of the settlement were cleared away and replaced by a wooden building with a *porticus* and a large, ditched yard. The relatively many Flavian and early Roman imports from this part of the settlement suggest that this house, and perhaps one or more of its predecessors, was the main building.[35] Around the mid-2nd century, the

[34] Wesselingh 2000, 71 ff.

[35] Wesselingh 2000, 164-168, 218-221 (building H78).

porticus building fell into disuse and the rectangular ditch system lost its purpose (stage 6). These changes coincided with a declining habitation level, followed by abandonment of the settlement in about 225.

Because metal detection was not used systematically and metal tends to be poorly preserved in sandy soils, 'Westerveld' has yielded relatively few metal finds.[36] It is noteworthy that almost all the metal was recovered from deeper features such as pits and, in particular, wells. The identifiable objects include three coins, 37 fibulae and five possible military items (237.1-5). A fragment of a small, rectangular fitting can be attributed to a *cingulum* apron. The remaining objects – three rectangular decorative fittings and a figure-eight fitting – are horse gear items. All objects belong typologically to period 2.

The fittings come from wells (table 3.2). Two of the decorative fittings and the apron fitting came from the same feature dated to the fourth quarter of the 1st century. The two other fittings were recovered from wells in use during the mid-1st century and the first half of the 2nd century. We see overlap in both the context datings and the typological datings, with the decorative fitting from the oldest well being used for several decades at the most.

The wells containing belt and horse gear components can be associated with houses from different stages of the settlement. Interestingly, the two most recent wells are located in the yard of the *porticus* building; given the dating of this house (c. AD 75-150), they were probably in contemporaneous use.

object	period	find context	context dating	cat.nr.
strap fitting hg	2	well	25-75	237.4
apron fitting;				
strap fitting hg (2x)	2	well	75-100	237.1-2, 5
strap fitting hg	2	well	100-150	237.3

Table 3.2. Overview of the militaria from Oss-'Westerveld', with known find contexts and context datings (AD) (hg: horse gear). The datings are based on Wesselingh 2000, tables 6, 30.

Tiel-'Passewaaijse Hogeweg' and Tiel-'Oude Tielseweg'
Excavations of a Roman-era settlement complex have been carried out since 1996 on the site of the new housing development at 'Passewaaij'. The complex comprises a central cemetery flanked on either side by settlements. Intensive use of a metal detector during the excavation has led to substantial metal finds.[37]

The settlement of 'Passewaaijse Hogeweg', which extends east of the cemetery, has been excavated most fully (fig. 3.19).[38] A residual channel dividing the inhabited area in two is a key structural element within the settlement. It carried water until the beginning of Roman habitation, after which it rapidly filled up with sediment and habitation waste. After a period with single finds and several graves from the Iron Age (stage 1, c. 150-80 BC), the earliest habitation dates from the late Iron Age and early Roman period (stage 2, c. 50 BC-AD 40). Two or three contemporary farmyards were laid out on both sides of the residual channel during this stage. In the third (c. AD 40-150) and fourth stage (c. AD 150-210) the settlement size remained stable, but a clustering of houses can be seen. In the fouth stage, part of the settlement area was enclosed by a rectangular ditch system, which fell into disuse and was replaced by a long, curved ditch in stage 5 (c. AD 210-240). Habitation in this stage was confined to a ditched compound east of the former ditch system. The individual compound continued to be inhabited into

[36] Wesselingh 2000, 144-154.

[37] Not only the excavation planes, but also the topsoil was subjected to a systematic layer-by-layer search with a metal detector.

[38] Heeren 2006; Roymans/Derks/Heeren 2007.

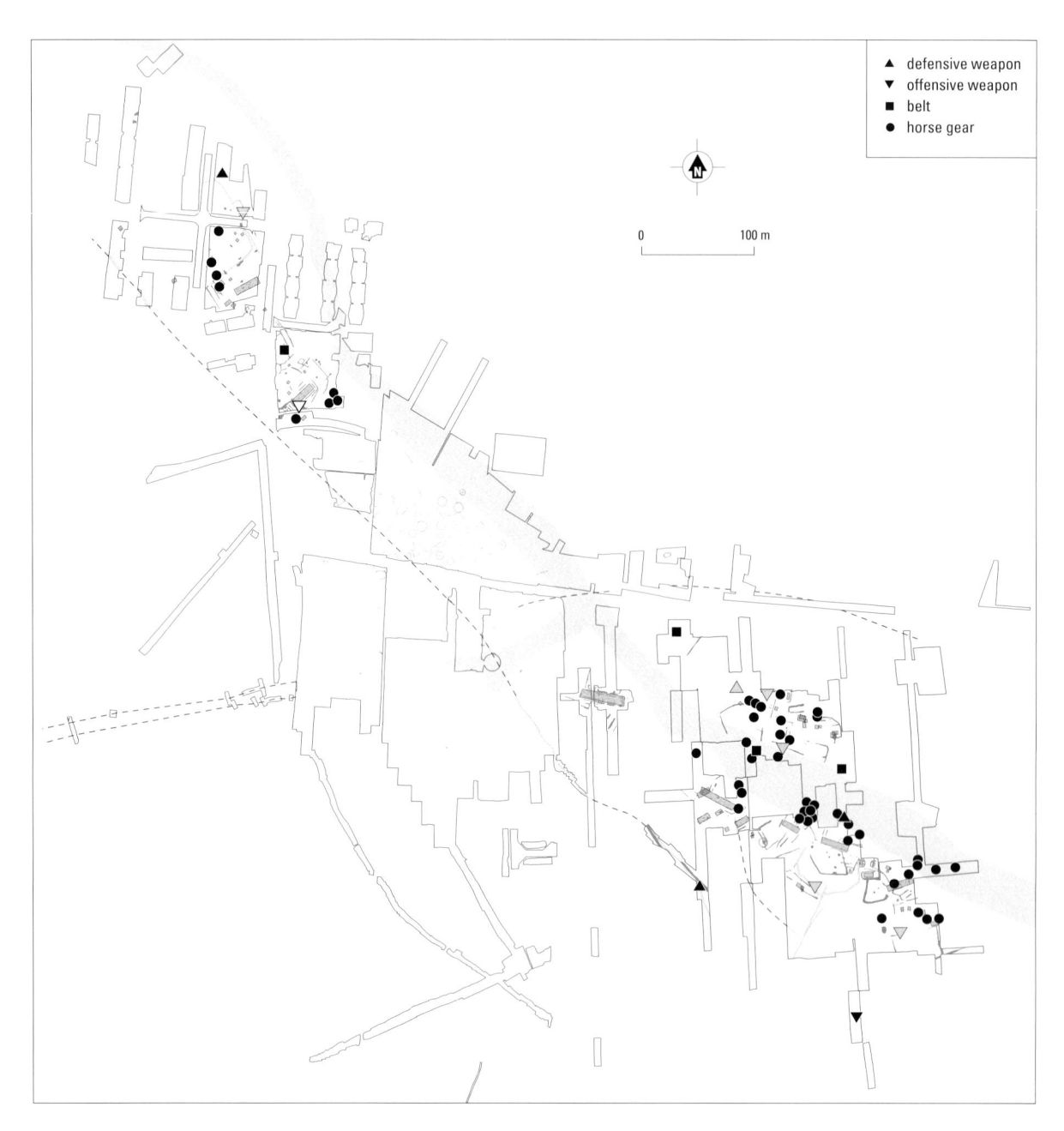

Fig. 3.19. Spatial distribution of militaria from the settlement complex of Tiel-'Passewaaij'. Above: periods 1 (white) and 2 (black), as well as non-securely-dated offensive weapons (grey) (settlement stages 1-3); next page: periods 3 (black) and 4 (white), as well as non-securely dated offensive weapons (grey) (stages 4-7).

the late Roman period (stages 6 and 7, c. 240-350), after which the settlement was abandoned in the 4th or 5th century.

Metal finds from the settlement include over 100 weaponry and horse gear components (242.1-106), including 45 finds from period 2.[39] The early weaponry consists of a *gladius* scabbard band, a plate armour tie loop (Corbridge type) and a semicircular, tinned helmet comb (Weiler type?). A simple buckle tongue and an atypical rectangular buckle can be attributed to the 1st-century *cingulum*. A tinned, rectangular

[39] Nicolay 2007; see also Verhelst 2006.

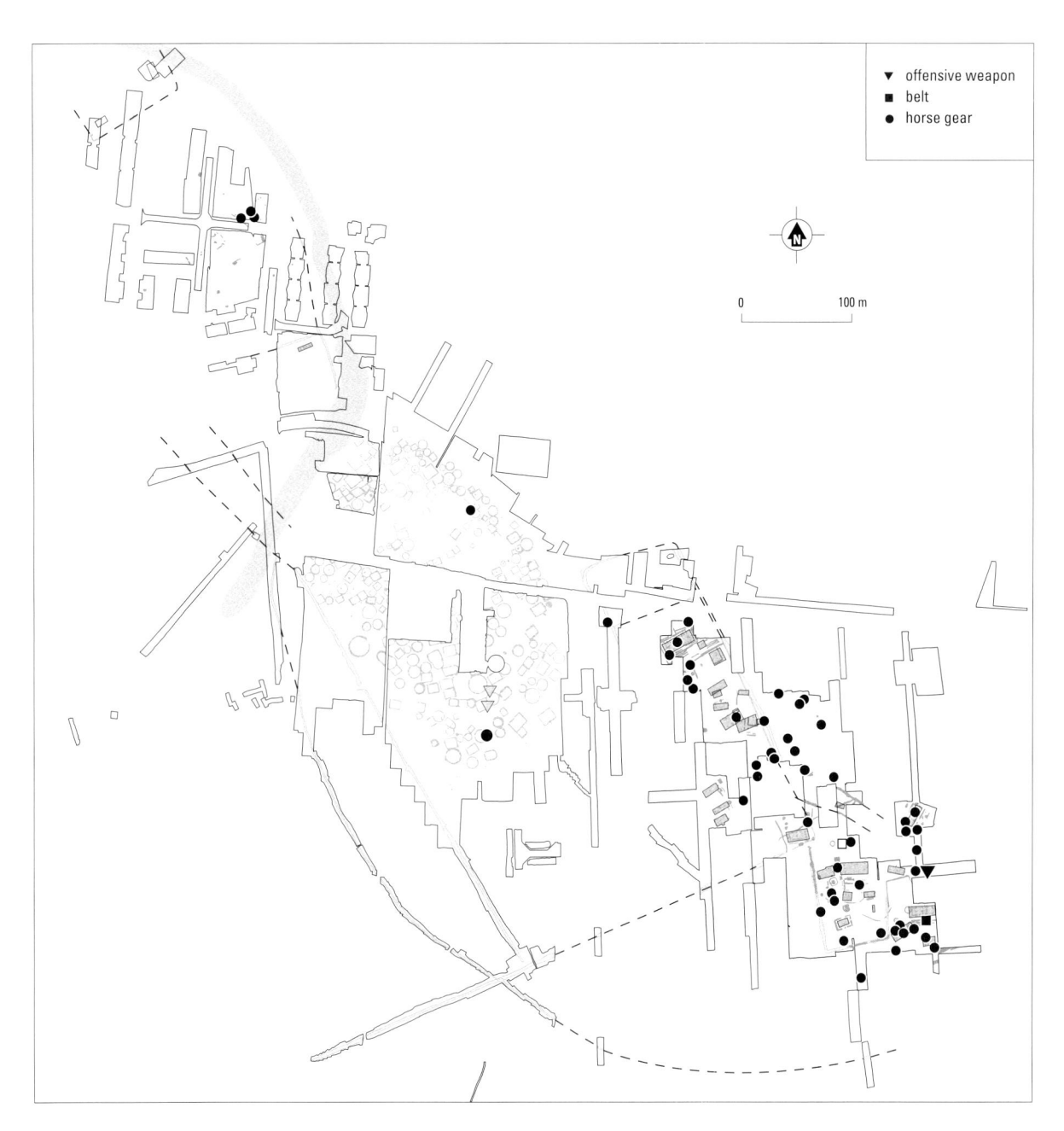

Fig. 3.19. Continued.

decorative fitting was part of the apron. The horse gear, which was in contemporaneous use, comprises two fasteners, three strap junction fittings, a strap terminal, 23 decorative fittings, six pendants and four bells.

A total of 54 finds are known from period 3. The only weaponry component is the peltate chape of a dagger sheath. A small baldric *phalera* and a rectangular ring buckle stud can be attributed to the suspension. The remaining finds are made up of horse gear, namely a fastener, a bell, two pendants and 47 decorative fittings. The T-shaped rivet indicates that a fragmentary spur fitting belongs to the same period.

site	object	period	find context	context dating	cat.nr.
'Passewaaijse Hogeweg'	strap fitting hg	2	house drainage ditch	120-175	242.58
	buckle	2	house drainage ditch	125-225	242.14
	strap fitting hg	3	house drainage ditch	125-225	242.91
	lancehead	-	pit	15-70	242.9
	looped strap fitting hg	2-3	pit	70-120	242.26
	strap fitting hg	2	pit	< 100	242.50
	strap fitting hg	2	pit	-	242.43
	baldric *phalera*	3	pit	-	242.12
	strap fitting hg	3	pit	-	242.46
	strap fitting hg	3	pit	-	242.75
	strap fitting hg	3	pit in residual channel	-	242.98
	bell hg	3	pit in residual channel	-	242.23
	strap fitting hg	3	well	150-225	242.72
	strap fitting hg	2	well	-	242.45
	strap fitting hg	2	ditch	50-100	242.38
	helmet crest	2	ditch	< 90-120	242.4
	strap fitting hg	2	ditch	100-150	242.40
	fastener hg	2	ditch	150-225	242.3
	spearhead	-	ditch	150-225	242.8
	strap fitting hg	3	ditch	150-225	242.104
	strap fitting hg	3	ditch	175-225	242.68
	strap fitting hg	3	ditch	225-270	242.81
	spearhead	-	ditch	270-350	242.7
	strap junction hg	2	ditch	-	242.37
	strap fitting hg	3	ditch	270-350	242.65
	plate armour closure	2	ditch in residual channel	150-200	242.2
	strap fitting hg	3	residual channel	175-225	242.61
	strap junction hg	2	residual channel	270-350	242.35
	strap fitting hg	2	residual channel	270-350	242.51
	strap fitting hg	2	residual channel	270-350	242.53
	strap fitting hg	2	residual channel	270-350	242.49
	pendant hg	2	residual channel	270-350	242.29
	pendant hg	3	residual channel	270-350	242.27
	strap fitting hg	2	residual channel	350-450	242.39
	strap fitting hg	2	residual channel	350-450	242.54
	strap terminal hg	2	residual channel	350-450	242.105
	strap fitting hg	3	residual channel	350-450	242.95
	spur	3	residual channel	350-450	242.106
	buckle tongue	2	residual channel	> 450	242.13
	pendant hg	2	residual channel	> 450	242.28
	bell hg	2	residual channel	> 450	242.19
	strap fitting hg	3	residual channel	> 450	242.90

'Oude Tielseweg'	pendant hg	2	pit	-	240.8
	strap fitting hg	2	pit	100-120	240.10
	sword hilt fitting	1	pit	140-170	240.3
	strap fitting hg (2x)	3	pit	145-170	240.12, 14
	butt spike	-	pit	150-170	240.2
	fastener hg	2	ditch	150-170	240.6
	buckle tongue	2	culture layer	130-165	240.4
	strap fitting hg	3	culture layer	150-170	240.13
	bell hg	2	residual channel	150-170	240.5
	looped strap fitting hg	2	residual channel	150-170	240.7
	strap fitting hg	2	residual channel	150-170	240.11
cemetery	strap fitting hg	3	disturbed grave?	90-140	241.3
	spearhead	-	ring ditch	200-260	241.1
	spear/lancehead	-	ring ditch?	200-260	241.2
	strap fitting hg	3	ring ditch	200-260	241.4

Table 3.3. Overview of the militaria from the settlement complex of Tiel-'Passewaaij' with known find contexts and context datings (AD) (hg: horse gear).

The only item from period 4 is a single belt fitting. A fragment of a bronze scale, that may have been part of scale armour, is less securely dated, as are a piece of lead slingshot, two spearheads and a lancehead.

The distribution of the material across the settlement area reveals that finds were made in similar numbers around the houses and in the residual channel (fig. 3.19). From northwest to southeast, we observe three concentrations in the material, which appear to be associated with the farmyards from stages 2 and 3. The material in the northern-most concentration was found primarily on the farmyards and to a lesser degree in the adjacent residual channel. The finds from the central concentration come chiefly from this creek, with almost no documented finds from the ditched farmyard. In the southern concentration, material has been recovered from around the houses and the associated outbuildings. Here too several objects were found in the residual channel. Period 3 shows a more regular distribution (fig. 3.19). The finds from the eastern-most part of the settlement can be associated with a farmyard from stage 4 located outside the ditch system and probably also with the compound from stage 5 or 6. The remaining objects show a link to the structures erected in the 2nd century inside the rectangular ditched enclosure. The same presumably applies to the finds discovered east of the settlement ditch. The belt fitting from period 4 comes from the single compound that was inhabited until well into the late Roman period.

A large portion of the objects come from the residual channel that runs through the centre of the settlement site (table 3.3). The remaining objects come from ditches and pits, and occasionally from wells. With the exception of the material from the residual channel, in most cases there is a correspondence between the typological and archaeological datings of the finds. The longer duration of use suggested in many instances by the context dating of the material from the residual channel is probably highly misleading. Drainage ditches were constantly being laid at the creek site throughout the Roman era, which means that the majority of the finds were not found in their original context.

The partially excavated settlement of 'Oude Tielseweg' is located on the western side of the cemetery (fig. 3.19).[40] Three farmhouses with ditched yards are known from c. 15 BC-AD 120 (stages 1-3); they

[40] Verhelst 2001.

succeeded one another around AD 45 and 70, shifting to the northwest over time. Although no house has been found, the ditched area between the two most recent farmyards was probably also inhabited in the earliest stage. A new house was built on one of the existing farmyards during the fourth stage (c. 120-170). Oude Tielseweg was now also incorporated into the ditch system enclosing the southern settlement. In around 170 the settlement was abandoned for a century (stage 5). Although no house floor plans from late Roman times have been uncovered, wells and ditches appear to be associated with the presence of at least one farmstead (from c. 270; stage 6). Coin finds show that this farmstead was inhabited into the late 3rd and possibly the first half of the 4th century.

A sizeable number of metal finds have also been documented from the settlement of 'Oude Tielseweg', including 14 coins, 116 fibulae and 16 weaponry and horse gear components (241.1-16).[41] An exceptional find is a weapon component from period 1: a bronze disc from the hilt of a Kessel type sword. A ribbed fitting, which had probably been attached to the brow of a Weisenau type helmet, belongs to the subsequent period. The *cingulum* is represented by a lily-shaped buckle tongue. The 1st-century horse gear comprises a fastener, five decorative fittings, a looped strap fitting, a pendant and a bell. Three decorative horse fittings are the only objects from period 3. The find context suggests the same dating for a butt spike (table 3.3). The fact that the site was abandoned between c. 170 and 270 would explain the small number of finds from this period. There are no finds at all from the late Roman phase of habitation.

The distribution of material from periods 1 and 2 shows that the possible military items were recovered from the central and southern pre-Flavian farmyards (fig. 3.19). The objects from period 3 were found in a part of the settlement where a farmyard was presumably located during the 2nd century (fig. 3.19). They could also be linked to earlier activities, given the discovery here of various pits and ditches dating to stage 3.

In addition to several finds from the residual channel, the material comes from two culture layers, a ditch and five pits (table 3.3). While some of the objects fell into disuse during the production period, others did so long thereafter. A duration of use of 60 years or longer can be established for the pre-Flavian buckle tongue (240.4), whereas the context dating indicates that a Claudio-Neronian looped strap fitting was in use for at least 80 years (240.7). Lastly, the sword from period 1 comes from a pit dated one and a half centuries later (240.3). Although it is quite possible that this is part of a weapon handed down as an heirloom over several generations, we cannot rule out that it originated from an older find layer. This was certainly the case with material from the residual channel.

Although the finds show a marked concentration in both settlement areas, several weaponry and horse gear components come from the cemetery (fig. 3.19, table 3.3). The material from the southern part of the cemetery comprises a spearhead, a lance- or spearhead and a horse gear fitting from period 3. The spearhead (241.1) and the decorative fitting (241.4) were found in the backfill of a ring ditch. The lance- or spearhead comes from an arable layer directly above a ring ditch (241.2). Going by the surrounding graves, these finds can be dated to between 200 and 260. Only the ring ditch with the decorative fitting has yielded a central interment. The cremation remains suggest that it was a young adult of indeterminate sex. Lastly, a second decorative fitting from period 3 was found in the topsoil at the site of a disturbed grave, which appears to have been constructed between 90 and 140 (241.3). Given the lack of settlement features on this site, we can assume that the objects were associated with the funerary ritual and in three cases were deliberately placed in the ring ditches after the burial.

Oosterhout-'Van Boetzelaerstraat'
Many excavations have been carried out in the past decade in connection with a new housing development in the 'Waalsprong', north of the Waal at Nijmegen.[42] In three instances, this involved Roman

---

[41] Verhelst 2001, 57-62; Nicolay 2007.

[42] For an overview, see Van den Broeke 2002.

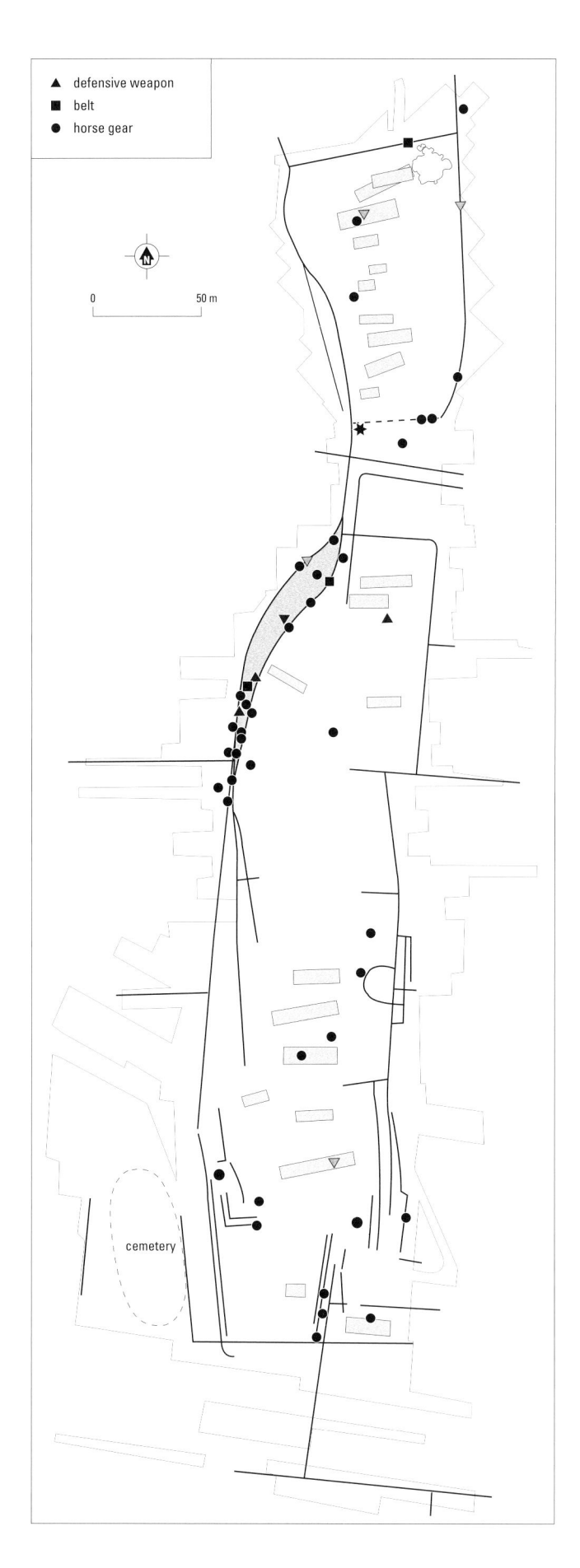

Fig. 3.20. Spatial distribution of militaria from the rural settlement of Oosterhout-'Van Boetzelaerstraat'. The find location of the weapon hoard containing a *gladius* and butt spike is marked by a star (period 2). Left: period 2 (black) and non-securely-dated offensive weapons (grey); next page: period 3. Based partly on unpublished data from Gemeente Nijmegen, Bureau Archeologie.

settlements containing finds of weaponry and horse gear: Oosterhout-'Van Boetzelaerstraat', Lent-'Steltsestraat' and Lent-'Laauwikstraat-Zuid'. The excavations have yet to be processed.

Only the finds from Oosterhout, the most extensively excavated site, will be discussed here (fig. 3.20).[43] This site was probably inhabited continuously from the late Iron Age until the mid-3rd century AD. Only a handful of stray finds date from the 4th century. The inhabited area reached its maximum extent about the beginning of the first millennium, from which time it was enclosed by an elaborate system of ditches. Despite the extensive inhabited area, five or six native houses at most were in use at any one time during the Roman period. Within the settlement there were two habitation nucleii separated by ditches.[44] The unearthed buildings and the spatial distribution of import goods does not suggest any social differentiation. Immediately west of the settlement is a small, contemporary cemetery.

Thanks to intensive metal detection, approximately 120 weaponry and horse gear components have been found in Oosterhout (222.1-119). Weapons are only documented for period 2. The most exceptional is a complete sword blade

[43] Van den Broeke 2002, 12-18.
[44] Recent research has shown that a third habitation core may have existed on the south side (Peter Van den Broeke, pers. comm.).

105

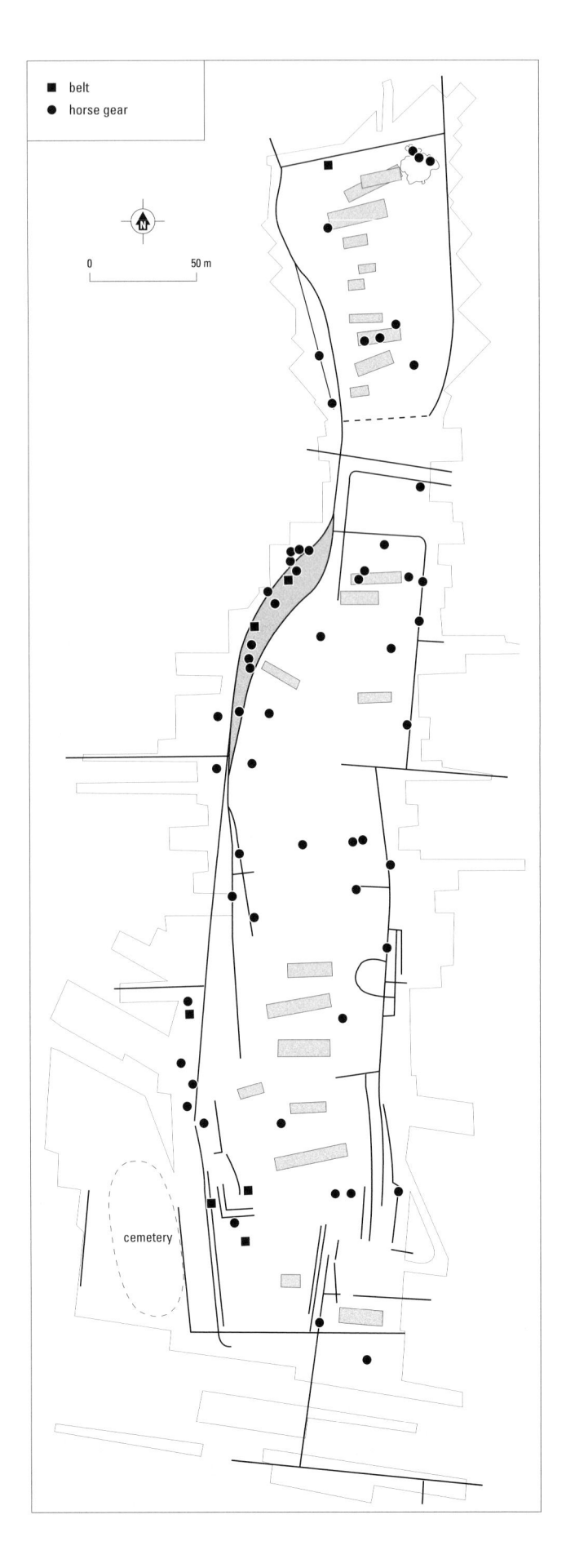

Fig. 3.20. Continued.

discovered in an oval pit together with a butt spike (fig. 5.15). The sword is a Pompeii type *gladius*. A fragment of a tinned scabbard band belonged to the scabbard of a second *gladius*. Dating from the same period are two fragments of elongated fittings, which had probably been fastened as decoration to a Weisenau type helmet. Plate armour is also represented among the early material in the form of a rectangular fitting. Two peltate buckles, one of which is inlaid with enamel, come from the 1st-century *cingulum*. A rectangular casing that was attached to the bottom of one of the suspended straps forms part of the apron. Horse gear from this period is represented by 40 objects: four fasteners, five strap junction fittings, two strap terminals, a looped strap fitting, five pendants, three bells and 20 decorative fittings.

Finds from period 3 are confined to belt and horse gear components. For the belt, this is a buckle and five round studs for ring buckles. The identification of two openwork fittings as part of a contemporaneous belt is uncertain. The horse gear consists of 53 decorative fittings, three looped strap fittings and three pendants. The dates of two spearheads, a lance- or spearhead and a winged arrowhead are less secure.

The spatial distribution of the period 2 finds shows a clear concentration in a broad ditch zone west of the central inhabited area (fig. 3.20). The sword hoard was located a little to the north near this western settlement ditch. Surprisingly few objects have been found around the farmhouses. In the subsequent period, we continue to see a concentration of finds in the ditch zone (fig. 3.20). A larger number of objects were also found across the settlement site. Three decorative fittings from period 3 come from a cluster of pits on the northern side of the settlement. There are no finds at all from the cemetery. Because the excavation is still being processed, context datings are not available.

Groesbeek-'Klein Amerika'

Finds made at the 'Klein Amerika' site using a metal detector suggest that a cult place or a special native settlement was located here. The exceptional character of the site is apparent not just from the metal finds (about 530 in all), but from the large quantity of material dating to before AD 70. Test trenches were dug in 1997 in order to establish the nature of the site (fig. 3.21).[45] This exploration showed that the site can be divided into at least two zones, each perhaps with a specific function: a western zone that may have served as a cult place and an eastern zone where a Flavian-era farmstead was located. A byre house, several outbuildings and the southern and eastern enclosure ditch formed part of the farmstead. The only older structure is a nine-post granary dating from the late Iron Age or early Roman period.

The metal finds from 'Klein Amerika' include 173 coins and over 200 fibulae. Twenty-four belt and horse gear components were also found, only one of them during the archaeological excavation (104.1-24). The material from period 2 includes a lily-shaped buckle tongue from the pre-Flavian *cingulum*. The remaining finds are all horse gear items: two fasteners, a strap junction fitting, three strap terminals, seven decorative fittings, two looped strap fittings, two pendants and a bell. Two decorative fittings found approx. 40 metres apart are identical in shape and appear to have belonged to the same set. Three pendants and a decorative horse gear fitting date from period 3.

The horse gear components from period 2 were distributed across the excavated site, with the majority concentrated in the eastern zone (fig. 3.21).[46] Although only a few objects come from the farmyard itself, most were found immediately west of there. Several horse gear items and the only *cingulum* component from period 2 were found in the western zone. The decorative fittings from the subsequent period exhibit no specific clustering, with objects occurring both on the farmyard and the western-most section of the site.

Although some of the belt and horse gear components may have been ritually deposited, their spatial distribution appears to contradict this. Moreover, 1st-century weaponry, the find category characteristic of the ritual complex from Empel-'De Werf', is absent altogether.[47] It is more likely that the majority of finds relate to the excavated farmyard.

Houten-Zuid, site '8A'

Various Roman sites are located south of Houten, including a rural settlement designated '8A', which has been fully excavated (fig. 3.22).[48] The site was inhabited from the beginning of Roman times, with five distinct stages. In the first stage (c. AD 1-50), we find traces of habitation mainly in the northern part of the excavated site. Two or three house sites have been found. In the second and third stages (c. 50-100), habitation features are concentrated on the higher part of the site further to the south. The settlement was enclosed by ditches during this period and consisted of one or two contemporaneously inhabited farmhouses. In the last two stages (c. 100-200), we observe greater structuring of the settlement. There were now two successive houses in the southeastern corner of the farmyard. The most recent earthenware dates from the late 2nd century, after which the site was no longer used for habitation.

A metal detector was used during the excavation, resulting in finds of 12 coins, 32 fibulae and nine items of weaponry and horse gear (128.1-9).[49] A straight piece of edging probably belongs to a shield

---

[45] Hiddink 2000.

[46] The detector finds made before the excavation were measured accurately, making it possible to establish their spatial relationship to the excavated structures.

[47] See below (chapter 3.3.3).

[48] Vos 2000.

[49] Van der Chys 2000.

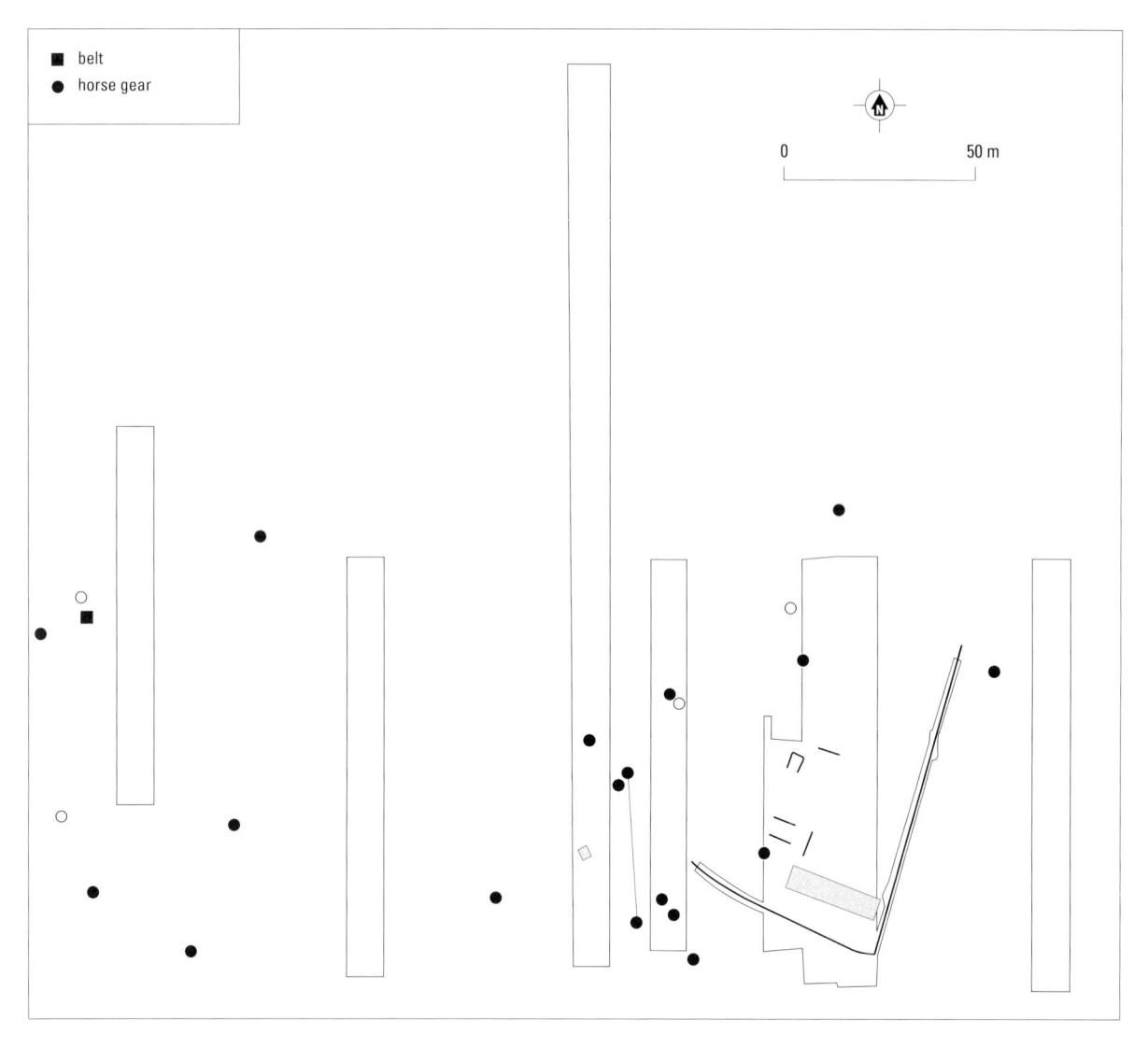

Fig. 3.21. Spatial distribution of militaria from the rural settlement of Groesbeek-'Klein Amerika' (period 2: black, period 3: white). Two rectangular horse gear fittings belonging to the same set are joined by a line. Based partly on Hiddink 2000, fig. 31.

from period 2. A rectangular fitting decorated with engraved lines comes from a *cingulum* in contemporaneous use. The irregular shape and crude decoration point to local production. Lastly, a strap junction and a trefoil horse pendant can be dated to period 2. The finds from the subsequent period consist solely of decorative horse gear fittings (3x). Two lance- or spearheads cannot be satisfactorily dated in typological terms but the context dating places them both in the 2nd century (table 3.4).

Although the number of objects is too small to observe spatial patterns, we can say that the majority were concentrated on or immediately around the southern farmyard. Regarding the material from period 2, the strap junction was found in the farmyard itself, while a piece of decorative fitting and the *cingulum* fitting came from the peripheral zone of the eastern farmyard ditch or just outside it (fig. 3.22). The probable shield edging was found north of the inhabited area, in the vicinity of a house from the first habitation stage. For the subsequent period, a lancehead and two decorative fittings came from the western farmyard ditch and a spearhead from a well in the northern part of the farmyard (fig. 3.22). Some of the objects come from a dated context (table 3.4). In all cases there is an overlap between the available context dating and the typological dating.

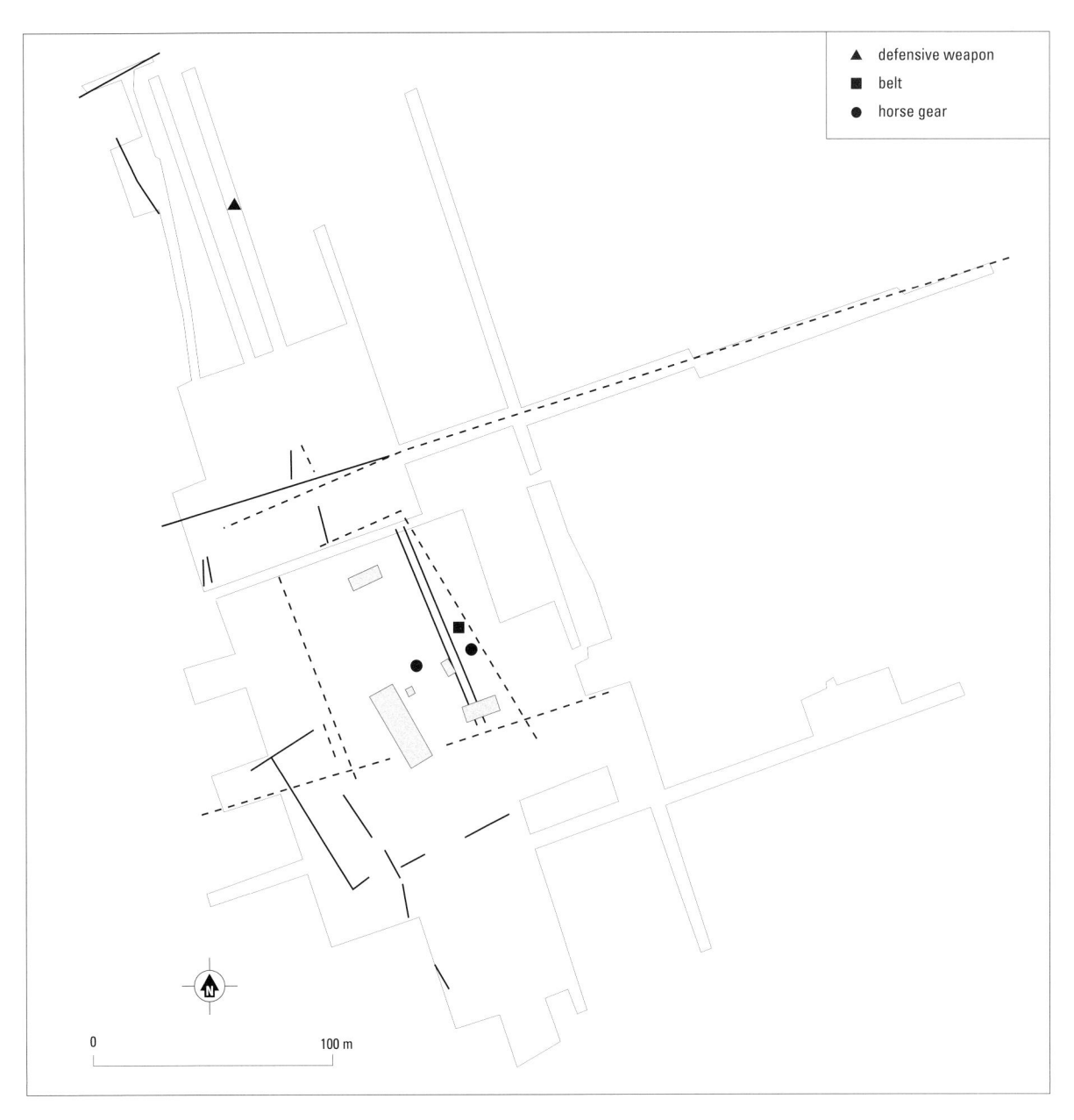

Fig. 3.22. Spatial distribution of militaria from the rural settlement of Houten-Zuid, site '8A'. The addition of a new ditch system in settlement stage 3 and the extensions in stage 5 are indicated by dotted lines. Above: period 2 (settlement stages 2-3); next page: period 3 (black) and non-securely-dated offensive weapons (grey) (stages 4-5). Based partly on Vos 2000, figs. 19-22.

object	period	find context	context dating	cat.nr.
strap junction hg	2	pit	0-100?	128.6
fitting *cingulum*	2	pit	-	128.4
spearhead	-	well	100-150	128.2
spearhead	-	ditch	100-200	128.3
strap fitting hg (2x)	3	ditch	100-200	128.8-9

Table 3.4. Overview of the militaria from Houten-Zuid, site '8A', with known find contexts and context datings (AD) (hg: horse gear).

109

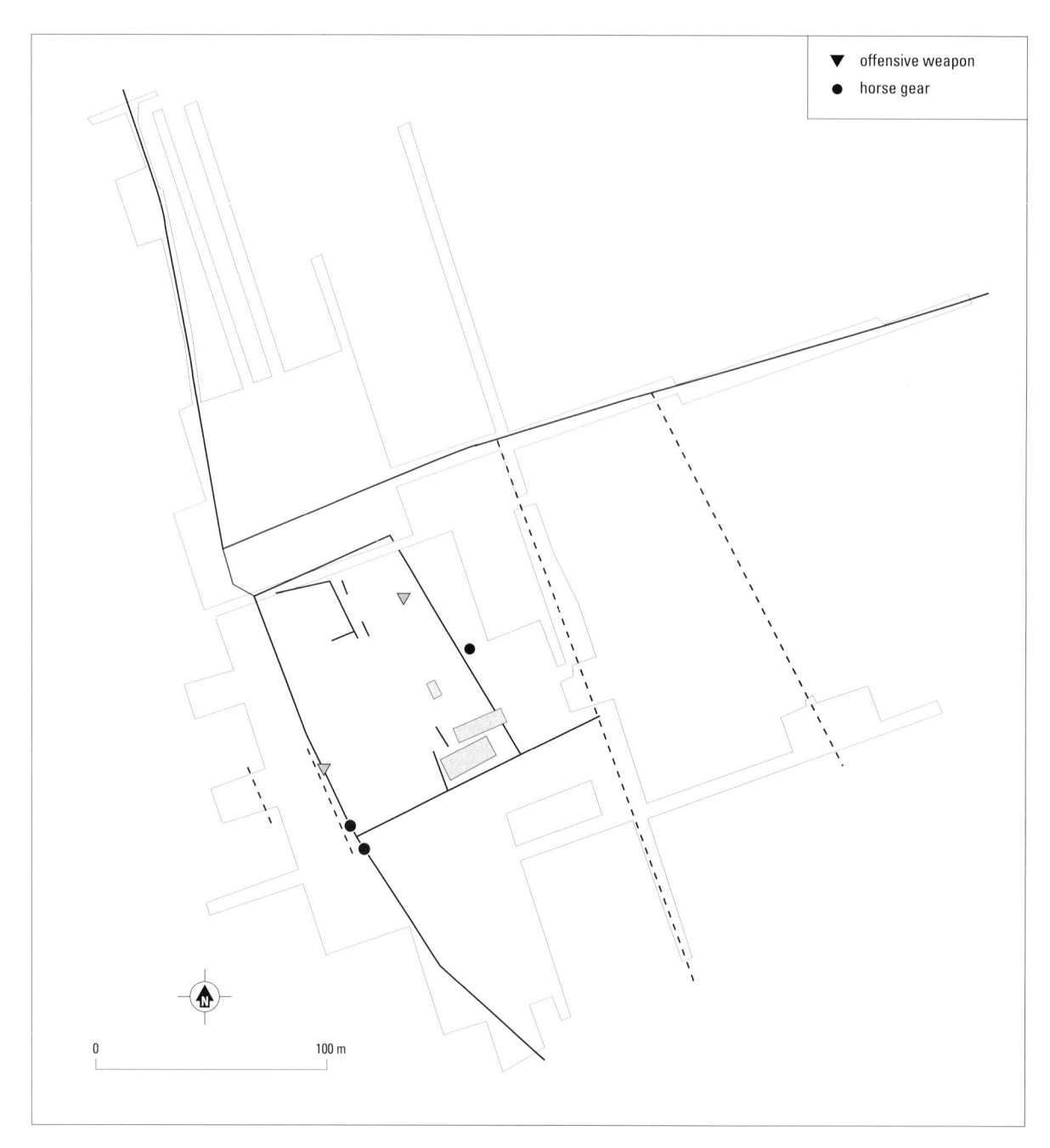

Fig. 3.22. Continued.

Beuningen-'Molenstraat'
A small excavation was carried out in 1997-1998 immediately west of Beuningen in connection with a new housing development.[50] The excavated site was inhabited from the second half of the 1st century AD, with the majority of the Roman features dating to the end of the 2nd and the beginning of the 3rd centuries. Two groups of parallel ditches mark the boundary of a rectangular plot. Between the ditches is a rectangular structure, probably an outbuilding for storage or artisanal activities. The remaining features consist of three wells and pits distributed across the sites. The recovery of a large quantity of building material, including several hypocaust tiles, suggests that a stone building stood in the immediate vicinity.

[50] Van der Kamp/Polak 2001.

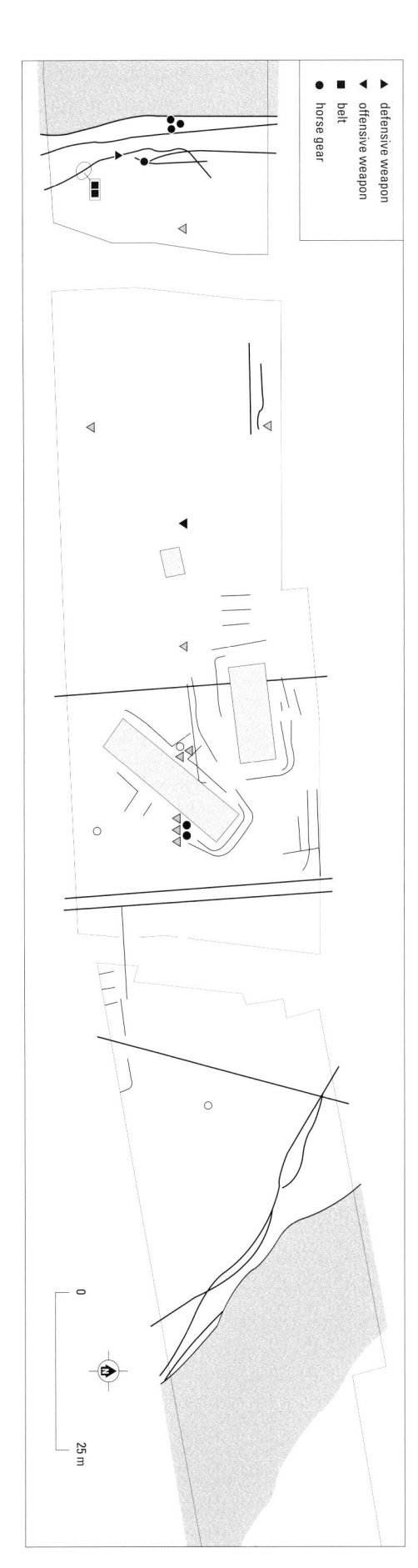

Fig. 3.23. Spatial distribution of militaria from the rural settlement of Kesteren-'De Woerd' (period 2: black, period 3: white, non-securely-dated offensive weapons: grey). Based partly on Sier/Koot 2001, appendix 4.2.

Although no stray finds of weaponry and horse gear were discovered during the excavation, one of the pits yielded a complete horse skeleton, as well as the accompanying horse gear. The irregularly shaped pit is located directly north of the rectangular structure and is interpreted as a ritual deposition.[51] The horse gear consists of 14 decorative fittings (including one of bone), a bell, a pendant and two bronze rings (27.1-16, fig. 6.12). The objects were located around the horse's head and were part of the bridle. What is interesting about this find is that some of the horse gear can be placed in period 2 and some in period 3. As both niello and enamel decoration occur, the most likely date for this assemblage is the early 2nd century AD, the transitional stage between the two periods.

Kesteren-'De Woerd'
A small-scale excavation was carried out at 'De Woerd' near Kesteren in 1961 in connection with the construction of a highway. A section of the site was excavated again later as part of a railway project (1998-2000).[52] The work focused on the northern zone of a larger settlement that extended across part of a natural levee and two adjacent crevasse ridges. About a third of this settlement was excavated during the most recent investigation (fig. 3.23). A find layer was uncovered across the central and western part of the site, which contained a mixture of material from both the Iron Age and the Roman period.

Roman habitation began around the beginning of the first millennium. A byre house and several outbuildings belong to the first Roman habitation stage (c. AD 1-40/50). In the Claudian stage, the settlement and probably also the surrounding land were shaped by the laying of a regular ditch system. No house sites are known from this period. The subsequent building of a farmhouse a little to the north of the pre-Claudian building can be dated at around 70/80. Although the settlement was inhabited until the beginning of

---

[51] Van der Kamp/Polak 2001, 23-25; for the horse gear, see Zwart 1998b; 2001, 44-49.
[52] Willems 1984, 118 (nr. 43); Sier/Koot 2001; Hessing 2001, 144-171.

111

the 3rd century, no obvious structures are documented from the period after c. 110. Habitation now shifted toward the natural levee to the south, where a villa-like complex probably evolved during the 2nd century. Evidence for this are painted wall plaster and roof tile fragments from a well that was discovered in 1961.

Use of a metal detector during the investigation yielded four coins, 56 fibulae and 23 weaponry and horse gear components.[53] When the excavation debris was combed with a metal detector after the excavation, more metal objects were uncovered, including 12 possible military items (fig. 5.17).[54] This brings the total number of objects of a military nature to 35 (166.1-35). The earliest finds are the scabbard chape of a Mainz type *gladius* and two rectangular plate armour hinges (Corbridge type). Two peltate buckles and a tinned, rectangular fitting with raised circles are part of the *cingulum*. Of the horse gear, a fastener, a ring junction fitting, three strap terminals, ten decorative fittings and two bronze bells can be placed in period 2. Only an arrowhead and two decorative horse gear fittings belong to period 3. The almost total absence of finds from this period is related to the lack of dwellings from the period after c. AD 110-130. The remaining finds comprise iron weaponry that occurs throughout the Roman period: a spearhead, a lancehead, two butt spikes, a winged arrowhead and four boltheads.

Figure 3.23 shows that the finds from the archaeological investigation occur across the inhabited area. A portion of the material is concentrated around the southern, pre-Claudian farmhouse. Interestingly, these are primarily weaponry components. We see a second concentration in the western peripheral zone of the farmyards, where material originates from various features. Of the excavated material, 17 objects were recovered from the find layer, and five from two ditches and two pits (table 3.5). Both ditches form part of the western boundary of the inhabited area, transected by an oval pit, containing both *cingulum* buckles. The context datings reveal that the pre-Flavian *cingulum* buckles and one of the armour fittings were deposited at the earliest 30 to 80 years after they were made.

object	period	find context	context dating	cat.nr.
buckle (2x)	2	pit	150-270	166.14, 16
butt spike	-	pit	0-270	166.12
strap fitting hg	2	ditch	100-150	166.28
plate armour fitting	2	ditch	150-270	166.1

Table 3.5. Overview of the militaria from Kesteren-'De Woerd', with known find contexts and context datings (AD) (hg: horse gear).

Wijchen-'Tienakker'
Part of a Roman villa complex was excavated in 1999-2000 on a building site on the northern side of the Wijchense Meer (fig. 3.24).[55] Although 1st-century material was uncovered (stage 1), the earliest structures date from the 2nd and 3rd centuries AD (stage 2). Two native farmhouses occupied the centre of the site. A simple stone building stood to the south, constructed around a well. It might have functioned as a type of water tower. The whole is surrounded by a rectangular ditch. A concentration of rubble and murals, found a little to the west, can also be associated with stone construction. However, the foundation of this structure has been disturbed. Dating from the same period is a large barrow in the southwestern corner of the excavated site. With the exception of the wooden houses, the barrow and the stone

[53] Koster/Joosten 2001, 185 ff.

[54] Among the metal finds are 48 Roman and three La Tène fibulae, as well as 13 Roman coins (Van Renswoude private collection, Oud Zuilen).

[55] The site description is based on unpublished data (Harry Van Enckevort, pers. comm.).

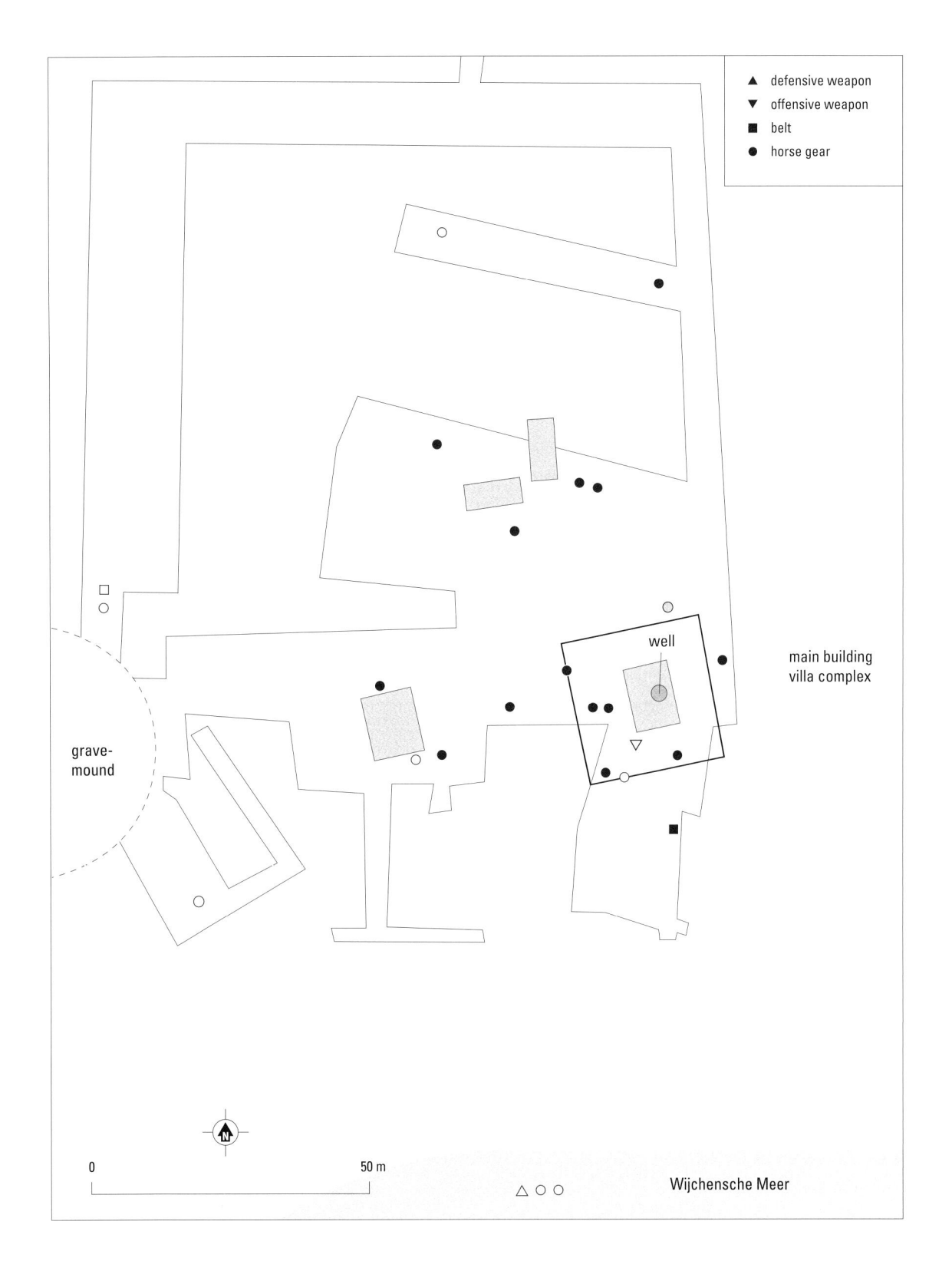

Fig. 3.24. Spatial distribution of militaria from the rural settlement of Wijchen-'Tienakker'. Above: periods 2 (black) and 3 (white) (settlement stage 2); next page: period 4 (stage 3). The find of a lead patrix is indicated by a grey circle (above, period 3). Based partly on unpublished data from Gemeente Nijmegen, Bureau Archeologie.

113

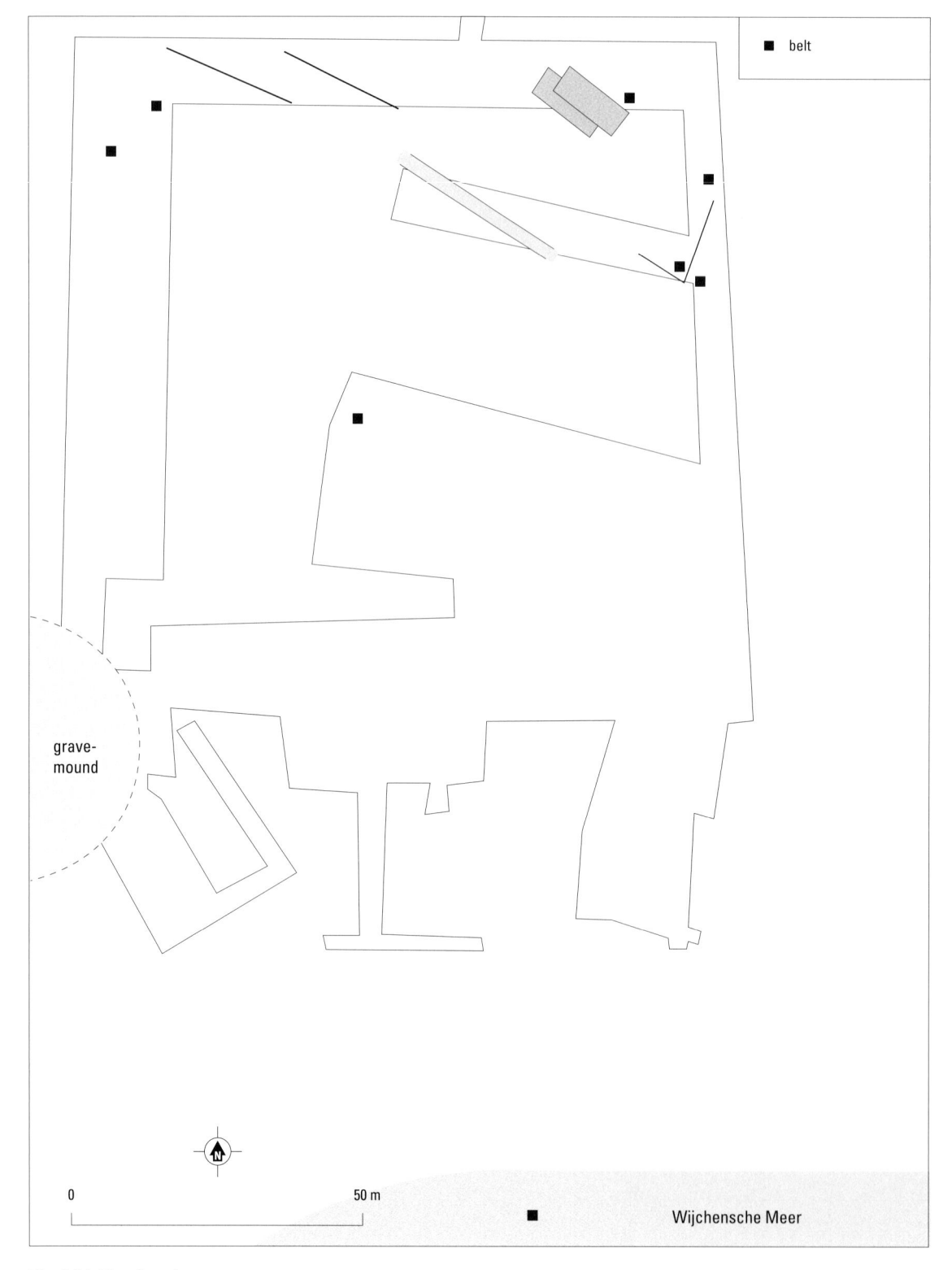

Fig. 3.24. Continued.

buildings were located in a straight line along the northern shore of the Wijchense Meer. This line can presumably be extended towards the east, where the main building in the villa complex must have stood. In the late Roman era, the settlement shifted to the north, where two successive houses have been found (stage 3). The houses have the same alignment as a road that borders the farmyard on the south.

During and before the excavation, many items were found using a metal detector, including over 40 weapon, suspension and horse gear components (284.1-43). Relatively few finds are documented from period 2. As well as a fragment of shield edging and a *cingulum* fitting, seven horse gear items can be attributed to this period: a fastener, two strap junction fittings, two decorative fittings, a looped strap fitting and a pendant. Horse gear makes up the bulk of the finds in period 3 as well. In addition to a round ring buckle stud, a round strap junction, a looped strap fitting and 18 decorative fittings can be assigned to this period. Four of these items come from a scrap hoard, which also contained a simple ring bit (fig. 5.16).[56] Dating from the same period is a lead patrix probably used for making moulds for oval, openwork fittings with trumpet-shaped motifs (fig. 4.4, nr. 2). An exceptional buckle, peltate and with a wide, rectangular loop at the back, can be placed typologically in the transition from period 2 to period 3. Eight objects belong in period 4. A rectangular belt plate, three elongated decorative fittings, a tear-shaped strap terminal and two tweezers come from the wide belt, and a rectangular decorative fitting from a narrower type F belt.

Interestingly, various metal objects probably associated with this settlement have been dredged up in the immediate vicinity of the Wijchense Meer assemblage (287.1-4). They include an ornamented *gladius* scabbard band, two decorative fittings from period 2 and tweezers from a late Roman belt.

Figure 3.24 presents the finds from the settlement site in distribution maps. Finds from period 2 are too small in number to identify spatial patterns. More material is documented from period 3. The finds are concentrated in the southeastern part of the excavated site, around the unearthed structures. The relatively large number of finds from around the possible water tower lends support to the idea that the principal building of the villa complex stood nearby. The distribution of the late Roman finds also ties in well with the features from this period. The specific find context is known for three objects. A decorative fitting from period 2 and another from period 3 were found in the ditch surrounding the stone building with the well. A belt component from period 4 comes from a well on one of the late Roman farmyards.

3.3.2 THE URBAN CENTRES AT NIJMEGEN

Excavations carried out in Nijmegen since the early 20th century have revealed the presence of two successive centres with an urban character: the pre-Flavian *oppidum Batavorum*, as well as the later Batavodurum and Municipium Batavorum Ulpia Noviomagus. Recent excavations (from c. 1990) have made systematic use of metal detectors in both settlements, resulting in substantial finds. As these excavations are still unpublished, we have no complete overview of the metal categories found.[57]

Oppidum Batavorum
Traces of a settlement identified as *oppidum Batavorum*, or Batavodurum, have been unearthed in recent decades in the centre of present-day Nijmegen.[58] Although only small areas have been excavated, a picture is emerging of a settlement with a regular layout and a find spectrum deviating from that of rural sites. The settlement was probably founded by the Romans along Roman lines as the political and administrative centre of the *civitas Batavorum*.[59] It was laid out in about the beginning of the first millennium

---

[56] The scrap hoard is a metal detector find. The exact find location in the settlement site is unknown.

[57] For a preliminary survey of the militaria, see Van Enckevort/Thijssen 2001/2002. The late Roman finds are omitted from this study.

[58] Bloemers 1990, 75 ff.; Willems 1990, 31-39. Van Enckevort and Thijssen (2001, 93-98) assume that Batavodurum was another settlement that was located in Nijmegen-West. However, there is insufficient empirical evidence to support this.

[59] See recently Roymans 2004, 195 ff.

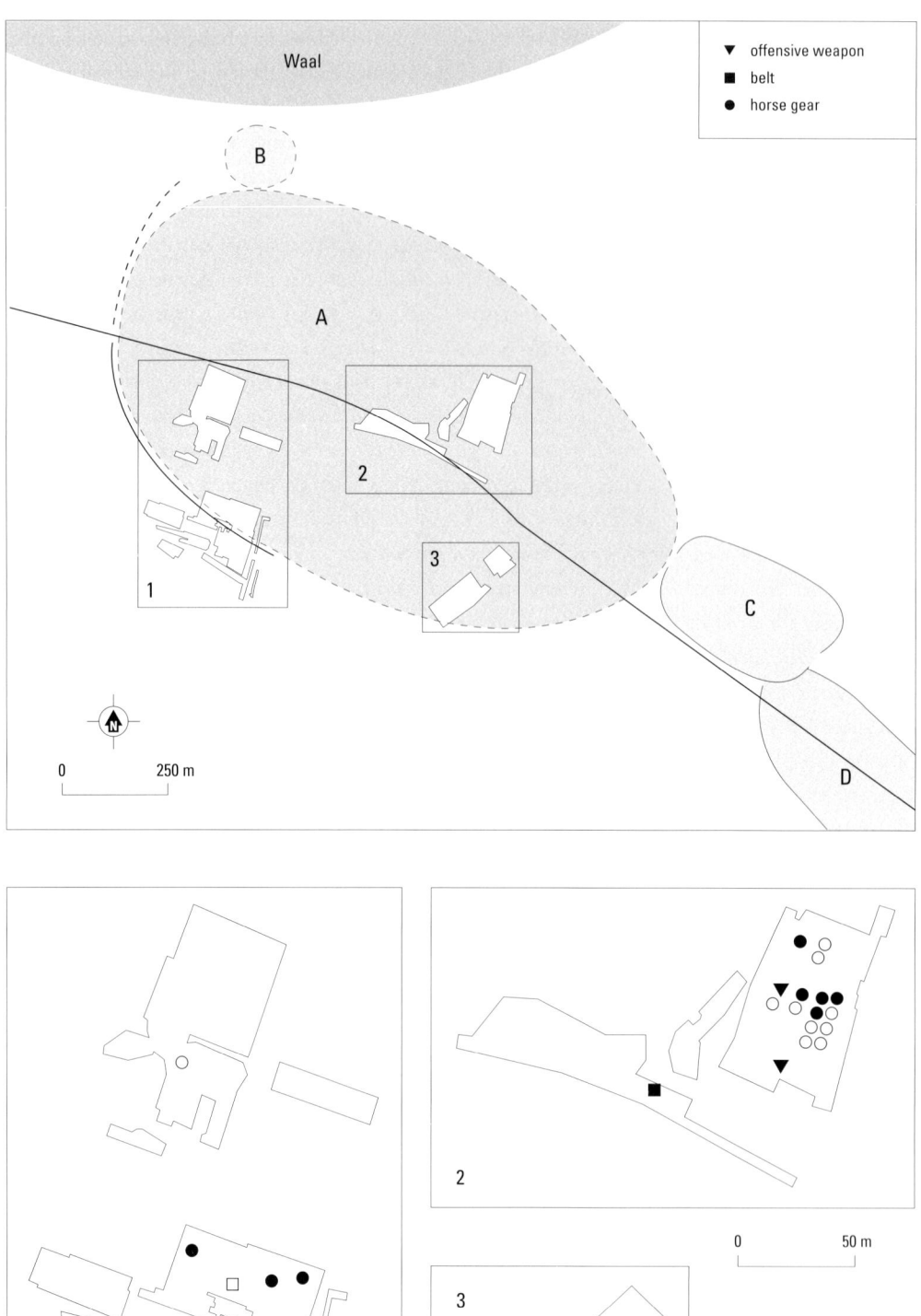

Fig. 3.25. Spatial distribution of militaria from the urban settlement of *oppidum Batavorum* (period 2: black, period 3: white). A star marks the location of the stone cellar where two silver medallions from exclusive *phalerae* were found. Based partly on Van Enckevort/Thijssen 2001, fig. 1. A *oppidum Batavorum*, B cemetery on the 'Waalkade', C military fortification on the 'Trajanusplein', D legionary cemetery on the 'Hunerberg'.

and set alight and abandoned during the Batavian revolt. We can distinguish at least two construction phases, with stone construction occurring for the first time in the more recent, Neronian stage. Directly east of the settlement is a fortification that was in use between c. AD 10 and 20, and subsequently partially encroached upon by the expanding settlement.[60]

The metal finds from the settlement include 52 objects belonging to weaponry and horse gear (208.1-52). Weaponry is known only from period 2. In addition to a rectangular fitting with a plate armour buckle, this is a straight piece of shield edging. Three scale armour fragments, comprising several rectangular scales still attached with bronze wire, are less easily dated (fig. 2.4). A C-shaped buckle once belonged to a *cingulum*. There are 32 early horse gear components: a fastener, two ring junction fittings, a strap terminal, 21 decorative fittings and seven pendants. Of the decorative fittings, nine small *phalerae* and a round fitting with a domed central section form a set (208.27-35, 40). Two fragmented, silver bosses from exclusive *phalerae* that were probably issued as part of *dona militaria* constitute an exceptional find (208.8-9, fig. 5.14). The bosses feature the high-relief bust of a male figure in military attire. Although the settlement was abandoned around AD 70, a strap terminal from a belt and 11 horse gear components can be dated to period 3. The horse gear consists of a strap junction, six decorative fittings, a looped strap fitting and two bells (fig. 2.23). A second looped strap fitting is too fragmentary to be assigned specifically to period 2 or 3.

Figure 3.25 presents the distribution of weaponry and horse gear across the excavation area. Only the material from period 2 can be associated with *oppidum Batavorum*. The western part of the settlement has yielded the smallest number of finds (area 1). Several horse gear items from the southern site were found at the back of long, narrow farmyards. The associated dwellings probably stood directly north of the excavation pits. No early objects are documented from the northern site, with almost no ground features found there. There is no immediate explanation for the two later finds from this part of the settlement.

Excavations conducted in the centre of the settlement between 1979 and 1981 have shown that this part of *oppidum Batavorum* was a housing area (area 2).[61] The houses are situated close to the central road that cuts through the settlement from east to west. The finds consist of two scale armour fragments, a *cingulum* buckle and several horse gear items. Interestingly, period 3 is represented by various pieces of horse gear in this part of the settlement. There may be a connection with the road a little to the south, linking the legionary camp on the 'Hunerberg' with Ulpia Noviomagus.

The bulk of the finds come from the southeastern part of the settlement (area 3). Remains of wooden buildings and the presence of a wooden and stone cellar show that the material was located on the house yards.[62] The objects from the southern settlement zone date exclusively from period 2. The weaponry includes a scale armour fragment, a plate armour closure and a shield edging. The remaining finds comprise horse gear, including the two silver bosses from exclusive *phalerae*. These come from the stone cellar, which is attributed to the Neronian construction phase and which was covered by a burn layer in AD 70. We can only comment on the duration of use for material from this securely dated context. If we assume that the *phalerae* to which the bosses belonged were made in around AD 40 at the earliest, these items would have been used for 30 years at most.

Batavodurum; Municipium Batavorum Ulpia Noviomagus
Following the destruction of *oppidum Batavorum* during the Batavian revolt, a new urban centre named Batavodurum was established 1500 metres to the west on the Waal.[63] Shortly after 100 under Emperor Trajan, the town was probably granted market rights and the status of *municipium* simultaneously, and

---

[60] Willems 1990, 21-22.
[61] Bloemers 1990, 75, fig. 6.3.
[62] Van Enckevort/Thijssen 1996, 146.
[63] Van Enckevort/Thijssen 2001, 100-105, with references; for the nomenclature of this town, see Haalebos 2000a, 35-39.

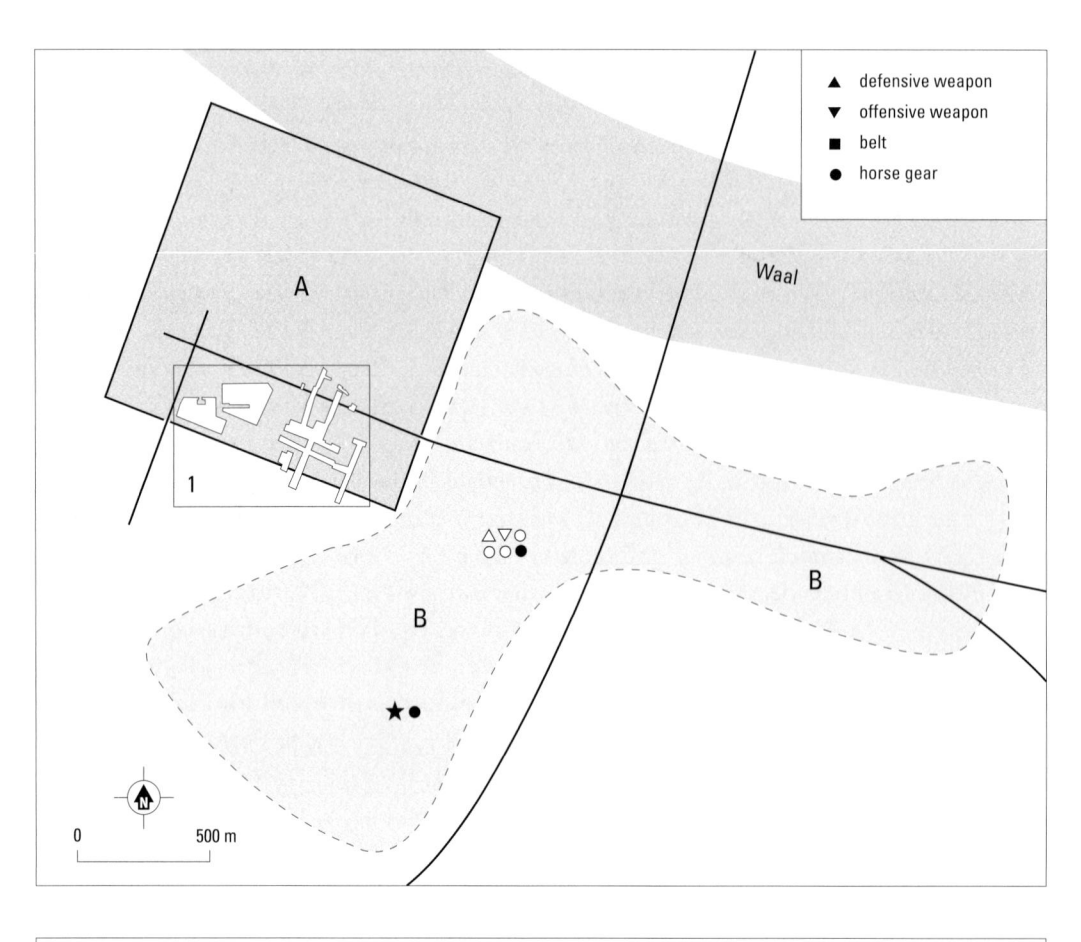

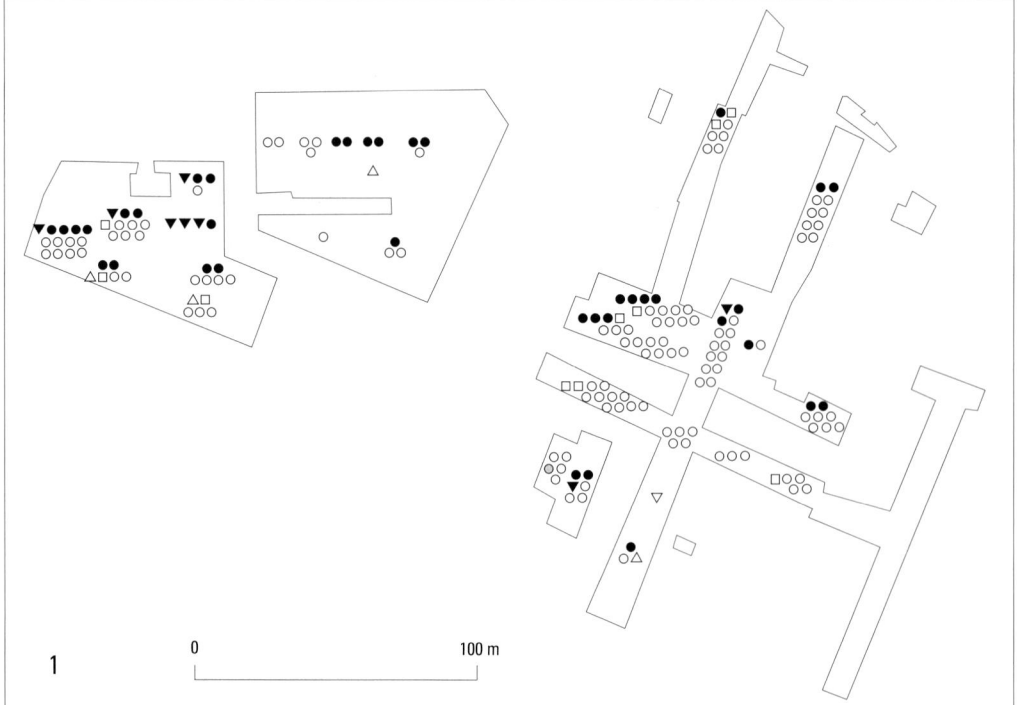

Fig. 3.26. Spatial distribution of militaria from the urban settlement of Ulpia Noviomagus (period 2: black, period 3: white). The find of a lead patrix is indicated by a grey symbol (period 3). Based partly on Van Enckevort/Thijssen 2001, fig. 3.
A Ulpia Noviomagus, B 'Onder Hees' cemetery (the monumental weapon grave on the 'Krayenhofflaan' is marked by a star).

118

henceforth bore the official name of Municipium Batavorum Ulpia Noviomagus.[64] Archaeological excavations have been conducted at various locations in the settlement since the 1970s, the most recent focusing on the town's southern zone (fig. 3.26). Although large areas have been excavated in the past few decades, they represent only a fraction of the total municipal area. On the basis of the current data, we can assume that Batavodurum was largely open in character, with predominantly wooden houses. Coinciding with the elevation to *municipium*, parts of the town were redesigned and we see evidence of growing monumentalisation, for example the construction of stone *domi* or urban villas and the temple complex on the 'Maasplein'. Like most of the rural settlements in the study region, the urban centre was abandoned in the second half of the 3rd century. Running along the town's eastern arterial road is an extensive cemetery, where an estimated 12,500 bodies are buried. The graves include several walled garden tombs with pillars, which can be associated with an urban elite.

Ulpia Noviomagus is one of the richest sites in the eastern Rhine delta, with 184 weapon, suspension and horse gear components (209.1-184). The weaponry from period 2 consists of seven tie hooks and a rectangular fitting with a plate armour buckle (Corbridge type). The early material also includes 39 horse gear components. In addition to 15 decorative fittings, these are two fasteners, five strap junction fittings, a strap terminal, six looped strap fittings, five pendants and five bells. A fragment of a bronze cavalry helmet bowl, decorated with locks of hair, comes from period 3. The *spatha* is represented by three bronze scabbard slides, one in the form of a stylised dolphin, and a bone chape. The belt fittings are four decorative fittings, two strap terminals and three ring buckle studs. A tinned openwork strap terminal featuring letters and a second, simpler example come from a baldric. Horse gear makes up most of the period 3 finds. In addition to 99 decorative fittings, these are four looped strap fittings, 13 pendants and three bells (fig. 2.23). Two oval examples identically inlaid with enamel were part of the same set. The recovery of a lead patrix, probably used to make moulds for round, openwork fittings with trumpet motifs, shows that horse gear was also produced in Nijmegen (fig. 4.4, nr. 3). A scale armour fragment, made up of three scales fastened together with bronze wire, is less easily dated.

All identified material comes from the southern part of the settlement excavated since 1992 (fig. 3.26). The finds from periods 2 and 3 show a fairly regular distribution pattern. Only for defensive weaponry from the 1st century AD is there a marked concentration in the western-most excavation pits. Insofar as can be established, the early material was situated on long, narrow compounds, where living and artisanal activities were combined. Because the excavations are yet to be published, it is not clear to what extent the finds can be associated with the presence of specific structures. The same applies to the subsequent period, when the town's southern zone was initially established as a residential area and where later, from about 170 onward, compounds combining houses and workshops appeared once again. Notably few finds have been documented from the site of the temple complex at the 'Maasplein'.[65] Their relationship to the cult building is uncertain.

In the case of Ulpia Noviomagus, a sizeable quantity of military objects has been found not only in the settlement, but also in the associated cemetery (204.1-8, fig. 3.26). Although most were collected in an unverifiable manner, the nature of the documented site makes it likely that these were grave finds.[66] Firstly, there is a cavalry sword (period 2) and a spear- or lancehead, both published as originating from the cemetery.[67] There is also a complete tie hook from chain mail or scale armour (period 2), various horse gear components (period 2) and a strap terminal from a belt (period 3). In addition to two decora-

---

[64] I generally refer in this book to Ulpia Novimagus; this is also the name often used in private inscriptions of individual Batavians.

[65] This can perhaps be partly explained by the fact that Daniëls (1927) had already excavated the site in 1920-1921, without a metal detector.

[66] This applies to the finds listed as coming from '(Onder) Hees' or 'Heeseveld'.

[67] Brunsting 1937, 165.

tive fittings, the horse gear consists of a pendant and a bell. The only objects whose find context is well documented are several weapons from a monumental, late 1st-century grave in the southern part of the cemetery.[68] These are three spearheads, a shield boss and an accompanying shield grip (207.1-4, fig. 5.20). A horse bell (period 2) comes from the site where the monumental grave is located (207.5).

3.3.3 CULT PLACES

The excavation of the monumental temple complex at Empel has shown that militaria and horse gear also occur at cult places within the research region. Recent finds recovered from the site of the monumental temples in the centre of Elst and from the nearby cult place of Elst-'Westeraam' reveal that the Empel finds are not unique.[69] In both cases, however, militaria are particularly rare, an indication that weapons deposition was not a uniform practice at all cult places in the study region.[70] Only the finds from Empel will be described here at site level.

Empel-'De Werf'
The large number and special character of the metal finds collected by an amateur detectorist from a site known as 'De Werf' prompted an archaeological investigation between 1989 and 1991.[71] The excavation revealed traces of an open-air sanctuary from the late Iron Age and a monumental temple complex from the Roman period (fig. 3.27). The sanctuary is dedicated to Hercules Magusanus, who was probably the chief deity of the Batavians.

Traces of a dozen rows of closely positioned stakes determined the appearance of the earliest, pre-Roman stage (from c. 100 BC). These palisades appear to have demarcated an open-air sanctuary. Inside that area are two rows of poles, which – in view of the concentration of votive offerings around them – probably had a ritual significance. A monumental temple complex was erected on the site of the older sanctuary in the Flavian period. Although no predecessor in the form of a simple, wooden cult building has been found, we can assume that one did exist.[72] The stone temple is of the Gallo-Roman type and stood within a walled temple courtyard with a large hall. Building material from several wells reveals that the temple was at least partly demolished in the late 2nd or early 3rd century. The lack of coin finds suggests that the end of the cult place can be placed at around 235. Several late Roman finds and two wells dating from the same period were no longer associated with ritual transactions and should be regarded as the deposit of normal settlement activities.

Both before and after the excavations, amateur archaeologists have collected a large quantity of metal finds at 'De Werf'. If we add this material to the excavation finds, we arrive at a total of about 2,000 metal objects, including over 1,000 coins, almost 500 fibulae and over 200 weapon, suspension and horse gear components (82.1-208).[73] The earliest military finds belong typologically in period 1. Kessel type swords

---

[68] Koster 1993; 1994; see also Bogaers/Haalebos 1987, 47; Haalebos 1990b, 199.

[69] Elst-centre: Ton Derks, pers.comm; a publication is in preparation (Derks, Van Kerckhove & Hoff, in press). Elst-'Westeraam': Van Enckevort/Thijssen 2005; Van Enckevort, in press.

[70] Open-air sanctuaries containing military finds are less well known: the possible examples from the eastern Rhine delta have yielded too little information to establish with certainty the type of site. For the identification of open-air sanctuaries, see Derks 1998, 166. A possible example is Groesbeek-'Klein Amerika' (see above).

[71] Roymans/Derks 1990; 1993; 1994.

[72] Coins and fibulae show that the site was still in use during the pre-Flavian period (Reijnen 1994; Pulles/Roymans 1994). Compare the development of the temple complex near Elst (Van Enckevort/Thijssen 2005; Van Enckevort, in press).

[73] A portion of the militaria and horse gear has already been published by Van Driel-Murray (1994).

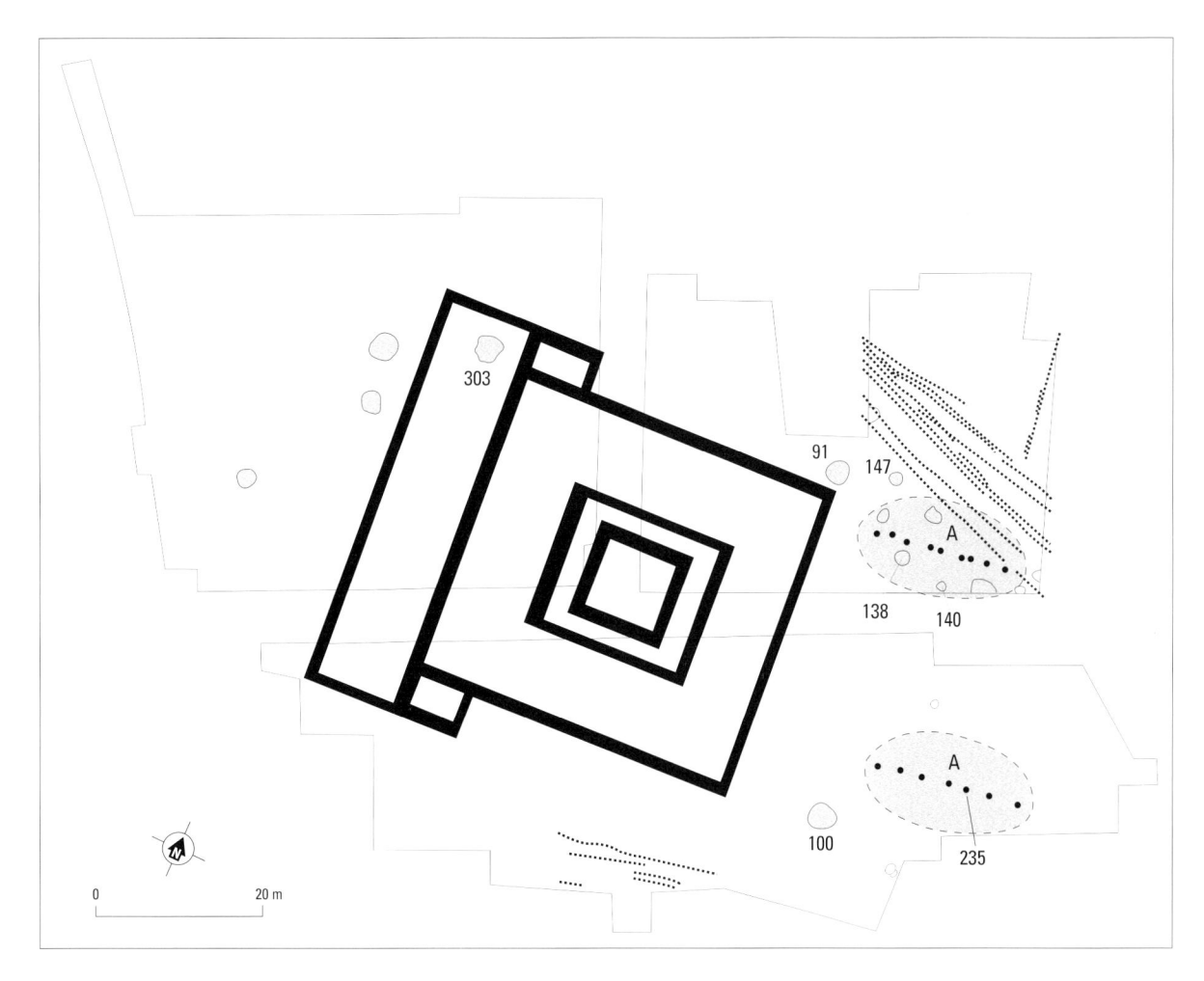

Fig. 3.27. The most important find locations of militaria at the cult place of Empel-'De Werf'. The numbers refer to the find contexts in table 3.6. Based partly on Roymans/Derks 1994, fig. 6.
A concentration of metal finds around both palisades of the open-air sanctuary.

are represented by a scabbard plate fragment and four almond-shaped discs from the hilt.[74] The variation in form suggests that the discs belonged to different swords. Dating to the same period is the butt end of a Roman *pilum* shaft. The round ferrule that is fastened around the wooden shaft is characteristic of the late Republican period.

The bulk of the finds can be dated to period 2. There are relatively many plate armour (22x) and shield (12x) components. For plate armour, these are four components of the Kalkriese type and 18 of the Corbridge type. An elongated chain mail fragment has been preserved, made up of three rows of bronze rings. Although armour of this type occurs throughout the Roman period, the diameter of the rings points to a date in period 2. The shield components consist of a 'German' type grip and various fragments of bronze edging. With regard to the edging, only a corner piece can be attributed to a specific type of shield, namely a rectangular legionary shield. The sword finds include two narrow blade fragments from early *spathae*. The 1st-century *gladius* is represented by two chapes (Mainz type), a leaf-shaped edging (Pompeii type) and three scabbard bands. Two cruciform bands have a special design. For

[74] The less securely dated La Tène weapons are discussed in chapter 7.1.

object	period	find context	context dating	cat.nr.
plate armour (type C2)	2	pit (140)	25-40	82.9, 17, 19-21, 23
spatha blade	2	idem.	25-40	82.54
lancehead (?)	LT	pit (138)	40-50	82.53
lancehead (2x)	-	idem	40-50	82.47-48
catapult bolt	-	idem	40-50	82.41
lance/spearhead	-	pit (147)	-	82.46
spearhead	LT	post hole (235)	-	82.52
shield grip, 'Germanic'	3	well (100)	150-175	82.34
lancehead	-	idem.	150-175	82.49
apron fitting	2	idem.	150-175	82.73
ring buckle fastener	3	idem.	150-175	82.85
pendant hg	2	idem.	150-175	82.119
looped strap fitting hg (2x)	2	idem.	150-175	82.111-112
bell hg	2	idem.	150-175	82.96
pendant hg	3	idem.	150-175	82.123
bit hg	-	idem.	150-175	82.89
gladius scabbard fitting	2	well (91)	c. 200	82.63
set of hg (10 or 13x)	2	idem.	c. 200	82.127-128, 138-145 (82.106, 109-110)
complete helmet	3	well (303)	c. 200	82.25
'Germanic' *umbo*	3	idem.	c. 200	82.33
chainmail fragment	2	idem.	c. 200	82.1
bit fitting hg	2	idem.	c. 200	82.91
strap fitting hg	3	idem.	c. 200	82.178
bit hg	-	idem.	c. 200	82.88

Table 3.6. Overview of the militaria from Empel-'De Werf', with known find contexts and context datings (AD) (LT: La Tène, hg: horse gear). The well datings are based on Hiddink 1994.

the *cingulum*, two buckles and six decorative fittings have been preserved. Seven decorative fittings and a lunate pendant are part of the apron. Lastly, many horse gear items date from period 2: five fasteners, five strap junctions, two strap terminals, 40 decorative fittings, seven looped strap fittings, seven pendants and two bells.

To a lesser degree, objects of a military nature were deposited at the cult place during period 3. One special find is a complete cavalry helmet of the Niederbieber type (fig. 5.9). Although there are no direct parallels, a rectangular fitting with a T-shaped closure stud can perhaps be attributed to Newstead type plate armour. A miniature bronze *umbo* belongs typologically to the same period. Atypical in shape is a 'Germanic' shield boss with a long, narrow point terminating in a conical knob. A bone pommel and a bronze scabbard chape belonged to *spathae*. Three ring buckle studs are part of the belt from period 3. Lastly, horse gear is represented by 26 decorative fittings, two looped strap fittings, a pendant and a spur.

Although the cult place fell into disuse in the 3rd century, several belt fittings – a decorative fitting, two fittings from the bottom edge and a strap terminal – can be placed in period 4. The remaining finds are two probable *pilum* heads, six spear- and lanceheads, two boltheads and a lead sling shot that in typological terms cannot be dated with greater accuracy than to the Roman period. The same applies to four components of the bit. A complete hackamore and fragments of three more were in use during periods 2 or 3. Nor can three horse gear fasteners and three looped strap fittings be assigned specifically to either of the two periods.

Given the presence of a cult building and the complete absence of settlement features from the sanctuary's hey-day, we can assume that the metal finds from 'De Werf' were left at the site as votive offerings, probably to Hercules Magusanus. Their ritual nature is apparent from the damage on some items, which should be seen as a form of 'ritual destruction'.[75] The best example is the round miniature shield boss, whose domed central section has been damaged with a sharp object. The back left-hand side of the complete cavalry helmet also shows signs of damage, which may have been deliberate. The same applies to a spearhead that is broken off at the transition to the blade and to a *pilum* that is broken at the shaft.

Further evidence of ritual deposition is the presence of various matching objects that were deposited as part of the same item of equipment or the same set of horse gear. A pit on the temple site has yielded substantial numbers of fragments of iron plating from plate armour (table 3.6, fig. 2.5). The hoard includes various bronze hinge elements and buckle closures that are characteristic of the Corbridge type of armour. Remains of iron plating show that three matching fittings come from a second set of plate armour (Kalkriese type) that was probably intact at the time of deposition (82.3-4, 10).[76] Further, we can point to two cruciform scabbard bands whose near-identical shape suggests that they belonged to the same *gladius* scabbard (82.61-62). A similar picture emerges with horse gear. We see this most clearly with a group of two *phalera* junctions and eight decorative fittings (type A2) found in and around well 91; their similar shape and decoration suggests that they were part of the same harness (fig. 2.22, table 3.6). The same applies to a set of possibly nine *phalera*-shaped fittings found together in the topsoil (82.148, 151-158). A final example comprises three rectangular fittings, including one with a fastener; their similar niello work indicates that they form a matching set (82.99, 129, 131). The washers and back plates of part of the fittings from 'De Werf' are still in situ, which indicates that they were attached to the leather harness when dedicated.

With regard to the specific archaeological context, it should be pointed out that the temple site was levelled during recent land consolidation, severely affecting the cult building located at the highest point. We can therefore only assume that the large number of finds from the topsoil were buried in shallow pits or stored aboveground.[77] Various larger pits have only been found outside the temple courtyard; they are concentrated around the northern-most palisade of the open-air sanctuary (fig. 3.27, table 3.6). A full set of plate armour, an early *spatha*, a spearhead and a bolthead probably come from two pits dating to the second quarter of the 1st century AD. Interestingly, one of the pits has also yielded a triangular lancehead, whose prominent midrib suggests a late Iron Age date. Small quantities of early Roman earthenware have been found in two other pits, one of which also contained a large number of cattle, goat and pig bones.[78] The pottery and bone material can be regarded as the remains of ritual meals, whereas the spearheads and other metal finds indicate that weaponry and other items were dedicated in the open-air sanctuary. In view of the early dating of the pits, the recovered items were in use for three to five decades at most before being offered at the cult place.

A substantial portion of the excavated material comes from three wells located outside the temple courtyard (fig. 3.27, table 3.6).[79] The most noteworthy finds include a complete cavalry helmet and a 'Germanic' shield boss from the bottom of one of the wells. In addition, various items of both weaponry and horse gear were found in and around two other wells. The presence of building débris dates the

[75] Van Driel-Murray 1994, 102. We see a similar picture with the fibulae and bracelets, some of which are clearly twisted (Pulles/Roymans 1994, 135-137, figs. 5-6).

[76] The same picture emerges for the remaining, stray components of both types of armour.

[77] Roymans and Derks (1994, 112) believe that the dedicated objects come from find layers and shallow pits located inside the cult place enclosure.

[78] Klomp 1994, 152 (pits e, f (=148): earthenware); Seijnen 1994, table 2 (pit 148: bone material).

[79] For the wells on the temple site, see Hiddink 1994.

wells to a period in which the sanctuary was already in decline. Hiddink believes that the finds were old votive offerings thrown into the wells during a clean-up operation.[80] This would explain the occurrence of 1st-century material in a late 2nd-century context. However, we cannot rule out the possibility that the helmet and shield boss, which date from the 2nd century, were primary depositions.

3.3.4 RIVERS

Rivers constitute a third context within the research region where weaponry and horse gear finds are common. This material can be regarded as the by-product of intensive sand and gravel dredging since the end of the 19th century. In addition to material from active rivers, the inventory includes finds from many dredge pits. Dredging operations are designed to extract sand and gravel deposited by rivers, which often involves riverbeds or cut-off loops (table 3.7). The uncertain nature of the find context and the fact that the data on the find location is not always consistently reliable has meant that Roman weaponry and horse gear from rivers and dredge pits have been subjected to only limited scrutiny. In view of their possible ritual character, however, river and dredge pit finds are an important category when it comes to interpreting finds from the research region.[81] I will discuss here several larger assemblages in order to gain an understanding of the composition of river finds.

Lower Rhine at Doorwerth
A large number of bronze objects were recovered during dredging operations in 1895, at the Drielsche Veer in the Lower Rhine, near Doorwerth.[82] In addition to domestic ware, a 2nd or 3rd-century shield boss (55.1, fig. 2.6) and other items, the assemblage is made up of more than 170 tinned, partially niello-inlaid horse gear components (55.2-173).[83] The finds, which are among the most exclusive from the study region, were part of 1st-century parade gear. Holwerda associates the finds with the Batavian revolt and believes them to be goods plundered by 'Germans'.[84] Fleeing from Cerialis and his army, they will have lost part of their booty while crossing the Rhine.

The harness components mainly comprise 15 strap junctions and 64 looped strap fittings in the form of *phalerae* (fig. 5.11). In the centre of two *phalera* junctions is a silver rivet with a raised bust of Victoria (fig. 4.14). Further parts of the harness are five fasteners, six strap terminals, and 20 decorative fittings, as well as two stray pendants. Judging by the shape and decoration of the *phalerae*, we can distinguish at least five matching sets in the assemblage.[85] The presence of washers and backplates is a key indication that these sets ended up in the water together with the leather harness. The assemblage also included 64 tinned saddle fittings, which decorated the leather straps that hung from under the saddle. These fittings are rectangular in shape and can be broken down typologically into five groups.[86] The similarity in width suggests that the different types of decorative fitting occur in combination, giving us a probable four sets.[87] Once again, the presence of washers and back plates indicate that these are objects that were still attached to the leather harness or saddle straps when they were lost or deposited.

---

[80] Hiddink 1994, 61, 64.

[81] The nature of this material will be discussed in more detail in chapter 5.3.2.

[82] Holwerda 1931; Brouwer 1982.

[83] A Pompeii type *gladius* with accompanying scabbard from the Lower Rhine at Oosterbeek (220.1) may come from the same find location. Roymans (1996, 104: B8) points out that there may have been a second *gladius*.

[84] Holwerda 1931, 26; Brouwer (1982, 167) agrees with this.

[85] Holwerda 1931, 2-8, 13-15.

[86] Bishop 1988, table 3, figs. 37-38.

[87] Holwerda 1931, 8-11, 15. The decorative fittings that he attributes to a fifth set (Holwerda's group M) are horse gear fittings.

Alem-'Marensche Waarden'	former Meuse arm
Amerongen-''t Spijk'	-
Angeren-'Loowaard/Kandia'	near a former Rhine arm
Arnhem-'Immerlooplas'	-
Dreumel-'Dreumelsche Waard'	former Waal arm?
Kerkdriel-'De Zandmeren'	former Meuse arm
Kessel/Lith-'De Bergen/De Kesselsche Waarden'	former Meuse arm
Lobith-'De Bijland'	former Oude Waal
Maurik-'Het Eiland van Maurik'	former Lower Rhine arm
Megen-'De Gouden Ham'	former Meuse arm
Pannerden-'Lobberdensche Waard'	-
Plasmolen-'Mokerplas'	former Meuse arm
Wijchen-'Wijchensche Meer'	former Meuse arm
IJzendoorn-'De Waard'	former Waal arm?

Table 3.7. The relationship between dredge pits yielding Roman weaponry and horse gear and original river courses.

Assuming that the decorative harness and saddle elements were worn in combination, we can distinguish four, possibly five, sets of horse gear in the assemblage. Two saddle fittings bear an ownership inscription: *M. Muttieni* (table 5.3). The two plaques differ in width, perhaps indicating that this soldier owned two horses. Another possibility is that the front and back saddle straps were of differing widths, and that the fittings belonged to a single set of horse gear. Holwerda favours the first option, interpreting ownership of two horses as evidence that the soldier was an officer.[88] He also believes that the exclusive horse gear was issued in the form of military distinctions. If the remaining owners were officers as well, this would mean that the assemblage contained the horse gear of two or three cavalrymen.

Kessel-Lith
Large quantities of material dating predominantly from the late Iron Age, the Roman period and the early Middle Ages were recovered during dredging operations west of Kessel and Lith.[89] The first finds were collected during regulation work on the Meuse in the 1930s. By far the largest share of the material comes from the 'De Kesselsche Waarden' and 'De Bergen' dredge pits, where sand and gravel was extracted from the 1950s to the 1990s. Although the material comes from different locations, the specific composition and dating suggest that the material from the Meuse and the two dredge pits belongs to a single assemblage. The finds come from a long, narrow find zone (approx. 2 km x 500 m) that extends along the site of a former arm of the Meuse, with a distinct concentration at Kessel. This cut-off river bed runs along an extensive settlement site, perhaps the location of Vada, known to us known from Tacitus' *Histories*, during the early Roman period.[90] It is believed that this cult place developed into a monumental temple complex in Roman times.

The finds from Kessel-Lith include many objects of a military nature (163.1-13, 164.1-41, 165.1-6). A total of 12 Kessel type sword finds make up the material from period 1.[91] In addition to five sword blades

[88] Holwerda 1931, 17-18.
[89] Roymans/Van der Sanden 1980; Verhart/Roymans 1998; Roymans 2004, 103 ff.
[90] Roymans 2004, 144-146.
[91] A further 10 swords and (accompanying?) scabbards of other types belong to the late La Tène period (see chapter 7.1). These are less easily dated than the Kessel type examples and cannot be assigned with certainty to period 1.

and six scabbards, an almond-shaped hilt disc can be attributed to this type of sword. The uniformly executed weapons are of native origin and can perhaps be associated with the earliest auxiliary. The same applies to an iron, Port type helmet bowl embellished with stylised eye and eyebrow designs.

Most of the Roman material can be placed typologically in period 2 (12x). The weaponry consists of three sword blades (early *spathae*) and part of a sword scabbard (Mainz type *gladius*), while two conical bosses, a grip and a rounded piece of edging are part of the shield. The shield bosses, and presumably the edging and grip as well, belonged to auxiliary shields. The remaining find categories are represented in small numbers. The *cingulum* components are a bone, C-shaped buckle and a dagger frog. And lastly, the horse gear consists of two strap terminals.

The only documented finds from period 3 are two rectangular belt fittings, as well as two decorative horse gear fittings and two horse gear pendants. A belt plate with a buckle, a fitting from the bottom edge of the belt, a strap terminal and tweezers are part of the wide belt from period 4. A leaf-shaped arrowhead can be placed in the same period. Three hackamores, which occur in both period 2 and 3, are less securely dated. Four spearheads cannot be dated more specifically than to the Roman period.

The Waal River at Nijmegen

An enormous quantity of material going back to the Stone Age has been found since the 1930s during the course of dredging operations in the Waal at Nijmegen. Whereas for most of the finds, the inventories list their place of origin as 'Waal at Nijmegen', in some instances their location is described more precisely. This is the case with the objects found at 'De Winseling', 'Fort Kraayenhoff' and the railway bridge across the Waal. Van Enckevort and Thijssen suspect that the majority of finds were ritual depositions associated with a monumental cult building on the riverbank at 'De Winseling'.[92] As with Kessel-Lith, the dredge finds appear to be part of a larger find zone, and here too we are probably looking at a single assemblage.

The river finds include over 80 objects of a military nature (211.1-75, 212.1-8). In contrast to Kessel-Lith, there is no weaponry at all from period 1, with the bulk of the finds dating from the subsequent period (46x). The weaponry consists of 12 helmets, a plate armour component, a shield boss and three swords. The helmets or helmet components are of the Hagenau (4x), Weisenau (2x) and Weiler types (3x) (fig. 2.3). There is also an iron helmet clad in tinned bronze with a face shield (fig. 4.9), a separate face shield (fig. 2.3) and the bowl of a bronze gladiator's helmet (fig. 2.3). The browbands of two Weiler type cavalry helmets are fashioned into an impressive laurel wreath with human busts (fig. 4.8). The rectangular armour fitting is of the Kalkriese type. The bronze shield boss has a vulviform thickening and probably belongs to a 1st-century auxiliary shield. The swords are two Mainz type *gladii* and an early cavalry *spatha*. The bone grip of the *gladii* is still in situ. There are 30 documented horse gear components, namely four ring junctions, a *phalera* junction, three decorative fittings, two strap terminals, four pendants and 16 bells. They include three complete ring junctions, a decorative fitting and two strap terminals which, given the matching decoration, make up a set. The centre of the *phalera* junction features a silver boss with the raised bust of Victoria.

Twenty-seven finds of a military nature are documented from period 3. The weaponry comprises five helmets, two shield bosses and three sword components. Two helmets, a browband and a cheekpiece are of the Niederbieber type (fig. 2.3). The helmets and browband can be attributed specifically to decorative helmets worn by the cavalry, as can a 'crown-shaped' browband that was attached to an ornate Guisborough type helmet. Both bronze shield bosses have a domed central section, in one case decorated with concentric grooves. The sword scabbard is represented by two peltate chapes as well as a scabbard slide.

---

[92] Van Enckevort/Thijssen 2001, 88-91; however, the assumed continuity in ritual use of this location from the Stone Age onward and the interpretation of a stone building on 'De Winseling' as a cult building are uncertain.

A C-shaped buckle and a ribbed fitting that hung from the end of the strap belong to the belt. There are 15 finds of horse gear components that were in contemporaneous use: five decorative fittings, four pendants and six bells.

A fully gilded crossbar can be attributed to a guard helmet from period 4. Four spear- and lanceheads and a bone 'amulet' (fig. 2.26) are more difficult to date. A hackamore and a *pilum* shaft with a socket-shaped, square cross-section base occur in both periods 2 and 3, as does a bronze disc with a high-relief Medusa head. With eight other discs, this piece formed part of a military distinction that was worn on leather straps on the chest.

Lobith-'De Bijland'
Since 1938, innumerable Roman finds associated with the washed-out fort of Carvium have come from the 'De Bijland' dredge pit.[93] The pit is located on the inner bank of the Oude Waal and can be linked to a cut-off loop of the Waal. The dredge finds comprise building material (including roof tiles with military stamps), gravestones and votive stones, bronze domestic ware, tools, as well as weaponry and horse gear (176.1-12).

Six sword finds and a horse gear item can be attributed to period 2. Four sword blades belong to *gladii* of the Mainz type. One of the swords still has the wooden guard and pommel in situ. The scabbard of a second sword is preserved in the form of a rectangular plate. The damaged plate depicts an armed Mars astride a chariot. A fifth, heavily damaged sword blade can probably be identified as belonging to a *gladius* of an indeterminate type. A bronze, partly tinned scabbard plate featuring a standing Mars belongs to a Mainz type *gladius*. The reverse still bears traces of the wooden scabbard and the iron blade, indicating that both scabbard and sword ended up in the Waal river bed. The sole horse gear item from period 2 is a rectangular fitting with a T-shaped fastener. The perimeter of the fitting is inlaid with silver wire. A complete Hagenau type helmet from the Rhine at Lobith may have been part of the same assemblage (177.1).

The only objects that can be attributed with certainty to period 3 are a complete sword blade and the ivory grip of two *spathae*. Less securely dated is a complete *pilum* head that terminates on the reverse in a socket with a square cross-section. This *pilum* type occurs in both period 2 and 3. A long, narrow point with a square cross-section may belong to a second example. Finally, there is a lancehead that cannot be dated more precisely than to Roman times.

Angeren-'Loowaard/Kandia'
The material found during dredging operations since the 1970s in the 'Loowaard' is also associated with a washed-out army camp.[94] The finds consist primarily of earthenware and building material, including *terra sigillata* with graffiti and, once again, roof tiles bearing military stamps. A new dredge pit ('Kandia') was dug in the 1980s and 1990s, once again yielding a large quantity of Roman material. The sand and gravel extracted from both locations was examined with a metal detector, producing over 70 metal objects.[95] The material from 'Loowaard' and 'Kandia' appears to be part of the same assemblage that came from a cut-off loop of the Rhine.

The metal finds include a total of 31 weaponry, suspension and horse gear components, 18 of which can be dated to period 2. The early weaponry includes four bronze shield edgings, including a curved fragment of an oval auxiliary shield. A notable find is an iron dagger sheath, with the front entirely clad in openwork silver leaf. The only *cingulum* component is a peltate buckle. Most finds are of horse gear,

[93] Vollgraff/Roes 1942; Bogaers/Rüger 1974, 90-92; Willems 1984, 97-98.
[94] Willems 1984, 96-97.
[95] Only a *cingulum* buckle is documented from the dredging operations in the 1970s (Willems 1984, fig. 73).

namely two fasteners, a strap junction fitting, four decorative fittings, a looped strap fitting and four pendants.

A scabbard slide and two *spatha* scabbard chapes are documented from the following period. In addition to the customary peltate chape, there is a round, iron example. An openwork fragment in the form of letters is part of a baldric. A looped strap fitting and eight fittings of horse gear make up the remaining material from this period.

3.4 CONCLUSION

The analysis presented here of weapons, suspension components and horse gear from non-military contexts in the eastern Rhine delta has revealed several patterns that we also observe in a broader, northwest European context. Of significance are the differences in the composition of the material, evident in both the typological periods and the specific types of context.

The earliest finds (period 1) consist of helmets and native swords of the Kessel type that can be associated with legionaries on the one hand and probably early auxiliary soldiers on the other. The finds come primarily from rivers and the cult place of Empel-'De Werf'. Conspicuously few items are documented from rural settlements.

In period 2 the material comprises relatively many weapons, in particular helmets, armour and shields. Belts and above all horse gear also make up a substantial portion of the finds. As in the previous period, finds from cult places and rivers occupy a prominent place. We see this continuity most clearly in Empel and Kessel-Lith, where there is a direct match between the dating of material from both periods. A new element in period 2 is the frequent occurrence of finds in rural settlements and the urban centre of *oppidum Batavorum*.

The following period saw a marked decline in the number of weapons, with the remaining categories displaying their own distinct trends. Particularly striking is the fact that defensive weaponry is found in smaller numbers, whereas offensive weapons – mainly swords – continue to appear in fairly substantial numbers. Belt (and baldric) finds remain about the same, while horse gear peaks in this period. There are also interesting differences between the contexts. We can distinguish between cult places and rivers on the one hand, and rural settlements and Ulpia Noviomagus on the other. Characteristic of cult places and rivers is a sharp drop in period 3 not only in defensive weaponry, but also in offensive weapons, suspension and horse gear components. Swords continue to occur frequently in settlements, with belts and above all horse gear being well represented in this period.

Weapon numbers continue to be low in period 4 and are disproportionate to the large number of belt finds documented for this time. Conspicuous for the eastern Rhine delta is that for the first time we encounter belts and weapons quite regularly in graves. In addition, belt items and occasionally weapons occur in rural settlements. By contrast, river finds are scarce, and there are no indications of ritual deposition at rural cult places.

4 Production and symbolic imagery

Chapter 3 presented an overview of the chronological, geographical and site-level spatial patterns evident in weaponry and horse gear finds from non-military contexts in the eastern Rhine delta. Before proceeding in subsequent chapters to link these patterns with specific types of use and significance, I shall first examine how weaponry and horse gear production was organised during the Roman period and discuss the symbolic significance of the decorative elements. These two aspects are important because production underpinned possibilities for use, while symbolic imagery enhanced the significance that soldiers and other users attached to weaponry and horse gear. They also help us to identify the extent to which 'military' objects were manufactured specifically for the Roman army or were also intended for civilian use.

4.1 THE PRODUCTION OF WEAPONRY AND HORSE GEAR

The early 5th-century *Notitia Dignitatum* mentions 35 *fabricae,* manufacturing centres for military equipment during the late Roman period.[1] The specialist nature of these centres and their spread across the empire points to a centralised system of production in the 4th and 5th centuries. Although this picture was initially thought to apply to the entire Roman period, there is evidence of a more diverse system, involving production in army camps, *canabae,* towns and rural settlements in the frontier region itself.[2] Clues to the nature of regional and local production are quite wide-ranging. For instance, there is epigraphic evidence of private weapons producers, while finds from army camps point to self-sufficiency.[3] Oldenstein has developed a useful model that satisfactorily integrates the range of production levels (private, self-sufficient and empire-wide).[4] He believes that supplies of weaponry and horse gear to the imperial frontier zones evolved in a rather uniform fashion, with four distinct stages.

The first three stages cover the early and middle Roman period. The first begins with the Roman army's occupation of a particular region. Because newly conquered territories were not in a position to immediately embark on large-scale production of military equipment, weaponry and horse gear were imported from Italy or Southern Gaul.[5] In the second stage, which is linked to the end of the offensive phase, arms supply gradually became less dependent on imported material. Increasingly, military items were both manufactured and repaired in the army camps and *canabae*. Nevertheless, imports from the Mediterranean region were still essential for satisfying the army's needs. Characteristic of the third stage is the partial takeover of production by private, local workshops. For the first time, it is correct to speak of a more or less self-sufficient frontier region. The fourth and final stage is associated with Diocletian's reforms, when production was taken over by the state and carried out in controlled, centralised state workshops.

---

[1] James 1988.

[2] For a survey of ideas about weapons production, see Bishop/Coulston 1993, 183-188.

[3] See MacMullen (1960) and Bishop (1985) respectively.

[4] Oldenstein 1985.

[5] 'Imports' refers here to weaponry and horse gear produced elsewhere in the Roman empire and destined for soldiers in the frontier zones.

4.1.1 MEDITERRANEAN IMPORTS

In order to establish the validity of Oldenstein's model for the northern provinces, I shall attempt to reconstruct the supply of weapons and horse gear using archaeological and historical sources.[6] Clues to the importation of military equipment in the pre-Flavian period can be found in references to the manufacturer on the weapons themselves. The inscriptions on two scabbards for Mainz type *gladii* mention the place of production. In the first example, the text on a rectangular scabbard-plate fragment from Vindonissa reads *C. Coelius Venust(us) Lugud(uno)* (fig. 4.1, nr. 3).[7] Significant here is the fact that this was a Roman citizen who names *Lugudunum*, the present-day Lyons, as the place of manufacture. The second example also involves a rectangular scabbard plate, this time from Strasbourg, which mentions both the maker and place of production: *Q. Nonienus Pude(n)s ad Ara(m) f(ecit)*.[8]

In other cases, only the maker's name is known and we are sometimes able to determine the origin indirectly. The hilt of an early 1st-century dagger from Oberammergau bears the inscription *C. Antonius fecit [...]* (fig. 4.1, nr. 2).[9] In view of the niello work, Ulbert suspects that the dagger was an imported item, probably made in Italy or *Gallia Cisalpina*.[10] A second inscription is found on the base of the guard of a Mainz type *gladius* from Rheingönheim (fig. 4.1, nr. 1).[11] The inscription reads *L. Valerius fec(it)*, followed by a possible reference to the weight of silver used for the hilt and probably the scabbard.[12] We do not know where L. Valerius' workshop was located. Also of interest are workshop stamps on Mainz type swords. One example is a sword from Bonn, with *Sabini* stamped on the hilt tang and *Sulla [f(ecit)]* on the blade.[13] These stamps point to production in private workshops, possibly in Italy or Southern Gaul.

Significant for the reconstruction of weapons supply is the fact that these items can be dated to the first half of the 1st century and, insofar as we can ascertain, were imported from the Mediterranean region. At this stage, private traders played a key role in distribution to army camps at the frontier.[14] The existence of a private sector dealing in military equipment is evident from funerary and votive inscriptions referring to professions such as *gladiarius*, *spatharius* and *scutarius*. The inscription of C. Gentilius Victor, a *negotiator gladiarius*, shows that these men were dealers rather than specialist weaponsmiths.[15]

This picture is perhaps distorted in that some of the weapons may have been associated, as personal property, with the transfer of officers and men from the Mediterranean to the frontier zone.[16] Also, weapons may have been produced in the frontier region and its hinterland without the practice of putting the name of the producer and his workshop on the items.[17] For example, there is evidence of quite large-scale metalworking on the Magdalensberg in the Augustan period, apparently involving the production

---

[6] The sources may relate to the Roman empire as a whole.

[7] Ettlinger/Hartmann 1985.

[8] *CIL* XIII, 10027, 197; Fremersdorf 1963, 39, Taf. 14. Although the *ara* is associated with present-day Strasbourg (MacMullen 1960, 36-37) and Cologne (Fremersdorf 1963, 39; see also Ulbert 1971a, 48-49), Ettlinger and Hartmann (1985, 38) assume that the Altar of Rome and Augustus in Lyons is meant here.

[9] Ulbert 1971a. The hilt is broken off after '*fecit*'; an abbreviated reference to the workshop may have followed.

[10] Ulbert 1971a, 44. In addition, the name Antonius occurs frequently in *Gallia Cisalpina* (Ulbert 1971a, 45). For the production of 1st-century daggers in Gaul, as well as northern Italy, see also Scott 1985b, 175-179.

[11] *CIL* XIII, 10026, 17; MacMullen 1960, 38 (nr. 74); Ulbert 1971a, 46-48.

[12] Ulbert 1971a, 47-48, note 13.

[13] *CIL* XIII, 10028, 9; MacMullen 1960, 37-38 (nr. 69); see also Biborski 1994a, 173. The name *Sabinus* is also stamped on a fibula from Nancy (*CIL* XIII, 10027, 120).

[14] MacMullen 1960, 25-26; see also Ettlinger/Hartmann 1985, 40.

[15] *CIL* XIII 6677 (Mainz).

[16] For the possession of weapons, see chapter 5.2.1.

[17] Compare the absence of votive inscriptions on ritually deposited pieces from cult places and rivers (see chapter 5.3.1).

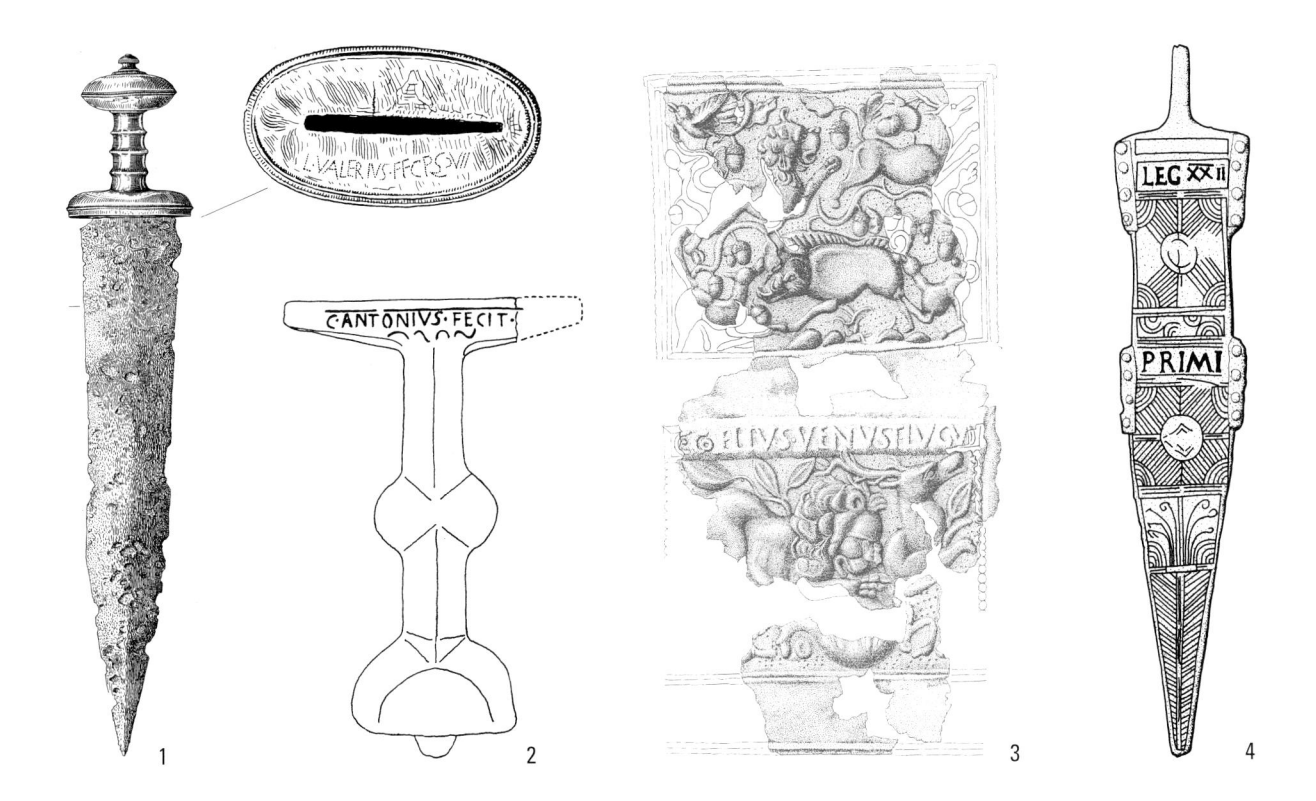

Fig. 4.1. Weaponry with inscriptions by the producer. Not to scale. After Ulbert 1971a, Abb. 1-2; Ettlinger/Hartmann 1984, Abb. 2; Bishop/Coulston 1993, fig. 16 (nr. 5).
1 Mainz type *gladius* from Rheingönheim; 2 dagger hilt from Oberammergau; 3 plate from a *gladius* scabbard (Mainz type) from Vindonissa; 4 dagger sheath from the Rhine at Mainz.

of offensive and defensive weapons as well as belt and horse gear components.[18] Finds from Cologne show that similar centres may have operated in the Rhineland.[19] A marble die for a phallic pendant with the maker's name (Gnatus) shows that in any event horse gear was manufactured on this site. Also found were crucibles which, like the die, date from the early 1st century, the time of the settlement of *oppidum Ubiorum*.

We may conclude that weapons supply in the first half of the 1st century AD was probably based largely on imports from Italy and Southern Gaul. However, urban workshops in the imperial frontier region also began – more rapidly than Oldenstein assumes – to produce weaponry and horse gear.

4.1.2 SELF-SUFFICIENT ARMY UNITS: PRODUCTION IN MILITARY FABRICAE

The organisation of the Rhine *limes* under Claudius meant a shift from an offensive to a defensive focus for the Roman army (Oldenstein's stage 2). This change in strategy meant that soldiers could be deployed for a wide range of duties besides battle. In his description of the early Roman legions, Vegetius points

[18] Dolenz/Flügel/Öllerer 1995; Dolenz 1998, 15 ff., 127-128.
[19] Riedel 1987, 43, fig. 1. Tacitus (*Hist.* IV, 12.3) reports that the Batavians supplied the Romans with weapons, in addition to manpower, during the 1st century AD. However, no further information is available about this weapons production.

to the large number of men responsible, among other things, for weapons production and repair: 'The legion had a train of joiners, masons, carpenters, smiths, painters, and workmen of every kind for the construction of barracks in the winter camps and for making or repairing the wooden towers, arms, carriages, and the various sorts of machines and engines for the attacks or defence of places. The legion had also *fabricae* for making shields, breast-plates, and bows, and in which arrows, javelins, helmets, and all sorts of armour were shaped.'[20] Relevant for our purposes is Vegetius' emphasis on the self-sufficiency of the legions in terms of both production and repair.

This picture of legionaries largely capable of meeting their own needs is substantiated by references on 1st-century writing tablets from Vindonissa. A *scutarius* is named on the outside of a writing tablet from the *Schutthügel*.[21] A second tablet from the *Schutthügel* bears the name and address of the weapon-smith (*ad armamentarium*) Agilis, possibly the same person who calls himself a *gladiarius* on a bronze votive inscription from Vindonissa: *Marti votum Tib(erius) Iul(ius) Agilis gladiarius s.l.l.m.*[22] Writing tablets from Vindolanda suggest that the auxiliary too was self-sufficient. One document lists the men working in the military workshops on a particular day.[23] There were 343 in all, but we have no details about the work they were engaged in. The fact that their number included soldiers involved in weapons manufacture is evident from another list of men, some of whom are referred to as *scutarius* and *gladiarius*.[24]

We can also deduce from traces of metalworking in army camps that legionaries and auxiliary soldiers were involved in arms production. Moulds provide the most direct evidence here. For instance, moulds for artillery, recovered from a cistern probably belonging to a military *fabrica*, are known from the Auerberg.[25] A second clue is provided by the frequent finds of production waste (crucibles, slag etc.) and tools.[26] An exceptional find is a stamp from Sheepen, used for imprinting animal motifs onto belt plates (fig. 4.2, nr. 1).[27] Finally, we can point to the presence of semi-manufactured items. With the exception, however, of pieces that were clearly miscast, we cannot rule out that these were items produced elsewhere and requiring finishing in the army camps. Semi-manufactured items in the form of belt components, decorative plate armour fittings and crest holders are known from Rheingönheim,[28] while unfinished fasteners and decorative fittings for horse gear occur in Mainz and Straubing.[29] From Haltern there is an unfinished Weisenau type helmet and a miscast, peltate buckle.[30] The early dating of the last two items is interesting as it could indicate that Roman troops began producing their own equipment shortly after their arrival.[31]

The large quantity of bronze slag and remains of casting material, together with various concentrations of scrap found on the 'Kops Plateau' at Nijmegen, reveal that the army was engaged in metal production in the research region during the 1st century AD.[32] The mould for a figure-of-eight strap junction fitting shows that horse gear featured among the items manufactured on site (fig. 4.2, nr. 2).[33] In the case of the adjacent 'Hunerberg', crucibles and slag point to the presence of smiths in the legionary fortress.[34] In

[20] Vegetius, *ERM* 2.11; translated by MacMullen 1960, 27-28.
[21] M.A. Speidel 1996, nr. 35.
[22] M.P. Speidel 1984b, 31-34; 1996, nr. 34.
[23] Bowman/Thomas 1983, 77-79 (inv. nrs. 195, 198).
[24] Bowman/Thomas 1983, 81-83 (inv. nr. 82.i).
[25] Drescher 1994.
[26] See Van Daele 1999; there is also the presence of leather finds that can be linked to shield makers (Van Driel-Murray 2002, 113).
[27] Bishop/Coulston 1993, 192, with references.
[28] Ulbert 1969a, 19-20, Taf. 26 (nrs. 19-21, 23-24), 29 (nrs. 5-7), 30 (nrs. 10-11).
[29] Oldenstein 1974, 188-190, Abb. 1 (nr. 16), 2 (nrs. 1-2).
[30] Von Schnurbein 1973; Müller 2002, 75, Taf. 43 (nr. 465).
[31] See also Oldenstein 1974, 192-193, 195.
[32] Bogaers/Haalebos 1975, 156; Bakker 1997.
[33] Bogaers/Haalebos 1975, 156; two other moulds are designed to produce cruciform and round objects, whose function is unknown. For a second mould for a horse gear item, see Breuer 1931, 93, fig. 27.
[34] Van Daele 1999, 127.

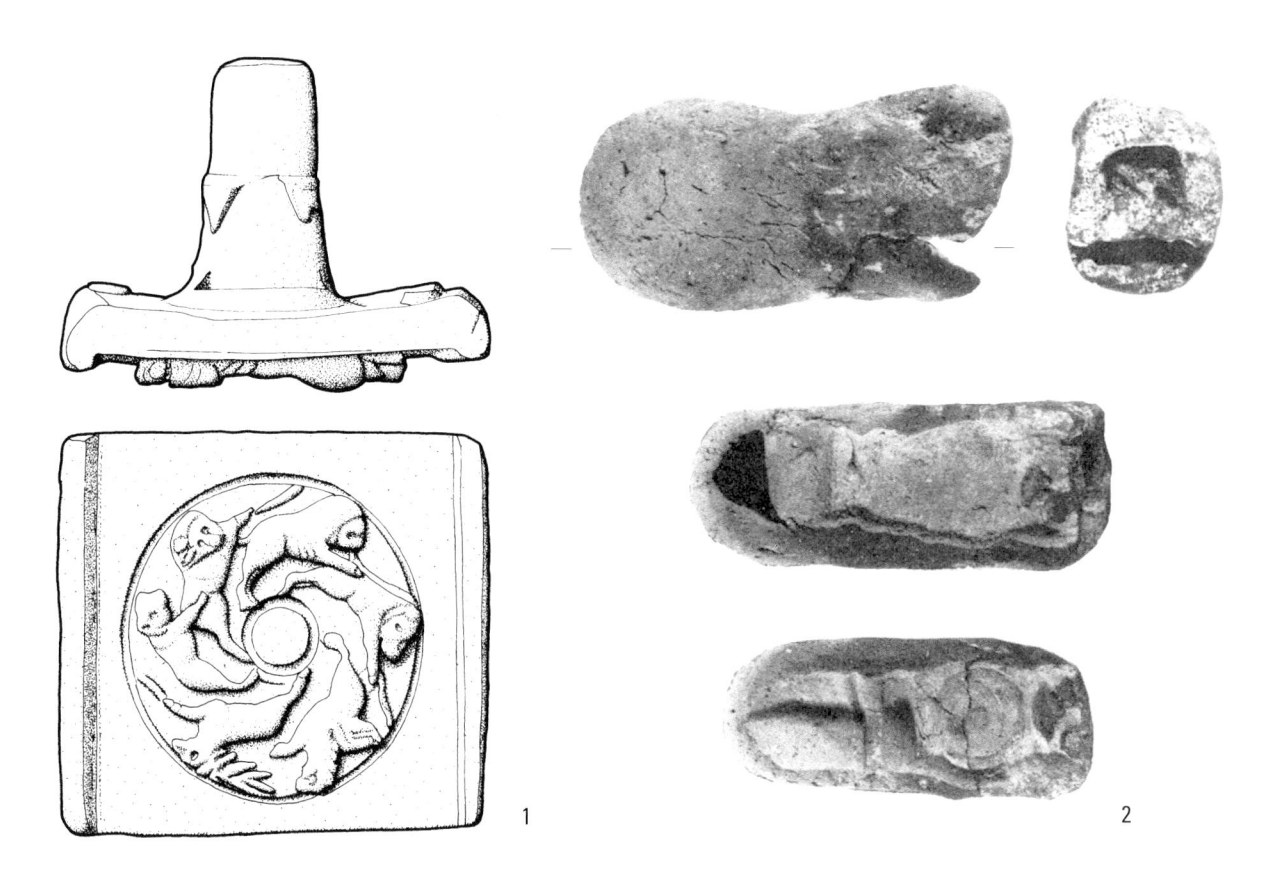

Fig. 4.2. Evidence of 1st-century production of weaponry and horse gear in military *fabricae*. Scale 1:1. After Bishop/Coulston 1993, fig. 138 (nr. 1); Bogaers/Haalebos 1975, pl. LII (nr. 1).
1 stamp for belt fitting (type A3) from Sheepen; 2 mould for a figure-eight strap junction (type A3) from the Kops Plateau, Nijmegen.

addition, a large quantity of slag and other manufacturing waste comes from the river bed near the fort at Albaniana (Alphen aan de Rijn), suggesting the presence of a military *fabrica* in the Claudio-Neronian camp.[35] In the last two instances, however, there is no evidence of the specific production of weaponry or horse gear.

The supply of daggers to the army illustrates the transition from weapons importing to local production in military workshops.[36] Significant here are the differences in quality and design between pre-Claudian and Claudian examples. The early daggers display the same superior quality and are generally inlaid with at least two materials (a metal and enamel). Decoration was simpler in the Claudian period, and the quality of the daggers varied considerably. According to Scott, this distinction is explained by the fact that in the first half of the 1st century daggers were manufactured by specialist artisans in private workshops in Northern Italy and Gaul, as is attested by the inscription on the sheath from Oberammergau. In about the mid-1st century, production was taken over by military *fabricae*, which had a major impact on quality. The probable Flavian dagger sheath from the Rhine at Mainz offers a clue to the rise of local workshops. The inlaid inscription, *Leg(io) XXII Primi(genia)*, points to its manufacture in the unit's own military workshop (fig. 4.1, nr. 4).[37]

[35] Anjolein Zwart, pers. comm.; more generally, see Haalebos et al. 2000.

[36] Scott 1985b, especially 175-179.

[37] Scott 1985b, cat. nr. 51 (for the Flavian dating, see cat. nrs. 47-50, 53-54).

Although Bishop stresses that army units, and the legions in particular, were at this stage completely self-sufficient in terms of arms manufacture, Oldenstein suspects that there was a continuing need for imports in the latter half of the 1st century in order to meet demand.[38] Wierschowski goes a step further, claiming that Mediterranean artisan centres continued to play a leading role in weapons supply in Roman times.[39] He believes that the only items manufactured in the army camps themselves were those requiring limited technical investment, such as spearheads and slingshot. Findings to date would suggest that a combined system is more likely. Firstly, historical and archaeological data show that weapons, belts and horse gear were produced in military *fabricae*. Army-based production, which will have been small in scale, particularly in the smaller auxiliary forts, was probably supplemented by imports from the traditional, Mediterranean production regions and possibly urban artisan centres in the frontier zone.

4.1.3 THE RISE OF PRIVATE WORKSHOPS

In the third stage of Oldenstein's model, we see an evolution toward quite self-sufficient frontier regions, with local non-military workshops increasingly supplying equipment to the army during the Flavian period. In this stage, the rise of private workshops is evidenced first and foremost by the prominent role of military *vici* and *canabae* in metalwork production. There are also indications of 'military' objects being produced in both towns and the countryside.

For the 2nd and 3rd centuries in particular, the archaeological record is able to confirm that military equipment was produced in camp villages. We know of five semi-manufactured horse gear components from the auxiliary *vicus* at Eining.[40] Traces of several workshops probably belonging to the camp village have been found to the north and east of the auxiliary camp in Tibiscum.[41] In addition to a large number of crucibles, 'Workshop II' yielded moulds for a Flavian belt buckle and a heart-shaped horse gear pendant.[42] Although specific evidence for equipment production is generally scarce, these finds appear to reflect a general pattern that applies to other camp villages as well.[43]

We can also attest to the emergence of private workshops in camp villages in the research region. One example is the legionary *canabae* on the 'Hunerberg'.[44] The large quantity of metal slag, and fragments of moulds, semi-manufactured items and crucibles found here point to iron and bronze working. The semi-manufactured items include a bronze statuette, with the sprues still in situ.[45] Although there are no finds of moulds or semi-manufactured items to indicate the production of militaria, we can assume that this did occur in the 'Hunerberg' *canabae*. With regard to the Cananefatian *civitas*, finds from The Hague-'Scheveningseweg' point to the importance of camp villages for metalworking. Moulds for a signet ring and a bronze rivet, crucibles and the remains of casting material have been recovered from a probable military *vicus* there.[46] Of special interest is an earthenware mould still containing a bronze scabbard slide (fig. 4.3), which tells us that private workshops produced not only horse gear and belt components, but also items of weaponry.

[38] Bishop 1985, 13, 17; Oldenstein 1985, 83, 89. Finds of moulds and semi-manufactured pieces of Claudio-Neronian horse gear from Alesia lend archaeological support to Oldenstein's claim that goods were imported from the Gallic region (Rabeisen 1990).

[39] Wierschowski 1984, 177 ff.

[40] Gschwind 1997, 610-614.

[41] Benea/Petrovszky 1987.

[42] Benea/Petrovszky 1987, 230-235, Abb. 5 (nrs. 4, 9); we can perhaps discern the imprint of a second belt buckle in a fragment of a third mould (nr. 5).

[43] Gschwind 1997, 619-620; various examples are given in the *Katalog*. Although the precise origin of the semi-manufactured items is unknown, it appears that the same pattern is present in Brigetio (Bónis 1986).

[44] Haalebos 1998, 35-36; Anjolein Zwart, pers. comm.

[45] Haarhuis 1995, 375-377.

[46] Waasdorp 1999, 99-103.

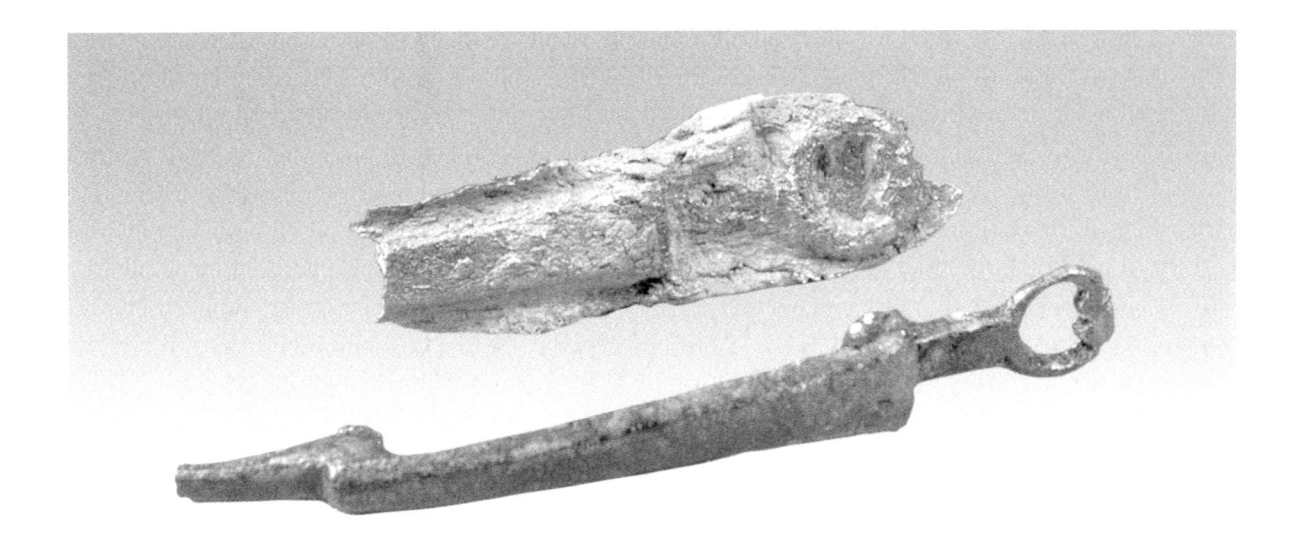

Fig. 4.3. Mould with miscast scabbard slide, as well as a complete example from the probable military *vicus* on the 'Scheveningseweg' in The Hague. Not to scale. After Waasdorp 1999, fig. VI (nr. 3).

Unlike the *fabricae*, workshops in military *vici* and *canabae* were organised around civilian artisans.[47] Returned soldiers who had worked in military *fabricae* and who then set up their own workshop in the camp village were probably critical to these ventures.[48] It seems we can distinguish between workshops in forts and camp villages on the basis of what they produced. Whereas the manufacture of decorative elements for swords, belts/baldrics and horse gear was largely the preserve of artisans in the military *vici* and *canabae*, it would appear that essential offensive and defensive weapons continued to be manufactured in the forts themselves.[49] One exception is a complete Niederbieber type helmet from the military *vicus* of Rainau-'Buch'.[50] However, as the unfinished helmet shows signs of wear, we cannot say for certain that it was manufactured there.

With regard to metalwork production, we observe differences not only between workshops in army camps and the neighbouring *vici* and *canabae*, but also between these camp villages and the towns and rural settlements located further afield. Characteristic of camp villages is the manufacture of decorative elements associated with military equipment, which points to the army as the principal market. In towns and *vici* in the hinterland, on the other hand, the emphasis was on goods such as fibulae that were not specifically military in nature.[51] Although horse gear and belt components do occur, they appear to have

[47] Gschwind 1997, 619-621; Bishop and Coulston (1993, 186), however, point out that the presence of finds in camp villages says nothing about the military or civilian status of the craftsmen; military workshops may also have been located outside the walls of the camp.

[48] Van Driel-Murray 2002, 113-114. See also chapter 5.1.2.

[49] See Jacobi 1897 (mould for arrowhead from Saalburg); Fischer 1985 (semi-manufactured cheekpiece from Eining); Bishop/Coulston 1993, fig. 134, nr. 6 (failed scabbard chape from Corbridge); Gschwind 1997, cat. nr. 79, Abb. 4.1 (semi-manufactured buckle from Künzing). The role of military workshops in the production of weapons is also evident from a 3rd-century papyrus document from Egypt describing two days' work at a legionary workshop. The goods produced include *spathae*, shields and bows (P. Berlin 6765; for a description, see Bishop 1985, 3).

[50] Planck 1983, 142-144, fig. 101; Gschwind 1997, cat. nr. 4.

[51] Gschwind 1997, 624-627; for the civilian nature of the produced goods, see for example Augst (Martin 1978) and Blicquy (Amand 1975).

Fig. 4.4. Evidence of the production of horse gear and belt components (period 3) in urban and rural settlements. Scale 1:1. After Bloemers/Louwe Kooijmans/Sarfatij 1981, 97; photos Bureau Archeologie, Gemeente Nijmegen (nrs. 2-3).
1 peltate fitting with remains of a sprue from Elst-'Merm' (79.27); 2 patrix for making moulds for almond-shaped fittings from Wijchen-'Tienakker' (284.43); 3 patrix for making moulds for round fittings from Ulpia Noviomagus (209.164); 4 mould for a *cingulum* buckle from Rijswijk-'De Bult'.

targeted the civilian market. This would also explain the find of a lead patrix from Ulpia Noviomagus (209.164, fig. 4.4, nr. 3), probably used to manufacture moulds for large, round horse gear fittings with trumpet motifs.[52]

Evidence that decorative belt and horse gear elements were also manufactured at rural sites are a peltate fitting with the remains of a sprue from Elst-'Merm' (79.27, fig. 4.4, nr. 1, pl. 75), a lead patrix for making moulds for almond-shaped fittings with trumpet motifs from Wijchen-'Tienakker' (284.43, fig. 4.4, nr. 2) and a mould for a Flavian belt buckle from Rijswijk (fig. 4.4, nr. 4). In addition, manufacturing waste is documented from many settlements in the research region, suggesting that metal production was quite common at rural sites.[53] Given the small-scale nature of this production, we can assume that it was primarily geared towards private use.

Although the evidence for metal manufacturing in military forts and their adjoining *vici* or *canabae* points to a largely independent system of production, self-sufficiency would only have been possible under normal circumstances. Various historical sources refer to crises in which the army was obliged to turn to workshops in Gaul and Italy for large-scale arms supply. Tacitus reports that Vespasian, for his battles against Vitellius (AD 69), arranged for his army's weapons to be produced in large, prosperous cities.[54] In addition, an early 3rd-century inscription from Mainz states that soldiers were recruited and weapons produced in Milan, actions which should be seen in relation to the power struggle between Maximinus Thrax and Balbinus.[55]

[52] Van Enckevort/Thijssen 2001/2002, fig. 8.
[53] No overview is available of manufacturing waste from rural sites. For metal production in rural settlements, see Slofstra 1987, 74-75, 81-82 (Hoogeloon-'Kerkakkers'); Sier/Koot 2001, 201-205 (Kesteren-'De Woerd').
[54] Tacitus, *Hist.* II, 12; see also MacMullen 1960, 26.
[55] *CIL* XIII, 6763; see also Oldenstein 1976, 80.

4.1.4 CENTRALISED PRODUCTION IN STATE WORKSHOPS

The system described above for supplying weaponry and horse gear was particularly successful during the 2nd and 3rd centuries, but came to an end following Frankish incursions in about 270. Once the frontier defences were restored under Diocletian, we observe significant changes in the production of equipment. In contrast to the previous period, the principle of self-sufficiency only partially applied to military and private workshops, with weapons – and probably belts – being manufactured in centralised workshops controlled by the state (Oldenstein's stage 4).[56]

Thanks to the *Notitia Dignitatum*, we know a great deal about the location and specialisation of these *fabricae*. There were 35 production centres altogether, specialising in the production of swords (*spatharia*), shields (*scutaria*), spears (*hastaria*), military saddles (*scordisci*) and weapons in general (*arma*), which probably included helmets.[57] The centres were primarily located in the larger towns, with a systematic distribution across the frontier regions and the hinterland of the northern and eastern provinces.[58] This meant that each region could produce the number of weapons it needed. A production centre for shields and swords was located close to both German provinces, while the remaining equipment was supplied from more centrally located workshops. The only weapon with a more or less convincing workshop stamp, situated on the gilded silver cladding of an iron shield boss, comes from a weapon grave at Misery.[59] Next to the abbreviated name of the owner's army unit (*mar*) is a standing figure, probably the emperor, in full battle dress. Semi-manufactured arrowheads from Housesteads and bows from Intercisa show that not all weapons were produced in central workshops.[60] The forts appear to have manufactured only the simpler items that soldiers could make themselves.

Although the wide belt characteristic of the 4th and 5th centuries is not specifically mentioned in the *Notitia Dignitatum*, Böhme believes that the depictions of belts suggest that they too were manufactured in the first instance in centralised workshops.[61] These are the belts with chip-carved buckles and decorative fittings from *Zeitstufen* I-II (type D). Centralised production for this type of belt is evidenced by the uniformity of components, the frequently recurring decorative details and the complex production technique. Occurring at the same time are belt types (including type F) which, given the specific distribution of variants, were probably manufactured in private workshops.[62] From about 430 onward, we see a greater variety of buckles and belt fittings, which seems to be associated with increasing differentiation in production (*Zeitstufe* III, belt type E).[63] The presence of moulds and unfinished belt parts at different military sites shows that at least the later belt components were manufactured locally.[64] Additionally, a mould for strap terminals was found in the rural settlement of Gennep-'De Maaskemp'.[65]

We have no data on the production of horse gear in this period. All decorative elements documented from 4th- and 5th-century contexts belong typologically to the previous period.[66]

[56] James 1988.

[57] Specifically for helmets, see also Klumbach 1973a, 12-13.

[58] James 1988, 262-265; for location in towns, p. 274-275.

[59] Werner 1958, 406; Böhme 1974, 113. Stamps giving only the name of a unit are not included here.

[60] Bishop/Coulston 1993, 188, with references.

[61] Böhme 1974, 97; see also Simpson 1976, 203-204. For a review of the literature on belt production in the 4th and 5th centuries, see Swift 2000, 1-2, 185 ff.

[62] Böhme 1974, 93-97; see also Swift 2000, 185 ff. Of interest here is the presence of regional variants of this belt type in Spain (Fernandéz 1999: 'pseudo-Hispanic belts').

[63] For the modified dating of Böhme's *Zeitstufen* from 1974, see Böhme 1989.

[64] Bishop/Coulston 1993, 188, fig. 134 (nrs. 4, 8).

[65] Heidinga/Offenberg 1992, 109; for metalworking at rural sites, see also Luik 1999, 211-214.

[66] Gschwind 1998.

4.2 DECORATION AND SYMBOLISM

Roman weaponry and horse gear were adorned in a wide variety of ways. In addition to its purely decorative value, some of the ornamentation had an important symbolic value as well. To understand the special significance that equipment had for Roman soldiers or other users, it is important to examine the imagery expressed on weaponry and horse gear during the Roman period. Although themes were sometimes combined, the initial emphasis was on political propaganda, aimed at the issue of succession and the glorification of the imperial house. From the time of Claudius, the invincibility of the Roman army was a central theme, followed in the early 2nd century by a symbolism, continuing until the late Roman period, with a protective value for the owner.

4.2.1 POLITICAL PROPAGANDA:
THE GLORIFICATION OF THE IMPERIAL FAMILY

Images of members of the imperial house, together with gods from the Roman pantheon and their distinctive attributes, dominated the decoration of military equipment in the first half of the 1st-century AD.[67] There appear to have been specific combinations of themes, with the images on decorative elements of the infantryman's *gladius*, belt and apron constituting a single symbolic entity.[68] For the cavalry, we see a narrower repertoire, with the symbolism centring on the helmet and more exclusive horse gear components. We can regard these themes as a form of political propaganda designed to glorify the Julio-Claudian emperors and to legitimise their power. Other key themes are the promotion of imperial succession and references to Rome as the centre of power. Political propaganda was not confined to military equipment in this period; it was also expressed in architecture, sculpture and coins, frequently employing the same themes. The official nature of the imagery is evident in the origins of the motifs, which were based in part on images on Italic state monuments, such as the *Ara Pacis*.[69] This highlights the fact that the propaganda was introduced under the central authority, with the aim of swaying public opinion in favour of the newly established autocracy of Emperor Augustus and his successors.

The most striking decoration on the Mainz type *gladius* and 1st-century belt is a small group of rectangular plates portraying members of the imperial family. There are also round fittings in the form of medallions with an imperial bust that could be attached to the sword scabbard or apron. The emperors depicted were Tiberius, Caligula and Claudius, who are portrayed either alone or together with their intended successor or successors. The representation of members of the imperial house aimed first and foremost at glorifying the imperial family and in so doing at legitimising their power. We see a clear example of this in the portrait of Tiberius on a series of standard belt fittings, in which the frontal bust of the emperor is portrayed atop a globe and flanked by crossed horns of plenty (fig. 4.5, nr. 1). Tiberius is presented here as the bringer of prosperity and fortune, while the globe symbolises the emperor's worldwide power.[70]

The medallions show the bust of Augustus and in one case Tiberius.[71] Some of them were probably affixed to the sword scabbard, whereas those with a central rivet would have adorned the apron. In most

[67] Groundbreaking research into the imagery on 1st-century weapons has been carried out by Von Gonzenbach (1966b) and Künzl (1994; 1997; 1998); see also Ettlinger/Hartmann 1985.
[68] Von Gonzenbach 1966b; 183; Künzl 1998, 408.
[69] Von Gonzenbach 1966b.
[70] Von Gonzenbach 1966b, 192-194.

[71] Ulbert 1971b; Feugère 1985; Künzl 1998, 433-434; Deschler-Erb 1999b, 234-236. Examples bearing a pendant characteristic of apron fittings are relevant for interpreting them as such (Ulbert 1971b, Abb. 5.10-12); medallions with an attachment loop on the reverse could have been fastened to either a belt or clothing (Deschler-Erb 1999b, 235-236).

Fig. 4.5. Belt and sword scabbard plates featuring political imagery. Scale 1:1. After Künzl 1998, Taf. 48 (nr. 3), 49 (nrs. 1-2), 53 (nr. 2).
1-2 belt plates from Rheingönheim; 3 scabbard plate from Vindonissa; 4 scabbard plate from Ptuj-Poetovio.

instances, a small Victoria is portrayed behind the profile bust of the emperor, a reference to the glory of the Julio-Claudian emperors. This is Victoria Augusti, Emperor Augustus' personal goddess of victory.[72] A round apron decoration probably showing Augustus was recovered from the *castra* on the 'Hunerberg'.[73] A similar example comes from the harbour complex at Velsen (harbour site II).[74] Traces of soldering on the reverse show that this medallion is akin to the one on the 'Sword of Tiberius' (fig. 4.12). The person depicted is Augustus, or perhaps Caligula.

Under Tiberius, the glorification of the emperor also took the form of establishing a parallel with Alexander the Great. Relevant here are iron Weiler type helmets clad in sheet bronze moulded in the shape of locks of hair. On an example from Xanten-'Wardt', the bronze work is replaced by a plaited horsehair cover.[75] Contemporaneous with this type of helmet were the masked helmets, which could also be covered with organic material (human or animal hair), as revealed by finds from the 'Kops Plateau' at Nijmegen.[76] Künzl assumes that this covering was introduced by Germanicus, who was inspired by finds from what is believed to be the grave of Alexander the Great.[77] By reintroducing the covered helmet,

[72] Von Gonzenbach 1966b, 193, 200.
[73] Zadoks-Josephus Jitta/Peters/Gerhartl-Witteveen 1973, nr. 139.
[74] Diederik 1985.
[75] Schalles/Schreiter 1993, cat. nr. Mil. 16, Taf. 28; Künzl 1999, 155.
[76] Van Enckevort/Willems 1994, 127; Künzl 1999, 155.
[77] Künzl 1997, 77-82; references to historical equipment were also an important feature of Roman art (Waurick 1983).

Fig. 4.6. *Gladius* plate from Bonn depicting Julia and her sons Gaius and Lucius Caesar. Scale 3:2. After Künzl 1998, Taf. 44 (nr. 1).

Germanicus was identifying himself with this illustrious predecessor. There is also evidence of elements from Alexander the Great's time on 1st-century face shields, in which the classical face and contoured locks of hair on the brow appear to be copies of Alexander's portrait.

Another central theme of the imagery was the promotion of a successor. We see this on a scabbard mount from Bonn depicting not an emperor, but Julia, Agrippa's widow, and her sons Gaius and Lucius Caesar (fig. 4.6).[78] Both sons had been adopted by Augustus and were therefore relevant in terms of the dynastic succession. We can view their portrayal as propaganda for Augustus' desire to have Gaius or Lucius succeed him in the Julian line.

It is interesting to note that changes in the planned succession were also echoed in the imagery. This is evident on several items with Tiberius' succession as their subject. The portrayal of Tiberius flanked by crossed horns of plenty (fig. 4.5, nr. 1) is familiar to us from coins featuring Germanicus and Tiberius Gemellus. Künzl suspects that the symbolism on belt fittings relates to the succession by Drusus II and his sons Germanicus and Tiberius and that the intention was to promote the Tiberius-Drusus-Gemellus line of succession.[79] However, the death of his son Drusus forced Tiberius to look to his adopted son Germanicus as a possible heir, as is reflected in the imagery on the 'Sword of Tiberius'.[80]

The browband of a Weiler type helmet from the Rhine at Amerongen (11.1, fig. 4.7) shows that the succession issue was also a key theme on cavalry equipment. In the centre and at each end of an olive wreath, we see three frontal busts probably representing members of the imperial family. Klumbach

[78] Künzl 1994, 39-40; 1998, 401-402.
[79] Künzl 1994, 45.
[80] See below.

Fig. 4.7. Tinned browband from the Rhine at Amerongen, probably with portraits of members of the imperial house (11.1). Length 23.5 cm. After Braat 1961, pl. XIV; Stuart 1986, fig. 147.

believes it is Drusus II flanked by his sons.[81] A cheekpiece from Frankfurt-Heddernheim (fig. 4.15, nr. 1), on which a young prince is portrayed with a laurel wreath and torque, also appears to show the planned successor from the Julio-Claudian family. The same central theme is perhaps evident on a highly ornate cavalry helmet from Xanten-'Warth'.[82] An olive wreath encircles the helmet bowl, meeting at the brow in a round medallion with the bust of a young man in high relief, decked with a laurel wreath and in military attire – perhaps Claudius portrayed as a prince.[83]

Besides the browband from Amerongen, we know of several helmets with busts from the *civitas Batavorum*, although it is not clear who is represented. In the case of a cavalry helmet from the Waal at Nijmegen (Weiler type), the browband is composed of a high-relief oak wreath with a central female bust (211.8, fig. 4.8). A stray browband from the same site shows a similar laurel wreath (211.10), with male faces flanking a central, female bust.[84] No fewer than five busts adorn the browband of a 1st-century masked helmet, also from the Waal at Nijmegen (211.13, fig. 4.9). The central and the two outermost busts are of female figures, the remaining two male.[85] The figures on the different helmets are probably members of the imperial family, including intended successors, featured for the purposes of political propaganda. The *corona* is a reference to the glory of the imperial house.

[81] Klumbach 1974, 52-53 (nr. 39); for alternatives, see Braat 1961, 61-62; Stuart 1986, 113-D.
[82] Von Prittwitz und Gaffron 1990; 1991; 1993.
[83] Another possibility is Tiberius as reigning emperor.
[84] Although Klumbach (1974, 47-48) and Stuart (1986, 113-C) assume that the two outermost figures are women, they appear to be young men.
[85] Kam (1915, 261-262) believes the busts are Vespasian and Titus with female members of the imperial family; Klumbach (1974, 61) considers this unlikely and believes them to be part of Dionysus' retinue.

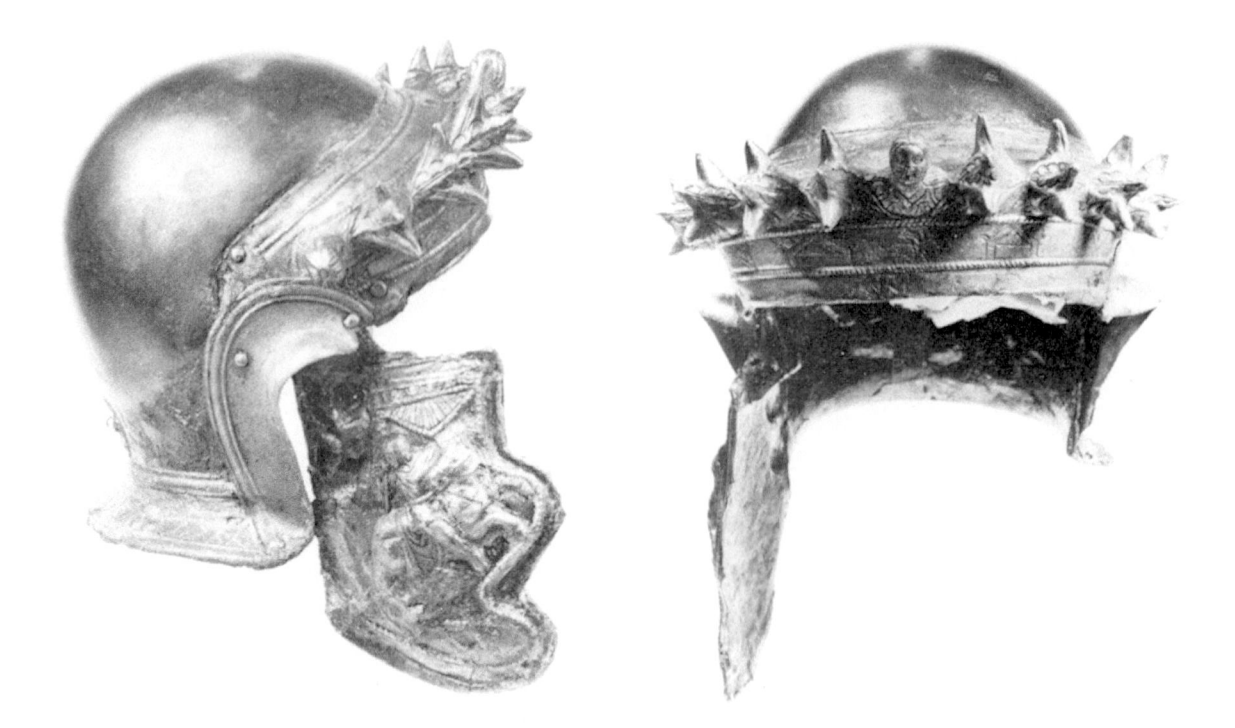

Fig. 4.8. Front and side view of a cavalry helmet with a high-relief browband in the form of a laurel wreath and with a central female bust from the Waal at Nijmegen (211.8). Height 29 cm. After Stuart 1986, fig. 155.

The depiction of the imperial family on horse gear, as in the case of a set of four *phalerae* from Xanten-'Wardt', is exceptional.[86] In the centre of the exclusive *phalerae* that can be attributed to parade gear is a high-relief bust of a male figure (fig. 4.10). As with the cheekpiece from Frankfurt-Heddernheim, the man is wearing a laurel wreath and what appears to be a torque on his chest. The subject is possibly Nero, Caligula or the young prince Germanicus.[87] Two sheet-silver medallions, recovered from a stone cellar in the Nijmegen *oppidum Batavorum*, belong to similar *phalerae* (208.8-9, fig. 5.14).[88] They show the bust of a toga-clad male raising his right arm and crowned with what looks like a laurel wreath. This is probably also a member of the imperial house, either a reigning emperor or his intended successor.

Succession as a dominant theme is more clearly apparent in the decorative discs attached to leather straps and awarded as *dona militaria*. Some of these *phalerae* are made up of round, glass medallions set in bronze, with the medallions portraying either mythical figures or members of the imperial family (fig. 4.11).[89] In the latter case, the importance of the succession issue is demonstrated by the fact that the medallions of Claudius always show him accompanied by his three children, while those of Tiberius generally depict him together with his sons Drusus II and Germanicus. The instances in which Germanicus and Agrippa I are depicted alone appear to relate to the succession of Caligula. Examples from the eastern Rhine delta are fragments of glass medallions from the legionary fortress on the 'Hunerberg' and the auxiliary camp at Vechten, both featuring Tiberius with Germanicus and Drusus II (fig. 4.11, nrs. 5-6).[90]

Finally, motifs such as the Lupa Capitolina and Roma-Victoria were also used for political propaganda purposes. Both arose out of the official state mythology and are references to Rome as the centre

[86] Jenkins 1985, 143-146.
[87] Künzl 1983, note 19; see also Jenkins 1985, 145, with references.
[88] Van Enckevort/Thijssen 2001/2002, 36.
[89] Boschung 1987; Künzl 1998, 413-415.
[90] Boschung 1987, *Kat.* 13, 17; Abb. 58, 63.

Fig. 4.9. Tinned masked helmet from the Waal at Nijmegen (211.13). The browband features two male and three female busts, probably of members of the imperial family. Height 24 cm. Photo Museum het Valkhof, Nijmegen.

of power.[91] The first examples are belt fittings with the *Lupa* motif, the crest of Rome. We see the twins Romulus and Remus, founders of Rome and ancestors of the imperial house, suckling from the she-wolf Lupa (fig. 4.5, nr. 2). A further reference to Rome is the goddess Roma, personifying the city as an armed Amazon (fig. 4.5, nr. 3). Surrounded by booty, she is shown together with a globe and the horn of plenty, alluding to the universal and luck-bringing power of Rome. This image is reinforced by the association with Victoria, goddess of victory.

A combination of the above themes is most clearly expressed in the scabbard of the 'Sword of Tiberius' from Mainz (fig. 4.12).[92] Germanicus, clad as a general, is portrayed on the rectangular plate at the top

---

[91] Von Gonzenbach 1966b, 190-193.
[92] Künzl 1998, 402-406; see also M.J. Klein 2003b, 43. The illustration probably relates to Germanicus' campaigns in Germania, 14-16 AD (Von Gonzenbach 1966b, 200-201).

Fig. 4.10. *Phalerae* from Xanten-'Wardt' with a central bust, probably of an emperor or prince. Scale 1:2. After Jenkins 1985, figs. 2-3.

of the scabbard; he stands before a seated Tiberius, who is depicted as a divine emperor, flanked by Mars and Victoria (*Victoria Augusti*, according to the inscription on her shield). Tiberius' role as a bringer of fortune and prosperity is apparent from the inscription – *felicitas Tiberi* – on the shield that he holds. In the centre of the scabbard is a medallion with the profile bust of Augustus, encircled by a laurel wreath, while the scabbard chape features a temple façade and a standing figure. The presence of the legionary eagle and two banners in the temple-shaped chamber suggest that this was probably the sanctuary of the legion's standard. The standing figure beneath, holding a double-headed axe and a spear, can be interpreted as the personification of a particular region. Between the scabbard plates and the medallion of Augustus are bronze strips with embossed laurel wreaths. The decorative elements belong to the imagery characteristic of the Julio-Claudian period: in addition to the symbols of war and triumph referring to Rome's invincibility and the imperial house, the scabbard depicts the glorification of Tiberius and the desired succession in the person of Germanicus.

Direct references to the imperial family cease to be customary after the reign of Claudius, the sole exception being the fragment of a silver sword scabbard from Leiderdorp.[93] At the bottom is a medallion with profile busts of Trajan and Hadrian on the front and back. Surrounding one portrait are the words *Imp(erator) Caes(ar) Nerva Traian(us) Aug(ustus)* and around the other *Aug(ustus) Caes(ar) Hadrianus*. This scabbard shows that weapons were only used incidentally as propaganda tools during the 2nd century, in this case by Emperor Hadrian to promote his succession. In view of the changing imagery on

[93] Stuart 1986, 109-110, fig. 145; see also Künzl 1998, 434-435.

Fig. 4.11. Glass medallions from *dona militaria* depicting members of the imperial house. Scale 1:1. After Boschung 1987, figs. 46, 54, 58, 63, 75, 84.
1 Tiberius (Istanbul); 2, 5, 6 Tiberius with Germanicus and Drusus minor (Cologne, Nijmegen-'Hunerberg', Vechten); 3 Germanicus (Aquileia); 4 Claudius with his children (Poetovio).

military equipment, it is likely that the bronze masked helmets with their classical masks known from this period had lost their original significance and were no longer consciously associated with Alexander the Great.

4.2.2 THE INVINCIBILITY OF ROME

Alongside references to the imperial house, other frequently occurring images in the pre-Flavian period were triumphant cavalrymen, booty and symbols of victory (palm leaves and wreaths) which, like Roma-Victoria, alluded to the might and invincibility of Rome. The historical value of such images is perhaps apparent from a series of scabbard fittings from *gladii* (Mainz type), showing captured Gallic barbarians kneeling amidst war booty (fig. 4.5, nr. 4). Künzl points out the severed hands visible behind the kneeling figure and beneath the booty on the right of the fitting.[94] In contrast to the frequently raised and outstretched hands signifying loyalty and friendship, the downward-pointing, severed hands have negative overtones. This imagery is perhaps linked to the quashing of the rebellion that broke out in Gaul and Germania Superior in AD 21 under the leadership of the Aeduan Julius Sacrovir.[95] In response, the imagery on sword scabbards appears to have been used to deter rebellious groups while at the same time displaying Rome's supremacy.

Whereas symbols of triumph supported the political imagery in the previous period, Rome's invincibility began to occupy a more prominent place from the mid-1st century on. Another change from the

[94] Künzl 1994, 45-49; 1998, 411-412.
[95] Künzl 1994, 49; 1998, 411-412.

Fig. 4.12. The 'Sword of Tiberius' from the Rhine at Mainz. Length 57 cm. After Künzl 1998, Taf. 45.

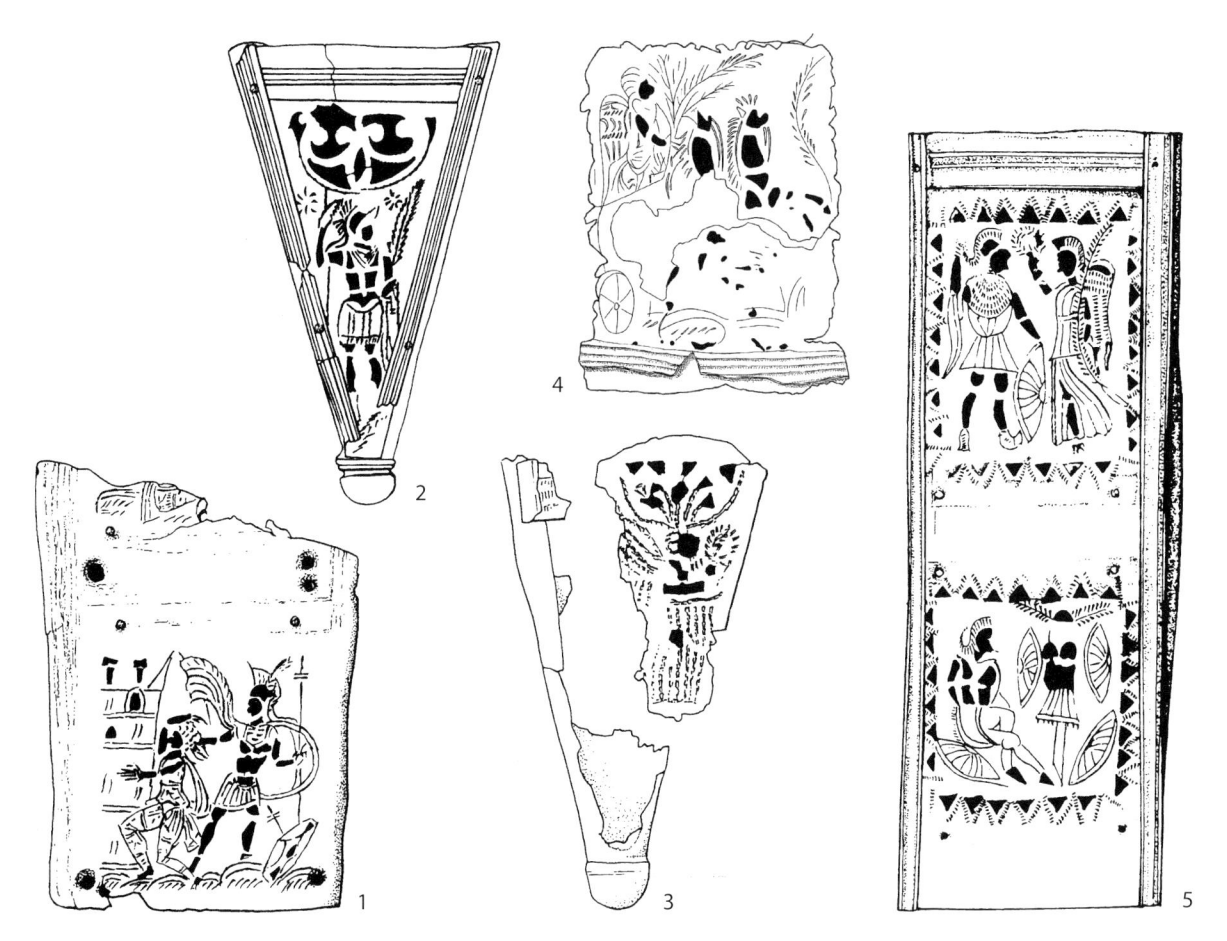

Fig. 4.13. Scabbard fittings from Pompeii type *gladii* with images that appear to refer to the capture of Jerusalem in AD 70. Scale 2:3. After Haalebos et al. 1998, figs. 42, 44-45; drawing Gemeente Nijmegen, Bureau Archeologie (nr. 4).
1-4 Nijmegen-'Hunerberg'; 5 site unknown (Nijmegen?).

previous period is that decoration became less ornate, with the Pompeii type *gladii* and to a lesser extent horse gear *phalerae* becoming the principal vehicles.

The decoration of swords takes the form of engraved and often partly openwork figures on scabbard fittings.[96] About 20 fittings are documented, with two key themes – the deities Victoria and/or Mars and a Roman soldier with a captive and/or booty – often appearing in combination.[97] Additionally, almost all fittings feature palms, which would appear to have been a rather general symbol of victory. The image on a decorative fitting from the legionary fortress at Nijmegen, however, suggests that these refer to a specific event, namely, the sack of Jerusalem by Titus in AD 70 (fig. 4.13, nr. 1).[98] Mars is shown on the bottom of a rectangular plate together with a kneeling captive before a city tower. As the siege of Jerusalem was Rome's only significant capture of a city in the second half of the 1st century, the tower can be identified as the Fortress of Antonia on the Temple Mount. Other references to this particular battle are palms and the trousers worn by the prisoners, both elements associated with the Near East. The Roman authorities probably used Pompeii type swords, just as they had several decades earlier after the revolt of Julius Sacrovir, to show Rome's supremacy, this time over Jerusalem.

[96] Künzl 1994, 51-53; 1998, 426-428.

[97] Künzl 1998, Tab. 5, Abb. 19-21; we can add a recent find from the 'Hunerberg' fortress, found by the Gemeente Nijmegen, Bureau Archeologie (see below).

[98] Haalebos et al. 1998, 52-58; Künzl 1998, 428, cat. nr. P15.

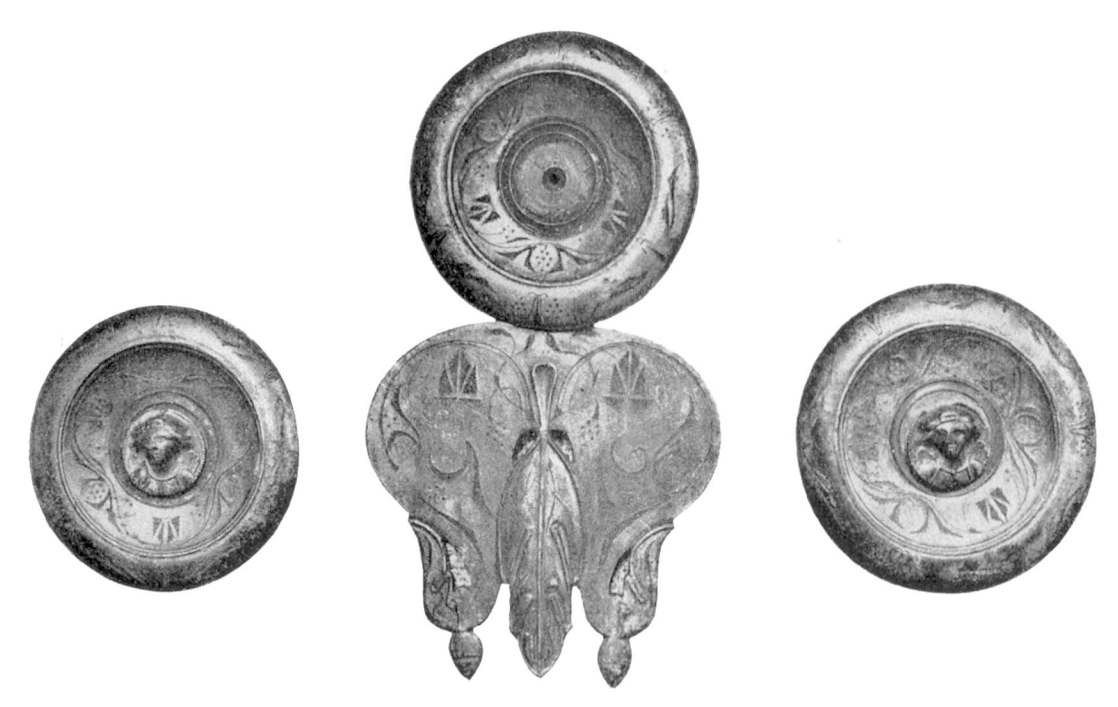

Fig. 4.14. *Phalerae* with relief bust of Victoria as the central medallion, from the Lower Rhine at Doorwerth (55.34-35, 77). The medallion is missing from the central *phalera* with a pendant. Diameter 8.9 cm. After Holwerda 1931, fig. 4.

In addition to the rectangular fitting depicting the city tower, five other examples of this type of decoration are known from the eastern Rhine delta, three of which also come from the 'Hunerberg' legionary fortress. First of all, there are two triangular fittings, one with a standing Mars and the other a standing Victoria (fig. 4.13, nrs. 2-3).[99] A recently found, rectangular fitting shows Victoria astride a horse-drawn chariot (fig. 4.13, nr. 4). A second rectangular fitting from an unknown site features Mars and Victoria in the upper zone (fig. 4.13, nr. 5).[100] Beneath is a seated, trouser-clad captive surrounded by the spoils of war. Mars features twice on an example from the Lower Rhine at Oosterbeek – standing between two banners in the upper scene and in a chariot drawn by two horses in the lower one (220.1, pl. 17). Finds from the legionary base at Nijmegen (4x) suggest that this symbolism was particularly favoured by *legionarii*.[101]

To a limited extent, the symbolism of victory was also a feature of 1st-century horse gear. Although ornamentation was usually confined to vegetal elements, from the Claudian period in particular, we see the appearance on parade equipment of oak leaves and acorns, which appear to be a reference to the *corona*. On a *phalera* from Wijk bij Duurstede-'De Horden' (291.51, pl. 81), this is expressed in a stylised laurel wreath inlaid with niello. Such imagery is most clearly apparent in the case of several *phalerae* from the Lower Rhine at Doorwerth (55.34-35, 77, fig. 4.14). The long hair and diadem suggest that the busts on the silver medallions in the centre of the *phalerae* should be interpreted as female, while the presence of wings shows that this is Victoria.[102] A similar piece is known from the Waal at Nijmegen (211.63). Here too a silver medallion with the bust of Victoria occupies the centre of an exclusive *phalera*.

Although we can discern a shift in the 2nd and 3rd centuries towards symbolism with a protective value, the invincibility of Rome continued to be an important theme on swords from this period. This included

[99] Künzl 1998, cat. nrs. P5-6.
[100] Gerhartl-Witteveen/Hubrecht 1990, nr. 5; Künzl 1998, cat. nr. P7. The site could also be Nijmegen.
[101] Compare the legionary fortress at Vindonissa (3x): Künzl 1998, 426-428, cat. nrs. P12-14.
[102] Brouwer 1982, 151; Stuart 1986, 119.

Fig. 4.15. Cheekpieces from Frankfurt-Hedderheim with the bust of an imperial prince (left) and from IJzendoorn-'De Waard' depicting a standing Hercules (139.1) (right). Not to scale. After Baatz/Herrmann 1982, Abb. 237; Stuart 1986, fig. 158.

both realistic and highly stylised motifs that could adorn both sides of the sword blade.[103] The primary subjects were gods such as Victoria, Mars and to a lesser extent Diana and Minerva. Wreaths and palm branches also occur, as do legionary eagles, in some cases flanked by standards. Again, Rome's invincibility is the dominant theme, centring on symbols of war (Mars and the legionary eagle) and triumph (Victoria, wreaths and palm branches).

4.2.3 APPEALS FOR DIVINE PROTECTION

Compared to members of the imperial house, the gods of the Roman pantheon were portrayed less frequently on weapons during the 1st century AD. With the exception of Victoria and the occasional depiction of Mars, Minerva and Fortuna, we primarily see attributes referring to the gods: Jupiter's thunderbolt, Bacchus' crater and vine, Apollo's griffin and Amor as companion to Venus.[104] Images of gods are also rare on 1st-century weapons from the research region. A Weiler type cheekpiece from IJzendoorn-'De Waard' depicts Hercules (139.1, fig. 4.15, nr. 2), while Mars is the central figure on two Mainz type *gladius* scabbards from Lobith (176.2, 9, pl. 16, 22). A further reference is the stylised temple façade sometimes depicted on *gladii* scabbards (Mainz type) and dagger sheaths.[105] A comparable temple façade is added as a bronze mount to an iron cheekpiece (Weisenau type) from the Meuse at Venlo.[106]

---

[103] Biborski 1994a; 1994b, 179-185.
[104] Künzl 1998, 425.
[105] Swords: Von Gonzenbach 1966a; Künzl 1998, 394; daggers: Obmann 2000, 11.
[106] Klumbach 1974, 55 (nr. 41), Taf. 41.

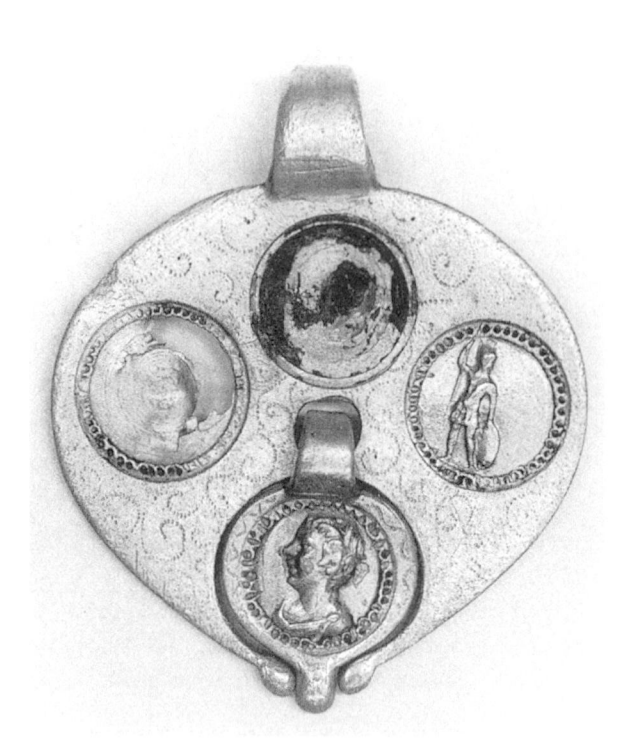

Fig. 4.16. Apron pendant from Cologne, with medallions showing the bust of a member of the imperial house and a standing Mars still in situ. Height 5.2 cm. After Schleiermacher 1996, 294-295.

Although these motifs seem to refer to the protective world of the gods in general, the exclusive apron pendant from Cologne reveals that they could be employed to underpin political imagery; both a member of the imperial family and Mars are portrayed on round medallions (fig. 4.16).[107] The depiction of Amor can also be explained in this light: as the son of the goddess Venus, whom the Julian house regarded as an ancestor, Amor is an indirect reference to the divine status of the emperor and his family.

Not until the 2nd century do we see the ascendancy of an imagery that was no longer politically charged, but which was intended to protect individual soldiers, both during their time in the army and after their death. The symbolism relating to the life of a soldier centred primarily on the baldric *phalera*, strap terminal and pendant.[108] Although images of imperial figures and gods do not feature on baldric fittings, there are several examples of references to Jupiter. One involves a uniform openwork group comprising a *phalera*, strap terminal and pendant that together make up a set (fig. 4.17, nrs. 1-3).[109] We find the words *Optime Maxime con(serva)* encircling an eagle on the *phalera*, while *numerum omnium* figures on the strap terminal, and *militantium* on the pendant. In the inscription, 'Jupiter, the greatest and best' is called upon to protect all the soldiers of this unit. Beneath the eagle is a thunderbolt which, like the bird itself, is a reference to Jupiter. Petculescu points out that baldrics bearing these symbols were worn exclusively by soldiers, with the eagle as the legionary standard indicating use by legionary soldiers.[110] Finds from auxiliary forts, however, suggest a more widespread use within the army.

---

[107] Schleiermacher 1996, 294-295.

[108] Finds from wet contexts in Scandinavia show that decorative motifs could also be stamped on leather baldrics (see Stjernquist 1954, Abb. 4).

[109] Oldenstein 1976, 223-226; Petculescu 1991a, 394-395; Bishop/Coulston 1993, 130-135.

[110] Petculescu 1991a, 394-395. Since the openwork text relates to the protection of the entire unit, she suggests that they were used specifically by standard bearers. There is no hard evidence for this, however.

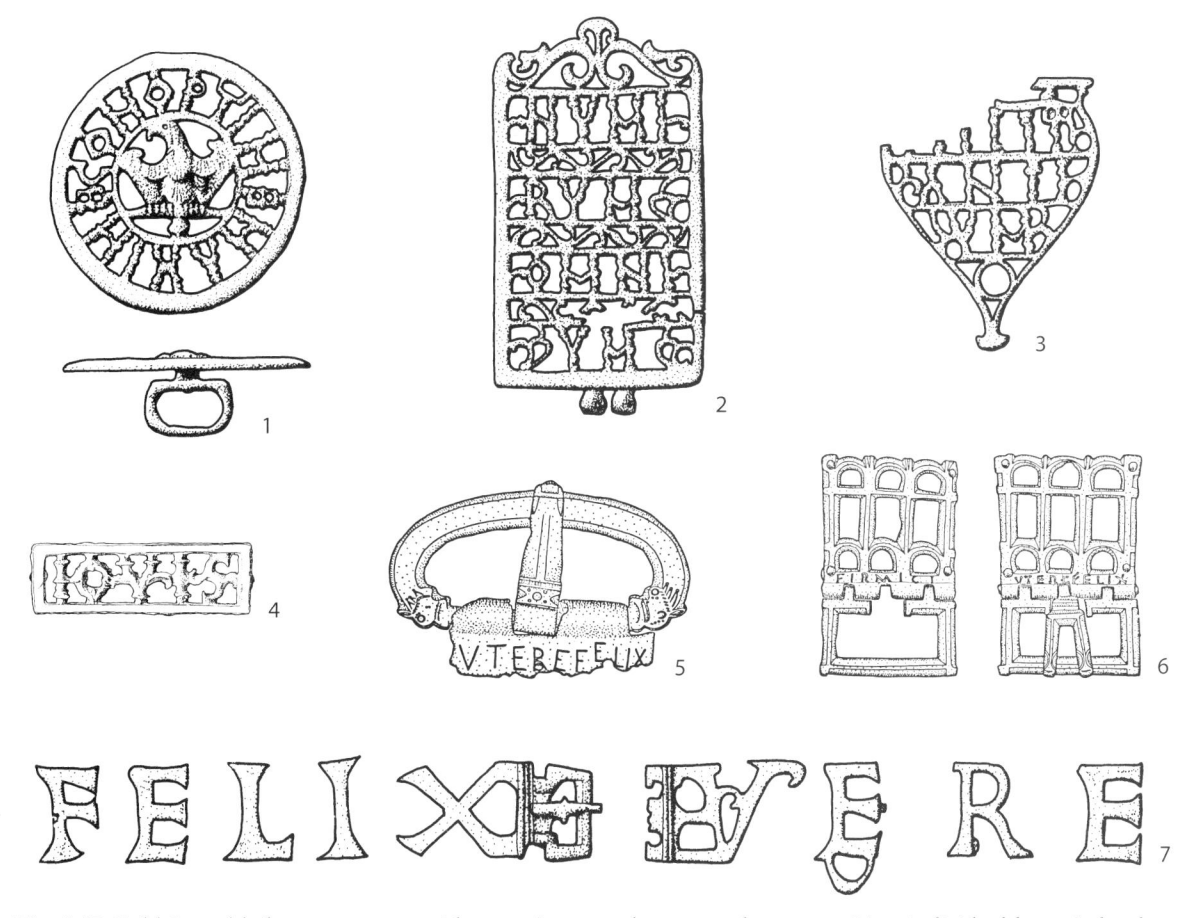

Fig. 4.17. Baldric and belt components with texts (openwork, engraved or comprising individual letters) that have a protective value. Scale 2:3. After Bullinger 1972, fig. 1; Bishop/Coulston 1993, figs. 91 (nrs. 2, 10, 13), 92 (nr. 1); Laser/Schulze 1995, Taf. 9 (nr. 5).
1-3 *phalera*, terminal and pendant from a baldric from Zugmantel; 4 belt fitting from Wiederau; 5 buckle from Würtemberg; 6 set of buckles from Dujmovaca; 7 belt fittings from Lyons.

Four baldric *phalerae* from Vimose feature a motif akin to the central part of the openwork examples (fig. 4.18).[111] In the centre of the discs is a round gold-leaf medallion showing an eagle atop a thunderbolt and flanked by two legionary standards. Beneath the eagles and encircling a globe, we can make out several letters, whose significance is unknown.[112] Similar to these central images are five round, gilded fittings with a standing eagle in relief, recovered from settlements in the Batavian countryside (fig. 2.15, pl. 48). This symbolism probably also relates to Jupiter, with the widening at the base of the feet perhaps representing a thunderbolt. The resemblance to the *phalerae* already mentioned suggests that they too are likely to be baldric components.

A protective value can also be demonstrated for a belt fitting from a 3rd-century cremation burial at Wiederau (fig. 4.17, nr. 4).[113] This is a rectangular openwork fitting with the text *iovis* ('(of) Jupiter'), which, judging by the inscription on decorative parts of the baldric, seems to be an appeal to Jupiter to

---

[111] Stjernquist 1954, Abb. 3 (nrs. 1-4).

[112] Stjernquist 1954, 62: *[..]om*; the first letter is possibly a *d* or an *i*.

[113] Laser/Schultze 1995, 28-29 (XIII-01-4/1.4), with references. It is not known whether the decorative fitting was originally part of a series of fittings making up a longer text.

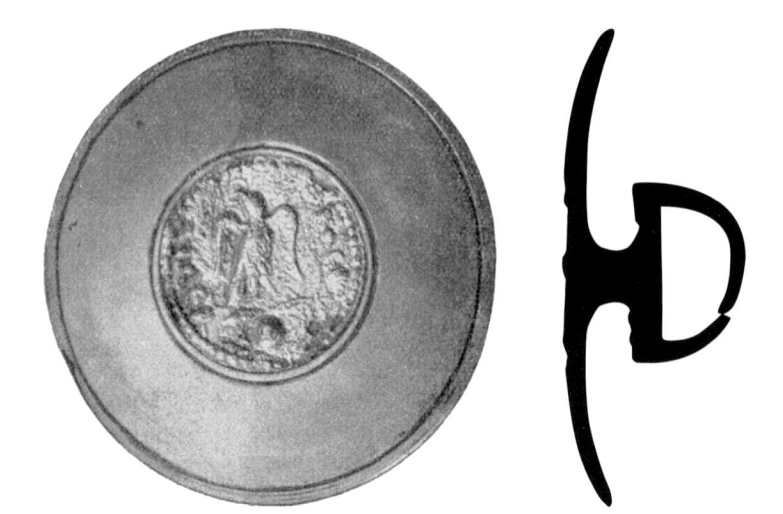

Fig. 4.18. A baldric *phalera* from Vimose (left). In the centre is a gold-leaf medallion with an eagle in relief. Scale 1:1. After Stjernquist 1954, Abb. 3 (nr. 2).

protect the owner. The presence of a sword in the same grave and the reference to Jupiter suggest that the deceased was probably a soldier.

Although they carry no specific reference to Jupiter, a series of belt fittings comprising individual letters can be assigned to a similar group of protective symbols.[114] Finds of complete belt sets in 3rd-century graves reveal that these letters make up the text *vtere felix*, which translates as 'use with luck' (fig. 4.17, nr. 7). The finds to date of bronze and occasionally silver letters are concentrated in the eastern part of the Roman empire. They appear to have been part of belts worn by soldiers from both the legions and auxiliary.[115] Buckle inscriptions from the 4th and 5th centuries show that this protective symbolism retained its significance right up to the end of the Roman era. In addition to the incised inscription *vtere felix* on a buckle from Württemberg (fig. 4.17, nr. 5), a set of two rectangular examples from Dujnovaca feature the words *vtere felix* on one buckle and *Firmici* on the other (fig. 4.17, nr. 6). In the latter case, this is the name of the person to whom the request to 'use with luck' refers.

Finally, decorative horse gear elements occur in the 1st and above all 2nd and 3rd centuries as a kind of amulet with a protective value for the cavalry.[116] The principal motifs were the lunula, phallus and vulva, which may occur in combination, for example as a vulvate fitting with a phallic pendant.[117] In contrast to the decorative baldric and belt fittings, there is nothing to suggest that these symbols related specifically to soldiers, which seems to tie in with the picture of a more general, military-civilian use of horse gear in this period.

Also found on cavalry helmets and parade equipment are motifs with a protective value seeking protection not during life itself but on the journey to the afterlife. The bronze elements on a decorative helmet (Niederbieber type) from the Waal at Nijmegen are embellished with incised female busts, mythological figures (Amor on two occasions, once flanked by two dolphins) and plants (211.15, fig. 2.3). A helmet of the same type from Bodegraven is decorated in a similar fashion.[118] The images consist

[114] Bullinger 1972; Petculescu 1991a, 392-394.

[115] Petculescu 1991a, 393.

[116] The protective symbolism on horse gear is discussed in greater depth in chapter 6.3.3.

[117] Lunate and phallic pendants, worn around the neck by adults and children as a kind of amulet, show that the protective value of these symbols was not confined to horsemen and their mounts (see Zadoks-Josephus Jitta/Gerhartl-Witteveen 1977, 172-175)

[118] Klumbach 1974, 43-54 (nr. 40), Taf. 40; Stuart 1986, 112-113, fig. 154.

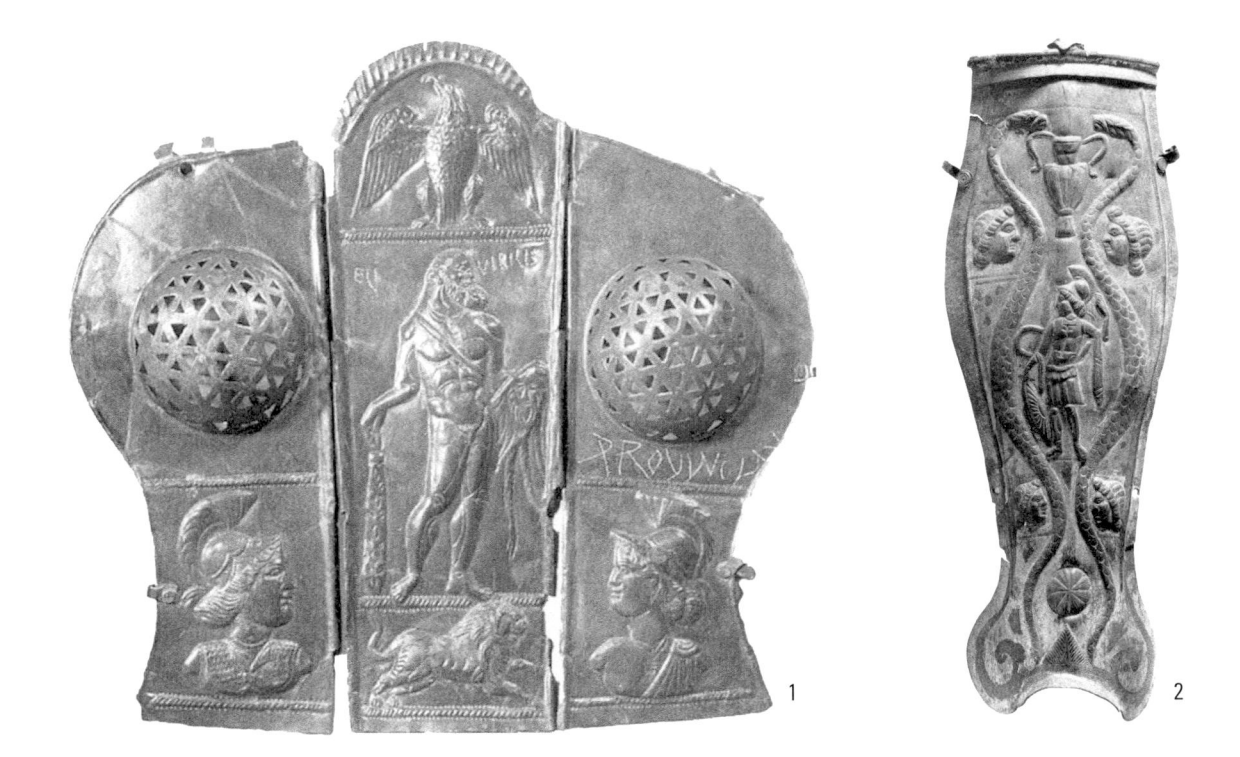

Fig. 4.19. Highly ornate parade gear components depicting Hercules and Mars. Not to scale. After Garbsch 1978, Taf. 11 (nr. 1); Kemkes/Scheuerbrandt 1997, Abb. 78.
1 chamfron from Eining; 2 greave from Regensburg-'Kumpfmühl'.

of a crater flanked by two outward-facing dolphins, three naked (dancing?) figures, each with a crooked staff or sickle, and plant motifs. According to Klumbach, the symbolism is Dionysian in nature. However, as the soul's companions on the journey to the afterlife, the dolphins would appear to be a reference to life after death.[119]

In the contemporaneous parade equipment, Garbsch distinguishes four themes with a significant mythological component.[120] The first is the frequent portrayal of gods associated with acts of war, such as Jupiter, Minerva, Mars, Victoria and Hercules (fig. 4.19). The second relates to the journey to the afterlife, with the key symbols being marine and mythical animals, together with Medusa. The third theme concerns images relating to war and to cult practices. The relationship to the world of the gods is once again paramount. Finally, we encounter different animals symbolising a particular legion (a bull, lion, wild boar, ibex and the wolverine Lupa). Although symbols of war and victory continued to play an important role in the imagery, there seems to have been a link to the text on baldric fittings from the 2nd and 3rd centuries. Seen in this light, the depicted gods have a significant protective function, not just during military service, but on the journey to the afterlife as well.

In the 4th and 5th centuries, the production of weapons in specialised *fabricae* was accompanied by a declining investment in decoration, resulting in a loss of symbolic expression. Although the guard helmets were clad in gilded silver leaf and were sometimes richly inlaid with glass imitation gems, references to the imperial house or Roman pantheon disappeared almost completely. The sole exception is a helmet from Budapest depicting the gods Victoria and Jupiter, as well as lions (in two instances flanking a crater).

[119] Klumbach 1974, 54; Garbsch 2000.   [120] Garbsch 1978, 29-32; 2000.

Fig. 4.20. Reconstruction of a late Roman guard helmet with Chi-Rho appliqué from the Meuse valley in Limburg. Not to scale. After Prins 2000, fig. 10.

Thomas points out that these symbols refer to the victory of life over death, with divine protection once again a key theme.[121] Interestingly, several guard helmets feature an appliqué with a Chi-Rho monogram at the brow.[122] In addition to stray appliqués, including finds from rural settlements near IJzendoorn (138.3, pl. 7) and Lienden (174.6, pl. 7), a helmet with the same monogram is documented from the Meuse valley in Limburg (fig. 4.20).[123] Like the depictions of the gods, this Christian symbol appears to have been added for its protective function.

The late Roman period saw the introduction of a new, broad belt, richly ornamented with bronze fittings. Although the decoration was chiefly geometric, the protomes on the buckles allude to an animal symbolism of 'Germanic' origin. The text *vtere felix* on several buckles (fig. 4.17) suggests that these may have been references to 'Germanic' gods who were intended to protect the wearer against misfortune.

---

[121] Thomas 1973.

[122] A. Alföldi 1932.

[123] Stray appliqués from outside the Rhineland are known from Richborough, England (Lyne 1994, 104) and especially from Pannonia (Migotti 1999).

4.3 CONCLUSION

The above survey shows that there is a relationship between the way in which the production of weapons, belts/baldrics and horse gear was organised, the specific symbols inherent in the images and the intended user. Equipment was imported from the Mediterranean region in the 1st century AD and quite soon came to be manufactured in the military *fabricae* as well. In this period, the imagery was dominated by political propaganda and subsequently by more general symbols of victory clearly targeting the military user. The imperial family's use of propaganda to glorify itself and thus legitimise its power was linked to a formative stage in the development of the young emperorship.[124] Military items were a logical vehicle for this, given that control of the army was a key power factor. Although imposed by the central authority, the imagery used – particularly military symbols of invincibility – would most certainly have appealed to soldiers as well.

The rise of local, private workshops in the Flavian period meant that soldiers and civilians alike could purchase belts and horse gear in the camp villages. There are also signs of the production of these 'military' items in towns and in the countryside. Coinciding with the increasingly differentiated levels of production was the rise of an imagery centring on the protection of the individual owner rather than on political propaganda. Although the text on openwork baldric fittings – and in one case a belt fitting – relates to soldiers, the remaining belt and horse gear finds feature more general symbols that could be meaningful both inside and outside the army.

Military equipment was produced in centralised, government-controlled *fabricae* for the first time in the 4th and 5th centuries. Private workshops, however, soon played a key role once again in the manufacture of belts. The few decorative elements with a specific imagery reveal a far-reaching fusion of Roman, Christian and 'Germanic' symbols. These were not specifically aimed at soldiers, but had a rather general, protective value.

---

[124] Interestingly, after Claudius, the imperial house rarely used military equipment for propaganda purposes such as promoting an heir. We have no clear explanation for this.

5 Military equipment and the life cycle of a Roman soldier

Chapter 3 showed that significant changes took place in the composition of 'military' finds from non-military contexts in the eastern Rhine delta during the Roman period. The early material (c. 50 BC – AD 120) is characterised by relatively large quantities of helmets, armour and shields, all of them militaria associated with soldiers. Judging by the organisation of production and the imagery used, this was also the period in which weapons and horse gear were intended for military users.[1] From the 2nd to the 5th centuries, specifically military items largely gave way to items that could have belonged to soldiers and non-soldiers alike.[2]

The aim of this chapter is to present a model that explains the presence of predominantly early, military items in non-military contexts.[3] Central to the model is the life cycle of a Roman soldier (fig. 5.1). By examining how weaponry and horse gear were used in the different stages of the cycle, we can identify the times during a soldier's life when his equipment could have ended up in non-military contexts. I will first discuss the key stages in the life of a Roman soldier, before going on to explore the question of ownership and the use of military equipment. By linking the kinds of use to specific stages in a soldier's life, we can distinguish between a period of military use by *milites* and one of 'social use' by *veterani*. Although the life-cycle model has been especially developed for finds from the research region, it has a more general validity for both legionary and auxiliary soldiers.[4]

5.1 THE LIFE CYCLE OF A ROMAN SOLDIER

Using historical and epigraphic sources, it is possible to reconstruct the life cycle of males during the Roman period. Key stages connected with specific rites of passage include birth, reaching maturity, and death.[5] For Roman soldiers, other significant stages are the beginning and end of their period of military service. Thus, in addition to birth and death, an epitaph from Lyons erected for the legionary veteran Vitalinius Felix emphasises entry into service and discharge as important moments in his life.[6] And funerary inscriptions of Roman officers often refer to their military careers, with promotions marking the different stages for each individual soldier.

Below I will briefly discuss entry into the army, military career options and discharge. To help in the interpretation of finds from non-military contexts, I will further examine the places where veterans preferred to settle, the trades they chose, as well as their origins in the case of soldiers who served in the *civitas Batavorum*.

---

[1] See chapter 4.
[2] See chapter 6.
[3] A summarised version of this chapter has already been published (Nicolay 2002). The ideas presented here are based in part on studies by Roymans (1996, 13-41) and Derks (1998, 45-54).
[4] In the case of auxiliary troops, 'Roman soldiers' means the professional soldiers organised in regular units from the time of Augustus onward. For some time to come, they may continue to have been recruited in accordance with native traditions (see chapter 7.2).
[5] For soldiers with Roman citizenship, see Laurence 2000, especially 444.
[6] *CIL* XIII, 1906 (Lyon): ...*natus est die Martis / die Martis proba/tus die Martis missionem / percepit die Martis defu/nctus est*...

MILITARY EQUIPMENT AND THE LIFE CYCLE OF A ROMAN SOLDIER

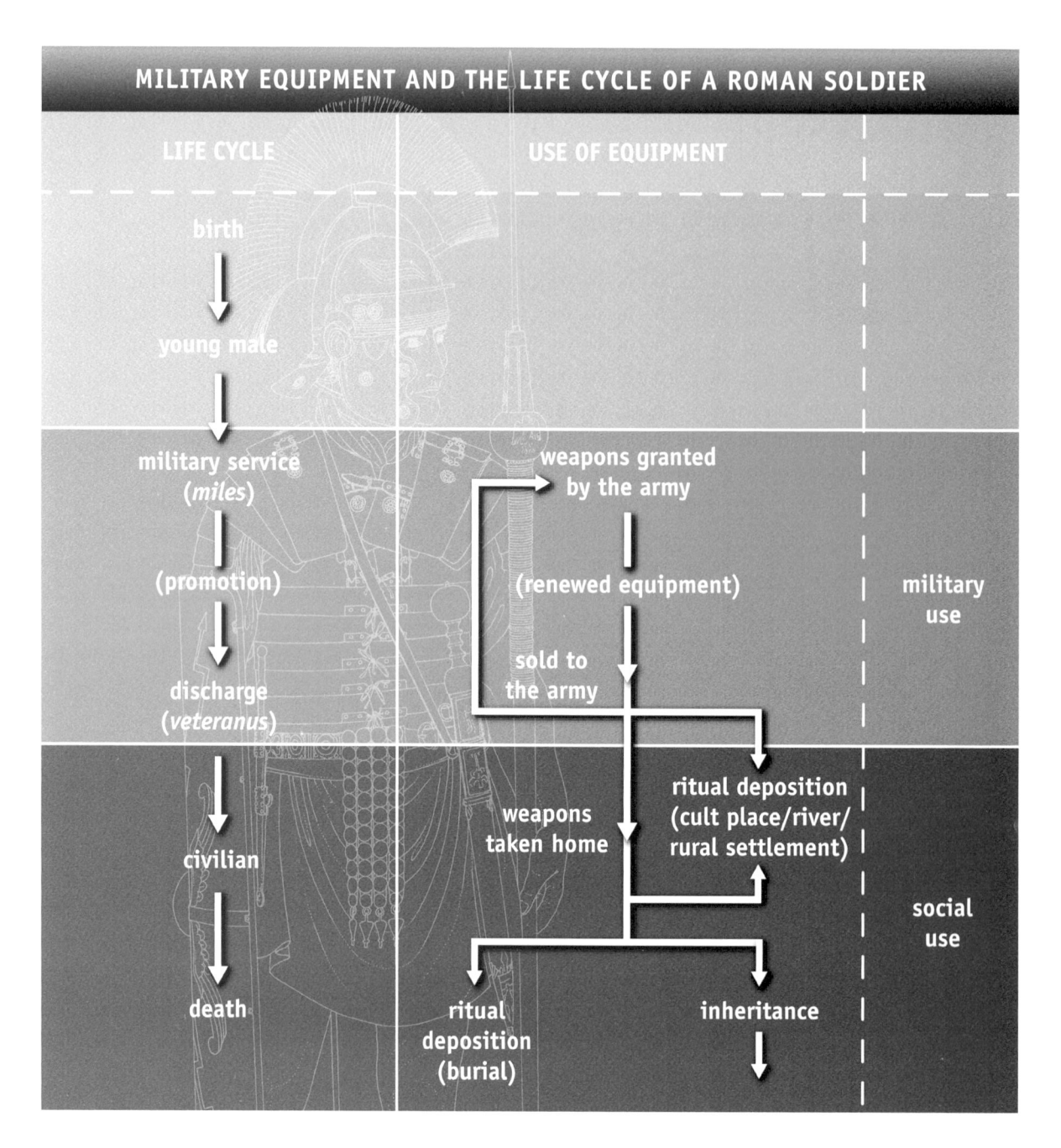

LIFE CYCLE

birth → young male → military service (*miles*) → (promotion) → discharge (*veteranus*) → civilian → death

USE OF EQUIPMENT

weapons granted by the army → (renewed equipment) / sold to the army

weapons taken home → ritual deposition (cult place/river/rural settlement) / inheritance

ritual deposition (burial)

military use / *social use*

Fig. 5.1. The use of military equipment during the life of a Roman soldier.

5.1.1 ENLISTMENT, MILITARY SERVICE AND HONOURABLE DISCHARGE: PROBATUS, SIGNATUS, MILES AND VETERANUS

A man's life as a soldier began from the moment he entered military service. Recruits were usually about twenty years old, although in exceptional cases boys of barely fifteen and men in their late thirties were accepted.[7] Admission to the army was preceded by a rigorous examination; a young man's physical con-

---

[7] Legions: R.W. Davies 1989, 7 (min. 13, max. 36, average 21); auxiliary: Alföldy 1968, 96-99 (min. 14, max. 36, average 22).

dition, as well as his background and citizenship status determined whether he should be admitted and, if so, to which unit.[8]

The first step was a medical examination to establish the recruit's age, height and health. If he passed the medical, he became a *probatus*, which meant that he was sent to his intended unit to undergo a physical, designed to test his speed, strength, weapons handling and courage. If he passed this stage, he would receive a *signaculum*, a lead identification disc worn on a cord around his neck, and would attain the status of *signatus*. This was also the time when he swore the military oath, the *sacramentum*. The recruit was then formally admitted to his future unit, having finally achieved the status of soldier (*miles*).

Assignment to a particular unit depended on a soldier's health and physical attributes and, just as importantly, the right references. Soldiers preferred units that offered the greatest prestige, the shortest term of service and the highest pay, the most prestigious being the Praetorian Guard and the imperial bodyguard[9]. However, until the end of the 2nd century, admission to these units was almost the exclusive preserve of men of Italian origin on the one hand, and in particular Batavians, Ubii and – later – more Eastern groups on the other.[10] For men born elsewhere, the legion offered the best prospects. But to be admitted, a recruit had to have Roman citizenship in addition to certain physical qualities. Men without citizenship and those who failed the rigorous test for the legions had no option but to join the auxiliary. Preference here went to the *alae* because the cavalry were more highly paid than the cohorts. A man's height was critical in this respect. Short men were not admitted to the cavalry and could only join the relatively poorly-paid cohorts.

Given that the size of the salary and various other payments made to troops as professional soldiers was dependent on their status and rank, promotion was the best way for a soldier to improve his position.[11] But career opportunities were limited for simple soldiers without connections or the right background. In general, such men could aspire no higher than to the rank of *centurio* or *decurio*, and in particular *principales* as the more senior officer positions were reserved for the sons of senators and knights. Also privileged were the sons of influential families and former officers; they could be appointed directly as a *centurio* or *decurio*. The same applied to members of the native elite who, certainly until the Batavian revolt, could command their own 'national' units.[12]

Around the beginning of the first millennium, the period of military service was 16 years for the Praetorian Guard, while legionary soldiers were awarded honourable discharge after 20 years.[13] Although a shortage of recruits meant that legionaries regularly served for up to 30 to 40 years, a standard term of 25 years was introduced under Tiberius. In the 1st and 2nd centuries, this term was made up of 20 obligatory years plus an additional five years *sub vexillo*. However, legionary soldiers who refused this were able to take honourable discharge after 20 years. From Claudius onward, it also became customary for auxiliary soldiers to serve for 25 years, although they were not entitled to *missio honesta* unless they served the full term.[14] A term similar to that of the auxiliary troops is assumed for the emperor's personal bodyguard.[15]

---

[8] For a description of the admission procedure, see R.W. Davies 1989, chapter 1; see also Watson 1969, chapters 2-3. The process was the same for potential officers (R.W. Davies 1989, 25).

[9] R.W. Davies 1989, 23-24.

[10] A key difference is that members of the Praetorian Guard were direct appointments, whereas the bodyguard were selected from the best cavalrymen from the *alae* (Bellen 1981; M.P. Speidel 1994).

[11] For an overview of rankings and promotion opportunities within the army, see Von Domaszewski 1967; E. Birley 1988 (several contributions); recently Wesch-Klein 1998, chapter 1. Maxfield (1981, fig. 40) presents a diagrammatic summary.

[12] See chapter 7.2.

[13] Mann 2000, 153-155; for the legions, see also H.M.D. Parker 1985, 212-214. Legionaries also faced a 16-year term prior to AD 5.

[14] Alföldy 1968, 105-110; Holder 1980, 46-48; Mann 2000, 155.

[15] M.P. Speidel 1994, 89-90.

Fig. 5.2. Front and back of *tabella* I of a military diploma from the rural settlement of Elst-'Lijnden' (AD 98). The diploma relates to a Batavian from the *ala Batavorum* who moved to the Batavian countryside after discharge. Height approx.13 cm. Photos Museum het Valkhof, Nijmegen.

On completion of the average term of 25 years, a soldier's time as a *miles* came to an end and he left the army as a *veteranus* at the age of about 45. Legionaries customarily received a reward at their *missio honesta*, initially a grant of land (*missio agraria*), and later a sum of money (*missio nummaria*).[16] For auxiliary soldiers, Roman citizenship (*civitas Romana*) and the right to contract a legal marriage with a peregrine woman (*conubium*) were the key rewards.[17] Although auxiliary veterans were not entitled to a discharge payment, they did enjoy the same privileges as legionaries, including exemption from various forms of taxation (including poll tax) and several forms of punishment.[18]

From the mid-1st century, auxiliary soldiers could be given a document setting out their honourable discharge and accompanying privileges (fig. 5.2). This military diploma comprised two bronze tablets bound together, containing the literal text of the imperial decree granting *civitas Romana* and *conubium*.[19] Although Augustus had granted citizenship in exceptional cases, this privilege – like the *conubium* – was introduced more systematically under Claudius.[20] Soldiers initially received both privileges following 25 years of service, which did not necessarily coincide with the ending of military service. From Trajan onwards, these privileges were linked to honourable discharge, and only veterans were eligible.[21]

[16] Keppie 2000; see also Watson 1969, 147-149.

[17] Mann 1986; Maxfield 1986, 37-42; Mirković 1986; Vittinghoff 1986; Link 1989, 4-5, 7 ff.; Phang 2001, 57-65

[18] For an overview of these privileges, see Wolff 1986; Link 1989.

[19] However, diplomas were not recognised as an official discharge document (Mann/Roxan 1988). Special discharge certificates (*tabulae honestae missionis*) served this purpose.

[20] For the evolution of citizenship, see Behrends 1986.

[21] Mirković 1986, 173-175.

5.1.2 VETERANS' WORK AND PLACE OF RESIDENCE AFTER THEIR MISSIO HONESTA

Using the archaeological contexts of military diplomas and other inscriptions linked to veterans, we can sketch a picture of the places in the frontier provinces where legionary and auxiliary veterans preferred to settle. In this respect, it is interesting to examine how veterans used their *depositum* and, in the case of legionary veterans also their discharge pay, to build up a life in the civilian world after 25 years in the army. But first I will investigate where veterans chose to live after discharge; did they return to their homeland or did they prefer the region where they had spent most of their soldiering life?

Epigraphic sources are by no means a representative data set. For example, the monumental inscriptions outside Italy are found primarily in the frontier regions of the empire, with centres of an urban nature – as arenas for 'monumental competition' – forming the chief find sites.[22] On the other hand, monumental inscriptions rarely occur in the countryside, making it almost impossible to trace veterans there through epitaphs and votive inscriptions.[23] Although military diplomas are documented from urban centres (including camp villages) and countryside alike, these too are a poorly representative category of finds. There are two reasons for this. First of all, diplomas relate almost solely to auxiliary soldiers and secondly, a sizeable portion of the bronze tablets will have been melted down, as is attested by the many such items found as scrap. Just as importantly, a fairly expensive diploma would have been superfluous for many veterans. Because they lived close to where they had last been stationed, it would have been easy for them to verify their veteran status.[24]

Despite the unrepresentative nature of epigraphic finds, they remain a key source of information for identifying the province and type of settlement where veterans lived. In Caesar's time, legionary veterans tended to return to Southern Gaul, and especially to Italy. This changed at the end of the 1st century, which saw a shift toward the frontier zone, primarily as the result of new recruitment areas, with the frontier provinces supplying an increasingly large share of manpower.[25] Additionally, soldiers recruited in other regions also favoured the area where they had been stationed. It is interesting to note that Tacitus confirms this preference, reporting that the veterans who settled in Italian towns under Nero preferred to return to the provinces where they had been stationed.[26] Tacitus presents the same picture for legionary veterans from Pannonia who complained that they were accommodated elsewhere than in the area where they had been based.[27]

The situation was much the same for auxiliary veterans. Inscriptions and military diplomas reveal that soldiers recruited both locally and elsewhere preferred the region where they ended their army days.[28] If we take into account the distribution of military diplomas, we see that over 90% of the auxiliary diplomas have been found in the frontier provinces, the majority (79%) in the same province where their owners completed their service.[29] In roughly half the cases, these veterans were stationed in their homeland; the other half were ex-soldiers who remained in the area where they had been based, often despite having come from far afield.[30]

The specific archaeological context of veteran inscriptions and diplomas also gives us an idea of the types of settlement favoured by veterans. As a case study, I will examine the situation in Germania Inferior. A review of inscriptions of legionary veterans shows that the vast majority of legionaries settled in camp

---

[22] Woolf 1996, 36-37; see also Lenz 2006.

[23] Roymans/Derks 2006.

[24] Mann/Roxan 1988, 343; Van Driel-Murray 2003, 211.

[25] Mann 1983, 56 ff., tables 12, 14 (German provinces); Keppie 2000; see also Demougin 1999; Bridger 2006.

[26] Tacitus, *Ann.* 14, 27; see also E. Birley 1982/1983, 272.

[27] Tacitus, *Ann.* 1, 17; see also Mann 1983, 58.

[28] E. Birley 1982/1983, 276-278; Kellner 1986; Roxan 1997; 2000.

[29] Kellner 1986, 242-243. A total of 217 diplomas relate to auxiliary soldiers.

[30] Roxan 1997, 483.

Fig. 5.3. Gravestone of a veteran from Southern Gaul from an unknown cohort. The stone was found near the villa site of Houten-'Molenzoom'. Preserved height 94.5 cm. After Derks 2003, fig. 9.

villages and especially towns in the region where they had been quartered.[31] One of the few pointers to legionaries also settling in the countryside is a 1st-century horse pendant bearing the inscription *leg(io) IX Hisp(ana)*, recovered from a villa site at Ewijk (93.13, fig. 5.4, nr. 5, pl. 85). Haalebos suggests that the pendant belonged to a possible Spanish legionary cavalryman who bought a villa close to his last post when discharged ('Hunerberg', Nijmegen).[32] Although monumental inscriptions are almost unknown in the countryside, the choice of location revealed by the data at hand does appear logical. These were soldiers who had largely been recruited elsewhere and who had little access to a network in the countryside.

Among epigraphic sources relating to auxiliary veterans, there is an important distinction between soldiers recruited locally and those recruited elsewhere (table 5.1). The preferred location for veterans from the latter group – urban centres or camp villages in the immediate vicinity of their army post – seems to match that of legionaries. The sole exception is a soldier from Fréjus in southern France, whose gravestone location suggests that he established a villa in the countryside (nr. 16, fig. 5.3).[33] Like the choice of the legionary cavalryman from Ewijk, this would appear to have been in the vicinity of his army base (perhaps Vechten). A diploma from a *canabae legionis* at Tokód in northern Pannonia Inferior, belonging to the cavalryman C. Petillius Vindex (nr. 8), shows that we can expect the same for Batavian soldiers garrisoned outside their own region. After receiving his *missio honesta* in AD 110, this Batavian did not return to the Lower Rhine region but settled in a camp village probably close to his army camp. The diplomas of two probable Batavian veterans who completed their service in Britannia reveal that veterans could also choose to return home (nrs. 4, 6).[34] After their discharge, one went to live in the Batavian countryside and the other in Ulpia Noviomagus.

[31] Mann 1983, table 12; compare the remaining tables. See also Demougin 1999.
[32] Haalebos 2000c, 23-24; 2000d, 472-473.
[33] Derks 2003. Traces of a villa or villa-like building found at the same location date from the early 2nd century AD.

The incorporation of spolia into the building's foundation stones suggests that at least one predecessor was fully or partially built of stone (Van Dockum/Hessing 1994, 224-225, fig. 184).

[34] Compare the choice made by two Thracians from the

	find site	dating	unit	post	origin	place of settlement	type of site
1.	Wiesbaden	78	*ala Moesica*	Germ. inf.	*civ. Trever.*	Germ. sup.	army camp
2.	Kamensko	80	*coh. IIII Thracum*	Germ. inf.	Thracia	Thracia	rural settlement
3.	Elst	98	*ala I Batavorum*	Germ. inf.	*civ. Batav.*	Germ. inf.	rural settlement
4.	Nijmegen-West	98-117?	*coh. Batavorum*?	Britannia	*civ. Batav.*?	Germ. inf.	*municipium*
5.	Nijmegen?	98-117?	-	-	-	Germ. inf.	*municipium*?
6.	Delwijnen	98-114	*coh. Batavorum*?	Britannia	*civ. Batav.*?	Germ. inf.	rural settlement.
7.	Kalkar	107-114	-	-	-	Germ. inf.	*vicus*
8.	Tokód	110	*ala Frontoniana*	Pann. inf.	*civ. Batav.*	Pann. inf.	*canabae leg.*
9.	Regensburg	113	*coh. I Batavorum*	Pann. sup.	*civ. Batav.*	Raetia?	mil. *vicus*
10.	Glava	127	*coh. IIII Thracum*	Germ. inf.	Thracia/Dacia	Thracia/Dacia	rural settlement
11.	Rimburg	130-140	-	Germ. inf or Pann. inf.	-	Germ. inf.	rural settlement?
12.	Xanten	158	*coh. I Pann. et Delmat.*	Germ. inf.	local recruit?	Germ. inf.	*colonia*
13.	Poeldijk	160-167	*ala I Noricorum*	Germ. inf.	*civ. Cannan.*	Germ. inf.	rural settlement
14.	Neuss	Tiberian	*coh. III Lusitanorum*	Germ. inf.	Spain?	Germ. inf.	*canabae leg.*
15.	Asberg	Tiberian	*coh. Silaucensium*	Germ. inf.	*domo* Turo	Germ. inf.	mil. *vicus*?
16.	Houten	mid-1st	unknown *cohors*	Germ. inf.	Narbonensis	Germ. inf.	villa?
17.	Neuss	pre-Flavian	*ala Frontoniana*	Germ. inf.	Belgica?	Germ. inf.	*canabae leg.*
18.	Cologne-Deutz	late 1st	*ala Moesica*	Germ. inf.	-	Germ. inf.	*colonia*
19.	Kalkar	1st	*ala I Voconitorum*	Germ. inf.	Gallia	Germ. inf.	*vicus*
20.	Cologne	1st/2nd	*ala I Noricorum*	Germ. inf.	Noricum/Illyria	Germ. inf.	*colonia*
21.	Xanten	early Trajan	*ala Afrorum vet.*	Germ. inf.	local recruit?	Germ. inf.	*canabae leg.*?
22.	Dodewaard	Trajan	*ala Afrorum*	Germ. inf.	local recruit	Germ. inf.	-
23.	Utrecht	mid-2nd	*ala I Thracum*?	Germ. inf.	Thracia	Germ. inf.	*vicus*
24.	Cologne	mid-2nd?	*ala Classiana*	Germ. inf.	Galata	Germ. inf.	*colonia*
25.	Remagen	3rd	*coh. I Hispanorum*	Germ. inf.	local recruit?	Germ. inf.	army camp

Table. 5.1. Data about veterans from the *auxilia* based on military diplomas (nrs. 1-13) and monumental inscriptions (nrs. 14-25) relating to men who came from or served in Germania inferior. This is supplemented by the diploma of a Batavian soldier from Regensburg (nr. 9). After Roxan 2000, tables 1A-B; Haalebos 2000b, 33; supplemented by *CIL* XVI (suppl.), 164 (nr. 8); Roxan 1985, nr. 86 (nr. 9); Derks 2003 (nr. 16).[37]

A different pattern emerges for veterans of local origin. While some bought a house in the town or camp village, a sizeable number went to live in the countryside.[35] The places where veterans settled are spread across the frontier zone of the empire, and there does not appear to be any direct geographical relationship to the army base where the veterans had served.[36] This was probably because locally recruited

cohors IIII Thracum (table 5.1, nrs. 2, 10). One exception is the chosen location of a Batavian veteran who had served in Pannonia and went to live in Raetia (nr. 9).

[35] See also Haalebos 2000a, 19.

[36] This is particularly apparent from the distribution of 1st-century weapons (figs. 3.9, 3.12).

[37] Both fragments from Nijmegen may have been part of the same military diploma.

soldiers, when discharged, could simply return home to be reunited with their family. By going home, they could also claim their inheritance and thus acquire their own plot of land.

For legionary veterans, we see a clear division in the type of work they took on after leaving the army.[38] Some will have used the money awarded at their *missio honesta* to buy a piece of land and to earn their living as farmers. Others bought a house in a town or in the camp village and set up business as artisans or merchants. An inscription from Mainz, for example, tells us that the legionary veteran Gentilius Victor began a trade in *gladii* after his honorary discharge.[39] In his business dealings, he was able to make good use of the contacts built up during his time in the army. What stands out is the small number of veterans who, in addition to these activities, held public office at an urban or provincial level.[40]

Although auxiliary veterans did not receive a discharge payment, we see a similar pattern to that of legionary veterans.[41] A substantial portion of the diplomas have been recovered in the countryside, which suggests that the recipients established farms after leaving the army. Excavations in the Lower Rhine region have shown that these were not new settlements founded by veterans; instead, the soldiers – often local recruits – returned to their homes to resume their lives as civilians, this time with Roman citizenship. Military diplomas and most notably monumental inscriptions are also documented from *vici* and towns. As with legionary veterans, auxiliary veterans will have been engaged in trades and crafts, including supplying the army's needs. When it came to holding public positions, auxiliary veterans were even less active than legionaries.

5.1.3 THE ORIGIN OF VETERANS WHO SETTLED IN THE EASTERN RHINE DELTA

Lastly, I shall examine whether the veterans who settled in the *civitas Batavorum* were Batavians or soldiers recruited elsewhere. We know that the Batavians supplied men for the Roman army on a vast scale. There were no fewer than eight *cohortes Batavorum* and one *ala Batavorum* in the pre-Flavian period (fig. 1.2).[42] In addition, substantial numbers served in the emperor's personal bodyguard and there are records of Batavian oarsmen in the Rhine fleet. The nine Batavian units (totalling about 4500 men) were probably stationed in their own territory during the pre-Claudian period. Although there are no inscriptions relating to veterans for this period, the majority will have stayed on there and returned home.

This all changed in AD 43 when the Batavian cohorts took part in the conquest of Britannia, remaining there until shortly before 70. After the units left, forts in the eastern Rhine delta were garrisoned by unknown units from other regions, with the possible sole exception of the base on the 'Kops Plateau' at Nijmegen, which is believed to have been occupied by the *ala Batavorum* until the Batavian revolt.[43] The many soldiers from other areas significantly altered the composition of the group of veterans who settled in the Batavian territory after their term of service. In addition to the Batavians stationed in their own region and especially Batavians returning home, a significant number will have been of foreign origin.

Following the Batavian revolt, most Batavian units were sent first to Britannia and then to the Danube provinces (Pannonia, Raetia and Noricum).[44] It was probably only the *ala Batavorum* and the first and sec-

[38] E. Birley 1982/1983, 265-268. Some of the veterans will also have retired.

[39] *CIL* XIII, 6677 (Mainz): *C. Gentilius Victor vet(eranus) leg(ionis) XXII Pr(imigeniae) p(iae) f(idelis) m(issus) h(onesta) m(issione) negotiator gladiarius*. Compare the veteran Vittalinius Felix, who started a earthenware business in Lyons (*CIL* XIII, 1906: *negotia(to)ri Lugdunensi artis cr(e)tariae*).

[40] Wesch-Klein 1998, 196-197.

[41] E. Birley 1982/1983; specifically for the Germanic provinces, see Roxan 2000; compare Mirković 2000.

[42] Alföldy 1968, 13-14, 45-48.

[43] Van Enckevort/Thijssen 2001, 95-96.

[44] Alföldy 1968, 102-104; Strobel 1987, 273 ff.

army camp	before AD 69	after AD 69	origin	after c. AD 80/90	origin
Nijmegen-'Kops Plateau'	ala Batavorum?	abandoned	-	abandoned	-
Woerden	?	?	-	coh. XV volunt. civium Romanorum	?
Vleuten-'De Meern'	?	coh. XV volunt. civium Romanorum	?	coh. I classica pia fidelis Domitiana	S France
Utrecht (Traiectum)	?	?	-	coh. II Hispanorum peditata pia fidelis	Spain
Vechten (Fectio)	?	coh. II Brittonum (or Britannorum)	England	coh. I Flavia Hispanorum equitata	Spain
				ala I Thracum (from c. 150)	Bulgaria
Wijk bij Duurstede (Levefanum)	?	coh. I Thracum equitata	Bulgaria	?	-
Maurik (Mannaricium)	-	coh. II Thracum equitata	Bulgaria	?	-
		coh. II Hispanorum equitata	Spain		
Herwen en Aerdt (Carvium)	?	coh. II civium Romanorum equitata	?	coh. II civ. Rom. eq. pia fidelis (Antoniniana?)	?

Table 5.2. Possible manning of the auxiliary camps in the eastern Rhine delta. After Bogaers/Rüger 1974, with additions.

ond Batavian cohorts that stayed on for a time in Lower Germania before being transferred to Pannonia and subsequently to Dacia.[45] The forts in the Batavian territory were now manned by units from England, Southern France, Spain and Bulgaria, marking the beginning of a second phase in which veterans from other regions came to settle in the Lower Rhine region (table 5.2).[46] Presumably, new recruits were for the most part enlisted in the area where they would be stationed, representing a partial return to the pre-Claudian situation, with units gradually becoming composed once again of Batavian soldiers who remained in their own region after discharge.[47] We can imagine a similar trend for the Claudian period.

[45] Haalebos 2000b, 42-43, 63-64; see also Holder 1999.
[46] For an overview of the units stationed in the Lower German region after the Batavian revolt, see Holder 1999; Haalebos 2000b.
[47] See Alföldy 1968, 102-103; Holder 1980, 121-123.

A change occurred during the 2nd century, when some of the forts were manned by Thracian units and supplemented by Thracian recruits rather than by Batavians.[48] The proportion of Batavians in the Roman army declined still further when, following a spate of Frankish attacks, the Lower Rhine region was inhabited by Gauls and by Germans from beyond the Rhine.[49] These 'new Batavians' became the principal suppliers of recruits in the late Roman period and will have made up the bulk of the returning veterans during the final stage of Roman occupation.[50]

5.2 USE OF WEAPONRY AND HORSE GEAR DURING THE LIFE OF A SOLDIER

To understand how weapons and horse gear were used during a Roman soldier's lifetime, we need to distinguish between military use in the context of the Roman army and 'social' use in other, non-military contexts. For the former, I will examine the extent to which serving soldiers were armed and the symbolic value that their military equipment had for them. I will then address the role of soldiers and ex-soldiers in the use of militaria in civilian contexts. For the interpretation of military finds, it is important first of all to clarify the question of ownership: was the equipment personal property or did it belong to the state?

5.2.1 THE ACQUISITION OF MILITARY EQUIPMENT AND THE QUESTION OF OWNERSHIP

For all recruits, life as a soldier began at the moment they enlisted and, following a period of weapons training, when they were first issued with arms.[51] With the exception of the pre-Augustan and possibly Tiberian period, when auxiliary soldiers were equipped in part with their own traditional weapons, Roman soldiers were given standard-issue equipment by the army.[52] It is often assumed that this fairly uniform equipment belonged to the state and was given on loan to soldiers during their term of service.[53] Various evidence suggests, however, that the equipment was private property, and that soldiers had to pay for it themselves.[54]

According to MacMullen, the sum that soldiers needed for weapons and other equipment was advanced by the army and deducted in instalments from their pay during their term of service.[55] This enabled soldiers who would otherwise have lacked the means to do so to purchase arms as soon as they enlisted. Central to this procedure was the *custos armorum*, who was in charge of both the weapons stores and payment arrangements.[56] A papyrus document from AD 183 appears to relate to payment to this

---

[48] Bogaers 1974.

[49] For the ethnic background of the late Roman inhabitants of the Lower Rhine region, see Willems 1984, 272 ff.; see also chapter 7.4.

[50] See Dobson/Mann 1973, 195-196.

[51] M.P. Speidel 1992b, 134-135.

[52] For the standard nature of military equipment, see chapter 2.

[53] See, for example, Horn 1984 (164-165) on the frequent absence of weapons in graves: 'Die römischen Soldaten erhielten keine Waffen mit ins Grab, da diese nicht ihr Eigentum, sondern im Besitz der Truppe und damit Staatseigentum waren.' Compare Keller 1979, 55; Wiedemann 1993, 522; Van Driel-Murray 1994, 105.

[54] For the discussion on ownership claims to Roman weaponry, see MacMullen 1960; Gilliam 1967, 237-238; Nuber 1972; Breeze 1976; Wesch-Klein 1998, 63-67. For the late Roman period, see Woods 1993.

[55] *P.Fouad* 45; MacMullen 1960, 24. The salary deductions only relate to equipment purchased via the *custos armorum* (see below).

[56] M.P. Speidel 1992b; see also MacMullen 1960, 24.

armourer.[57] It describes a loan of 50 denarii taken out by a cavalryman to pay off the advance for his weapons.

In addition to the purchase of arms and horse gear, soldiers were also responsible for the repair and, where necessary, replacement of their equipment. A writing tablet from Vindolanda reports that salary was withheld for mending weapons (*refec(tio) ar[m](orum)*).[58] Regular checks were carried out by the centurion or decurion to establish whether equipment was in need of repair or replacement.[59]

We can examine papyrus documents and ownership inscriptions on the equipment itself to establish whether, once paid off, weapons and horse gear actually became the property of individual soldiers. A document from Egypt refers to a mother taking possession of the inheritance left by her son, Ammonius, a soldier from the *cohors II Thracum* who died in AD 143.[60] The inheritance amounted to 235 denari and 14½ obols. In addition to a *depositum* (savings) of 100 denari, this sum was made up of 21 denari and 27½ obols for *armis* and 20 denari for the *papilio*.[61] Lastly, a damaged part of the document mentions 93 denari and 15 obols, but we have no further information on this.

Another document from Egypt (c. AD 120-140) mentions the cavalryman Dionysus, who received 1563 denari at his discharge.[62] Part of this sum comprised a payment of 103 denari for his weaponry. The large discrepancy between the amounts received for military equipment in the same period by Dionysus and by Ammonius' mother may be because Ammonius died shortly after enlisting. In that case, the weapons will not have been fully paid off, and his family will have received only part of their value.

The third document is the will of Antonius Silvanus, a cavalryman from the *ala I Thracum Mauretana*, who left all his 'military and household possessions' to his son (AD 142).[63] Judging by the sums paid out, this was an inheritance amounting to at least 1350 denari. The 'military possessions' probably included his weapons, although it is not clear whether this refers to the weapons themselves or to their equivalent value.

These documents provide indirect evidence that soldiers themselves had to pay for their equipment and that the value was paid out either to them or to their surviving relatives when they died or were discharged. Also of interest is a document of a different nature from Alexandria (AD 27).[64] It relates to a loan of 400 drachmes which cavalryman L. Caesilius Secundus borrowed from soldier C. Pompeius, using as security his silvered helmet, a silvered military award and a silver dagger sheath with ivory inlays. Using military equipment as security for a loan only makes sense if the objects belonged to the soldier in question.

Ownership inscriptions have always figured prominently in discussions on weapons possession.[65] We regularly come across these inscriptions on helmets, shields, and to a lesser extent on swords, lances/spears and horse gear. In most cases the owner's name is given, preceded by the name of the unit and/or the officer of the *centuria* or *turma* to which he belonged.[66] Sometimes there is only the soldier's name or that of his unit.[67] It is interesting to note that in some instances two, three or even four names of successive

---

[57] MacMullen 1960, 24. Also of interest is a report by Tacitus (*Ann.* 1, 17) that salary was withheld for clothing, weapons and tents; see also Hanel 1999, 118-119.

[58] *P.Vindob.* L 72/82; Fink 1971, nr. 71; see also M.P. Speidel 1992b, 132, note 8.

[59] Tomlin 1999, 137-138.

[60] *P.Columbia* 325; Gilliam 1967.

[61] Given that an army tent held eight men, the 20 denari for the *papilio* probably represents one eighth of the tent's total value (Gilliam 1967, 238).

[62] *P.Fay.* 105ii; Fink 1971, nr. 73; Breeze 1976, 94.

[63] *FIRA* III, nr. 47, 4-6: *bona castrensia et domestica*.

[64] *P.Vindob.* L 135; Harrauer/Seider 1979; see also Obmann 1999, 195-196.

[65] MacMullen 1960; Nuber 1972.

[66] Nuber 1972, *Fundliste*.

[67] Based on the type of ownership inscription, Nuber (1972, 498-501) distinguishes between state property (reference to the army unit/*centurio*) and private property (only the owner's name). However, references to the army unit and/or commander appear to be arbitrary.

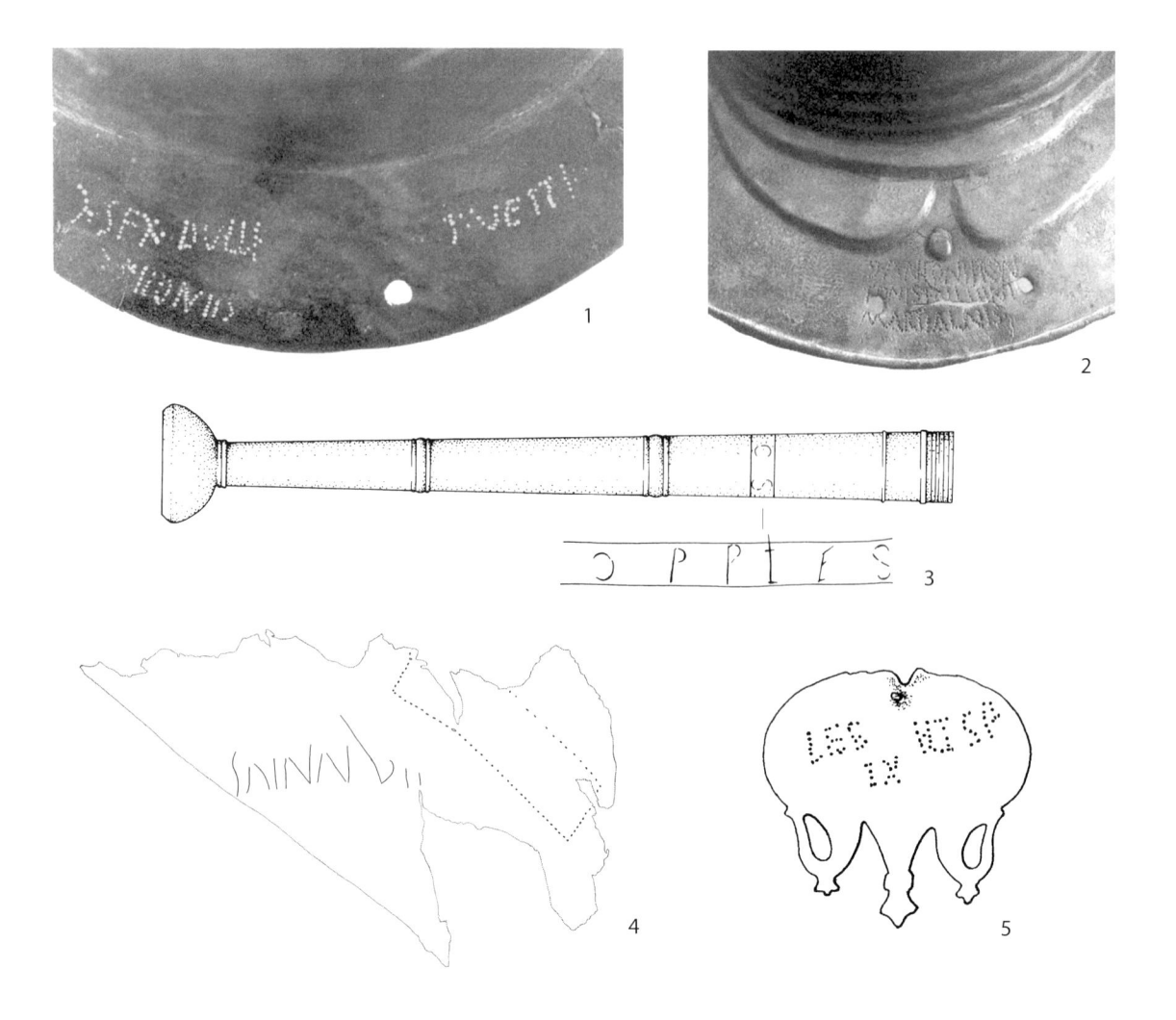

Fig. 5.4. Ownership inscriptions on weapons and horse gear from the Lower Rhine region. Not to scale. After Klumbach 1974, nr. 23; Van Es/Hessing 1994, fig. 128; Hulst 1986, fig. 1; Groenman-Van Waateringe 1967, fig. 9-5; Haalebos 2000c, fig. 11. 1 helmet from the Waal at Nijmegen (211.5); 2 helmet from the Lower Rhine at Rijswijk (254.3); 3 mouthpiece of a wind instrument from the military *vicus* at Kesteren; 4 fragment of a leather shield cover from the auxiliary camp at Valkenburg; 5 *phalera* pendant from the villa site of Ewijk-'De Grote Aalst' (93.13).

generations of owners are given.[68] The weapons in question will have been sold back to the army when soldiers ended their term of service and will have been re-issued to a new recruit, who – like the previous owner – then inscribed his name.[69]

Various items of weaponry and horse gear bearing ownership inscriptions are also known from the research region (table 5.3, fig. 5.4), with several owners mentioned in some instances. Interestingly, in the case of two helmets, the soldiers recorded the same *centuria*, suggesting that the items were passed from one soldier to another within the same unit (table 5.3, nrs. 14-15). In each instance, the equipment of the discharged or deceased soldier appears to have been handed in to the unit's *custos armorum* and then re-issued to a new recruit in that unit. In the case of a sword scabbard from Lobith-'De Bijland' (nr. 16),

[68] MacMullen 1960, 23, 36 (nrs. 39-49); Nuber 1972, 498-499; Breeze 1976, 94.

[69] Another possibility is that weapons were passed on to friends within the ranks following honourable discharge. A pointer in this direction could be reference to the same *centuria* on some items.

site	object	unit	subunit/commander	owner
1. Ewijk-'De Grote Aalst' (93.13)	pendant (horse)	Leg(io) IX Hisp(ana)	-	-
2. Nijmegen-Waal (211.19)	helmet gladiator	L(egio) XV (Primigenia)	-	-
3. Nijmegen-'Hunerberg'	chamfron (horse)	L(egio) XV (Primigenia)	-	-
4. Nijmegen-'Hunerberg'	tabula ansata	L(egio) X G(emina)	(Centuria) [...]cinnae	[...]amonius [...]iullus
5. Nijmegen-'Hunerberg'	tabula ansata	[Leg(io) X] Gem(ina)	-	M. S[...] Strate[gus]
		-	C(enturia) Flavi(i) Amadis (?)	Acil(ius) Secundus
6. Lobith-Rhine (177.1)	helmet	-	C(enturia) Firvi (?)	Iuni(us) Sencudus
7. Kesteren	tuba / cornu (?)	-	C(enturia) P.	Pli(...) Es(...) (?)
8. Nijmegen-'Hunerberg'	tabula ansata	-	C(enturia) Epotis	C(aius) Marcius Materni(us)
9. Vechten	tabula ansata	-	C(enturia) Luci Victoris	A[te]gnius
10. Arnhem-'Meinerswijk'	tabula ansata	-	C(enturia) Sabin[...]	Regil(lus?)
11. Amerongein-"t Spijk' (12.1)	helmet	-	C(enturia) Reburri	?
12. Nijmegen-Waal (211.5)	helmet	-	C(enturia) Sex(ti) Dulli(i)	T. Vettius
		-	C(enturia) Piionii	?
13. Alem-'Marensche Waarden' (8.1)	helmet	-	C(enturia) Servati	V(alerius) M(a)xumus
		-	C(enturia) Grati	M. Rufus
14. Nijmegen-Waal (211.3)	helmet	-	C(enturia) Q. Petroni(i)	Q. Valerius
		-	C(enturia) Catuli	C. Apius
		-	C(enturia) Catuli	L. Cornelius
15. Rijswijk-Lower Rhine (254.3)	helmet	-	C(enturia) Antoni Frontonis	T. Allienus Martial<n>is
		-	C(enturia) Antoni Front(onis)	Statorius Tertius
		-	C(enturia) Antoni Frontonis	Statorr(ius) (Ter)tius (sic)
16. Lobith-'De Bijland' (176.9)	gladius scabbard	-	C(enturia) Reburi	Acio (?)
		-	C(enturia) L. Boni	Acio
17. Vechten	saddle horn	-	T(urma) Calpurni	(H)ilarius
18. Nijmegen-Waal (211.8)	helmet	-	-	Vannus
19. Nijmegen-Waal (211.13)	face mask	-	-	Marcian[u]s
		-	-	C. N(...) T(...)
20. Nijmegen-Waal (211.20)	shield boss	-	-	Verinius Rufus
21. Doorwerth-Lower Rhine (55.141, 169)	saddle fitting (2x)	-	-	M. Muttieni(us)

Table 5.3. Ownership inscriptions on weaponry and horse gear from military and non-military contexts in the study region.

Legionary fort: nrs. 3-5, 8 (Haalebos 1994b, 16-19, fig. 5.1; Brunsting/Bogaers 1962, ★4-5, ★79-80; Brunsting 1966, ★16-17; Bogaers et al. 1979, fig. 47).
Auxiliary camp: nrs. 9, 10, 17 (Hulst 2000/2001, 416-417, fig. 8; nrs. 9 and 17 are unpublished).
Military *vicus:*   nr. 7 (Hulst 1986, 37-41, fig. 1).
River: nrs. 2, 6, 11-16, 18-21 (Klumbach 1974, nrs. 19, 22-24, 33, 51, 57; Van Tent/Vogelzang 1996, 4-5; Braat 1967, 57-58 (nr. 4); Van Es 1984b, 259-265, figs 7-10; Brouwer 1982, 165-166, Taf. 9 (nrs. 216, 236); nr. 16 is unpublished).
Rural settlement: nr. 1 (Haalebos 2000c, 23-24, fig. 11).

it was the arrival of a new *centurio* rather than a change of owner that seems to have prompted the new inscription. A helmet from Rijswijk (nr. 15) shows that attempts to add an inscription did not always succeed the first time round. After an unsuccessful first attempt, the soldier Statorius Tertius managed to add his name correctly the second time.

Ownership inscriptions reveal that not just standard equipment but also the often finely-crafted parade gear items probably belonged to the soldiers themselves. For example, judging by the inscriptions, exclusive 1st-century horse gear from Doorwerth (nr. 21) and Xanten was the property of individual soldiers.[70] The same applies to a *phalera* pendant with a legionary inscription from Ewijk (nr. 1). We see a similar picture for 2nd- and 3rd-century cavalry helmets, greaves and horse parade gear executed in relief. Although Garbsch believes that the presence of inscriptions confirms state ownership, it seems more logical to link these inscriptions to the recycling of equipment that was private property.[71]

Although soldiers generally had to buy their own weapons and horse gear, in exceptional cases they were presented with weaponry as *donativa*. We know from several bronze name plates of weaponry and a shield boss from the Wetterau, bearing the text *Imp(eratore) Com(modo) Aug(usto)*, that this form of reward consisted not only of money but of weapons as well.[72] The uniform nature of the inscriptions, their limited geographical distribution and the reference to an emperor – Commodus in all cases – would suggest that some of the auxiliary units in the Wetterau were equipped with new weaponry by the emperor. This exceptional reward was probably given in appreciation for loyalty shown to Rome during the unrest that broke out under Commodus' rule of Germania Superior (AD 185-186).

Further examples of equipment presented to soldiers are 1st-century helmets, swords, belts and horse gear depicting members of the imperial family. Künzl has demonstrated convincingly that this was a form of political propaganda aimed at the glorification of the imperial house and the question of succession.[73] The fact that similar busts occur on the glass medallions of military distinctions suggests that these weapons and horse gear were gifts as well.[74] Further evidence is the *corona*, an important form of distinction found on various helmets with these busts.[75] Although the similarities to *dona militaria* would suggest that items featuring political propaganda were awarded as distinctions, they could also have been *donativa*. It is likely that both officers and simple soldiers were eligible for such gifts.[76] In the case of Wetterau, entire units appear to have acquired weapons in this way.

As well as receiving arms through the *custos armorum* or as incidental rewards, a soldier could buy individual pieces from private workshops in the camp village or could have some of his equipment repaired there.[77] This was particularly true of the Flavian and later period when finds of moulds and semi-manufactured items show that the production of bronze components for sword scabbards, belts and horse gear was fairly much the preserve of artisans in the military *vici* and *canabae*.

It seems that the Praetorian Guard was an exception when it came to obtaining arms. Speidel assumes that these soldiers were issued with equipment for which they did not have to pay.[78]ABut Unlike items that soldiers did have to pay for, this weaponry was reclaimed as state property when a soldier died or left the army. A 3rd-century papyrus fragment from Egypt, which reports the purchase of a wooden shank – prob-

---

[70] Jenkins 1985, 154-156 (Xanten).

[71] Garbsch 1978, 33-34. We see a similar picture with gladiators (Junkelmann 2000, 87-89, 269-270).

[72] Nuber 1972, 486-489, 501-503; see also Hanel 1999, 120.

[73] Künzl 1994; 1998. For the symbolism of this group of weapons, see chapter 4.2.1.

[74] See also Obmann 1999, 196-197.

[75] See Von Prittwitz und Gaffron 1991, 236; for the *corona* as a military distinction, see Maxfield 1981, 67 ff.

[76] In the form of traditional *dona militaria*, *coronae* were given only to higher-ranking officers and distinctions with glass medallions to centurions and soldiers of lower rank (Neumann 1976, 51 ff.; Maxfield 1981, 67 ff.). There was no such distinction for *donativa*.

[77] See chapter 4.1.

[78] M.P. Speidel 1992b, 134-135.

ably for a spear – shows that the state was responsible for both supply and maintenance of equipment for the imperial guard.[79] The cavalryman did not bear the cost of this purchase; it was paid for out of the state coffers. Although there is little evidence to substantiate this, it is highly likely that the situation was similar for legionary and auxiliary officers.[80]

We may conclude that regular soldiers in the Roman army had to bear the cost of their own weapons which, once paid off, became their own property. This applied not just to standard weaponry and horse gear, but also to parade gear. The equipment was made available by the *custos armorum* and, from the Flavian period onward, some components could also be purchased in the camp villages. Soldiers in the Praetorian Guard, and probably legionary and auxiliary officers, were privileged in that they appear to have been issued with equipment free of charge.

5.2.2 MILITARY USE: FUNCTIONAL OBJECTS AND SYMBOLS OF RANK, WEALTH AND STATUS

The presence of ownership inscriptions has led MacMullen to surmise that soldiers did not have free access to their equipment, but were only issued with weapons on particular occasions: 'The soldier, whether praetorian, legionary, or auxiliary, did not ordinarily keep his own arms by him. They were stored instead in a room or rooms usually opening off the praetorium, under charge of the *custos armorum*... There they remained till needed for parade or war, no doubt jumbled together a good deal, and hence marked with their owners' name and unit.'[81] Here inscriptions are linked to the question of storage, probably for weapon types that were indistinguishable without a specific identification mark. Although not all items of equipment bear such marks, they probably did originally. It is precisely the organic materials, frequently not preserved, that lent themselves to ownership inscriptions, as examples on leather shield covers demonstrate.[82]

Von Petrikovits and Nuber suspect that the *armamentaria* held only weapon stocks needed for replacement purposes and for arming future recruits.[83] They would also have housed munitions in the form of arrows, spears, lances and boltheads. Personal equipment, on the other hand, was kept in the barracks, where a special area was set aside adjacent to the sleeping quarters for the storage of weaponry, horse gear and other items. Speidel also believes that, for troops in the frontier regions, weapons were not held by the *custos armorum* as they had to be ready to hand in the event of attack.[84] It would also be highly impractical to have to take in, store and re-issue the various arms on a regular basis.

For storage purposes, we probably need to distinguish between heavier arms (artillery and perhaps *pila*, helmets, shields and armour) and lighter arms (swords, daggers, military belts and horse gear). In peacetime, the heavier equipment will have been stored in the *armamentaria* under the care of the *custos armorum*. As the remaining items were worn on daily patrol and short expeditions, a soldier will have needed them close at hand, and they were therefore more likely to have been stored in the barracks. For parade gear, both storage options are possible, but given the infrequency with which it was used, storage in the *armamentaria* is most probable.

Although some of the arms were probably stored for long periods and hence out of sight, they nevertheless had an important symbolic value. In imitation of Hellenistic and La Tène examples, equipment was often richly ornamented, with the decoration taking the form of feather crests, niello inlay and the use of more expensive materials. To understand the significance that military objects had for soldiers

---

[79] M.P. Speidel 1981, 405.
[80] MacMullen 1960, 24.
[81] MacMullen 1960, 23.
[82] Nuber 1972, 492; for shield covers, see Van Driel-Murray 1988, 53, figs. 2a, 4; 1999b.
[83] Von Petrikovits 1970, 245-246; Nuber 1972, 493.
[84] M.P. Speidel 1992b, 132.

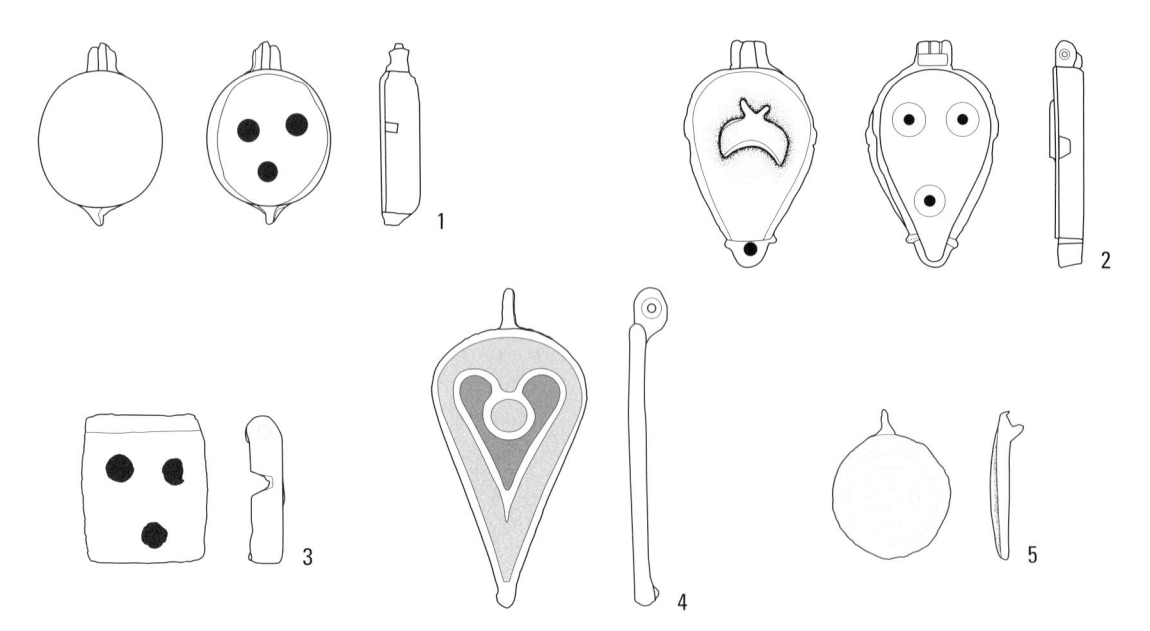

Fig. 5.5. Seal boxes from the rural settlement of Tiel-'Passewaaijse Hogeweg'. Scale 1:1. After Derks/Roymans 2003, pl. 7.IX (nrs. 45.1-5).

and those around them, I shall examine the extent to which the style and workmanship expressed the owner's rank, wealth and status.

It has proven extremely difficult to link types of equipment, on the basis of their type of decoration, to specific ranks in the Roman army and hence to social status.[85] The general view is that the equipment of centurions was characterised by a transverse helmet crest (*crista transversa*), greaves and, less importantly, a vine stave (*vitis*) and golden finger ring.[86] However, the helmet type referred to by Vegetius and portrayed on several gravestones does not appear in the archaeological record, while conversely the many archaeological examples of greaves cannot be unequivocally ascribed to this group of officers.[87] The same problem arises with other equipment. Exclusive weaponry and horse gear featuring political imagery were probably awarded in the 1st century as *dona militaria* or *donativa* to both officers and lower-ranking soldiers, while the manufacture of belt components in gold, silver or bronze during the 2nd and 3rd centuries was not tied to a specific rank.[88] An exception is the late Roman guard helmet which, in imitation of the imperial helmet, features gilded or ungilded silver leaf and is set with stones. These exclusive helmets were probably only worn by members of the Praetorian Guard and by high-ranking officers.[89]

Despite the limited extent to which weaponry and horse gear were linked to rank, they were nevertheless an important way in which soldiers could distinguish themselves from others – from fellow soldiers on the one hand and non-soldiers on the other. In the first instance, soldiers purchased fancier equipment to set themselves apart from their fellows. The document from Alexandria referred to above

---

[85] See Obmann 1999, 189-200; Ortisi 2006, 379.

[86] Obmann 1999, 192-194; for the *crista transversa*, see also Robinson 1975, 141-143.

[87] The greaves in the archaeological record are bronze components of the parade gear of 2nd- and 3rd-century cavalrymen (Garbsch 1978, 9-12).

[88] For 1st-century *donativa*, see above; one of the few examples of a possible officer's weapon is a sword scabbard from Kalkriese, which has silver scabbard bands inset with semi-precious stones (Franzius 1999, especially 599-602; see, however, Mackensen 2000, 141). For the discussion on the rank-related nature of the belt from the 2nd and 3rd centuries, see Fischer 1988; Petculescu 1991b, 210-211.

[89] Klumbach 1973a, 10-12.

– which mentions the simple cavalryman Caecilius Secundus and his possessions, including a silver dagger sheath with ivory inlays – shows that regular soldiers too could have exclusive pieces. This example confirms that an object's exclusivity was a direct reflection of the owner's financial circumstances rather than his rank. However, given that a soldier's income depended on the unit to which he belonged, and to his position within the unit, we can speak of an indirect relationship between an object's exclusivity and the rank of its owner. Thus Caecilius Secundus' purchase of the lavish dagger sheath can be explained by the fact that, as a cavalryman, he ranked among the more highly paid soldiers.

Bearing arms was also significant for expressing membership of a particular group, in this case professional soldiers. Military objects can be viewed as symbols of military status, used by soldiers to distinguish themselves from non-soldiers. The role of equipment in expressing this status –both during a soldier's lifetime and after his death – is most noticeable in the often detailed depiction of weapons and horse gear on soldiers' gravestones.

5.2.3 'SOCIAL USE' AFTER COMPLETING MILITARY SERVICE: PERSONAL MEMORABILIA

In addition to the military-symbolic use of equipment by Roman soldiers, it is important when interpreting finds from non-military contexts in the eastern Rhine delta to identify the extent to which equipment could have ended up there during military service. The widespread occurrence of bronze seal boxes in rural settlements suggests that Batavian soldiers maintained close contacts with their families (fig. 5.5).[90] Although soldiers, certainly those stationed in their own region, will have made regular visits home, it is highly unlikely that they left their weapons behind or deposited them in a cult place while on leave. A soldier simply could not manage without his equipment, and would have had to pay for any new weapons or horse gear. Moreover, there were penalties for serving soldiers who lost or sold their weapons.[91]

It was a different story for veterans. Papyrus documents suggest that it was customary for Roman soldiers to sell their weaponry and horse gear back to the army when they completed their term of service. Different ownership inscriptions on the same piece of equipment indicate that usable components were recycled in order to furnish new recruits with weapons. The presence of full sets of equipment in graves, cult places and rural settlements shows that this was not the only option, however. Soldiers wishing to keep all or part of their equipment were able to do so. It even appears that they were at liberty to decide what to do with it: return it to the army in exchange for a sum of money or retain it in order to dedicate it at a cult place or keep it at home.[92]

The second option was clearly very popular in the *civitas Batavorum* during the 1st century AD in particular, as is attested by the many finds of weaponry and horse gear in cult places, rivers and almost 250 rural settlements. In order to establish *why* so many veterans chose to take their equipment home rather than accept its monetary value, we need to distinguish between a stage of military use and one of

---

[90] Derks/Roymans 2003. In addition, applications for leave from Vindolanda show that Batavians stationed outside their own region were able to visit their homeland (A. Birley 2002, 85; generally, see M.P. Speidel 1985). For the importance of maintaining contacts with family, see Van Driel-Murray 2003, 208: 'The ability to write and maintain contacts with home would ease the acceptance of individuals back into the community after long absences and Egyptian letters reveal serving soldiers taking an active interest in the running of the family farms as well as in family affairs.'

[91] Tomlin 1999, 137.

[92] It should be borne in mind that veterans, particularly legionary veterans, could still be called up for quite some time, in which case some of the equipment brought home by ex-soldiers can be associated with 'active veterans' (Carol van Driel-Murray, pers. comm.).

'social use'. Although equipment also had a social significance – as a symbol of wealth and status – for serving soldiers, the emphasis here is on the shift from a predominantly functional use within the army to a non-military one on completion of military service, with the social aspect being central.

When interpreting military finds from non-military contexts, it is important to bear in mind that an object's significance is not only determined by the type and manner of decoration, but to a significant extent by its cultural biography, its individual history: 'Not only do objects change through their existence, but they often have the capability of accumulating histories, so that the present significance of an object derives from the persons and events to which it is connected'.[93] During their history, objects acquire a significance which can be associated with ideas and emotions for both the owner and bystanders.

With regard to an object's cultural biography, we can distinguish between the generalised biography of objects and the specific history of an individual object.[94] The generalised biography refers to a comparable history observable in the same kind of objects in a specific cultural context over a given period.[95] In fact, we are dealing here with an ideal biography, in which the object passes through culturally accepted and desired stages of use. A specific biography, on the other hand, refers to the particular history of one specific object. This history deviates from the general pattern and evokes memories of a particular person or event.

Two examples of objects with a specific history are mentioned in Suetonius' biography of Vitellius. The first is a *gladius*, which was placed as an offering in a Mars sanctuary near the *Ara Ubiorum*. According to Suetonius, after a group of soldiers proclaimed Vitellius emperor, probably in the present-day Cologne, they carried him around with Julius Caesar's sword, taken from the sanctuary of Mars: 'Then he was carried about the most populous villages, holding a drawn sword of the Deified Julius, which someone had taken from a shrine of Mars and handed to him during the first congratulations.'[96] The second is the dagger used by Otho, who had been embroiled in a power struggle with Vitellius, to commit suicide.[97] By way of thanks for his victory, Vitellius decided to send Otho's dagger to Cologne to be sacrificed to Mars. Both cases involve weapons that were significant because of their specific cultural biography. Although we cannot rule out the possibility that these personal weapons belonging to a military elite were exceptional examples of craftsmanship, they nevertheless derived their special significance from their association with the actions of two key figures in Roman history.

In the case of weaponry and horse gear from non-military contexts in the *civitas Batavorum*, however, these appear to have been large numbers of items belonging to regular veterans. We can observe a general pattern that prevailed for some time in the context of the Batavian frontier. After a period of military use, it was customary for Batavian soldiers to dedicate all or part of their equipment at a cult place or to take it home, thus making the social use of weapons a key stage in the ideal, culturally valued history of military equipment. Whereas the exceptional objects mentioned above were meaningful for many people other than the original bearers, the items taken home by ordinary veterans had value above all for the bearers themselves. As personal objects, the militaria were associated with the owner and his life as a soldier. They evoked stories and memories of the veteran's time in the army and can be viewed as 'personal memorabilia', with considerable emotional value for their owner.

Because of this biographical history, equipment played a key role in the outward display of the personal history of veterans and hence their identity. Inscriptions relating to veterans on graves and other monuments, which almost always refer to the term of service, demonstrate the importance that veterans and their families attached – in their expression of identity – to a career as a soldier. The use of weapons

[93] Kopytoff 1986, chapter 2; Gosden/Marshall 1999 (quotation p. 170).
[94] Gosden/Marshall 1999, 169-178; see also Fontijn 2003, 26 ff.
[95] However, this does not mean that each individual object cannot at the same time have a specific history and significance for the owner.
[96] Suetonius, *Vitellius* 8.
[97] Suetonius, *Vitellius* 10.

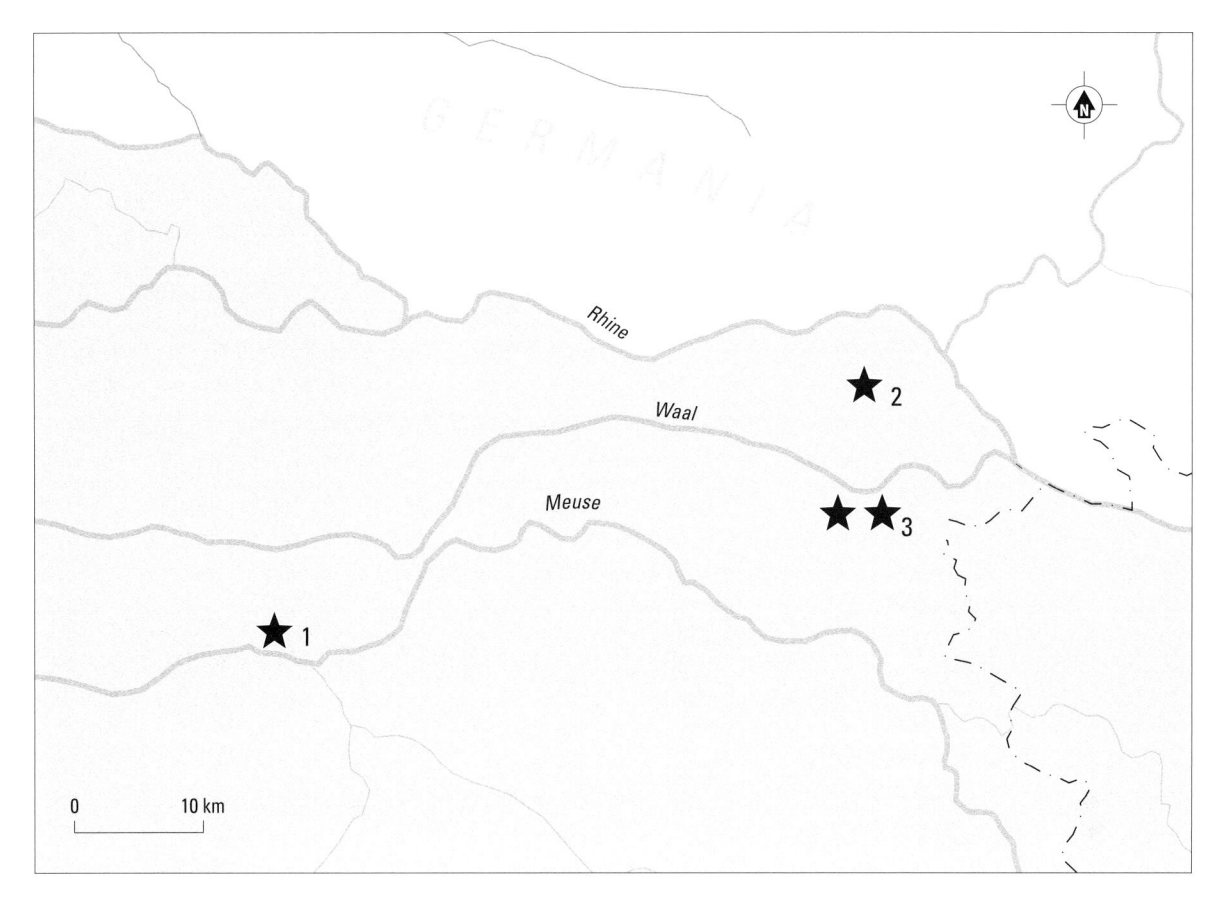

Fig. 5.6. Distribution of military diplomas in the *civitas Batavorum* (table 5.1, nrs. 3-6).
1 Delwijnen-'Eendenkade'; 2 Elst-'Lijnden'; 3 Nijmegen(-West).

and horse gear in the Batavian territory can be explained in a similar fashion. Just as it did during military service, the equipment brought home expressed membership of a certain group, namely veterans. This emphasis on the status of veteran was important for announcing to outsiders their newly acquired citizen status and its attendant privileges.[98]

The possession of Roman weaponry and horse gear will also have bestowed prestige on their owners within the local community where veterans settled. This was particularly true of the earliest stage of recruitment, when the items will have been viewed as exclusive and unique. However, they will have quickly lost their significance as prestige goods thanks to the heavy recruitment of young men among the Batavians and the fact that many brought their weapons home. Only exceptional objects like *dona militaria* and *donativa* will then have conferred prestige on their owners.

The role of veterans in the social use of military equipment in non-military contexts is confirmed in various diplomas found in rural and urban settlements within the research region, where military equipment is also documented (fig. 5.6).[99] The best example is the site of Delwijnen-'Eendenkade', where – in addition to an early 2nd-century diploma fragment (table 5.1, nr. 6) – over 60 weaponry and horse gear components from the 1st-3rd centuries have been found (51.1-61). The weaponry includes many

[98] Discharge certificates and military diplomas officially setting out a veteran's status and/or his legal privileges had a similar function.

[99] We should bear in mind that the small number of diplomas does not reflect the number of veterans who settled in this region, as we know from finds of military equipment (see chapter 5.1.2).

Fig. 5.7. Bronze plate armour components from the rural settlement of Delwijnen-'Eendenkade' (51.1-9, 11-12). Remains of the iron plating suggest that at least one full set of armour was deposited at the site. Not to scale.

bronze components of one or more sets of Corbridge type plate armour (fig. 5.7). Also known from Ulpia Noviomagus are an early 2nd-century diploma (table 5.1, nr. 4), as well as weaponry and horse gear (209.1-184).[100] The weaponry includes various plate armour components and a scale armour fragment. A second diploma may have come from the same site (table 5.1, nr. 5).

An interesting question is whether veterans opted to take home all their equipment or just certain parts. Although the concentration of symbolic imagery on particular components suggests the latter, the composition of finds from the various non-military contexts shows that *all* components of equipment were brought home. It is difficult to establish the extent to which soldiers chose to retain their full equipment or seemingly random components, given the uncertain relationship between single finds from settlements, cult places and rivers. However, the frequent occurrence at the same site of different components dating from the same period suggests that in most cases probably complete sets of weaponry and horse gear were brought home.

The many finds from non-military contexts show that militaria had an important symbolic value not only during active service, but also thereafter. Especially during the 1st century AD, many veterans in the *civitas Batavorum* chose to take their full equipment home as both a reminder of 25 years of service and a symbol of their veteran status and the associated privileges. The social use of military objects was not confined to weapons and horse gear. Veterans also took other objects of significance as personal memorabilia to be offered at a cult place or to be kept at home, but this takes us beyond the bounds of this study.[101]

---

[100] For an overview, see chapter 3.3.2; see also chapter 5.3.3.

[101] This includes all manner of consumer goods such as domestic ware, coins and earthenware. For example, the graffiti on a *terra sigillata* plate from a 2nd-century grave in the rural cemetery of Oosterhout-'Van Boetzelaerstraat' can be linked to a Batavian who took the plate as a souvenir after his term of service (Van den Broeke 2002, 18).

5.3   TYPES OF SOCIAL USE IN THE DIFFERENT
       NON-MILITARY CONTEXTS

In order to test the idea of social use of weapons and horse gear as personal memorabilia, I shall now examine – largely on the basis of archaeological data – the types of use of military objects in the different non-military contexts, as well as the involvement of soldiers, veterans and non-soldiers. The central question I will address is whether specific patterns of use prevailed in Batavian society and if these can be interpreted as part of the concluding, 'social' phase of use of military objects by veterans.

5.3.1   RITUAL DEPOSITIONS AT CULT PLACES

According to Derks, to qualify as a cult place, a site must be separated from its profane surroundings and have a ritual focus.[102] In the temple complexes that sprang up in Germania Inferior in the 1st century, the cult building – and to a lesser degree the walls enclosing the temple precinct (*temenos*) – marked the boundary with the profane outside world, while one or more statues of deities were the ritual focus of the sanctuary in the *cella*. The situation is less clear with the cult places known as open-air sanctuaries.[103] For such sites, the boundaries could comprise a simple ditch, with a palisade or tree as the ritual focus. In archaeological terms, we can identify this category of cult place in particular by the spectrum of finds, in this case large numbers of coins and fibulae.[104]

The deposition of weaponry and horse gear at cult places in the late Iron Age is well documented.[105] A survey of published finds from temple complexes and open-air sanctuaries in Northern Gaul, the neighbouring 'German' area and Britannia (appendix 4) shows that this tradition continued into the Roman period. The material is primarily from the 1st century, with both weaponry (helmets, plate armour, shields and *gladii*) and belts being represented. Horse gear also occurred simultaneously at various sanctuaries. Despite the fragmentary state of some objects, the shield components from Matagne-la-Petite (fig. 5.8, nr. 1) and the remains of iron platework on armour fittings from Harlow (fig. 5.8, nrs. 2-3) show that complete items were originally deposited there.[106]

The survey shows that equipment must have been widely used as votive offerings during the 1st century AD. For the most part, however, these are incidental finds, so that we cannot conclude that weapons were frequently deposited; this was only the case in Ober-Olm, Velserbroek and perhaps Vindonissa.[107] Insofar as we can ascertain, the cult places where weaponry and horse gear were deposited during the 1st century were dedicated primarily to Mars (6x). There are also individual instances of depositions at cult places devoted to Jupiter, Minerva and the otherwise unknown goddess Nodens.

We observe a sharp decline in the number of weapon finds from the 2nd and 3rd centuries in cult places. The few specifically military items include scale-armour scales from Matagne-la-Grande, a baldric *phalera* with openwork letters from Uley and perhaps the mouthpiece of a wind instrument from Lydney Park.[108] Two swords (Möhn, Kontich) and two scabbard chapes (Genainville and Lydney Park) are not unequivocally military in nature and may also have been deposited by civilians. The same applies to the

---

[102] Derks 1998, 133.

[103] Slofstra/Van der Sanden 1987; Wesselingh 2000, 126-128; Gerritsen 2003, 150 ff.

[104] Derks 1998, 132-133.

[105] See chapter 7.1.

[106] The fragmentation does not appear to be due to the kind of ritual destruction that occurred during the late Iron Age. Deliberately damaged objects (bent or pierced) rarely appear in Roman cult places.

[107] Oberammergau does not belong here because the consecrations seem to relate to a single specific event (appendix 4, B1)

[108] The mouthpiece could also have been part of a temple instrument.

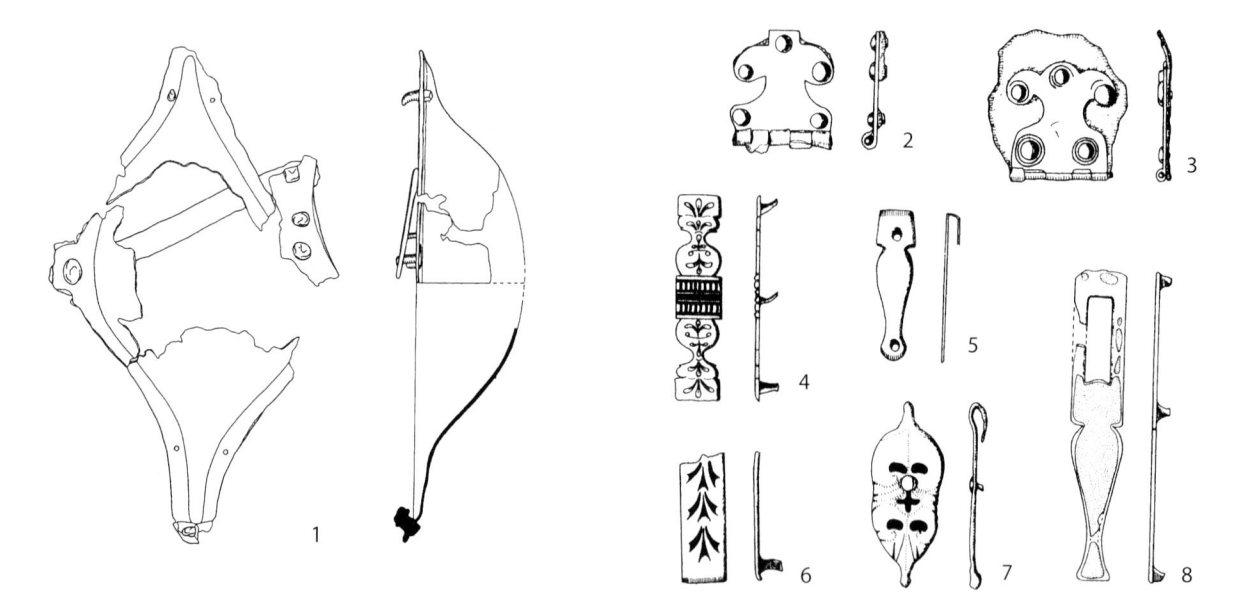

Fig. 5.8. Components of military equipment from Roman cult places (periods 1-2). Scale 1:2, 1:5 (nr. 1). After De Boe 1982, fig. 5 (nr. 1); France/Gobel 1985, fig. 46 (nrs. 117, 121-122, 123-124).
1 late La Tène shield boss from Matagne-la-Petite; 2-8 components of plate armour and horse gear from Harlow.

many spearheads, lanceheads and butt spikes which to a significant degree were probably hunting weapons. Another feature of finds from this period is the rather frequent occurrence of belt components and horse gear, which could have belonged to soldiers and civilians alike.[109] We see a similar pattern in the late Roman period. Finds from the English cult places of Uley, Lamyett Beacon and Woodeaton are primarily made up of spears and lances, some in miniature, which once again may have had a civilian use. The only suggestion of military involvement in this period is a probable late Roman *spatha* from Uley.

The consecration of military items at Roman cult places is also documented in literary sources and votive inscriptions. An inscription on a *tabula ansata* from Sint-Huibrechts-Hern in Belgium mentions the legionary centurion Q. Catius Libo Nepos, who offered a shield and lance to the native goddess Vihansa (3rd century).[110] That simple soldiers also dedicated their weapons is evidenced by a votive inscription of a soldier who sacrificed his shield, sword and helmet to Mars.[111] These same weapons are depicted in the image above the inscription. A similar offering, this time of a shield and *spatha*, together with a writing tablet, is documented from Silistra in Bulgaria (AD 297).[112] The status of the dedicant is unknown.

An inscription from the sanctuary of Venus Erycina in Sicily tells us the actual reason for the offering. The dedicant was the legionary tribune L. Apronius Caesianus, who dedicated his *felicem gladium* after winning a military victory.[113] Suetonius mentions a similar act in his biography of Emperor Vitellius. At the Mars sanctuary in present-day Cologne, to symbolise his victory, Vitellius dedicated the dagger used by his rival Otho to commit suicide.[114] This was not a unique act on his part: we know of a second

[109] For the non-military use of swords, spears/lances, belts and horse gear, see chapter 6.

[110] *CIL* XIII, 3592: *Vihansae / Q. Cattus Libo Nepos / centurio leg(io) III / Cyrenaicae scu/tum et lanceam d.d*; see Bogaers 1972, 331-332; Deman/Raepsaet-Charlier 2002, 54-58 (nr. 29).

[111] M.P. Speidel 1992b, 4, fig. 1; the site of the 'stèle of Ares' is not reported by Speidel.

[112] *CIL* III, 14433: *scutu(m) spat(h)a(m) pugellares / arg[en]to tectas d(omino) n(ostro) / [M]ax(imiano) Aug(usto) et Ma(ximiano) / [C(aesare)] co(n)s(ulibus)*; see Thiel/Zanier 1994, 69.

[113] *CIL* X, 7257; see Thiel/Zanier 1994, 69; Mackensen 2000, 127.

[114] Suetonius, *Vitellius* 10.

instance in which he sought to dedicate a dagger, this time in the Temple of Concord.[115] Suetonius also mentions Caesar's sword that had earlier been offered at the Temple of Mars.[116] Finally, when the Pisonian conspiracy had been quashed, Nero offered the conspirator's dagger, with a votive inscription, to Jupiter Capitolinus.[117]

Archaeological finds and information from historical sources enable us to distinguish the following four groups of dedicants of Roman weaponry and horse gear.

1. Active soldiers from army command
The first group comprises army officers who deposited weaponry at cult places following a military victory, as in the case of L. Apronius Caesianus, who sacrificed his 'luck-bringing sword'.[118] Vitellius also dedicated a weapon to mark his victory, namely the dagger Otho had used to commit suicide. Significant here is the fact that this group of dedicants contains members of the army leadership (also true of Vitellius before his victory over Otho), who deposited a weapon at a cult place *while* on active service. As already mentioned, it was not customary for regular serving soldiers to dedicate parts of their equipment at cult places. Unlike officers, they had to pay for new equipment themselves and risked punishment if their weaponry was incomplete at the time of inspection.[119]

2. Regular veterans
The second group consists of individual veterans who sacrificed all or part of their military equipment at a cult place upon leaving the army. Judging by the finds, these were both legionary and auxiliary veterans. In most cases, the dedication will have followed immediately upon discharge, and served to thank the relevant deity for the protection the soldiers had enjoyed.[120] This gesture of thanks could be made at a cult place in the homeland, but also in the immediate vicinity of their last post.[121] Votive inscriptions naming veterans provide clues to the involvement of ex-soldiers.[122] Although none of the inscriptions mention the dedicated item, we should assume an association with the equipment found at the site. This applies above all to dedications to Mars, the god of war, where an offering of a military nature would appear self-evident.

3. Private weapons producers and dealers
There is evidence that non-soldiers were also involved in depositions of military items at cult places. Some will have had links with the army through weapons production or dealing, and direct access to military equipment. For example, it may have been a weapons producer who dedicated an unfinished parade shield boss in a sanctuary at Brigetio in Hungary.[123] And the *gladiarius* Tiberius Julius Agilis, named on a bronze votive plaque from Vindonissa, had access to arms as a weapons dealer. It is altogether conceivable that he offered a sword to Mars, in gratitude, say, for a thriving business.

---

[115] Suetonius, *Vitellius* 15.
[116] Suetonius, *Vitellius* 8.
[117] Tacitus, *Ann.* 15, 74.
[118] The consecration of *benificiarius* lances from Ober-Olm may also be associated with a military victory (M.J. Klein 1999, 87, 92-93); see appendix 4, A5.
[119] The early 1st-century finds from Oberammergau form an exceptional assemblage. The deliberate damage suggests that these were weapons collected after a battle between a native group and the 19th legion, and dedicated at a local open-air sanctuary.
[120] We cannot rule out that some equipment was dedicated by next of kin following the death of veterans, although there is no concrete evidence for this.
[121] See below.
[122] Appendix 4, A2 (Grand St. Bernard), A7 (Vindonissa).
[123] Klumbach 1977. The usual attachment holes on the corners of the rectangular *umbo* are absent.

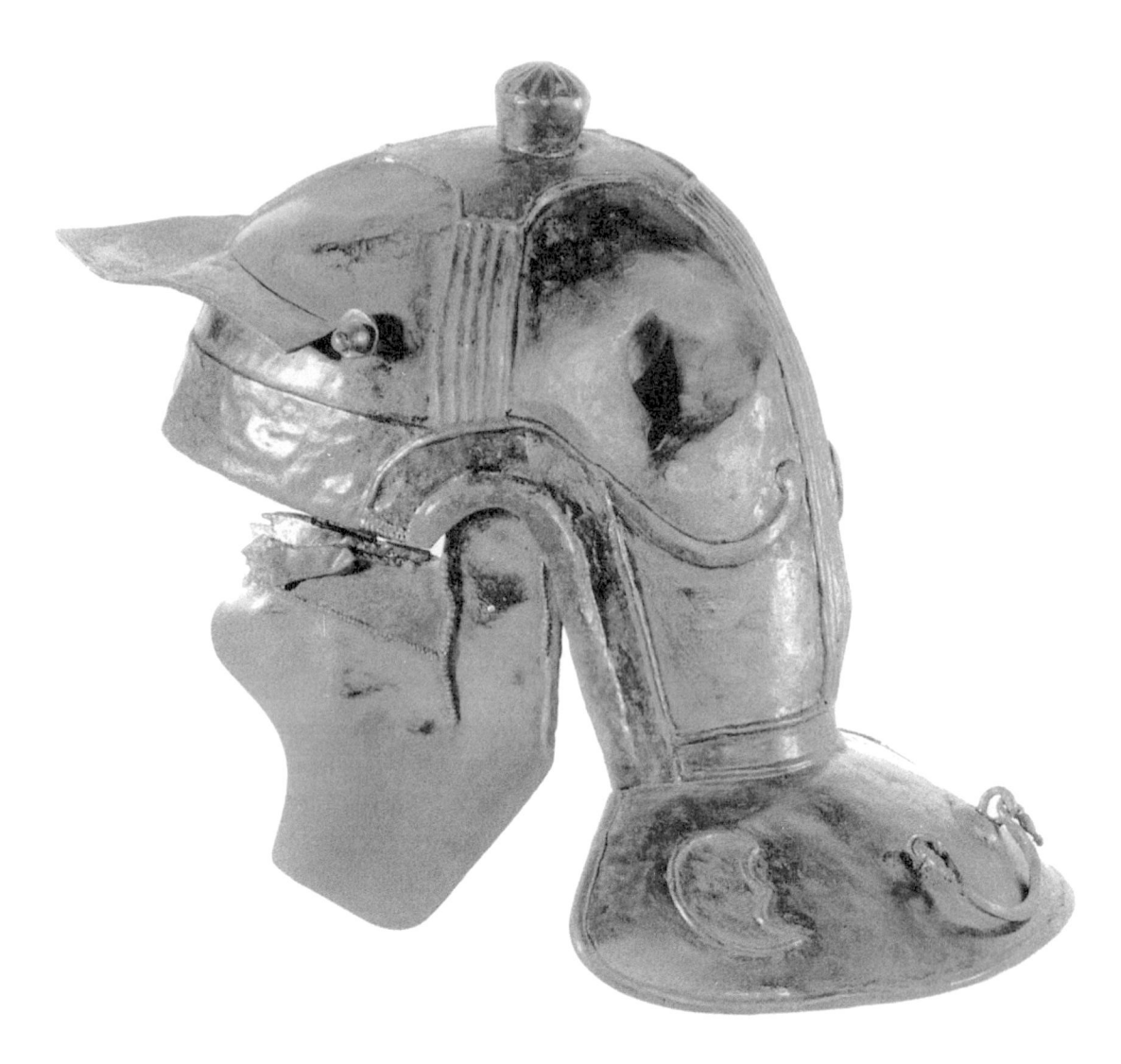

Fig. 5.9. Helmet of the Niederbieber type from a 3rd-century well in the temple precinct of Empel-'De Werf' (82.25). Not to scale.

4. Other non-soldiers
The last group of dedicants comprises non-soldiers with a purely civilian background who made offerings of weapons, belts and horse gear. This happened primarily in the 2nd-5th centuries, when the less frequent occurrence of specifically military objects points to a decline in rituals involving weapons and horse gear among dedicants with a military background.

With over 200 examples, the cult place of Empel-'De Werf' is the most important non-military site for weaponry and horse gear finds in the research region (82.1-208).[124] The nature of the Empel dedicants is evidenced first of all in the martial qualities of Hercules Magusanus, the principal deity worshipped there. Secondly, among the 1st-century AD finds are large numbers of weapons, including plate armour, shields and swords. Of particular significance are the defensive weapons, as these were worn only by soldiers. We can perhaps associate the swords dating from before the beginning of the first millennium with soldiers from the earliest, as yet irregular, auxiliary troops.

[124] For an overview, see chapter 3.3.3.

Veterans are the most likely candidates among dedicants with a military background.[125] Interestingly, the only person known to us from a votive plaque is a veteran (fig. 5.10). Although no dedications of weapons are mentioned, the inscription is an important indicator that ex-soldiers did visit the cult place. Military items may also occasionally have been deposited as booty by high-ranking soldiers, as was possibly the case with a 'German' shield boss (82.33, pl. 12). Van Driel-Murray associates the *umbo* with the Marcoman wars (AD 166-180), believing that it was brought back as a 'souvenir'.[126] Although booty generally fell to the state, it is possible that this memento belonged to a Batavian officer.[127] The sharp decline in the number of weapon finds from the 2nd and 3rd centuries, with almost no specifically military items, suggests a changing group of dedicants. Unlike the previous period, ritual transactions now seem to have been carried out by a group of non-soldiers whom we cannot further identify. Nevertheless, the finds of a complete cavalry helmet (82.25, fig. 5.9) and the 'Germanic' shield boss in a well dating to about AD 200 show that veterans continued for quite some time, albeit only occasionally, to dedicate parts of their equipment to the Batavian Hercules.

We can conclude that it was mainly during the 1st century AD that military dedicants deposited equipment at cult places both inside and outside the Batavian territory. Most of them were probably veterans who, when discharged, made their offerings chiefly to Mars and, in the Batavian *civitas*, to Hercules. The time of deposition probably coincided with a key moment in a Roman soldier's life, namely the end of his active military career. It seems to have been associated with an individual rite of passage, in which the conclusion of the military phase was marked in ritual terms by consecrating, say, a helmet or a sword. At the same time, these were offerings to thank the deity for the protection given to the veteran during his time in the army.[128]

Finds from an open-air sanctuary near the fort of Rocester perhaps make a case for this transition ritual having been carried out immediately after discharge at a cult place near the soldier's last post.[129] However, the fact that the remaining sanctuaries were located in or near towns and in the countryside shows that it was more usual for veterans to first go home and then make an offering. The practice of ritually depositing equipment seems to have largely faded out in the 2nd century, with the transition ritual now being associated with the consecration of other, not specifically military, votive offerings like coins, statues or altars. In addition, spear- and lanceheads, belts and horse gear continue to occur at cult places, although it seems that the main dedicants were no longer veterans, but civilians. Nevertheless, finds from Empel and also the votive inscriptions from Sint-Huibrechts-Hern and Silistra testify to the occasional continued deposition of militaria.

5.3.2 RIVER FINDS: DELIBERATE DEPOSITIONS, LOST ITEMS AND WASHOUT MATERIAL

Roman river finds were long regarded as washout debris from settlements or as lost items.[130] But as in prehistoric archaeology, recent decades in particular have seen a shift towards an interpretation as ritual finds.[131] A key argument is the fact that river finds exhibit a number of chronological peaks, with the same

---

[125] Roymans/Derks 1993; 1994; Roymans/Aarts 2005.

[126] Van Driel-Murray 1994, 104.

[127] Despite this hypothesis, it is possible that a Batavian soldier bought a new 'Germanic' shield on the spot.

[128] Finds of seal boxes from Empel-'De Werf' show that soldiers may have been honouring a pledge probably made in writing when they enlisted (Derks/Swinkels 1994; Roymans/Aarts 2005, 355; generally, see Derks 1998, 215 ff.).

[129] Appendix 4, B5.

[130] See Holwerda 1931, 26; Klumbach 1961, 98; Schalles 1994a, 162; 1999, 215-216.

[131] See Pauli 1987, 294 ff.; Thiel/Zanier 1994; Roymans 1996, 32-34; Haynes 1997, 116 ff.; Derks 1998, 140; Thiel 2000.

Fig. 5.10. Votive inscription from the temple complex of Empel-'De Werf', dedicated by the legionary veteran Julius Genialis to Hercules Magusenus. Height approx. 9 cm.

basic features in evidence from the Mesolithic through to the Middle Ages.[132] Secondly, finds are not evenly distributed along the course of the rivers, but are concentrated in specific, often prominent, locations. Thirdly, there is a clear relationship between the types of object found. Thus we often encounter a military element, with celts – and later – swords, daggers and spears occurring frequently. And finally, the categories of finds that predominate in rivers are virtually unknown in contemporaneous graves and/or settlements.

If we test the Roman finds for these features, the same pattern emerges. River finds date mainly from the 1st century AD, thus tying in with the evident peak in the late La Tène period. In terms of geographical distribution, the Roman material is concentrated in specific locations, often in the vicinity of forts. For the rest, apart from bronze domestic ware, jewellery, coins and earthenware, the finds are made up of military objects. Although similar items have been found in many Batavian settlements, there is a marked difference from contemporaneous burial practices. With some exceptions, weapon graves are unknown in the Lower Rhine region.

Besides the possible ritual deposits, river finds may include lost objects. This is material that found its way into the water when people crossed rivers, or following a shipwreck or military conflict. However, the archaeological record contains few concrete examples, apart from several shipwrecks where weapons form part of the ship's inventory.[133] The enormous assemblage dredged up in a former arm of the Rhine at Neupotz may also have comprised lost objects. The finds are believed to be booty lost by Alamanni when crossing the Rhine.[134]

[132] Driehaus 1970; Zimmermann 1970; Maringer 1974; see also Torbrügge 1960; Pauli 1987; Wirth 2000.

[133] A.J. Parker 1992, nrs. 307, 610, 1141, 1206 (swords).

[134] Künzl 1993a; specifically for weapons, see Künzl 1993b.

River finds can also include waste that was deliberately deposited. Excavations at the foot of the natural rises on which the fortresses of Nijmegen ('Kops Plateau') and Vindonissa were located have unearthed waste layers containing a large number of military components.[135] These were not ritual depositions, but items discarded as waste. Part of the river finds can be similarly interpreted since military camps were frequently situated on rivers and waste could simply be dumped in the water. Such 'waste dumps' are documented from the Rhine bed at Zwammerdam (Nigrum Pullum) and Alphen aan de Rijn (Albaniana).[136] Relevant here is that not only broken but also intact objects seem to have been discarded, which means that an object's condition is not an argument for interpreting river finds as votive offerings. This would require an analysis of assemblages as a whole.

Finally, river finds could be washout material from settlements, army camps, graves and cult places. Rivers in the Lower Rhine delta have shifted frequently over time, with formerly inhabited areas regularly falling victim to the flowing water. This material from different types of context acts as a kind of 'static', further hampering our interpretation of river finds. In addition to some possible ritually deposited helmets dating from the same period, the Lower Rhine at Rijswijk, for example, has yielded earthenware, coins, roof tiles and building material that would suggest washout debris from a flooded army camp.[137] Material from settlements, cult places and graves may also be represented in the river finds. Of relevance when distinguishing deliberately deposited objects from washout material is the fact that metalwork from settlements tends to be highly fragmentary, and that the Lower Rhine region did not have a tradition of weapon graves.

Despite the tendency towards ritual interpretation of weaponry and horse gear finds from rivers, Künzl has recently adopted an opposing point of view. He considers it more likely that the equipment was lost: 'Die römischen *gladii* und wohl überhaupt die römischen Waffen aus Flüssen sind normalerweise keine Votive, sondern profane Phänomene; es dürfte sich meist um schlichte Transportverluste und Verkehrsverluste handeln.'[138] Künzl puts forward a number of arguments to support his interpretation; I will now discuss the four main ones.

Firstly, Künzl points to the prevalence of weapons in broader rivers, where crossing will have involved a greater chance of loss. In Künzl's view, the 1st-century dating of the bulk of the finds is linked to bridge construction in the Flavian period, which led to a smaller risk of weapons being lost.[139] This early dating is no argument for abandoning a ritual interpretation, however, as becomes clear if we compare the finds with material from different rural cult places, including Empel-'De Werf'. Weapon finds from rural settlements also peak for the 1st century, so that we can speak of a general pattern. A further argument against a general interpretation as lost material is the distinctly regional character of river finds in general. For example, in Northern Gaul we see a clear concentration in the eastern Rhine delta and the neighbouring Rhineland as far as Xanten (figs. 3.9, 3.12).[140] There appears to have been a regional tradition of depositing weapons in rivers which, in view of the presence of La Tène weaponry in the same context, dates back to pre-Roman times.[141]

---

[135] Kops Plateau: Breuer 1931; Bogaers/Haalebos 1975; Vindonissa: Laur-Belart 1935, 60-67; Künzl 1998, 408 (complete *gladius* and accompanying *cingulum*).

[136] Zwammerdam: Haalebos 1977, 82 ff., 217 ff.; the finds include components of shields, spearheads, swords and a rolled-up piece of chain mail. Alphen aan de Rijn: Anjolein Zwart, pers. comm.

[137] Van Es 1984b, 277-281.

[138] Künzl 1999/2000 (quotation p. 564); see also Künzl 1998, 438 ff.

[139] Künzl 1999/2000, 549-551.

[140] Similar, regional concentrations are evident for finds from the Saône (Bonnamour 1990).

[141] For the pre-Roman origin, see Thiel/Zanier 1994, 69; Roymans 1996, 13 ff.; Haynes 1997; Nicolay 2002. Chapter 7 takes a closer look at continuity and discontinuity in the ritual use of weaponry and horse gear during the late Iron Age/Roman period.

A second argument against a ritual interpretation of river finds is that, unlike coin offerings, weapon depositions in wells and springs barely feature in the archaeological record.[142] One of the few examples involves three 1st-century daggers with ornate sheaths, deposited with their associated belts in a reservoir on the Auerberg.[143] The find of a dagger with sheath, wrapped in a *cingulum*, from a second reservoir on the same site shows that these were not exceptions; Ulbert regards them as ritual depositions.[144] By contrast, most of the militaria from wet contexts have been recovered from rivers. The preference for this specific context is probably linked to the native origin of weapon sacrifices, with cult places and rivers being the key ritual foci from the late La Tène period onward.[145]

A third argument, and one to which Künzl attaches considerable importance, is that – unlike ownership inscriptions – votive inscriptions are altogether absent. However, we see a similar situation for weapons and horse gear deposited at Roman cult places. These items do not carry votive inscriptions either, despite their obviously ritual nature. Once again, this appears to be linked to the pre-Roman origin of weapon deposition at cult places and in rivers, which did not involve the addition of inscriptions to votive offerings.

Künzl's final argument is the lack of historical references to weapon depositions in rivers. However, although weapons are not specifically mentioned, there is both archaeological and historical evidence for consecrations in rivers, for example when a bridge was built or a river crossed.[146] The ritual significance of rivers is also expressed in their association with gods. Various votive inscriptions refer to the Rhine as Rhenus, the divine personification of the river.[147] Significant too is Tacitus' report that the low level of the Rhine benefited Julius Civilis and was interpreted as the Rhine god supporting the rebellious Batavians.[148] According to Thiel, the absence of references to weapon sacrifices in the literature is explained by the fact that actions of a private nature are seldom documented in historical sources.[149] He cites coin offerings as an example; although familiar to us from the archaeological record, there are few historical references to this ritual.

Although some of the river finds are made up of lost objects, waste and washout material, the arguments put forward by Künzl are not convincing enough to rule out ritual deposition. Critical to such an interpretation is the existence of a pre-Roman tradition that continued into the 1st century AD, even peaking in the Roman period. The survival of this native tradition in a Roman context can be associated with the heavy recruitment of soldiers among local groups.[150] Ownership inscriptions on helmets show that not only auxiliary troops but probably legionaries too featured among the dedicants.[151] This would appear to suggest that the pre-Roman tradition of depositing weapons in rivers gained widespread currency in Roman army circles, thanks to local recruitment.

Assuming that offerings are present among the Roman militaria from rivers, it is important to further define assemblages of a ritual nature. Zimmermann distinguishes three types of deposition among river or peat bog finds:[152]

---

[142] For the deposition of coins in wells and springs, see Künzl 1999/2000, 558 ff., with references.

[143] Ulbert 1985, 72-74; see also Thiel/Zanier 1994, 67, cat. nrs. 39-42.

[144] Ulbert 1985, 72-74; see, however, Künzl 1999/2000, 554-555. For the find location, see Ulbert/Zanier 1997, 71 ff.

[145] Roymans 1990, 84-90; for rivers, see also Fitzpatrick 1984.

[146] See Künzl 1999/2000, 557; Thiel 2000, 72.

[147] Derks 1998, 140-141; see also Haynes 1997, 117-118, note 22.

[148] Tacitus, *Hist.* 4, 26.

[149] Thiel 2000, 72.

[150] Roymans 1996, 37-41; Nicolay 2002. See also chapter 7.2.

[151] For legionary inscriptions, see, for example, Bogaers 1959 (Meuse at Buggenum); Klumbach 1961 (Rhine at Mainz); Schalles/Schreiter 1993, cat. nr. Mil.1 (Xanten-'Wardt').

[152] Zimmermann 1970, 67.

1. Deposition of a single object by a single individual.
2. Deposition of various objects by one or more groups of people at a random location. It is not the place of action, but the act itself that is relevant here.
3. Deposition of one or more objects at the same location. The objects may be deposited by either individuals or groups. Both the act and the place of action are important for the ritual.

Derks adopts a different approach, distinguishing between assemblages made up of several offerings and those that were deposited on a single specific occasion.[153] Combining this distinction with Zimmermann's deposition types, we arrive at two categories of river assemblages. The first contains various depositions made at the same location: these could be either individual offerings by one person or collective depositions. In both instances, it is not only the specific act, but the place of action that is significant. The second category contains various depositions of a one-off nature. Although these might involve a specific location, it is the ritual act that is of primary relevance.

It is possible, despite the complexity of river finds, to assign different assemblages from the eastern Rhine delta to one or both categories on the basis of their size and composition. The first category contains the larger assemblages that were deposited in specific zones of a river, often over a lengthy period. Examples are the finds from the Meuse at Kessel-Lith, the Waal at Nijmegen and the Rhine at Lobith.[154]

In the case of Kessel-Lith, weaponry and horse gear from the late La Tène and early Roman period was dredged up over a long, narrow zone in a former bed of the Meuse (163.1-3, 164.1-41, 165.1-6).[155] The site also yielded building material from a monumental temple complex that probably stood on the river bank.[156] Roymans assumes that the deposition of military objects in this part of the Meuse is attributable to the presence of the cult place, which was possibly dedicated to Hercules Magusanus. The dredge finds can be dated in the main to La Tène D2 (60-30/15 BC). Also occurring are Roman weapons, as well as several *cingulum* and horse gear components. To a significant extent, the Roman weapon finds appear to be associated with the 1st-century auxiliary. Some of the La Tène swords may also have been worn by soldiers from the early auxiliary.[157] The securely dated items show that the Roman material ties in chronologically with the assemblage from the late Iron Age, suggesting a continuity in ritual dealings with military objects.

The Waal at Nijmegen is a second location where military equipment was repeatedly deposited over a longer period. The finds dredged up here come from an extensive zone of finds, which has yielded over 80 items of Roman weaponry and horse gear (211.1-75, 212.1-8).[158] Van Enckevort and Thijssen feel that the assemblage should be interpreted in relation to a monumental cult place erected on the bank of the Waal near a ford.[159] The find site stretches along the *oppidum Batavorum*, the later Ulpia Noviomagus,

---

[153] Derks 1998, 140.

[154] Although an overview is presented here of 'military' items, the different assemblages also frequently contain categories of items that are not specifically military in nature, such as bronze domestic ware, earthenware and bone material.

[155] Roymans/Van der Sanden 1980, 191-203; Verhart/Roymans 1998; Roymans 2004, 103 ff. For an overview of the finds, see chapter 3.3.4.

[156] The building components were incorporated as spolia in a late Roman fortification located there. For the assignment of this material to a temple building, see Roymans 2004, 134-144.

[157] Compare the assemblage from a cut-off loop of the Rhine at Xanten (Schalles/Schreiter 1993). Although most of the finds can be dated to the 1st century AD, two swords (one with the accompanying scabbard), a shield boss and four spearheads almost certainly date from the late Iron Age (cat. nrs. Mil 24, 26, 35, 35, 39, 43-45); they were most likely weapons belonging to early auxiliary troops.

[158] For an overview, see chapter 3.3.4.

[159] Van Enckevort/Thijssen 2000; 2001, 88-90. However, there are doubts surrounding the interpretation as a cult building of a stone construction discovered at the 'De Winseling' site.

Fig. 5.11. Several sets of horse gear dredged from the Lower Rhine at Doorwerth. Not to scale. After Holwerda 1931, fig.11.

the fortification on the 'Trajanusplein', as well as the more outlying fortresses on the 'Hunerberg' and the 'Kops Plateau'. Although the bulk of the finds can be dated to the 1st century AD, the helmets show that the site may have survived as a cult place into the 4th or 5th century. In contrast to Kessel-Lith, La Tène weaponry is completely absent. The types of weapon recovered and the ownership inscriptions reveal that the depositions were made by auxiliary, and to a lesser extent legionary, soldiers.

Finds from a cut-off loop of the Rhine at the site of a dredge pit ('De Bijland') near Lobith make up a third assemblage of river finds.[160] This has been interpreted as washout material from an army camp that was originally located there.[161] Various swords, mainly from the 1st century, have been recovered at this site

---

[160] For an overview, see chapter 3.3.4.

[161] Bogaers/Rüger 1974, 90-92; Willems 1984, 97-98.

Fig. 5.12. Three helmets of the Weisenau type from the Lower Rhine at Rijswijk (254.1-3). Not to scale. After Van Es/Hessing 1994, fig. 36.

(176.1-12). A helmet dredged from the present-day course of the Rhine adjacent to the dredge pit can perhaps be attributed to the same assemblage (177.1). Of the *gladii*, a Mainz type scabbard is exceptionally well preserved (176.9, pl. 22). The state of preservation of the wooden scabbard plates and remains of the leather cover indicates that the scabbard was consigned to the water soon after it ceased being used. The same applies to one of the swords, whose wooden guard and pommel are still in situ (176.7, pl. 16). The good state of preservation is evidence that at least a portion of the assemblage was primarily deposited, possibly as offerings, while the recovered building material suggests that this happened in the vicinity of an army camp.

In addition to the larger assemblages, some river finds should be viewed as one-off depositions. One such find consists of tinned and niello-inlaid parade horse gear from the Lower Rhine at Doorwerth.[162] Over 180 horse gear components, made up of *phalerae*, and strap and saddle fittings from the Claudio-Neronian period, have been dredged from a bend in the river (55.2-173, fig. 5.11). We can identify at least four sets that were probably consigned to the water at the same time. Other items dredged from this site are a *gladius* (220.1) and a 1st-century *umbo* (55.1), suggesting that the depositions may have been part of a river assemblage from the first category.[163]

Three helmets from the Lower Rhine at Rijswijk should also be interpreted as one-off depositions (254.1-3, fig. 5.12). The relationship between the finds is evident not only from the similar find site, but especially from the specific dating of the helmets to the late 1st century AD. With the exception of a fragmentary helmet from ''t Spijk' at Amerongen (12.1), these three helmets are the only examples from the research region that feature the late stylistic elements of the Weisenau type. We can assume that the helmets were deposited at the same time, with the lack of other weapon finds pointing to the one-off nature of the action. The assemblage was mixed up with finds that probably came from a washed-out army camp, suggesting that the helmets were deposited in the immediate vicinity of the camp.[164]

---

[162] Holwerda 1931; Brouwer 1982; see also chapter 3.3.4. A similar assemblage has been discovered in Xanten (Jenkins 1985); given the good state of preservation, it too comprises river finds – in this case a single horse gear set.

[163] A second *gladius* may have come from the same location (Roymans 1996, 104: B8).

[164] Van Es 1984b.

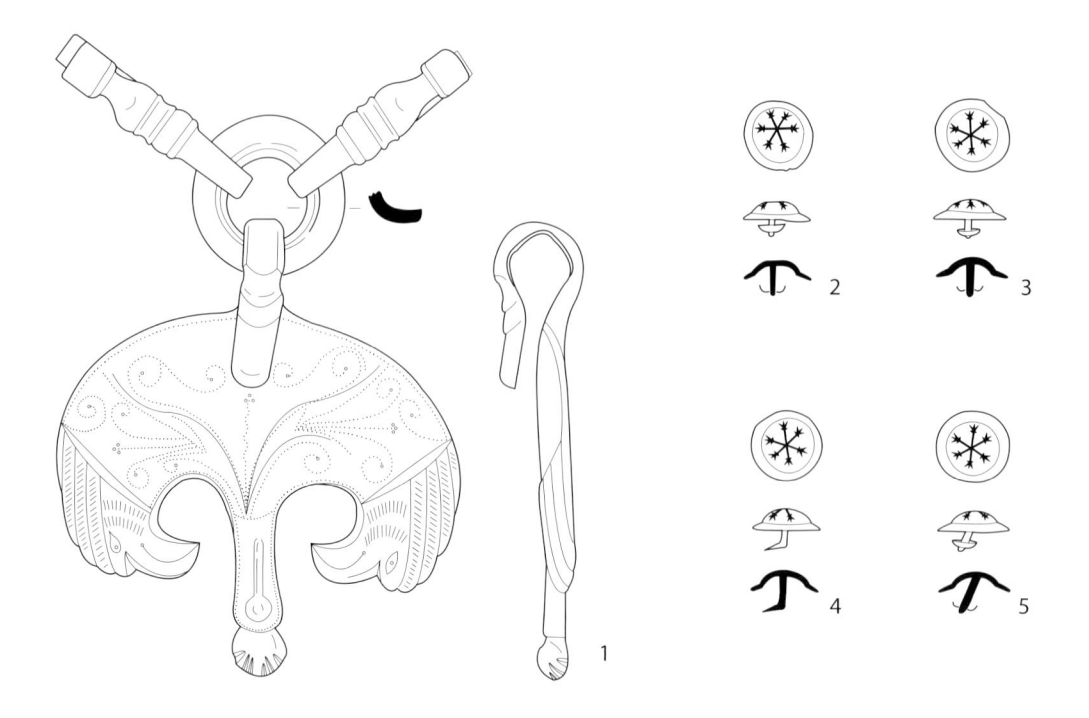

Fig. 5.13. A lunate pendant and four niello-inlay fittings belonging to a set of horse gear, from a creek near the rural settlement of Empel-West (83.1-8). Scale 2:3.

Although from a different context, we can also regard a set of 1st-century horse gear from a site near Empel as a one-off 'river deposition' (83.1-8, fig. 5.13). The find was discovered on the fringes of a rural settlement in the bank zone of a creek. The good state of preservation and the presence of a fishing trap in the same find layer suggest that the horse gear had originally been deposited in water.[165] The horse gear comprises a large lunate pendant, whose arms terminate in two eagles' heads. The pendant is attached to a bronze ring with two junctions. The assemblage included seven convex, niello-inlay decorative fittings. The presence of washers and backplates among the junctions and decorative fittings show that the bronze work was still attached to the leather strapping at the time of deposition and was probably deposited as a set.

Lastly, a sizeable portion of the river finds belong in the category of 'other'. Characteristic of this group are stray finds and various objects, dredged from the same location, whose interrelationship is difficult to pinpoint. Given their dating and composition, many of these objects seem to tie in with the picture that emerges from the probable ritual assemblages. The finds, mainly weapons, can be dated primarily to the 1st century AD. Some may belong to the larger, ritual assemblages that we cannot identify as such because they were used for such a short time or were later washed away. One-off depositions, which are even harder to identify, will also be included in the finds.

We can conclude from the presented data that not all river finds are lost or washout objects. The finds comprise 1st-century items of equipment, at least some of which appear to have been ritually deposited in accordance with pre-Roman tradition. The assemblages that give rise to problems of interpretation are those whose composition suggests that they were made up of washout material. For these assemblages, however, we cannot rule out in advance the presence of primary depositions of a ritual nature. Despite

---

[165] This is a metal detector find; the physical relationship of the objects in the creek has not been documented.

the 'static' of washout material, the finds from 'De Bijland' and the Rhine at Rijswijk show that some of the objects may have been ritual depositions.

Given the absence of votive inscriptions from river finds, there are no epigraphic clues to the identity of the dedicants. The composition of the finds can provide an initial indication as to whether soldiers, ex-soldiers or civilians were involved. As with rural cult places, the 1st-century finds tend to be specifically military items that can be associated with soldiers. The involvement of soldiers is also evident in the close proximity of many of the sites to army camps. Lastly, the presence of military ownership inscriptions shows that soldiers from the auxiliary and legions alike numbered amongst the dedicants.

Not active soldiers but veterans are likely to have figured prominently in the deposition of weaponry and horse gear in rivers; they will have done so by dedicating part of their equipment to the god associated with that particular river in order to mark the end of their soldiering career.[166] The location of the river sites may provide a clue as to when such depositions occurred. The recovery of some items close to an army camp suggests that veterans deposited equipment within sight of their former post immediately after discharge.[167] In other cases, the veterans presumably took their equipment home before depositing all or part of it in a river.

A further possibility could be the consecration of booty by high-ranking soldiers. It is interesting to note that the exclusive set of horse gear from the Lower Rhine at Doorwerth dates from the time of the Batavian revolt. In the light of Tacitus' report, this may have been an offering to Rhenus to thank her for her role in the success of the revolt. It may have comprised equipment captured from Roman soldiers or officers, which was then dedicated by leaders of the rebel forces.[168]

Lastly, non-military dedicants may have been involved in the depositions. This applies in particular to the period from the 2nd century onward, when the number of weapon finds fell in relation to those of horse gear and, later, belt components. However, helmet finds show that veterans may have continued to make occasional equipment depositions in rivers into the late Roman period.

5.3.3 URBAN CENTRES: LOST OBJECTS, DELIBERATE DEPOSITIONS AND KEPT OBJECTS

Many publications report 'military' finds from towns and *vici*, including both weapons and horse gear.[169] Excavations in Nijmegen (*oppidum Batavorum* and *Ulpia Noviomagus*) show that such material also circulated in urban contexts in the Batavian territory. Before discussing the use and patterns of deposition and/or loss of the finds from the Nijmegen centres, I will describe the ways in which 'military' items might have ended up in urban centres. The following possible explanations have been put forward by Fischer and others.[170]

---

[166] Roymans 1996, 34; see also Thiel/Zanier 1994, 69; Derks 1998, 140. Van Enckevort and Hazenberg (1997, 39) interpret a face shield from Corbulo's canal at the Matilo fortress (Leiden-'Roomburg') in a similar fashion: 'One of the cavalrymen from Matilo may have relinquished his most precious possession, sacrificing the exquisite mask to a god in gratitude for the protection he had received during 25 years of service.'

[167] A further possibility is that fellow soldiers dedicated a comrade's equipment after his death. This is particularly plausible if the equipment went to a fellow soldier. Generally, however, family members were the principal heirs, which means offerings could have been made both near the army camp and the family's home.

[168] A similar explanation is possible for the parade gear assemblage from Xanten (Jenkins 1985).

[169] See, for example, Bogaers 1971, 132 (Voorburg); Brulet 1981, fig. 40 (Braives); De Clerck 1983, nrs. 291-293, 299, 316 (Tienen); Wickenden 1988 (English towns); Bishop 1991 (English towns); Cordie-Hackenberg 1998, Abb. 4 (Belgium); Liesen 1999 (Cologne); Voirol 2002 (Avenches); Lenz 2000; 2001; 2002 (Xanten); Deschler-Erb 2001 (Oberwinterthur); Joly 2001, 158-159 (Langres).

[170] Fischer 2002; see also Lenz 2001, 77-78; Voirol 2002.

1. The presence of military guard posts
Urban guard posts were probably garrisoned by small groups of soldiers who operated as a kind of police force to maintain order. Such units (*cohortes vigiles*) are familiar to us from Rome, where they combined the duties of militia and fire brigade.[171] Pointers to the presence of military posts are concentrations of equipment in certain parts of the town.[172]

2. Short-term deployment of soldiers in construction work
Soldiers could also be quartered temporarily in towns for construction duties. Various towns show evidence of army involvement in the initial laying out of the town and the building of monumental works.[173]

3. Military conflicts
Military conflicts leave behind little tangible evidence in the archaeological record. Clues are burn layers and human bone material found in association with weaponry and horse gear.[174]

4. 'Trophies' brought home
Veterans figure prominently here. Military diplomas and inscriptions tell us that it was most notably the legionaries and auxiliary soldiers recruited elsewhere who chose urban centres as places to settle after discharge. A link to veterans is especially plausible in the case of *coloniae*.[175]

5. The presence of metal workshops
Fabricae are known from the Gallic and Italic area, where military equipment was produced from the very beginning of the Roman period.[176] We can also assume metalworking in the northwestern frontier zone, some of which will have been intended for army consumption. If military objects are linked to the presence of a workshop, we can expect an association with scrap, semi-manufactured items and waste products.[177]

6. Use by non-soldiers
This applies above all to the 2nd and 3rd centuries, when private artisans partly took over the production of 'military objects' and when belt and horse gear components in particular were more readily available to civilians. The late Roman belt also appears to have been worn in both military and civilian contexts.[178]

7. The deposition of militaria in urban sanctuaries
The example of the Mars sanctuary in present-day Cologne, where Caesar's sword and Otho's dagger were deposited, shows that weapons were dedicated in urban sanctuaries. As mentioned above, the possible dedicants were high-ranking soldiers and veterans, as well as non-soldiers. We can often deduce a function as votive offering from an association with a cult building and/or a specific spectrum of finds (votive inscriptions, statuettes of gods, coins, etc.).

---

[171] Le Bohec 1994, 22-23, fig. 4; see also Ortisi 2006.
[172] See Bishop 1991, 25-26; 2002b, 10-11 (English towns); Lenz 2000, 77-79; 2001, 588-590 (Xanten).
[173] See Vanderhoeven 1996, 210, 231 ff.
[174] See Deschler-Erb/Deschler-Erb 2002, 23-24 (Augst).
[175] See Voirol 2002 (*colonia* Aventicum).
[176] See chapter 4.1.
[177] See Deschler-Erb/Deschler-Erb 2002, 25-28 (Augst).
[178] For the non-military use of belts and horse gear, see chapter 6.2-3.

Fig. 5.14. One of the two silver medallions from exclusive *phalera* junctions from *oppidum Batavorum* (208.8). The *phalerae* were probably awarded as part of *dona militaria*. Scale 4:1. Photo Bureau Archeologie, Gemeente Nijmegen.

To what extent do these possible explanations relate to the material from the two Nijmegen centres?[179] In the case of *oppidum Batavorum*, the finds were unearthed during excavations in the central and southern part of the *civitas* capital (fig. 3.25). The town has a regular layout, with Gallo-Roman houses occurring at least in the centre. Over 50 weaponry and horse gear components have been recovered, scattered across the excavated sites (208.1-52).[180] Of these, pieces of plate armour (1x), scale armour (3x) and a shield (1x) can be associated with the 1st-century army, while a *cingulum* buckle and 35 horse gear components may have been of military origin. A belt terminal and 11 horse gear items are the only finds dating from the 2nd and 3rd centuries. In a brief find report, Van Enckevort and Thijssen link the early material to the Batavian revolt, when the *oppidum Batavorum* was set alight and abandoned once and for all.[181] They point out that the objects dating to the period after the abandonment of the settlement were recovered close to the road linking the 'Hunerberg' to Ulpia Noviomagus and may have been lost by travellers.

Although few context datings are available, some of the finds may be linked to the revolt of AD 70. I should point out here that, according to Tacitus, it was the Batavians themselves who set fire to the town; he makes no reference to a military conflict at this site.[182] However, the concentration of finds in the southeastern part of the town – including a plate armour closure, three linked scales from scale armour and a large fragment of shield edging – might suggest that a confrontation did in fact occur there. A guard post in this part of the town is a further possibility, but excavations have failed to substantiate this. Nor have they demonstrated the presence of metal workshops or a sanctuary where the objects could have been deposited. And what about veteran involvement? Relevant in this regard is the discovery of two silver medallions with imperial (?) busts from *phalerae* that were probably awarded as *dona militaria* or *donativa* (208.8-9, fig. 5.14). The once richly executed *phalerae* will have belonged to a veteran who took his military distinction or reward with him from the army. The remaining 1st-century items can perhaps be similarly accounted for, although we cannot rule out civilian use of some of the horse gear. Given the absence of contemporaneous weapon components, the horse gear from the 2nd and 3rd centuries is probably connected with non-soldiers. Alongside stray objects found scattered across the town, there was a limited concentration in the centre of the settlement. As the town appears to have been uninhabited at that time, the suggested association with the road to Ulpia Noviomagus is the most likely explanation.

---

[179] As the excavations in the two Nijmegen centres have yet to be analysed in full, the ideas presented here remain tentative.

[180] For the settlement layout and composition of the finds, see chapter 3.3.2.

[181] Van Enckevort/Thijssen, 2001/2002, 35-36.

[182] Tacitus, *Hist.* 5, 19.

After the Batavian revolt, a new urban centre was established west of the abandoned *oppidum Batavorum*, which under Trajan acquired the name Municipium Batavorum Ulpia Noviomagus. The finds examined here originate from the southern part of the town (fig. 3.26), which initially had a rather open character and combined residential and artisanal activities (pottery-making and metalworking). In the 2nd century, this part of town was set up for housing and a monumental temple complex appeared on the site of the 'Maasplein'. After a town fire at the end of the century, the site was once again organised around artisanal activities (pottery-making and meat processing). The present study has compiled over 180 weaponry and horse gear components (209.1-184).[183] The 1st-century finds comprise eight fasteners and plate armour hinges, a scale armour fragment and 39 pieces of horse gear. Once again, the bulk of the 2nd- and 3rd-century finds are horse gear (119x). Dating from the same period are a masked helmet fragment, and three slides and a chape from sword scabbards, nine belt components and two baldric fittings. According to the excavators, the 1st-century finds could point to the involvement of soldiers from the 10th legion in the construction of the temple complex on the 'Maasplein', while the later material could indicate that soldiers were engaged in meat processing.[184] . It has also been suggested that small military detachments were garrisoned in Ulpia Noviomagus after the legionary base on the 'Hunerberg' was abandoned.

The finds show a fairly regular distribution over the area surveyed. Only the western-most excavation pits revealed a clustering of 1st-century defensive weapons. These were found at the site of several civilian farmsteads, which show no further evidence of a military presence. As conspicuously few finds come from the temple complex established on the 'Maasplein' in the early 2nd century, any ritual deposition of military items there will have been at most occasional. Given the lack of evidence of a military conflict, three possible explanations remain. Firstly, some of the finds may be associated with one or more workshops. The evidence here is a lead die for manufacturing decorative 2nd- and 3rd-century horse gear fittings found in the southeastern part of the town (209.164, fig. 4.4). Secondly, veterans may have taken part of their equipment with them. This applies particularly to the 1st-century material, some of which are specifically military items. The cavalry helmet and a baldric fitting composed of openwork letters must also have belonged to soldiers.[185] Thirdly, the many horse gear finds from the 2nd and 3rd centuries point to everyday use by non-soldiers. The same is true of the contemporaneously used belts and *spathae*, which civilians were able to purchase in this period.[186]

Both Nijmegen centres show little evidence of the deliberate, possibly ritual, deposition of weapons and horse gear. The only convincing example from *oppidum Batavorum* is a set of ten Claudio-Neronian decorative horse gear fittings (208.27-35, 40). The washers are still in situ, suggesting that they had been deposited as part of the leather strapping. In the case of Ulpia Noviomagus, we can point to a set of two identical, enamel-inlay fittings from the 2nd and 3rd centuries (209.90, 114). The decorative fittings come from the 'Maasplein' and may have been dedicated at the cult place there. Also recovered from both settlements are plate armour components with remnants of iron sheeting and fragments of scale armour. As in Empel-'De Werf', the items may have been wholly or virtually intact at the time of deposition. The remaining finds are largely of a fragmentary nature and appear to have been discarded as waste across the inhabited area. Loss is also a possibility for the horse gear, especially for the 2nd and 3rd centuries, when decorative fittings were fastened less firmly than in the previous period. The key pointer to loss is the concentration of finds along the thoroughfare that cuts through the excavation pits of both settlements.

Assuming that veterans brought some of the weaponry and horse gear back with them, the question remains as to how this memorabilia was then used within each of the urban centres. Although perhaps

---

[183] For the settlement layout and composition of the finds, see chapter 3.3.2.

[184] Van Enckevort/Thijssen, 2001/2002, 37-40.

[185] The openwork letters of the baldric fitting form part of a protective text that was of special significance for soldiers (see chapter 4.2.3).

[186] For the use of swords, belts and horse gear by non-soldiers, see chapter 6.

worn at certain gatherings or ceremonies, generally speaking these military symbols will have been kept in the veterans' homes, where they might have been on prominent display, as is well attested in the late Republic. Written sources reveal that weapons, largely booty, were openly displayed on the walls of the *atrium* in order to show off and to honour the military prowess of the owners and their forebears. In Fischer's view, a parade helmet and a military distinction in the form of a torque from the villa of Treuchtlingen-'Weinbergshof' should similarly be viewed as '...martialischen Zimmerschmuck, der an die militärische Karriere des letzten Bewohners der Villa erinnern sollte.'[187]

Veterans may also have chosen to hide from view the objects they brought home. We find several instances of this in the archaeological record. For example, two silver medallions from exclusive *phalerae* were found in the stone cellar of a private dwelling in *oppidum Batavorum*. The cellar was covered with a burn layer during the Batavian revolt, a sign that the objects' owner had not deliberately deposited them but was forced to leave them behind. An interesting parallel is scale armour with bronze breastplates, as well as shield edging from a stone cellar of a civic building that formed part of a villa complex on the 'Bemelerveld' at Maastricht.[188] These objects were also stored in a cellar, and were left behind because of a fire.

5.3.4 RURAL SETTLEMENTS: RITUAL DEPOSITIONS AND DISCARDED ITEMS

Finds of weapons and horse gear have been recovered from rural settlements both inside and outside the Roman empire. Although few regional inventories are available, finds from various villa sites reveal that 'military' objects are also widespread in the countryside.[189] Finds from the research region confirm this, with weaponry and horse gear documented in almost 250 rural settlements to date. The settlements are generally simple in nature, comprising several byre houses enclosed by a system of ditches. A key difference from the southern loess soils is that villa complexes built of stone are rare in the Lower Rhine region.

We can gain an idea of the frequency and composition of 'military' finds in rural settlements by looking at table 5.4, which presents the weaponry and horse gear excavated in recent decades. We see that almost all excavations have yielded early – predominantly 1st-century – items, with finds of helmets and armour pointing to the specifically military character of some of the material. Given the many sites where amateur detectorists have made similar finds, we can extrapolate this pattern for most of the settlements in the Batavian countryside (fig. 3.8). Significantly less weaponry is known from period 3, which is typified by finds of belts/baldrics and especially horse gear. The almost complete absence of defensive weapons shows that these items were no longer predominantly military in nature. We see a similar picture in period 4, with belts now forming the principle category of finds.

The possible interpretations are less complex than for the urban centres. There is no evidence at all of a military presence in the form of guard posts or construction activity, and simple, rural settlements will seldom have witnessed military conflicts. From the Flavian era onwards, local production seems to have

---

[187] Fischer 2002, 17; see also Koch/Grabert 1986; Grabert/Koch 1986.

[188] Van Daele 2001.

[189] The inventory of Pfahl/Reuter (1996) is an exception here. Also available are regional studies for Germania (Tejral 1994; Erdrich 1994; 2001a; 2002). For weaponry and horse gear from individual sites (period 2-3), see for example Bloemers 1978, Abb. 127 (Rijswijk); Willems 1985 (Rijckholt); Grabert/Koch 1986 (Treuchtlingen); Maisant 1990, Taf. 92 (Altforweiler); Burmeister 1995, Abb. 1 (nr. 6) (Andechs); Fischer 1995, Abb. 1 (nrs. 1-3) (Affecking); Stoepker et al. 2000, fig. 55 (Venray); Lenz 2006, 88, Abb. 9 (vicinity of Köln).

	helmet	armour	shield	sword	dagger	belt	horse gear
periods 1-2							
Oosterhout-'Van Boetzelaerstraat'	2	1	-	2	-	3**	40
Tiel-'Passewaaijse Hogeweg'	1	1	-	1	-	3**	39
Tiel-'Oude Tielseweg'	1	-	-	1*	-	1	9
Beneden-Leeuwen-'De Ret'	-	3	2	1	-	2	11
Wijk bij Duurstede-'De Horden'	-	2	-	1	-	9	44
Kesteren-'De Woerd'	-	2	-	1	-	3	17
Wijk bij Duurstede-'De Geer'	-	1	-	-	-	-	7
Wijchen-'Tienakker'	-	-	1	-	-	1	7
Houten-'Zuid 8A'	-	-	1	-	-	1	2
Arnhem-'De Laar 6/7'	-	-	-	1	-	1	9
Echteld-'Medel'	-	-	-	1	-	-	12
Lent-'Steltsestraat'	-	-	-	1?	-	-	12
Groesbeek-'Klein Amerika'	-	-	-	-	-	1	18
Oss-'Westerveld'	-	-	-	-	-	1**	4
Geldermalsen-'Rijs en Ooyen'	-	-	-	-	-	1	13
Arnhem-'De Laar 4'	-	-	-	-	-	-	8
Houten-'Zuid 8A'	-	-	-	-	-	-	3
Oss-'Vijver'	-	-	-	-	-	-	1
period 3							
Arnhem-'De Laar 6/7'	-	1	-	1	1	-	4
Tiel-'Passewaaijse Hogeweg'	-	-	-	-	1	2***	51
Oosterhout-'Van Boetzelaerstraat'	-	-	-	-	-	6	59
Wijk bij Duurstede-'De Geer'	-	-	-	-	-	1***	21
Wijk bij Duurstede-'De Horden'	-	-	-	-	-	1	28
Beneden Leeuwen-'De Ret'	-	-	-	-	-	-	3
Wijchen-'Tienakker'	-	-	-	-	-	1	21
Echteld-'Medel'	-	-	-	-	-	-	14
Lent-'Steltsestraat'	-	-	-	-	-	-	10
Arnhem-'De Laar 4'	-	-	-	-	-	-	6
Groesbeek-'Klein Amerika'	-	-	-	-	-	-	4
Kesteren-'De Woerd'	-	-	-	-	-	-	2
Tiel-'Oude Tielseweg'	-	-	-	-	-	-	3
Houten-'Zuid 8A'	-	-	-	-	-	-	3
Hatert-'Hulzen'	-	-	-	-	-	-	1
period 4							
Wijk bij Duurstede-'De Geer'	-	-	-	-	-	24	-
Wijchen-'Tienakker'	-	-	-	-	-	8	-
Arnhem-'De Laar 4'	-	-	-	-	-	8	-
Arnhem-'De Laar 6/7'	-	-	-	-	-	1	-
Tiel-'Passewaaijse Hogeweg'	-	-	-	-	-	1	-
Geldermalsen-'Rijs en Ooyen'	-	-	-	-	-	1	-
Beneden-Leeuwen-'De Ret'	-	-	-	-	-	1	-

Table 5.4. An overview of weaponry and horse gear recovered during excavations in rural settlements in the eastern Rhine delta. Amateur finds from the same sites are included (*: La Tène sword; **: including apron; ***: including baldric).

been confined to decorative belt and horse gear elements, which does not explain the bulk of the 1st-century finds, particularly the early weaponry.[190] Moreover, the excavation finds display a fairly regular distribution over the inhabited area, rendering unlikely a link with private sanctuaries at the settlement level. Although none of these possibilities can be ruled out entirely, the material is more likely to have belonged to veterans, as is underlined by finds of military diplomas from a few rural settlements (table 5.1, fig. 5.6). Also, civilians themselves – especially during the 2nd and 3rd centuries – could have produced 'military items' or have purchased them in the camp villages.

Loss does not explain the 2700 objects recovered from Batavian settlements. These appear to have been deliberately deposited, and we can distinguish between ritual deposition, the burial of material as scrap and the discarding of objects as waste. Despite the large settlement areas investigated in recent decades, closed hoards occur infrequently in the research region. Characteristic of the 1st-century assemblages is their affinity in terms of (1) location in the peripheral zone of settlements, (2) deposition in a purpose-dug pit, and (3) the incomplete nature of the set of objects deposited. The following four hoard finds are documented:

1. *Oosterhout-'Van Boetzelaerstraat'*. Spread across the flat floor of an oval pit near the western settlement ditch were a Pompeii type sword blade (222.9), a butt spike (222.5), several iron nails and fragments of animal bone (figs. 3.20, 5.15). A sword scabbard and the spear-, lance-, or *pilum* head belonging to the butt spike were not found. The hoard is part of a group of pits with an unusual fill which was probably of a ritual nature.[191] In two instances the fill comprised human skeletons and in a third a horse buried in several pieces.

2. *Kesteren-'De Woerd'*. Two pre-Flavian *cingulum* buckles were found in an oval pit inside the western enclosing ditch (166.14-15, fig. 3.23). The tongue of the buckle and any decorative belt fittings are missing. The placing of the two buckles in an otherwise clear pit suggests deliberate deposition.

3. *Arnhem-'De Laar 6/7'*. The disturbed assemblage consists of three pendants, two identical and one of a similar type (15.10-12). The openwork pendants are of the trefoil type (type A1) and date from the Claudio-Neronian period. They were found together, and their similar level of corrosion suggests that they were buried as a set. Although the settlement has only been partially excavated, the assemblage appears to have been located in the peripheral zone.

4. *Beuningen-'Molenstraat'*. The hoard was discovered in the vicinity of an outbuilding on a narrow farmstead. The small-scale nature of the excavation makes it difficult to work out where the farmstead was located within the settlement site. The find comprises a complete horse skeleton that was buried in a pit in the early 2nd century.[192] A number of decorative fittings, a bell and a pendant were found around the horse's head; these were attached to the leather bridle at the time of burial (27.1-16, fig. 6.12). We can deduce from the horse's shoulder height that it was probably a military mount (approx. 150 cm).

---

[190] For production in rural settlements, see chapter 4.1.3.
[191] Van den Broeke 2002, 16-17.
[192] Zwart 1998b; 2001, 44-49.

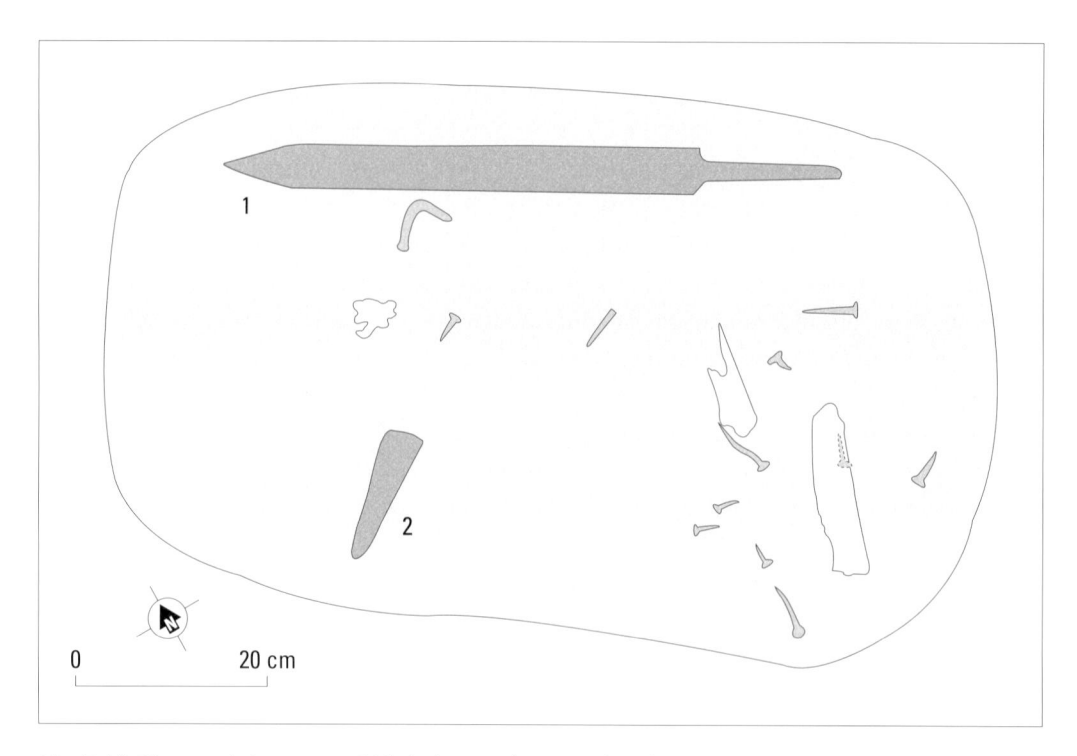

Fig. 5.15. Pit containing a sword blade, butt spike, several nails and animal bone fragments from the rural settlement of Oosterhout-'Van Boetzelaerstraat'. Redrawn from Van den Broeke 2002, 18.
1 *gladius* of the Pompeii type (222.9); 2 butt spike of a spear, lance or *pilum* (222.5).

We know from various assemblages which seem to have been disturbed that the number of early hoard finds is underrepresented. For example, a large number of plate armour components have been found together in Delwijnen-'Eendenkade' (fig. 5.7). The reverse of the bronze buckles and hinge components shows traces of iron plating, which suggests that they were buried as part of one or more complete sets of armour. We can also point to decorative horse gear fittings, which have the round washers or rectangular back plates still in situ, suggesting that they were attached to a leather strap at the time of deposition.

Finds from army camps offer interesting clues to the interpretation of 1st-century hoard finds from rural settlements. Illustrative here are some unusual depositions from the cavalry camp on the 'Kops Plateau' at Nijmegen, where the *ala Batavorum* may have been based during the pre-Flavian period. These were eight helmets, three with a face shield, as well as two assemblages containing a total of ten saddle horns.[193] Earthenware, in one case together with chicken, was buried with some of the helmets. Four of the saddle horns appear to have been deposited with poultry and pieces of meat. Two complete hackamores, a dagger and sheath, and a bent shield, as well as three exclusive horse gear pendants found together, were probably part of similar assemblages.[194] Like some of the helmets, the shield was buried together with earthenware.

Van Enckevort and Willems believe that these finds are offerings that include the remains of ritual meals, deposited by soldiers at a key moment in their military career.[195] Although no clue is given as

---

[193] Van Enckevort/Willems 1994; see also Willems 1991; Van Enckevort 1998/1999. An isolated example was probably part of a third assemblage containing saddle horns.

[194] Willems 1991, 14-15; Van Enckevort/Willems 1994, 133. Compare the find of a helmet and a shield boss in a pit immediately outside the legionary fortress on the 'Hunerberg' (Brunsting/Steures 1991). For other examples, both inside and outside the Batavian *civitas*, see Van Enckevort/Willems 1994, 131-133; Van Enckevort 1998/1999, 142, 149-151; both with references.

[195] Van Enckevort/Willems 1994, 133-134; see also Van Enckevort 1998/1999, 149-151.

to when that was, honourable discharge would appear most likely. Presumably, before leaving their last post for good, soldiers offered some of their equipment to Mars or Hercules in thanks for successfully completing their term of service.

Such a ritual interpretation is also likely for the above hoards from rural settlements. The 1st-century finds can be regarded as evidence of veterans who, on quitting the army, settled in the countryside throughout the territory of the Batavians. As with cult places and rivers, we can link these depositions to the conclusion of a key stage in soldiers' lives and to their return to the civilian world. Especially in the peripheral zone of their 'new' home, the weapon sacrifices by veterans were probably part of a transition ritual. Given that soldiers, who were often recruited locally, tended to return to their former home, the choice of location for the offering can be linked to their safe return.

The settlement finds are conspicuously incomplete. Missing from the Oosterhout assemblage are the scabbard and spearhead, from Kesteren the buckle tongue and possible belt fittings, and from Arnhem and Beuningen the remainder of the horse gear. We see the same pattern in what are probably ritual hoards from the 'Kops Plateau'. For example, in two instances the silver cladding has been removed from the face shields and one of the saddle hoards is incomplete. In contrast to the often intact items from cult places and rivers, there seems to have been a conscious decision to bury specific, not necessarily fully complete pieces of equipment. Perhaps the gesture of consecration was considered more important than whether or not the object was intact.

The 2nd century marks a distinct shift in the use of weaponry and horse gear and there is no evidence of specific veteran involvement. Unlike the preceding period, there are no documented finds from the *civitas Batavorum* that are unequivocally ritual in nature. An exceptional find from the Lower Rhine region is a suspected ritual hoard from the *civitas Cananefatium*; a pit containing two complete drinking vessels, a tin plate, a Neolithic axe and two vulvate horse gear fittings was found within the presumed military *vicus* on the 'Scheveningseweg' in The Hague.[196] In general, however, the assemblages contain fragmentary objects that we can interpret as scrap. Outside the research region, such scrap hoards are known primarily from the 3rd century and are traditionally associated with 'Germanic' incursions.[197] The sole example from the research region is an assemblage from Wijchen-'Tienakker' (fig. 5.16), which consists of decorative fittings, some of them fragmentary, and a slightly bent horse bit. Recovered from the bottom of a small pit, the objects appear to have been buried for later melting down.[198] Possible ritual hoards are also virtually unknown from the 4th and 5th centuries. The complete blade of a *semispatha* from Druten-'Klepperhei' (58.1, pl. 20) is one of the few objects that may have been deposited as an offering.

Most finds from rural settlements are isolated, fragmentary items which were found scattered across the settlement site and which can ultimately be viewed as waste (fig. 5.17). Excavation finds reveal specific patterns of spatial distribution for the 1st century AD. Firstly, finds occur around dwellings. This is most apparent in the well-preserved settlement of Wijk bij Duurstede-'De Horden' (fig. 3.16), where the finds are concentrated, especially inside the eastern boundary ditch, on the farmsteads of several farms. Secondly, the material is frequently recovered from ditches or depressions in the peripheral zones of settlements. For instance, most of the weaponry and horse gear from Oosterhout-'Van Boetzelaerstraat' comes from

---

[196] Waasdorp 1999, 157-158.

[197] See Garbsch 1878, 45 ff.; Fasold/Weber 1987; Lodewijckx et al. 1993; for the 3rd-century find horizon, see also Kellner/Zahlhaas 1993, 145-146.

[198] An interpretation as scrap also applies to the fragment of a contemporaneous cavalry helmet from Ede-'Op den Berg', situated north of the Rhine. The folded helmet fragment was buried in a pit from the second half of the 3rd century together with a large number of metal fragments, presumably as a smith's hidden metal supply (Ernst Taayke, pers. comm.).

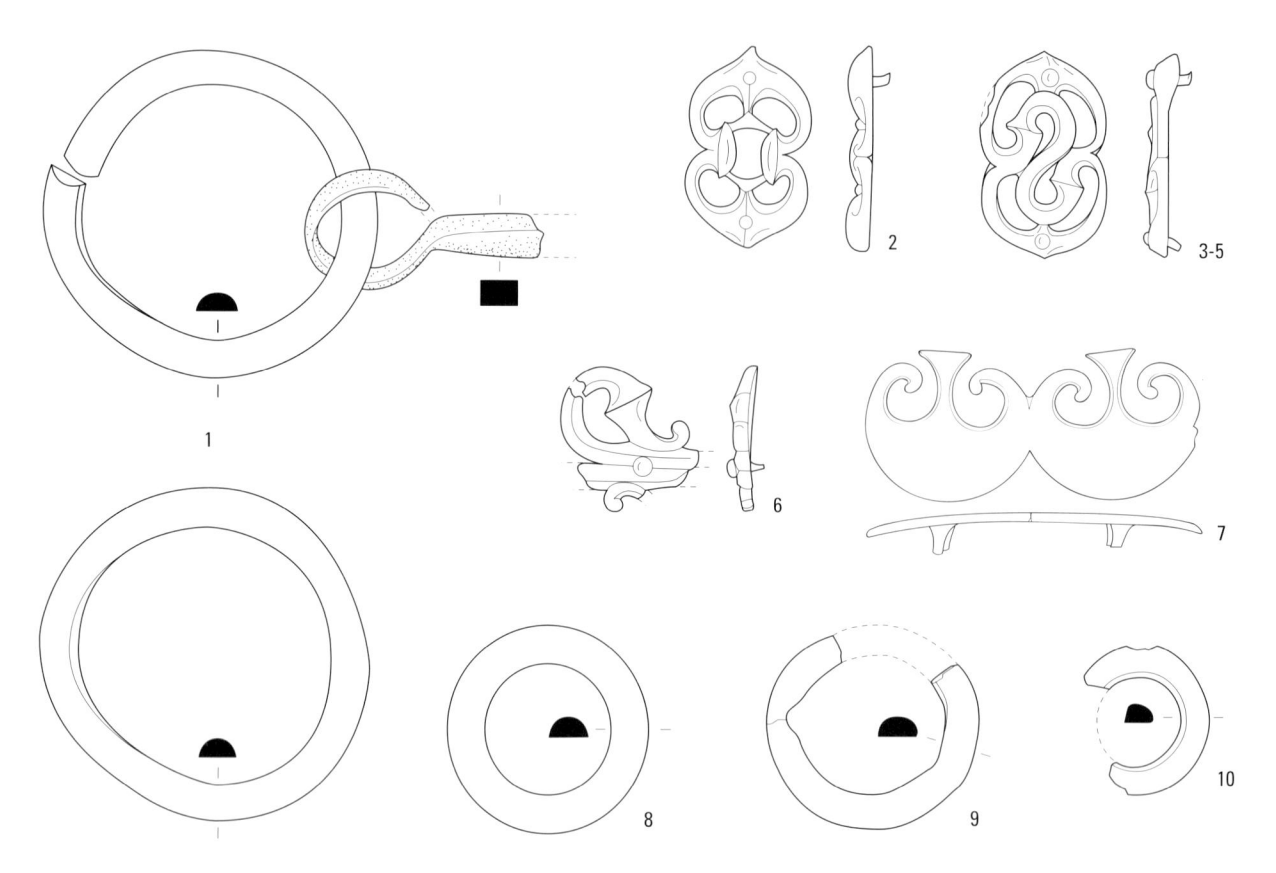

Fig. 5.16. Horse gear bit, fittings and rings from a pit on the villa site of Wijchen-'Tienakker'. Scale 2:3.
1 two bronze rings and iron mouthpiece from a bit (284.13); 2-7 bronze fittings (284.29, 32-34, 36-37); 8-10 bronze rings.

a broad ditch zone on the western side of the settlement (fig. 3.20). We encounter both patterns in the settlement 'Passewaaijse Hogeweg' at Tiel: analogous parts of the finds are distributed over the farmsteads and in the adjacent ditch (fig. 3.19).

The context datings for the 1st-century material give an impression of the duration of use of the militaria before the items were discarded as waste. This tells us that a substantial portion of the objects were already deposited (or sometimes lost) several decades after their manufacture. We also observe a longer period of use of up to 100-150 years. Examples here are the finds from Oss-'Westerveld' (table 3.2) and Tiel-'Oude Tielseweg' (table 3.3). The partial overlap between the typological and context datings suggests a relatively short use. In other cases, the context datings are 30-50 years after the objects went out of production, indicating that they were used for at least one or two generations.

As with the material from urban centres, we can ask ourselves how the equipment brought by veterans was used within the rural settlements and what significance was ascribed to it by successive generations. Given that some of the items were distributed around the dwellings, we can assume that here too the military symbols were displayed or stored in the veterans' homes. They may have been worn on particular occasions, when their owners could show off their status as veterans and Roman citizens. It is interesting to think that veterans' sons who entered military service may have re-used any usable items. However, there is a lack of evidence – for instance, in the form of different ownership inscriptions citing the same family name – to substantiate this. Using context datings, we can only establish indirectly the extent to which memorabilia constituted a cherished memory of a father or grandfather for subsequent generations. While some objects were thrown away quite soon, underlining the idea that they were of special significance to the owners themselves, others were kept for several generations by

Fig. 5.17. Fragmentary components of plate armour, the *cingulum* and horse gear, from the rural settlement of Kesteren-'De Woerd' (166.2, 16-17, 20, 23-25, 29, 33-34). Not to scale.
1 bronze plate armour hinge; 2 *cingulum* fitting; 3-10 strap junction loop, strap terminals, decorative fittings and bell fragment from horse gear.

next of kin. This latter group may constitute a selection of heirlooms that evoked a special memory for the family. Nevertheless, these too ceased to be meaningful after a certain time and ended up as waste on the farmsteads or on the fringes of the settlements.

From the 2nd century onward, the changing composition of the finds points to the growing involvement of non-soldiers. The distribution of this later material closely matches that of finds from the previous period. Given the fragmentary nature of the 'military' objects, these are once again largely waste that was discarded both at farmsteads and in the peripheral zones of the settlements. Complete items – especially horse gear, which was fastened less securely than in the previous period – may also have been lost from time to time. The typological dating of the objects is insufficiently accurate to allow us to comment reliably on duration of use. Occasionally, veterans continued to be involved in the use of weapons and horse gear in rural settlements. Thus several finds of openwork baldric fittings from the 2nd and 3rd centuries and the above-mentioned *semispatha* from the late Roman period are probably still instances of military symbols brought home by veterans as a personal reminder of their years in the army.

5.3.5 GRAVES: GIFTS FOR THE DEAD

The use of military objects as grave goods is a native tradition that survived within the borders of the empire in the early Roman period.[199] As with river finds, we can identify regional patterns. While rela-

[199] Roymans 1996, 34.

tively many weapon graves are documented in the Treverian territory, they are rare in the Lower Rhine region (fig. 3.12). The Trier finds furnish the best clues for interpreting weapons and horse gear from graves. In the cemetery of Wederath, in use from the 4th century BC until the end of the 4th century AD, we are able to trace the funerary tradition over a longer period.[200] From the beginning of La Tène D, swords, lances and shields occur frequently in graves for the first time.[201] Characteristic of this stage is that the interred weapons were bent and broken, a practice that can be explained in terms of ritual destruction.[202] Although weapons were still commonly buried during La Tène D2, the practice died out altogether at the beginning of the Roman period. The two most recent weapon graves date to around the mid-1st century AD, with a Mainz type sword included among the weaponry in each case. This trend in Wederath seems to reflect that of the Middle Rhine region, where Roman equipment in particular continues to occur in funerary contexts until the mid-1st century.[203]

It is generally assumed that the soldiers buried in these graves were from the auxiliary.[204] Important clues are the continuity of burial practices, the presence of imitation Roman weapons and the combination of Roman and native weaponry. For example, grave 2214 in Wederath contained both a Roman *gladius* and a native spearhead with a pronounced midrib.[205] The atypical *pilum* head from the other grave that contained a *gladius* is also of native origin (grave 1344, fig. 7.5).[206] The weapon graves containing native elements were probably those of soldiers from the earliest, as yet irregular, auxiliary troops who to some extent were armed with their own weapons.

Although the interment of weapons in the Lower Rhine region was not rooted in local tradition and was rather infrequent during the 1st century AD, the weapon graves found there do fit the Middle Rhine pattern. All the graves date from the pre-Flavian period, and contained both Roman and native weapons, as well as imitations. For example, a grave from Mehrum yielded – in addition to a Roman spearhead and shield boss – a sword, a dagger and military belt components that were imitations of Roman examples (fig. 5.18).[207] The native origin of the deceased is also apparent in the 'Germanic' shield. Roymans points out that the weapon graves from the Lower Rhine region, including the Mehrum grave, are among the richest in the region, and suspects that the deceased were highly-placed members of the Lower Rhine auxiliary.[208]

All this leads us to conclude that the 1st-century weapon graves were those of soldiers, and probably primarily auxiliary officers. Most of the graves are situated in native cemeteries, suggesting that the deceased were often veterans interred with military symbols in accordance with native custom. It is also possible that some graves held soldiers who had died while on active service and who were brought home with their equipment by their next of kin, to be buried alongside their ancestors. The latter applies in particular to soldiers who had served in their home territory.[209]

[200] Haffner 1971; 1989a.

[201] For the chronological development, see Haffner 1989b, 44 ff.

[202] Haffner 1989c; for ritual destruction in general, see also Derks 1998, 46-47. Crucial to this interpretation is an analogous use in contemporaneous cult places.

[203] For an overview, see Schönberger 1953; De Laet/Van Doorselaer 1962; Van Doorselaer 1963/1964; 1965; Engels 1972.

[204] Schönberger 1953, 53, note 4; Van Doorselaer 1965, 128; Haffner 1989b, 103-108; Schumacher 1989b; Waurick 1994; Krier/Reinert 1991; Reinert 2000.

[205] Schumacher 1989b; for other examples, see Waurick 1994. Although Schumacher (1989b, 274) assumes that the soldier from grave 2215 had served in a cavalry unit, the *gladius* used by infantrymen points to a position in a cohort (see also Waurick 1994, 21-22).

[206] Haffner 1989b, 105. Compare the *pilum* in grave 689 (Haffner 1971, Taf. 184).

[207] Gechter/Kunow 1983.

[208] Roymans 1996, 35, note 77; compare Gechter/Kunow 1983, 454-455.

[209] However, it was customary for soldiers who died while on active service to be buried close to their army camp. Examples are given by Waurick (1994, 5-12).

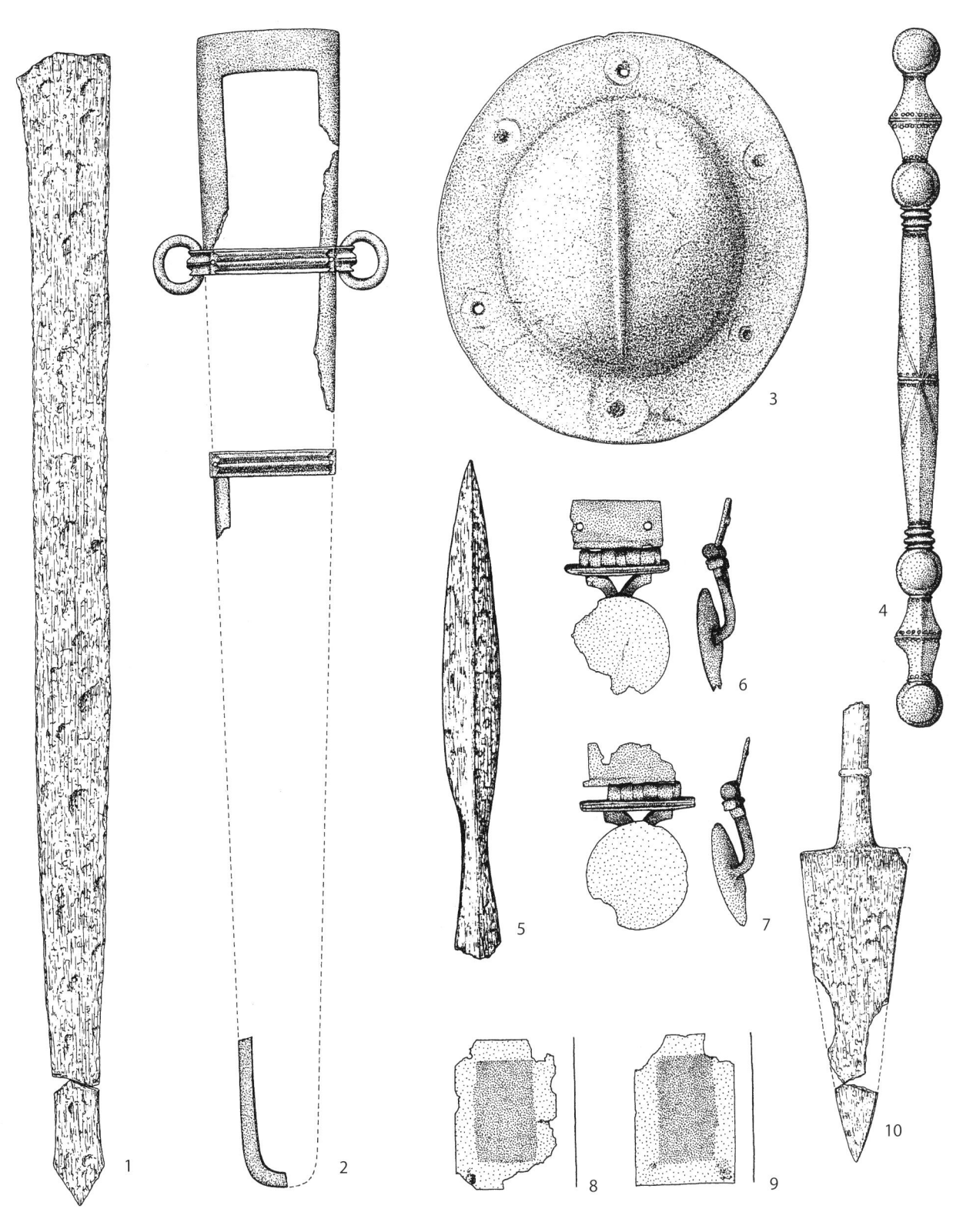

Fig. 5.18. Components of military equipment from a weapon grave at Mehrum. Scale 1:3, 1:2 (nrs. 4-7). After Gechter/Kunow 1983, figs. 16-17.
1-2 sword blade and scabbard; 3-4 shield boss and grip; 5 spearhead; 6-7 dagger frogs; 8-9 belt plates; 10 dagger.

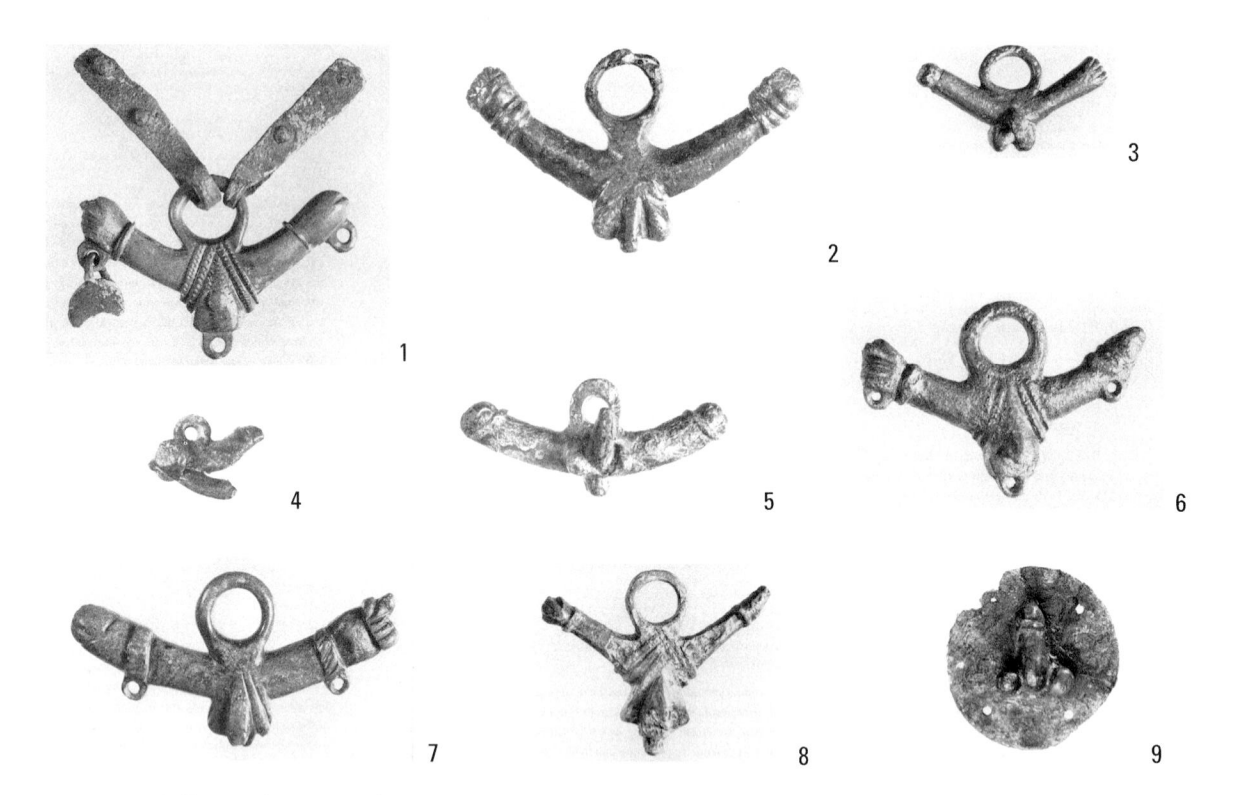

Fig. 5.19. Phallic pendants and a fitting from suspected funerary contexts in the vicinity of Nijmegen. Scale 1:2. After Zadoks-Josephus Jitta/Peters/Gerhartl-Witteveen 1973, cat. nrs. 79, 80-81, 83, 85-86, 96, 102.
1-5 pendants from the pre-Flavian cemetery of *oppidum Batavorum* (203.1-5); 6-7 pendants from the pre-Flavian cemetery of the cavalry camp on the 'Kops Plateau' (206.1-2); 8-9 pendant and decorative fitting from the Flavian and later cemetery of Ulpia Noviomagus (204.6, 8).

Although weapon graves are especially numerous during the 1st century AD, De Laet and Van Doorselaer emphasise that the practice of burying weapons by no means fell out of favour in the following period.[210] During the 2nd and 3rd centuries, 'military' grave goods consisted of swords, spears/lances and sometimes daggers, *pila* and arrows. Belts were also characteristic of some of the weapon graves.[211] In a few instances, stray items or complete sets of horse gear also occur.[212] Unlike in the previous period, however, these were no longer specifically military objects that can be linked unequivocally to deceased soldiers or veterans. A grave assemblage from Lyons, which includes a sword, belt and baldric (fig. 2.14), demonstrates that soldiers and veterans continued to be buried along with their equipment.[213] We can identify the status of the deceased from the belt fittings in the shape of openwork letters, whose protective text is especially relevant to soldiers.

The 4th and 5th centuries saw a resurgence of the practice of interring 'military' items. Due to the growing role of 'Germanic' groups in the Roman army, new types of equipment were introduced and 'military' objects were deposited more frequently in graves (figs. 3.12-13).[214] Unlike in the 1st century, the interred

---

[210] De Laet/Van Doorselaer 1962, 61; see also Schönberger 1953, 55-56.

[211] Hübener 1963/1964; Petculescu 1995.

[212] Stray finds: Fasold 1993, grave 41 (Seebruck); Liéger 1997, grave T.461 (Cutry); Hintermann 2000, graves 93.66, 93.100 (Vindonissa); complete sets: Lehner 1923 (Frenz); Massart 2000 (Celles-lez-Waremme).

[213] Oldenstein 1976, 88-89; compare the weapon grave from Zauschwitz (Hübener 1963/1964).

[214] Böhme 1974; see also Werner 1958; Ypey 1969; Swift 2000, 185 ff.

Fig. 5.20. Inventory of a rich weapon grave from a walled garden tomb located in the cemetery of Ulpia Noviomagus. In the foreground the bronze boss and iron grip from a shield (207.1) and in the centre at the back three iron spearheads (207.2-4). After Koster 1993, Abb. 2.

items were no longer just a sword, shield and one or more spears, but also a broad belt, often richly decorated with plates. Although Theuws interprets the 'weapons' from this period as symbols of hunting and authority, and associates them with newcomers to the areas abandoned in the 3rd century, the presence of swords and shields suggests that at least some of the graves are military ones.[215] In the case of graves containing only a spear or lance, axe and/or belt, the deceased could have been either a soldier or a civilian.

If we examine the few weapon finds from graves in the eastern Rhine delta, we see a chronological trend that largely fits in with this picture. Here too, weapon finds can be linked to burial practices, especially during the 1st century AD. An iron dagger blade was recovered from the ring ditch of a cremation grave (AD 90-120) in Hatert-'Hulzen' (109.1, pl. 26).[216] The fact that the adult individual was buried in a native cemetery probably shows that he was a veteran. As daggers were only worn by infantrymen, this would have made him a veteran from a cohort.

We also find 1st-century weapon graves in the cemetery of Flavian and later date that extends east of Ulpia Noviomagus (fig. 3.26). The weapons include a *gladius* (204.3), an S-shaped chain-mail hook (204.1), and a less securely dated spear- or lancehead (204.2). The sword's long, narrow blade indicates that it belonged to a cavalryman. The chain mail and the throwing weapon were also worn primarily by

[215] Theuws, in print; see also Theuws/Alkemade 2000, 448 ff.

[216] Haalebos 1990a, 58 (grave 403.BA.108).

the cavalry, suggesting that the deceased served in an *ala* or a *cohors equitata*. As these are stray finds, no further data on the interment is available. The cemetery also incorporates a monumental weapon grave (c. AD 80-100) within a walled garden tomb.[217] The grave goods included three spearheads and a shield, typical equipment for a cavalryman (207.1-4, fig. 5.20).[218] The richness of the grave goods and the style of the monument suggest that this person would have belonged to the Nijmegen aristocracy.[219] In addition to weapons, the cemetery has yielded several stray 1st-century horse gear finds: a phallic pendant, two round fittings, one of which bears a phallic appliqué, and a bell (204.5-8, fig. 5.19). In the case of the weapon graves, we can assume that these were veterans buried with some of their equipment in accordance with 1st-century practice. The horse gear finds are more difficult to interpret and may also have come from the graves of non-soldiers.

A round disc featuring Amor or Eros in relief has been recovered (205.1, fig. 2.17) from the eastern branch of the cemetery that encompasses a large part of the Flavian *castra* and the surrounding *canabae* on the 'Hunerberg'.[220] It was part of *dona militaria* worn on the chest with another eight *phalerae* attached to leather straps. Bogaers believes that the decorative disc came from a grave which – judging by the associated earthenware – dates to the last quarter of the 1st or the early 2nd century.[221] The military distinction was certainly interred with a soldier or ex-soldier.

Two phallic pendants have been recovered from the nearby cemetery of the pre-Flavian auxiliary camp on the 'Kops Plateau' (206.1-2, fig. 5.19).[222] The location of the cemetery makes it likely that both stray pendants were buried as grave goods together with soldiers.[223] Because cavalrymen, possibly from the *ala Batavorum*, were stationed on the 'Kops Plateau', these items were probably deliberately selected pieces of horse gear belonging to the deceased; the choice was presumably dictated by the symbolic, protective value of the phallus.[224]

Also of interest are five phallic horse gear pendants from the pre-Flavian cemetery located west of the *castra*, where the inhabitants of *oppidum Batavorum* were probably buried (203.1-5, fig. 5.19).[225] Although we have no information about the specific find context, we can assume that these objects too were interred as grave goods.[226] In one case, two strap fittings are attached to the pendant loop, indicating that the pendant was still attached to a piece of leather strapping at the time of deposition. The pendants might have belonged to ex-cavalrymen who settled in the Batavian *civitas* capital after completing their term of service, but could equally have been given to civilians as grave goods.

A stray horse gear item from the 1st-century is the only documented 'military' find from the two cemeteries in the rural settlement complex of Arnhem-'De Laar' (16.1). The looped strap mount came from a cremation grave and had been placed in an earthenware bowl buried in the grave. This piece could have belonged to a deceased soldier, an ex-soldier or a civilian.

[217] Koster 1993; 1994.

[218] Koster (1994, 296) believes the shield to be a hunting weapon. However, the three interred spearheads are characteristic of the cavalry, while the shield can also be regarded as a military item (see also Haalebos 1990b, 199; 2000a, 39). The same site also yielded a 1st-century horse bell (207.5).

[219] See Bogaers/Haalebos 1987, 47; Haalebos 1990b, 199; Koster 1994, 246.

[220] A 'grave find' from the Hunerberg published by Brunsting and Steures (1991) has been omitted here because of its atypical character.

[221] Bogaers 1970/1971, 183-184.

[222] The cemetery on the 'Kruisweg' (Van Enckevort/Thijssen 2001, 96-98, fig. 1).

[223] We should bear in mind that these protective 'amulets' may have been buried with the wives or children of soldiers; for the non-military use of horse gear, see chapter 6.3.

[224] See chapter 6.3.3.

[225] The cemetery on the 'Museum Kamstraat' (Van Enckevort/ Thijssen 2001, 96-98, fig. 1).

[226] We cannot rule out that the objects were lost along the thoroughfare that bisected the cemetery. However, the uniform nature of the recovered items and similar finds from other cemeteries suggest a link to burial practices.

site	sword	shield	dagger/ knife	spear/ lance	axe	belt	cat. nr.
Lent-'Steltsestraat' *	-	-	-	-	-	+	170.3-4
Teeffelen *	-	-	-	-	-	+	264.1
Nijmegen-'Broerstraat'	-	-	-	-	-	+	202.1
Rhenen, grave 821	1	-	-	-	-	-	253.1
grave 833	-	1	1	1	1	+	253.2
grave 842	-	-	3	2	-	+	253.3
grave 846	-	-	2	-	-	+	253.4
grave 356	-	-	1	1	1	+	253.5
grave 835	-	-	1	-	-	+	254.6
grave 818	-	-	-	1	1	+	253.7
grave 839	-	-	-	1	1	+	253.8
grave 819	-	-	-	1	-	+	253.9
grave 829	-	-	-	1	-	+	253.10
grave 834	-	-	-	-	-	+	253.11
Wageningen, grave 155	-	-	-	1	-	+	277.1
grave 67	-	-	-	-	-	+	277.2
Wijchen, grave A	-	-	1	-	-	+	285.1
grave B	-	-	-	-	-	+	285.2

Table 5.5. Weaponry and belt elements from 4th- and 5th-century 'weapon graves' from the *civitas Batavorum* and the neighbouring 'Germanic' area (*: stray finds).

It is interesting to note that, insofar as can be ascertained, the above-mentioned graves containing weaponry and horse gear are more recent than those in the Trier region. This suggests that the graves from the *civitas Batavorum* belonged to the final phase of the 1st-century 'horizon' of weapon graves from the Rhine region. There is also an interesting pattern in the choice of grave goods: not complete equipment but instead often a specific piece of weaponry or horse gear, indicating that the symbolic significance of the items was paramount.

Weapons from funerary contexts are almost unknown in the 2nd and 3rd centuries. The few examples include two spearheads and two decorative horse gear fittings from the cemetery of Tiel-'Passewaaij' (241.2-4, table 3.3). Both throwing weapons and one of the fittings were recovered from the ring ditches of 3rd-century graves, and the other fitting from the site of a disturbed grave that was laid out in the late 1st or first half of the 2nd century AD. The complete absence of specifically military elements in the remaining graves and the settlements associated with the cemetery from this period suggests that these items had been used by civilians. A similar interpretation applies to the horse gear and a possible arrowhead from a rich 2nd-century *tumulus* grave at Esch (87.1-13).[227] The female nature of the remaining grave goods, including jewellery and a case containing (knitting) needles, demonstrates that no soldier was buried there.[228]

The late Roman revival of the practice of placing 'military objects' in graves can also be seen in the Batavian territory (table. 5.5). In addition to graves located north of the Rhine at Rhenen (11x) and Wageningen (2x), five 'weapon graves' are known in the research region. As most of the graves did not

[227] In general, see Van den Hurk 1973 (grave II).
[228] Van den Hurk 1984, 19.

contain any swords or shields, either soldiers or civilians could have been buried there. Exceptions are graves 821 and 833 from Rhenen, where a *spatha* and conical shield boss respectively feature among the grave goods (fig. 7.9). The owners of these weapons may have served in the auxiliary and have been buried along with parts of their equipment.[229]

5.4 CONCLUSION

This chapter has used a life-cycle model in an attempt to reconstruct the use of military equipment during the life of a Roman soldier. I have distinguished two key stages associated with specific uses of weapons and horse gear. The first, which coincides with active military service, can be described as military use in the context of the Roman army. Critical to the interpretation of militaria from non-military contexts is the second stage of 'social use' by ex-soldiers. Following their honourable discharge, it seems that large numbers of veterans – especially in the 1st century AD – elected not to sell their equipment back to the army, but to keep it and take it home as a reminder of an important stage in their lives. Some of the equipment brought home in this way was ritually deposited at cult places, in rivers and in the settlements where they lived in order to mark the end of their soldiering days. The remaining items were kept at home as personal memorabilia and perhaps worn on special occasions as symbols of their newly acquired veteran and citizen status. In specific regions, it was customary when a veteran died for parts of his equipment to be buried alongside him. That the items brought home had particular significance for the owners themselves is revealed by the many finds that were discarded in settlements as waste one or two generations later. Only in exceptional cases does the equipment appear to have been handed down as heirlooms over a longer period, presumably in special commemoration of an ancestor.

[229] See also Ypey 1973, 307-308.

6 Non-military use of weaponry and horse gear in urban and rural settlements

I argued in the previous chapter that part of the finds from non-military contexts were the property of Roman soldiers. After completing their term of service, they would take their equipment home to keep as personal memorabilia or make a ritual deposition to mark the end of their soldiering days. The key pointer here is the frequent occurrence of what are clearly military items (including helmets, armour and shields) in settlements and ritual contexts, especially during the 1st century AD. In the following period, we see marked changes in the composition of the material.[1] Specific types of offensive weapons, belts and above all horse gear are the chief find categories for the 2nd and 3rd centuries (period 3), while belt components are almost the only documented finds from the 4th and the first half of the 5th century (period 4). This chapter seeks to explain the changing composition of 'military' finds from the Batavian territory. Did these objects still belong to veterans or might they have been purchased by civilians for day-to-day use in the town and countryside? One reason why this question is difficult to answer is that we cannot distinguish typologically between items used by civilians and those used contemporaneously by the military. In order nevertheless to make a distinction between 'military' and 'civilian', we need to analyse larger assemblages. The finds from the research area would appear to constitute a useful data set for this purpose.[2]

6.1 THE BEARING OF ARMS BY NON-SOLDIERS

Although we tend to automatically associate Roman weaponry with soldiers or veterans, civilian use is a further possibility when it comes to offensive weaponry. These weapons were not only used by the army, they could also have played a role in civilian hunting expeditions and in self-defence. Before elaborating further on the non-military types of use of offensive weaponry, I shall first examine Roman legislation to establish whether civilians were permitted to bear arms inside the imperial borders.

6.1.1 THE CORPUS JURIS CIVILIS: A BAN ON WEAPONS POSSESSION BY CIVILIANS?

The *Corpus Juris Civilis*, drawn up in around 530 under the Byzantine Emperor Justinian I (527-565), is a unique source of information about the legal position of those living in the Roman empire with regard to weapons possession. The code is a collection of existing laws in the field of civil law, dating from the 1st century BC to the 3rd century AD.[3] Relevant for our purposes is the *Lex Julia de Vi Publica*, which sets out the instances when non-soldiers were permitted to possess arms or prohibited from doing so. The antecedents of this law are 2nd- and 3rd-century codes, drafted by Marcian, Scaevola and Paul, with the following articles dealing specifically with weapons possession:[4]

---

[1] For an overview, see chapter 3.1.

[2] For the terms 'military' and 'civilian' in a Roman context, see chapter 1.3.

[3] Mommsen/Krueger/Watson 1985, vol. I, xi.

[4] *Dig. Just.*, 48.6.1-3, 11; translation Mommsen/Krueger/Watson 1985, vol. VI, 816-817. Each article is preceded by the name of the writer, the work and the scroll number from which the text in question has been taken.

1. Marcian, Institutes, book 14. *A man is liable under the* lex Julia *on* vis publica *on the grounds that he collects arms or weapons at his home or on his farm or at his country house beyond those customary for hunting or for a journey by land or sea.*

2. Scaevola, Rules, book 4. *But those arms are excepted which someone has by way of trade or which come to him by inheritance.*

3. Marcian, Institutes, book 14. *Under the same heading come those who have entered into a conspiracy to raise a mob or a sedition or who keep either slaves or freemen under arms. 1. A man is also liable under the same statute if, being of full age, he appears in public with a missile weapon. 2. Under the same heading come those who, assembling seditiously in the most wicked manner, attack country houses and seize property with missile and hand weapons. 3. Also liable is the man who seizes anything from a fire, excepting building materials. 4. Furthermore, anyone who forcibly violates boy or woman or any other person is punished by the penalty of this statute. 5. Anyone who has been present at a fire with a sword or a missile weapon for the purpose of robbery or of preventing the owner from rescuing his property is liable to the same penalty. 6. Also liable under this statute is anyone who with armed men expels someone having possession from his home, his farm, or his ship, or attacks him.*

11. Paul, Views, book 5. *Those who loot, break open, or storm the homes or country houses of others, if, indeed, they gathered an armed mob, receive capital punishment. 1. In the term "weapons" all objects from which injury can result to a man's health are included. 2. Persons who bear weapons for the purpose of protecting their own safety are not regarded as carrying them for the purpose of homicide.*

This last article clearly shows that 'weapons' (*tela*) means all objects that can be used to inflict injury on another person. The prohibition on bearing arms relates first of all to individuals in armed groups. For fear of riots and uprisings, it was not permitted to maintain or belong to such groups. The ban on stockpiling weapons is directly linked to this fear. Civilians were also prohibited from carrying weapons and missiles in public places or using them improperly against others.

Other references cover situations in which non-soldiers were permitted to possess weapons. The first relates to civilians using weapons for hunting. The second involves travellers, who were entitled to protect themselves with a weapon. Article 11, which states that *every* person may carry a weapon for their own safety, shows that the same applied to other civilians. Finally, civilians were allowed to possess one or more weapons if these were merchandise or inherited items. Interestingly, this means that the next-of-kin of veterans who had taken their equipment home were permitted by law to keep these memorabilia at home.

The *Lex Julia* shows clearly that the purchase of weapons was not the privilege of soldiers alone; perhaps as early as the 1st century BC, civilians too could carry arms in certain situations. Using finds from the eastern Rhine delta, I will now elaborate further on the extent to which the presence of weaponry in non-military contexts can be explained by civilian use of weapons for hunting and self-protection.

6.1.2 LANCES, SPEARS, ARROWS AND SLING SHOT: HUNTING WEAPONS

Wild animal skeletal material from rural settlements shows that hunting played only a marginal role in food supply during the Roman era; instead, the significance of hunting may have lain in the recreational and symbolic spheres.[5] Initially, hunting was not a privilege of the upper class, but was open to all.[6] This appeared to change in the late Roman period, when hunting increasingly became a vehicle by which the aristocracy could display leadership and courage, as well as claims to land.[7] Mosaic images reveal lances,

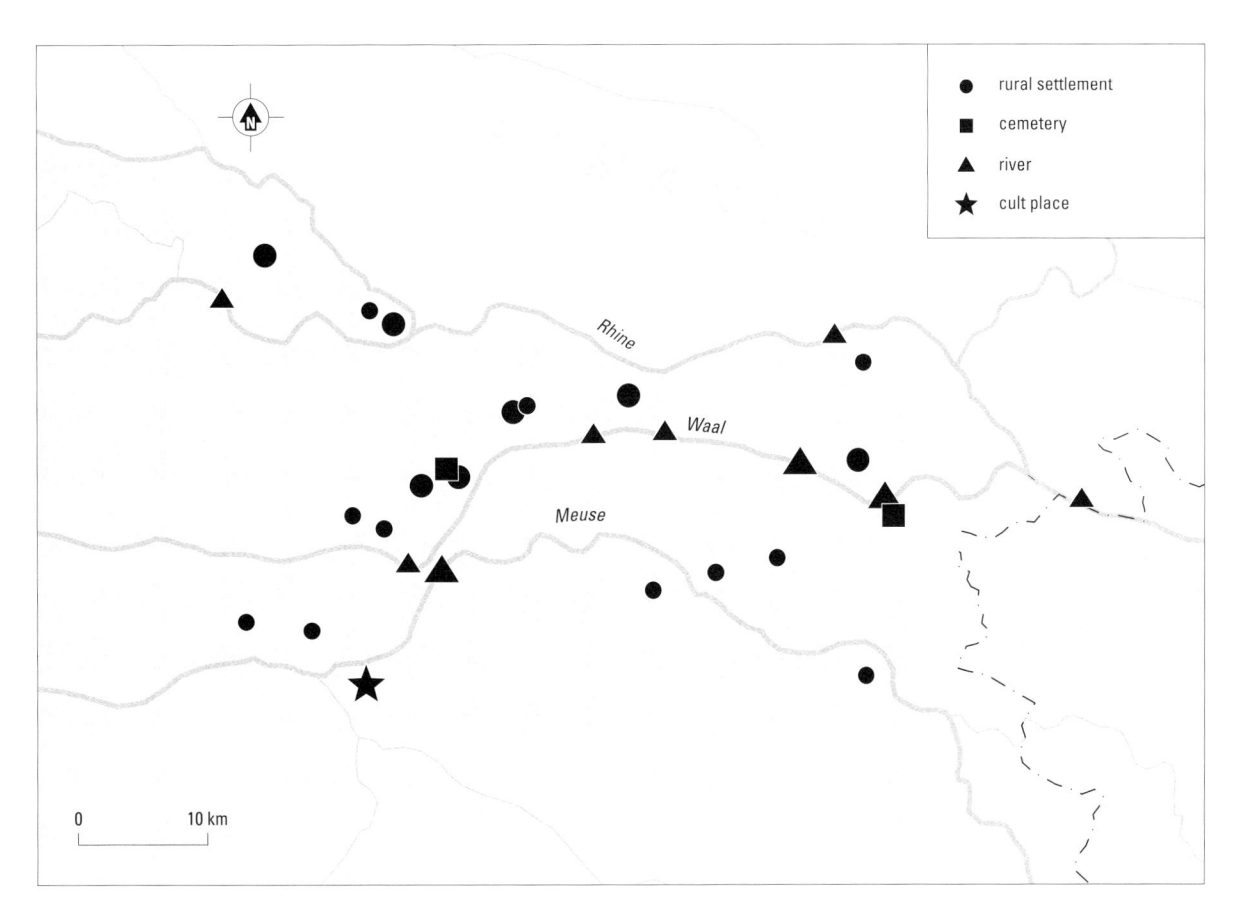

Fig. 6.1. Distribution of lance-, spear- and arrowheads from non-military contexts in the Batavian region (large symbols: 2 or more objects).

spears, slings, bows and arrows, and nets to be the most frequently used hunting weapons.[8] When in pursuit of beasts of prey, hunters could also carry shields, as well as large knives, swords or axes.[9] For the archaeologically traceable lance- and spearheads, arrowheads and sling shot, I will successively determine whether these can be viewed as military items or as hunting weapons.

Lance- and spearheads from non-military contexts are well documented in the research area, despite the frequently poor state of preservation of iron objects. There are 69 examples in total, chiefly from rural settlements (fig. 6.1, pl. 29-33).[10] We cannot establish with certainty the original function of stray finds as these could be used for both military and hunting purposes. The composition of larger, reliably dated assemblages offers more clues. The finds from the eastern Rhine delta are ill-suited for this pur-

[5] See Lauwerier 1988, 90 ff.; Kooistra 1996. The most commonly hunted animals were wild boars, roe deer and red deer.

[6] Pfahl/Reuter 1996, 137, with references. A clue here is the large number of finds of votive inscriptions relating to the Diana cult (Pfahl/Reuter 1996, note 76).

[7] Theuws/Alkemade 2000, 456 ff.; Theuws, in print. See also chapter 7.4.

[8] Pfahl/Reuter 1996, 137-138, with references. See for example. Levi 1971, figs. 89 (lance, sword), 91 (spear/lance, axe), 148 (lance), 151 (spear/lance, bow and arrow, sword, shield); see also Dunbabin 1999, with several examples.

[9] Junkelmann 2002, 19; see also Fischer 2002, 13.

[10] In addition, some of the boltheads could be part of light spears used for hunting (see Baatz 1966, 206). The iron butt spikes attached to the base of a lance or spear are omitted here as these could also be part of *pila*. There are 11 documented examples of such spikes from the Batavian region (pl. 34).

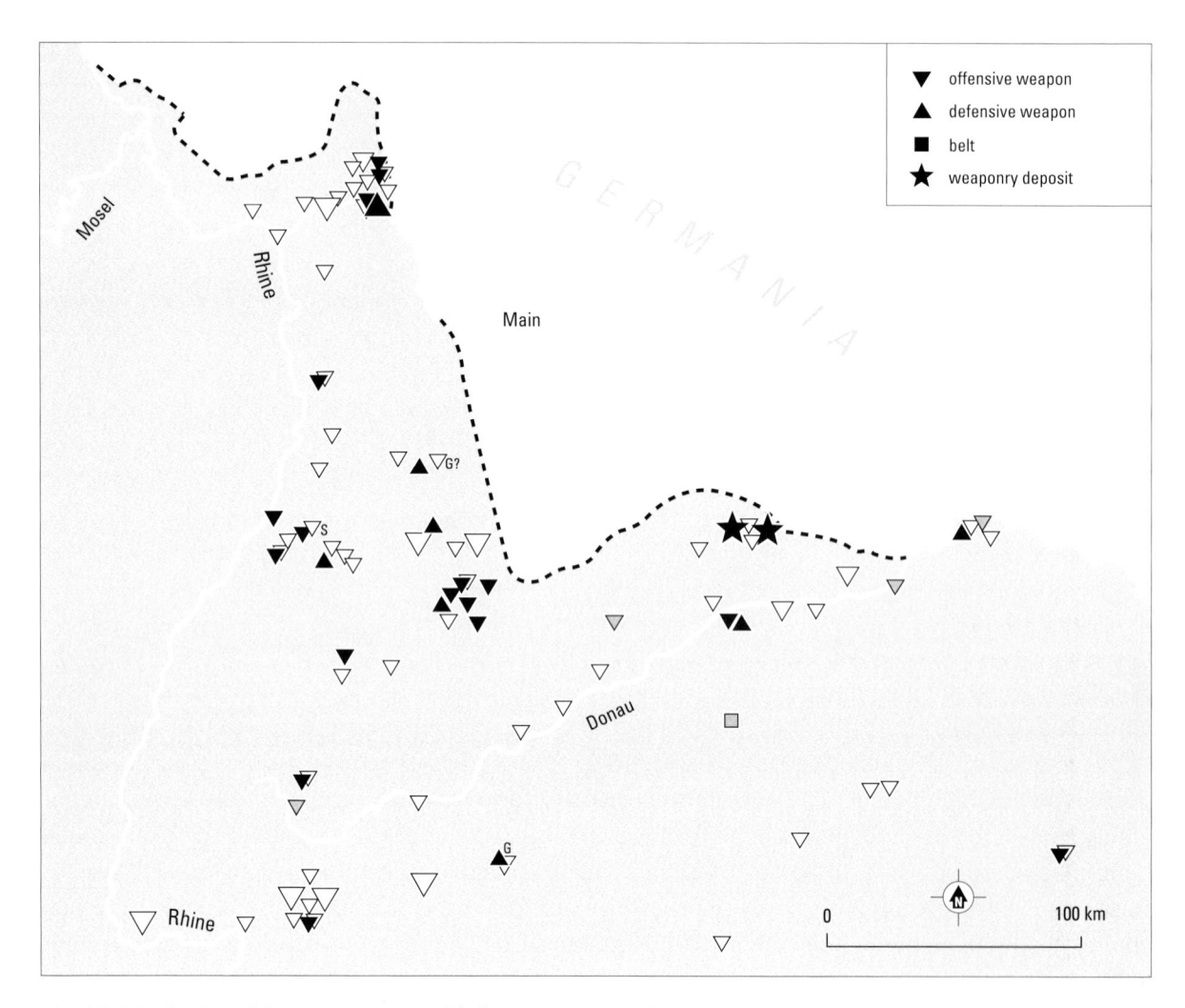

Fig. 6.2. Distribution of Roman weapons and belt components in the Agri Decumates and neighbouring area south of the Danube (grey symbols: period 2; black: period 3; white: non-securely dated spear-, lance-, arrow- and boltheads and butt spikes; G: grave; S: military standard; large symbols: 2 or more finds). Partially redrawn from Pfahl/Reuter 1996, *Beilage* 1.

pose, however, because they comprise almost exclusively stray material with no context dating. Exceptions are five lance- and spearheads from a cemetery and two associated settlements at Tiel-'Passewaaij' (241.1-2, 242.7-9, table 3.3). The find contexts suggest that four of these objects date from the 2nd and 3rd centuries, the period for which no distinctly military finds are documented from these sites. We see the same picture in Houten-'Zuid 8A', where both spearheads date from the 2nd century (128.2-3, table 3.4).[11] For the purpose of comparison, we can examine the situation in the Agri Decumates and the neighbouring region south of the Danube (fig. 6.2). Lance- and spearheads feature in roughly half of the over 80 rural settlements from the 1st to the 3rd century AD where weaponry and horse gear have been found. As almost no defensive weaponry occurs, we can safely conclude that the majority of the finds were civilian hunting weapons.[12] This picture appears to be confirmed by finds from the rural settlement of Breda-'Steenakker', in what was probably the territory of the Frisiavones.[13] The deep-litter barn of

---

[11] Also from Wijk bij Duurstede-'De Horden' are two dateable lanceheads, one from the 1st century AD and one from the 2nd (291.24-25, table 3.1).

[12] Pfahl/Reuter 1996, 136-138.

[13] Brandenburgh et al. 2002; Harry Van Enckevort, pers. comm. (dating).

a 3rd-century byre house yielded arrow-, spear- and lanceheads, which – given their association with a large fish hook – were probably used for hunting.

Arrowheads are represented to a lesser extent in finds from the research region (9x, pl. 35). Unlike the previous category of finds, these corroded objects are difficult to identify, and as a result are probably strongly underrepresented. Because the number of typologically dateable arrowheads from the research area is too small to observe chronological patterns, interpretation becomes problematical. Also, context datings are not available in most cases. The only indication of non-military use is a possible arrowhead from a *tumulus* grave at Esch (87.1). In view of the other grave goods, this grave dates from the second half of the 2nd century and belongs to a civilian.[14] Finds from the Agri Decumates and the neighbouring area once again make for an interesting comparison. As with spear- and lanceheads, arrowheads occur here fairly regularly in the countryside (14x), again making an interpretation as hunting weapons the most plausible. A relevant find is an unfinished arrowhead, which was probably produced locally for private use.[15]

Sling shot comprises the last type of hunting weapon, with a distinction between lead and baked clay shot. The lead shot is primarily known from army camps, with military use also evident in references to the army unit on some of the shot.[16] Since surprisingly few of these objects, which are often well-preserved and easy to identify, have been found in the Batavian countryside (13x, pl. 36), this would seem to rule out their general use as a hunting weapon.[17] This is in contrast to the baked clay examples, which occur frequently in rural settlements up until the pre-Flavian period.[18] It has been suggested that the shot is linked to local conflicts.[19] This is unlikely in the context of the Roman empire, however, and we should assume a primary function as a hunting weapon.

The interpretation of spear-, lance- and arrowheads as hunting weapons does not preclude the possibility that some were brought home by veterans. Three spearheads from a rich grave in a walled garden tomb at Ulpia Noviomagus (c. 80-100 AD) probably belonged to a veteran (207.2-4, fig. 5.20).[20] A similar interpretation is probable for an example with an octagonal cross-section from the Lek at Hagestein (105.1, pl. 32). Spearheads of this type date from the late 2nd or 3rd century and are documented above all in Dacia. This particular example may have been a weapon brought home after discharge by a Batavian stationed outside his home region. Finally, a 'military' interpretation is likely for the spear-, lance- and arrowheads from Empel-'De Werf'. Given the composition of the remaining finds, we can assume that at least some of the recovered weapons had been dedicated by veterans.[21]

6.1.3 SWORDS AND DAGGERS: WEAPONS FOR CIVILIAN SELF-DEFENCE

The two most likely categories of weapons carried by civilians for the purpose of self-defence are swords and daggers. For both weapon types, however, civilian use is difficult to confirm archaeologically. One of

---

[14] Van den Hurk 1984, 19. Some of the grave goods are 'female'.
[15] Pfahl/Reuter 1996, cat.nr. 56.
[16] See Bishop/Couston 1993, fig. 25.
[17] Most sling shot is documented from the rural settlement of Wijk bij Duurstede-'De Horden' (291.10-15). One example comes from the cult place of Empel-'De Werf' (82.45).
[18] For the dating, see Van den Broeke 1987, 38. Clay sling shot has been omitted in the inventory of weapon finds from the Batavian *civitas*.
[19] See Schinkel 1994, 165.
[20] Koster (1993, 295-296), however, also interprets the arrowheads as hunting weapons; for an interpretation as memorabilia, see chapter 5.3.5.
[21] See chapters 3.3.3 and 5.3.1.

the few pieces of concrete evidence is finds from the wrecks of merchant ships. A key assumption here is that these vessels belonged primarily to private entrepreneurs.[22]

Parker's inventory reveals that weapons are documented from 11 ships that sank between 25 BC and the 2nd century AD.[23] In seven instances, these are swords. On one occasion, a sword was found together with a dagger, once with a corresponding military belt, and once with a legionary helmet.[24] Further, one or more helmets are documented from four ships. A sword found in a shipwreck at Valle Ponti in Italy tells us that this weapon was not part of the ship's cargo.[25] It was found in the crew's quarters, as was apparently also the case with a sword from La Luque in France. Given the weapon's location in relation to the ship's cargo, in association with earthenware showing signs of use, this object too can be associated with the crew.[26] Parker is probably correct in interpreting the swords and dagger as private property for defending the ship against pirates.[27] This explanation does not seem to hold true for the helmets, which must have belonged to soldiers who were on board as travellers or as captives, or whose job it was to protect imperial goods or military facilities. A further possibility is that the helmets were being transported as military merchandise.

Given the danger of piracy, it is unsurprising that sailors carried weapons. But how essential was it for the inhabitants of towns and the countryside to purchase swords or daggers? The specific reference in the *Lex Julia* to the fact that 'travellers by land and sea' had the right to bear arms leads us to deduce that this was generally not really necessary for inhabitants of the Roman empire. Once a regular series of forts was established under Claudius, the *limes* for a long time provided a secure border. Public order was maintained by means of military and semi-military posts in towns and along major roads. In addition, the Roman government sought to prevent revolts from breaking out by imposing a ban on maintaining armed groups and stockpiling weapons.

This all came to an end when the empire was threatened by incursions from 'Germanic' groups – initially in about 170 and again during the 3rd century.[28] In the frontier regions of the empire, we see archaeological evidence of this threat in the fortification of urban settlements, several find horizons of metal hoards and ultimately the abandonment of many settlements in the 3rd century.[29] A period of unrest also dawned for the eastern Rhine delta. It is significant that Ulpia Noviomagus was fortified with a canal, a stone wall and a rampart at the end of the 2nd century, yet was nevertheless struck by fire several years later.[30] Following renewed attacks, the town was abandoned once and for all in the third quarter of the following century. The cult place of Empel-'De Werf' was also partly destroyed towards the end of the 2nd century and appears, in view of the coin finds, to have been in operation until about 235 at the

---

[22] For the involvement of private individuals in shipping, see Von Petrikovits 1985, 323-328. See also the mentions of merchants on votive inscriptions to Nehalennia, from the Oosterschelde at Coleinsplaat (Stuart/Bogaers 2001, 34-37); in none of the cases did this involve military dealers or shipmasters.

[23] A.J. Parker 1992, nrs. 126 (Cabrera: three bronze helmets), 307 (Chrétienne: short sword, dagger), 610 (La Luque: sword), 1017 (Ses Salines: helmet, sword), 1141 (Terrasini: two swords), 1176 (San Domino: short sword?), 1206 (Comacchio: sword); Feugère 1993, 266 (Gruissan: bronze helmet; Moro Boti: two iron helmets; Saint Jordi: iron helmet); Bernard et al. 1998 (Porto-Vecchio: sword and belt). Parker has examined the inventory of about 500 ships from the Roman period. The small number of weapon finds can be explained by the fact that the weapons were the personal property of the crew and will generally have been brought to safety.

[24] The military origin of the belt is attested to by the decoration on both fittings of a standing Mars in military attire (Bernard et al. 1998, 80).

[25] A.J. Parker 1992, nr. 1206.

[26] A.J. Parker 1992, nr. 610.

[27] For possible interpretations, see A.J. Parker 1992, 30, 82, 410; Feugère 1993, 267-268; Bernard et al. 1998, 81.

[28] For an overview, see Van Es 1981, 44 ff.

[29] See MacMullen 1967, 129 ff.; Fischer 1999, 129 ff.

[30] Van Enckevort/Thijssen 2001, 105.

Fig. 6.3. Iron knife and sheath from the 'Grote Markt' in Nijmegen. The wooden, leather-clad sheath is held together by two bronze bands, to which are attached pelta-shaped decorations. Length 25.5 cm. Photo Museum het Valkhof, Nijmegen.

latest.[31] The impact of attacks on rural settlements is more difficult to demonstrate, given that the original surface with possible burn layers has been frequently disturbed. Nevertheless, it is clear that the majority of the settlements were abandoned in the second half of the 3rd century.[32]

Interestingly, it is precisely in the 2nd and 3rd centuries that we see changes in the composition of 'military' finds from the research area. In contrast to the previous period, the finds are now characterised by an almost complete absence of defensive weaponry, with swords and to a lesser extent daggers constituting the principal categories of weapon. The sword finds consist of two blades, two ivory hilts, a bone pommel, as well as 11 scabbard chapes and 17 scabbard slides (pl. 20-21, 24-25). The dagger is represented by three chapes (pl. 26). Most of the weapons were recovered from rural settlements (16x), and three scabbard slides and a scabbard knob from Ulpia Noviomagus. The find of a single-edged knife in a grave from c. 200 AD at the site of the 'Grote Markt' in Nijmegen (fig. 6.3) also demonstrates that the inhabitants of Ulpia possessed weapons.[33] The knife and accompanying sheath strongly resemble a dagger in shape and appear to have been worn as a weapon on a belt around the waist. Finally, six sword finds are documented from rivers and a scabbard chape was found in Empel-'De Werf'.

The arming of civilians can also be demonstrated for the Cananefatian region. Until about 100 AD, there were military harbours on the 'Marktveld' and 'De Woerd' sites located at Valkenburg south of the army camp.[34] Native farms appeared on the 'Marktveld' site in the 2nd century, whereas 'De Woerd' was organised as a military *vicus*. Several sword components made of bone date from this phase (fig. 6.4).[35] In addition to two hilts, these are five rectangular scabbard chapes. With the exception of a scabbard knob from a ditch near the *vicus*, the objects were found in the rural settlement and an adjacent ditch.

The Agri Decumates and neighbouring area are once again a good parallel for the situation in the Lower Rhine (fig. 6.2). With the exception of the throwing weapons, the weaponry consists primarily of swords and scabbard components that belong typologically to the 2nd and 3rd centuries (13x). Two daggers and a dagger chape date from the same period. Although some of the weapons may be linked to veterans, this does not explain the sizeable quantity of sword finds.[36] The weapons have been dated primarily to the second half of the 3rd century, the final habitation phase of the rural settlements. Pfahl

---

[31] Roymans/Derks 1993, 482; 1994, 25.

[32] See the settlements discussed in chapter 3.3.1.

[33] Den Boesterd 1959; Gerhartl-Witteveen/Hubrecht 1990, nr. 11. In both publications, this object has incorrectly been labelled a dagger; the 1993 restoration revealed it to be a knife (Louis Swinkels, pers. comm.).

[34] Van Dierendonck/Hallewas/Waugh 1993.

[35] Verhagen 1993, 366-372; cat. nr. 74 has incorrectly been interpreted as a scabbard slide.

[36] An indication of the military origin of some of the swords is four hoards containing clearly military material, as well as two stray finds of parade helmets. Also documented from this region are three military diplomas dating to about the mid-2nd century (Pfahl/Reuter 1996, *Anhang*).

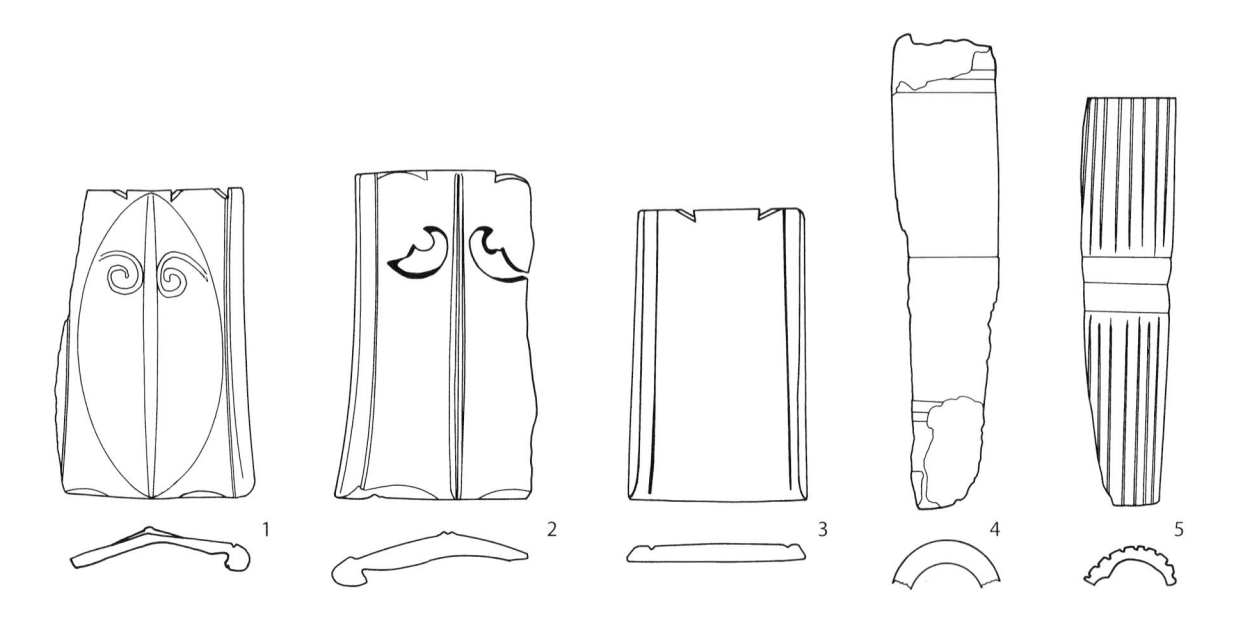

Fig. 6.4. Bone *spathae* components (period 3) from two rural settlements at Valkenburg. Scale 2:3. After Verhagen 1993, figs. 15-17. 1-2, 4-5 scabbard chapes and sword hilts from Valkenburg-'Marktveld'; 3 scabbard chape from Valkenburg-'De Woerd'.

and Reuter point out that the weakened *limes* offered little guarantee of security in this period, forcing the rural population to seek protection against raids by arming itself.[37]

We see a comparable situation in Xanten (Colonia Ulpia Trajana), which has yielded over 300 weaponry and horse gear components from the 2nd and 3rd centuries. With 24 finds, swords make up the principal weapon group.[38] Lenz emphasises that the weapon components originate mainly from the most recent find horizon and date from the period AD 250 to 276. He suggests that the concentration of finds in certain parts of the town indicates that small military units were garrisoned there.[39] Although this interpretation would explain the finds from *insulae* 20 and 27, eleven finds were distributed more widely across the town and in the harbour immediately to the north. The dating of the finds suggests that they were components of swords worn by the town's inhabitants to protect themselves in a time of unrest.

The picture just described ties in well with that painted by MacMullen of the imperial frontier zones.[40] After the army camps along the Rhine were destroyed by invading 'Germans' in the course of the 3rd century, Rome could no longer guarantee the security of its provinces. Urban centres like Nijmegen and Xanten were fortified and, presumably, continued to be protected by military detachments and possibly armed civilians for some time.[41] With the collapse of the *limes*, however, the rural population was left to fend for itself. Their response, particularly in the hinterland of Cologne, is evident in the fortification of villas, with *burgi* often erected on the villa sites.[42] Of interest for the interpretation of weapon finds is that wealthier farmers established small, private militias to protect their families and estates from being plundered.[43] It seems reasonable to assume that farmers who did not have these militias also armed

[37] Pfahl/Reuter 1996, 138-140, 143; see also Fischer 2002, 14.
[38] Lenz 2000, 38-47, Taf. 61-64.
[39] Lenz 2000, 77-79, Taf. 65 (compare Taf. 66-67: other weapon types and horse gear); 2001, 588-590.
[40] MacMullen 1967, 129 ff.; see also Luttwak 1976, 159 ff.
[41] Veterans may have played an important role here (MacMullen 1967, 129-130).
[42] For an overview, see Van Ossel 1992, 161-168. The construction of *burgi* occurred between c. AD 275 and 315. As in the Lower Rhine region, many settlements were already abandoned before 275.
[43] MacMullen 1967, 135-139.

themselves and their sons with swords or daggers. We do not know to what extent the finds from the research region are associated with armed militias or with individually armed farmers. The small number of finds from individual sites suggests that the latter is perhaps the more likely (fig. 3.9).

Given the threat of incursions in the second half of the 3rd century, demand for weapons will have been greatest in this period. This does not mean, however, that all the weapons from previous centuries were memorabilia brought back by veterans. Although veterans appear to have played the largest role in the circulation of military items in non-military contexts in the 1st century AD, shipwreck finds show that civilians also carried weapons in this period. This leaves the issue of whether the population of the towns and countryside felt the need to protect itself with swords or daggers in a period of relative calm. As we also see indirectly in the *Lex Julia*, it was above all vulnerable groups like travellers and traders who, as early as the Augustan period, carried weapons for the purpose of self-defence.

6.2 MILITARY–CIVILIAN USE OF THE CINGULUM AND BALDRIC

Since possession of a *cingulum* or baldric did not pose a threat to public order, no legislation exists concerning the bearing of this type of arms by civilians. As with weaponry, items used by civilians cannot be distinguished from the contemporaneous belt and baldric used by the military. The key pointers to military and/or civilian use are the way in which production was organised, and the presence or absence of military imagery on decorative elements.[44]

During the 1st century AD, the *cingulum* was the military belt soldiers used for carrying their sword and dagger. We can see from the evolution of production that the *cingulum* must have become increasingly available to civilians in the course of the 1st century. While we can assume for the pre-Flavian period that the belt was manufactured in military *fabricae* and perhaps initially in Mediterranean towns as well, for the subsequent period we observe the growing role of local, private artisans. The find of a mould for a *cingulum* buckle in the Cananefatian Rijswijk-'De Bult' suggests that belts were made not just in camp villages, but even at the level of rural settlements, probably for private use (fig. 4.4, nr. 4). Different imagery also points to a changing type of use: into the Claudian period, the symbolism specifically targeted the military user, after which more general, often purely decorative elements began to predominate.

Although it is safe to say that belts may have belonged to soldiers and civilians alike, certainly during the Flavian period, the overwhelming majority of 1st-century finds from the eastern Rhine delta appear to be military in nature. This involves a total of 55 buckles and decorative fittings, primarily from rural settlements (fig. 3.10, pl. 37-39). Almost all components are of a pre-Flavian type and therefore date from the period in which belts were produced specifically for soldiers. Military use is underlined by contemporaneous finds of aprons (19x, pl. 47) and dagger frogs (6x, pl. 38). Significantly, several *cingulum* components, including the apron, were probably dedicated in association with military items (shields, plate armour etc.) at the cult place of Empel-'De Werf'; for the most part, these appear to have been brought by veterans.

The *cingulum* continued to be used by soldiers in the 2nd and 3rd centuries. Besides this narrow belt, a wider type occurred that could be fastened with a ring buckle. A total of 65 finds are documented for both belt types (pl. 40-41), once again mainly from rural settlements. Excavations in Ulpia Noviomagus have also yielded various belt components (9x). As in the Flavian period, belts were largely manufactured in private workshops, and the fittings tended to be purely decorative in nature. Only the *vtere felix* fittings,

---

[44] For an overview of production and symbolism, see chapter 4.

designed to protect the belt's wearer against evil and misfortune, have a specific symbolic meaning (fig. 4.17).[45] As this text does not relate specifically to soldiers, belts with these fittings could have belonged to either soldiers or non-soldiers. The same applies to examples with the purely decorative fittings.[46]

In the 2nd and 3rd centuries, the sword was carried on an additional strap, the *balteus* or baldric. Assuming that civilians could also purchase swords in this period, a combined military/civilian use seems feasible for the baldric too. Notably, the finds show a different picture. For the baldric, three *phalerae*, five strap terminals and a pendant are documented in the research area (fig. 3.10, pl. 48). Five round fittings featuring a standing eagle were probably also part of the baldric (fig. 2.15, pl. 48). The presence of part of the text *Optime Maxime con(serva) numerum omnium militantium* ('Jupiter, protect all warriors') on two of the terminals and the pendant indicates that these items belonged to military baldrics.[47] The eagle on the fittings ties in with this military symbolism. Despite the fact that most of the baldric finds can probably be associated with veterans, we can expect a blurring of the dividing line between military and civilian use during the course of the 2nd and especially the 3rd century. It seems that civilians bought swords for the purpose of self-defence, and these swords, as in the army, will have been suspended from baldrics.

In the second half of the 4th century, a broad belt – often richly decorated with bronze fittings– made its appearance.[48] Böhme assumes that the chip-carved buckles and decorative fittings were initially centrally manufactured in state workshops.[49] At the same time, we see simpler belt types which, given the specific distribution of variants, were probably made in private workshops. The greater variation in types and decoration from about AD 400 then points to a further differentiation in production.[50] Characteristic of the bronze decorative elements of the different belt types are stylised 'Germanic' animal motifs that may have had a general, protective function.[51] It is assumed that the centrally manufactured belt was part of the insignia of high-ranking soldiers and civilian officials, while the simpler belts were more commonly worn by soldiers and civilians.[52] This picture seems to be substantiated by the finds from the research region. Chip-carved belts occur only incidentally in rural settlements and graves, while the less exclusive examples, in addition to a few grave and river finds, are documented from no less than 43 rural settlements (fig. 3.10, pl. 42-46). The first instance may involve members of the local elite who held a high military or civilian post, while the remaining finds could have belonged to soldiers and civilians alike. The virtual absence of weaponry from the same period makes a civilian interpretation more likely.

We may conclude that the *cingulum* gradually lost significance as a symbol of military status during the 1st century AD. From the Flavian period onward, belts were manufactured in private workshops and appear to have been worn by civilians. The symbolism of the decorative elements confirms the change in user patterns; only in the pre-Flavian period is it correct to speak of imagery of a distinctly military nature. The situation is different with regard to the 2nd- and 3rd-century baldric, which appears to have been primarily used by soldiers. However, like the growing civilian use of swords following the collapse of a stable frontier defence, we can assume that baldrics too showed a gradual shift from military to combined military/civilian use.

---

[45] See chapter 4.2.3. These fittings have not yet been documented in the research area.

[46] For military versus non-military use of the ring buckle belt, see James 1999, 18-21 and Von Schnurbein 1995 respectively.

[47] See chapter 4.2.3.

[48] The baldric was replaced by a narrow belt also worn around the waist. However, this belt has not yet been identified in the archaeological record.

[49] Böhme 1974, 92-97; see also Swift 2000, 201-202.

[50] See chapter 4.1.4.

[51] See chapter 4.2.3.

[52] For an overview, see Swift 2000, 2-3; compare Clarke 1979, 289-291.

6.3 NON-MILITARY USES OF HORSE GEAR

During the Roman era, horses served as breeding animals, as draught animals for pulling light loads, carts or chariots, and as mounts for soldiers and civilians.[53] Horse gear finds from army camps, as well as rural and urban settlements, show that it was customary to richly embellish the leather straps of the harness with bronze fittings and pendants. For the 1st and 2nd/3rd centuries (periods 2 and 3), 397 and 737 horse gear components respectively are documented from non-military contexts in the eastern Rhine delta. Most of the finds come from settlements in the countryside and from the urban centres at Nijmegen. Alongside pieces which will have been brought back by veterans, mainly during the 1st century AD, these appear to largely involve horse gear used by civilians. In order to build up a picture of the non-military types of use of 'military' horse gear in rural and urban settlements, I will explore the following questions:

1. To what extent did the Batavian territory specialise in the breeding and training of horses for the Roman army, with the young animals being harnessed for their first training session in accordance with military practice?
2. Is there a relationship between finds of horse gear and yoke fittings, with horses caparisoned with decorative fittings and pendants used as draught animals?
3. Was it customary to harness civilian mounts with bronze decorative elements, and if so, was this for decorative reasons or for symbolic reasons as well?

6.3.1 LOCAL HORSE BREEDING TO SUPPLY THE ROMAN ARMY

In recent years, the local breeding of horses for the Roman army has been a recurring theme in Dutch archaeology. This has been prompted by finds of rather large quantities of horse bones in rural settlements in the research region. The assumption is that there was a specialisation in horse breeding, alongside cattle raising, possibly one of the pillars of the Lower Rhine economy.[54] This would link horse gear finds to the training of young horses before they were sold to the army.[55] To test this hypothesis, I will first briefly discuss the army's acquisition of horses. I will then outline the existing evidence for specialist horse breeding in the research area, before exploring its relationship to horse gear finds from rural and urban settlements.

As a rule, cavalrymen were equipped with mounts through the army.[56] An exception is the period leading up to the Augustan reforms, when soldiers from the irregular auxiliary had to supply their own equipment and presumably their own horses. The military acquisition of horses followed a standard procedure that began with an application to the provincial governor or a high-ranking official.[57] The approval of such an application by the governor of Syria Coele shows that these animals were not supplied by the soldiers or units themselves, but that a central application had to be made for a specific soldier:[58]

---

[53] See White 1970, 288 ff.; Toynbee 1973, 167 ff.

[54] See Laarman 1996, 377; Roymans 1996, 82; Hessing 1994, 229; 2001, 162.

[55] Above all Hessing 2001, 168.

[56] R.W. Davies 1969; 1989, chapter 7; Hyland 1990, chapter 5.

[57] R.W. Davies 1969, 435-437, 449-452; 1989, 154-158; compare the admission procedure for troops (see chapter 5.1.1). Given the large number of new horses that must have been requested each year, the animals will not have been assigned by the governor or another high official himself, but by a lower-ranking official acting on his authority.

[58] *P. Dur.* 56 (= Fink 1971, nr. 99a); translation R.W. Davies 1969, 436. Compare *P. Dur.* 56, 58 (= Fink 1971, nrs. 99b-c, 100).

Marius Maximus to Valentinus
Received 16 March, AD 208

Enter in the records according to the regular procedure a horse, four years old, reddish, masked, without brands, approved by me; assign it to Julius Bassus, trooper of cohors XX Palmyrenorum under your command, at one hundred and twenty-five denarii, and make note [in the records?] with effect from 29 May(?), AD 208.

Once horses had passed the initial military inspection, they were consigned with a letter like this to the relevant unit. The animals now had the status of *probatus*, as attested by a list of animals from Dura Europos.[59] The same list reveals that the horses were about four years old at the time, the age at which they are fully grown and can be trained. Training would take place at a training ground (*campus*) near an army camp and under the supervision of the *magister campi*.[60] After successfully completing a lengthy course of military training, the horse became a *signatus*. This is also the time when the intended horseman first received his horse.

During the first half of the 3rd century, horses deemed suitable could be purchased by a cavalryman for a fixed sum of 125 *denarii*.[61] As with weaponry and horse gear, this amount was probably deducted in instalments from the soldier's pay. Once paid off, the horse became the property of the cavalryman, and on discharge or death, its value – if the horse was still serviceable – will have been paid out to the soldier or his next of kin respectively.[62] As we assume to have been the case with military equipment, a veteran probably also had the option of keeping his mount and taking it home.[63]

Hyland points out that there were several ways of obtaining the horses supplied through the army.[64] The brand marks mentioned in the list from Dura Europos show that the horses came from at least three different stud farms. Most of the animals will have been supplied by local stud farms, with the horses acquired as tribute (later taxation) on the one hand and through regular trading on the other. Imperial stud farms may also have been involved in supplying horses. Although we only have evidence of this from Spain, Thracia and Asia Minor during the late Roman period, such stud farms presumably played a role in previous centuries as well.[65] Finally, as in the period of the earliest *auxilia*, it was customary for some recruits to provide their own horse during the late Roman period.

In the case of the Batavians, we know that they were exempt from taxation and supplied large numbers of troops for the auxiliary instead. Although it is not clear whether supplying horses was part of this exemption, skeletal material from rural settlements shows that the organisation of the Rhine *limes* went hand in hand with intensified horse breeding. The chief evidence for this is the sharp increase in the percentage of horses compared with cattle, sheep/goats and pigs. Whereas horses made up an average 5% of domestic animals kept during the Iron Age, a figure of 20% was not unusual in the Roman period.[66] In

---

[59] *P. Dur.* 97 (= Fink 1971, nr. 83); R.W. Davies 1989, 159. Some of the horses listed here were already trained and had attained the status of *signatus*. For the status of *aestimatum*, see R.W. Davies 1989, 164-165.

[60] R.W. Davies 1989, 93 ff., 163-164.

[61] R.W. Davies 1989, 164; Hyland 1990, 85-86; in the late Roman period the value of a horse was set at 20 *solidi* (Hyland 1990, 85-86, table 1). M.P. Speidel (1994, 109) assumes that the cavalrymen in the imperial bodyguard also had to pay for their mounts themselves.

[62] Compare chapter 5.2.3 for weaponry and horse gear.

[63] In view of the shoulder height (150 cm), Van der Kamp and Polak (2001, 23-24) believe that a horse from the rural settlement of Beuningen-'Molenstraat' was brought by a veteran. It may also have been a breeding horse acquired through the army.

[64] Hyland 1990, chapter 5, for an overview, p. 77.

[65] See R.W. Davies 1989, 167-168; Hyland 1990, 76-77.

[66] Roymans 1996, table 5; Lauwerier/Robeerst 2001, table 1. Compare the situation in the Cananefatian settlement Rijswijk-'De Bult' (Clason 1978, fig. 210).

a few settlements, we even observe a jump to over 30%.[67] Data from Kesteren-'De Woerd' shows that this represented a rapid acceleration: horses there accounted for 9% of domestic animals in the pre-Claudian period, and for 20-30% in the 3rd century.[68] Finds from Tiel-'Oude Tielseweg' and Houten-'Zuid 21' demonstrate that horses are not equally represented in all Batavian settlements.[69] In the case of Tiel, the percentage of horse bones remains below 15%, while the figure in Houten does not rise above 10%.

A second clue to intensified horse breeding was the changing shoulder height of horses after the Roman occupation. Fluctuating between 125 and 140 cm during the middle and late Iron Ages, we observe a marked increase in the Roman period, with horses of over 150 cm occurring.[70] The role of larger horses in local breeding can be linked to the army's need for mounts that were bigger than the native breeds.[71] The large number of smallish horses documented from Batavian settlements until well into Roman times shows that horses were not bred exclusively according to Roman standards.[72] The army also needed smaller horses for use as draught animals.[73]

Finally, the presence of foals can be associated with horse breeding. For example, Druten-'Klepperhei' (7x), Wijk bij Duurstede-'De Horden' (6x), Kesteren-'De Woerd' (1x) and Tiel-'Passewaaijse Hogeweg' (1x) have yielded bones of horses that died before the age of 15 months.[74] It is conspicuous, however, that young animals are entirely absent from some of the rural settlements with a relatively high percentage of horses. The assumption is that these locations were used for training animals from neighbouring studs, and not for breeding.[75] Although a differentiated breeding and training programme remains a possibility, there may be another explanation for the absence of young animals. It is probable that the horses grazed for most of the year in the floodplain areas, with the foals often born in the wild.

We can conclude that horse breeding intensified in the eastern Rhine delta shortly after the Roman occupation. However, the number of horses is too small to speak of *specialised* breeding. Besides horses, a significant part of the livestock was made up of cattle and to a lesser extent sheep and goats. We should therefore speak in terms of mixed animal husbandry, with a partial shift in emphasis toward horse breeding in the Roman period. The rapid increase in the shoulder height of horses in the Lower Rhine region tells us that farm practices were adapted in response to army demand. Finds of military equipment brought home by veterans in settlements where horse bones have been found in sizeable quantities show that former soldiers probably played a crucial role in this development. Not only did this group have the right contacts for setting up trade in horses, they also had access to the right breeding stock.

The key question is whether there is a link between intensified horse breeding and the presence of horse gear in almost every rural settlement in the research region. The idea is that the farms were involved not only in breeding horses, but also in training them before they were sold on to the army. Hessing even speculates about whether the horse gear, as well as some of the weapons found, can be associated with mock battles held in and around the settlements as part of training.[76] However, with regard to training, we need to distinguish between the initial, basic training on the farms, and specific military training under army supervision. Significantly, most of the horses in the list from Dura Europos

---

[67] These are Wijk bij Duurstede-'De Horden' (Laarman 1996, table 67), Druten-'Klepperhei', phase III (Lauwerier 1988, table 37) and Kesteren-'De Woerd', phase d (Zeiler 2001, table 9.12).

[68] Zeiler 2001.

[69] Maaike Groot, pers. comm. (Tiel); De Vries/Laarman 2001, table 7 (Houten).

[70] Lauwerier/Robeerst 2001, table 2.

[71] Roymans 1996, 82; Lauwerier/Robeerst 2001, 277-279.

[72] Some of these may have been mules.

[73] R.W. Davies 1989, 153 ff.; for the military use of smaller horses and mules, see Junkelmann 1990, 42-43.

[74] Lauwerier 1988, table 76 (Druten); Laarman 1996, table 63 (Wijk bij Duurstede); Zeiler 2001, table 9.41 (Kesteren); Maaike Groot, pers. comm. (Tiel).

[75] See Lauwerier 1988, 163.

[76] Hessing 2001, 168.

Fig. 6.5. Image of two oxen with a Gallo-Roman double yoke and a horse with a simpler, probable leather yoke on a grave relief of the *negotiator* Securius from Neumagen (Germany). Dated late 2nd century AD. After Raepsaet 1982, pl. IX, 1 (nr. 21).

are referred to as *probatus*, which means that they had at most undergone basic training. Since it is hard to imagine that horses wore harness richly decorated with bronze work at this initial stage, this cannot explain the enormous number of horse gear components known from rural sites in the eastern Rhine delta. Only functional harness components, like bits and strap junctions, will have been used in the training of young horses.

6.3.2 FINDS OF THE GALLO-ROMAN DOUBLE YOKE AND THE ROLE OF HORSES AS DRAUGHT ANIMALS

Although it was customary for oxen and mules to be employed as draught animals, illustrations on monumental reliefs and coins show that horses were also used, especially for light coaches and carts.[77] Finds of the Roman double yoke at military and non-military sites that have yielded horse gear could suggest that

[77] Raepsaet 1982; 2002; Junkelmann 1990, 64 ff. for a description of the different types of cart, see Junkelmann 1990, 68-72; Schleiermacher 1996, 212-214.

the harness of these draught horses was also embellished with bronze work. Before elaborating further on this use, I will first describe the Roman double yoke on the basis of iconography and archaeological finds. I will then discuss the typochronology of the bronze yoke components and examine the yoke finds from the research region. Finally, I will look at whether draught horses were harnessed with bronze decorative elements in the Roman era and whether there is a relationship between yoke and horse gear finds from the research region.[78]

In Roman times, the same yoke, known as a Gallo-Roman double yoke, was used for harnessing a pair of oxen, mules or horses to a cart. This yoke is well-documented iconographically, for example on a grave relief from Neumagen depicting two oxen attached by a wooden yoke (fig. 6.5). The yoke has a characteristic triangular shape where it rests on the neck of each animal, with bronze loops at the top to guide the reins. The horse shown behind the oxen is not part of this harness system; a simpler yoke, probably made of leather, is used.

The archaeological record contains only a few examples of the double yoke. Partially preserved yokes are documented from cart burials at Inota (ca. 50-120 AD) and Zsámbék, both in Hungary.[79] The yokes are made of wood and the underneath side is reinforced with a thin strip of lead.[80] The whole thing is then covered with leather. As we also see on the grave relief from Neumagen, the yoke is raised at the neck of both draught animals. In the centre of the raised parts is a bronze yoke ring, with two more rings or decorative knobs on the oblique sides. These latter elements penetrate through the yoke and are used to fasten the V-shaped, iron collar that hangs under the horse's neck.[81] Lastly, decorative fittings or additional rein guides are attached to both ends of the yoke.

Because the wooden and iron collars are only preserved under exceptional conditions, finds of the Roman double yoke consist almost solely of bronze components. Here we can distinguish between functional fittings, which terminate at the top in a round loop to guide the rein, and similar fittings with no loop that are purely decorative. Based on securely dated finds from army camps, the yoke fittings can be subdivided typochronologically into the following four groups (fig. 6.6):

A. The first group is derived from late La Tène examples and comprises a rectangular, ribbed fitting (A1) which, in the case of rein guides, terminates at the top in an openwork, heart- or tear-shaped loop (A2). At the base is a semi-circular or rectangular loop for fastening to the yoke. In the light of the finds from Haltern, Kalkriese and Augsburg-Oberhausen, this type is of Augustan origin.[82] The type A fittings probably remained in use during the first half of the 1st century AD.

B. The Claudian period saw the appearance of a new type of yoke fitting that was also rectangular.[83] In addition to examples with a domed centre and a narrow edge at the base (B1), there are more exclusive fittings with a widened foot terminating in six rosette knobs (B2). In the case of the rein guides, the plate on type B1 terminates at the top in a round ring (B3). The yoke fittings were fastened in the same way as the previous type.

---

[78] It is not clear whether the mule harness was also adorned with bronze. This does not appear to be the case with oxen.

[79] Palágyi 1981; 1986 (Inota); 2000, 540-544 (Zsámbék).

[80] For the reconstruction of the yoke, see Palágyi 1981, Taf. XXIV-XXV.

[81] The ends of these collars consist of oval, wooden discs that prevented the draught animal's neck from being pinched (see Junkelmann 1990, 72-77; Alföldy-Thomas 1993, 331 ff.).

[82] Müller 2002, Taf. 93; Franzius 1993, Abb. 42; Hübener 1973, Taf. 13 (nr. 24); for La Tène yoke fitting, see Van Endert 1991, Taf. 18; Schlott 1999, Taf. 9 (nr. 6), 13 (nrs. 10-11).

[83] Ritterling 1904, Taf. III (nr. 38); 1909, Taf. X (nr. 44, 48); Ulbert 1969a, Taf. 35 (nrs. 11-12); Frere/Wilkes 1989, fig. 74 (nr. 51).

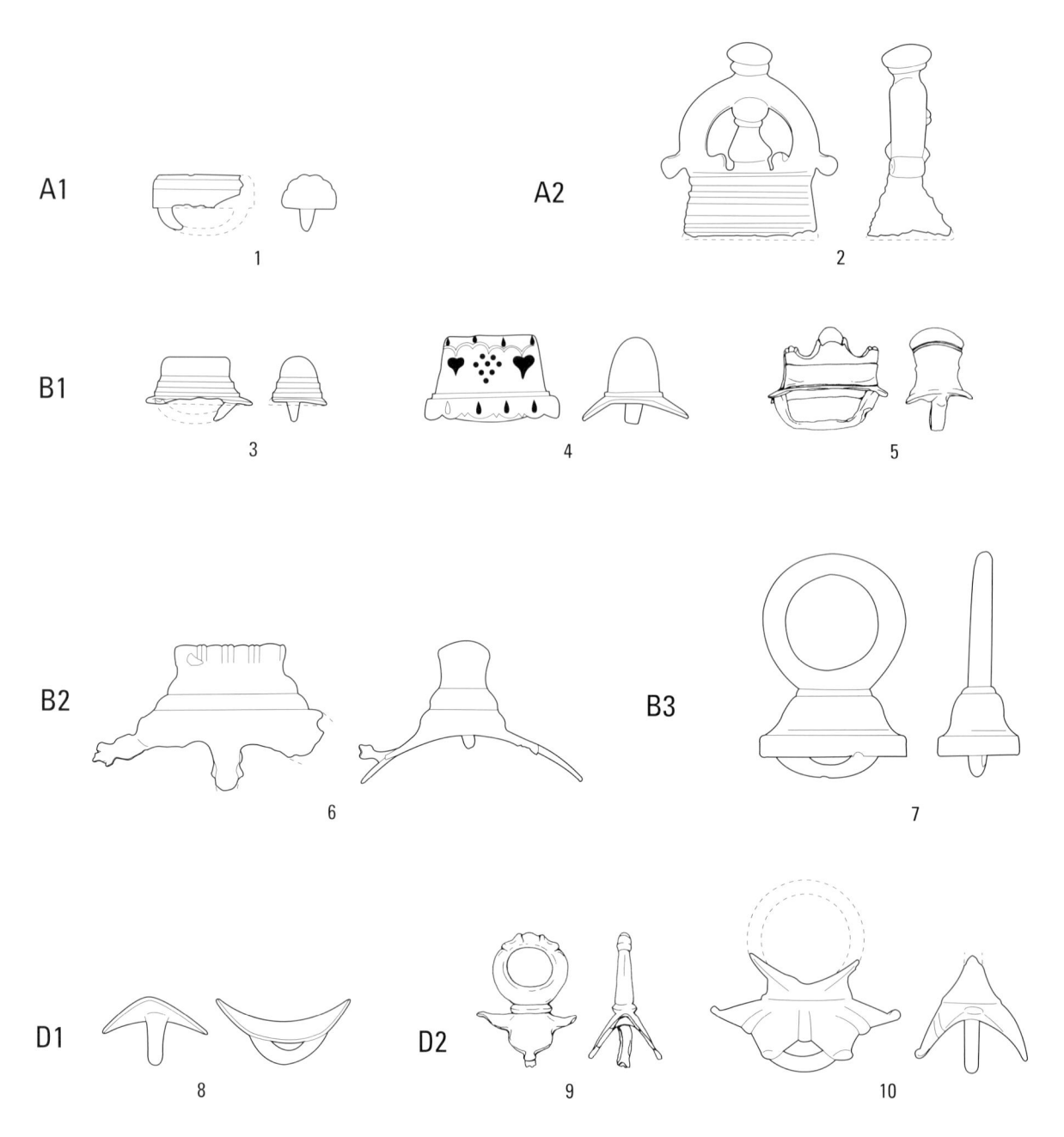

Fig. 6.6. Finds of bronze rein rings and yoke fittings for a wooden double yoke from rural settlements in the research region (no drawings of type C available). Scale 1:2. Based partly on Krist/De Voogd/Schoneveld 2002, figs. 9.11-12; partly redrawn from Wesselingh 2000, figs. 155, 159.
1 Maurik-'Parkstraat'; 2, 10 Oss-'Westerveld'; 3 Altforst; 4 Erichem-'Hooge Korn'; 5, 9 Houten-'Loerik'; 6-7 Tiel-'Oude Tielseweg'; 8 Ommeren-'Oude Eng'.

C. In the early 2nd century, type B was replaced by a yoke fitting with a round and flattish base (type C).[84] The base and the loop were joined by a narrow 'neck'. An example from Neupotz shows that this yoke fitting was used until well into the 3rd century.[85] Decorative fittings of this type are unknown.

D. In the last type, the fitting is composed of four leaf-shaped motifs: a suspended leaf at the front and back, and on each side a projecting leaf terminating in a round knob (D1).[86] The rein guides feature simple, round (D2) or more complex, openwork loops (D3). This type was certainly in use from the Flavian period and appears to have occurred until the 3rd century.[87]

Bronze components of the Gallo-Roman double yoke are well documented from military and non-military contexts in the Lower Rhine region (table 6.1, fig. 6.6). There are 65 rein guides and decorative fittings in total, most belonging to type B (41x). For instance, most of the yoke fittings from the *canabae legionis* on the 'Hunerberg' and all from army camps (Vechten and Leiden) and the cult place of Empel-'De Werf' can be assigned to this type. Of the finds from rural settlements (30x), a little over half can be ascribed to type B (16x). The dating of type B fittings to the Claudio-Flavian period is confirmed by the niello decoration, typical for this period, on three examples, as well as the Flavian find context of the pieces from the Nijmegen *canabae*. Finds from rural settlements (type A: 5x) show that the wooden double yoke must already have been in use in the Batavian countryside during the Augustan period. Compared with the 1st-century yoke components, the number of finds that can be dated with certainty to the 2nd and 3rd centuries is extremely small: in addition to one example from a rural settlement, a further three examples of type C are known from Ulpia Noviomagus. The less securely dated examples of type D occur more frequently (16x).

It is vital when interpreting horse gear from the eastern Rhine delta to determine whether the harness of draught horses was embellished with bronze work. A clue here is assemblages with a clear association between yoke and horse gear components in contemporaneous use. Several cart burials that are relevant here have been unearthed in Pannonia. Firstly, there is the above-mentioned burial at Inota, where two draught horses were interred with decorative trappings.[88] The decorative elements comprise *phalera*-shaped strap junctions and similar looped strap mounts with a tear-shaped pendant, all of them tinned and inlaid with niello. The location of the objects in the burial pit suggests that they were decorative bridle components. We encounter a comparable situation with a 3rd-century grave assemblage in Kozármisleny (Hungary), where a cart and two draught horses were interred.[89] Here too, several strap junctions and decorative bridle elements were found around the heads of both animals.

Finds from a grave at Frenz (Germany) demonstrate that the rich adornment of draught horses with bronze was not only customary in the eastern provinces.[90] There the remains of a cart and several horse gear components were found against the outer wall of a tufa coffin from the 2nd or 3rd century.[91] The horse gear consists of a series of decorative fittings, a strap junction and a strap terminal, all in openwork, peltate motifs. We know that these objects adorned horse harness because of two hackamore fragments that were part of the same assemblage.

These examples demonstrate that harness richly embellished with fittings and pendants was used not only for Roman cavalry mounts, but also for draught horses. The research region has not yet yielded any assemblages that show a definite association between the double yoke and horse gear. The only clue to the use of horse gear for draught animals is the presence of contemporaneous horse gear in most of the settlements where yoke components have been found. We see this same picture in the cult place of Empel-'De Werf', which has yielded – in addition to horse gear – several rein rings and the wheel rims and nave

---

[84] Jacobi 1897, Taf. LIX (nrs. 4, 6); M.R. Alföldi et al. 1957, Taf. XLVII (nrs. 1, 6, 18, 22), XLIX (nrs. 1, 4); Jütting 1995, Abb. 15 (nr. 202); compare Junkelmann 1990, Abb. 78.

[85] Alföldy-Thomas 1993, 338, cat.nr. G.22.

[86] Jacobi 1897, Taf. LIX (nrs. 1-3); Swinkels 1993, fig. 7b.

[87] Anjolein Zwart, pers. comm. (context datings Nijmegen-'Hunerberg').

[88] Palágyi 1981, Taf. XXVII-XVIII; for the reconstruction, see Taf. XXIV (nr. 2).

[89] Palágyi 1997; for the dating, see Schleiermacher 1996, 212.

[90] Lehner 1923.

[91] Lehner (1923, 47-53) suspects that the grave had been robbed, with the unattractive metal remains ending up outside the actual burial chamber.

site	type	number	comment	collection/reference
army camp				
Vechten	B3	3	1x lozenge-shaped base; 1x loop with round knob	unknown
canabae legionis				
Nijmegen-'Hunerberg'	B1	2	1x niello inlay	pers. comm. A. Zwart
	B2	1	central, peltate knob	pers. comm. A. Zwart
	B3	16	fixing bar can be replaced by round loops for studs on corners of base	pers. comm. A. Zwart
	D1	4	1x pelta with round knob instead of loop	pers. comm. A. Zwart
urban centre				
Ulpia Noviomagus	C	1	base burnt; fixing bar missing	GNBA, find nr. WW1, 13.0.412
	C misc.	1	peltate loop and round fixing bar	GNBA, find nr. WW1, 4.0.8
	D	1	three leaves and fixing bar missing	GNBA, find nr. MP1, 4.2.123
rural settlement				
Maurik-'De Hucht'	A1	1	fragment	Van Renswoude priv. coll.
Maurik-'Parkstraat'	A1	1	fragment	Vroon priv. coll.
Oss-'Schalskamp'	A1	1	fixing bar broken off	Wesselingh 2000, fig. 202
Oss-'Westerveld'	A2	1	intact; peltate loop with double knob	Wesselingh 2000, fig. 159
	D2	1	loop broken off	Wesselingh 2000, fig. 155
Tiel-'Passewaaijse Hogeweg'	A2?	1	loop fragment with round knob	HBS, find nr. 177.0.11
Altforst	B1	1	bottom side ribbed; fixing bar partly broken off	Vroon priv. coll.
Arnhem-'De Laar 6/7'	B1	1	-	municipality of Arnhem
precise find site unknown	B1	1	intact	unknown
Aalst-'Lienden'	B1	1	fixing bar broken off	Vroon priv. coll.
Erichem-'Hooge Korn'	B1	1	intact; ribbed edge, niello inlay	Vroon priv. coll.
Wijk bij Duurstede-'De Horden'	B1	1	intact, ribbed edge, niello inlay	ROB, find nr. 529.1.15
Houten-'Loerik'	B1	1	intact; upper side in shape of stylised pelta	Krist et al. 2002, fig. 9.12
	D2	1	intact	Krist et al. 2002, fig. 9.11
Tiel-'Oude Tielseweg'	B2	1	ribbed upper side	HBS, find nr. 16.1.1
	B3	1	intact	HBS, find nr. 29.2.1
Wijk bij Duurstede-'De Geer'	B3	1	intact	ROB, find nr. 816.5.44
Ophemert-'Westerbroek I'	B3	1	loop and fixing bar broken off	Vroon priv. coll.
Buren-'Hooge Korn'	B3	1	loop and fixing bar broken off	Van Wiggelinkhuizen priv. coll.
Ophemert-'Westerbroek I'	B3	1	loop and fixing bar broken off	Vroon priv. coll.
Puiflijk	B3	1	intact; iron fixing bar	Zwart 1998a, fig. 12
	D2 misc.	1	pointed knobs along perimeter of loop; iron fixing bar broken off	Zwart 1998a, fig. 13
Tiel-'Passewaaijse Hogeweg'	B3?	1	loop fragment with knob	HBS, find nr. 11.1.999
Groesbeek-'Klein Amerika'	B3?	1	loop and fixing bar broken off	De Jong priv. coll.

Gasperen-'De Stern'	C	1	base and fixing bar broken off	V.d. Brandhof priv. coll.
Rumpt-'De Worden'	D1	1	loop broken off	Wakker priv. coll.
Ommeren-'Oude Eng'	D1 misc.	1	intact; almond-shaped with upright ends	Vroon priv. coll.
Waardenburg-'De Vergt'	D1 misc.	1	intact; almond-shaped with upright ends	Vroon priv. coll.
Bruchem	D2	1	intact	Verhagen priv. coll.
Waardenburg-'De Woerden'	D2?	1	fixing bar fragment, terminating in heavy pin	Vroon priv. coll.
cult place				
Empel-'De Werf'	B3	4	partial set (find nrs. 561, 916); 2x fixing bar broken off	GD'sH, find nrs. 561, 916-917, 949
	B3 misc.	1	intact; lozenge-shaped base	GD'sH., find nr. 520
river				
Loowaard/Kandia	D1	1	intact; single leaf	Kuijpers priv. coll.
	D2	1	loop broken off	Kuijpers priv. coll.
Waal bij Nijmegen	B1	1	intact	RMO, inv.nr. NS 440
	D2	1	round loop and peltate fixing bar	MhV, inv.nr. BE VI.23a

Table 6.1. Decorative fittings and rein rings of the Gallo-Roman double yoke from military and non-military contexts in the eastern Rhine delta.

boxes of a four-wheeled, wooden (cult) cart from the second half of the 2nd century AD.[92] Also found across the cult place were an iron axle arm, as well as decorative elements that were probably attached to a cart: a bronze bust of the moon goddess Luna, a solid, lunate fitting and an elongated, rectangular fitting with a lunate terminal (fig. 6.7).

Despite the possible association between yoke fittings and horse gear from the research region, we see a marked difference if we compare the two find categories chronologically. Whereas the yoke components can be dated primarily to the second half of the 1st century, the horse gear from the eastern Rhine delta exhibits a peak in the 2nd and 3rd centuries. This suggests that increasing use of horses to pull light carts is no explanation for the large number of horse gear finds from period 3. An exception is Ulpia Noviomagus, where both the yoke finds and most of the horse gear items date from the 2nd and 3rd centuries. The situation is different for the early finds. As with the yoke fittings, a significant portion of the 1st-century horse gear appears to belong to the Claudio-Flavian period. If we assume that the yoke is associated not only with oxen and mules, but also with draught horses, some of the decorative elements from this period may have been used for draught horses. The same might apply to the richer, niello-inlay items which – in the light of the burial assemblage at Inota – sometimes embellished the harness of draught animals.

6.3.3 PROTECTIVE SYMBOLS FOR CIVILIAN MOUNTS

A third possible explanation for the large number of Roman horse gear finds from non-military contexts is the use of horses as mounts by civilians. Although some finds may be linked to horses being used as

[92] Roymans/Derks 1994, 30. None of the finds have been published as yet.

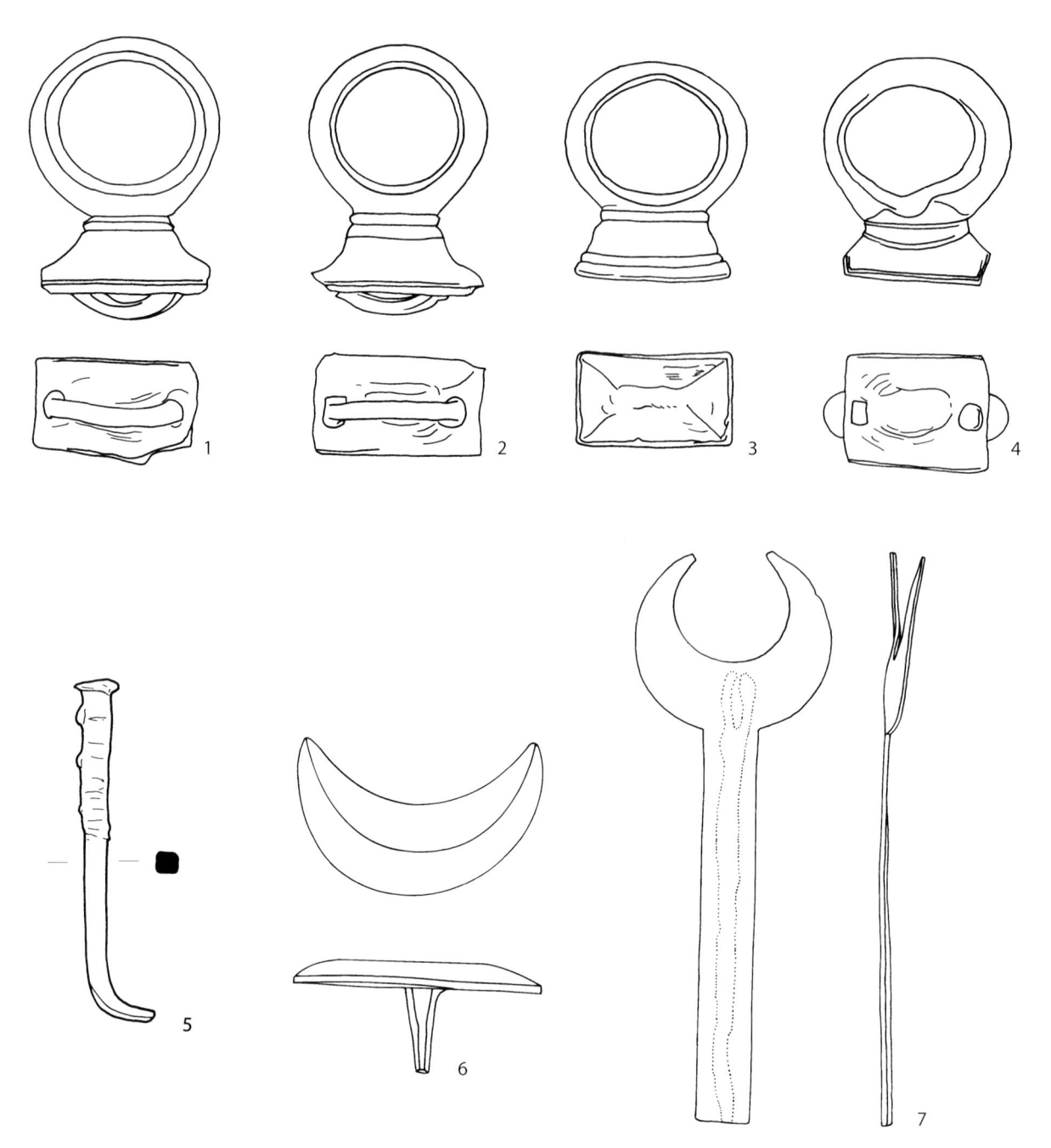

Fig. 6.7. Components of the Gallo-Roman double yoke and a possible cult wagon from the cult place of Empel-'De Werf'. Scale 2:3.
1-4 bronze rein guides from the yoke, 5 iron axle arm, 6-7 bronze decorations with lunula motif.

draught animals, this does not explain the high incidence of horse gear in the 2nd and 3rd centuries (fig. 3.11). It is likely that these finds reflect the everyday use of horses as mounts in towns and in the countryside. In order to discover *why* horse gear was so popular among civilians, I will investigate which motifs occur most frequently in periods 2 and 3 and whether these had a special significance.

A survey of the imagery employed in decorative elements of military equipment reveals that there were several principal themes during the Roman period.[93] Whereas 1st-century finds can be characterised by

[93] See chapter 4.2.

political imagery, with an emphasis on glorification of the imperial family and the symbolism of victory, we see a preference in the following period for a more general, protective symbolism. Subsequently, the late Roman period can be characterised by a fusion with 'German' animal symbolism and Christian motifs, which probably had a protective value as well. I will now use the motifs that occur on *phalerae*, decorative fittings and pendants from the research region, to see whether the symbolism on horse gear shows a similar development.[94]

Like the decoration on contemporaneous swords, belts and helmets, a portion of the 1st-century horse gear bears political imagery. These are the highly prominent *phalerae* and accompanying pendants of exclusive parade gear. Examples are several *phalerae* from Xanten with central busts, probably of a member of the imperial house (fig. 4.10). The accompanying pendants are fashioned in the form of oak leaves, a reference to the *corona* and hence to the symbolism of victory. The busts of Victoria on *phalerae* from the Rhine at Doorwerth (55.34-35, fig. 4.14) and the Waal at Nijmegen (211.63) can be explained in the same way, as can the stylised laurel wreath on a *phalera* from Wijk bij Duurstede-'De Horden' (291.51, pl. 81).

Alongside the exclusive items that feature political imagery, some of the simpler decorative fittings also had a symbolic significance (fig. 6.8). Firstly, these are round fittings decorated with knobs along the outer edge and terminating at the base in a crescent or lunula (A10). The lunula refers to Luna, the goddess of the night, who is often portrayed together with Sol, the sun god.[95] In Roman times, lunula pendants were worn around the neck, especially by women and children, to ward off evil.[96] The moon-shaped motif also symbolised the female sex and was associated with fertility because of the moon's supposed influence on the menstruation cycle. Interestingly, for the fittings, the lunula is often attached to a round upper section, a possible reference to Sol. Fittings referring to the male sexual organ and shaped like a phallus (A13) had a similar significance to the lunula. These symbols were also worn around the neck, this time by men.[97] The overlapping symbolism is underlined by fittings which feature the lunula and phallus in combination. Because of their protective qualities, these symbols were popular not only as pendants, but also as part of military-civilian horse gear; they were supposed to protect cavalrymen and their horses from evil and misfortune.

The protective symbolism of 1st-century horse gear was also expressed in 'bone amulets' worn on a horse's chest. These objects were cut from red deer antler, which was reputed to have the power to ward off misfortune.[98] This power could be strengthened by the addition of certain symbols, the most common of which was the phallus. Among finds from the research region, we encounter this motif on several examples from Vechten (fig. 6.9, nrs. 1-2). The 'Hunerberg' at Nijmegen has yielded an example with an incised vulva (fig. 6.9, nr. 3), a motif whose significance parallels that of the phallus and lunula. Although most of the amulets were probably attached to horse harness in the 1st and 2nd centuries, an example from London with plasterwork on the reverse shows that they could also be affixed to walls.[99]

In the 2nd and 3rd centuries we see an increase in horse gear with a protective symbolism. A number of motifs clearly stand out among the decorative fittings (fig. 6.8). Firstly, simple, round examples, some inlaid with enamel (type B1-B2), were popular decorations. Other common motifs are the pelta (B9),

---

[94] For the 1st-century fittings, the strap junctions and terminals have been omitted, as this permits a better comparison with the material from the 2nd and 3rd centuries.

[95] For the symbolism of the lunula, see *RE* XIII/2 (1927), 1811-1812 (Wickert); Zadoks-Josephus Jitta/Witteveen 1977, 173; Swinkels 1994, 88-89; Kemkes/Scheuerbrandt 1997, 43-44.

[96] For the lunula as a neck ornament, see Zadoks-Josphus-Jitta/Gerhartl-Witteveen 1977, 171-174, pl. 26-28.

[97] See Zadoks-Josephus Jitta/Gerhartl-Witteveen 1977, 174, pl. 28-29. For the symbolism of phalluses, see *RE* XIX/2 (1938), 1681 ff. (Herter). Oldenstein (1976, 158-160) refers to 'persönliche Glücksbringer'.

[98] Hottentot/Van Lith 1990, 187; Greep 1994, 82-84.

[99] Greep 1994, 85; Haalebos 1994c, 705.

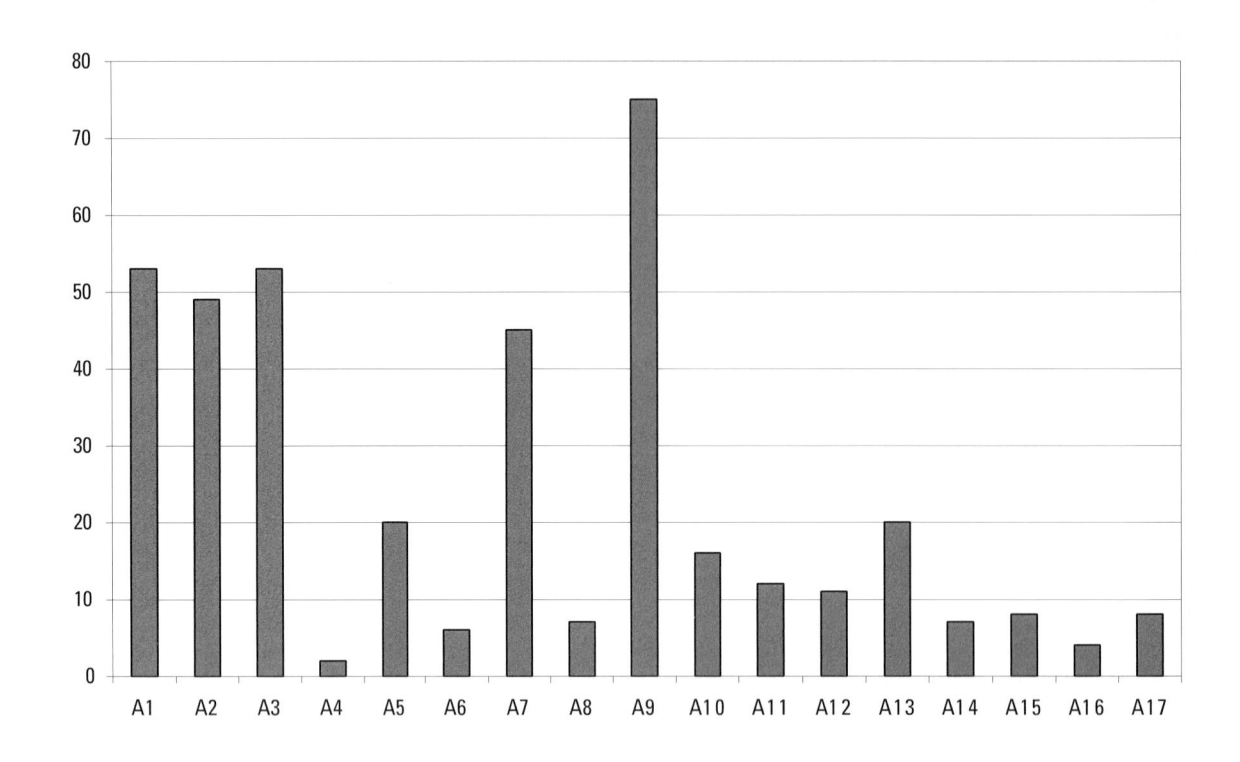

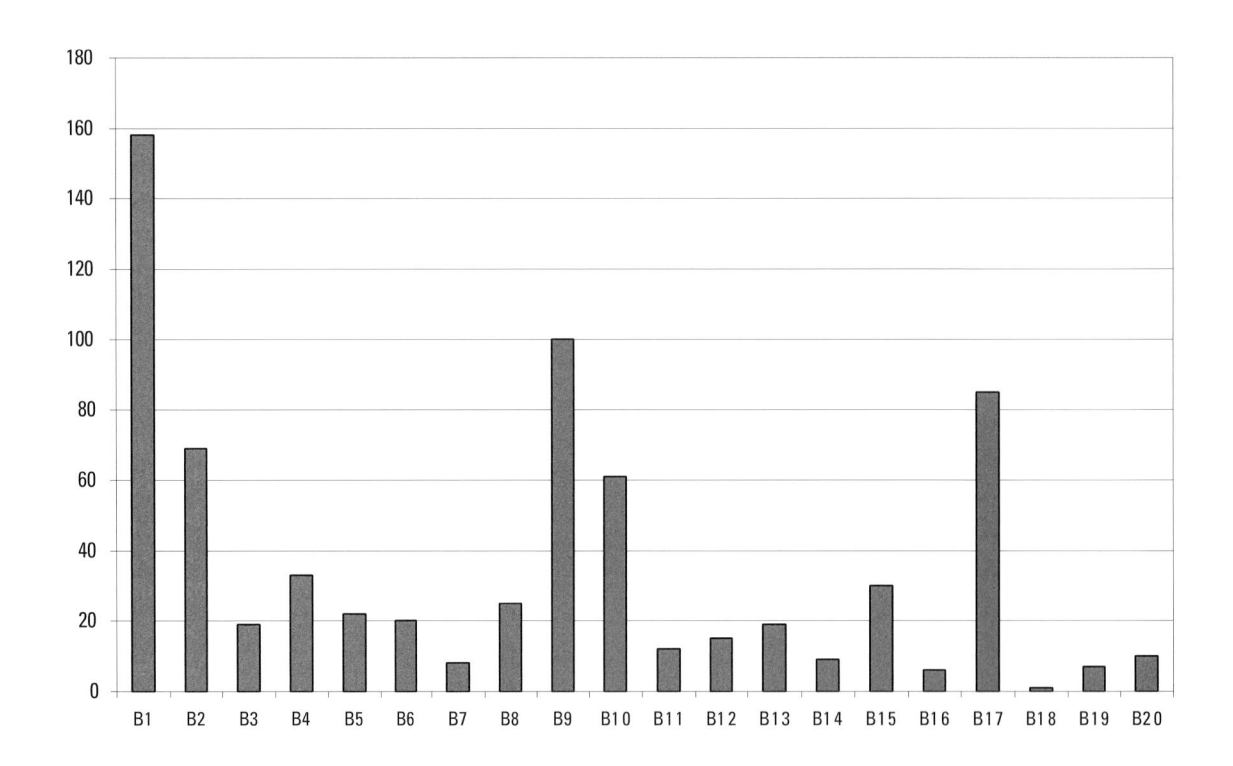

Fig. 6.8. Typological composition of decorative horse fittings from non-military contexts in the Batavian region. Periods 2 (above) and 3 (below).

Fig. 6.9. 'Bone amulets' with phallus and vulva motifs that were probably attached at the horse's chest. Scale 1:1. After Hottentot/ Van Lith 1990, nrs. 6, 8, 11.
1-2 Vechten, 3 Nijmegen-'Hunerberg'.

almond (B10) and vulva (B17). Like the phallic symbols from the previous period, the frequent use of fittings with a vulva motif can be explained by their protective value.[100] It is conspicuous that the lunula (B16) and phallus (B18) occur much less often from the 2nd century onward, and appear to have been replaced by the vulva. The significance of the remaining motifs is unclear; presumably their function was primarily decorative.

If we compare the symbolism of the decorative fittings and pendants, the material from period 2 reveals a similar picture (fig. 6.10). Trefoil and winged pendants (A1-A3), which were tinned and sometimes inlaid with niello and which were part of parade gear, occupy a prominent position. With the exception of the finds from Doorwerth, oak leaves do not occur on these *phalera* pendants, so we can only assume an indirect reference to the symbolism of victory. In addition to decorative, round and tear-shaped pendants (A7), the lunula (A8) and the phallus (A9) are frequently occurring motifs for this horse gear component.[101] The phallic pendants consist of a male sex organ terminating on the reverse in an arm with a stylised hand. The hand is closed, with the index finger extended or the thumb inserted between the index and middle fingers.[102] In the latter case, this is a reference to the sexual act and hence to fertility. The centre of the pendant features a second, frontal phallus, which further emphasises the object's symbolism. As with decorative fittings, the pendants with lunate and phallic motifs may be regarded as protective symbols.[103]

[100] In some of the almond-shaped fittings too, a stylised vulva is depicted by means of a central rib (pl. 76).

[101] The lunula can also be made up of two wild boar teeth attached back to back (Kemkes/Scheuerbrandt 1997, 44, fig. 8).

[102] See Zadoks-Josephus Jitta/Peters/Gerhartl-Witteveen 1973, 52-57.

[103] See also Deschler-Erb 1999a, 54-55.

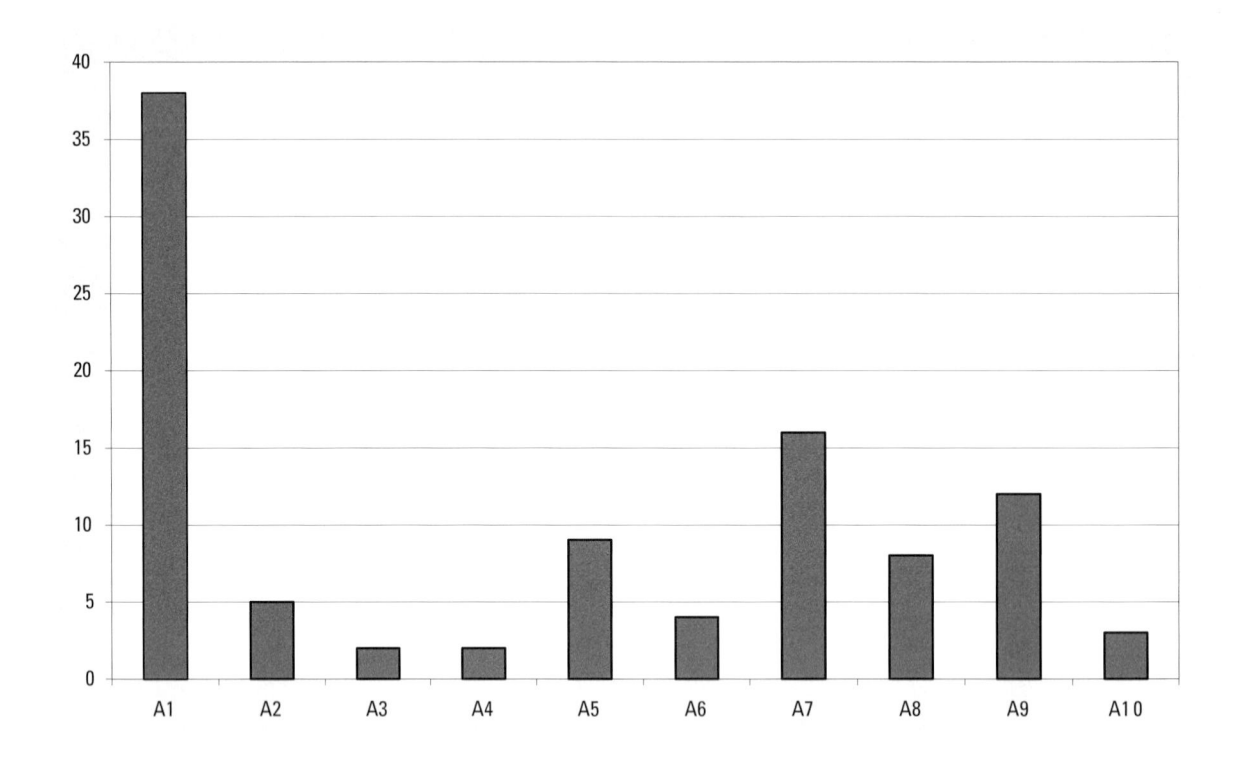

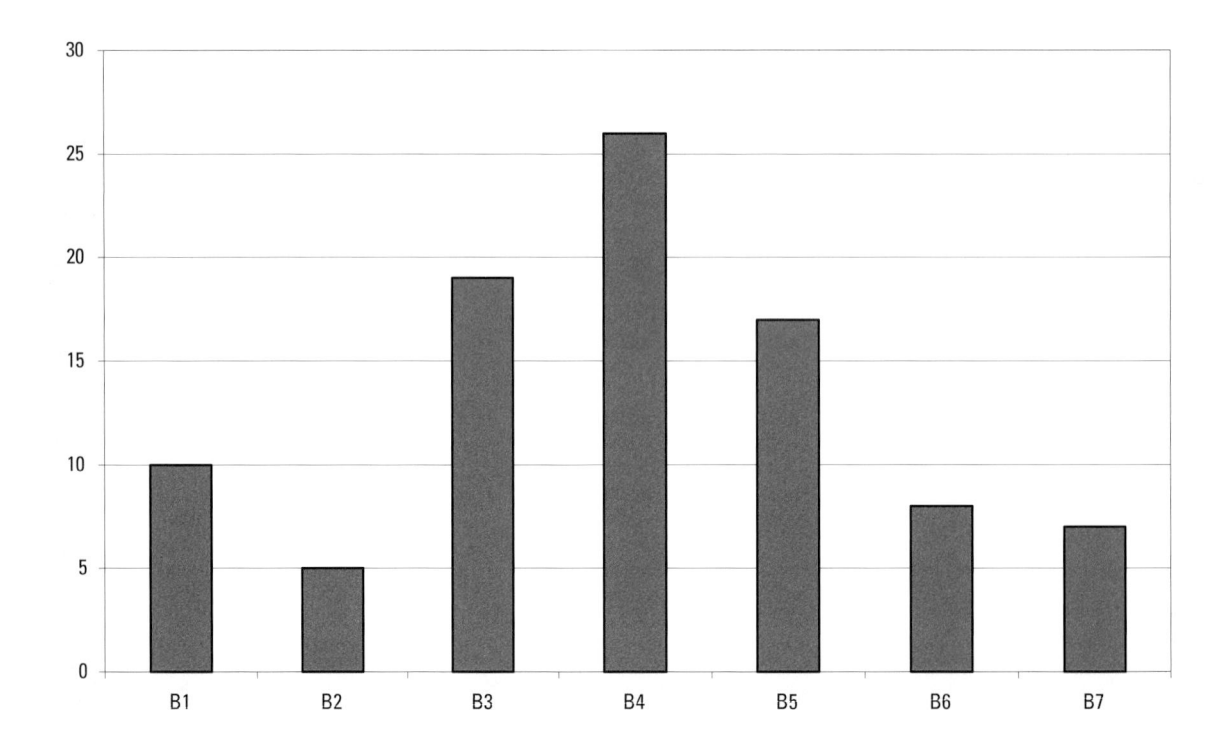

Fig. 6.10. Typological composition of horse pendants from non-military contexts in the Batavian region. Periods 2 (above) and 3 (below).

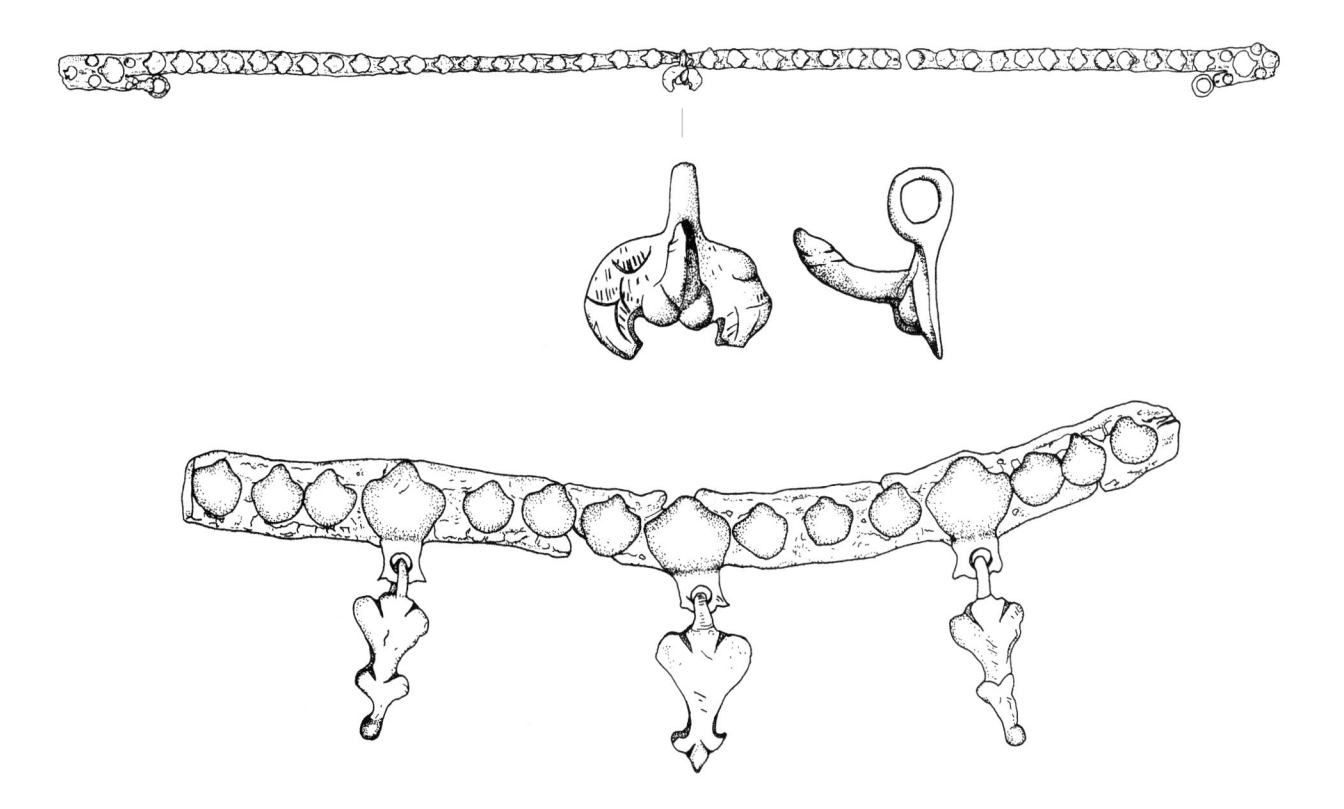

Fig. 6.11. Leather horse straps with central lunula-phallus pendant and three heart-phallus pendants from a horse burial at Celles-lez-Waremme (Belgium). Scale 2:3 (pendant above), 1:2 (below). After Massart 2000, figs. 9, 10, 13.

Among pendants from the 2nd and 3rd centuries, we see a marked contrast to the contemporaneous decorative fittings (fig. 6.10). Whereas a significant portion of the fittings feature a vulva motif, this does not occur among the pendants. As in the previous period, the phallus (B4) and lunula (B5) are the primary motifs.[104] Besides horizontal phalluses attached by a large, round loop or a central opening, there are pendants in the form of human figurines, in which the lower body is replaced by a scrotum and phallus. The heart-phallus pendant (B3), with the heart-shaped upper part terminating in a stylised phallus, is also well documented from this period. A different group comprises solid examples in the shape of an acorn (B6). These examples could perhaps be regarded as a last reference to the *corona* and hence to the symbolism of victory from the previous period.

An analysis of the decorative motifs used in Roman horse gear reveals that their symbolism corresponds largely to that of military equipment. For example, in the 1st century there was an emphasis on motifs referring directly or indirectly to the glory of Rome. Earlier than is the case with weaponry, from the Augustan period onward we see the emergence of a protective symbolism in the addition of lunate and phallic motifs.[105] In the 2nd and 3rd centuries too, fittings and pendants had an important protective value as symbols warding off evil and misfortune. The vulva occurs conspicuously frequently among the decorative fittings, whereas the lunula and phallus are the principal motifs among the pendants. Given that both fittings and pendants are horse gear components, we can assume that this combination of motifs offered maximum protection to the rider and his horse. We see this combined use most clearly in the heart-phallus pendants, which were often attached to fittings bearing a vulva motif.

[104] In a lunate pendant from Zugmantel (D), an additional phallic pendant is attached to a loop, underlining the similar symbolism of the two motifs (Oldenstein 1976, Taf. 45, nr. 446).

[105] For the dating, see chapter 2.2.3.

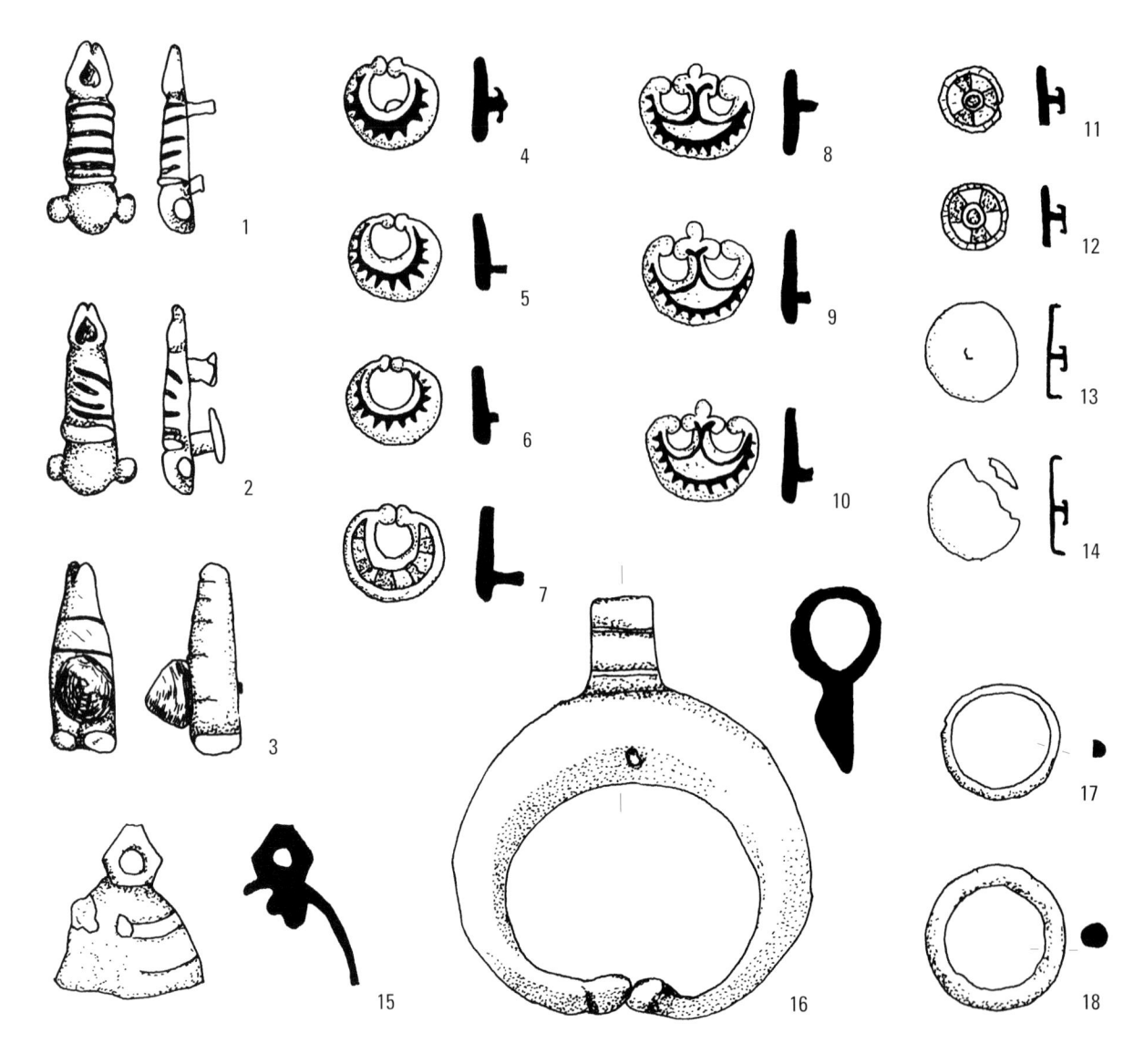

Fig. 6.12. Bridle components from a horse burial at Beuningen-'Molenstraat' (27.1-16). Scale 1:1. After Zwart 2001, fig. 32.

Horse gear sets from funerary contexts are a key source of information to determine whether fittings and pendants with a protective value were attached to specific parts of the harness. Although the leather straps are seldom preserved, in some cases we are able to reconstruct the original rigging by means of the location of the different metal components in relation to the horse's skeleton. The harness decoration was concentrated around the head of the horse in a burial at Tihany (Hungary).[106] In addition to fittings, the decoration comprised four heart-phallus pendants, which probably adorned both sides of the head and chest. The grave of a richly caparisoned horse is known from Celles-lez-Waremme in Belgium.[107] Of special interest here is the partially preserved leatherwork. The bronze decoration included three heart-phallus pendants on the chest or behind the saddle (fig. 6.11). A lunate pendant with a phallus had an important position in the middle of the horse's chest (fig. 6.11).

[106] Palágyi 1990.
[107] Massart 2000; for a free-hand reconstruction, see Junkelmann 1996, fig. 177.

With regard to the research area, the situation of harness decoration can be reconstructed from a horse burial in the rural settlement of Beuningen-'Molenstraat' (fig. 6.12).[108] The phallic fittings were part of the bridle, whereas a large lunula hung on the forehead or neck.[109] Also relevant is the discovery of a horse gear set from a creek bordering the rural settlement of Empel-West (fig. 5.13).[110] Alongside nine decorative fittings, this comprised a large lunate pendant. The presence of a bronze ring with two junctions placed on the diagonal suggests that the pendant hung from the horse's chest. Of special interest is the termination of both ends of the lunula in an eagle's head, a possible reference to the protective role of Jupiter.[111]

Although we cannot in every case establish with certainty the original position of the fittings and pendants on the harness, objects with an important symbolic significance appear to have been prominently displayed on the horse's head and chest. That the lunula also played a key role here is shown by images on 1st-century cavalry gravestones.[112] Illustrative is the well-known funerary monument of T. Flavius Bassus from Cologne, which depicts several lunate pendants on the chest of the rider's horse (fig. 6.13). Lunulas are also attached behind the saddle and on the hanging straps on either side of the neck. Finally, we can refer to a round decorative disc made of antler. Together with one of the lunate pendants, this was positioned in the middle of the chest of Bassus' horse. The bone disc and the pendants will have been placed around the horse, and especially on the animal's chest, offering maximum protection to rider and horse by forming a shield of symbols to ward off evil.

A category yet to be discussed, but which may have had a protective value similar to some of the decorative fittings and pendants, is that of bronze bells. The horse burial from Beuningen shows that one or more bells could be attached to the harness of military or civilian mounts (fig. 6.12). Junkelmann points out that the noise of these bells was designed not only to impress adversaries, but also to drive away evil spirits.[113] Most of the bells from non-military contexts in the eastern Rhine delta date from period 2 (58x), although several examples are also documented from period 3 (17x). The fewer finds from the 2nd and 3rd centuries may indicate that civilians were less inclined to use bells to ward off evil, and that this practice was largely confined to the army. If this assumption is correct, the examples from non-military contexts in the research area can be primarily associated with veterans.

Of particular interest is the occurrence of horse gear with a protective value in human graves. For example, two phallic pendants were found in the cemetery of the cavalry camp on the 'Kops Plateau' (fig. 5.19). The cemeteries of *oppidum Batavorum* and Ulpia Noviomagus have also yielded a total of six phallic pendants, as well as a round fitting with a phallic appliqué (fig. 5.19).[114] The objects can be placed typologically in the 1st century AD. In the case of the cemetery on the 'Kops Plateau', we may assume that the objects were interred along with the deceased soldiers. The finds from both urban cemeteries are more difficult to interpret. Although the deceased may have been veterans who settled in *oppidum Batavorum* or Ulpia Noviomagus after leaving the army, they could also be civilians. In the case of cavalrymen or ex-cavalrymen, a horse gear pendant belonging to the deceased may have been buried to offer protection during the soldier's trip to and sojourn in the hereafter. The comparable nature of these grave

---

[108] Zwart 1998b; 2001; see also Van der Kamp/Polak 2001, fig. 16.

[109] Zwart (1998b, figs. 4-5) assumes that the pendant was placed on the forehead.

[110] This is a metal detector find. Unfortunately, the relative positions of the harness components in the creek were not documented.

[111] See chapter 4.2.3.

[112] See Bishop 1988, figs. 1-13; for a similar use of the lunula up until the 4th century, see Junkelmann 1992, Abb. 99.

[113] Junkelmann 1992, 85.

[114] All the phallic symbols referred to are stray finds, lacking any specific information about the find context. Although the pendants may have been lost along the roads that run through the cemetery, the find location, the early dating and the uniform nature of the finds argues for a function as grave goods (see also chapter 5.3.5).

Fig. 6.13. Funerary monument of cavalryman Flavius Bassus in Cologne (Germany), with several lunula pendants and an antler disc attached in the centre of the horse's chest. Photo T. Derks (ACVU).

goods indicates that objects were deliberately chosen for their special significance. In the case of civilians, this could be either an item of horse gear from their civilian mount, or a necklace placed in the grave for the same protective reason. One clear aspect at least of the grave finds is that because of their symbolic value phalluses were not only significant for the living but also offered protection to the dead.[115]

Victoria's role, and that of Mars and Hercules in the case of weapons, in the symbolism of victory during the 1st century AD shows that such propaganda mainly targeted soldiers. Given the general, protective value of the less exclusive decorative fittings and pendants from period 2 and in particular period 3, this 'military' horse gear was ideally suited to urban and rural contexts as well. For this reason, we can assume that a period of military use was fairly rapidly followed by one of a combined military/civilian use in the course of the 1st century. Interestingly, bronze decoration was popular both inside and outside the army not only for its decorative role, but also for its protective function. The same picture emerges with draught animals, as is attested by two vulvate fittings from the above-mentioned cart burial at Frenz.[116]

The question remains as to what exactly we should understand by the equestrian use of horses in the Nijmegen centres and in particular in the Batavian countryside. The general view is that travel on horseback played only a minor role in the Roman period.[117] Horses were used almost exclusively by soldiers and the couriers of the *cursus publicus*. For other forms of transport over land, both couriers and civilians employed carts. This was possible thanks to the extensive road network, initially built for military purposes, but which civilians could also use.[118] Given that there were almost no paved roads in the Batavian countryside, we can assume that horses were the principal means of transport there in Roman times for short journeys to a neighbouring settlement or to an urban centre. This is attested to above all by the presence in virtually every Batavian settlement of both horses and the harness needed to equip them as mounts. It is also possible that horses were ridden for activities such as hunting, as shown by images on mosaics and monumental reliefs.[119]

6.4 CONCLUSION

Following a period in which items were distinctly military in nature, the 2nd and 3rd centuries heralded a major change in the composition of weaponry and horse gear from non-military contexts in the eastern Rhine delta. For instance, helmets and armour are noticeably less common, with swords and daggers, belts and *baltei*, and horse gear from now on forming the principal find categories. I have established for each group of objects the extent to which they could have been purchased by non-soldiers during the Roman period and the role they played in the everyday life of the town or countryside.

As far as weaponry is concerned, swords and daggers were worn by traders and travellers as early as the Augustan period. Although civilians were permitted to purchase weapons for the purpose of self-defence, this presumably did not happen on a large scale during times of relative calm. This situation changed when the frontier defence came under pressure from 'German' incursions, even collapsing entirely during the 3rd century. Civilians in towns and the countryside were forced to protect their families and their possessions by taking up arms. In the archaeological record, this is reflected in the relatively large number of sword finds. Images on mosaics and monumental reliefs show that some of the throwing weapons – the spears, lances and arrows often found in non-military contexts – could also have been used by civilians, namely for hunting.

---

[115] Compare the symbolism on weaponry from the 2nd and 3rd centuries, in which the afterlife also featured prominently (see chapter 4.2.3).

[116] Lehner 1923, Taf. IIIb (nrs. 11-12).

[117] See Bender 1978, 27-28; Junkelmann 1990, 80

[118] In general, Laurence 1999.

[119] Junkelmann 1990, 157 ff.

The belt appears to have been commonly worn by non-soldiers from the Flavian period onward, continuing in use as a 'military-civilian belt' into the late Roman period. The main evidence for this is the production of belt components in private workshops and the disappearance of decorative elements with a specific military imagery after Claudius. Although the *balteus* will also have been used to carry civilian swords, the finds reveal a different picture, with the items primarily being associated with veterans. The fact that baldrics were not in general civilian use is evident from the few finds from non-military contexts and from the openwork text on some of the *phalerae*, strap terminals and pendants, which specifically targets military users. This would mean that, unlike the *cingulum*, the baldric retained its significance as a symbol of military status until well into the 2nd century.

There are several possible explanations as far as horse gear is concerned. Firstly, parts of the functional harness, like strap junctions and bits, may point to horse breeding. However, it is hardly likely that the horses were already equipped as military mounts during the initial basic training in the Batavian countryside. This did not happen until the animals were sold to the army to undergo further military training. A second explanation is that the finds are linked to the use of horses as draught animals. However, the dating of most of the yoke finds in the Claudio-Flavian period does not correspond to the horse gear peak in the 2nd and 3rd centuries. A third and more likely explanation is that decorative horse gear elements were widely used for civilian mounts and, given the presence of lunula, phallus and vulva symbols, were intended to offer the rider and his horse protection against evil and misfortune on short trips or hunting expeditions.

7 Warriors, soldiers and civilians. Use and significance of weaponry and horse gear in a changing socio-political context

The *civitas Batavorum* was of great military significance throughout the Roman period, initially as a base of operations for the conquest of Germania and, from the mid-1st to the early 5th centuries AD, as part of the Roman *limes*. The Rhineland's military significance was not only strategic in nature. It appears to have been determined in part by the importance of warriorship in pre-Roman tribal societies and the way in which Rome capitalised on this in the frontier zones of the empire. The aim of this chapter is to explain the use and significance of weaponry and horse gear from non-military contexts against the changing socio-political backdrop. My starting point is the importance of warriorship in the pre-Roman situation and the transformation of late Iron Age traditions in the context of the Roman empire.

7.1 THE PRE-ROMAN SITUATION: THE IMPORTANCE OF WARRIORSHIP

Thanks to historical reports, in particular Caesar's *Commentarii de Bello Gallico* and Tacitus' *Germania*, it is widely accepted that warriorship and the acquisition of glory were key values in the 'German' and pre-Roman, Gallic world. Van Driel-Murray has recently emphasised how Rome exploited the 'martial' character of Batavian and other frontier societies in order to use them to best advantage for the purposes of frontier defence.[1] Here she joins Enloe in the perception that states often contain politically and economically peripheral zones where tribal groups tend to play a military role. For purely strategic reasons, these marginal groups are defined as *martial races* that were largely dependent on the central authority for their identity and the way they operated.[2] In order to establish whether martial values were already significant in the 'Celtic-German' world or whether they became so in response to Roman frontier policy, this section will compare the historical and archaeological data on warriorship in the period before and during Caesar's conquests.

My starting point is the socio-political structure of pre-Roman, northern Gallic societies. Patron-client relationships were a key element that shaped this tribal world.[3] Here, the socio-political structure was based on personal relationships between a king or other leader (*rex* or *princeps*) and his followers (*clientes*).[4] The understanding is that clients offered their leader loyalty and military and other support in return for protection and material compensation. These relationships were asymmetrical, in that they expressed differences in status and power between a leader and his followers. At the same time, the patron-client system had an important integrating function. It established a network of dependency relationships, not only between tribal leaders and lower social groups, but also between tribal elites themselves.

---

[1] Van Driel-Murray 2003.

[2] Enloe 1980, 23 ff. Van Driel-Murray (2003, 201 ff.) points to the example of the British government's exploitation of Nepalese societies for Ghurkha units.

[3] See Roymans 1990, 17 ff.; Hiddink 1999, 65 ff.

[4] For several tribes at the time of Caesar's campaigns we see the emergence of new political institutions in the form of a *senatus* and annually appointed magistrates (Roymans 1990, 30-36).

237

It would appear that a leader's political power within this system was directly linked to the size of his following. To guarantee loyalty, he was obliged to uphold the relationship with gifts (in particular torques, gold and silver ornaments or coins and weapons) or to regularly confirm it in some other way. Thus the number of followers a leader could call upon was also dependent on the material resources at his disposal. Key ways of acquiring valuables were to wage war and above all to conduct raids.[5] Because the groups of followers that leaders maintained could be deployed as military bands, they were at the same time a vital tool for securing new resources and thus maintaining the patron-client system.

According to Dobesch, in the late Iron Age the core of these military groups was made up of one or more *ritterliche Gefolgschaften*, groups of young warriors of noble birth who acted as a kind of personal bodyguard to the key leaders.[6] In particular, these *comitatus* – as Tacitus calls them – took the form of mounted units.[7] In his report on the Gallic wars, Caesar mentions various probable examples of *comitatus*, including the small group of *comites familiaresque* of the Eburonean leader Ambiorix, referred to later in the text as *equites*.[8] According to Creighton, the growing importance of the horse in English hill forts and *oppida* was linked to the rise of these mounted units from about 100 BC.[9] Clues here are finds of sizeable quantities of horse gear and a sharp increase in the proportion of horse bones in the skeletal material. Although almost no late Iron Age horse gear is documented from the eastern Rhine delta, here too the percentage of horse bones in rural settlements shows a marked increase during that period.[10] Roymans sees a link with the presence of gold staters and especially the *triquetrum* coins made of silver and bullion, and points to the role of these currencies in maintaining client networks and above all in the creation of the *comitatus*.[11]

In his study of relationships between leaders and their *Gefolgschaft* in the Anglo-Saxon epic *Beowulf*, Bazelmans points out that our understanding of the patron-client system should not rely too heavily on a modern, political-economic perspective.[12] An aspect that has tended to be overlooked is the fact that warfare and raids furnished not only loot but – no less importantly – glory, and were crucial in the life cycle of male individuals. Using the life story of Beowulf, a descendant of the royal line of the Geats, Bazelmans has reconstructed the life cycle of noble 'warrior-followers'.[13] These members of the *ritterliche Gefolgschaft* were expected to pass through a number of fixed, culturally valued stages, at the heart of which lay participation in heroic deeds to display their military prowess and courage and hence to acquire glory. In the case of Beowulf, this was symbolised by his fight against the dragon Grendel and Grendel's mother in the land of the Danes. By killing both monsters, he proved himself to be a fully-fledged member of the elite, a precondition for eligibility for the kingship.

The transition to each new stage in Beowulf's life is accompanied by ceremonial gift exchanges in which weapons featured prominently. For young warriors, this involved items of equipment usually given by their fathers, whereas for members of the *Gefolgschaft* it also included gifts from a king or other leader.

---

[5] For an overview of the material resources at a leader's disposal, see Roymans 1990, 41-43. Tacitus (*Germ.* 14) states that large groups of followers could only be maintained through plunder and violence.

[6] Dobesch 1980, 419 ff.; see also Roymans 1990, 40; Creighton 2000, 14-21.

[7] Tacitus, *Germ.* 13-14.

[8] Caesar, *BG* 6.30, 6.43; compare *BG* 1.18, 3.22.

[9] Creighton 2000, 15-18.

[10] Roymans 1990, 82, table 5.

[11] Roymans 2004, 88 ff. These coins are dated to between c. 50 and 15 BC (Roymans 2001, 105-111).

[12] Bazelmans 1999; 2000.

[13] Bazelmans (1999, 156 ff.) assumes that a person is made up of different 'constituents', which are brought together during his lifetime and which separate again after his death. He distinguishes between 'body', 'soul', 'life' and 'image/honour', with a person being able to supplement the inherent constituents of body, soul and life with 'image' and 'honour' during his life time; see also Theuws/Alkemade 2000, 413-417, 446-448.

In addition, displays of bravery by successful warriors were rewarded with weapons of a more exclusive nature, which were a reference to this newly-acquired prestige. Thus as a young warrior-follower, Beowulf received a sword, probably from his father, and chain mail from his king. After his 'military' successes, he was given various highly ornate pieces of equipment, including regalia from the *thesaurus* of the Danish king. Whereas the weapons that Beowulf initially received show his *potential* qualities, his reward of valuable items can be seen as a confirmation of his status as an honourable warrior and hence as a fully-fledged member of the elite.

What is special about the weapons given to Beowulf as gifts is that they are in all instances 'old' objects, frequently with a specific biography and their own name.[14] The anthropologist Mauss was the first to point out that gifts in tribal societies cannot be viewed separately from the people who gave them.[15] The gifts can be seen as animate entities with their own qualities that are directly associated with the cultural biography of these objects, or with their use by one or more previous owners.[16] Weiner refers here to inalienable valuables, objects with "[an] exclusive and cumulative identity with a particular series of owners through time."[17] Because they represent the identity of individual or group owners, such objects may only be exchanged in exceptional cases and then primarily between heirs.[18]

I should point out that the picture described here relates to a select group of warriors of aristocratic descent, who formed part of a king or leader's immediate retinue. A military lifestyle was less a matter of course for warriors of lower social status. Only in times of war, as reinforcements for the *Gefolgschaft*, did they have an opportunity to acquire booty and glory. Their leaders will not have supplied them with fine weapons that were significant for the group's identity. They are likely to have been given simpler weapons by their father or another member of the family, weapons which cannot be ranked among the inalienable valuables referred to by Weiner.[19]

Relevant to this study is the finding, in the light of references in classical sources, that values central to the early medieval *Beowulf* must also have played a key role in the lives of pre-Roman warriors. The life cycle of men in 'Celto-Germanic' societies was made up of several comparable stages, each marked by the ritual exchange of weapons and other gifts.[20] A key stage in a young man's life was the moment in which he was admitted into the warrior class and presented with military equipment. According to Tacitus, this happened at a public gathering, in which his leader, father or other family member presented him with weapons:

> *"…no one shall carry arms until the state authorities are satisfied that he will be competent to use them. Then, in the presence of the Assembly, either one of the chiefs or the young man's father or some other relative presents him with a shield and a spear. These, among the Germans, are the equivalent of the man's toga with us – the first distinction publicly conferred upon a youth, who now ceases to rank merely as a member of a household and becomes a citizen."*[21]

---

[14] Bazelmans 1999, 150-156; see also Theuws/Alkemade 2000, 419-427.

[15] Mauss 1991; for the application of Mauss' ideas in anthropology, see Bazelmans 1999, 13 ff.

[16] See also chapter 5.2.3.

[17] Weiner 1992, 33. These objects may also be significant because supernatural powers were involved in their production. Examples are the chain mail given to Beowulf as a young warrior by his king, which according to tradition was fashioned by Weland, the renowned smith of German legends, and the sword, made by Giants, which Beowulf used to kill Grendel (Bazelmans 1999, 155-156).

[18] Such an exceptional situation is the Danish King Hrothgar's gift of the sword and golden standard to Beowulf (Bazelmans 1999, 178-179). These objects were part of the Danish regalia and would normally go to a member of the Danish royal house.

[19] Hiddink (1999, 81) does not even consider the weapons that Beowulf receives as 'real' inalienable goods; only land and a group name constitute this.

[20] See also Roymans/Aarts 2005, 354-356.

[21] Tacitus *Germ*. 13; see also Caesar, *BG* 6.18.

From this moment youths were members of the *iuventus*, or group of young warriors, and able to take part in public life. In tribal societies, rites of passage are often of a group nature, with new groups of boys initiated at frequent intervals. According to Roymans and Aarts, this rite took place in sanctuaries and was accompanied by a ritual vow, intended to protect the participants and bring them military success during their active life as warriors.[22] We know that the presented weapons were important symbols of warrior status from a practice described by Caesar and Tacitus whereby the *iuventus* and older warriors would attend public gatherings *armed*. It was by rattling these military symbols that they demonstrated their approval of the speaker.[23]

As with Beowulf, it was also important for the 'Celto-Germanic' *iuventus* to display military skills and courage by taking part in hazardous undertakings.[24] Of interest here are the 'barbarian invasions' that constantly threatened the imperial frontier. Although large-scale investment in the *limes* reveals just how much Rome regarded the invading Germans as a threat to its territory, Hiddink points out that the 'Germans' were not particularly intent on territorial expansion. He views the attacks first and foremost as raids, brief plundering expeditions designed to capture booty and in particular to win military prestige and glory.[25] A clue to the importance of warriorship and glory can be found in a practice described by Tacitus, whereby newly initiated warriors of the Chattian tribe did not cut their beard and hair until they had killed their first opponent.[26] The bravest wore an iron ring, a token of self-abasement that was not removed until the death of the first adversary.[27] Elsewhere, Tacitus describes the speaking order at public gatherings. It is significant that, together with age, position and eloquence, this was decided by the military successes of those present.[28]

It is difficult to demonstrate to what extent late Iron Age weapons also constituted significant heirlooms. As in the early Middle Ages, these will have largely been simple items presented by fathers to sons during a rite of passage. This picture appears to be confirmed by weapon graves in the Treveri territory.[29] A sword, shield and often one or more lance- or spearheads were interred in a large number of La Tène graves. These were fairly ordinary objects that do not equate with the inalienable valuables familiar to us from *Beowulf*. In addition, the simple nature of the grave goods and especially the large number of weapon graves show that the deceased were members of the group of warriors with lesser social standing than the *ritterliche Gefolgschaft*. Inalienable valuables remaining in circulation as heirlooms would explain the almost complete absence of exclusive weapon sets. They will only occasionally have been interred as grave goods.[30]

A study by Roymans based on archaeological finds makes an important contribution to the discussion of warriorship in the pre-Roman period.[31] The springboard for his analysis is the fact that in tribal societies martial traditions frequently coincided with specific, ritualised dealings with weapons. An inventory of swords and helmets from northern Gaul and trans-Rhenish Germania shows that during the middle and especially late La Tène periods (c. 150-15 BC) these are primarily documented from what we can regard as ritual contexts: cult places, rivers and in some regions graves as well (fig. 7.1). Although we

---

[22] Roymans/Aarts 2005, 355; for the ritual vow, see Derks 1995; 1998, 215 ff.

[23] Tacitus, *Germ.* 11; *Hist.* 5.17; Caesar, *BG* 7.21.

[24] Although members of the *ritterliche Gefolgschaft* were expected to demonstrate their bravery through heroic deeds, it was warfare in particular that gave warriors of lower social status an opportunity to distinguish themselves militarily.

[25] Hiddink 1999, 76-77, 190-191; for the late Roman situation, compare Elton 1996, 45 ff.

[26] Tacitus, *Germ.* 31.

[27] There may be a link to the practice of head-hunting, as known from classical sources and perhaps archaeological finds (Roymans 1996, note 17); see below.

[28] Tacitus, *Germ.* 11.

[29] See Haffner 1989b, 61 ff.

[30] For example, Haffner 1992.

[31] Roymans 1996, 13 ff.; see also Derks 1998, 45 ff.

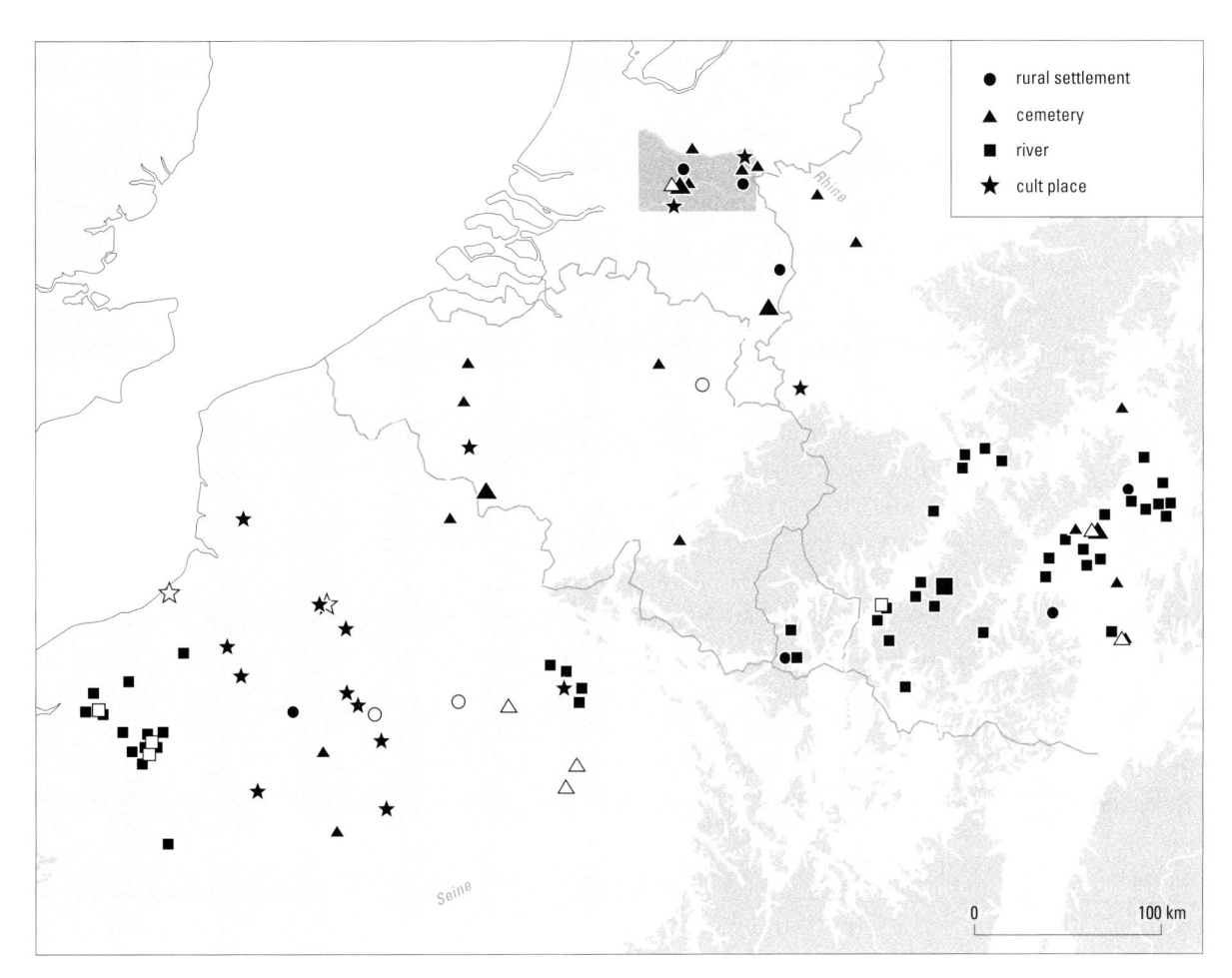

Fig. 7.1. Geographical distribution of La Tène swords (black) and helmets (white) from northern Gaul and the adjacent 'German' area (large symbols: more than 5 objects). The research area is shown in dark grey. After Roymans 1996, figs. 1-2, with supplements (77.1, 240.2).

observe regional differences in terms of preferences for a particular context, the different kinds of deposition can be seen as the expression of an overarching 'martial ideology'. Apart from the specific context in which the objects have been recovered, the ritual nature of the depositions is apparent from the broken or bent condition in which swords in particular are found. The damage constitutes 'ritual destruction', in which objects are destroyed in order to render them unsuitable for everyday use and in this way to deliver them permanently to the gods.[32]

The ritual weapon depositions include some of a distinctively collective nature that can be associated with raids. Various rural cult places in northern Gaul have yielded large numbers of deliberately damaged weapons, as well as human and animal skeletal material.[33] The best known are Ribemont-sur-Ancre and Gournay-sur-Aronde.[34] In Ribemont, the decapitated bodies of about 100 armed warriors were placed on a wooden structure just outside the cult place. In addition, a selection of long human and horse bones have been incorporated in rectangular structures (*ossuaria*), which may have functioned as

[32] Haffner 1989c; Roymans 1990, 82-83; Derks 1998, 46-47.

[33] For an overview, see Roymans 1990, 75 ff.

[34] Ribemont: Cadoux 1984; Fercoq du Leslay 1996; Brunaux et al. 1999; Gournay: Rapin et al. 1982; Brunaux/Meniel/Poplin 1985; Brunaux/Rapin 1988; Lejars 1994. For an overview of both sites, see Brunaux 1995.

241

a kind of 'shrine'. At Gournay, weapons are displayed in or above the entrance and on poles at the cult place, while decapitated bodies were deposited in the ditch enclosing the site. Human skulls appear to have been attached to the gateway at both cult places. The assumption is that the material at these sites constitutes booty and the bodies are those of slain opponents or prisoners, dedicated in gratitude for a military victory.[35] The dedications date predominantly from La Tène C (c. 300-150 BC) and are important evidence for the existence of a martial way of life in pre-Roman Gaul.[36] Roymans assumes that, as the owner of the largest share of the booty, the ruling aristocracy was responsible for organising these collective rituals. He views the dedications not only as a gesture to the gods, but at the same time as an important socio-political investment designed to boost the prestige of the military elite.[37]

Most of the weapon finds are simpler in nature and are associated with individual dedications of swords, spears and shields. The explanation for these finds is less unequivocal. Firstly, the weapons may have been deposited by active warriors, for example as thanks for a victory or a safe return after a military conflict.[38] They may also have been objects dedicated as part of a rite of passage when a man ceased being an active warrior.[39] Or the weapons may not have been presented to the gods until after the warrior's death. Interestingly, the areas where weapons were deposited in graves or in another ritual context tend to be mutually exclusive (fig. 7.1). It may have been customary in one region to inter a warrior's body together with his weapons, but in another region to inter the body and all or part of the deceased's military equipment separately.

La Tène weaponry from the eastern Rhine delta is relatively scarce. Here too, the weapons generally appear to be ritual depositions.[40] The same applies to the contemporaneous horse gear that, in view of the mounted *comitatus*, was also significant in the military domain. Firstly, finds from several cult places are of a ritual nature. Five sword components and two throwing weapons are documented from the open-air sanctuary at Empel-'De Werf'.[41] The sword components were probably part of Kessel type swords and date from the second half of the 1st century BC (82.57-60, 68, pl. 2). Also belonging to the late La Tène period is a narrow spearhead (82.52, pl. 3) and the triangular tip of a second throwing weapon (82.53, pl. 3). The find of a sword component during recent investigations at the Roman temple complex in the centre of Elst reveals that the situation in Empel is not exceptional (77.1, pl. 2). The sword is probably also of the Kessel type and appears to be associated with the presence of a pre-Roman open-air sanctuary.[42] Less clear is the interpretation of a sword find from the vicinity of Nijmegen (210.1, pl. 2). The corrosion on the sword and accompanying scabbard (Kessel type) suggests that it came from a dry location. As the interment of weapons in graves is completely undocumented for the Lower Rhine region, this find can be linked to the presence of a cult place. Finally, we can point to a set of at least nine bronze horse

---

[35] For dedications of booty following a military victory, see Caesar, *BG* 6.17; Tacitus, *Ann.* 13.57.

[36] Brunaux et al. 1999, fig. 63. Weapons deposition continued in Ribemont into La Tène D2; however, the more recent depositions do not compare with the material from La Tène C in terms of scale.

[37] Roymans 1990, 84. This also explains why the military trophies were displayed so prominently inside and outside the cult place.

[38] Roymans 1990, 83; 1996, 19.

[39] Roymans 1996, 19; Roymans/Aarts 2005, 355-356.

[40] Weaponry and horse gear also occur occasionally in rural settlements, as demonstrated by a sword component from Tiel-'Oude Tielseweg' (240.3, pl. 2), a twisted horse bit from Bijsterhuizen-'Bijsterhuizenstraat' (30.1, pl 4) and a spur from Wijk bij Duurstede-'De Horden' (291.116, pl. 4). The assumed ritual interpretation of the finds from Lith-'Oijensche Hut' is uncertain (175.1-2, pl. 3; Jansen/Fokkens/Van der Linde 2002, 179-188); it would appear to be settlement waste.

[41] Roymans/Derks 1990; 1993; 1994. See also chapters 3.3.3, 5.3.1.

[42] Also dating from the pre-Roman phase of the sanctuary are fibulae and coins of the *triquetrum* type (Roymans 2004, fig. 7.10, appendix 6.1), as well as a large quantity of animal bone material (Lauwerier 1988, 120).

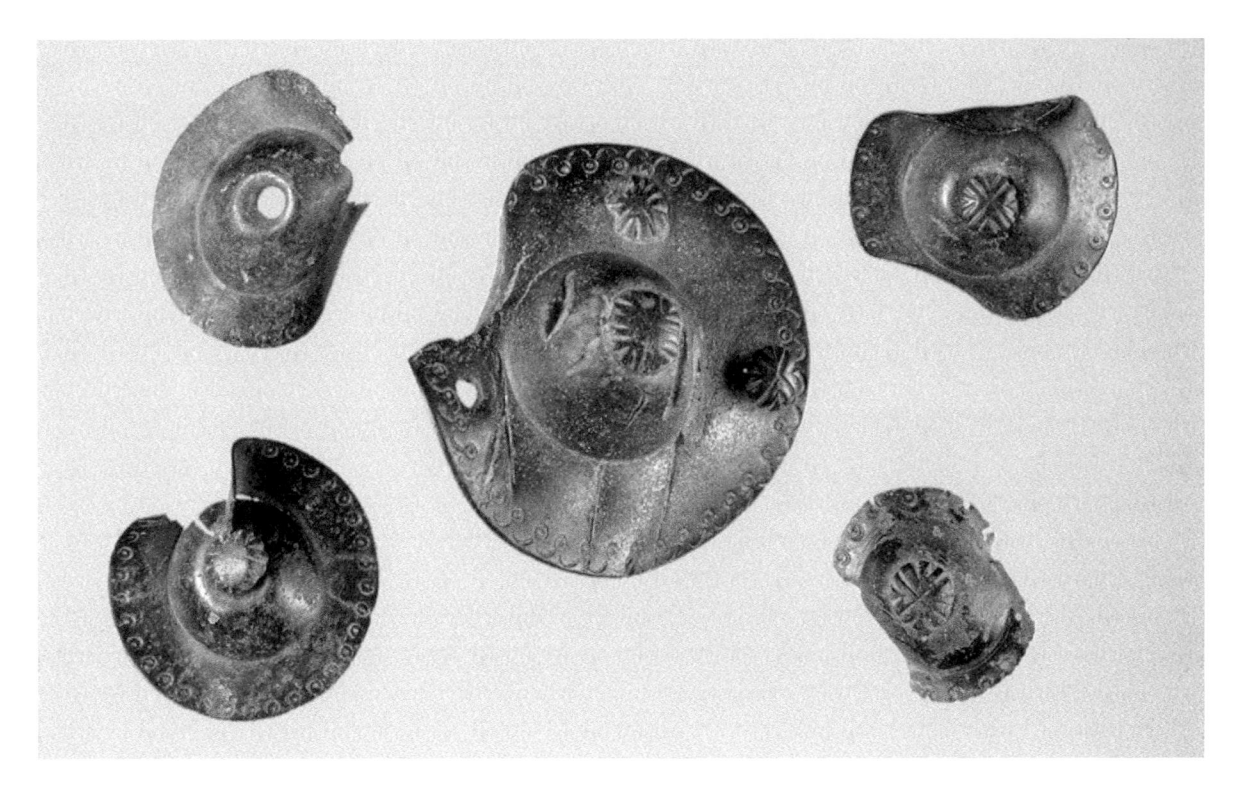

Fig. 7.2. Bronze *phalerae* from a set of La Tène horse gear from a possible cult place at Deil (46.2-6). Diameter of large *phalera* 5.7 cm.

phalerae that were recovered from what was presumably a cult place at Deil (46.1-8, pl. 5, fig. 7.2).[43] The rosette-shaped rivets are inlaid with red enamel, a form of decoration that is typical of the late La Tène period.[44]

Dredge finds from an old bed of the Meuse at Kessel-Lith can be interpreted as ritual depositions as well.[45] These weapons comprise 12 Kessel type swords and scabbard plates (163.2, 164.6-16, pl. 1) and a Port type helmet bowl (164.1, pl. 6). Also from the late Iron Age are 10 swords and scabbards of unknown types (163.3-7, 164.17-21), a horn-shaped decoration that was probably attached to a helmet (164.2, pl. 3), four spearheads (163.8, 164.26-28, pl. 3), and a horse bit and looped strap mount (164.36, 40, pl. 4). Some of the swords were rendered unusable by being deliberately bent. Relevant to the interpretation of this assemblage is the sizeable quantity of unburnt human bones found at the same location.[46] Primarily the remains of adult males, some exhibit signs of having met a violent death. Unlike the bone material from Ribemont and Gournay, the different parts of the skeleton are fairly evenly represented, a possible indication that the bodies had not been decapitated.[47] The ^{14}C datings of the finds from Kessel-Lith show a distinct peak in the late Iron Age and a smaller one in the Merovingian period, suggesting that a significant proportion of the individuals ended up in the water at the same time as the weapons and horse gear.

---

[43] Given the find of 31 *triquetrum* coins at the same site, Roymans (2004, appendix 6.1) also assumes it was a cult place. A parallel to this type of *phalerae* is known from the Dünsberg (Schulze-Forster 2002, Taf. 21, nr. 476).

[44] Compare the occurrence of enamel in the rosette-shaped rivets of belt hooks dated to the 1st century BC (Roymans/Derks 1994, 14; Verhart/Roymans 1998, 76).

[45] Verhart/Roymans 1998; Roymans 2004, 103 ff. See also chapters 3.3.4, 5.3.2.

[46] Ter Schegget 1999.

[47] See Ter Schegget 1999, 210, fig. 6.

The Kessel-Lith assemblage includes swords in numbers unprecedented for the eastern Rhine delta, some bearing traces of ritual damage. The presence of human skeletal material makes it likely that the swords were deposited as part of collectively dedicated booty. An argument against this, however, is that the geographical distribution shows that most of the Kessel type swords were manufactured in that particular region.[48] If the assemblage consisted of booty, a series of weapons characteristic of one or more surrounding areas would have been found.[49] It is more likely that Kessel-Lith was a central cult place where, alongside possible collective offerings of slain opponents, there were individual depositions of military objects during the 1st century BC. The same interpretation is likely for the finds from Empel-'De Werf'. Here too the deposition of weapons and horse gear and the absence of human skeletal material can be associated with individual warriors.

We may conclude that, together with the ceremonial exchange of weapons between leaders, followers and the gods, warfare and raids during the late La Tène period were part of a socio-political and ideological system that largely centred on warriorship and the acquisition of glory. The most concrete evidence is provided by specific, ritualised dealings with weapons. Classical sources and the early medieval *Beowulf*, together with archaeological finds, demonstrate that warriorship was not a temporary *Roman* construct specific to a single ethnic group, but instead represented a central value in the northwest European tribal world over a longer period of time. It was part of a 'martial ideology' supported not only by the elite, but one which appealed to warriors of lesser social standing as well, as attested by individual depositions of weapons in the various ritual contexts. A martial way of life was possible because there was no central authority – like the Romans – with a clear monopoly on force in the pre-Roman, 'Celto-Germanic' world, in Germania during the Roman era and in the early medieval world.[50] This was the ideal setting for a martial lifestyle offering both young men and their leaders an opportunity through warfare and raids to acquire booty and to win glory as a warrior.

7.2 CONSEQUENCES OF THE ROMAN TAKEOVER: CONTINUITY AND DISCONTINUITY OF LATE IRON AGE TRADITIONS

When Gaul became part of the Roman empire following Caesar's conquests (58-51 BC) and Augustus' political and administrative restructuring (27-12 BC), it was important to the Romans to first of all put an end to the violence caused by tribal warfare and raids. The Augustan pacification of Gaul was no uniform process; there were significant regional differences. The most important evidence is the distribution of 1st-century weapons (fig. 3.12).[51] Based on the presence and absence of helmets and swords, northern Gaul can be roughly divided into two zones: the Gallic interior and the Rhineland frontier zone.

First-century weapons from the Gallic interior are virtually unknown, pointing to a break with the pre-Roman tradition of depositing weapons in sanctuaries, rivers and graves. As a consequence of pacification, a rapid demilitarisation seems to have occurred in the Gallic provinces, with – as its logical consequence – the disappearance of traditional martial values.[52] Finds of 1st-century miniature weapons

---

[48] Verwers/Ypey 1975; Roymans 2004, 111-112, fig. 7.5.

[49] The origin of the non-Kessel type swords is unknown; they may have been booty.

[50] Roymans 1990, 34, 44; 1996, 14.

[51] Roymans 1996.

[52] Although Roymans (1996, 40) believes that Gallic societies had already lost many of their military ideals at the time of Caesar's campaigns, Drinkwater (1978, 831) sees the revolts in Gaul following the provincialisation under Augustus as a reaction against the curtailment of the military exploitation of this region, which meant the end of native warrior traditions.

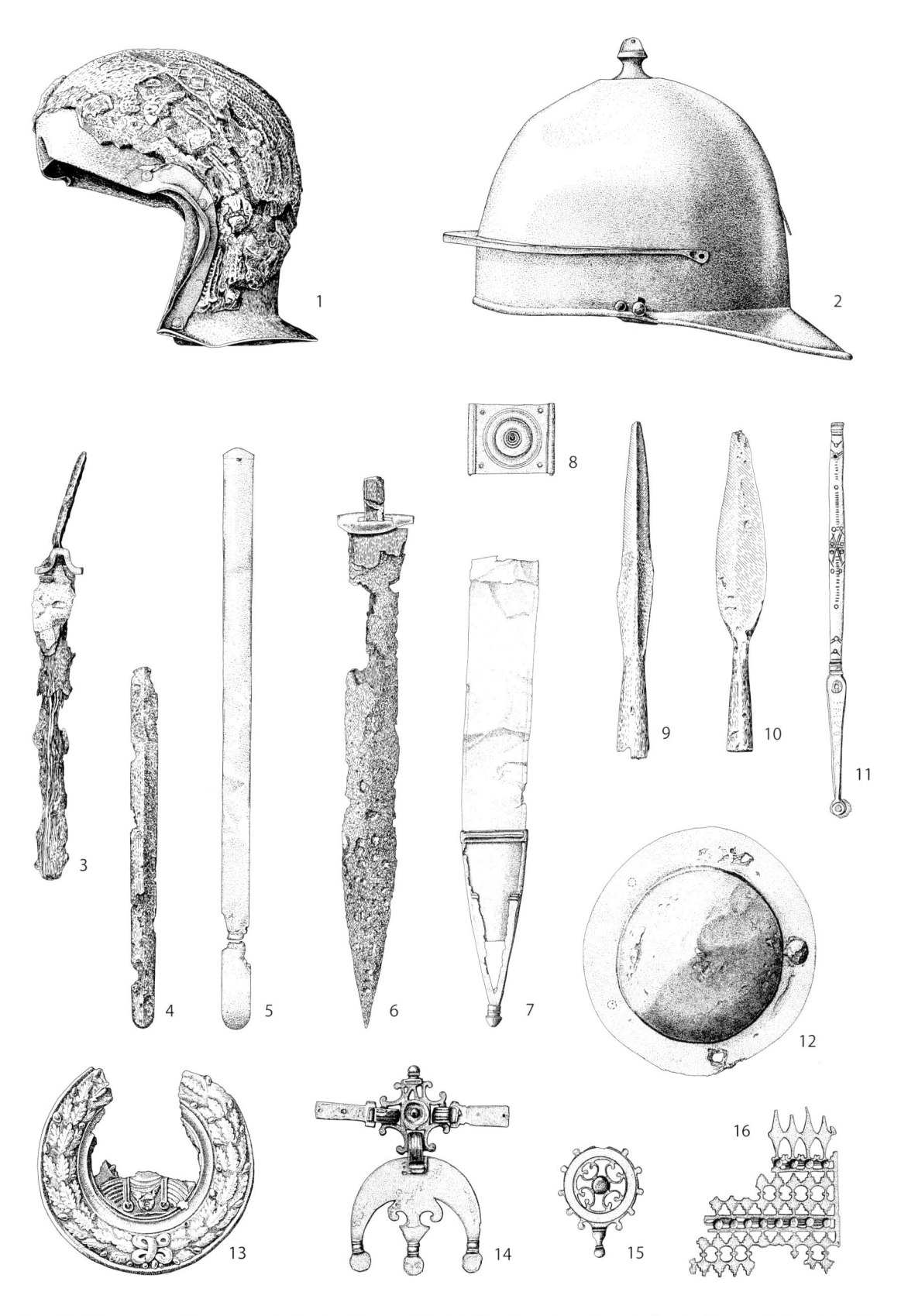

Fig. 7.3. Weaponry and horse gear dredged at Xanten-'Wardt'. The pieces date from the late La Tène period and the 1st century AD. Scale 1:4, 1:2 (nr. 13). After Schalles/Schreiter 1993, Taf. 20 ff.

1-2 helmets; 3-7 swords; 8 belt fittings; 9-10 spear-/lanceheads; 11-12 shield grip and *umbo*; 13 disc from *dona militaria*; 14-15 horse pendants; 16 saddle fitting.

in sanctuaries in the French Ardennes can be viewed as the final tangible expression of a martial ideology.[53]

The pacification process had a very different effect in the imperial frontier zone. For instance, the number of weapon finds from non-military contexts in the Rhineland peaked rather than declined in the 1st century AD. Documented for the same period is a large number of horse gear components, which can probably be associated with the Roman cavalry. As in the previous period, a sizeable portion of the objects were deposited in sanctuaries and rivers or interred in graves (fig. 3.12). There was continuity in ritual dealings with military objects, with weapons and horse gear apparently constituting the tangible markers of an ideology which continued to centre on martial values.

The survival of the pre-Roman practice of weapons deposition can be seen clearly in the different ritual contexts. Items of military equipment are documented in Empel-'De Werf' from both La Tène D2 and the 1st century AD.[54] In both periods this appears to involve similar, ritual depositions, pointing to the continuity of use and probably also significance of military objects. The same picture emerges from the river assemblage at Kessel-Lith.[55] Weaponry and horse gear items from the 1st century AD have been recovered alongside finds from the late Iron Age. A good parallel is the dredge assemblage of Xanten-'Wardt', which also contains swords and spears/lances from both periods (fig. 7.3).[56] Finally, we can point to the weapon graves from the Trier region. The native use of weapons as grave goods was not brought to an end by the Roman occupation but retained its significance into the Claudian period (fig. 7.5).[57]

Alongside finds from ritual contexts, military items also occur frequently in urban and above all rural settlements during the 1st century AD.[58] Although some of the finds have a ritual interpretation, the material is chiefly made up of fragmentary objects which were discarded as rubbish after being used for several decades or longer. These were presumably parts of military equipment brought home by veterans as 'personal memorabilia' after their term of service.[59] The equipment will have been stored or displayed in the veteran's home and perhaps worn during certain ceremonies. As with the weapons from the late Iron Age, these objects were important symbols of the owner's military career and status.

Before elaborating further on the survival of martial values in frontier societies, it is relevant to briefly outline their political and administrative structure in the light of their treaty relationship with Rome and the associated military exploitation. Opinions vary widely, however, as to how the Rhineland and in particular the Batavian territory were governed in the pre-Flavian period. Slofstra assumes that the later German provinces were not divided into formal *civitates* up until the time of the Batavian revolt, but were controlled by means of a system of alliances with native elites, in combination with a military presence. Characteristic of this 'frontier zone' is that existing socio-political structures were left largely intact. Political reorganisation was confined to the appointment of *praefecti* who, in the case of tribes like the Batavians who were friendly to Rome, belonged to the native elite. It was their job to monitor frontier groups, collect taxes and oversee the recruitment of auxiliary troops.[60]

Roymans believes that the restructuring was far more sweeping and that a *civitates* along Roman lines, administered from urban centres like the *oppidum Batavorum*, already existed under Drusus.[61] The existence of a Batavian *summus magistratus*, rather than the customary two-headed magistrature, demonstrates that there was not yet a uniform *civitates*, as was the case in the Gallic interior. This was presumably a continuation of a pre-Roman type of administration acceptable to Rome. It is not clear whether this institution operated alongside, instead of, or as the successor to a prefecture. Slofstra claims that both

[53] Roymans 1996, 30.
[54] For an overview of finds, see chapter 3.3.3.
[55] For an overview of finds, see chapter 3.3.4.
[56] Schalles/Schreiter 1993, 51-52, 199 ff.
[57] Waurick 1994, Abb. 15.
[58] For an overview, see chapter 3.3.1-2.
[59] See chapter 5 (especially 5.2.3).
[60] Slofstra 2002.
[61] Roymans 2004, 195 ff.

types of administration co-existed, with the magistrature perhaps being held by lower-ranking aristocrats, as the peregrine status of the above *summus magistratus* suggests.[62] Roymans, on the other hand, believes that the prefecture was merely a transitional stage during the Augustan period, after which the Batavian territory largely became integrated into the Roman state structure.

In both cases, treaty relations between Rome and the various imperial frontier societies were of paramount importance.[63] The many 'national' or 'ethnic' units known from the frontier zone show that the principal aim was military exploitation (fig. 1.2). The Batavians played a key role here, supplying one *ala* and eight *cohortes* in addition to featuring prominently in the emperor's personal bodyguard and the Rhine fleet. The Cugerni, Tungri and Nervii each supplied five units, and we know of one or two units for each of the remaining tribal areas in the frontier zone.[64] These auxiliary troops supposedly evolved out of the traditional *Gefolgschaften* and were initially of an irregular and temporary nature.[65] Under Augustus these detachments appear to have been transformed into regular *auxilia*, with soldiers serving for a fixed period in return for a salary.[66] In this way local warrior bands came under the supervision of the authorities in Rome and could be deployed in a controlled way for Roman purposes.

The central role of frontier societies in supplying troops meant that the native aristocracy could continue to present itself as a military elite. Firstly, members of the leading aristocratic families were entitled to hold the position of *praefectus*. This meant not only that they were able to consolidate their position of power as direct representatives of Rome, but perhaps also that they had small military units at their disposal in order to carry out their work.[67] This situation is reminiscent of the traditional leaders who maintained their own *Gefolgschaft* and it will have contributed significantly to the aristocracy's military status.

Secondly, we know that members of the Batavian and Treverian elite had the right to command their own 'national' units, which also meant in the context of the Roman army that they were able to maintain their position as military leaders.[68] Most of these commanders possessed the citizenship granted to them by the Julian emperors. Roymans believes that these Julii had already been granted citizenship in the time of Caesar or Augustus, as part of the above-mentioned alliance with Rome.[69] It is not clear to what extent the right to command their own units was part of such alliances. Alföldy suspects that it was customary for *civitates* who had demonstrated loyalty to Rome to themselves command the troops they supplied.[70] This is possibly also apparent from the command of Cananefatian, Nervian and Tungrian units by members of the native aristocracy.[71]

Thirdly, the Rhineland elite was responsible for recruiting new troops, presumably under the control of prefects and/or magistrates.[72] Recruitment will have been carried out among their own clientèle in accordance with the traditional system that maintained the position of native leaders as patrons of groups of 'warrior-followers'.

---

[62] Slofstra 2002, 28.

[63] See chapter 1.2.

[64] Roymans 1996, table 1 (after Alföldy 1968).

[65] For the origin of the *auxilia*, see Roymans 1996, 20-21.

[66] For the supposed reforms of the *auxilia* under Augustus, see chapter 2.3.

[67] Slofstra 2002, 28. In the case of the Batavians, he is thinking of the prestigious *ala Batavorum*.

[68] Roymans 1996, 25, note 49.

[69] Roymans 1996, 25; for the Batavian treaty relationship with Rome, see also Slofstra 2002, 24-25. Drinkwater (1978, 826) suspects that the Julii were the descendants of auxiliary soldiers who demonstrated their loyalty to Caesar during the Gallic wars.

[70] Alföldy 1968, 89-90, 110 ff.; see also Wolters 1990, 109 ff. Drinkwater (1978, 830), however, points out that the Batavians and Treveri were exceptions.

[71] For an overview, see Roymans 1996, 27, note 60. It is not clear how representative these examples are. They were irregular units, partly at the time of the Batavian revolt. We also know that the Ubii were already led by a prefect of Italic descent at the time of Tiberius (Alföldy 1968, 112, nrs. 139, 157).

[72] Alföldy 1968, 88, specifically for the Batavian situation p. 46-47; Roymans 1996, 25.

At the same time, pacification had far-reaching consequences for the military elites.[73] They could no longer instigate hostilities on their own initiative within the Roman structure. The local aristocracy had to adhere to army regulations and was under the surveillance of the Roman army command, which meant a curtailment of their power and authority. Moreover, the booty captured in times of war did not go to the elite, but to the Roman state. It seems likely that this loss was compensated by the payment of wages. These may have been disbursed indirectly via the elite, to enable them to maintain their position vis-a-vis their 'warrior-followers'. However, it is unlikely that such a system continued once the *auxilia* had been transformed into regular forces. Disbursement will gradually have been taken over by Rome, putting an end once and for all to the role of the native elite in this area.

The assimilation of the traditional *Gefolgschaft* system into the Roman army structure also had ambivalent consequences for warrior-followers. On the one hand, military exploitation meant that even after the Roman occupation men in the frontier region of the empire still had a chance to show off their military prowess and to win glory. On the other hand, the transformation of *Gefolgschaften* into regular units along Roman lines, and of warriors into professional soldiers, had sweeping consequences for the life cycle of men and the associated ritual transactions (fig. 7.4).

	warriors	**soldiers**
service	temporary warriorship	fixed term of service
formation	irregular *Gefolgschaften*	regular *auxilia*
activities	raids/warfare	military service (warfare)
rewards	a share of the spoils	pay/*dona militaria*
weapons acquisition	as gifts	as commodities
end of military stage of life	unknown rite of passage	*missio honesta*

Fig. 7.4. The key differences between warriors in the late Iron Age and professional soldiers in the Roman period.

Firstly, the change from warrior to soldier had implications for the time at which young men were equipped with weapons and the way in which this was done. Membership of the *iuventus* may still have been significant, with young men being prepared for a life as a soldier. However, the rite of passage that accompanied admission to this 'warrior class' was no longer the ceremonial issue of weaponry. From now on, the moment when a man was given his first weapons coincided with his admission to the army. These weapons were not gifts issued as part of an important rite of passage, but *commodities* supplied by the *custos armorum* of the army camp which a soldier had to pay for himself.[74] The start of his soldiering career will also have been the moment at which a new recruit made a ritual vow, which included a petition for military success and protection during his period of service.[75] In addition, when joining the army each soldier was expected to swear the *sacramentum*, the solemn oath of loyalty to the emperor.[76]

Secondly, there are essential differences between the active life of a warrior and a soldier, as well as the associated forms of reward. A young warrior was expected to take part in heroic deeds, often in the form of raids. Soldiers had fewer opportunities for displaying their skills and reputation, given that occasional military campaigns were the only means of doing so. In times of war or peace, the reward given to all soldiers was no longer a share of the spoils, but chiefly their pay. The way to acquire status – and a higher salary – was to hold a higher army post. Although the key positions were set aside for

---

[73] See also Derks 1998, 52-54.
[74] See chapter 5.2.1.
[75] Roymans/Aarts 2005, 355.
[76] Haynes 1999, 168.

Fig. 7.5. Inventory of a weapon grave from the mid-1st century AD, found at Wederath (grave 1344). After Haffner 1989b, fig. 72.

the sons of senators, knights and local aristocrats, simple soldiers were able to work their way up to the rank of *centurio* or *decurio*. They were also eligible for *dona militaria* as a reward for valour and bravery on the battlefield. These distinctions were an important substitute for the reward that warriors received after military victories.[77]

Finally, the moment a soldier completed his term of service and left the army as a *veteranus* marked the beginning of a new stage in his life cycle, one which was unknown in the late Iron Age. As a reward for 25 years of loyal service, soldiers were granted honourable discharge. For auxiliary soldiers, this meant that they became Roman citizens and could enter into a lawful marriage with a peregrine woman. This group ritual, which was held in the army camp, was highly political. The *missio honesta* was awarded each year on 7 January, the anniversary of Augustus' accession to the *imperium*.[78] The discharge ritual included making sacrifices to gods associated with the army and the emperor. It was also customary, probably in keeping with a late Iron Age tradition, for soldiers to deposit part of their equipment at cult places and/or in rivers. Presumably these were ritual transactions marking the end of a key stage in the life of a soldier and the return to the civilian world.[79] The objects may have been dedicated in fulfilment of the promise made earlier. The sharp increase in ritual dealings with weaponry and horse gear vis-à-vis the late Iron

[77] Maxfield 1986, 27-29.
[78] Derks 1998, 54.
[79] See chapter 5.2.3, 5.3.

Fig. 7.6. Reconstruction of the monumental cavalry reliefs erected in the Rhineland during the late Neronian and early Flavian periods. After Noelke 1998, Abb. 39.

Age can probably be explained by the fact that military service gave a larger proportion of the population access to military equipment and an opportunity to deposit it in a ritual fashion.

In contrast to these changes, the rite of passage associated with a soldier's death shows a remarkable degree of continuity in terms of the use of military symbols in a funerary context. Both in the late Iron Age and the 1st century AD, it was customary – among the Treveri in particular – to bury the dead warrior or soldier with part of his military equipment (fig. 7.5). Given that weapon graves are known exclusively from native cemeteries, the deceased would appear to be auxiliary veterans who took their equipment home after discharge and who, in keeping with native traditions, were buried alongside it.[80] A new element that entered the Rhineland funerary ritual was the erection of stone monuments. A characteristic of 1st-century gravestones is the depiction of infantrymen and cavalrymen in full battle dress.[81] The representation of cavalrymen is particularly interesting. Astride a galloping horse, the cavalryman is captured at the moment of triumph over a kneeling opponent shown beneath him. In the late Neronian and early Flavian periods, this theme was incorporated into large cavalry reliefs that formed part of imposing funerary monuments.[82] These show several Roman cavalry soldiers adopting an offensive stance toward a group of 'barbarian' cavalrymen (fig. 7.6). In the *civitas Batavorum*, a fragment of one such monument is known from Nijmegen (fig. 7.7). The symbolism of military triumph, which must have held great appeal for both native elites and simple cavalrymen, can be regarded as a new articulation of the traditional, martial lifestyle.

In summary, we can say that the Rhineland and the Gallic interior underwent specific political and military changes during the pre-Flavian period, with a continuation of a martial way of life on the one hand, and the development of a more 'civilian' lifestyle on the other.[83] A characteristic of the Rhineland frontier region is not only that traditional, martial traditions were able to survive but that for strategic

[80] See chapter 5.3.5.
[81] Gabelmann 1973, especially 156-175.
[82] Although Gabelmann (1973, 193 ff.), in view of the epitaph on a monument from Wesseling-'Keldenich', associates the large cavalry reliefs with officers from Italy who commanded cavalry units during and after the suppression of the Batavian revolt, the native military elite will certainly have erected such monuments as well. In general, see recently Krier 2003.
[83] Roymans 1996, 37-41.

Fig. 7.7. Fragment of a monumental cavalry relief, found in Nijmegen. Height 50 cm. Photo, Museum het Valkhof Nijmegen.

reasons they were actively encouraged by the Romans. Thanks to the heavy recruitment of men for 'national' units based on the native *Gefolgschaft*, native elites and young men continued to be able to acquire status through military means after the Roman conquest. Compared to the Gallic provinces, there was less need to express status in the civilian domain; new, Roman elements became integrated into the martial ideology and were used to express traditional values.

7.3 A 'CIVILIAN' LIFESTYLE AT THE IMPERIAL FRONTIER

Although the Rhineland and the Gallic interior can be characterised by military and 'civilian' lifestyles respectively following the Augustan reorganisations, this distinction seems to have been of quite short duration. In the course of the 1st century we also see sweeping changes in the use and significance of 'military' objects in the Rhineland frontier zone.

The changing composition of the finds from non-military contexts reveals different patterns of use (figs. 3.2-3). Compared with the previous period, weaponry finds from the 2nd and 3rd centuries decline sharply, with distinctly military items (helmets, armour and shields) occurring in negligible numbers. The fact that belt numbers remain roughly the same, yet horse gear shows a peak in this period, is linked to a shift in the Flavian period from objects with a strictly military use to ones with a military-civilian use.[84] Finds from non-military contexts no longer appear to be mainly associated with returning veterans, but increasingly with civilian use by civilians. This is confirmed by the geographical distribution of 'military' finds from the 2nd and 3rd centuries (fig. 3.12-13). Although there is only limited data available on the Gallic interior, there is no longer a concentration of finds in the frontier zone. Instead, they exhibit a broad distribution across the frontier region, the immediately adjacent areas and hinterlands, supporting the idea of a more general, military-civilian use.

The significance of weaponry and horse gear for their owners was also subject to change. This is demonstrated in the cessation of a long tradition of ritual weapons deposition. The dateable pieces from Kessel-Lith and Xanten-'Wardt' can be placed predominantly in the first half of the 1st century.[85] The same applies to grave finds from the Treveri territory, where the most recent graves date from the mid-1st century.[86] The exclusive horse gear sets from the Rhine at Doorwerth (fig. 5.11) and Xanten (fig.

[84] See chapter 6.
[85] Schalles/Schreiter 1993, 178 ff.
[86] Schumacher 1989a; 1989b; compare Waurick 1994, Abb. 15 (Wederath cemetery).

4.10), and the military finds from Empel-'De Werf', suggest that ritual disposal of militaria did not come to an abrupt halt in around AD 50, but persisted on a limited scale at least into the Claudio-Neronian period.[87]

The fact that weapons and horse gear declined in significance as personal memorabilia for veterans from the Claudio-Neronian period onward and barely featured in the once so important rites of passage for soldiers is linked to changes in lifestyle and ideology that were probably accelerated in the wake of the Batavian revolt.[88] Although old alliances with the Batavians and other frontier groups appear to have been restored once the revolt was suppressed, and the Batavians continued to be major suppliers of auxiliary troops, the event was not without its repercussions. Those most affected will have been the old elite families who had led or supported the revolt. A critical factor here is the fall of the Julio-Claudian house, the principal patron of the Rhineland Julii until Nero's death in AD 68. The elite, who remained loyal to Rome under the Flavian Emperor Vespasian during the Batavian revolt, will have seized its opportunity and – with the support of the Roman authorities – will have usurped the position of the old aristocracy.[89]

A key question is the degree to which the position of this 'new' elite changed vis-à-vis the traditional, military elite. If a prefecture did exist up until the time of the Batavian revolt, this position will definitely have been abolished thereafter. This means that from 70 onward, *praefecti* were no longer able to pose as military leaders with their own small military units. And presumably, the days were over in which the native elite could command their own units and recruit new soldiers.[90] Leadership will have been taken over by officers of Italic origin, with the Roman authorities taking responsibility for recruitment. The Batavians and Treveri seem to have occupied a unique position, for we know that they still, at least in part, commanded their 'national' units themselves.[91] In general, however, the role of the Rhineland aristocracy as military leaders recruiting troops from among their own clientele had come to an end.

The repercussions of the Batavian revolt were no less far-reaching for the regular auxiliary soldiers. The units that took part in the revolt were stationed in distant provinces, where in general they appear to have been reinforced by local recruits.[92] In this way the Roman authorities sought to prevent the creation of too strong a bond between soldiers and their homeland. A major consequence of this measure is that soldiers no longer belonged to highly homogenous, 'national' units, putting an end to opportunities for displaying military prowess in the 'traditional' auxiliary. Rather than a privilege, military service was increasingly regarded as a regular profession, designed not to win glory and show off one's skills, but to better oneself financially and – as a key symbol of a civilian lifestyle – to acquire Roman citizenship.

Given that the native elite were no longer able to achieve status through the army, competition among the Rhineland elite also took on more of a 'civilian', or 'Roman' character. For the Flavian elite, investment in private and public buildings became the chief new means by which they could distinguish themselves. In the eastern Rhine delta, this manifested itself in the emergence of villas and villa-type complexes ('proto-villas') in the countryside.[93] In addition, monumental temple complexes were erected at Empel, Kessel-Lith and Elst, public works that were probably funded in full or in part by members of

---

[87] Brouwer 1982 (Doorwerth); Jenkins 1985 (Xanten); for Empel, see chapter 3.3.3.

[88] See also Roymans 1996, 40-41; Derks 1998, 54.

[89] Slofstra 2002, 30-35.

[90] Alföldy 1968, 98, 101-102.

[91] Strobel 1987, 287-292.

[92] Alföldy 1968, 102-104. It is believed that the first and second Batavian cohorts and the Batavian *ala* were stationed in Germania Inferior until the end of the 1st century and that they continued to be supplemented by Batavian recruits (Holder 1999; Haalebos 2000b, 42-43).

[93] Willems 1984, 112 ff.; Slofstra 1991, especially 178 ff; Van Enckevort 2001, 349 ff.

Fig. 7.8. Gravestone featuring *Totenmahlrelief* from Dodewaard. The stone was erected by Marcus Traianus Gumattius, a veteran from the *ala Afrorum*. Height 144 cm. After Derks 1998, fig. 2.8.

the native aristocracy.[94] We see from the way in which the deceased are presented on funerary monuments that martial values were also becoming less important for auxiliary soldiers. Characteristic of the pre-Flavian period are gravestones showing infantrymen and triumphant cavalrymen in full battle dress. In the Flavian period they were gradually replaced by monuments emphasising the deceased's civilian status.[95] From now on, soldiers and veterans preferred *Totenmahlreliefs*, which portrayed them as leading

[94] Recent research has shown that the most recent temple in Elst was built in around AD 100. Based on this new dating, the stone construction phase in Empel and Kessel-Lith can also be placed at the time of Trajan (Roymans 2004, 143-144; for the original datings of the temples of Elst and Empel, see Bogaers 1955; Roymans/Derks 1994).

[95] Noelke (1998, 409-411) emphasises that the uniform depiction of the deceased does not reflect reality. Only wealthy civilians and high-ranking officers possessed furniture, fine tableware and a slave, whereas the deceased were simple soldiers in almost all cases.

citizens, clad in togas and reclining on couches (fig. 7.8).[96] The only remaining reference to the military status of the deceased is found in the epitaph and, for cavalrymen, in a second relief beneath the epitaph featuring the deceased's horse and a slave carrying his weapons.[97] This points to a far-reaching change in the ideal image that *auxiliarii* had of themselves. Their model was no longer the traditional, military elite; this had been supplanted by the new, Flavian aristocracy who lived a more Roman lifestyle.

After the Batavian revolt, the tribal warrior ideology appears to have given way to a 'civilian ideology' in the frontier zone of the empire. Being a soldier was no longer regarded as a privilege, one associated with traditional values and prestige. This meant that it became less important for veterans to display their newly-won status by bringing equipment home and in this way shaping their identity. Only occasionally did veterans continue to take home their weapons and horse gear, presumably because these items were still relevant for some individuals as a reminder of an important part of their lives. Nor was it still customary for veterans, on their return to the civilian world, to ritually deposit part of their equipment in a river or cult place. And for the Treveri, there was an end to the long tradition of burying soldiers and veterans together with military symbols.[98]

7.4 'GERMANIC' NEWCOMERS AND A REVIVAL OF MARTIAL VALUES?

The development outlined in the previous section is characteristic of a period of relative calm and economic prosperity. This situation came to an end when the *limes* was breached by raiding Germans in around 170 and again in the 3rd century. Although the frontier defence was at first restored, the second wave of attacks led to many forts along the Rhine being abandoned once and for all. The fortification of towns and the construction of *burgi* on villa sites show that the northern Gallic population sought to take the defence of its territory upon itself.[99] In addition to small military and civilian detachments, deployed to protect the towns, there appear to have been private militias who defended the estates of the wealthier farmers.[100] The relatively many *spathae* from the 2nd and 3rd centuries found in rural settlements show that simpler farmers also tried to protect their family and property by arming themselves.[101]

The fortification of settlements and the arming of the northern Gallic population were to no avail. In the second half of the 3rd century, towns were destroyed and large tracts of countryside were abandoned for a period of almost fifty years. The situation was restored to some degree from the time of Diocletian (284-305), after which the northern provinces became repopulated in the 4th century. We see archaeological evidence of this in the appearance in urban fortifications, rural settlements, rivers and graves of late Roman weapons and belts richly decorated with bronze fittings. Studies of the late Roman era always pay particular attention to weapon graves. The traditional interpretation of these graves as being

---

[96] Noelke 1998. Interestingly, this type of gravestone was also erected for auxiliary soldiers who died while on active service and who had therefore not yet acquired Roman citizenship.

[97] These military reliefs no longer occur after the beginning of the 2nd century (Noelke 1998, 414); the same applies to gravestones featuring triumphant cavalrymen (Gabelmann 1973, 172).

[98] The dedications by veterans may have acquired a more 'civilian' character at cult places. An example here is a late 1st- or early 2nd-century votive plaque of a legionary veteran from Empel-'De Werf', which may originally have been affixed to the base of a statue (fig. 5.10). The statue was presumably dedicated after completion of the term of service to honour a vow made to Hercules Magusanus (Roymans/Aarts 2005, 356).

[99] For an overview, see chapter 6.1.3.

[100] MacMullen 1967, 129 ff.; see also Luttwak 1976, 169-170. These militias are highly reminiscent of the pre-Roman *Gefolgschaften*.

[101] See chapter 6.1.3.

associated with 'German' newcomers who served in the Roman army has come under fire recently.[102] Theuws presents an alternative model, based on new ideas about the ethnic background and status of the deceased, as well as the symbolic significance and dating of the grave goods.[103]

Firstly, the 'Germanic' origin of the deceased is called into question. Although some grave finds (especially fibulae) appear to have been inspired by trans-Rhenish examples, they are predominantly Roman products.[104] For instance, most of the swords are Roman *spathae* and there are clear indications that the 'Germanic belt' was manufactured inside the imperial borders. For this reason, the weapon graves are classified as 'Gallo-Germanic' or 'Gallo-Frankish' in the more recent literature.[105] Theuws supports this interpretation, pointing out that the deceased could just as well have come from the Gallic interior as from Germania.

Secondly, it seems incorrect to regard the deceased as soldiers in all instances. We know that, as in the previous periods, the population of northern Gaul furnished the Roman army with large numbers of troops. Archaeological evidence for this are Chi-Rho appliqués from guard helmets from rural settlements near IJzendoorn (138.3, pl. 7) and Lienden (174.6, pl. 7), and several guard helmets from wet contexts that had presumably been ritually deposited.[106] Once again, these objects can be associated with veterans who took them home when completing their military service. This leaves open the possibility, however, that weapons could also have belonged to local leaders and their warrior-followers, particularly in the 5th century. Nor do 'military' belts present an unequivocal picture. As in the previous period, belts were worn by soldiers and civilians alike during the 4th and 5th centuries.[107]

Halsall interprets grave goods more generally as 'symbols of authority' and the funerary ritual as a form of competition between local leaders following the collapse of effective Roman control over northern Gaul.[108] He believes that these leaders recruited from among their clientèle warrior-followers to form military bands to protect the population against raids.[109] According to Theuws, their protective role is also evident in the location of some of the weapon graves close to walled towns and on or near fortified hilltops. These locations have an important symbolic value in that they express the protective capability of the elite.

Thirdly, the general interpretation of the interred 'weapons' as military objects has been called into question. It is conspicuous that the weaponry comprises an axe and/or lance in almost 80% of the graves. There seems to have been a conscious choice of objects that were not used exclusively in a military context. Lances, as well as bows and arrows, constitute hunting weapons in Theuws' view, while the axe is associated with wood cutting and clearing land. He points out that hunting was a favourite pastime of

---

[102] Werner (1950/1951; 1958) interprets the weapon graves above all in ethnic terms, associating them with Germanic Laeti. Böhme (1974, 195 ff.) thinks more generally of German *foederati*, which continues to be the widely accepted view (e.g. Fischer 1999, 127).

[103] Theuws, in print; see also Theuws/Alkemade 2000.

[104] See Halsall 1982; Whittaker 1994, 235.

[105] See Theuws, in print, with references.

[106] Wet context finds are documented from the Waal at Nijmegen (211.18), 'De Peel' at Deurne (Braat et al. 1973), Augsburg-'Pfersee' (Klumbach 1973b, 95-101) and Worms-'Schildergasse' (Klumbach 1973c, 111-114).

[107] The examples with uniform, chip-carved plates are regarded as insignia belonging to officers, as well as to high-ranking civilian officials (see chapter 6.2).

[108] Halsall 1982, 205-207. Illustrative of the elite's role is their appropriation in the 5th century of the imperial privilege of minting coins, as is evident in the distribution of silver imitations, especially in areas containing weapon graves (King 1982). Theuws (in print) points out, however, that it is not competition but the staking of claims to land that is central to the rhetoric of the funerary ritual; in particular the small number of graves (amounting to one grave per year for the 4th and 5th centuries) and the simplicity of the bulk of the grave goods would contradict this.

[109] Cf. Halsall 1982, 206.

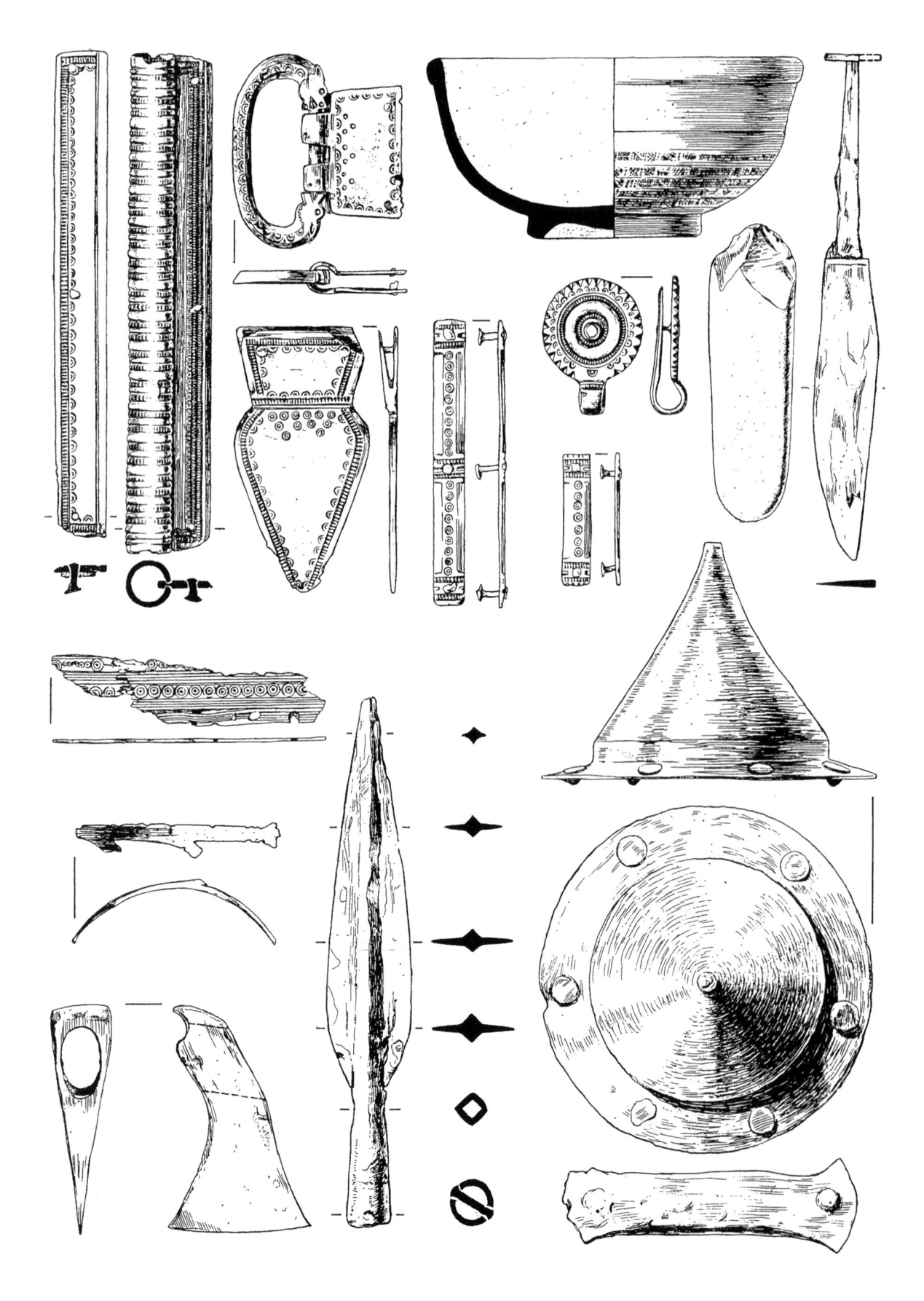

Fig. 7.9. Inventory of a late Roman weapon grave including a shield, a spearhead and an ornate belt from the cemetery on the 'Donderberg' at Rhenen (grave 833, 253.2). After Böhme 1974, Taf. 63.

the aristocracy in the late Roman era – not only for relaxation, but in particular because it gave them an opportunity to display courage and hence, indirectly, dominance over nature and control of their world. The ritual deposition of axes, lances, and bows and arrows in a funerary context gives expression to the elite's dominant position and can be regarded as a confirmation of their claims to an area of land.

Fourthly, the deposition of weapons and other precious objects in ritual contexts is linked to a fairly unstable socio-political situation.[110] It is precisely at such times that positions of authority need to be constantly redefined through ritual transactions. The weapon graves are concentrated in the fertile loess regions that were largely abandoned in the 3rd century and reinhabited once again in the 4th century.[111] The lack of a stable power base meant that new leaders in these areas were obliged to shape their position with the help of a new ritual repertoire. The absence, or scarcity, of weapon graves in other areas can firstly be explained by the relatively stable socio-political situation there. This was particularly true of the estates controlled by the emperor in Trier until well into the 4th century. Secondly, some of these areas were not yet inhabited during this period.

Finally, it has been pointed out that the 4th- and 5th-century graves are not a fairly homogenous group, but instead can be classified chronologically on the basis of the types of weapon finds.[112] Graves containing swords and shields belong to the most recent stage and date primarily from the late 4th and 5th centuries.[113] For the remaining graves, the weapons consist of axes, lances and/or bows and arrows, dating roughly from the 4th century. A problem with this classification is that the late Roman weapon graves can be dated at the earliest to around the mid-4th century and probably not until the last quarter of the 4th century.[114] This means that it is hardly possible to distinguish chronologically graves containing hunting weapons, axes and 'real' weapons, which for the most part occur contemporaneously. A distinction can only be made on the basis of the grave locations: the 'real' weapon graves tend to be associated with defensible locations.

We may conclude that the appearance of the late Roman weapon graves is associated with the repopulation of large parts of northern Gaul during the 4th century, probably by people from both Gaul and across the Rhine. The settlement of these 'Gallo-Germans' went hand in hand with the introduction of a new funerary ritual, whereby the deceased were interred as cultivators (axe) and hunters (lance, bow and arrow). This expressed the local aristocrats' role in the recultivation of tracts of land and the staking of territorial claims, not only during their lifetime, but in particular as ancestors after their death. The same period saw the appearance of 'real' weapon graves containing swords and shields. In Theuws' view, these military symbols refer not so much to an army career, but to the native elite's protective role after the collapse of an effective frontier defence. This interpretation is supported by the specific choice of location for some of the weapon graves. The graves symbolise an elite which trod in the footsteps of the Roman authority, not only as political leaders, but also as military, protective leaders.

Finds from the *civitas Batavorum* and the adjacent area across the Rhine tie in well with this picture. After Nijmegen and most of the settlements in the Batavian countryside were abandoned during the 3rd century, weapon graves appeared here too in the 4th century, accompanying the arrival of new inhabitants (table 5.5). The majority come from a single cemetery at Rhenen.[115] Here we find the only graves for which there are documented finds of 'real' weapons – one containing a *spatha* and one a shield (fig. 7.9). The weapons in the

---

[110] Theuws/Alkemade 2000, 464-466; compare Hedeager 1992. However, ritual dealings with valuables are not always associated with instability; compare the 1st-century AD when simple soldiers deposited parts of their equipment at cult places or rivers in the socially and politically stable Rhine zone.

[111] Theuws, in print; this is especially the area between the Loire and Meuse rivers. Compare the deposition of valuables in the second half of the 5th and the 6th century (Theuws/Alkemade 2000, 464-466).

[112] Theuws/Alkemade 2000, 450 ff.; Theuws, in print.

[113] Here, graves containing swords of the 'Krefeld type' make up the last phase (mid-5th to early 6th century).

[114] Böhme 1974 (from c. 350); 1989 (from c. 390); see also Swift (2000) who adheres to a dating from c. 360/370.

[115] Ypey 1973; 1978; Wagner 1994.

remaining graves are hunting weapons (spears and lances), axes and/or a dagger or knife. Additionally, almost all graves contain a belt. Interestingly, the cemetery occupies a prominent position on the edge of a moraine immediately north of the Rhine. Although there is no data on the associated settlement, a fortification may have been present.[116] Outside this cemetery, several stray graves have been found at Wageningen and across the research region in the vicinity of settlements. In all cases, the grave goods included a belt.

A question that remains is the extent to which the late Roman funerary ritual can be regarded as the renewed expression of a martial ideology. In contrast to the 1st-century graves, the grave goods do not seem to point to the military prowess and glory of the deceased, but to his specific roles following the collapse of Roman authority.[117] Although *Beowulf* shows that taking part in heroic deeds and gaining glory continued to be important values, an interesting shift can be discerned vis-à-vis the late Iron Age and the 1st century AD with regard to ritual dealings with weapons. In the funerary ritual the emphasis was not on the military status of the deceased as a warrior or soldier, but more specifically on his skills as a cultivator of land and a protector.

7.5 CONCLUSION

We have seen different kinds of use and significance of weaponry and horse gear during the Roman period. Finds can be associated with either a military or a more civilian lifestyle, depending on the specific socio-political context. The springboard for the survey presented here was the importance of warriorship in the tribal, 'Celto-Germanic' world. In this martial world, native leaders presented themselves as military elites and young men were expected to prove themselves as warriors. Weapons were important symbols of the actual or potential status and skills of warriors, and played a key role in male rites of passage.

From Augustus onward, Gaul was divided along politico-military and ideological lines. Whereas the demilitarisation of the Gallic interior resulted in a more civilian lifestyle, the military way of life was able to survive thanks to the heavy recruitment of men for the Roman army in the imperial frontier region. At the same time, however, the transformation of tribal warriors into professional soldiers had far-reaching consequences. Weapons lost their value as important gifts, and admission to and discharge from the army became the new key moments in a man's life. Characteristic of this period is the fact that large numbers of veterans chose to take part of their equipment home as personal memorabilia or to ritually deposit it, thus marking the end of their active soldiering days.

This difference between the Gallic provinces and the Rhineland was of short duration, however. From the Claudio-Neronian period onward, traditional, martial values also went into decline at the imperial frontier. This was probably accelerated by the consequences of the Batavian revolt, when the native aristocracy's role as military leaders was curtailed and it became increasingly difficult for auxiliary soldiers to display their skills and bravery in their 'own' units. In imitation of the elite, we see the rise of a civilian lifestyle among the *auxiliarii*, most evident on soldiers' gravestones featuring *Totenmahlreliefs*. Weaponry and horse gear were only occasionally brought home by veterans as a reminder of their time in the army and these appear to have no longer played a key role in male rites of passage.

Not until the Roman authorities lost their hold on power from the late 4th century onward can we assume a revival of martial values in northern Gaul. However, the emphasis in ritual dealings with 'military' items was no longer on military prowess and glory, but on the role of the elite in cultivating land and providing protection.

---

[116] Evidence for this could be the probable location along a road to the German area across the Rhine (Ypey 1973, 304-305).

[117] We see a similar picture throughout the Merovingian period, with swords as the principal grave goods (Theuws/Alkemade 2000, 461 ff.).

ABBREVIATIONS

Archaeological and other organisations

AAC	Amsterdams Archeologisch Centrum
ACVU	Archeologisch Centrum Vrije Universiteit, Amsterdam
ADC	Archeologisch Diensten Centrum, Amersfoort
ARC	Archaeological Researsch & Consultancy, Groningen
BATO	Beoefenaren Archeologie Tiel en Omstreken
GD'sH	Gemeentelijk depot Bouwhistorie, Archeologie en Monumenten, 's-Hertogenbosch
GNBA	Gemeente Nijmegen, Bureau Archeologie
HBS	Hendrik Brunsting Stichting, Amsterdam
IPL	Instituut voor Prehistorie, Leiden
MhV	Museum het Valkhof, Nijmegen
RAAP	RAAP Archeologisch Adviesbureau, Weesp
RMO	Rijksmuseum van Oudheden, Leiden
ROB	Rijksdienst voor het Oudheidkundig Bodemonderzoek (= Rijksdienst voor Archeologie, Cultuurlandschap en Monumenten), Amersfoort
RUN	Radboud Universiteit Nijmegen
UvA	Universiteit van Amsterdam
UL	Universiteit Leiden
VU	Vrije Universiteit, Amsterdam

Classical sources

Ann.	*Annales* (Tacitus)
BG	*De bello Gallico* (Caesar)
Cod. Just.	*Codex Justinianus*
Cod. Theod.	*Codex Theodosius*
Dig. Just.	*Digest Justinianus*
Hist.	*Historiae* (Tacitus)
Germ.	*Germania* (Tacitus)
ERM	*Epitoma Rei Militaris* (Vegetius)
FIRA	*Fontes Iuri Romani Antejustiniani*

Journals and series

AAS	Amsterdam Archaeological Studies
AB	Archaeologia Belgica
AD	*Archaeological Dialogues*
AK	*Archäologisches Korrespondenzblatt*
APL	Analecta Praehistorica Leidensia
BAR	British Archaeological Reports, British Series
BAR Int. Ser.	British Archaeological Reports, International Series
BMVG	*Bijdragen en Mededeelingen, Vereeniging Gelre*
BROB	*Berichten van de Rijksdienst voor het Oudheidkundig Bodemonderzoek*
BRGK	*Berichte der Römisch-Germanischen Kommission*
BJ	*Bonner Jahrbücher*
BVB	*Bayerische Vorgeschichtsblätter*
CIL	*Corpus Inscriptionum Latinarum*

HABES	Heidelberger Althistorische Beiträge und Epigraphische Studien
JberGPV	Gesellschaft pro Vindonissa, Jahresbericht
JRA	Journal of Roman Archaeology
JRS	Journal of Roman Studies
JRGZM	Jahrbuch des Römisch-Germanischen Zentralmuseums Mainz
JRMES	Journal of Roman Military Equipment Studies
KJ	Kölner Jahrbuch
LCL	Loeb Classical Library
NAR	Nederlandse Archeologische Rapporten
OMROL	Oudheidkundige Mededelingen uit het Rijksmuseum van Oudheden te Leiden
RAM	Rapportage Archeologische Monumentenzorg
RAP	Revue Archéologique de Picardie
RE	Paulys Real-Encyclopädie der klassischen Altertumswissenschaft
SJ	Saalburg Jahrbuch
ZAR	Zuidnederlandse Archeologische Rapporten
ZPE	Zeitschrift für Papyrologie und Epigraphik

BIBLIOGRAPHY

Classical sources

Arrianus, Die 'Taktik' des Flavius Arrianus, text and translation F. Kiechle, 1965, *BRGK* 45, 87-129.

Codex Justinianus, translation C. Pharr, 1952: *The Theodosian Code and novels and the Sirmondian Constitutions*, Princeton.

Codex Theodosius, text and translation H. Hulot et al., 1979, Aalen (Corps de Droit Civil Romain 9).

Digest Justinianus, text and translation T. Mommsen, 1985, Pennsylvania.

Caesar, *De bello Gallico*, text and translation H.J. Edwards, 1970, London/Cambridge (LCL 72).

Tacitus, *Annales*, text and translation J. Jackson, 1979-1986 (3 vols), London/Cambridge (LCL 249, 312, 322).

Tacitus, *The Agricola and the Germania*, translation H. Mattingly (Penguin Classics 28).

Tacitus, *Historiae*, text and translation C.H. Moore, 1968-1969 (2 vols), London/Cambridge (LCL 111, 249).

Vegetius, *Epitoma Rei Militaris*, translation N.P. Milner, 1993: *Vegetius: Epitome of Military Science*, Liverpool.

Modern sources

Aarts, J., 1994: Romeinse munten op De Horden, in W.A. van Es/W.A.M. Hessing (eds.), *Romeinen, Friezen en Franken in het hart van Nederland. Van Traiectum tot Dorestad (50 v. Chr.-950 n. Chr.)*, Utrecht/Amersfoort, 138-144.

Aarts, J., 2000: *Coins or money? Exploring the monetization and functions of Roman coinage in Belgic Gaul and Lower Germany, 50 BC-AD 450*, Amsterdam (unpublished dissertation, VU).

Aarts, J., 2003: Monetisation and army recruitment in the Dutch river area in the early 1st century AD, in Th. Grünewald/S. Seibel (eds.), *Kontinuität und Diskontinuität. Germania inferior am Beginn und am Ende der römischen Herrschaft*, Berlin/New York (Ergänzungsbände zum Reallexikon der germanischen Alterumskunde 35), 162-180.

Abeleven, H.A.J./C.G.J. Bijleveld, 1895: *Catalogus van het Museum van Oudheden te Nijmegen*, Nijmegen.

Abeleven, H.A.J./C.G.J. Bijleveld, 1902: *Bijlage tot den vierden druk van den catalogus van het Museum van Oudheden te Nijmegen*, Nijmegen.

Alföldi, A., 1932: The helmet of Constantine with the Christian monogram, *JRS* 22, 9-23.

Alföldi, M.R. et al., 1957: *Intercisa II (Dunapentele). Geschichte der Stadt in der Römerzeit*, Budapest.

Alföldy, G., 1968: *Die Hilfstruppen in der römischen Provinz Germania inferior*, Düsseldorf (Epigraphische Studien 6).

Alföldy-Thomas, S., 1993: Anschirrungszubehör und Hufbeschläge von Zugtieren (G 1-54), in E. Künzl (ed.), *Die Alamannenbeute aus dem Rhein bei Neupotz. Teil 1: Untersuchungen*, Mainz, 331-344.

Allason-Jones, L./R. Miket, 1984: *The catalogue of small finds from South Shields Roman fort*, Gloucester.

Amand, M., 1975: *Atelier de bronzier d'époque romain à Blicquy*, Brussels (AB 171).

Baatz, D., 1963/1964: Die Grabungen im Kastell Echzell 1962, *SJ* 21, 32-58.

Baatz, D., 1966: Zur Geschützbewaffnung römischer Auxiliartruppen in der frühen und mittleren Kaiserzeit, *BJ* 166, 194-207.

Baatz, D./F.-R. Herrmann (eds.), 1982: *Die Römer in Hessen*, Stuttgart.

Bakker, A.M., 1997: Een smid in het kamp: Romeinse ijzeren wapens van het Kops Plateau te Nijmegen (Gld.), *Paleo-Aktueel* 9, 60-64.

Bazelmans, J., 1999: *By weapons made worthy. Lords, retainers and their relationship in Beowulf*, Amsterdam (AAS 5).

Bazelmans, J., 2000: Beyond power. Ceremonial exchanges in Beowulf, in F. Theuws/J.L. Nelson (eds.), *Rituals of power. From Late Antiquity to the Early Middle Ages*, Leiden (The transformation of the Roman world 8), 311-375.

Bazelmans, J./D. Gerrets/A. Pol, 2002: Metal detection and the Frisian kingdom. Questions about the central place of northern Westergo in the Early Middle Ages, *BROB* 45, 219-241.

Bechert, T., 1986: Die 'Einfriedungen' von Krefeld-Gellep – militärisch oder zivil?, in C. Unz (ed.), *Studien zu den Militärgrenzen Roms III. 13. Internationaler Limeskongreß, Aalen 1983*, Stuttgart (Forschungen und Berichte zur Vor- und Frühgeschichte in Baden-Württemberg 20), 96-100.

Bechert, T./W.J.H. Willems (eds.), 1995: *Die römische Reichsgrenze zwischen Mosel und Nordseeküste*, Stuttgart.

Behrends, O., 1986: Die Rechtsregelungen der Militärdiplome und das die Soldaten des Prinzipats treffende Eheverbot, in W. Eck/H. Wolff (eds.), *Heer und Integrationspolitik. Die römischen Militärdiplome als historische Quelle*, Cologne/Vienna, 116-166.

Bellen, H., 1981: *Die germanische Leibwache der römischen Kaiser des julisch-claudischen Hauses*, Wiesbaden.

Benea, D./R. Petrovszky, 1987: Werkstätten zur Metallverarbeitung in Tibiscum im 2. und 3. Jahrhundert n.Chr., *Germania* 65, 226-239.

Bender, H., 1978: *Römischer Reiseverkehr. Cursus publicus und Privatreisen*, Stuttgart (Schriften des Limesmuseums Aalen 20).

Bennet, J., 1991: Plumbatae from Pitsunda (Pityus), Georgia, and some observations on their probable use, *JRMES* 2, 59-63.

Berghe, L. vanden, 1996: Some Roman military equipment of the first three centuries AD in Belgian museums, *JRMES* 7, 59-93.

Bernard, H. et al., 1998: L'épave romaine de marbre de Porto Novo, *JRA* 11, 76-81.

Biborski, M., 1994a: Römische Schwerter mit Verzierung in Form von figürlichen Darstellungen und symbolischen Zeichen, in C. von Carnap-Bornheim (ed.), *Beiträge zu römischer und barbarischer Bewaffnung in den ersten vier nachchristlichen Jahrhunderten. Akten des 2. Internationalen Kolloquiums in Marburg a.d. Lahn, 20. bis 24. Februar 1994*, Lublin/Marburg (Veröffentlichung des vorgeschichtlichen Seminars Marburg 8), 108-135.

Biborski, M., 1994b: Römische Schwerter im Gebiet des europäischen Barbaricum, *JRMES* 5, 169-197.

Birley, A., 2002: *A band of brothers. Garrison life at Vindolanda*, Stroud.

Birley, E., 1982/1983: Veterans of the Roman army in Britain and elsewhere, *Ancient society* 13/14, 265-276 (reprinted in E. Birley, 1988: *The Roman Army Papers 1929-1986*, Amsterdam, 272-283).

Birley, E., 1988: *The Roman army papers 1929-1986*, Amsterdam (Mavors 4).

Bishop, M.C., 1985: The military fabrica and the production of arms in the Early Principate, in M.C. Bishop (ed.), *The production and distribution of Roman military equipment*, Oxford (BAR Int. Ser. 275), 1-30.

Bishop, M.C., 1988: Cavalry equipment of the Roman army in the first century A.D., in J.C. Coulston (ed.), *Military equipment and the identity of Roman soldiers. Proceedings of the fourth Roman Military Equipment Conference*, Oxford (BAR Int. Ser. 394), 67-195.

Bishop, M.C., 1991: Soldiers and military equipment in the towns of Roman Britain, in V.A. Maxfield/M.J. Dobson (eds.), *Roman frontier studies 1989. Proceedings of the XVth International Congress of Roman Frontier Studies*, Exeter, 21-27.

Bishop, M.C., 1992: The early imperial 'apron', *JRMES* 3, 81-104.

Bishop, M.C., 2002a: *Lorica Segmentata. Volume 1: A handbook of articulated Roman plate armour*, Breamer et al., (JRMES Monograph 1).

Bishop, M.C., 2002b: A catalogue of military weapons and fittings, *JberGPV* 2001, 7-11,

Bishop, M.C./J.C.N. Coulston, 1993: *Roman military equipment. From the Punic Wars to the fall of Rome*, London.

Bloemers, J.H.F., 1978: *Rijswijk (Z.H.), 'De Bult'. Eine Siedlung der Cananefaten*, Amersfoort (Nederlandse Oudheden 8).

Bloemers, J.H.F., 1990: Lower Germany: *plura consilio quam vi*. Proto-urban settlement developments and the integration of native society, in T. Blagg/M. Millett (eds.), *The early Roman Empire in the west*, Oxford, 72-86.

Bloemers, J.H.F./L.P. Louwe Kooijmans/H. Sarfatij, 1981: *Verleden land. Archeologische opgravingen in Nederland*, Amsterdam.

Bockius, R., 1989: Ein römisches Scutum aus Urmitz, Kreis Mayen-Koblenz. Zu Herkunft und Verbreitung spindlerförmiger Schildbuckelbeschläge im Gebiet nördlich der Alpen, *AK* 19, 269-282.

Boe, G. de, 1982: *Le sanctuaire gallo-romain dans la Plaine de Bieure à Matagne-la-Petite*, Brussels (AB 251).

Boesterd, M.H.P. den, 1959: Romeins Nijmegen. Een graf op de Grote Markt te Nijmegen, *Jaarboek Numaga* 6, 117-126.

Bogaers, J.E., 1952: Bewoning uit de Romeinse tijd, 2e helft van de 2e en 1e helft van de 3e eeuw na Chr., Rockanje (prov. Zuid-Holland), *BROB* 3, 4-8.

Bogaers, J.E., 1955: *De Gallo-Romeinse tempels te Elst in de Over-Betuwe*, 's-Gravenhage (Nederlandse Oudheden 1).

Bogaers, J.E., 1959: Twee vondsten uit de Maas in Midden-Limburg, *BROB* 9, 85-97.

Bogaers, J.E., 1960/1961: Civitas en stad van de Bataven en Cannanefaten, *BROB* 10/11, 263-317.

Bogaers, J.E., 1970/1971: Een medaille, *Jaarboek Numaga* 17/18, 183-191.

Bogaers, J.E., 1971: Voorburg-Arentsburg: Forum Hadriani, *OMROL* 52, 128-138.

Bogaers, J.E., 1972: Civitas und Civitas-Hauptorte in der nördlichen Germania inferior, *BJ* 172, 310-333.

Bogaers, J.E., 1974: Thracische hulptroepen in Germania inferior, *OMROL* 55, 198-220.

Bogaers, J.E. et al., 1979: *Noviomagus. Op het spoor der Romeinen in Nijmegen*, Nijmegen.

Bogaers, J.E./J.K. Haalebos, 1975: Problemen rond het Kops Plateau, *OMROL* 56, 127-178.

Bogaers, J.E./J.K. Haalebos, 1987: Einfache und reiche Gräber im römischen Nijmegen, *Antike Welt* 18, 40-47.

Bogaers, J.E./C.B. Rüger, 1974: *Der niedergermanische Limes. Materialien zu seiner Geschichte*, Bonn.

Bohec, Y. Le, 1994: *The imperial Roman army*, London/New York.

Böhme, H.W., 1974: *Germanische Grabfunde des 4. bis 5. Jahrhunderts zwischen unterer Elbe und Loire*, Munich (Münchner Beiträge zur Vor- und Frühgeschichte 19).

Böhme, H.W., 1986: Das Ende der Römerherrschaft in Britannien und die angelsächsische Besiedlung Englands im 5. Jahrhundert, *JRGZM* 33, 469-574.

Böhme, H.W., 1989: Gallien in der Spätantike. Forschungen zum Ende der Römerherrschaft in den westlichen Provinzen, *JRGZM* 34, 770-773.

Bónis, É.B., 1986: Das Militärhandwerk der Legio I Adiutrix in Brigetio, in C. Unz (ed.), *Studien zu den Militärgrenzen Roms III. 13. Internationaler Limeskongreß, Aalen 1983*, Stuttgart (Forschungen und Berichte zur Vor- und Frühgeschichte in Baden-Württemberg 20), 301-307.

Bonnamour, L. (ed.), 1990: *Du silex à la poudre... 4000 ans d'armement en val de Saône (exposition 1990-1991)*, Montagnac.

Borhy, L., 1990: Zwei neue Parade-Brustplatten im ungarischen Nationalmuseum, *BVB* 55, 299-307.

Boschung, D., 1987: Römische Glasphalerae mit Porträtbüsten, *BJ* 187, 193-258.

Bosman, A.V.A.J., 1992: Velserbroek B6, military equipment from a ritual site, *Arma* 4-1, 5-8.

Bosman, A.V.A.J., 1995a: Velserbroek B6-Velsen 1-Velsen 2. Is there a relationship between the military equipment from a ritual site and the fortresses of Velsen?, *JRMES* 6, 89-98.

Bosman, A.V.A.J., 1995b: Pouring lead in the pouring rain. Making lead slingshot under battle conditions, *JRMES* 6, 99-103.

Bosman, A.V.A.J., 1997: *Het culturele vondstmateriaal van de vroeg-Romeinse versterking te Velsen 1*, Amsterdam (unpublished dissertation, UvA).

Bosman, A.V.A.J./T. Looijenga, 1996: A runic inscription from Bergakker (Gelderland), the Netherlands, in E. Langbroek et al. (eds.), *Amsterdamer Beiträge zur älteren Germanistik* 46, Amsterdam, 9-16.

Bowman, A.K./J.D. Thomas, 1983: *Vindolanda: the Latin writing-tablets*, London (Britannia Monograph Series 4).

Braat, W.C., 1949: Drie inheemse nederzettingen uit de Romeinse tijd, *OMROL* 30, 23-46.

Braat, W.C., 1961: Das Stirnband eines römischen Paradehelmes, *OMROL* 42, 60-62.

Braat, W.C., 1967: Römische Schwerter und Dolche im Rijksmuseum van Oudheden, *OMROL* 48, 56-61.

Braat, W.C. et al., 1973: Der Fund von Deurne, Holland, in H. Klumbach (ed.), *Spätrömische Gardehelme*, Munich (Münchner Beitrage zur Vor- und Frühgeschichte 15), 15-83.

Brandenburgh, C.R. et al., 2002: Van woonstalboerderij tot legerkamp, *Brabants Heem* 54, 142-152.

Breeze, D.J., 1976: The ownership of arms in the Roman army, *Britannia* 7, 93–95.

Breeze, D.J./J. Close-Brooks/J.N.G. Ritchie, 1976: Soldiers' burials at Camelon, Stirlingshire, 1922 and 1975, *Britannia* 7, 73-95.

Breuer, J., 1931: Les objets antiques découverts à Ubbergen près Nimègue, *OMROL* 12, 27-122.

Bridger, C., 2006: Veteran settlement in the Lower Rhineland: the evidence from the *civitas Traianensis*, *JRA* 19, 137-149.

Broeke, P.W. van den, 1987: De dateringsmiddelen voor de IJzertijd van Zuid-Nederland, in W.A.B. van der Sanden/ P.W. van den Broeke (eds.), *Getekend zand. Tien jaar archeologisch onderzoek in Oss-Ussen*, Waalre (Bijdragen tot de studie van het Brabantse Heem 31), 23-43.

Broeke, P.W. van den, 2002: *Vindplaatsen in vogelvlucht. Beknopt overzicht van het archeologische onderzoek in de Waalsprong, 1996-2001*, Nijmegen (Archeologische Berichten Nijmegen 1).

Brouwer, M., 1982: Römische Phalerae und anderer Lederbeschlag aus dem Rhein, *OMROL* 63, 145-199.

Brulet, R., 1981: *Braives gallo-romain. 1. La zone centrale*, Louvain-la-Neuve (Publications d'histoire de l'art et d'archéologie de l'Université Catholique de Louvain 26).

Brunaux, J.-L., 1995: Die keltischen Heiligtümer Nordfrankreichs, in A. Haffner (ed.), *Heiligtümer und Opferkulte der Kelten*, Stuttgart (Archäologie in Deutschland, Sonderheft 1995), 55-74.

Brunaux, J.-L./P. Meniel/F. Poplin, 1985: *Gournay I. Les fouilles sur le sanctuaire et l'oppidum (1975-1984)*, s.l. (*RAP*, numéro special).

Brunaux, J.-L./A. Rapin, 1988: *Gournay II. Boucliers et lances depots et trophées*, Amiens/Paris (*RAP*, numéro special).

Brunaux, J.-L. et al., 1999: Ribemont-sur-Ancre (Somme). Bilan préliminaire et nouvelles hypothèses, *Gallia* 56, 177-283.

Brunsting, H., 1937: *Het grafveld onder Hees bij Nijmegen. Een bijdrage tot de kennis van Ulpia Noviomagus*, Amsterdam.

Brunsting, H., 1966: Nijmegen. Legerplaats van het 10de legioen. *Bulletin van de Koninklijke Nederlandse Oudheidkundige Bond* 65, ★16–17.

Brunsting, H./J.E. Bogaers, 1962: Nijmegen. Legerplaats 10de legioen, *Bulletin van de Koninklijke Nederlandse Oudheidkundige Bond* 15, ★4–5, ★79–80.

Brunsting, H./D.C. Steures, 1991: The lone watchman. The find circumstances of the Augustan iron helmet from Nijmegen and the date of the Augustan legionary fortress, *OMROL* 71, 101-111.

Buckland, P., 1978: A first-century shield from Doncaster, Yorkshire, *Britannia* 9, 247-269.

Bullinger, H., 1968: Punzverzierte spätkaiserzeitliche Gürtelbronzen aus Tongeren, Prov. Limburg, *Helinium* 8, 45-56.

Bullinger, H., 1972: *Utere felix*: à propos de la garniture de ceinturon de Lyon, *Gallia* 30, 276-283.

Bult, E.J./D.P. Hallewas, 1990: De opgravingscampagne op het Marktsveld te Valkenburg (Z.H.) in 1987 en 1988, in E.J. Bult/D.P. Hallewas (eds.), *Graven bij Valkenburg III, het archeologisch onderzoek in 1987 en 1988*, Delft, 1-36.

Buora, M., 2002: Militaria in Aquileia, *JberGPV* 2001, 41-52.

Burgers, J.Th.M, 1968: Twee Romeinse vondsten uit Mijnsherenland, *Westerheem* 17, 126-132.

Burmeister, S., 1995: Die römerzeitliche Besiedlung im Landkreis Starnberg, in W. Czysz et al. (eds.), *Provinzialrömische Forschungen. Festschrift für Günter Ulbert zum 65. Geburtstag*, Espelkamp, 217-231.

Büttner, A., 1957: Untersuchungen über Ursprung und Entwicklung von Auszeichnungen im römischen Heer, *BJ* 157, 127-180.

Cadoux, J.-L., 1984: L'ossuaire gaulois de Ribemont-sur-Ancre (Somme), premières observations, premières questions, *Gallia* 42, 53-78.

Campbell, D.B., 1986: Auxiliary artillery revisited, *BJ* 186, 117-132.

Carmiggelt, A. et al. (eds.), 1997: Archeologisch onderzoek in het tracé van de Willemsspoortunnel te Rotterdam, *Boor Balans* 3.

Chys, F.A. van der, 2000: Bijlage IV. Metaal, in W.K. Vos (ed.), *Houten-Zuid. Het archeologisch onderzoek op het terrein 8A*, Bunschoten (ADC Rapport 30), 113-122.

Clarke, G. (ed.), 1979: *The Roman cemetery at Lankhills II*, Oxford (Winchester Studies 3).

Clason, A.T., 1978: Animal husbandry and hunting at Rijswijk (Z.H.), in J.H.F. Bloemers, *Rijswijk (Z.H.), 'De Bult'. Eine Siedlung der Cananefaten*, Amersfoort (Nederlandse Oudheden 8), 424-437.

Clerck, M. de, 1983: *Vicus Tienen. Eerste resultaten van een systematisch onderzoek naar een Romeins verleden*, Tienen.

Connolly, P., 1986: A reconstruction of a Roman saddle, *Britannia* 17, 353-355.

Connolly, P., 1997: Pilum, gladius and pugio in the Late Republic, *JRMES* 8, 41-57.

Connolly, P./C. van Driel-Murray, 1991: The Roman cavalry saddle, *Britannia* 22, 33-50.

Cordie-Hackenberg, R., 1998: Die antike Siedlung von Belginum. Bericht über das Forschungsprojekt im Vicusareal, *Trierer Zeitschrift* 61, 81-91.

Couissin, P., 1926: *Les armes romaines*, Paris.

Coulston, J.C.N., 1990: Later Roman armour, 3rd-6th centuries AD, *JRMES* 1, 139-160.

Creighton, J., 2000: *Coins and power in Late Iron Age Britain*, Cambridge.

Crummy, N., 1983: *Colchester Archaeological report 2: The Roman small finds from excavations in Colchester 1971-9*, Essex.

Curle, J., 1911: *A Roman frontier post and its people. The fort of Newstead in the parish of Melrose*, Glasgow.

Daele, B. van, 1999: The military fabricae in Germania Inferior from Augustus to A.D. 260/270, *JRMES* 10, 125-136.

Daele, B. van, 2001: Romeinse militaria in een Romeinse kelder in het Bemelerveld te Maastricht, *Archeologie in Limburg* 89, 14-20.

Daniëls, M., 1927: Romeinsch Nijmegen II. Ulpia Noviomagus, *OMROL* 8, 65-115.

Davies, J.L., 1977: Roman arrowheads from Dinorben and the *sagittarii* of the Roman army, *Britannia* 8, 257-270.

Davies, R.W., 1969: The supply of animals to the Roman army and the remount system, *Latomus* 28, 429-459.

Davies, R.W., 1989: *Service in the Roman army*, Edinburgh.

Dawson, M., 1990: Roman military equipment on civil sites in Roman Dacia, *JRMES* 1, 7-15

Deman, A./M.-T. Raepsaet-Charlier, 2002: *Nouveau recueil des inscriptions latines de Belgique (ILB²)*, Bruxelles (Collection Latomus 264).

Demougin, S., 1999: Les vétérans dans la Gaule Belgique et la Germanie inférieure, in M. Dondin-Payre/M.-T. Raepsaet-Charlier (eds.), *Cités, municipes, colonies. Les processus de municipalisation en Gaule et en Germanie sous le haut Empire romain*, Paris (Histoire Ancienne et Médiévale 53), 355-380.

Derks, T., 1995: The ritual of the vow in Gallo-Roman religion, in J. Metzler et al. (eds.), *Integration in the Early Roman West. The role of culture and ideology*, Luxembourg (Dossiers d'Archéologie du Musée National d'Histoire et d'Art 4), 111-127.

Derks, T., 1998: *Gods, temples and ritual practices. The transformation of religious ideas and values in Roman Gaul*, Amsterdam (AAS 2).

Derks, T., 2003: Twee Romeinse grafstèles uit Houten-Molenzoom en hun betekenis voor de Romanisering van een grensstreek, *Jaarboek Oud-Utrecht* 2003, 2-32.

Derkst, T./J. van Kerckhove/P. Hoff, in press: *Nieuw archeologisch onderzoek rond de Grote Kerk van Elst, gemeente Overbetuwe*, Amsterdam (ZAR).

Derks, T./N. Roymans, 2003: Seal-boxes and the spread of Latin literacy in the Rhine Delta, in A. Cooley (ed.), *Becoming Roman, writing Latin? Literacy and epigraphy in the Roman West* (JRA, suppl. 48), 87-134.

Derks, T./N. Roymans, 2006: Returning auxiliary veterans: some methodological considerations, *JRA* 19, 121-135.

Derks, T./L.J.F. Swinkels, 1994: Bronzen doosjes en verzegelde geloften, in N. Roymans/T. Derks (eds.), *De tempel van Empel. Een Hercules-heiligdom in het woongebied van de Bataven*, 's-Hertogenbosch, 146-151.

Deschler-Erb, E., 1991: Römische Militaria des 1. Jahrhunderts aus Kaiseraugst. Zur Frage des frühen Kastells, in E. Deschler-Erb/M. Peters/S. Deschler-Erb (eds.), *Das frühkaiserzeitliche Militärlager in der Kaiseraugster Unterstadt*, Augst (Forschungen in Augst 12), 9-81.

Deschler-Erb, E., 1992: Ein germanischer Schildrandbeschlag des 1./2. Jahrhunderts n. Chr. aus Augst, *Archäologie der Schweiz* 15, 18-23.

Deschler-Erb, E., 1999a: *Ad arma! Römisches Militär des 1. Jahrhunderts n.Chr. in Augusta Raurica*, Augst (Forschungen in Augst 28).

Deschler-Erb, E., 1999b: Militaria aus Windisch-Vindonissa im Vergleich mit den Funden aus Kalkriese, in W. Schlüter/R. Wiegels, *Rom, Germanien und die Ausgrabungen von Kalkriese*, Osnabrück, 227-239.

Deschler-Erb, E., 2000: Niellierung auf Buntmetall: Ein Phänomen der frühen römischen Kaiserzeit, *KJ* 33, 383-396.

Deschler-Erb, E., 2001: Die Funde aus Buntmetall, in J. Gisler (eds.), *Beiträge zum römischen Oberwinterthur – Vitudurum 9. Ausgrabungen auf dem Kirchhügel und im Nordosten des Vicus 1988-1998*, Zürich/Egg (Monographien der Kantonsarchäologie Zürich 35), 225-239.

Deschler-Erb, E./S. Deschler-Erb, 2002: Der Nachweis militärischer Präsenz in der Koloniestadt Augusta Raurica/Schweiz aufgrund archäologischer und archäozoologischer Untersuchungen, *JberGPV* 2001, 23-29.

Diederik, F., 1985: Een siervoorwerp uit Romeins Velsen, *Westerheem* 34, 169-172.

Dierendonck, R.M. van/D.P. Hallewas/K.E. Waugh, 1993: *The Valkenburg excavations 1985-1988. Introduction and detail studies*, Amersfoort (Nederlandse Oudheden 15).

Dobesch, G., 1980: *Die Kelten in Österreich nach den ältesten Berichten der Antike. Das norische Königreich und seine Beziehungen zu Rom im 2. Jahrhundert v. Chr.*, Vienna/Cologne/Graz.

Dobson, B./J.C. Mann, 1973: The Roman army in Britain and Britons in the Roman army, *Britannia* 4, 191-205.

Dockum, G. van/W.A.M. Hessing, 1994: Houten-Dorp en Houten-Doornkade, in W.A. van Es/W.A.M. Hessing (eds.), *Romeinen, Friezen en Franken in het hart van Nederland. Van Traiectum tot Dorestad, 50 v.C.-900 n.C.*, Amersfoort, 219-225.

Dolenz, H., 1998: *Eisenfunde aus der Stadt auf dem Magdalensberg*, Klagenfurt.

Dolenz, H./C. Flügel/C. Öllerer, 1995: Militaria aus einer Fabrica auf dem Magdalensberg (Kärnten), in W. Czysz et al. (eds.), *Provinzialrömische Forschungen. Festschrift für Günter Ulbert zum 65. Geburtstag*, Espelkamp, 51-80.

Domaszewski, A. von, 1967: *Die Rangordnung des römischen Heeres*, Cologne/Graz.

Doorselaer, A. van, 1963/1964: Provinzialrömische Gräber mit Waffenbeigaben aus dem Rheinland und Nordfrankreich, *SJ* 21, 26-31.

Doorselaer, A. van, 1965: Le problème des mobiliers funéraires avec armes en Gaule septentrionale à l'époque du Haut-Empire Romain, *Helinium* 5, 118-129.

Downey, R./A. King/G. Soffe, 1980: The Hayling Island temple and religious connections across the Channel, in W. Rodwell (ed.), *Temples, churches and religion: recent research in Roman Britain with a gazetteer of Romano-Celtic temples in continental Europe, part 1* (BAR 77), Oxford, 289-304.

Drescher, H., 1994: Römische Giessereifunde vom Auerberg, in G. Ulbert, *Der Auerberg I. Topographie, Forschungsgeschichte und Wallgrabungen*, Munich (Münchner Beiträge zur Vor- und Frühgeschichte 45), 113-145.

Driehaus, J., 1970: Urgeschichtliche Opferfunde aus dem Mittel- und Niederrhein, in H. Jankuhn (ed.), *Vorgeschichtliche Heiligtümer und Opferplätze in Mittel- und Nordeuropa*, Göttingen, 40-54.

Driel-Murray, C. van, 1986: Shoes in perspective, in C. Unz (ed.), *Studien zu den Militärgrenzen Roms III. 13. Internationaler Limeskongreß, Aalen 1983*, Stuttgart (Forschungen und Berichte zur Vor- und Frühgeschichte in Baden-Württemberg 20), 139-145.

Driel-Murray, C. van, 1988: A fragmented shield cover from Caerleon, in J.C. Coulston (ed.), *Military equipment and the identity of Roman soldiers*, Oxford (BAR Int. Ser. 394), 51-66.

Driel-Murray, C. van, 1994: Wapentuig voor Hercules, in N. Roymans/T. Derks (eds.), *De tempel van Empel. Een Hercules-heiligdom in het woongebied van de Bataven*, 's-Hertogenbosch, 92-107.

Driel-Murray, C. van, 1999a: Dead men's shoes, in W. Schlüter/R. Wiegels (eds.), *Rom, Germanien und die Ausgrabungen von Kalkriese*, Osnabrück, 169-189.

Driel-Murray, C. van, 1999b: A rectangular shield cover of the *coh. XV Voluntariorum C.R.*, *JRMES* 10, 45-54.

Driel-Murray, C. van, 2000: More so-called 'liturgical brooches' from the Netherlands, *Instrumentum* 11, 22.

Driel-Murray, C. van, 2002: The leather trades in Roman Yorkshire and beyond, in P. Wilson/J. Price (eds.), *Aspects of industry in Roman Yorkshire and the north*, Oxbow, 109-123.

Driel-Murray, C. van, 2003: Ethnic soldiers: the experience of the Lower Rhine tribes, in Th. Grünewald/S. Seibel (eds.), *Kontinuität und Diskontinuität. Germania inferior am Beginn und am Ende der römischen Herrschaft*, Berlin/New York (Ergänzungsbände zum Reallexikon der germanischen Alterumskunde 35), 200-217.

Drinkwater, J.F., 1978: The rise and fall of the Gallic Iulii: aspects of the development of the aristocracy of the three Gauls under the early empire, *Latomus* 37, 816-850.

Dunbabin, K.M.D., 1999: *Mosaics of the Greek and Roman world*, Cambridge.

Dupraz, J., 2000: Sanctuaires et espaces urbains: Alba-la-Romaine, Ier s. av. – IIIe s. ap. J.-C. (Ardèche), in W. van Andringa (ed.), *Archéologie des sanctuaires en Gaule romaine. Textes réunis et présentés par William Van Andringa*, Saint-Étienne, 47-72.

Elton, H., 1996: *Warfare in Roman Europe, AD 350-425*, Oxford (Oxford Classical Monographs).

Enckevort, H. van, 1998/1999: Votivopfer und Paraderüstungen. Römische Sattelhörnchen vom Kops Plateau in Nijmegen, *BROB* 43, 141-153.

Enckevort, H. van, 2001: Bemerkungen zum Besiedlungssystem in den südöstlichen Niederlanden während der späten vorrömischen Eisenzeit und der römischen Kaiserzeit, in Th. Grünewald (ed.), *Germania inferior. Besiedlung, Gesellschaft und Wirtschaft an der Grenze der römisch-germanischen Welt*, Berlin/New York (Ergänzungsbände zum Reallexikon der germanischen Alterumskunde 28), 336-396.

Enckevort, H. van (ed.), in press: *De Romeinse cultusplaats. Een opgraving in het plangebied Westeraam te Elst – gemeente Overbetuwe (Gld.)*, Nijmegen (Archeologische Berichten Nijmegen – Rapport 4).

Enckevort, H. van/T. Hazenberg, 1997: Romeins masker uit de klei getrokken, *Spiegel Historiael* 32, 38-39.

Enckevort, H. van/J. Thijssen, 1996: *Graven met beleid. Gemeentelijk archeologisch onderzoek in Nijmegen 1989-1995*, Abcoude.

Enckevort, H. van/J. Thijssen, 2000: Batavodurum: een Bataafs heiligdom in Nijmegen-West?, in H. van Enckevort/J.K. Haalebos/J. Thijssen (eds.), *Nijmegen. Legerplaats en stad in het achterland van de Romeinse limes*, Abcoude, 61-63.

Enckevort, H. van/J. Thijssen, 2001: Der Hauptort der Bataver in Nijmegen im 1. Jahrhundert n.Chr. Von *Batavodurum* und *Oppidum Batavorum* nach Ulpia Noviomagus, in G. Precht (ed.), *Genese, Struktur und Entwicklung römischer Städte im 1. Jahrhundert n.Chr. in Nieder- und Obergermanien*, Mainz (Xanterer Berichte. Grabung-Forschung-Präsantation Band 9), 87-110.

Enckevort, H. van/J. Thijssen, 2001/2002: Militaria from the Roman urban settlements at Nijmegen, *JRMES* 12/13, 35-41.

Enckevort, H. van/J. Thijssen (eds.), 2005: *In de schaduw van het noorderlicht. De Gallo-Romeinse tempel van Elst-Westeraam*, Abcoude.

Enckevort, H. van/W.J.H. Willems, 1994: Roman cavalry helmets in ritual hoards from the Kops Plateau at Nijmegen, the Netherlands, *JRMES* 5, 125-137.

Enckevort, H. van/K. Zee, 1996: *Het Kops Plateau. Prehistorische grafheuvels en een Romeinse legerplaats in Nijmegen*, Abcoude/Amersfoort.

Endert, D. van, 1991: *Die Bronzefunde aus dem Oppidum von Manching. Kommentierter Katalog*, Stuttgart.

Engelhardt, C., 1869: *Vimose fundet*, Copenhagen.

Engels, H.-J., 1972: Frührömische Waffengräber aus dem pfälzischen Rheintal, *AK* 2, 183-189.

Enloe, C.H., 1980: *Ethnic soldiers. State security in divided societies*, London.

Erdmann, E., 1976: Dreiflügelige Pfeilspitzen aus Eisen von der Saalburg, *SJ* 33, 5-10.

Erdrich, M., 1994: Waffen im mitteleuropäischen Barbaricum: Handel oder Politik, *JRMES* 5, 199-209.

Erdrich, M., 1999: Continuity or discontinuity: native and Roman metal finds, in J.C. Besteman et al. (eds.), *The excavations at Wijnaldum. Reports on Frisia in Roman and Medieval times, volume 1*, Rotterdam/Brookfield, 171-183.

Erdrich, M., 2001a: *Rom und die Barbaren. Das Verhältnis zwischen dem Imperium Romanum und den germanischen Stämmen vor seiner Nordwestgrenze von der späten römischen Republik bis zum Gallischen Sonderreick*, Mainz (Römisch-Germanische Forschungen 58).

Erdrich, M., 2001b: Wirtschaftsbeziehungen zwischen der Germania inferior und dem germanischen Vorland – ein Wunschbild, in Th. Grünewald (ed.), *Germania inferior. Besiedlung, Gesellschaft und Wirtschaft an der Grenze der römisch-germanischen Welt*, Berlin/New York (Ergänzungsbände zum Reallexikon der germanischen Alterumskunde 28), 306-335.

Erdrich, M., 2002: *Corpus der römischen Funde im europäischen Barbaricum. Deutschland, Band 4: Hansestadt Bremen und Bundesland Niedersachsen*, Bonn.

Es, W.A. van, 1981: *De Romeinen in Nederland*, Haarlem.

Es, W.A. van, 1984a: Een Romeins bronzen beeldje uit de opgraving in De Horden bij Wijk bij Duurstede, in J.A. de Waele/L.J.F. Swinkels/E.M. Moormann (eds.), *Om de tuin geleid. Een feestbundel aangeboden aan prof.dr. W.J. Th. Peters ter gelegenheid van zijn vijfenzestigste verjaardag*, Nijmegen, 20-27.

Es, W.A. van, 1984b: Romeinse helmen uit de Rijn bij Rijswijk, in A.O. Kouwenhoven/G.A. de Bruijne/G.A. Hoekveld (eds.), *Geplaatst in de tijd. Liber amicorum aangeboden aan Prof. Dr. M.W. Heslinga bij zijn afscheid als hoogleraar in de sociale geografie aan de Vrije Universiteit te Amsterdam op vrijdag 12 oktober 1984*, Amsterdam (Bijdragen tot de Sociale Geografie en Planologie 9), 255-291.

Es, W.A. van, 1994: Wijk bij Duurstede-De Geer, in W.A. van Es/W.A.M. Hessing (eds.), *Romeinen, Friezen en Franken in het hart van Nederland. Van Traiectum tot Dorestad (50 v. Chr.-950 n. Chr.)*, Utrecht/Amersfoort, 231-233.

Es., W.A. van/S.G. van Dockum, 1991: Opgravingen Wijk bij Duurstede-De Geer (1989-2000), *Jaarverslag ROB* 1990, 50-54.

Es., W.A. van/S.G. van Dockum, 1992: Wijk bij Duurstede-De Geer (1989-2000), *Jaarverslag ROB* 1991, 42-48.

Es, W.A. van/W.A.M. Hessing (eds.), 1994: *Romeinen, Friezen en Franken in het hart van Nederland. Van Traiectum tot Dorestad (50 v. Chr.-950 n. Chr.)*, Utrecht/Amersfoort.

Es, W.A. van/R.E. Lutter/S.G. van Dockum, 1990: Wijk bij Duurstede-De Geer (putten 755-767), *Jaarverslag ROB* 1989, 48-49.

Es., W.A. van et al., 1995: De Geer (putten 847-879), *Jaarverslag ROB* 1994, 158-160.

Ettlinger, E./M. Hartmann, 1985: Fragmente einer Schwertscheide aus Vindonissa und ihre Gegenstücke vom Grossen St. Bernhard, *JberGPV* 1984, 5-46.

Exner, K., 1940: Römische Dolchscheiden mit Tauschierung und Emailverzierung, *Germania* 24, 22-28.

Fasold, P., 1993: *Das römisch-norische Gräberfeld von Seebruck-Bedaium*, Kallmünz (Bayerisches Landesamt für Denkmalpflege, Abteilung Bodendenkmalpflege 64).

Fasold, P./G. Weber, 1987: Ein römischer Metall-Sammelfund aus Kempten-Cambodunum, *BVB* 52, 37-55.

Fercoq du Leslay, G., 1996: Chronologie et analyse spatiale à Ribemont-sur-Ancre (Somme), *Revue Archéologique de Picardie* 1996-3/4, 189-208.

Fernández, J.A., 1998: Aprons fittings from Flavian times found in Spain, *JRMES* 9, 37-41.

Fernández, J.A., 1999: Late Roman belts in Hispania, *JRMES* 10, 55-62.

Ferris, I.M./L. Bevan/R. Cuttler, 2000: *The excavations of a Romano-British shrine at Orton's Pasture, Rocester, Staffordshire*, Oxford (BAR 314).

Feugère, M., 1985: Nouvelles observations sur les cabochons de bronze estampés du cingulum romain, in M.C. Bishop (ed.), *The production and distribution of Roman military equipment*, Oxford (BAR Int. Ser. 275), 117-141.

Feugère, M., 1993: *Les armes des Romains*, Paris.

Feugère, M/M. Poux, 2002: Gaule pacifiée, Gaule libérée? Enquête sur les *militaria* en Gaule civile, *JberGPV* 2001, 79-95.

Fink, R.O., 1971: *Roman military records on papyrus*, Princeton (Philological Monographs of the American Philological Association 26).

Fischer, T., 1985: Ein Halbfabrikat von der Wangkleppe eines römischen Reiterhelmes aus dem Lager von Eining-Unterfeld, Gde. Neustadt, Ldkr. Kelheim, *BVB* 50, 477-482.

Fischer, T., 1988: Zur römischen Offiziersausrüstung im 3. Jahrhundert n. Chr., *BVB* 53, 167–190.

Fischer, T., 1995: Ein römischer Hortfund aus Affecking, Stadt Kelheim, in W. Czysz et al. (eds.), *Provinzialrömische Forschungen. Festschrift für Günter Ulbert zum 65. Geburtstag*, Espelkamp, 339-347.

Fischer, T., 1999: *Die Römer in Deutschland*, Stuttgart.

Fischer, T., 2002, Waffen und militärische Ausrüstung in zivilem Kontext – grundsätzliche Erklärungsmöglichkeiten, *JberGPV* 2001, 13-18.

Fitzpatrick, A.P., 1984: The deposition of La Tène Iron Age metalwork in watery contexts in Southern England, in B. Cunliffe/D. Miles (eds.), *Aspects of the Iron Age in Central Southern Britain*, Oxford, 178-190.

Flokstra, L., 2004: Vroeg-Christelijke beslagstukken in het rivierengebied, *AWN jaarverslag 2004, afdeling Nijmegen en omstreken*, 40-42.

Fokkens, H., 1998, *The Ussen Project. The first decade of excavations at Oss*, Leiden (APL 30).

Fontijn, D.R., 2003: *Sacrificial landscapes. Cultural biographies of persons, objects and 'natural' places in the Bronze Age of the southern Netherlands, c. 2300-600 BC*, Leiden (APL 33).

France, N.E./B.M. Gobel, 1985: *The Romano-British temple at Harlow, Essex*, Gloucester.

Franzius, G., 1993: Die römischen Funde aus Kalkriese, in W. Schlüter (ed.), *Kalkriese – Römer im Osnabrücker Land. Archäologische Forschungen zur Varusschlacht*, Bramsche, 107-147.

Franzius, G., 1995: Die römischen Funde aus Kalkriese 1987-95 und ihre Bedeutung für die Interpretation und Datierung militärischer Fundplätze der augusteischen Zeit im nordwesteuropäischen Raum, *JRMES* 6, 69-88.

Franzius, G., 1999: Beschläge einer Gladiusscheide und Teile eines *cingulum* aus Kalkriese, Lkr. Osnabrück, *Germania* 77, 567-607.

Fremersdorf, F., 1963: *Urkunden zur Kölner Stadtgeschichte aus römischer Zeit*, Cologne (Die Denkmäler des römischen Köln 2).

Frere, S.S./J.J. Wilkes, 1989: *Strageath. Excavations within the Roman fort, 1973-86*, London (Britannia Monograph Series 9).

Gabelmann, H., 1973: Römische Grabmonumente mit Reiterkampfszenen im Rheingebiet, *BJ* 173, 132-200.

Garbsch, J., 1978: *Römische Paraderüstungen*, Munich (Münchner Beiträge zur Vor- und Frühgeschichte 30).

Garbsch, J., 1986a: Donatus torquibus armillis phaleris. Römische Orden in Raetien, *BVB* 51, 333-336.

Garbsch, J., 1986b: Ein Trense des 3. Jahrhunderts n. Chr., *BVB* 51, 337-340.

Garbsch, J., 2000: Römische Paraderüstungen, in L. Wamser (ed.), *Die Römer zwischen Alpen und Nordmeer. Zivilisatorisches Erbe einer europäischen Militärmacht*, Mainz, 53-57.

Gechter, M./J. Kunow, 1983: Der frühkaiserzeitliche Grabfund von Mehrum, *BJ* 183, 449-468.

Gerhartl-Witteveen, A.M./A.V.M. Hubrecht, 1990: Survey of swords and daggers in the Provincial Museum G.M. Kam, Nijmegen, *JRMES* 1, 99-107.

Gerhartl-Witteveen, A.M et al., 1989: *Schatkamer van Gelderse oudheden*, Nijmegen.

Gerritsen, F., 2003: *Local identities. Landscape and community in the late prehistoric Meuse-Demer-Scheldt region*, Amsterdam (AAS 9).

Giesler, U., 1978: Jüngerkaiserzeitliche Nietknopfsporen mit Driepunkthalterung vom Typ Leuna, *SJ* 35, 5-56.

Gilliam, J.F., 1967: The deposita of an auxiliary soldier, *BJ* 167, 233-243 (reprinted in J.F. Gilliam, 1986: *Roman Army Papers*, Amsterdam, 317-327).

Gonzenbach, V. von, 1966a: Schwertscheidenbleche von Vindonissa aus der Zeit der 13. Legion, *JberGPV* 1965, 5-36.

Gonzenbach, V. von, 1966b: Tiberische Gürtel- und Schwertscheidenbeschläge mit figürlichen Reliefs, in R. Degen et al. (eds.), *Helvetia Antiqua. Festschrift Emil Vogt*, Zürich, 183-208.

Gonzenbach, V. von, 1976: Ein Heiligtum im Legionslager Vindonissa, in P. Collart (ed.), *Mélanges d'histoire ancienne et d'archéologie offerts à Paul Collart*, Lausanne (Cahiers d'Archéologie Romande 5), 205-222.

Gosden, C./Y. Marshall, 1999: The cultural biography of objects, in Y. Marshall/C. Gosden (eds.), *The cultural biography of objects*, London (World Archaeology 31), 169-178.

Grabert, W./H. Koch, 1986: Militaria aus der villa rustica von Treuchtlingen-Weinbergshof, *BVB* 51, 325-332.

Greep, S., 1994: Antler roundel pendants from Britain and the north-western Roman provinces, *Britannia* 24, 79-97.

Grew, F./N. Griffiths, 1991: The pre-Flavian military belt: the evidence from Britain, *Archaeologia* 109, 47-84.

Groenman-Van Waateringe, W., 1967: *Romeins lederwerk uit Valkenburg*, Groningen (Nederlandse Oudheden 2).

Gschwind, M., 1997: Bronzegießer am raetischen Limes. Zur Versorgung mittelkaiserzeitlicher Auxiliareinheiten mit militärischen Ausrüstungsgegenständen, *Germania* 75, 607-638.

Gschwind, M., 1998: Pferdegeschirrbeschläge der zweiten Hälfte des 3. Jahrhunderts aus Abusina/Eining, *SJ* 49, 112-138.

Haalebos, J.K., 1977: *Zwammerdam Nigrum Pullum. Ein Auxiliarkastell am niedergermanischen Limes*, Amsterdam (Cingula 3).

Haalebos, J.K., 1990a: *Het grafveld van Nijmegen-Hatert. Een begraafplaats uit de eerste drie eeuwen na Chr. op het platteland bij Noviomagus Batavorum*, Nijmegen (Beschr. van de verz. in het Prov. Museum G.M. Kam te Nijmegen XI).

Haalebos, J.K., 1990b: Neues aus Noviomagus, *AK* 20, 193-200.

Haalebos, J.K., 1992: Archeologische kroniek van Gelderland 1990-1991: 6. Rijnwaarden, 7. Maurik, *BMVG* 83, 175-177.

Haalebos, J.K., 1994a: Hatert 1993, sporen van een gehucht uit de midden-Romeinse keizertijd bij Ulpia Noviomagus, *Jaarboek Numaga* 41, 35-42.

Haalebos, J.K., 1994b: Opgravingen op het terrein van het voormalige Canisiuscollege te Nijmegen, 1993, *Jaarboek Numaga* 41, 10-34.

Haalebos, J.K., 1994c: Review 'E. Deschler-Erb et al. (1991), Das frühkaiserzeitliche Militärlager in der Augster Unterstadt, Augst', *BJ* 194, 703-705.

Haalebos, J.K., 1995: *Castra und Canabae. Ausgrabungen auf dem Hunerberg in Nijmegen, 1987-1994*, Nijmegen (Libelli Noviomagenses 3).

Haalebos, J.K., 1998, Die Canabae der Legio X Gemina in Nijmegen, *JberGPV* 1997, 33-39.

Haalebos, J.K., 2000a: Mosterd na de maaltijd. Een vergeten jubileum: Traianus en het jaar 98 na Chr. in Nijmegen, *Jaarboek Numaga* 47, 9-41.

Haalebos, J.K., 2000b: Traian und die Hilfstruppen am Niederrhein. Ein Militärdiplom des Jahres 98 n. Chr. aus Elst in der Over-Betuwe (Niederlande), *SJ* 50, 31-72.

Haalebos, J.K., 2000c: Romeinse troepen in Nijmegen, *BMVG* 91, 9-36.

Haalebos, J.K., 2000d: Römische Truppen in Nijmegen, in Y. Le Bohec/C. Wolff (eds.), *Les légions de Rome sous le Haut-Empire. Actes du Congrès de Lyon (17-19 septembre 1998)*, Lyons (Collection du centre d'études Romaines et Gallo-Romaines, nouvelle série 20), 465-489.

Haalebos, J.K. et al., 1998: *Centuriae onder Centuriae Hof. Opgravingen achter het hoofdgebouw van het voormalig Canisiuscollege te Nijmegen, 1995-1997*, Nijmegen (Libelli Noviomagenses 5).

Haalebos, J.K. et al., 2000: *Alphen aan den Rijn, Albaniana, 1998-1999. Opgravingen in de Julianastraat, de Castellumstraat, op Het Eiland en onder het St.-Jorisplein*, Nijmegen (Libelli Noviomagenses 6).

Haarhuis, H.F.A., 1995: Recently found bronzes from the *canabae legionis* in Nijmegen, in S.T.A.M. Mols et al. (eds.), *Acta of the 12th International Congress on Ancient Bronzes, Nijmegen 1992*, Amersfoort/Nijmegen (NAR 18), 373-377.

Haffner, A., 1971: *Das keltisch-römische Gräberfeld von Wederath-Belginum. 1. Teil: Gräber 1-428, ausgegraben 1954/1955*, Mainz.

Haffner, A. (ed.), 1989a: *Gräber – Spiegel des Lebens. Zum Totenbrauchtum der Kelten und Römer am Beispiel des Treverer-Gräberfeldes Wederath-Belginum*, Mainz.

Haffner, A., 1989b: Das Gräberfeld von Wederath-Belginum vom 4. Jahrhundert vor bis zum 4. Jahrhundert nach Christi Geburt, in A. Haffner (ed.), *Gräber – Spiegel des Lebens. Zum Totenbrauchtum der Kelten und Römer am Beispiel des Treverer-Gräberfeldes Wederath-Belginum*, Mainz, 37-128.

Haffner, A., 1989c: Zur pars pro toto-Sitte und rituellen Zerstörung von Waffen während der Latènezeit, in A. Haffner (ed.), *Gräber – Spiegel des Lebens. Zum Totenbrauchtum der Kelten und Römer am Beispiel des Treverer-Gräberfeldes Wederath-Belginum*, Mainz, 197-210.

Haffner, A., 1992: Die keltischen Fürstengäber des Mittelrheingebietes, in R. Cordie-Hackenberg et al. (eds.), *Hundert Meisterwerke keltischer Kunst. Schmuck und Kunsthandwerk zwischen Rhein und Mosel*, Trier, 31-66.

Halsall, G., 1982: The origins of the *Reihengräberzivilisation*: forty years on, in J. Drinkwater/H. Elton (eds.), *Fifth-century Gaul: a crisis of identity?*, Cambridge, 196-207.

Hanel, N., 1999: Militär als Wirtschaftsfaktor in den Nordwestprovinzen in der frühen und mittleren Kaiserzeit, in H. von Hesberg (ed.), *Das Militär als Kulturträger in römischer Zeit*, Cologne, 117-133.

Harrauer, H./R. Seider, 1979: Ein neuer lateinischer Schuldschein: P.Vindob. L 135, *ZPE* 36, 109–120.

Haynes, I., 1997: Religion in the Roman army: unifying aspects and regional trends, in H. Cancik/J. Rüpke (eds.), *Römische Reichsreligion und Provinzialreligion*, Mohr/Siebeck, 113-126.

Haynes, I., 1999: Military service and cultural identity in the auxilia, in A. Goldsworthy/I. Haynes (eds.), *The Roman army as a community*, Portsmouth (JRA, suppl. 34), 165-174.

Hedeager, L, 1992: *Iron-Age societies. From tribe to state in Northern Europe, 500 BC to AD 700*, Oxford/Cambridge.

Heeren, S. (ed.), 2006: *De nederzetting aan de Passewaaijse Hogeweg. Opgravingen bij Tiel 1*, Amsterdam (ZAR 29).

Heidinga, H.A./G.A.M. Offenberg, 1992: *Op zoek naar de vijfde eeuw. De Franken tussen Rijn en Maas*, Amsterdam.

Herrmann, F.-R., 1969: Der Eisenhortfund aus dem Kastell Künzing, *SJ* 26, 129-141.

Hessing, W.A.M., 1994: Wijk bij Duurstede-De Horden, in W.A. van Es/W.A.M. Hessing (eds.), *Romeinen, Friezen en Franken in het hart van Nederland. Van Traiectum tot Dorestad (50 v. Chr.-950 n. Chr.)*, Utrecht/Amersfoort, 226-230.

Hessing, W.A.M., 1999: Building programmes for the Lower Rhine Limes. The impact of the visits of Trajan and Hadrian to the Lower Rhine, in H. Sarfatij et al. (eds.), *In discussion with the past. Archaeological studies presented to W.A. van Es*, Zwolle, 149-156.

Hessing, W.A.M., 2001: Paardenfokkers in het grensgebied. De Bataafse nederzetting op De Woerd bij Kesteren, in A. Carmiggelt (ed.), *Opgespoord verleden. Archeologie in de Betuweroute*, Abcoude, 142-171,

Hessing, W.A.M./R. Steenbeek, 1990: Landscape and habitation history of 'the Horden' at Wijk bij Duurstede. An overview, *BROB* 40, 9-28.

Hettner, F., 1901: *Drei Tempelbezirke im Trevererlande. Festschrift zur Feier des hundertjährigen Bestehens der Gesellschaft für nützliche Forschungen in Trier*, Trier.

Hiddink, H.A., 1994: Romeinse waterputten uit de nadagen van het heiligdom, in N. Roymans/T. Derks (eds.), *De tempel van Empel. Een Hercules-heiligdom in het woongebied van de Bataven*, 's-Hertogenbosch, 58-71.

Hiddink, H.A., 1999: *Germaanse samenlevingen tussen Rijn en Weser. 1ste eeuw voor-4de eeuw na Chr.*, Amsterdam (unpublished dissertation, UvA).

Hiddink, H.A., 2000: *Groesbeek-Klein Amerika. Prospectie en Aanvullend Archeologisch Onderzoek van bewoning uit de prehistorie en Romeinse tijd en een mogelijk pre-Flavisch openluchtheiligdom*, Amersfoort (RAM 74).

Hintermann, D., 2000: *Der Südfriedhof von Vindonissa. Archäologische und naturwissenschaftliche Untersuchungen im römerzeitlichen Gräberfeld Windisch-Dägerli*, Brugg (Veröffentlichungen der Gesellschaft pro Vindonissa 17).

Holder, P.A., 1980: *Studies in the auxilia of the Roman army from Augustus to Trajan*, Oxford (BAR. Int. Ser. 70).

Holder, P.A., 1999: *Exercitus pius fidelis*: the army of Germania inferior in AD 89, *ZPE* 128, 237-250.

Holwerda, J.H., 1931: Een vondst uit de Rijn bij Doorwerth, *OMROL* 12, 1-26.

Holwerda, J.H., 1936: Een nederzetting te Naaldwijk, *OMROL* 17, 19-37.

Horn, H.G., 1984: Totenkult und Grabsitten, in H. Chantraine et al. (eds.), *Das römische Neuss*, Stuttgart, 164–165.

Hoss, S./E. van der Chijs, 2005: Metaal en slakmateriaal. In: G. Tichelman (ed.), *Het villacomplex Kerkrade-Holzkuil*, Amersfoort (ADC Rapport 155), 221-247.

Hottentot, W./S. M. E. van Lith, 1990: Römische Amulette aus Hirschhorn in den Niederlanden, *Helinium* 30, 186-207.

Hübener, W., 1957: Ein römisches Gräberfeld in Neuburg an der Donau, *BVB* 22, 71-96.

Hübener, W., 1963/1964: Zu den provinzialrömischen Waffengräbern, *SJ* 21, 20-25.

Hübener, W., 1973: *Die römischen Metallfunde von Augsburg-Oberhausen*, Kallmünz.

Hulst, R.S., 1978: Druten-Klepperhei. Vorbericht der Ausgrabungen einer römischen Villa, *BROB* 28, 133-151.

Hulst, R.S., 1986: Een signaal van de limes, in R.M. van Heeringen (ed.), *Voordrachten gehouden te Middelburg ter gelegenheid van het afscheid van Ir. J.A. Trimpe Burger als provinciaal archeoloog van Zeeland*, Amersfoort (NAR 3), 37–41.

Hulst, R.S., 2000/2001: The castellum at Arnhem-Meinerswijk: the remains of period 5, *BROB* 44, 397-438.

Hundt, H.-J., 1953: Die spätrömischen eisernen Dosenortbänder, *SJ* 12, 66-79.

Hundt, H.-J., 1955: Nachträge zu den römischen Ringknaufschwertern, Dosenortbändern und Miniaturschwertanhängern, *SJ* 14, 30-59.

Hunt, P., 1998: *Summus Poeninus* on the Grand St Bernard Pass, *JRA* 11, 265-274.

Hurk, L.J.A.M. van den, 1973: The tumuli from the Roman period of Esch, Province of North Brabant, I, *BROB* 23, 189-236.

Hurk, L.J.A.M. van den, 1984: The tumuli from the Roman period of Esch, Province of North Brabant, V, *BROB* 34, 7-38.

Hyland, A., 1990: *Equus: The horse in the Roman world*, London.

Hyland, A., 1992: The Roman cavalry horse and its efficient control, *JRMES* 3, 73-79.

Impe, L. van/G. Creemers, 1991: Aristokratische graven uit de 4de/5de eeuwen v. Chr. en Romeinse cultusplaats op de 'Rieten' te Wijshagen (gem. Meeuwen-Gruitrode), *Archeologie van Vlaanderen* 1, 55-73.

Jacobi, L., 1897: *Das Römerkastell Saalburg bei Homburg von der Höhe*, Homburg.

Jahn, M., 1921: *Der Reitersporn. Seine Entstehung und früheste Entwicklung*, Leipzig (Mannus-Bibliothek 21).

James, S.T., 1988: The fabricae: state arms factories of the later Roman Empire, in J.C. Coulston (ed.), *Military equipment and the identity of Roman soldiers. Proceedings of the fourth Roman Military Equipment Conference*, Oxford (BAR Int. Ser. 394), 257-294.

James, S.T., 1999: The community of soldiers: a major identity and centre of power in the Roman Empire, in C. Forcey/R. Witcher (eds.), *Proceedings of the eighth annual Theoretical Roman Archaeology Conference, Leicester, 1998*, Oxford, 14-25.

James, S.T., 2001: Soldiers and civilians. Identity and interaction in Roman Britain, in S.T. James/M. Millett (eds.), *Britons and Romans. Advancing an archaeological agenda*, York (CBA Research Report 125), 77-89.

James, S.T., 2002: Writing the legions: the development and future of Roman military studies in Britain, *Archaeological Journal* 159, 1-58.

Jansen, R./H. Fokkens/C. van der Linde, 2002: Lith-Oijensche Hut en Haren-Spaanse Steeg. Lokale riviercultusplaatsen uit de Late IJzertijd in de Brabantse Maaskant, in H. Fokkens/R. Jansen (eds.), *2000 jaar bewoningsdynamiek. Brons- en ijzertijdbewoning in het Maas-Demer-Scheldegebied*, Leiden, 173-205.

Jenkins, I., 1985: A group of silvered-bronze horse-trappings from Xanten (*Castra Vetera*), *Britannia* 16, 141-164.

Joly, M., 2001: *Langres*, Paris (Carte Archeologique de la Gaule 52).

Junkelmann, M., 1986: *Die Legionen des Augustus. Der römische Soldat im archäologischen Experiment*, Mainz (Kulturgeschichte der Antiken Welt 33).

Junkelmann, M., 1990: *Die Reiter Roms. Teil 1: Reise, Jagd, Triumph und Circusrennen*, Mainz (Kulturgeschichte der Antiken Welt 45).

Junkelmann, M., 1992: *Die Reiter Roms. Teil III: Zubehör, Reitweise, Bewaffnung*, Mainz (Kulturgeschichte der Antiken Welt 53).

Junkelmann, M., 1996: *Reiter wie Statuen aus Erz*, Mainz (Sonderhefte der Antiken Welt).

Junkelmann, M., 2000: *Das Spiel mit dem Tod. So kämpften Roms Gladiatoren*, Mainz.

Junkelmann, M., 2002: Waffen für Jagd und Gladiatur, *JberGPV* 2001, 19-21.

Jütting, I., 1995: Die Kleinfunde aus dem römischen Lager Eining-Unterfeld, *BVB* 60, 143-230.

Kam, G.M., 1915: Antieke helmen in het Museum "Kam", *Bulletin van den Nederlandschen Oudheidkundigen Bond* 8, 258-266.

Kamp, J.S. van der /M. Polak (eds.), 2001: *Archeologisch onderzoek aan de Molenstraat te Beuningen (1997-1998)*, Amersfoort (RAM 92).

Keller, E., 1969: Zur Datierung des Reitersporns von Seebruck, *BVB* 34, 201-206.

Keller, E., 1979: *Das spätrömische Gräberfeld von Neuburg an der Donau*, Kallmünz.

Kellner, H.-J., 1966: Zu den römischen Ringknaufschwertern und Dosenortbändern in Bayern, *JRGZM* 13, 190-201.

Kellner, H.-J., 1986: Die Möglichkeit von Rückschlüssen aus der Fundstatistik, in W. Eck/H. Wolff (eds.), *Heer und Integrationspolitik. Die römischen Militärdiplome als historische Quelle*, Cologne/Vienna, 241-248.

Kellner, H.-J./G. Zahlhaas, 1993: *Der römische Tempelschatz von Weißenburg i. Bay.*, Mainz.

Kemkes, M./J. Scheuerbrandt, 1997: *Zwischen Patrouille und Parade. Die römische Reiterei am Limes*, Stuttgart.

Keppie, L., 2000: *Legions and veterans. Roman army papers 1971-2000*, Stuttgart.

Kimmig, W., 1940: Ein Keltenschild aus Ägypten, *Germania* 24, 106-111.

King, A./G. Soffe, 1991: Hayling Island, in R.F.J. Jones (ed.), *Britain in the Roman period: recent trends*, Sheffield, 111-113.

King, C.E., 1982: Roman, local and barbarian coinages in fifth-century Gaul, in J. Drinkwater/H. Elton (eds.), *Fifth-century Gaul: a crisis of identity?*, Cambridge, 184-195.

Klar, M., 1971: Musikinstrumente der Römerzeit in Bonn, *BJ* 171, 301-317.

Klein, J., 1897: Der Marberg bei Pommern an der Mosel und seine Kultstätte, *BJ* 101, 64-116.

Klein, M.J., 1999: Votivwaffen aus einem Mars-Heiligtum bei Mainz, *JRMES* 10, 87-94.

Klein, M.J., 2003a: Römische Helme aus dem Rhein bei Mainz, in M.J. Klein (ed.), *Die Römer und ihr Erbe. Fortschritt durch Innovation und Integration*, Mainz, 29-42.

Klein, M.J., 2003b: Römische Schwerter aus Mainz, in M.J. Klein (ed.), *Die Römer und ihr Erbe. Fortschritt durch Innovation und Integration*, Mainz, 43-54.

Klein, M.J., 2003c: Römische Dolche mit verzierten Scheiden aus dem Rhein bei Mainz, in M.J. Klein (ed.), *Die Römer und ihr Erbe. Fortschritt durch Innovation und Integration*, Mainz, 55-70.

Klomp, A., 1994: Feestgelagen en het gebruik van aardewerk, in N. Roymans/T. Derks (eds.), *De tempel van Empel. Een Hercules-heiligdom in het woongebied van de Bataven*, 's-Hertogenbosch, 152-161.

Klumbach, H., 1961: Ein römischer Legionarshelm aus Mainz, *JRGZM* 8, 96-105.

Klumbach, H., 1966: Drei römische Schildbuckel aus Mainz, *JRGZM* 13, 165-189.

Klumbach, H. (ed.), 1973a: *Spätrömische Gardehelme*, Munich (Münchner Beitrage zur Vor- und Frühgeschichte 15).

Klumbach, H., 1973b: Der Fund von Augsburg-Pfersee, Deutschland, in H. Klumbach (ed.), *Spätrömische Gardehelme*, Munich (Münchner Beitrage zur Vor- und Frühgeschichte 15), 95-101.

Klumbach, H., 1973c: Der Helm von Worms, Deutschland, in H. Klumbach (ed.), *Spätrömische Gardehelme*, Munich (Münchner Beitrage zur Vor- und Frühgeschichte 15), 111-114.

Klumbach, H., 1974: *Römische Helme aus Niedergermanien*, Cologne (Kunst und Altertum am Rhein 51).

Klumbach, H., 1977: Ein Paradeschildbuckel aus Brigetio, in J. Fitz (ed.), *Akten des XI. Internationalen Limeskongresses (Székesfehérvár, 30. 8.-6. 9. 1976)*, Budapest, 199-208.

Koch, H./W. Grabert, 1986: Zwei bemerkenswerte Funde aus der villa rustica von Treuchtlingen-Weinbergshof, *Das archäologische Jahr in Bayern 1985*, 111-113.

Koning, J. de, 2003: Why did they leave? Why did they stay? On continuity versus discontinuity from Roman times to the Early Middle Ages in the western coastal area of the Netherlands, in Th. Grünewald/S. Seibel (eds.), *Kontinuität und Diskontinuität. Germania inferior am Beginn und am Ende der römischen Herrschaft*, Berlin/New York (Ergänzungsbände zum Reallexikon der germanischen Alterumskunde 35), 53-82.

Kooistra, L.I., 1996: *Borderland farming. Possibilities and limitations of farming in the Roman period and early Middle Ages between the Rhine and Meuse*, Assen/Amersfoort.

Kopytoff, I., 1986: The cultural biography of things: commoditization as process, in A. Appadurai (ed.), *The social life of things. Commodities in cultural perspective*, Cambridge, 64-91.

Koster, A., 1993: Ein reich ausgestattetes Waffengrab des 1. Jahrhunderts n.Chr. aus Nijmegen, in M. Struck (ed.), *Römerzeitliche Gräber als Quellen zu Religion, Bevölkerungsstruktur und Sozialgeschichte*, Mainz (Archäologische Schriften des Instituts für Vor- und Frühgeschichte der Johannes Gutenberg-Universität Mainz 3), 293-296.

Koster, A., 1994: Zwei römische Gräber mit Bronzegefäßen aus Ulpia Noviomagus (Nijmegen, Niederlande), in J. Ronke (ed.), *Akten der 10. internationalen Tagung über antike Bronzen, Freiburg, 18.-22. Juli 1988*, Stuttgart (Forschungen und Berichte zur Vor- und Frühgeschichte in Baden-Württemberg 45), 245-250.

Koster, A.A./I. Joosten, 2001: Metaal en metaalbewerking, in M.M. Sier/C.W. Koot (eds.): *Archeologie in de Betuweroute: Kesteren-De Woerd. Bewoningssporen uit de IJzertijd en de Romeinse tijd*, Utrecht (RAM 82), 183-205.

Kraft, K., 1951: *Zur Rekrutierung der Alen und Kohorten an Rhein und Donau*, Bern (Diss. Bernenses I, 3).

Krier, J., 2003: Ein neuer Reliefblock aus Bartringen und die Grabmonumente mit Reiterkampfdarstellungen an Mosel und Rhein, in P. Noelke (ed.), *Romanisation und Resistenz in Plastik, Architektur und Inschriften der Provinzen des Imperium Romanum. Neue Funde und Forschungen*, Mainz, 255-263.

Krier, J./F. Reinert, 1991: La tombe au casque de Hellange (Grand-Duché de Luxembourg), in F. Beck/H. Chew (eds.), *Masques de fer. Un officier romain du temps de Caligula*, Paris, 130-153.

Krist, J.S./J.B. de Voogd/J. Schoneveld, 2002: *Een vindplaats uit de Late IJzertijd en vroeg-Romeine tijd aan de Schalkwijkseweg te Houten, terrein 14, provincie Utrecht*, Groningen (ARC-publicaties 48).

Kunow, J., 1987: Die Militärgeschichte Niedergermaniens, in H.G. Horn (ed.), *Die Römer in Nordrhein-Westfalen*, 27-109.

Künzl, E., 1983: Zwei silberne Tetrarchenporträts im RGZM und die römischen Kaiserbildnisse aus Gold und Silber, *JRGZM* 30, 381-402.

Künzl, E. (ed.), 1993a: *Die Alamannenbeute aus dem Rhein bei Neupotz. Teil 1: Untersuchungen*, Mainz.

Künzl, E., 1993b: Römerzeitliche Waffen (B 3-20), in E. Künzl (ed.), *Die Alamannenbeute aus dem Rhein bei Neupotz. Teil 1: Untersuchungen*, Mainz, 75-81.

Künzl, E., 1994: Dekorierte Gladii und Cingula: Eine ikonografische Statistik, *JRMES* 5, 33-58.

Künzl, E., 1997: Waffendekor im Hellenismus, *JRMES* 8, 61-89.

Künzl, E., 1998: Gladiusdekorationen der frühen römischen Kaiserzeit: dynastische Legitimation, Victoria und Aurea Aetas, *JRGZM* 43, 383-474.

Künzl, E., 1999: Fellhelme. Zu den mit organischen Material dekorierten römischen Helmen der frühen Kaiserzeit und zur *imitatio Alexandri* des Germanicus, in W. Schlüter/R. Wiegels (eds.), *Rom, Germanien und die Ausgrabungen von Kalkriese*, Osnabrück, 149-168.

Künzl, E., 1999/2000: Wasserfunde römischer *Gladii*: Votive oder Transportverluste?, *Caesarodunum* 33/34, 547-575.

Laarman, F.J., 1996: Organic material of the Iron Age, Roman period and Early Middle Ages at Houten-Tiellandt: the zoological remains, in L.I. Kooistra, *Borderland farming. Possibilities and limitations of farming in the Roman period and early Middle Ages between the Rhine and Meuse*, Assen/Amersfoort, 343-357.

Laet, S.J. de, 1948: Romeinse oudheden gevonden te Hofstade bij Aalst (O.Vl.), *L'Antiquité Classique* 16, 287-306.

Laet, S.J., de, 1960: Survivances prehistoriques à l'epoque gallo-romaine dans les cités des Nerviens et des Menapiens, *Analecta Archaeologica, Festschrift F. Fremersdorf*, Cologne, 115-120.

Laet, S.J. de/A. van Doorselaer, 1962: Gräber der römischen Kaiserzeit mit Waffenbeigaben aus Belgien, den Niederlanden und dem Großherzogtum Luxemburg, *SJ* 20, 54-61.

Laur-Belart, R., 1935: *Vindonissa. Lager und Vicus*, Berlin/Leipzig.

Laurence, R., 1999: *The roads of Roman Italy. Mobility and cultural change*, London/New York.

Laurence, R., 2000: Metaphors, monuments and texts: the life course in Roman culture, *World Archaeology* 31, 442-455.

Lauwerier, R.C.G.M., 1988: *Animals in Roman times in the Dutch eastern river area*, 's-Gravenhage (Nederlandse Oudheden 12).

Lauwerier, R.C.G.M./A.J.M.M. Robeerst, 2001: Horses in Roman times in the Netherlands, in H. Buitenhuis/ W. Prummel (eds.), *Animals and man in the past. Essays in honour of Dr. A.T. Clason, emeritus professor of archaeozoology, Rijksuniversiteit Groningen, the Netherlands*, Groningen (ARC-publicatie 41), 275-290.

Laser, R./E. Schultze, 1995: *Corpus der römischen Funde im europäischen Barbaricum. Deutschland, Band 2, Freistaat Sachsen*, Bonn.

Lawson, A.K., 1978: Studien zum römischen Pferdegeschirr, *JRGZM* 25, 131-172.

Leech, R., 1986: The excavations of a Romano-Celtic temple and a later cemetery on Lamyett Beacon, Somerset, *Britannia* 17, 259-328.

Lehner, H., 1923: Ein gallorömischer Wagen aus Frenz an der Inde im Kreis Düren, *BJ* 128, 28-62.

Lejars, T., 1994: *Gournay III. Les fourreaux d'épée. Le sanctuaire de Gournay-sur-Aronde et l'armement des Celtes de La Tène moyenne*, Paris.

Lenz, K.H., 2000: *Römische Waffen, militärische Ausrüstung und militärische Befunde aus dem Stadtgebiet der Colonia Ulpia Traiana (Xanten)*, Nijmegen (unpublished dissertation, RUN).

Lenz, K.H., 2001: Militaria und Militärlager der römischen Kaiserzeit im Stadtgebiet der Colonia Ulpia Traiana (Xanten). Ein Beitrag zur Entstehung und Entwicklung der Städte in den römischen Nordwestprovinzen, *AK* 31, 587-599.

Lenz, K.H., 2002: Die Deutung von Fundkomplexen frühkaiserzeitlicher Militaria am Beispiel von Xanten und weiteren römischen Zentralorten der Rheinzone – Archäologische und epigraphische Aspekte, *JberGPV* 2001, 67-78.

Lenz, K.H., 2006: Veteranen der römischen Armee im Siedlungsbild einer früh- und mittelkaiserzeitlichen Koloniestadt und deren Hinterland. Das Beispiel der *Colonia Claudia Ara Agrippinensium* (Köln), *Germania* 84, 61-91.

Levi, D., 1971: *Antioch mosaic pavements*, Rome.

Liéger, A., 1997: Le *nécropole gallo-romaine de Cutry (Meurthe-et-Moselle)*, Nancy (Études Lorraines d'Archéologie Nationale 3).

Liesen, B., 1999: Die Grabungen südlich und westlich des Kölner Doms. 1. Die Funde aus Metall, *KJ* 32, 343-431.

Link, S., 1989: *Konzepte der Privilegierung römischer Veteranen*, Stuttgart (HABES 9).

Lodewijckx, M. et al. 1993: A third-century collection of decorative objects from a Roman villa at Wange (Central Belgium), *JRMES* 4, 67-99.

Londen, H. van, 1996: *Archeologisch onderzoek naar een inheemse nederzetting uit de Romeinse tijd aan de Polderweg, gemeente Schiedam*, Amsterdam (unpublished report, UvA).

Luik, M., 1999: Gewerbliche Produktionsstätten in Villen des römischen Rheinlandes, in M. Polfer (ed.), *Artisanat et productions artisanales en milieu rural dans les provinces du nord-ouest de l'Empire romain*, Montagnac (Monographies Instrumentum 9), 209-216.

Luik, M., 2002: Militaria in städtischen Siedlungen der iberischen Halbinsel, *JberGPV* 2001, 97-104.

Luttwak, E.N., 1976: *The grand strategy of the Roman empire. From the first century A.D. to the third*, Baltimore/London.

Lyne, M., 1994: Late Roman helmet fragments from Richborough, *JRMES* 5, 97-105.

Mackensen, M., 2000: Ein vergoldetes frühkaiserzeitliches Gladiusortband mit figürlich verziertem Scheidenblech aus Kleinasien oder Nordsyrien, *BVB* 65, 125-142.

Mackensen, M., 2001: Militärische oder zivile Verwendung frühkaiserzeitlicher Pferdegeschirranhänger aus der Provinz *Africa Proconsularis* und den Nordwestprovinzen, *Germania* 79, 325-345.

MacMullen, R., 1960: Inscriptions on armor and the supply of arms in the Roman Empire, *American Journal of Archaeology* 64, 23-40

MacMullen, R., 1967: *Soldier and civilian in the later Roman Empire*, Cambridge/Massachusetts.

Maes, K./L. van Impe, 1986: Begraafplaats uit de IJzertijd en Romeinse vondsten op 'de Rieten' te Wijshagen (gem. Meeuwen-Gruitrode), *Archaeologia Belgica* N.S. 2, 47-56.

Maisant, H., 1990: *Der römische Gutshof von Altforweiler (Krs. Saarlouis)*, Saarbrücken (Bericht der Staatlichen Denkmalpflege im Saarland, Abteilung Bodendenkmalpflege 1).

Mann, J.C., 1983: *Legionary recruitment and veteran settlement during the Principate*, London.

Mann, J.C., 1986: A note on conubium, in W. Eck/H. Wolff (eds.), *Heer und Integrationspolitik. Die römischen Militärdiplome als historische Quelle*, Cologne/Vienna, 187-189.

Mann, J.C., 2000: Honesta missio from the legions, in G. Alföldy et al. (eds.), *Kaiser, Heer und Gesellschaft in der römischen Kaiserzeit. Gedenkschrift für Eric Birley*, Stuttgart (HABES 31), 153-161.

Mann, J.C./M.M. Roxan, 1988: Discharge certificates of the Roman army, *Britannia* 19, 341-347.

Manning, W.H., 1985: *Catalogue of the Romano-British iron tools, fittings and weapons in the British Museum*, London.

Maringer, J., 1974: Flußopfer und Flußverehrung in vorgeschichtlicher Zeit, *Germania* 52, 309-318.

Martin, M., 1978: Römische Bronzegiesser in Augst BL, *Archäologie der Schweiz* 3, 112-120.

Massart, C., 2000: Élements de char et de harnachement dans les tumulus Tongres du IIIe s. Les deux harnachements du tumulus de Celle (Waremme), Belgique, *KJ* 33, 509-522.

Mauss, M., 1991: *The gift. The form and reason for exchange in archaic societies*, London (translation of Mauss 1923/1924 by W.D. Halls).

Maxfield, V.A., 1981: *The military decorations of the Roman army*, London.

Maxfield, V.A., 1986: Systems of reward in relation to military diplomas, in W. Eck/H. Wolff (eds.), *Heer und Integrationspolitik. Die römischen Militärdiplome als historische Quelle*, Cologne/Vienna, 37-42.

Migotti, B., 1999: Liturgical(?) brooches from Pannonia, *Instrumentum* 10, 14.

Mirković, M., 1986: Die Entwicklung und Bedeutung der Verleihung des Conubium, in W. Eck/H. Wolff (eds.), *Heer und Integrationspolitik. Die römischen Militärdiplome als historische Quelle*, Cologne/Vienna, 167-186.

Mirković, M., 2000: Military diplomas from Viminacium and the settlement of auxiliary veterans: city or countryside?, in G. Alföldy et al. (eds.), *Kaiser, Heer und Gesellschaft in der römischen Kaiserzeit. Gedenkschrift für Eric Birley*, Stuttgart (HABES 31), 365-375.

Mitard, P.-H., 1993: *Le sanctuaire gallo-romain des Vaux-de-la-Celle à Genainville (Val-d'Oise)*, Guiry-en-Vexin.

Mommsen, T./P. Krueger/A. Watson, 1985: *The Digest of Justinian* I-V, Philadelphia/Pennsylvania.

Morel, J./W. Groenman-Van Waateringe, 1993: Opkomst en ondergang van een Romeins havenfort bij Velsen, in J.H.F. Bloemers et al. (eds.), *Voeten in de aarde. Een kennismaking met de Nederlandse archeologie*, Amsterdam, 45-60.

Müller, M., 2002: *Die römischen Buntmetallfunde von Haltern*, Mainz (Bodenaltertümer Westfalens 37).

Neumann, A.R., 1976: Die Ehrenzeichen des römischen Heeres, *Antike Welt* 7, 48-55.

Nicasie, M.J., 1997: *Twilight of empire. The Roman army from the reign of Diocletian until the battle of Adrianople*, Leiden (dissertation, UL).

Nicolay, J.A.W., 2002: Interpreting Roman military equipment and horse gear from non-military contexts. The role of veterans, *JberGPV* 2001, 53-66.

Nicolay, J.A.W., 2003: The use and siginificance of military equipment and horse gear from non-military contexts in the Batavian area: continuity from the Late Iron Age into the Early Roman period, in Th. Grünewald/S. Seibel (eds.), *Kontinuität und Diskontinuität. Germania inferior am Beginn und am Ende der römischen Herrschaft*, Berlin/New York (Ergänzungsbände zum Reallexikon der germanischen Alterumskunde 35), 414-435.

Nicolay, J.A.W., 2007: Wapens en paardentuig: een herinnering aan 25 jaar militaire dienst in het Romeinse leger, in N. Roymans/T. Derks/S. Heeren (eds.), *Een Bataafse gemeenschap in de wereld van het Romeinse Rijk. Opgravingen te Tiel-Passewaaij*, Utrecht, 99-114.

Noelke, P., 1986: Ein neuer Soldatengrabstein aus Köln, in C. Unz (ed.), *Studien zu den Militärgrenzen Roms III. 13. Internationaler Limeskongreß, Aalen 1983*, Stuttgart (Forschungen und Berichte zur Vor- und Frühgeschichte in Baden-Württemberg 20), 213-222.

Noelke, P., 1998: Grabreliefs mit Mahldarstellung in den germanisch-gallischen Provinzen – soziale und religiöse Aspekte, in P. Fasold et al. (eds.), *Bestattungssitte und kulturelle Identität. Grabanlagen und Grabbeigaben der frühen römischen Kaiserzeit in Italien und den Nordwest-Provinzen*, Cologne/Bonn (Xantener Berichte, Grabung-Forschung-Präsentation 7), 399-418.

Nuber, H.U., 1972: Zwei bronzene Besitzmarken aus Frankfurt/M.-Heddernheim, *Chiron* 2, 483-507.

Obmann, J., 1999: Waffen: Statuszeichen oder alltäglicher Gebrauchsgegenstand?, in H. von Hesberg (ed.), *Das Militär als Kulturträger in römischer Zeit*, Cologne, 189–200.

Obmann, J., 2000: *Studien zu römischen Dolchscheiden des 1. Jahrhunderts n.Chr.*, Rahden (Kölner Studien zur Archäologie der römischen Provinzen 4).

Oldenstein, J., 1974: Zur Buntmetallverarbeitung in den Kastellen am obergermanischen und rätischen Limes, *Bulletin des Musees Royaux d'art et d'histoire* 6, 185-196.

Oldenstein, J., 1976: Zur Ausrüstung römischer Auxiliareinheiten. Studien zu Beschlägen und Zierat an der Ausrüstung der römischen Auxiliareinheiten des obergermanisch-raetischen Limesgebietes aus dem zweiten und dritten Jahrhundert n. Chr., *BRGK* 57, 49-284.

Oldenstein, J., 1985: Manufacture and supply of the Roman army with bronze fittings, in M.C. Bishop (ed.), *The production and distribution of Roman military equipment*, Oxford (BAR Int. Ser. 275), 82-94.

Oldenstein, J., 1997: Mit *hasta* und *lorica* Wache schieben. Rekonstruktion der Ausrüstung eines Auxiliarsoldaten aus severischer Zeit, in E. Schallmayer (ed.), *Hundert Jahre Saalburg. Vom römischen Grenzposten zum europäischen Museum*, Mainz, 134-146.

Ortisi, S., 2006: *Gladii* aus Pompeji, Herculaneum und Stabia, *Germania* 84, 369-385.

Ossel, P. van, 1992: *Etablissements ruraux de l'Antiquité tardive dans le nord de la Gaule*, Paris (Gallia, suppl. 51).

Palágyi, S.K., 1981: Die römischen Hügelgräber von Inota, *Alba Regia* 19, 7-93.

Palágyi, S.K., 1986: Über Pferdegeschirr- und Jochrekonstruktionen von Inota, in C. Unz (ed.), *Studien zu den Militärgrenzen Roms III. 13. Internationaler Limeskongreß, Aalen 1983*, Stuttgart (Forschungen und Berichte zur Vor- und Frühgeschichte in Baden-Württemberg 20), 389-397.

Palágyi, S.K., 1990: Römerzeitliches Pferdegrab in Tihany, *Alba Regia* 24, 17-45.

Palágyi, S.K., 1995: Ein neuer Pferdegeschirrfund aus Pannonien und Möglichkeiten seiner Rekonstruktion, in S.T.A.M. Mols et al. (eds.), *Acta of the 12th International Congress on Ancient Bronzes, Nijmegen 1992*, Amersfoort/Nijmegen (NAR 18), 401-408.

Palágyi, S.K., 1997: Rekonstruktionsmöglichkeit des Zaumzeuges aus dem Wagengrab von Kozármisleny (Pannonia), in W. Groenman-Van Waateringe et al. (eds.), *Roman Frontier Studies 1995. Proceedings of the XVIth International Congess of Roman Frontier Studies*, Oxford (Oxbow Monograph 91), 467-471.

Palágyi, S.K., 2000: Joche aus Pannonien, *KJ* 33, 535-544.

Parker, A.J., 1992: *Ancient shipwrecks of the Mediterranean & the Roman provinces*, Oxford (BAR Int. Ser. 580).

Parker, H.M.D., 1985: *The Roman legions*, Chicago.

Pauli, L., 1987: Gewässerfunde aus Nersingen und Burlafingen, in M. Mackensen (ed.), *Frühkaiserzeitliche Kleinkastelle bei Nersingen und Burlafingen an der oberen Donau*, Munich, 281-312.

Peddie, J., 1994: *The Roman war machine*, Stroud.

Petculescu, L, 1991a: '*Vtere felix*' and '*optime maxime con(serva)*' mounts from Dacia, in A. Maxfield/M.J. Dobson (eds.), *Roman frontier studies 1989. Proceedings of the XVth International Congress of Roman Frontier Studies*, Exeter, 392-396.

Petculescu, L., 1991b: A note on military equipment of Roman officers in the 3rd century A.D., *BVB* 56, 207-212.

Petculescu, L., 1991c: Bronze spear heads and spear butts from Dacia, *JRMES* 2, 35-58.

Petculescu, L, 1995: Military equipment graves in Roman Dacia, *JRMES* 6, 105-145.

Petrikovits, H. von, 1970: *Die Spezialgebäude römischer Legionslager*, in A. Vinayo González (ed.), *Legio VII Gemina*, León, 227-252 (reprinted in H. von Petrikovits (ed.), *Beiträge zur römischen Geschichte und Archäologie, 1931 bis 1974*, Bonn (BJ, Beiheft 36), 519-545).

Petrikovits, H. von, 1985: Römische Handel am Rhein und an der oberen und mittleren Donau, in K. Düwel et al. (eds.), *Untersuchungen zu Handel und Verkehr der vor- und frühgeschichtlichen Zeit in Mittel- und Nordeuropa. Teil 1: Methodische Grundlagen und Darstellungen zum Handel in vorgeschichtlicher Zeit und in der Antike*, Göttingen (Abhandlungen der Akademie der Wissenschaften in Göttingen 143), 299-336.

Pfahl, S.F./M. Reuter, 1996: Waffen aus römischen Einzelsiedlungen rechts des Rheins. Ein Beitrag zum Verhältnis von Militär und Zivilbevölkerung im Limeshinterland, *Germania* 74, 119-167.

Pflug, H., 1988: Helm und Beinschiene eines Gladiators, in A. Bottini et al. (eds.), *Antike Helme. Sammlung Lipperheide und andere Bestände des Antikenmuseums Berlin*, Mainz, 365-374.

Phang, S.E., 2001: *The marriage of Roman soldiers (13 B.C.-A.D. 235)*, Leiden/Boston/Cologne (Columbia Studies in the Classical Tradition 24).

Pirling, R., 1986: Ein Mithräum als Kriegergrab. Neue Untersuchungen im Vorgelände des Kastells Galduba, in C. Unz (ed.), *Studien zu den Militärgrenzen Roms III. 13. Internationaler Limeskongreß, Aalen 1983*, Stuttgart (Forschungen und Berichte zur Vor- und Frühgeschichte in Baden-Württemberg 20), 244-246.

Planck, D., 1983: *Das Freilichtmuseum am rätischen Limes im Ostalbkreis*, Stuttgart (Führer zu archäologischen Denkmälern in Baden-Württemberg 9).

Pulles, I., 1988: *Brons uit Brabant. Een inventarisatie van Romeinse bronzen voorwerpen uit de Kempen*, Amsterdam (unpublished thesis, VU).

Pulles, I./N. Roymans, 1994: Mantelspelden en armringen als offerobject, in N. Roymans/T. Derks (eds.), *De tempel van Empel. Een Hercules-heiligdom in het woongebied van de Bataven*, 's-Hertogenbosch, 132-141.

Prins, J., 2000: The 'fortune' of a late Roman officer. A hoard from the Meuse valley (Netherlands) with helmet and gold coins, *BJ* 200, 309-328.

Prittwitz und Gaffron, H.-H. von, 1990: Ein römischer Reiterhelm aus Xanten-Wardt, in M. Hellenkemper et al. (eds.), *Archäologie in Nordrhein-Westfalen. Geschichte im Herzen Europas*, Cologne, 216-218.

Prittwitz und Gaffron, H.-H. von, 1991: Der Reiterhelm des Tortikollis, *BJ* 191, 225-246.

Prittwitz und Gaffron, H.-H. von, 1993: Der schiefe Prunkhelm, in H.-J. Schalles/C. Schreiter (eds.), *Geschichte aus dem Kies. Neue Funde aus dem Alten Rhein bei Xanten*, Cologne, 59-63.

Rabeisen, E., 1990: La production d'équipement de cavalerie au 1er s. après J.-C. à Alesia, *JRMES* 1, 73-98.

Raddatz, K., 1959/1961: Ringknaufschwerter aus germanischen Kriegergräbern, *Offa* 17/18, 26-56.

Raddatz, K., 1987: *Der Thorsberger Moorfund, Katalog. Teile von Waffen und Pferdegeschirr, sonstige Fundstücke aus Metall und Glass, Ton- und Holzgefäße, Steingeräte*, Neumünster.

Raepsaet, G., 1982: Attelages antiques dans le Nord de la Gaule. Les systèmes de traction par équidés, *Trierer Zeitschrift* 45, 215-273.

Raepsaet, G., 2002: *Attelages et techniques de transport dans le monde gréco-romain*, Brussels.

Rankov, B., 1999: The governor's men: the *officium consularis* in provincial administration, in A. Goldsworthy/I. Haynes (eds.), *The Roman army as a community*, Portsmouth (JRA, suppl. 34), 15-34.

Rapin, A. et al., 1982: Das keltische Heiligtum von Gournay-sur-Aronde, *Antike Welt* 13, 39-60.

Reichmann, C., 1979: *Zur Besiedlungsgeschichte des Lippemündungsgebietes während der jüngeren vorrömischen Eisenzeit und älteren römischen Kaiserzeit*, Wesel.

Reijnen, R., 1994: Romeinse munten en het offer als gebaar, in N. Roymans/T. Derks (eds.), *De tempel van Empel. Een Hercules-heiligdom in het woongebied van de Bataven*, 's-Hertogenbosch, 124-131.

Reinert, F., 2000: Das Reitergrab eines Veteranen aus Hellingen in Luxemburg, in L. Wamser (ed.), *Die Römer zwischen Alpen und Nordmeer. Zivilisatorisches Erbe einer europäischen Militärmacht*, Mainz, 44-47.

Reuter, M., 1999: Späte Militärdolche vom Typ Künzing. Anmerkungen zur Datierung und Verbreitung, *JRMES* 10, 121-124.

Riedel, M., 1987: Keulen als industrie- en exportcentrum, in P. Stuart/M.E.Th. de Grooth (eds.), *Langs de weg. De Romeinse weg van Boulogne-sur-Mer naar Keulen, verkeersader voor industrie en handel. Villa Rustica, het Romeinse boerenbedrijf in het Rijn/Maasgebied*, Heerlen.

Ritterling, E., 1904: *Das frührömische Lager bei Hofheim im Taunus. Ausgrabungs- und Fundbericht*, Wiesbaden (Annalen des Vereins für Nassauische Altertumskunde 34).

Ritterling, E., 1909: *Das Kastell Wiesbaden, Nach ältesten Untersuchungen des nassauischen Altertumsvereins*, Heidelberg.

Rober, A., 1983: *Le sanctuaire gallo-romain de Matagne-la-Grande*, Brussels (AB 252).

Robinson, H.R., 1975: *The armour of Imperial Rome*, London.

Roes, A., 1953: Een Romeinse zwaardschede onlangs gevonden te Herwen (Gelderland), *BROB* 4, 9-10.

Roest, J. van der, 1988: Die römischen Fibeln von 'De Horden', *BROB* 38, 141-202.

Roest, J. van der, 1991: *De collectie Wakker. Detectorvondsten uit de Nederbetuwe en de Tielerwaard*, s.l. (unpublished report).

Roest, J. van der, 1992: *De collectie Wakker. Detectorvondsten uit de Nederbetuwe en de Tielerwaard II – Rumpt-"De Worden"*, s.l. (unpublished report).

Roest, J. van der, 1994: Koper in militaire metaalwerkplaatsen, in W.A. van Es/W.A.M. Hessing (eds.), *Romeinen, Friezen en Franken in het hart van Nederland. Van Traiectum tot Dorestad, 50 v.C.-900 n.C.*, Amersfoort, 153-160.

Roxan, M., 1985: *Roman military diplomas 1978–1984*, London.

Roxan, M., 1997: Settlement of veterans of the auxilia – a preliminary study, in W. Groenman-Van Waateringe et al. (eds.), *Roman frontier studies 1995. Proceedings of the XVIth International Congress of Roman Frontier Studies*, Oxford (Oxbow Monograph 91), 483-487.

Roxan, M., 2000: Veteran settlement of the auxilia in Germania, in G. Alföldy et al. (eds.), *Kaiser, Heer und Gesellschaft in der römischen Kaiserzeit. Gedenkschrift für Eric Birley*, Stuttgart (HABES 31), 307-326.

Roymans, N., 1990: *Tribal societies in northern Gaul. An anthropological perspective*, Amsterdam (Cingula 12).

Roymans, N., 1996: The sword or the plough. Regional dynamics in the romanisation of Belgic Gaul and the Rhineland area, in N. Roymans (ed.), *From the sword to the plough. Three studies on the earliest romanisation of Northern Gaul*, Amsterdam (AAS 1), 9-108.

Roymans, N., 2004: *Ethnic identity and imperial power. The Batavians in the early Roman Empire*, Amsterdam (AAS 10).

Roymans, N./J. Aarts, 2005: Coins, soldiers and the Batavian Hercules cult. Coin deposition at the sanctuary of Empel in the Lower Rhine region, in C. Haselgrove/D. Wigg-Wolf (eds.), *Iron Age coinage and ritual practices*, Mainz (Studien zur Fundmünzen der Antike), 337-359.

Roymans, N./T. Derks, 1990: Ein keltisch-römischer Kultbezirk bei Empel (Niederlande), *AK* 20, 443-451

Roymans, N./T. Derks, 1993: Ein Hercules-Heiligtum im Batavergebiet, *AK* 23, 479-492.

Roymans, N./T. Derks (eds.), 1994: *De tempel van Empel. Een Hercules-heiligdom in het woongebied van de Bataven*, 's-Hertogenbosch.

Roymans, N./T. Derks/S. Heeren (eds.), 2007: *Een Bataafse gemeenschap in de wereld van het Romeinse Rijk. Opgravingen te Tiel-Passewaaij*, Utrecht.

Roymans, N./F. Kortlang, 1993: Bewoningsgeschiedenis van een dekzandeiland langs de Aa te Someren, in N. Roymans/F. Theuws (eds.), *Een en al zand. Twee jaar graven naar het Brabantse verleden*, 's-Hertogenbosch (Graven naar het Brabantse verleden 1), 22-41.

Roymans, N./W. van der Sanden, 1980: Celtic coins from the Netherlands and their archaeological context, *BROB* 30, 173-254.

Sanden, W.A.B. van der, 1988: The Ussen Project: large scale settlement archaeology of the period 700 BC-AD 250, a preliminary report, *APL* 20, 95-102.

Sanden, W.A.B. van der, 1993: Fragments of a *lorica hamata* from a barrow at Fluitenberg, Netherlands, *JRMES* 4, 1-8.

Sanden, W.A.B., van der, 2005: Een vroeg-Romeins ruitergraf uit Zuidoost-Drenthe, *Palaeohistoria* 45/46, 347-362.

Sanden, W.A.B. van der/P.W. van den Broeke (eds.), 1987: *Getekend zand. Tien jaar archeologisch onderzoek in Oss-Ussen*, Waalre (Bijdragen tot de studie van het Brabants Heem 31).

Schaaff, U., 1988a: Keltische Helme, in A. Bottini et al. (eds.), *Antike Helme. Sammlung Lipperheide und andere Bestände des Antikenmuseums Berlin*, Mainz, 293-317.

Schaaff, U., 1988b: Etruskisch-römische Helme, in A. Bottini et al. (eds.), *Antike Helme. Sammlung Lipperheide und andere Bestände des Antikenmuseums Berlin*, Mainz, 318-326.

Schalles, H.-J., 1994a: Frühkaiserzeitliche Militaria aus einem Altrheinarm bei Xanten-Wardt, *JRMES* 5, 155-165.

Schalles, H.-J., 1994b: Ein neuer Schildfesselbeschlag aus Xanten?, *Arma* 6, 18-19.

Schalles, H.-J., 1999: Beutegut oder Kampfplatzzeugnis? Ergänzende Überlegungen zu den frühkaiserzeitlichen Militaria aus Xanten-Wardt, in W. Schlüter/R. Wiegels (eds.), *Rom, Germanien und die Ausgrabungen von Kalkriese*, Osnabrück, 207-225.

Schalles, H.-J./C. Schreiter (eds.), 1993: *Geschichte aus dem Kies. Neue Funde aus dem Alten Rhein bei Xanten*, Cologne.

Schegget, M. ter, 1999: Late Iron Age human skeletal remains from the river Meuse at Kessel: a river cult place?, in F. Theuws/N. Roymans (eds.), *Land and ancesters. Cultural dynamics in the Urnfield period and the Middle Ages in the Southern Netherlands*, Amsterdam (AAS 4), 199-240.

Schinkel, K., 1994: *Zwervende erven. Bewoningssporen in Oss-Ussen uit de Bronstijd, IJzertijd en Romeinse tijd. Opgravingen 1976-1986*, Leiden.

Schleiermacher, M., 1996: Wagenbronzen und Pferdegeschirr im Römisch-Germanischen Museum Köln, *KJ* 28, 205-295.

Schlott, C., 1999: *Zum Ende des spätlatènezeitlichen Oppidum auf dem Dünsberg (Gem. Biebertal-Fellingshausen, Kreis Gießen, Hessen)*, Montagnac (Forschungen zum Dünsberg 2).

Schnurbein, S. von, 1973: Ein Helm von Weisenauer Typus aus dem Hauptlager von Haltern, *AK* 3, 351-352.

Schnurbein, S. von, 1995: Merkur als Soldat? Zur Gürtelmode des 3. Jahrhunderts n. Chr., in W. Czysz et al. (eds.), *Provinzialrömische Forschungen. Festschrift für Günter Ulbert zum 65. Geburtstag*, Espelkamp, 139-148.

Schönberger, H., 1953: Provinzialrömische Gräber mit Waffenbeigaben, *SJ* 12, 53-56.

Schulze-Forster, J., 2002: *Die latènezeitlichen Funde vom Dünsberg*, Marburg (unpublished dissertation, Universität Marburg).

Schumacher, F.-J., 1989a: Eine römische Kriegerbestattung mit Schildbuckel. Grab. 982, in A. Haffner (ed.), *Gräber – Spiegel des Lebens. Zum Totenbrauchtum der Kelten und Römer am Beispiel des Treverer-Gräberfeldes Wederath-Belginum*, Mainz, 255-264.

Schumacher, F.-J, 1989b: Ein Trevererkrieger in römischen Diensten. Grab 2215, in A. Haffner (ed.), *Gräber – Spiegel des Lebens. Zum Totenbrauchtum der Kelten und Römer am Beispiel des Treverer-Gräberfeldes Wederath-Belginum*, Mainz, 265-274.

Schumacher, K., 1911: Votivfunde aus einer römischen Tempelanlage bei Klein-Winternheim (Rheinhessen), *Altertümer unserer heidnischen Vorzeit* 5, 108-113.

Schönberger, H., 1953: Provinzialrömische Gräber mit Waffenbeigaben, *SJ* 12, 53-56.

Schwinden, L., 1987: Zur Trageweize der Metallhackamore bei römischen Pferden, *Funde und Ausgrabungen im Bezirk Trier* 19, 36-41.

Scott, I.R., 1985a: Daggers, in W.H. Manning, *Catalogue of the Romano-British iron tools, fittings and weapons in the British Museum*, London, 152-159.

Scott, I.R., 1985b: First century military daggers and the manufacture and supply of weapons for the Roman army, in M.C. Bishop (ed.), *The production and distribution of Roman military equipment*, Oxford (BAR Int. Ser. 275), 160-219.

Seijnen, M., 1994: Dierebotten en rituele maaltijden, in N. Roymans/T. Derks (eds.), *De tempel van Empel. Een Hercules-heiligdom in het woongebied van de Bataven*, 's-Hertogenbosch, 162-173.

Sier, M.M./C.W. Koot (eds.), 2001: *Archeologie in de Betuweroute: Kesteren-De Woerd. Bewoningssporen uit de IJzertijd en de Romeinse tijd*, Utrecht (RAM 82).

Simpson, C.J., 1976: Belt-buckles and strap-ends of the later Roman Empire: a preliminary survey of several new groups, *Britannia* 7, 192-223.

Slofstra, J., 1987: Een nederzetting uit de Romeinse tijd bij Hoogeloon, in W.C.M. van Nuenen et al. (eds.), *Drie dorpen, een gemeente. Een bijdrage tot de geschiedenis van Hoogeloon, Hapert en Casteren*, Hapert, 51-86.

Slofstra, J., 1991: Changing settlement systems in the Meuse-Demer-Schelde area during the early Roman period, in N. Roymans/F. Theuws (eds.), *Images of the past. Studies on ancient societies in Northwestern Europe*, Amsterdam (Studies in Prae- en Protohistorie 7), 131-199.

Slofstra, J., 2002: Batavians and Romans on the Lower Rhine. The romanisation of a frontier area, *AD* 9, 16-38.

Slofstra, J./W. van der Sanden, 1987: Rurale cultusplaatsen uit de Romeinse tijd in het Maas-Demer-Scheldegebied, *APL* 20, 125-168.

Speidel, M., 2000: Sold und Wirtschafsanlage der römischen Soldaten, in G. Alföldy et al. (eds.), *Kaiser, Heer und Gesellschaft in der Römischen Kaiserzeit. Gedenkschrift für Eric Birley*, Stuttgart (HABES 31), 65-94.

Speidel, M.A., 1996: *Die römischen Schreibtafeln von Vindonissa. Lateinische Texte des militärischen Alltags und ihre geschichtliche Bedeutung*, Brugg (Veröffentlichungen der Gesellschaft pro Vindonissa 12).

Speidel, M.P., 1976: Eagle-bearer and trumpeter. The eagle-standard and trumpets of the Roman legions illustrated by three tombstones recently found at Byzantion, *BJ* 176, 123-163 (reprinted in M.P. Speidel (ed.), *Roman army studies I*, Amsterdam (Mavors 1), 3-43).

Speidel, M.P., 1981: The prefect's horse-guards and the supply of weapons to the Roman army, in R.S. Bagnall et al. (eds.), *Proceedings of the XVI International Congress of Papyrology*, Chicago, 405-409 (reprinted in M.P. Speidel (ed.), *Roman army studies I*, Amsterdam (Mavors 1), 329-332)

Speidel, M.P. (ed.), 1984a: *Roman army studies I*, Amsterdam (Mavors 1).

Speidel, M.P., 1984b: Zum Aufbau der Legion und zum Handwerk in Vindonissa (Neulesung zweier Briefadressen auf Holztäfelchen aus dem Schutthügel), *JberGPV* 1983, 29-34 (reprinted in M.P. Speidel (ed.), 1992: *Roman army studies II*, Stuttgart (Mavors 8), 56-61).

Speidel, M.P., 1985: Furlough in the Roman army, *Yale Classical Studies* 28, 283-293 (reprinted in M.P. Speidel (ed.), 1992: *Roman army studies II*, Stuttgart (Mavors 8), 330-341).

Speidel, M.P. (ed.), 1992a: *Roman army studies II*, Stuttgart (Mavors 8).

Speidel, M.P., 1992b: The weapon keeper, the *fisci curator*, and the ownership of weapons in the Roman army, in M.P. Speidel (ed.), *Roman army studies II*, Stuttgart (Mavors 8), 134–135.

Speidel, M.P., 1994: *Riding for Caesar. The Roman emperors' horse guard*, London.

Stjernquist, B., 1954: Runde Beschlagplatten mit Befestigungsöse, *SJ* 13, 59-68.

Stoepker, H. et al., 2000: *Venray-Hoogriebroek en Venray-Loobeek. Nederzettingen uit de prehistorie, Romeinse tijd en late Middeleeuwen*, Amersfoort (RAM 46).

Strobel, K., 1987: Anmerkungen zur Truppengeschichte des Donauraumes in der hohen Kaiserzeit IV: zur Truppenliste des oberpannonischen Militärdiploms CIL XVI 64 von 116 n.Chr. mit einem Anhang zur Geschichte der *Ala I Ulpia contariorum milliaria c.r.*, *ZPE* 70, 259–292

Stuart, P., 1986: *Provincie van een imperium. Romeinse oudheden uit Nederland in het Rijksmuseum van Oudheden te Leiden*, Leiden.

Stuart, P./J.E. Bogaers, 2001: *Nehalennia. Römische Steindenkmäler aus der Oosterschelde bei Colijnsplaat. 1. Textband*, Leiden.

Swift, E., 2000: *Regionality in dress accessories in the late Roman West*, Montagnac (Monographies *instrumentum* 11).

Swinkels, L.J.F., 1993: Medaillon met Medusahoofd, in A.A.J.J. van Pinxteren et al. (eds.), *Goltzius. Pronkstukken Venlo 650 jaar stad*, Venlo, 25-27.

Swinkels, L.J.F., 1994: Een vergoddelijkte Hercules en enkele andere bronsfiguren, in N. Roymans/T. Derks (eds.), *De tempel van Empel. Een Hercules-heiligdom in het woongebied van de Bataven*, 's-Hertogenbosch, 82-91.

Taylor, A.K., 1975: Römische Hackamoren und Kappzäume aus Metall, *JRGZM* 22, 106-133.

Tejral, J., 1994: Römische und germanische Militärausrüstungen der antoninischen Periode im Licht norddanubischer Funde, in C. von Carnap-Bornheim (ed.), *Beitrage zu römischer und barbarischer Bewaffnung in den ersten vier nachchristlichen Jahrhunderten. Akten des 2. Internationalen Kolloquiums in Marburg a.d. Lanh, 20. bis 24. Februar 1994*, Lublin/Marburg (Veröffentlichung des Vorgeschichtlichen Seminars Marburg 8), 27-59.

Tent, W.J. van/F. Vogelzang, 1996: Amerongen: 't Spijk. *Archeologische kroniek van de provincie Utrecht over de jaren 1970-1979*, 4-5.

Theuws, F., in print: Ethnicity, grave goods and the rhetoric of the burial ritual in Late Antique Northern Gaul, in T. Derks/N. Roymans (eds.), *Ethnic constructs in antiquity: the role of power and tradition* (AAS).

Theuws, F./M. Alkemade, 2000: A kind of mirror for men: sword depositions in Late Antique Northern Gaul, in F. Theuws/J.L. Nelson (eds.), *Rituals of power. From Late Antiquity to the Early Middle Ages*, Leiden (The transformation of the Roman world 8), 401-476.

Thiel, A., 2000: Römische Wasserfunde der frühen Kaiserzeit aus Gewässern, in L. Bonnamour (ed.), *Archéologie des fleuves et des rivières*, Paris, 70-74.

Thiel, A./W. Zanier, 1994: Römische Dolche – Bemerkungen zu den Fundumständen, *JRMES* 5, 59-81.

Thoma, M., 2000: Der gallo-römische Kultbezirk auf dem Martberg bei Pommern an der Mosel, Kr. Cochem-Zell, in A. Haffner/S. von Schnurbein (eds.), *Kelten, Germanen, Römer im Mittelgebirgsraum zwischen Luxemburg und Thüringen. Akten des internationalen Kolloqiums zum DFG-Schwerpunktprogramm 'Romanisierung' in Trier vom 28. bis 30. September 1998*, Bonn, 447-483.

Thomas, E.B., 1973: Der Helmfund von Budapest, Ungarn, in H. Klumbach (ed.), *Spätrömische Gardehelme*, Munich, 39-50.

Thomas, N./M. Feugère/N. Dieudonné-Glad, 2001: Une épée Romaine découverte à Saintes (Charente-Maritime), *Gallia* 2001, 261-269.

Tomlin, R.S.O., 1999: The missing lances, or making the machine work, in A. Goldsworthy/I. Haynes (eds.), *The Roman army as a community*, Portsmouth (JRA, suppl. 34), 127-138.

Torbrügge, W., 1960: Die bayerischen Inn-Funde, *BVB* 25, 16-69.

Toynbee, J.M.C., 1973: *Animals in Roman life and art*, London (Aspects of Greek and Roman life).

Ulbert, G., 1969a: *Das frührömische Kastell Rheingönheim*, Berlin (Limesforschungen 9).

Ulbert, G., 1969b: Gladii aus Pompeji. Vorarbeiten zu einem Corpus römischer Gladii, *Germania* 47, 97-128.

Ulbert, G., 1971a: Gaius Antonius, der Meister des silbertauchierten Dolches von Oberammergau, *BVB* 36, 44-49.

Ulbert, G., 1971b: Römische Bronzeknöpfe mit Reliefverzierung, *Fundberichte aus Schwaben* N.F. 19, 278-297.

Ulbert, G., 1985: Die frühkaiserzeitliche Siedlung auf dem Auerberg, in E. Keller et al. (eds.), *Die Römer in Schwaben. Jubiläumsausstellung 2000 Jahre Augsburg*, Munich (Bayerisches Landesamt für Denkmalpflege, Arbeitsheft 27), 72-76.

Ulbert, G./W. Zanier, 1997: *Der Auerberg II. Besiedlung innerhalb der Wälle*, Munich.

Vanderhoeven, A., 1996: The earliest urbanisation in Northern Gaul. Some implications of recent research in Tongres, in N. Roymans (ed.), *From the sword to the plough. Three studies on earliest romanisation of northern Gaul*, Amsterdam (AAS 1), 189-260.

Verhagen, M., 1993: Bone and antler artefacts, in R.M. van Dierendonck/D.P. Hallewas/K.E. Waugh (eds.), *The Valkenburg excavations 1985-1988. Introduction and detail studies*, Amersfoort (Nederlandse Oudheden 15), 339-416.

Verhart, L.B.M./N. Roymans, 1998: Een collectie La Tène-vondsten uit de Maas bij Kessel, gemeente Lith (prov. Noord-Brabant), *OMROL* 78, 75-91.

Verhelst, E.M.P., 2001: *Passewaaij Oude Tielseweg. Chronologie, structuur en materiële cultuur van een inheemse nederzetting in het Bataafse stamgebied*, Amsterdam (unpublished thesis, UvA).

Verhelst, E.M.P., 2006: Metaal, in S. Heeren (ed.), *De nederzetting aan de Passewaaijse Hogeweg. Opgravingen bij Tiel 1*, Amsterdam (ZAR 29), 145-153.

Verwers, W.J.H., 1972: *Das Kamps Veld in Haps in Neolitikum, Bronzezeit und Eisenzeit*, Leiden.

Verwers, W.J.H., 1978: Romeinse vondsten uit de omgeving, *Spiegel Historiael* 13, 230-231.

Verwers, W.J.H., 1986: Romeinse tijd: Lith, Teeffelen, *Archeologische Kroniek van Noord-Brabant* 1981/1982, 39-41.

Verwers, G.J./J. Ypey, 1975: Six iron swords from the Netherlands, *APL* 8, 79-91.

Vittinghoff, F, 1986: Militärdiplome, römische Bürgerrechts- und Integrationspolitik der Hohen Kaiserzeit, in W. Eck/H. Wolff (eds.), *Heer und Integrationspolitik. Die römischen Militärdiplomen als historische Quelle*, Cologne/Vienna, 535-555.

Voirol, A., 2002: «Etats d'armes». Les *militaria* d'Avenches/*Aventicum*, *JberGPV* 2001, 31-40.

Vollgraff, C.W./A. Roes, 1942: Nieuwe oudheidkundige vondsten uit Lobith, *Mededeelingen der Nederlandsche Akademie van Wetenschappen* NR. 5, 283-326.

Vos, W.K. (ed.), 2000: *Houten-Zuid. Het archeologisch onderzoek op het terrein 8A*, Bunschoten (ADC Rapport 30).

Vos, W.K., 2002: *De inheems-Romeinse huisplattegronden van De Horden te Wijk bij Duurstede*, Amersfoort (*RAM* 96).

Vossen, I., 2003: The possibilities and limitations of demographic calculations in the Batavian area, in Th. Grünewald/S. Seibel (eds.), *Kontinuität und Diskontinuität. Germania inferior am Beginn und am Ende der römischen Herrschaft*, Berlin/New York (Ergänzungsbände zum Reallexikon der germanischen Alterumskunde 35), 414-435.

Vossen, I., in prep.: *Landschap en bewoning in de civitas Batavorum. Een reconstructie van het cultuurlandschap in het rivierengebied gedurende de Romeinse tijd*, Amsterdam (dissertation, VU).

Vries, L.S. de/F.J. Laarman, 2001: Bijlage III. Archeozoölogie, in W.K. Vos/J.J. Lanzing, *Houten-Zuid. Het archeologisch onderzoek op terrein 21*, Bunschoten (ADC Rapport 36), 89-95.

Waasdorp, J.A., 1999: *Van Romeinse soldaten en Cananefaten. Gebruiksvoorwerpen van de Scheveningseweg*, Den Haag.

Wagner, A., 1994: Rijke mannengraven in Rhenen, in W.A. van Es/W.A.M. Hessing (eds.), *Romeinen, Friezen en Franken in het hart van Nederland. Van Traiectum tot Dorestad, 50 v.C.-900 n.C.*, Amersfoort, 180-183.

Walser, G., 1984: *Summus Poeninus. Beiträge zur Geschichte des Grossen St. Bernhard-Passes in römischer Zeit*, Wiesbaden (Historia 46).

Warmenbol, E., 1993: *Les collections archéologiques du Musée du Monde Souterrain à Han-sur-Lesse*, Han-sur-Lesse.

Watson, G.R., 1969: *The Roman soldier*, London.

Watt, M., 1994: Gladii in Dänemark – Milieu und Zeitstellung, in C. Carnap-Bornheim (ed.), *Beiträge zu römischer und barbarischer Bewaffnung in den ersten vier nachchristlichen Jahrhunderten. Akten des 2. Internationalen Kolloquiums in Marburg a.d. Lahn, 20. bis 24. Februar 1994*, Lublin/Marburg, 303-317.

Waurick, G., 1983: Untersuchungen zur historisierenden Rüstung in der römischen Kunst, *JRGZM* 30, 265-301.

Waurick, G., 1988: Römische Helme, in A. Bottini et al. (eds.), *Antike Helme. Sammlung Lipperheide und andere Bestände des Antikenmuseums Berlin*, Mainz, 327-364.

Waurick, G., 1994: Zur Rüstung von frühkaiserzeitlichen Hilfstruppen und Verbündeten der Römer, in C. Carnap-Bornheim (ed.), *Beiträge zu römischer und barbarischer Bewaffnung in den ersten vier nachchristlichen Jahrhunderten. Akten des 2. Internationalen Kolloquiums in Marburg a.d. Lahn, 20. bis 24. Februar 1994*, Lublin/Marburg, 1-25.

Weiner, A.B., 1992: *Inalienable possessions. The paradox of keeping-while-giving*, Berkeley/Los Angeles/Oxford.

Werner, J., 1950/1951: Zur Entstehung der Reihengräberzivilisation. Ein Beitrag zur Methode der frühgeschichtlichen Archäologie, *Archaeologia Geographica* 1-2, 23-32.

Werner, J., 1958: Kriegergräber aus der ersten Hälfte des 5. Jahrhunderts zwischen Schelde und Weser, *BJ* 158, 372-413.

Werner, J., 1966: Spätrömische Schwertortbänder vom Typ Gundremmingen, *BVB* 31, 134-141.

Wesch-Klein, G., 1998: *Soziale Aspekte des römischen Heerwesens in der Kaiserzeit*, Stuttgart (HABES 28).

Wesselingh, D., 2000: *Native neighbours. Local settlement system and social structure in the Roman period at Oss (The Netherlands)*, Leiden (APL 32).

Wheeler, R.E.M./T.V. Wheeler, 1932: *Report on the excavation of the prehistoric, Roman and post-Roman site in Lydney Park, Gloucestershire*, Oxford (Reports of the research committee of the Society of Antiquaries of London 9).

White, K.D., 1970: *Roman farming*, London (Aspects of Greek and Roman life).

Whittaker, C.R., 1994: *Frontiers of the Roman empire. A social and economical study*, Baltimore/London.

Wickenden, N.P., 1988: Some military bronzes from the Trinovantian civitas, in J.C. Coulston (ed.), *Military equipment and the identity of Roman soldiers. Proceedings of the fourth Roman Military Equipment Conference*, Oxford (BAR Int. Ser. 394), 234-256.

Wiedemann, K., 1993: Die geplünderte Villa in Gallien – ein anderes archäologisches Modell, in E. Künzl (ed.), *Die Alamannenbeute aus dem Rhein bei Neupotz. Teil 1: Untersuchungen*, Mainz, 505-539.

Wierschowski, L., 1984: *Heer und Wirtschaft. Das römische Heer der Prinzipatszeit als Wirtschaftsfaktor*, Bonn (Habels Dissertationsdrucke 20).

Wild, J.P., 1970: Button-and-loop fasteners in the Roman provinces, *Britannia* 1, 137-155.

Willems, W.J.H., 1981: Romans and Batavians. A regional study in the Dutch Eastern River Area, I, *BROB* 31, 7-217.

Willems, W.J.H., 1984: Romans and Batavians. A regional study in the Dutch Eastern River Area, II, *BROB* 34, 39-332.

Willems, W.J.H., 1985: Archeologische kroniek van Limburg over 1984: Rijckholt, *Publications de la Société Historique et Archéologique dans le Limbourg* 121, 172.

Willems, W.J.H., 1990: *Romeins Nijmegen. Vier eeuwen stad en centrum aan de Waal*, Utrecht.

Willems, W.J.H., 1991: Een Romeins viziermasker van het Kops Plateau te Nijmegen, *Jaarboek Numaga* 38, 9-18.

Wirth, S., 2000: Die Funde aus der Donauschleife bei Schäfstall in Bayern, in L. Bonnamour (ed.), *Archéologie des fleuves et des rivières*, Paris, 84-92.

Wolff, H., 1986: Die Entwicklung der Veteransprivilegien vom Beginn des 1. Jahrhunderts v. Chr. bis auf Konstantin d. Gr., in W. Eck/H. Wolff (eds.), *Heer und Integrationspolitik. Die römischen Militärdiplome als historische Quelle*, Cologne/Vienna, 44-115.

Wolters, R., 1990: *Römische Eroberung und Herrschaftsorganisation in Gallien und Germanien. Zur Entstehung und Bedeutung der sogenannten Klientel-Randstaaten*, Bochum (Bochumer historische Studien, Alte Geschichte 8).

Woods, D., 1993: The ownership and disposal of military equipment in the Late Roman army, *JRMES* 4, 55-65.

Woodward, A./P. Leach, 1993: *The Uley shrines. Excavation of a ritual complex at West-Hill, Uley, Gloucestershire: 1977-9*, London (English Heritage Archaeological Report 17).

Woolf, G., 1996: Monumental writing and the expansion of Roman society in the early empire, *JRS* 86, 22-39.

Ypey, J., 1960/1961: Drei römische Dolche mit tauschierten Scheiden aus niederländischen Sammlungen, *BROB* 10/11, 347-362.

Ypey, J., 1969: Zur Tragweise frühfränkischer Gürtelgarnituren auf Grund niederländischer Befunde, *BROB* 19, 89-127.

Ypey, J., 1973: Das fränkische Gräberfeld zu Rhenen, Prov. Utrecht, *BROB* 23, 289-312.

Ypey, J., 1978: La chronologie du cimetière franc de Rhenen (Pays-Bas, provence d'Utrecht), in M. Fleury/P. Périn (eds.), *Problèmes de chronologie relative et absolute concernant les cimetières mérovingiens d'entre Loire et Rhin*, Paris, 51-57.

Ypey, J., 1982: Een Romeinse ijzeren helm uit het begin van onze jaartelling, gevonden bij Hedel (Gld.), *Westerheem* 31, 101-103.

Zadoks-Josephus Jitta, A.N./W.J.T. Peters/A.M. Gerhartl-Witteveen, 1973: *The Figural Bronzes*, Nijmegen (Descripion of the Collection in the Rijksmuseum G.M. Kam at Nijmegen 7).

Zadoks-Josephus Jitta, A.N./A.M. Gerhartl-Witteveen, 1977: Roman bronze lunulae from the Netherlands, *OMROL* 58, 167-195.

Zanier, W., 1988: Römische dreiflügelige Pfeilspitzen, *SJ* 44, 5-27.

Zanier, W., 1997: Ein einheimischer Opferplatz mit römischen Waffen der frühesten Okkupation (15-10 v. Chr.) bei Oberammergau, in W. Groenman-Van Waateringe et al. (eds.), *Roman frontier studies 1995. Proceedings of the XVIth International Congress of Roman Frontier Studies*, Oxford (Oxbow Monograph 91), 47-51.

Zee, K., 2005: Bronzen voorwerpen met een militair luchtje. In: H. van Enckevort/J. Thijssen (eds.), *In de schaduw van het noorderlicht. De Gallo-Romeinse tempel van Elst-Westeraam*, Abcoude, 109-110.

Zieling, N., 1989: *Studien zu germanischen Schilden der Spätlatène- und der römischen Kaiserzeit im freien Germanien*, Oxford (BAR Int. Ser. 505).

Zimmermann, W.H., 1970: Urgeschichtliche Opferfunde aus Flüssen, Mooren, Quellen und Brunnen Südwestdeutschlands, *Neue Ausgrabungen und Forschungen in Niedersachsen* 6, 53-92

Zeiler, J.T., 2001: Archeozoölogie, in M.M. Sier/C.W. Koot (eds.), *Archeologie in de Betuweroute: Kesteren-De Woerd. Bewoningssporen uit de IJzertijd en de Romeinse tijd*, Utrecht (RAM 82), 217-259.

Zwart, A.J.M., 1998a: Romeins paardentuig uit de regio Nijmegen, *Westerheem* 47, 245-255.

Zwart, A.J.M., 1998b: A bridled horse burial from Beuningen (NL), *JRMES* 9, 77-84.

Zwart, A.J.M., 2001: Metaalvondsten uit het Romeinse paardengraf, in J.S. van der Kamp/M. Polak (eds.), *Archeologisch onderzoek aan de Molenstraat te Beuningen (1997-1998)*, Amersfoort (RAM 92).

Appendix 1

Survey of sites for Roman weaponry and horse gear finds in the eastern Rhine delta and the adjacent area across the Rhine. Sites are divided into urban centres, rural settlements, cemeteries, cult places, rivers and dredge pits. The exact coordinates are not known for the sites marked with an asterisk.

site number	place name	toponym	site type
001	Aalst (Aalst district)	Eendenkade	rural settlement
002	Aalst (Aalst district)	Eendes	rural settlement
003	Aalst (Lienden district)	De Morgen	rural settlement
004	Aalst (Lienden district)	Nelly's Hof	rural settlement
005	Aalst (Lienden district)*	-	rural settlement
006	Aalst (Lienden district)*	Boutenburg II	rural settlement
007	Afferden*	-	rural settlement
008	Alem*	Marensche Waarden	dredge pit
009	Alphen aan de Rijn	Goudse Rijpad	rural settlement
010	Altforst	-	rural settlement
011	Amerongen*	Rhine	river
012	Amerongen*	't Spijk	dredge pit
013	Angeren*	Loowaard/Kandia	dredge pit
014	Arnhem	De Laar-4	rural settlement
015	Arnhem	De Laar-6/7	rural settlement
016	Arnhem	De Laar-8	cemetery
017	Arnhem	De Laar-9	rural settlement
018	Arnhem*	Immerlooplas	dredge pit
019	Asch	Hofkampsesteeg	rural settlement
020	Asch*	-	rural settlement
021	Asch*	Noord Asch	rural settlement
022	Beesd	Betuwestrand I	rural settlement
023	Beesd	Betuwestrand II	rural settlement
024	Bemmel	Den Heuvel	rural settlement
025	Beneden-Leeuwen	De Ret	rural settlement
026	Beuningen	De Heuve	rural settlement
027	Beuningen	Molenstraat	rural settlement
028	Beusichem	De Ronde	rural settlement
029	Beusingen	Pietersteeg	rural settlement
030	Bijsterhuizen/Nijmegen	Bijsterhuizenstraat	rural settlement
031	Boven-Leeuwen*	Waal	river
032	Bruchem	Broekseweg	rural settlement
033	Bruchem	De Burge	rural settlement
034	Bruchem	Kasteelterrein	rural settlement
035	Bruchem	Viaductweg I	rural settlement
036	Bruchem	Viaductweg II	rural settlement
037	Bunnik	De Beesd	rural settlement
038	Buren	Buurseveld	rural settlement
039	Buren	Hennisdijk	rural settlement

040	Buren	Hooge Korn	rural settlement
041	Buurmalsen	Nieuwe Steeg	rural settlement
042	Cothen	De Dom	rural settlement
043	Cothen	Trechtweg	rural settlement
044	Culemborg	Molenkade	rural settlement
045	Deil	Bulksteeg	rural settlement
046	Deil	Hazenhoek	cult place?
047	Deil	Hooiblok	rural settlement
048	Delwijnen	De Boosteren	rural settlement
049	Delwijnen	De Eng	rural settlement
050	Delwijnen	De Vorsten	rural settlement
051	Delwijnen	Eendenkade	rural settlement
052	Dodewaard	De Grote Wuust	rural settlement
053	Dodewaard	Trafostation	rural settlement
054	Dodewaard	Wuuste Graaf	rural settlement
055	Doorwerth*	Lower Rhine (Drielse Veer)	river
056	Dreumel*	Dreumelsche Waard	dredge pit
057	Driel*	Rhine	river
058	Druten	Klepperhei	rural settlement
059	Druten*	Hooge Bobbert	rural settlement
060	Druten*	Waal	river
061	Echteld	De Wilmert	rural settlement
062	Echteld	Medel	rural settlement
063	Echteld	Medelse Kop	rural settlement
064	Echteld	Saneringsweg	rural settlement
065	Echteld	Westering	rural settlement
066	Echteld*	-	rural settlement
067	Eck en Wiel	De Hoge Eng	rural settlement
068	Eck en Wiel	De Kniphoek	rural settlement
069	Ede	Op den Berg	rural settlement
070	Ede*	Kreelsche Zand	rural settlement
071	Ede*	Kwadenoordsebeek	rural settlement
072	Ede*	Langenberg/Drieberg	rural settlement
073	Ede*	Maanderzand	rural settlement
074	Eimeren	Eimeren-Zuid	rural settlement
075	Eimeren	Village	rural settlement
076	Elst	Aam	rural settlement
077	Elst	St.-Maartenskerk	cult place
078	Elst	Lijnden	rural settlement
079	Elst	Merm	rural settlement
080	Elst	Viaduct	rural settlement
081	Elst	Westeraam	cult place
082	Empel	De Werf	cult place
083	Empel	Empel-West	rural settlement
084	Erichem	Aardkuil	rural settlement
085	Erichem	Burenwal	rural settlement
086	Erichem*	-	rural settlement
087	Esch	De Kollenberg	cemetery

088	Escharen	Village	rural settlement
089	Est/Opijnen	De Lieverij	rural settlement
090	Est	Diepersestraat	rural settlement
091	Est	Snelleveld	rural settlement
092	Est	De Steendert	rural settlement
093	Ewijk	De Grote Aalst	rural settlement
094	Ewijk	Doddendaal	rural settlement
095	Gameren/Nieuwaal	De Epen	rural settlement
096	Gameren/Nieuwaal	Middelkampse Weg	rural settlement
097	Gassel	Overlaat	rural settlement
098	Geldermalsen	Hoge Weide	rural settlement
099	Geldermalsen	Middengebied	rural settlement
100	Geldermalsen	Rijs en Ooyen	rural settlement
101	Gellicum	Boutenstein	rural settlement
102	Gennep	De Maaskemp	rural settlement
103	Grave	Escharensche Veld	rural settlement
104	Groesbeek	Klein Amerika	cult place?/rural settlement
105	Hagestein*	Lek	river
106	Halder	Village	rural settlement
107	Haren	Het Broek	rural settlement
108	Hatert	Hulzen I	rural settlement
109	Hatert	Hulzen II	cemetery
110	Hedel	Adelseweg	rural settlement
111	Hedel	De Appert (= site nr. 112)	rural settlement
112	Hedel	Achterdijk (= site nr. 111)	rural settlement
113	Hedel	De Woerd	rural settlement
114	Hedel*	-	rural settlement
115	Hedel*	Meuse	river
116	Heeswijk*	-	rural settlement
117	Hemmen	Kobelwei	rural settlement
118	Hemmen	Kasteelsweide	rural settlement
119	Hernen	De Fleerde	rural settlement
120	Hernen	De Wijnakker	rural settlement
121	Herveld-Noord	Binnenstraat	rural settlement
122	Herveld-Noord*	-	rural settlement
123	Houten	Binnenweg	rural settlement
124	Houten	De Veste	rural settlement
125	Houten	Heemstede	rural settlement
126	Houten	Houten-Zuid 21	rural settlement
127	Houten	Houten-Zuid 24	rural settlement
128	Houten	Houten-Zuid 8A	rural settlement
129	Houten	Houtenseweg	rural settlement
130	Houten	Kniphoek	rural settlement
131	Houten	Leebrug	rural settlement
132	Houten	Loerik I	rural settlement
133	Houten	Loerik II/Houten-Zuid 9	rural settlement
134	Houten	Oud Wulven	rural settlement
135	Houten	Schalkwijkseweg	rural settlement

136	Houten	Tiellandt	rural settlement
137	Houten	Veerwagenweg	rural settlement
138	IJzendoorn	Het Hof	rural settlement
139	IJzendoorn*	De Waard	dredge pit
140	Ingen*	-	rural settlement
141	Ingen*	-	rural settlement
142	Ingen*	Tabaksland	rural settlement
143	Kapel-Avezaath	Hoge Hof	rural settlement
144	Kekerdom-Millingen*	Waal	river
145	Kerk-Avezaath	Bergakker I	rural settlement
146	Kerk-Avezaath	Bergakker Noord	rural settlement
147	Kerk-Avezaath	De Lente/Teisterbant	rural settlement
148	Kerk-Avezaath	De Nije Graaf	rural settlement
149	Kerk-Avezaath	Village	rural settlement
150	Kerk-Avezaath	Hamperk	rural settlement
151	Kerk-Avezaath	Hamse Biezen	rural settlement
152	Kerk-Avezaath	Heuvelakker	rural settlement
153	Kerk-Avezaath	Malburg	rural settlement
154	Kerk-Avezaath	Stenen Kamer	rural settlement
155	Kerk-Avezaath*	-	rural settlement
156	Kerk-Avezaath*	Bergakker II	rural settlement
157	Kerk-Avezaath*	Burense Dijk	rural settlement
158	Kerkdriel	De Zandmeren	dredge pit
159	Kerkwijk	Achter de Vameren	rural settlement
160	Kerkwijk	De Hof van Aalderwijk	rural settlement
161	Kerkwijk	Het Paradijs	rural settlement
162	Kerkwijk	Walderweg	rural settlement
163	Kessel/Lith*	De Bergen	dredge pit
164	Kessel/Lith*	Kesselsche Waarden	dredge pit
165	Kessel/Lith*	Meuse at Heerewaarden	river
166	Kesteren	De Woerd	rural settlement
167	Kesteren*	-	rural settlement
168	Kesteren*	Hoogeveld	rural settlement
169	Lent	Laauwikstraat-Zuid (La-2)	rural settlement
170	Lent	Steltsestraat (Sl-1)	rural settlement
171	Lienden (Buren district)	Boutenburg	rural settlement
172	Lienden (Buren district)	Hoogmeien	rural settlement
173	Lienden (Wijchen district)	Kapelhof	rural settlement
174	Lienden (Wijchen district)	Liendensestraat	rural settlement
175	Lith	Oijensche Hut	cult place
176	Lobith*	De Bijland	dredge pit
177	Lobith*	Rhine	river
178	Maasbommel*	-	rural settlement
179	Haren	De Peppelen	rural settlement
180	Macharen	Delenkanaal	rural settlement
181	Maurik	De Hucht	rural settlement
182	Maurik	Valentijn	rural settlement
183	Maurik	De Woerd	rural settlement

184	Maurik	Het Eiland van Maurik	dredge pit
185	Maurik	Hornixveld	rural settlement
186	Maurik	Parkstraat I	rural settlement
187	Maurik	Parkstraat II	rural settlement
188	Maurik*	Parkstraat III	rural settlement
189	Maurik*	Parkstraat IV	rural settlement
190	Maurik*	Rhine	river
191	Maurik*	Rijnbaandijk	rural settlement
192	Medel/Echteld	Oude Weiden	rural settlement
193	Megen*	De Gouden Ham	dredge pit
194	Meteren	Blankertseweg/De Dell	rural settlement
195	Meteren	Hondsgemet/Zes Morgen	rural settlement
196	Meteren*	-	rural settlement
197	Meteren*	Bergakker	rural settlement
198	Millingen aan de Rijn	Vruchtenoord	rural settlement
199	Millingen*	Waal	river
200	Mook	Bank of the Meuse	rural settlement
201	Nieuwaal*	-	rural settlement
202	Nijmegen	Broerstraat (Ulpia Noviomagus cemetery)	cemetery
203	Nijmegen	Canisius College/Hugo de Grootstraat (*castra* cemetery)	cemetery
204	Nijmegen	Hees (Ulpia Noviomagus cemetery)	cemetery?
205	Nijmegen	Heuvellust (*castra/canabae* cemetery)	cemetery
206	Nijmegen	Kleine Kopse Hof (Kops Plateau cemetery)	cemetery
207	Nijmegen	Krayenhofflaan (Ulpia Noviomagus cemetery)	cemetery
208	Nijmegen	Valkhof (*oppidum Batavorum*)	urban centre
209	Nijmegen	Waterkwartier (Municipium Ulpia Noviomagus Batavorum)	urban centre
210	Nijmegen*	-	rural settlement?
211	Nijmegen*	Waal	river
212	Nijmegen*	Waal at Winseling	river
213	Ommeren	Achterstraat	rural settlement
214	Ommeren	Kroonheuvel/Ommerse Veldweg	rural settlement
215	Ommeren	Ommerense Veldweg	rural settlement
216	Ommeren	Oude Eng	rural settlement
217	Ommeren*	-	rural settlement
218	Ommeren*	-	rural settlement
219	Ommerenveld	Blauwe Kamp	rural settlement
220	Oosterbeek*	Lower Rhine	river
221	Oosterhout	Akkerstraat	rural settlement
222	Oosterhout	Van Boetzelaerstraat (Bo-5)	rural settlement
223	Ophemert	Elzevier (= site nr. 230)	rural settlement
224	Opijnen	Keizershof	rural settlement
225	Ophemert	Kerkakkers	rural settlement
226	Ophemert	Kleine Mastmolen	rural settlement
227	Ophemert	Schuddegaffel	rural settlement
228	Ophemert	Veelust/Bommelsestraat	rural settlement
229	Ophemert	Wilhelminahoeve	rural settlement

230	Opijnen	Elzevier (= site nr. 223)	rural settlement
231	Opijnen	Esterweg	rural settlement
232	Opijnen	Oude Zandstraat	rural settlement
233	Opijnen	Westerbroek I/Wilhelminahoeve	rural settlement
234	Opijnen	Westerbroek II	rural settlement
235	Opijnen	Elzevierstraat	rural settlement
236	Oss	Vijver	rural settlement
237	Oss	Westerveld	rural settlement
238	Pannerden*	Lobberdensche Waard	dredge pit
239	Pannerden*	Waal	river
240	Tiel	Oude Tielseweg	rural settlement
241	Tiel	Passewaaij	cemetery
242	Tiel	Passewaaijse Hogeweg	rural settlement
243	Tiel	Zennewijnenseweg	rural settlement
244	Plasmolen*	Mokerplas	dredge pit
245	Plasmolen*	Mokerplas(?)	dredge pit
246	Randwijk	De Asterd	rural settlement
247	Randwijk	De Stern	rural settlement
248	Randwijk	Hokkerden	rural settlement
249	Remmerden	Plantage Willem III/Defensieweg	rural settlement
250	Remmerden	Noord-Remmerden	rural settlement
251	Ressen	Kerkenhof	rural settlement
252	Ressen	Kerkerakker	rural settlement
253	Rhenen	Donderberg	cemetery
254	Rijswijk*	Lower Rhine	river
255	Rossum*	Waal(?)	river
256	Rumpt	Boutenstein	rural settlement
257	Rumpt	De Worden	rural settlement
258	Slijk-Ewijk*	Waal	river
259	Snelleveld/Neerijnen	De Tieflaar I	rural settlement
260	Snelleveld/Neerijnen	Tieflaarse Straat	rural settlement
261	't Goy	Groenedijkje/Beusichemseweg	rural settlement
262	Teeffelen	De Honig	rural settlement
263	Teeffelen	Kennedybaan	rural settlement
264	Teeffelen*	-	cemetery?
265	Tiel*	Waal	river
266	Velddriel	Veilingweg	rural settlement
267	Veldhuizen	Kasteelterrein	rural settlement
268	Waardenburg	De Vergt	rural settlement
269	Waardenburg	De Woerden	rural settlement
270	Waardenburg*	-	rural settlement
271	Waardenburg/Neerijnen*	De Tieflaar II	rural settlement
272	Wadenoijen	De Breeuwert I	rural settlement
273	Wadenoijen	De Ouweling I	rural settlement
274	Wadenoijen	Ophemertsestraat	rural settlement
275	Wadenoijen*	De Breeuwert II	rural settlement
276	Wadenoijen*	De Ouweling II	rural settlement
277	Wageningen	Geertjesweg	cemetery

278	Wageningen	Wageningscheberg	rural settlement
279	Wehl	Oldershove	rural settlement
280	Wehl*	Hessenveld	rural settlement
281	Werkhoven	Achterdijk/De Klaproos	rural settlement
282	Werkhoven	Van Breugelhoeve/Oostromsdijkje	rural settlement
283	Wijchen	Mussenberg	rural settlement
284	Wijchen	Tienakker	rural settlement
285	Wijchen	Valendries	cemetery
286	Wijchen*	Wijchensche Meer I	dredge pit
287	Wijchen*	Wijchensche Meer II	dredge pit
288	Wijk bij Duurstede	De Geer-Trekweg I	rural settlement
289	Wijk bij Duurstede	De Geer-Trekweg II	rural settlement
290	Wijk bij Duurstede	De Heul	rural settlement
291	Wijk bij Duurstede	De Horden	rural settlement
292	Wijk bij Duurstede	De Lage Maat	rural settlement
293	Wijk bij Duurstede*	Lower Rhine	river
294	Winssen	De Grote Woerd	rural settlement
295	Woezik/Wijchen	Wezelsche Berg	rural settlement
296	Zennewijnen	De Hoogekamp	rural settlement
297	Zetten	Vloedschuur	rural settlement
298	Zetten	Zettensepad	rural settlement
299	Zoelen	Beneden Terwei	rural settlement
300	Zoelen	De Beldert	rural settlement
301	Zoelen	De Hevel	rural settlement
302	Zoelen	Uiterdijk	rural settlement
303	Zoelen	Vergarde	rural settlement
304	Zoelen*	-	rural settlement?
305	Zoelen*	Beneden Strijmen	rural settlement
306	-	(exact site not known)	rural settlement

Appendix 2

Functional and typochronological categories of weaponry and horse gear from the Roman period as described in chapter 2 and used in the database of finds from non-military contexts in the eastern Rhine delta.

functional groups in catalogue		type categories		type/variant/features	period
militaria	defensive weapons	helmet	A	Buggenum type	1
			B	Port type	1
			C	Hagenau type	2
			D1	Weisenau type	2
			D2	Weisenau type – late	2
			E1	Weiler variant	2
			E2	Guisborough variant	3
			F1	masked helmet – Weiler variant	2
			F2	masked helmet – Guisborough variant	3
			G1-3	Niederbieber type	3
			H	guard helmet	4
			I1	gladiator helmet – early	(1-)2
			I2	gladiator helmet – late	3
		armour	A	chain mail	1-4
			B	scale armour	1-4
			C1	plate armour – Kalkriese type	2
			C2	plate armour – Corbridge type	2
			C3	plate armour – Newstead type	3
		shield	A	rectangular/(flattened) oval	1-2
			B	oval	(1-)2
			C	round/oval	3
			D	'Germanic' type	2-3
	offensive weapons	sword (scabbard)	A1	*gladius* – Hispaniensis type	1
			A2	*gladius* – Mainz type	2
			A3	*gladius* – Pompeii type	2
			A4	*gladius*-like sword	2
			B1	*spatha* – Newstead type	2
			B2	*spatha* – Straubing/Nydam type	3-4
			C	*semispatha*	4
		dagger (sheath)	A	Republican type	1
			B1	Mainz type	2
			B2	Vindonissa type	2
			C	Künzing type	3
			D	peltate chape	3

		pilum/plumbata	A	*pilum* – tongue-shaped shaft	1-2
			B	*pilum* – socketed shaft	1-3
			C	*plumbata*	4
		spear/lance	A1/2	leaf-shaped	1-4
			B	triangular/square	3-4
			C	multi-faceted	3
		bow and arrow	A	trilobate	1-4
			B	round	2-3
			C	lozenge-shaped	(3-)4
			D	leaf-shaped	(3-)4
		artillery	A	lozenge-shaped	1-4
			B	round	1-4
		sling shot	A	almond-shaped	1-3
	suspension/apron	belt	A	narrow belt, buckle (pelta-shaped)	2
			B	narrow belt, buckle (pelta-shaped)	3
			C	wide belt, ring buckle	3
			D/E	wide belt, buckle (animal head)	4
			F	narrow belt, buckle (dolphins)	4
			G	narrow belt, buckle (C-shaped)	4
		baldric	-	-	3
		apron	-	-	2
	various	signalling instrument	A	*tuba*	-
			B	*lituus*	-
			C	*cornu*	-
			D	*bucina*	-
		distinction	A	torque	2-3
			B	armband	2-3
			C	*phalera* (worn on soldier's chest)	2-3
			D	*phalera* (horse gear)	2-3
horse gear	bridle	hackamore	A	rhomboid	2-3
			B	rhomboid with pointed tip	2-3
			C1/2	round/rosette	2-3
		bit	A	ring type	1-4
			B1	curb, straight	1-2
			B2	curb, omega-shaped	1-3
			C1	variant B1	1-2
			C2	variant B2	2-3
			D	semicircular shank, ring with loops	2

	chamfron	A	leather, round eyeguard	2
		B	leather, pointed eyeguard	2
		C	bronze	3
saddle	saddle fitting	A	openwork	2
		B	raised circles	2
harness	fastener	A	C-shaped buckle	2
		B1/2	T-shaped fastener	2
		C	disc-shaped fastener	2
		D	small (ring) buckle	3
		E	heart-shaped fitting with loop	3
		F	fitting with two strap holders	3
	strap junction	A	ring junction	2
		B	*phalera* junction	2
		C	openwork, with loops	3
		D	front and back plate	3
	strap terminal	A	oblong, solid	2
		B	various, openwork	3
	decorative fitting	A1	rectangular	2
		A2	waisted rectangular	2
		A3	figure eight	2
		A4	double figure eight	2
		A5	ribbed	2
		A6	acorn-shaped	2
		A7	*phalera*-shaped	2
		A8	lozenge-shaped	2
		A9	round	2
		A10	round with knobs	2
		A11	peltate	2
		A12	rectangular with round knobs	2
		A13	phallic	2
		A14	elongated with rosette knobs	2
		A15	rectangular with hinge	2
		A16	heart-shaped	2
		A17	lunate	2
		B1	round/oval	3
		B2	round, enamel inlay	3
		B3	rosette-shaped	3
		B4	mushroom-shaped	3
		B5	shell-shaped	3
		B6	rectangular/square	3
		B7	lozenge-shaped	3
		B8	shield-shaped	3
		B9	peltate	3
		B10	almond-shaped	3

	B11	almond-shaped, oblate ends	3
	B12	elongated	3
	B13	elongated and ridged	3
	B14	winged	3
	B15	trumpet motifs	3
	B16	lunate	3
	B17	vulvate	3
	B18	phallic	3
	B19	heart-shaped	3
	B20	tear-shaped	3
looped strap mount	AA	*phalera*	2
	A	various	2
	B	various	3
pendant	A1	leaf-shaped (trefoil)	2
	A2	winged, with rosette	2
	A3	winged, with animal head	2
	A4	oval with pelta/rosette	2
	A5	leaf-shaped (single leaf)	2
	A6	peltate	2
	A7	round/oval/tear-shaped	2
	A8	lunate	2
	A9	phallic	2
	A10	lancet-/lozenge-shaped	2
	B01	round/oval/tear-shaped	3
	B02	heart-shaped/peltate	3
	B03	heart-shaped/phallic	3
	B04	phallic	3
	B05	lunate	3
	B06	acorn-shaped	3
	B07	openwork	3
bell	A	tall, concave central part	2
	B	hemispherical, incised lines	2
	C	conical, square base with knobs	2
	D	conical, square base	3
	E	conical, faceted	3
bone 'amulet'	A	round, cut from antler	1-4
	B	lunate, wild boar teeth	1-3
spurs	A	U-shaped, rectangular loops	2
	B	semicircular, knobs/stray fittings	3
	C1/2	semicircular, shanks of unequal length	4

Appendix 3.1

Overview of weaponry that belongs typologically in periods 1 and 2 (helmet, shield, armour, sword and dagger) or that can be assigned to this period on the basis of context dating.

site	context	description of find	reference
Amay-Meuse (B)	river	*gladius*, Mainz type; g*ladius*, Pompeii type	Vanden Berghe 1996, 61-63
Andernach (D)	burial	*gladius*(-like sword); conical *umbo*	Schumacher 1989a/b, Karte 1
Bell (D)	burial	*gladius*(-like sword)	Schumacher 1989b, Karte 1
Bingen-Büdesheim (D)	burial	*gladius*(-like sword)	Schumacher 1989b, Karte 1
Bladel-'Kriekeschoor'	settlement	shield edging	Pulles 1988, nr. 233
Böbingen (D)	burial	*gladius*(-like sword)	Schumacher 1989b, Karte 1
Büderich (D)	river?	helmet cheekpiece, Hagenau type	Robinson 1975, pl. 236
Buggenum-Meuse	river	helmet, Buggenum type	Klumbach 1974, nr. 6
Conflans (F)	burial	helmet face shield	Krier/Reinert 1991, 145
Dhrönecken (D)	cult place	*gladius*?	Hettner 1901, 51.
	burial	*gladius* scabbard; *gladius* or dagger blade	Hettner 1901, 51, Taf. VI.37
Doncaster (GB)	burial	shield	Buckland 1978
Düsseldorf-Rhine (D)	river?	helmet, Buggenum type	Klumbach 1974, nr. 3
Eich (D)	river?	2 helmets, Hagenau/Weisenau types	Waurick 1988, 329
Ensdorg (D)	burial	*gladius*(-like sword)	Schumacher 1989b, Karte 1
Flüren-Rhine (D)	river	helmet, Hagenau type	Klumbach 1974, nr. 12
Heddernheim-Main (D)	river	2 helmets, Hagenau type	Waurick 1988, 329, Abb. 2.4
's Gravenvoeren (B)	river?	dagger with bone grip	Vanden Berghe 1996, 66
Goeblingen-Nospelt (L)	burial	*gladius*(-like sword); two conical *umbones*	Schumacher 1989a/b, Karte 1
Grimbergen-Schelde (B)	river	*gladius*, Pompeii type	Vanden Berghe 1996, 84
Grügelborn (D)	burial	conical *umbo*	Schumacher 1989a, Karte 1
Haldern-Banningsberg (D)	burial	terminal knob of *gladius* scabbard	Reichmann 1979, pl. 35.5
Harlow (GB)	cult place	2 plate armour fittings, Corbridge type	France/Gobel 1985, fig. 46
Heimbach-Weis (D)	burial	conical *umbo*	Schumacher 1989a, Karte 1
Hellingen (L)	burial	helmet face shield	Krier/Reinert 1991/Reinert 2000
Hirstein (D)	burial	*gladius*(-like sword)	Schumacher 1989b, Karte 1
Hofheim (D)	burial	*gladius*(-like sword)	Schumacher 1989b, Karte 1
Hofstade (B)	cult place?	*gladius*, Pompeii type	Vanden Berghe 1996, 80-82
Hönnepel-Rhine (D)	river	helmet, Hagenau type	Klumbach 1974, nr. 17
Izier (B)	settlement?	*gladius*, Mainz type	Vanden Berghe 1996, 72
Katwijk-'Zanderij'	settlement	plate armour fitting, Corbridge type	unpublished (private coll.)
Kelvedon (GB)	*vicus*	shield edging	Wickenden 1988, 241
Keulen-Rhine (D)	river	helmet, Hagenau type	Klumbach 1974, nr. 9
Keulen-Marienburg (D)	burial	*gladius*	Van Doorselaer 1963/64, 29
Koblenz (D)	burial	*gladius*(-like sword)	Schumacher 1989b, Karte 1
Koblenz-Bubenheim (D)	burial?	helmet, Weiler type	Klumbach 1974, nr. 32
Koblenz-Neuendorf (D)	burial	*gladius*(-like sword); two conical *umbones*	Schumacher 1989a/b, Karte 1
Lautenbach (D)	burial	conical *umbo*	Schumacher 1989a, Karte 1
Lautzkirchen (D)	burial	*gladius*(-like sword)	Schumacher 1989b, Karte 1
Lebach (D)	burial	*gladius*(-like sword); two conical *umbones*	Schumacher 1989a/b, Karte 1

Limbach (D)	burial	*gladius*(-like sword)	Schumacher 1989b, Karte 1
Maasbree-'De Boekend'	burial?	terminal knob of *gladius* scabbard	Roymans 1996, 105, C25
Klein-Winterheim (D)	cult place	*gladius*, Pompeii type; dagger; shield edging	Schumacher 1911, Taf. 21
Mainz-Rhine (D)	river	9 *gladii*, Mainz type; 14 helmets, Hagenau/Weisenau types	Ulbert 1969b, 127; Robinson 1975, pl. 33, 230-232, 235
Melle-Schelde (B)	river	helmet, Buggenum type	Vanden Berghe 1996, 84
Merhrum (D)	burial	*gladius*-like sword, dagger, shield	Gechter/Kunow 1983, fig. 16
Möhn (D)	cult place	iron *umbo* (dating uncertain)	Hettner 1901, 30, Taf. VI.27
Mühlbach (D)	burial	two *gladii* (or *gladius*-like swords)	Schumacher 1989b, Karte 1
Mülheim-Kärlich (D)	burial	two *gladii* (or *gladius*-like swords)	Schumacher 1989b, Karte 1
Mülheim-Rhine (D)	river	helmet, Hagenau type	Klumbach 1974, nr. 10
Nattenheim (D)	burial	*gladius*(-like sword)	Schumacher 1989b, Karte 1
Neeritter	burial	*gladius*, Mainz type; conical *umbo*	Roymans 1996, fig. 9
Neunkirchen (D)	burial	*gladius*(-like sword)	Schumacher 1989b, Karte 1
Niedermörmter (D)	river	helmet, Weisenau type	Klumbach 1974, nr. 27
Nienbüttel (D)	burial	*gladii* scabbard	Erdrich 2002, XXI-10-6/1.22-23
	burial?	plate armour fastener and fitting	Erdrich 2002, XXI-10-6/1.24-25
Olfen-Lippe (D)	river	helmet, Buggenum type	Klumbach 1974, nr. 4
Pommern-'Martberg' (D)	cult place	folded *gladius*	J. Klein 1897, 110
Radwinter (GB)	*vicus*?	plate armour fitting, Corbridge type	Wickenden 1988, 243
Ronchin (F)	burial	*gladius*	Roymans 1996, 105, C-30
Saarbrücken (D)	burial	*gladius*(-like sword)	Schumacher 1989b, Karte 1
Seehausen-Weser (D)	river	*gladius* scabbard, Mainz type	Erdrich 2002, XVIII-**-1/17.2
Septfontaines (L)	burial	*gladius*	Krier/Reinert 1991, fig. 38
Someren	burial	*gladius*, Mainz type	Roymans 1996, fig. 8
Sötern (D)	burial	*gladius*(-like sword)	Schumacher 1989b, Karte 1
Speyer (D)	burial	*gladius*(-like sword)	Schumacher 1989b, Karte 1
Temse (B)	burial	*gladius*, Pompeii type	De Laet 1960, 118, pl. 26
Texel	beach	helmet, Hagenau type	Klumbach 1974, nr. 25
Uitgeest-'Dorregeest'	settlement	helmet cheekpiece, Weisenau type	De Koning 2003, fig. 6a
Urmitz (D)	burial	*gladius*(-like sword)	Schumachter 1989b, Karte 1
Valkenburg-'De Woerd'	river	terminal knob of *gladius* scabbard, Mainz type; plate armour fitting, Corbridge type	Bult/Hallewas 1990, fig. 14a/f
Velserbroek	cult place	dagger; *pilum*; spear/lance; catapult bolt; scale armour	Bosman 1992; 1995a
Venlo-Meuse	river	helmet cheekpiece, Weisenau type	Klumbach 1974, nr. 41
Wahnwegen (D)	burial	conical *umbo*	Schumacher 1989a, Karte 1
Wardt-Lüttingen (D)	river	2 helmets, Buggenum/Hagenau types	Klumbach 1974, nr. 5, 16
Weiler (B)	burial	helmet face shield	Krier/Reinert 1991, 145
Wederath (B)	burial	two *gladii*, Mainz type; seven conical *umbone*s	Haffner 1971
Wijshagen (B)	cult place	*gladius* scabbard fitting, Mainz type	Impe/Creemers 1991, fig. 12
Wissel-Rhine (D)	river	helmet, Hagenau type	Klumbach 1974, nr. 18
Xanten-Rhine (D)	river (?)	2 helmets, Hagenau type	Klumbach 1974, nr. 13-14
Xanten-Wardt (D)	river	18 helmets, Hagenau/Weisenau/Weiler types; 10 swords (*gladii*, Mainz/Pompeii types and early *spathae*)	Schalles/Schreiter 1993

Appendix 3.2

Overview of weaponry that belongs typologically in period 3 (helmet, shield, armour, sword and dagger) or that can be assigned to this period on the basis of context datings.

site	context	description of find	reference
Adendorf (D)	burial?	*spatha* scabbard chape (pelta)	Erdrich 2002, XXI-5-1/1.1
Anthée (B)	settlement	weapon hoard (including ring sword, convex *umbo*)	Vanden Berghe 1996, 66-70
Barnstorf (D)	burial	convex *umbo*, repaired	Erdrich 2002, XX-2-1/2.30
Bavai (F)	*vicus*?	*spatha* sword blade	Vanden Berghe 1996, 78
Bodegraven	river	helmet, Niederbieber type	Klumbach 1974, nr. 40
Boltersen (D)	burial	*spatha* scabbard chape (pelta)	Erdrich 2002, XXI-5-8/1.1
Chelmsford (GB)	*vicus*	*spatha* scabbard chape (pelta)	Bishop 1991, 27
Colchester (GB)	urban centre	*spatha* guard fitting, scabbard slides (3x) and scabbard chapes (2x)	Bishop 1991, 26
Colmschate	settlement	*spatha* scabbard chape (pelta)	Erdrich 1994, 205
Dronrijp	settlement	*spatha* scabbard chape (pelta) and dagger	Erdrich 1994, 205
Ede-'Op den Berg'	settlement	helmet face shield fragment (mask?)	unpublished (69.1)
Famars (F)	river?	*spatha* with ivory guard fitting	Vanden Berghe 1996, 78
Gestingthorpe (GB)	*vicus*?	*spatha* scabbard chape (pelta)	Wickenden 1988, 243
Grimbergen-Schelde (B)	river	ring sword fragment	Vanden Berghe 1996, fig. 16.1
Holzhausen (D)	burial	*spatha* scabbard chape (pelta) and scabbard slide	Erdrich 2002, XIX-13-6/1.2-3
Hoogeloon-'Kerkakkers'	settlement	outer rim *umbo*	Pulles 1988, nr. 180; fig. 3.15
Hönnepel (D)	river	helmet, Niederbieber type	Klumbach 1974, nr. 30
Jemelle (B)	near settlement	*spatha* fragment	Vanden Berghe 1996, fig. 10.1
Juslenville (B)	settlement?	*spatha* bone grip	Vanden Berghe 1996, fig. 7.1
Kontich-'Steenakker' (B)	cult place	*spatha* sword blade	Vanden Berghe 1996, fig. 12.1
Liberchies I (B)	*vicus* (military?)	*spatha* sword blade and bone scabbard chapes (3x)	Vanden Berghe 1996, 80
Mahlstedt (D)	settlement	*spatha* scabbard slide	Erdrich 2002, XIX-13-7/1.29
Matagne-la-Grande (B)	cult place	2 scale armour fragments	Rober 1983, fig. 16 (nr. 70)
Möhn (D)	cult place	ring sword	Hettner 1901, Taf. VI.35
Naaldwijk-'Hooge Werf'	settlement	*spatha* scabbard chape (rectangular, pelta motif)	Holwerda 1936, fig. 23
Polleur-Hoegre (B)	river	*umbo*	Vanden Berghe 1996, fig. 6.2
Poortugaal-'Hofterrein'	settlement	*spatha* bone scabbard slide	unpublished
Remmerden	settlement	*spatha* scabbard chape (pelta)	unpublished (250.1)
Rotterdam-'Willemsspoor'	residual channel	bronze *umbo*	Carmiggelt et al. 1997, p. 88
Schagen-'Muggenburg'	settlement	*spatha* scabbard slide	Erdrich 1994, 206
Schiedam-'Polderweg'	settlement	bronze *umbo*; dagger scabbard chape (pelta)	Van Londen 1996, 21
Schwarmstedt (D)	burial?	*umbo* fragment	Erdrich 2002, XXI-8-3/1.6
Silchester (GB)	*vicus*	*spatha* bone scabbard chape and scabbard slide	Bishop 1991, 26
St. Albans (GB)	*vicus*	*spatha* scabbard chape (pelta)	Bishop 1991, 26
Tienen (B)	*vicus*	*spatha* bone guard fitting	De Clerck 1983, 315
Uitgeest-'Dorregeest'	settlement	*umbo* fragment (imitation?)	De Koning 2003, fig. 6c
Valkenburg-'Marktveld'	settlement	several *spatha* scabbard parts (bone)	Verhagen 1993, figs. 71-78
Wehden (D)	burial?	*spatha* scabbard slide	Erdrich 2002, XXI-2-25/1.6
Wijnaldum-'Tjitsma'	settlement	dagger scabbard chape (pelta)	Erdrich 1999, fig. 3.33
Xanten (D)	urban centre	*spatha* sword blade and several scabbard parts	Lenz 2000, Taf. 61-64

Appendix 3.3

Overview of belt components and horse gear that belong typologically in periods 1 and 2 (hg: horse gear).

site	context	description of find	reference
Amiens 1 (F)	settlement	*cingulum* fitting (niello)	unpublished (fig. 3.14)
Amiens 2 (F)	settlement	*cingulum* buckle tongue; strap junction and 2 strap fittings hg (niello)	unpublished (fig. 3.14)
Bladel-'Kriekeschoor'	settlement	strap fitting hg	Pulles 1988, nr. 159
Braives (B)	settlement	strap fitting hg	Brulet 1981, fig. 40
Chelmsford (GB)	*vicus*	several parts hg	Wickenden 1988, 235-237
Cologne (D)	urban centre	several parts hg	Liesen 1999, Abb. 15, 28
Dalheim (L)	*vicus*	several strap fittings hg	unpublished
Drögennindorf (D)	burial	*cingulum* buckle (imitation?)	Erdrich 2002, XXI-5-3/1.1
Ede-'Kreelsche Zand'	settlement	2 strap fittings hg (niello)	unpublished (70.1-2)
Ede-'Kwadenoordsebeek'	settlement	pendant hg (niello)	unpublished (71.1)
Ede-'Langenberg/Drieberg'	settlement	strap junction hg	unpublished (72.1)
Ede-'Maanderzand'	settlement	strap terminal hg	unpublished (73.1)
Emmen-'Barger-Oosterveld'	burial	strap junction hg	Van der Sanden 2005, fig. 3
Great Dunmow (GB)	*vicus*	strap fitting hg (niello)	Wickenden 1988, 239
Hamme-Durme (B)	river	pendant hg (niello)	Vanden Berghe 1996, fig. 17.4
Harlow (GB)	cult place	pendants and strap fittings hg (niello)	France/Gobel 1985, fig. 46
Heybridge (GB)	*vicus*	strap terminal hg	Wickenden 1988, 238
Hoogeloon-'Kerkakkers'	settlement	strap fitting (*phalera*) hg	unpublished (fig. 3.15)
Katwijk-'Zanderij'	settlement	dagger frog; 2 strap fittings hg	unpublished (private coll.)
Kelvedon (GB)	*vicus*	pendant hg	Wickenden 1988, 241
Kerkrade-'Holzkuil'	settlement	several parts hg	Hoss/Van der Chijs 2005, 230-231
Klein-Winterheim (D)	cult place	2 belt fittings hg (niello)	M.J. Klein 1999, 87
Krefeld-Gellep (D)	cult place	several parts hg	Bechert 1986, Abb. 3
Naaldwijk-'De Lier/Leehove'	settlement	*cingulum* buckle	unpublished
Nienbüttel (D)	burial?	*cingulum* buckles and single buckle tongue	Erdrich 2002, XXI-10-6/1.26-30
Rijckholt	settlement	pendant hg (niello)	Willems 1985
Rijswijk-'De Bult'	settlement	mould *cingulum* buckle; 2 strap junctions hg	Bloemers 1978, fig. 127
Schelde (B)	river	exclusive pendant hg (niello)	Vanden Berghe 1996, fig. 17.3
Sottorf (D)	burial?	*cingulum* buckle	Erdrich 2002, XXI-5-2/3.6
Texel	burial	2 strap junctions and strap fitting hg	Erdrich 2001b, Abb. 4
Tongeren-'Clarissenstraat' (B)	urban centre	pendant hg	unpublished (private coll.)
Trier-'Viehmarkt' (D)	urban centre	hinged strap fitting hg	Landesmuseum Trier (unpub.)
Uitgeest-'Dorregeest'	settlement	2 *cingulum* fittings; strap junction hg	De Koning 2003, fig. 6a; unpublished
Velserbroek	cult place	several parts hg	Bosman 1992; 1995a
Xanten (D)	urban centre?	several *cingulum* parts and hg	Lenz 2000, Taf. 22 ff.
Xanten-'Wardt' (D)	river	several *cingulum* parts and hg	Schalles/Schreiter 1993

Appendix 3.4

Overview of belt components and horse gear that belong typologically in period 3 (hg: horse gear).

site	context	description of find	reference
Altforweiler (D)	settlement	strap fitting and fastener hg	Maisant 1990, Taf. 92
Amiens 1 (F)	settlement	2 strap fittings and pendant hg	unpublished (fig. 3.14)
Amiens 2 (F)	settlement	3 strap fittings hg	unpublished (fig. 3.14)
Bonsin (B)	settlement?	strap fitting and looped strap fitting hg	Vanden Berghe 1996, 72
Borg (D)	settlement	c.15 strap fittings hg	unpublished
Braives (B)	vicus	several strap fittings hg	Brulet 1981, fig. 40
Chelmsford (GB)	vicus	baldric pendant; strap fittings and pendants hg	Bishop 1991, 27
Chichester (GB)	vicus	mount and terminal fitting belt; 2 strap fittings hg	Bishop 1991, 26-27
Colchester (GB)	urban centre	belt fitting; 3 strap fittings and pendant hg	Bishop 1991, 26
Dongjum	settlement	3 strap fittings hg	Erdrich 1994, 206
Dronrijp	settlement	2 strap fittings hg	Erdrich 1994, 206
Ede-'Op den Berg'	settlement	strap fitting hg	unpublished (69.2)
Franeker	settlement	strap fitting hg	Erdrich 1994, 206
Friesland	settlement?	belt fastener; 3 strap fittings hg	Erdrich 1994, 207-208
Gestingthorpe (GB)	vicus?	3 strap fittings hg	Wickenden 1988, 243
Han-sur-Lesse (B)	river	belt buckle; c. 20 strap fittings hg	Warmenbol 1993, 44; partly unpublished
Hapert-'Hoogpoort'	settlement	strap junction hg	Pulles 1988, nr. 175
Hemelingen (D)	settlement	strap fitting hg	Erdrich 2002, XVIII-**-1/7.1
Herxen	settlement	strap fitting hg	Erdrich 1994, 206-207
Holwerd	settlement	2 strap fittings hg	Erdrich 1994, 207
Hoogeloon-'Kerkakkers'	settlement	5 strap fittings and looped strap fitting hg	Pulles 1988, nrs. 119, 153, 155-157, 198; fig. 3.15
Hoogeloon-'Kerkakkers-Zuid'	settlement	strap fitting hg	Pulles 1988, nr. 118
Jemelle (B)	settlement	several strap fittings hg	Vanden Berghe 1996, fig. 10
Juslenville (B)	settlement?	pendant hg	Vanden Berghe 1996, fig. 7.2
Kerkrade-'Holzkuil'	settlement	belt fastener; strap fitting and bit hg	Hoss/Van der Chijs 2005, 230-231, fig. 7.9-10
Keulen (D)	urban centre	several strap fittings hg	Liesen 1999, Abb. 16-17, 28
Knegsel	settlement?	strap fitting and bell hg	Prins 2000, 45
Leidschendam-'Leeuwenbergh'	settlement	strap fitting hg	unpublished
Les Avins (B)	settlement?	several strap fittings hg	Vanden Berghe 1996, 72-74
Mahlstedt (D)	settlement	strap fitting hg	Erdrich 2002, XIX-13-7/1.28
Matagne-la-Grande (B)	cult place	strap fitting hg	Rober 1983, fig. 16 (nr. 69)
Modave (B)	settlement?	3 strap fittings hg	Vanden Berghe 1996, 72
Peins	settlement	strap fitting hg	Erdrich 1994, 207
Riethoven-'Heesmortel'	settlement	belt fastener; strap fitting, pendant and bell hg	Pulles 1988, nrs. 152, 154, 199, 231
Rijswijk-'De Bult'	settlement	strap fitting hg	Bloemers 1978, fig. 127
Rockanje-'Helhoek'	settlement	strap fitting hg	Bogaers 1952, fig. 3.12
Scole (GB)	vicus	belt buckle; fitting *balteus*	Bishop 1991, 27

Sebbenhausen (D)	settlement?	bone fitting belt(?)	Erdrich 2002, XX-7-1/2.2
Silchester (GB)	*vicus*	4 parts belt and *balteus*	Bishop 1991, 26
St. Albans (GB)	*vicus*	belt fitting and terminal fitting; 2 strap fittings and pendant hg	Bishop 1991, 26
Tienen (B)	*vicus*	2 strap fittings hg	De Clerck 1983, 295
Uitgeest-'Dorregeest'	settlement	strap fitting hg	unpublished
Venray-'Hoogriebroek'	settlement	belt fastener; strap fitting hg	Stoepker et al. 2000, fig. 55
'From the Weser' (D)	river	strap fitting hg	Erdrich 2002, XVIII-**-1/22.1
Wickford (GB)	urban centre	strap junction and strap fitting hg	Bishop 1991, 27
Wijnaldum-'Tjitsma'	settlement	11 strap fittings hg	Erdrich 1994, 207
Woodcock Hall (GB)	urban centre	4 strap fittings hg	Bishop 1991, 27
Xanten	urban centre	several belt and hg components	Lenz 2000, Taf. 71ff.

Appendix 4

This is a survey of the cult places in Northern Gaul, the neighbouring 'German' area and Britannia that have yielded Roman weaponry and horse gear. The temple complexes (A) and open-air sanctuaries (B) are presented in chronological order, based on the typological datings of the 'military' finds. Wherever possible, in addition to a brief description of the finds, the specific find context and interpretations of the material are provided.

A. TEMPLE COMPLEXES:

1. *Matagne-la-Petite (Belgium). Period 1?*
   The finds from this sanctuary, in use from the Augustan period to the mid-2nd century AD, include a late La Tène shield boss (fig. 5.8, nr. 1).[1] The presence of the grip suggests that the iron boss was deposited as part of a complete shield. The shield may have belonged to a soldier from the earliest auxiliaries who were still partially armed with their own weapons.

2. *Grand St. Bernard (Switzerland). Period 2*
   Alongside spear- and lanceheads, two richly ornamented scabbard fittings of Mainz type *gladii* were found in a temple dedicated to Jupiter Poeninus on the Grand St. Bernard Pass.[2] The weapons were probably votive offerings dedicated to Jupiter for a safe crossing. Over fifty votive plaques point to soldiers and civilians as possible dedicants. Three veterans are included among the civilians.[3]

3. *Harlow (Great Britain). Period 2*
   A spearhead, lobate shoulder hinges from two different sets of plate armour, as well as three decorative fittings and a horse pendant were recovered from the sanctuary of Harlow (fig. 5.8, nrs. 2-8).[4] The spearhead has a raised midrib and may be of pre-Roman origin. The remaining objects belong typologically to the 1st century AD, with the horse gear being partly Claudio-Flavian. Remains of the iron sheeting on the back of the armour hinges show that they were probably deposited as part of complete sets of armour. Although the earliest known temple was built around AD 80, given the context datings, the military finds appear to be associated with pre-Flavian and perhaps even pre-Roman forerunners. The military objects are interpreted as dedications by the soldiers themselves or as a collective offering of booty.[5]

4. *Hofstade (Belgium). Period 2*
   The complete blade of a Pompeii type *gladius* was discovered in a pit near Hofstade.[6] Later excavations have unearthed traces of a cult building and other votive offerings, including a large quantity of earthenware, fibulae and fragments of terracotta figurines.

---

[1] De Boe 1982, 14-16, fig. 5.

[2] In general, Hunt 1998; for the scabbard plates, see Ettlinger/Hartmann 1985, 8-10. The votive plaques are discussed by Walser (1984).

[3] Walser (1984, 78) believes that the veterans may have crossed the pass as traders.

[4] France/Gobel 1985, 21-23 (nr. 6), 89-90 (nrs. 117, 120-124); figs. 46, 48, with context datings.

[5] France/Gobel 1985, 82.

[6] Vanden Berghe 1996, 81-82, fig. 13.1; see also De Laet 1948. Roymans (1996, appendix 1, C-29) views it as a grave find.

5. *Ober-Olm (Germany). Period 2*

    Votive plaques show that this sanctuary was dedicated to Mars Loucetius.[7] The military finds consist of a Pompeii type *gladius*, several iron and bone sword fragments, a dagger, parts of shield edgings, the shank of a *pilum* and two niello-inlay *cingulum* fittings. Of special interest are three large lanceheads (complete item 87.2 cm long, remaining damaged heads 72 and 50 cm) which were probably part of what are called '*beneficiarius* lances'.[8] As with two smaller spearheads, the edges are blunt, rendering a military use of these 'weapons' impossible in Schumacher's view.[9] The belt fittings date to the Claudian period; the majority of the weapons can also be assigned typologically to the 1st century. A clue to the ritual nature of the finds is a bronze plaque, found together with the spearheads, bearing a votive inscription from Fabricius Veiento, consul and key military advisor to Emperor Domitianus. Klein has pointed out the finds may be linked, in which case they might have been dedicated in connection with a battle against the Chatti (c. AD 83).[10]

6. *Alba-la-Romaines-'Bagnols' (France). Period 2*

    The only weapon finds from this sanctuary are an iron bolthead and a helmet bowl fragment of the Weisenau type.[11] The finds are associated with the 1st-century phase of the sanctuary.

7. *Vindonissa (Switzerland). Period 2*

    The sanctuary of Vindonissa is located inside the legionary fort. References in votive inscriptions show that it was visited by both legionaries and civilians, including a *gladiarius*.[12] Although there is no precise description of the weapon finds, they include daggers, swords, spear- or lanceheads and arrowheads.[13] Some of the objects appear to have been collected and buried in the course of alterations at the end of the 1st century. The military equipment is probably dedicated to Mars, with a bronze votive plaque suggesting the involvement of a legionary veteran.[14]

8. *Hayling Island (Great Britain). Period 2?*

    In contrast to the large numbers of items of native weaponry and horse gear from the late 1st century BC and the early 1st century AD, there are almost no Roman items.[15] Possible exceptions are a few chain mail fragments.[16] A fragment of a shrine erected by a legionary shows that soldiers numbered among the visitors to the sanctuary.

9. *Pommern-'Martberg' (Germany). Period 2(-3)*

    Excavations of this sanctuary dedicated to Lenus Mars have yielded various military finds. The weaponry comprises a bent sword (*gladius*?), approx. 20 lanceheads, five arrowheads and an atypical, possibly native, *pilum*.[17] In addition, there are some items of horse gear: a bit, a bell and possibly a phallic pendant. With the exception of the possible *gladius* (1st-century), none of the objects can be dated more accurately than to within the Roman period. We know that the sword, one arrowhead,

---

[7] K. Schumacher 1911; M.J. Klein 1999.

[8] Rankov 1999; see K. Schumacher (1911, 109), however, who regards them as votive lances; for other possible interpretations, see M.J. Klein 1999, 90-91.

[9] K. Schumacher 1911, 109-110; for a fourth example from this site, see p. 110.

[10] M.J. Klein 1999, 87, 92-93; see also K. Schumacher 1911, 109.

[11] Dupraz 2000, 55.

[12] Von Gonzenbach 1976, 309, 319.

[13] Von Gonzenbach 1976, 311, 315, note 48.

[14] Von Gonzenbach 1976, 310-311, 315, 318, fig. 13.

[15] Downey/King/Soffe 1980; King/Soffe 1991.

[16] Ton Derks, pers. comm..

[17] J. Klein 1897, p. 110-111, Taf. V. For the most recent interpretation of the structures, see Thoma 2000.

the pendant and the bit were found in buildings outside the *temenos* wall, so we are unable to demonstrate that they were deposited as votive offerings.[18] Ritual deposition appears more likely in the case of the spearheads, which were found between the two walls enclosing the temple precinct. The origin of the remaining objects is unknown.

10. *Möhn (Germany). Period 2-3*

Traces of a pre-Roman phase comprising a charcoal layer rich in finds have been discovered in addition to a stone cult building from the Flavian period. The 'military' finds comprise a sword, a shield boss fragment, a large number of lance- and arrowheads and several horse gear items.[19]. The probable 'ring pommel sword' can be placed in the 2nd and 3rd century.[20] The remaining weaponry cannot be dated more accurately than to the Roman period. Of the horse gear items, a *phalera* belongs to the 1st century and three decorative fittings to the 2nd and 3rd centuries.[21] The sanctuary was probably dedicated to Mars Smertrius or Mars Smertulitanus.[22]

11. *Dhronecken (Germany). Period 2-3*

The series of bronze statues recovered from the sanctuary at Dhronecken suggests that it was dedicated to Mars. The cult place has yielded a sword blade, several lance- and arrowheads and a round horse gear fitting (2nd/3rd century), as well as weapon finds from four graves.[23] The dating of the weaponry is problematical as the presence of medieval spurs points to a blending with post-Roman material.[24] The fragmentarily preserved sword blade (*gladius*?) was found immediately outside the temple porticus.[25] Most of the lance- and arrowheads were found between the central temple (building 'A') and a neighbouring cult building (building 'B'), and were probably votive offerings that were collected and buried in the course of a clean-up.[26] Finally, one of the lanceheads and the horse gear fitting were recovered from a building outside the *temenos*, rendering ritual deposition improbable.

12. *Genainville-'Vaux-de-la-Celle' (France). Period 2-3*

A total of 32 weaponry and horse gear components were recovered at the cult place of Vaux-de-la-Celle.[27] The earliest find is a rectangular, niello-inlay belt fitting of a type that predominated in the Claudian period. The remaining dateable finds come from the 2nd and 3rd centuries. In addition to 11 horse gear components, these are a disc-shaped chape of a *spatha* scabbard. A shield boss can probably be placed in the same period. Three spearheads, three butt spikes of spears, lances or *pila* and 12 smaller (arrow?) heads can be dated less reliably.

13. *Uley-'West Hill' (Great Britain). Period 2-4*

The weapon finds from the temple precinct consist of a *spatha*, 15 lance- or spearheads and 25 boltheads.[28] Two buckles, a round fastener for a ring buckle and a fitting inlaid with millefiori can be

---

[18] However, we cannot rule out that this is a secondary context.

[19] Hettner 1901; for the military finds, p. 22, 29-20, Taf. IV, VI.

[20] Hettner 1901, Taf. VI (nr. 35); compare Raddatz 1959/1961; Kellner 1966. The blunt tip and especially the rectangular, projecting guard are features of this type of sword.

[21] The finds may contain a second *phalera* (Hettner 1901, Taf. IV, nr. 70).

[22] Derks 1998, 250 (nr. 42).

[23] Hettner 1901, 49, 51-52, Taf. V-VI.

[24] Hettner 1901, Taf. VI, nrs. 44-46 (medieval spurs).

[25] There is a Roman burn layer here that has been interpreted as a votive layer (Hettner 1901, 44).

[26] Hettner 1901, 44.

[27] Mitard 1993, 358 (nr. 4), 375 (nrs. 67-75), 390, 393 (nrs. 69-83).

[28] Woodward/Leach 1993, figs. 91 (nr. 3), 97 (nr. 3), 110-113, 126 (nrs. 1, 3), 135 (nrs. 11-12), 151 (nr. 4), 152 (nr. 9), with context datings.

ascribed to belts, and a *phalera* fragment comprising openwork letters belongs to a baldric. The horse gear consists of a niello-inlay fitting, a strap junction fragment with vulvate motifs and an enamel-inlay phallic fitting. Finally, the finds include 14 ritually damaged miniature spear- and lanceheads. The iron throwing weapons can be dated to the 1st century AD on the basis of the find context. The round horse gear fitting belongs typologically in the Claudio-Flavian period. One of the buckles, the belt closure and fitting, the baldric *phalera*, as well as the strap junction and the phallic horse gear fitting date from the 2nd and 3rd centuries, while the *spatha*, a second buckle and the miniature weapons are late Roman. Although Mercurius was the principal deity from the 2nd century onward, several inscriptions and the weapon finds suggest that the temple may originally have been dedicated to Mars Silvanus.[29]

14. *Kontich-'Steenakker' (Belgium). Period 3*
    A complete sword blade from a 2nd- or 3rd-century spatha and a spearhead come from a pit located directly in front of a temple.[30] This was probably a ritual deposition associated with transactions at the cult precinct. A statuette of Minerva comes from the cult building.

15. *Matagne-la-Grande (Belgium). Period 3(-4)*
    A decorative 2nd- or 3rd-century horse gear fitting and scales from at least two sets of scale armour are known from the temple precinct.[31] The presence of bronze thread still attaching several scales suggests that they may have been deposited as part of complete sets of armour. Given the dating of the cult place, this would have been between the late 2nd century and the end of the 4th century.

16. *Lydney Park (Great Britain). Period (3-)4*
    This temple complex from the late 3rd and the 4th century is dedicated to an otherwise unknown goddess Nodens.[32] The finds encountered in the vicinity of the cult building include the mouthpiece of a military (or religious) wind instrument, the bone chape from a *spatha* scabbard, a *cingulum* buckle, as well as four decorative fittings and a horse gear pendant.[33] With the exception of the mouthpiece, which cannot be securely dated, the finds belong typologically to the 1st century (*cingulum*) and 2nd and 3rd centuries.

17. *Lamyett Beacon (Great Britain). Period (3-)4*
    The finds from Lamyatt Beacon show that Roman weapon components continued to be dedicated at cult places until the 5th century. A large quantity of iron objects were found here, including eight spearheads and butt spikes, a trilobate arrowhead and five miniature spear- and lanceheads.[34] The objects cannot be assigned typologically to a specific period but the dating of the sanctuary suggests that they were deposited between the late 3rd and early 5th centuries.

---

[29] Woodward/Leach 1993, 333.
[30] Vanden Berghe 1996, 78-80, fig. 12.1.
[31] Rober 1983, fig. 16 (nrs. 69-70).
[32] There are no traces of earlier cult buildings, although Wheeler and Wheeler (1932, 25) comment that these may have been disturbed.
[33] Wheeler/Wheeler 1932, cat. nrs. 47, 94-95, 97, 101, 131, 133, 150.
[34] Leech 1986, figs. 26 (nrs. 9-10), 29-30 (nrs. 43-54).

B. OPEN-AIR SANCTUARIES:

1. *Oberammergau-'Döttenbichls' (Germany). Period 2*
A systematic search at the foot of the Alps using a metal detector has unearthed no fewer than 700 metal objects, including 330 arrowheads, 23 boltheads (three with an identical *Legio XIX* stamp), 12 lanceheads and a dagger.[35] Earlier, two daggers with richly decorated sheaths had been found at the same location. The majority of the weapon components are so uniform in their design that Zanier believes they were used by the same army unit.[36] He conjectures that the finds were 'pick-ups' from a battlefield that were then offered at a native sanctuary by the local population. It is likely that the battle coincided with the earliest habitation phase in this region (15-10 BC). As there are no traces of a temple complex at this location, it may have been an open-air sanctuary.

2. *Velserbroek-'B6' (Netherlands). Period 2*
Almost 60 weaponry and horse gear components were found distributed across a sand ridge in the peat at Velsen.[37] The site can be regarded as a 1st-century open-air sanctuary, with the transition to the peat marking the sacral zone. The finds include *pila*, spearheads and boltheads, decorative rivets from dagger sheaths, scales from scale armour, as well as horse gear strap junctions, strap terminals, decorative fittings and pendants. The deposition of military objects is probably associated with the occupation of the nearby army camp (AD 15-30 and 40-50). Bosman assumes that these were 'pick-ups' collected by the native population after the army camp was abandoned and which were then deposited as an offering on the sand ridge.[38] However, he does not rule out offerings by Roman soldiers. Soldiers from the Frisian area returning home after their term of service may have been involved.[39]

3. *Wijshagen-'Rieten' (Belgium). Period 2*
Excavations have yielded a large number of metal finds, including the bronze terminal knob of a *gladius* scabbard (type Pompeii).[40] Although there are no other weapon finds, the knob is part of a special assemblage consisting of a large quantity of coins, fibulae and bronze armbands. The finds were concentrated around a rectangular pole structure that may have had a religious function. Slofstra and Van der Sanden believe that this structure was part of an open-air sanctuary.[41]

4. *Krefeld-Gellep (Germany). Period 2(-3)*
To the southeast of the camp and military *vicus* of Krefeld-Gellep are three rectangular ditch structures that may have been part of an open-air sanctuary at the adjoining cemetery. Various stray finds of a military nature appear to be associated with these structures.[42] The finds include seven boltheads, an arrowhead and two spearheads probably dating from the Roman period. Five 1st-century horse gear components are more securely dated. As the ditches were dug at the end of the 1st century, we can at least place the horse gear in the initial phase of the sanctuary. The remaining objects could have been dedicated up until the 3rd century.

---

[35] Zanier 1997.
[36] Zanier 1997, 49-51.
[37] Bosman 1992; 1995a.
[38] Bosman 1995a, 94.
[39] Bosman 1995a, 94.
[40] Van Impe/Creemers 1991, 69-70, fig. 12; cf. also Maes/Impe 1986.
[41] Slofstra/Van der Sanden 1987, 145-147.
[42] Bechert 1986. Some of the iron objects may have come from Frankish graves.

5. *Rocester-'Orton's Pasture' (Great Britain). Period 2-3*

Two rectangular ditch structures, apparently enclosing an open-air sanctuary, were discovered immediately to the south of the fort at Rocester. Inside the southern ditch is a stone foundation, probably of an altar. A round apron fitting, a figure-eight fitting from a strap junction and a tear-shaped pendant were found in the ditch and a pit.[43] The round fitting depicts an imperial bust and can be dated, together with the strap junction, to the 1st century. The pendant belongs in the 2nd-century phase of the presumed sanctuary. The presence of graffiti, as well as the earthenware and bone spectrum, shows that soldiers visited the cult place.[44] However, given the damaged state of the militaria, we cannot rule out that these were litter from the nearby army camp.

[43] Ferris/Bevan/Cuttler 2000, fig. 28 (nrs. 15-16, 18).
[44] Ferris/Bevan/Cuttler 2000, 72-79.

About the plates and the catalogue

In order to present an overview of the weaponry and horse gear circulating in the eastern Rhine delta during the late Iron Age and the Roman period, the range of finds is presented as comprehensively as possible in plates 1-96. Following the typochronology explained in chapter 1, the objects are arranged in functional categories, with a further subdivision within each functional group based on the basic form (appendix 2). The letter and number combination on the left-hand side of the page refers to this subdivision. The catalogue number, comprising the site number (which refers to appendix 1) and one or more serial numbers for each site, is given under each object.

The plates primarily show drawings that were made specifically for this study. The figures are supplemented with unpublished drawings from the Bureau Archeologie, Gemeente Nijmegen (sites 208, 209 and 284) and the Rijksdienst voor het Oudheidkundig Bodemonderzoek (site 288).

Finally, the plates include already published drawings. In addition to the figures from an article by Van Driel-Murray (1994), these illustrations come from the following books or articles:

Böhme 1974, Taf. 70 (nr. 13), 83 (nrs. 2-4).
Gerhartl-Witteveen et al. 1989, 33 (fig. 3).
Haalebos 1990a, fig. 98 (nr. 2).
Haalebos 1992, fig. 4 (nr. 1).
Haalebos 1994a, fig. 4.
Haalebos 2000c, fig. 11.
Hulst 1986, fig. 2.
Van den Hurk 1973, figs. 30, 37.
Roes 1953, fig. 1.
Van der Roest 1991, pl. 3-XIX.
Van der Roest 1992, pl. 10 (nr. 420).
Roymans/Derks 1994, fig. 5 (nrs. 1-5).
Roymans 1996, fig. 3b.
Roymans 2004, pl. 4-9, 19, 26-27.
Verwers 1986, fig. 29b (nr. 5).
Verwers/Ypey 1975, figs. 2, 4-5.
Volgraff/Roes 1942, fig. 1b-c.
Ypey 1960/1961, Abb. 12.
Ypey 1982, fig. 1.

The catalogue containing the full inventory of finds is available as an Excel document on the web page of the Archaeological Centre of the Vrije Universiteit (www.acvu.nl/nicolay).

163.2 164.8 164.9

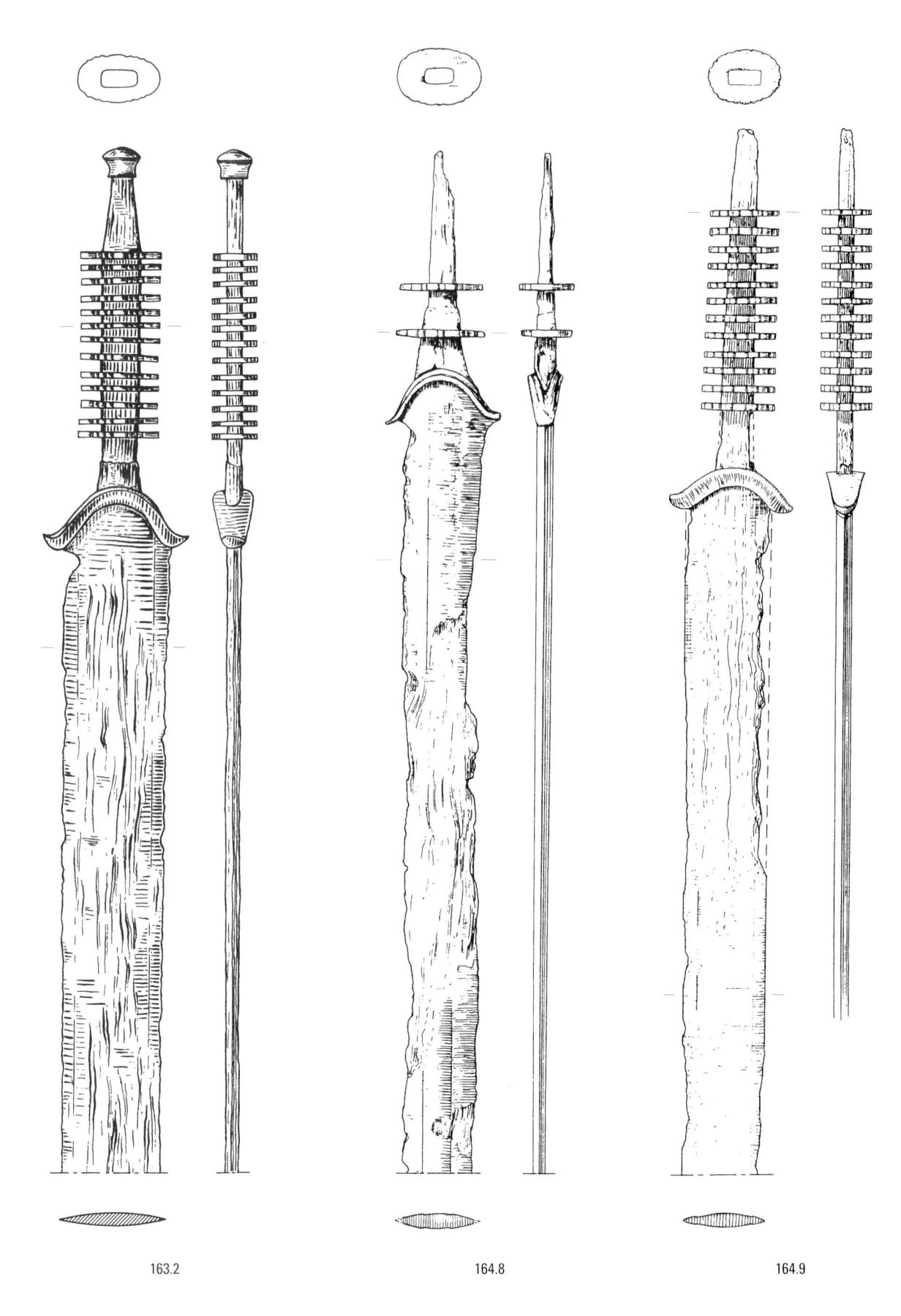

Pl. 1 Swords, La Tène period. Scale 1:2.

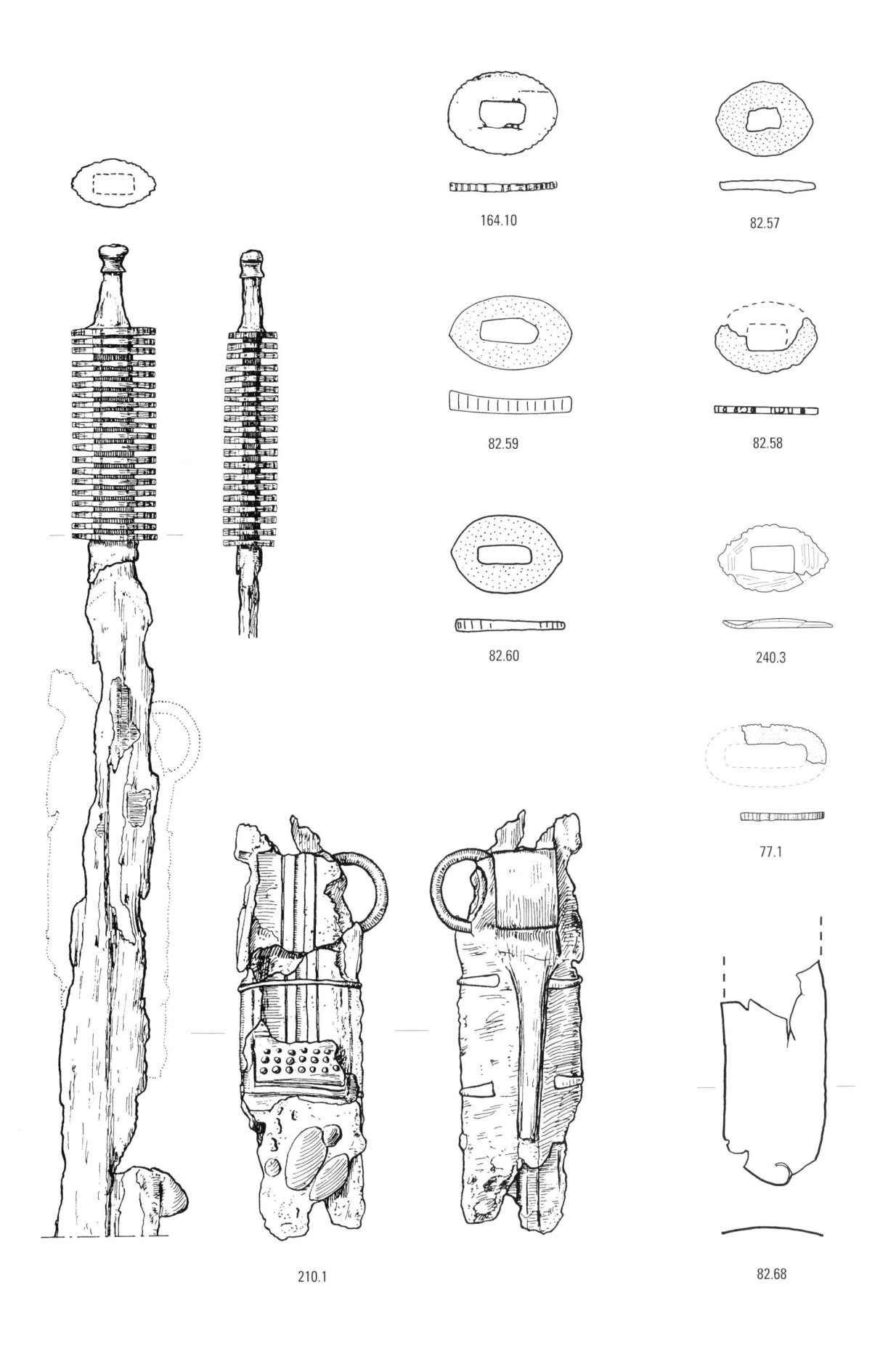

Pl. 2 Swords, stray discs from hilt, and scabbard plates, La Tène period. Scale 2:3; 1:2 (nr. 210.1).

164.2

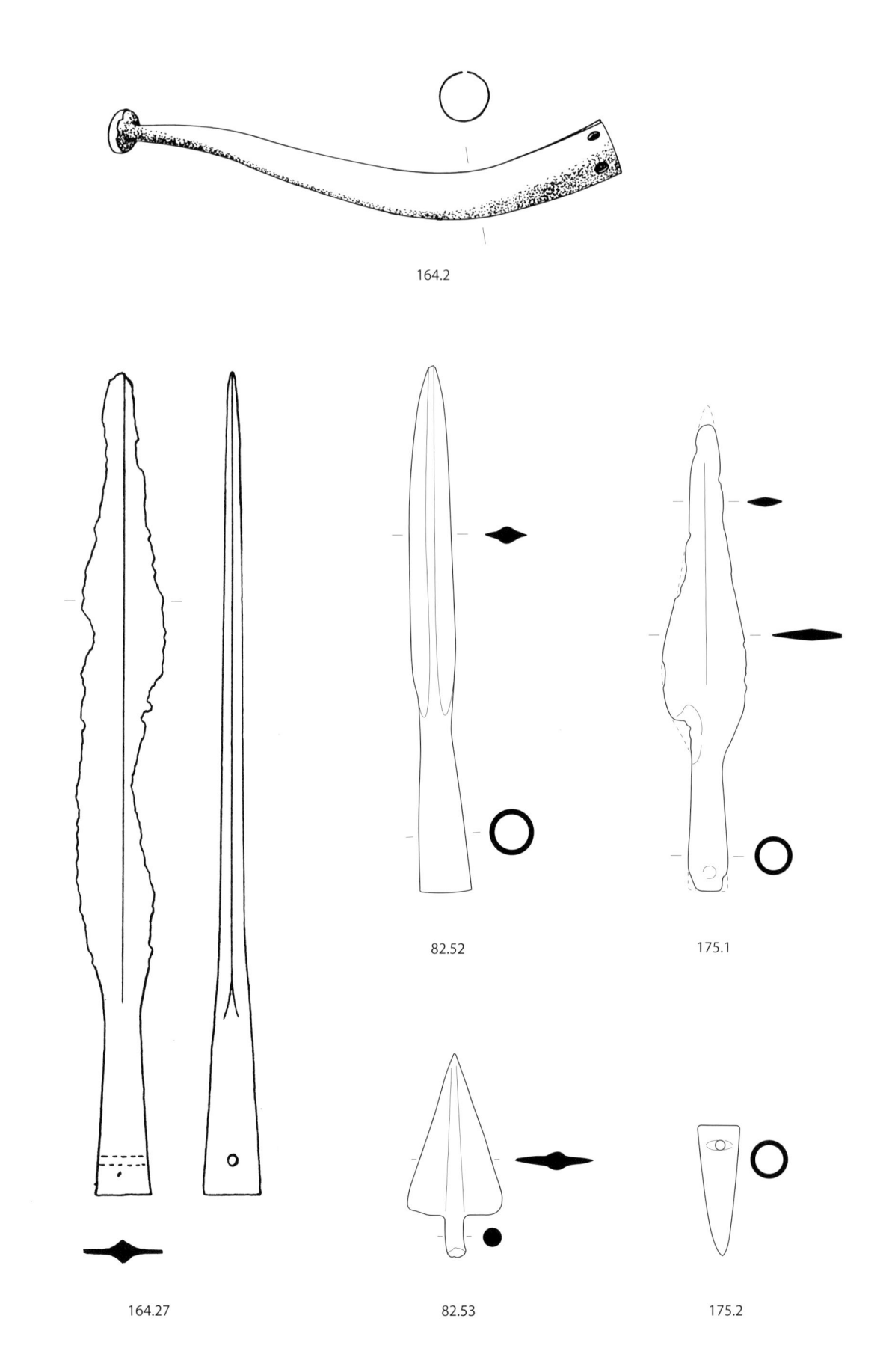

164.27   82.52   175.1

82.53   175.2

Pl. 3 Helmet appliqué, spear-/lanceheads and butt spike, La Tène period. Scale 1:2; 3:4 (164.2).

314

164.36

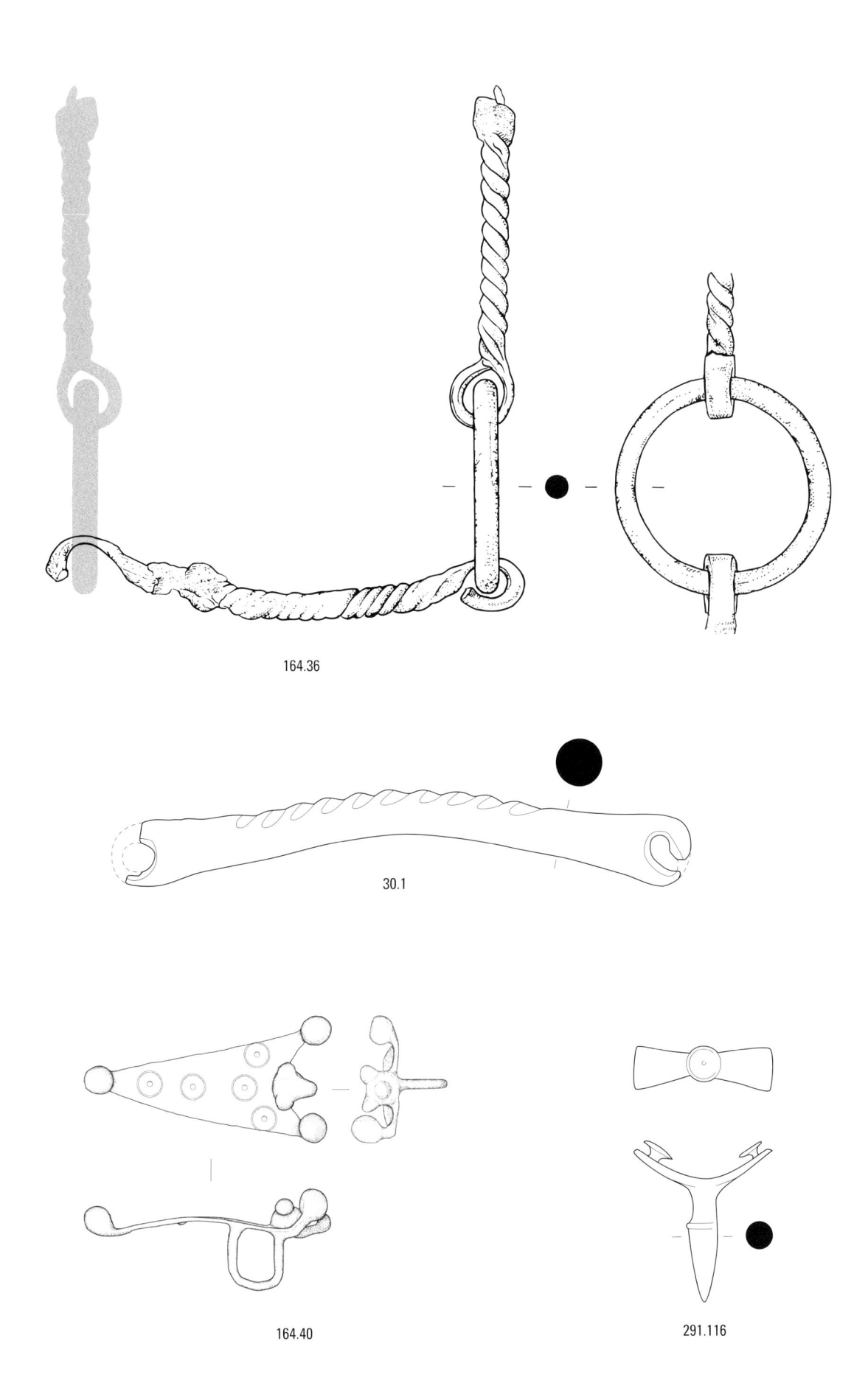

30.1

164.40

291.116

Pl. 4 Horse gear bits, looped strap mount and spur, La Tène period. Scale 2:3; 1:2 (164.36).

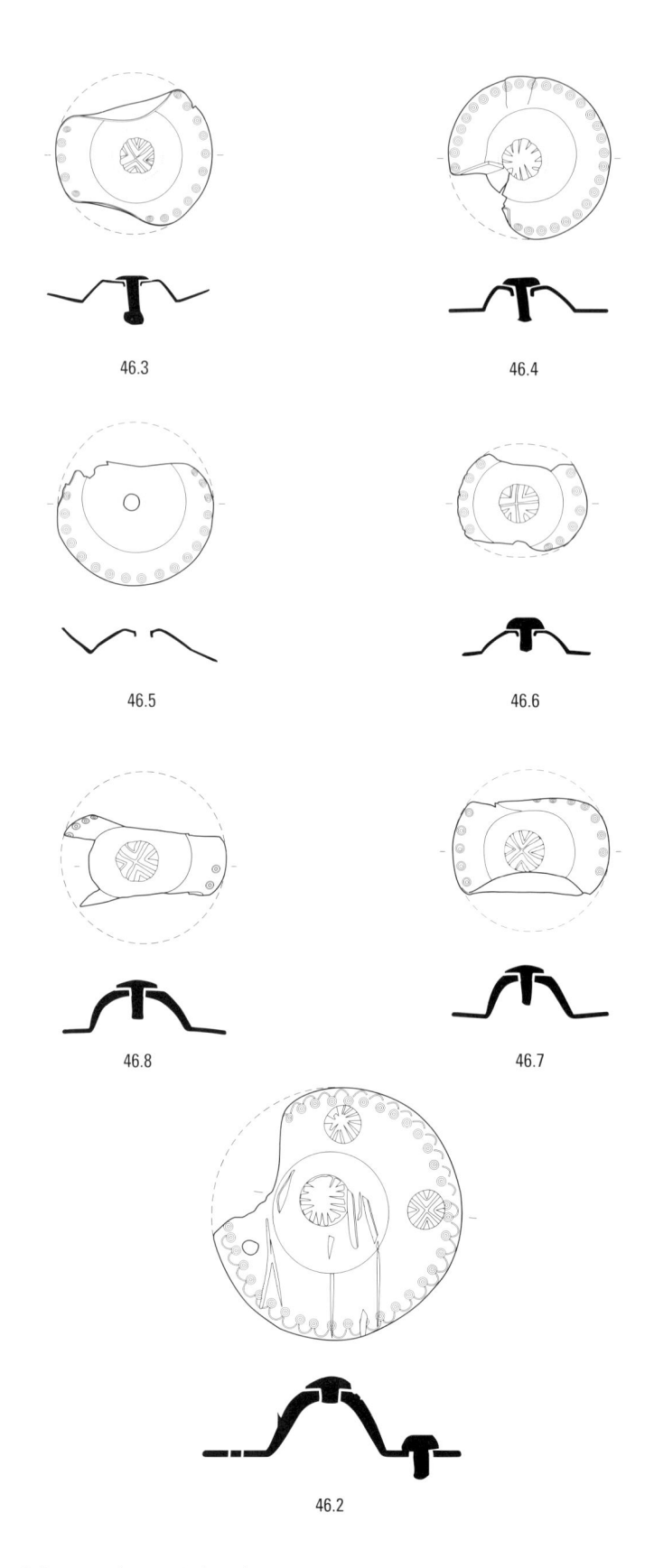

Pl. 5 Horse gear *phalerae*, La Tène period. Scale 2:3.

316

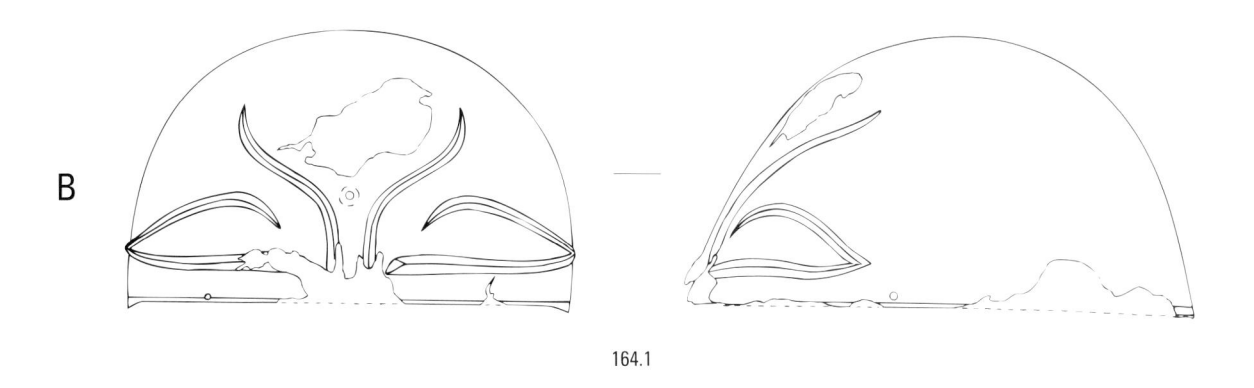

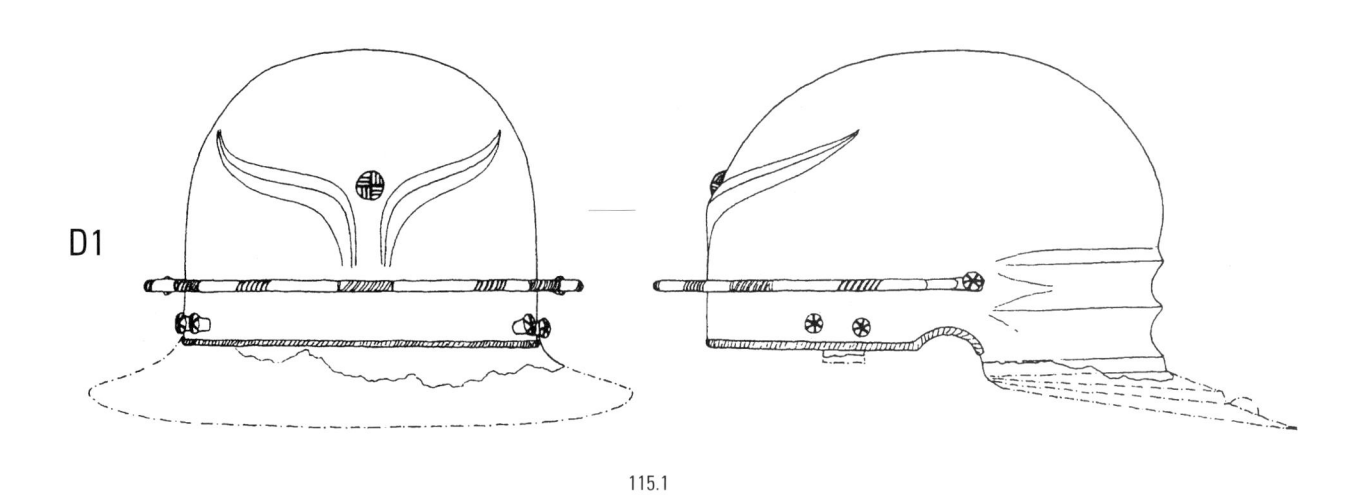

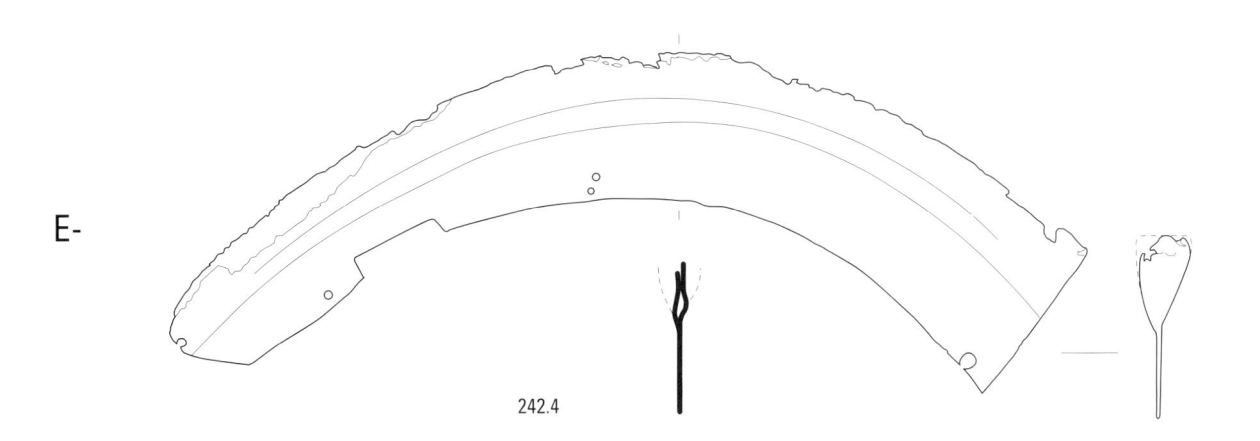

Pl. 6 Helmets and helmet comb, periods 1–2. Scale 1:2 (242.4); 1:3 (164.1); 1:4 (115.1).

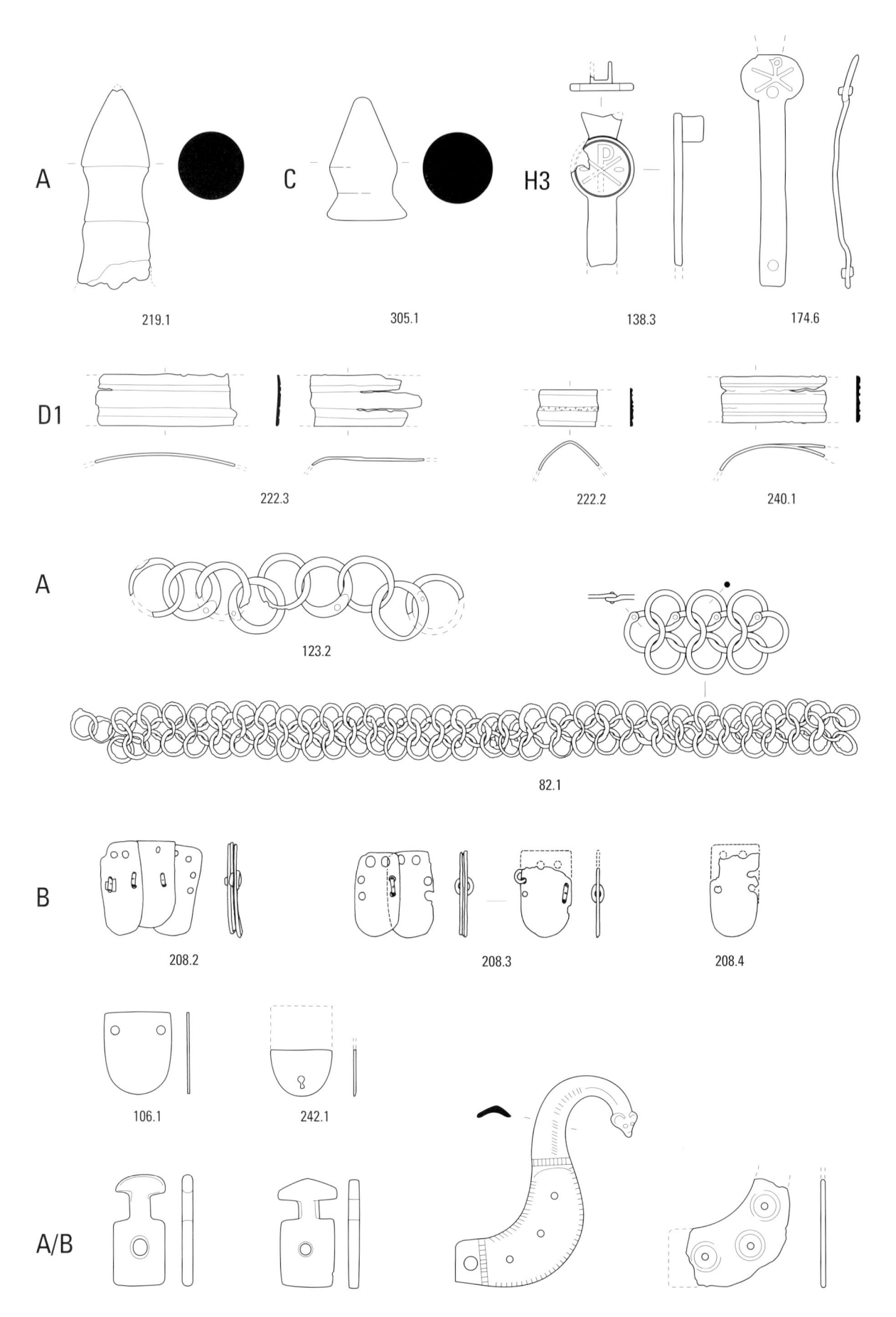

Pl. 7 Various components of the helmet, chain mail and scale armour, periods 1-4. Scale 2:3.

318

C1-A

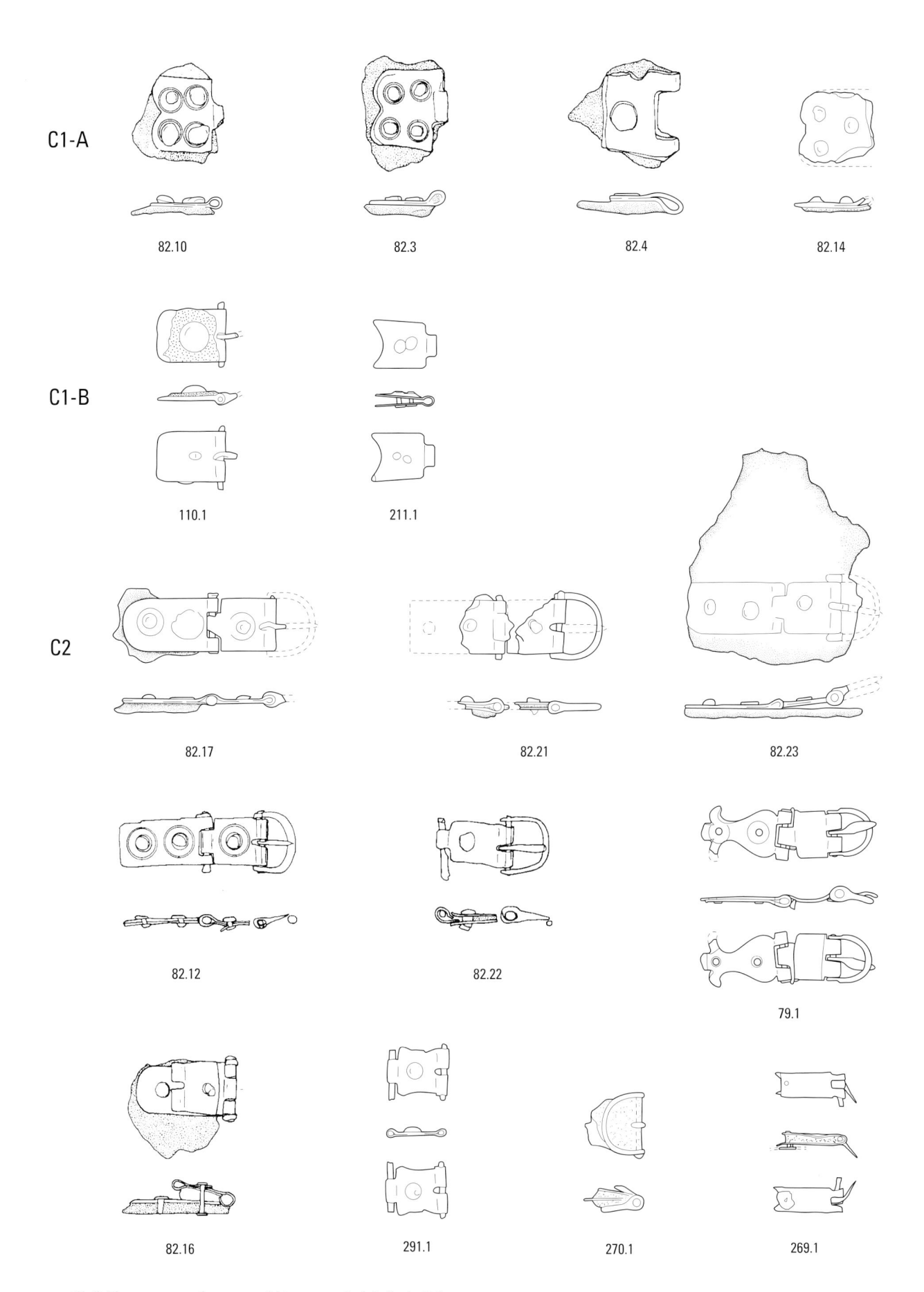

82.10   82.3   82.4   82.14

C1-B

110.1   211.1

C2

82.17   82.21   82.23

82.12   82.22   79.1

82.16   291.1   270.1   269.1

Pl. 8 Plate armour closures and hinges, period 2. Scale 2:3.

319

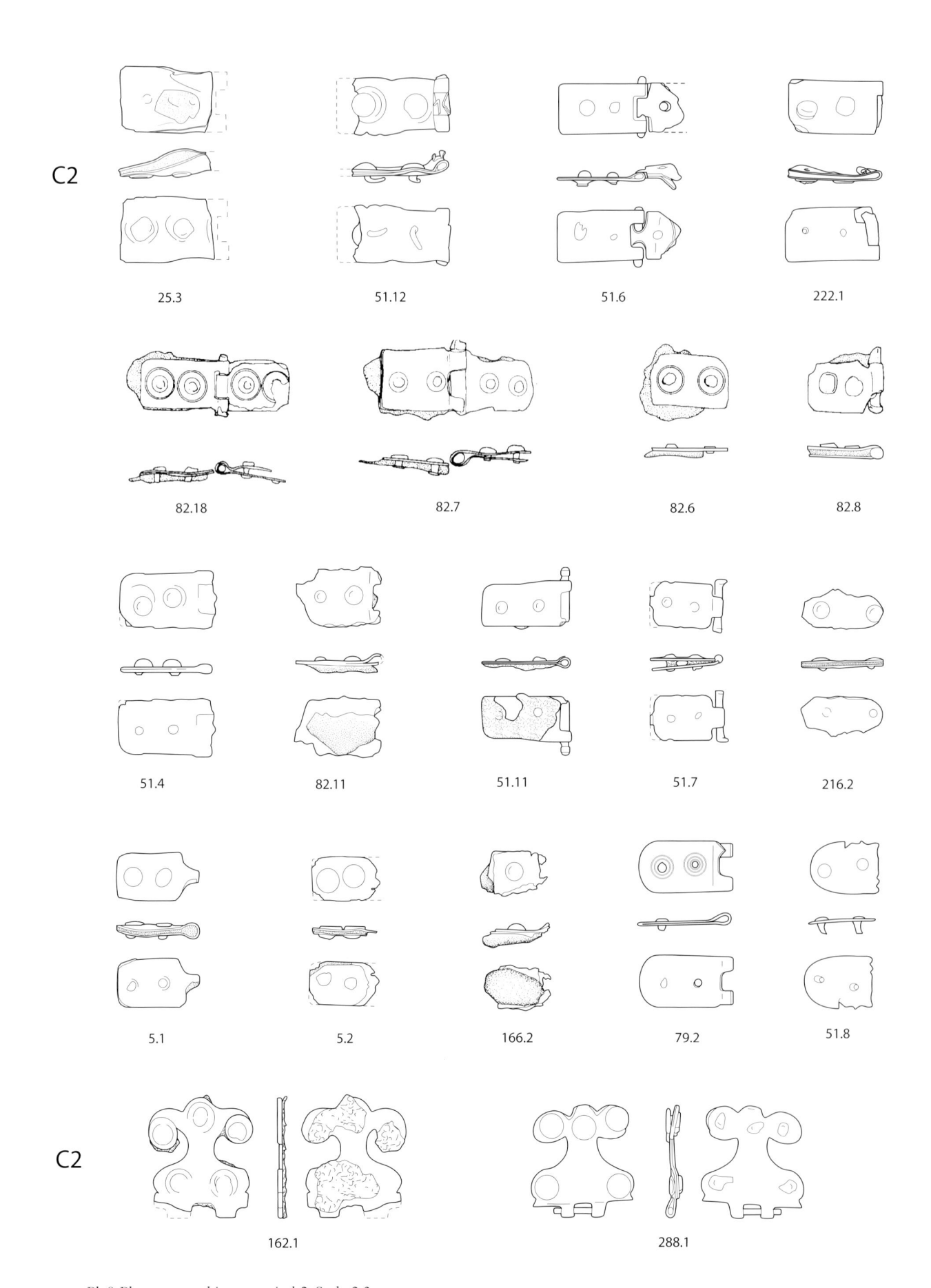

C2

25.3 51.12 51.6 222.1

82.18 82.7 82.6 82.8

51.4 82.11 51.11 51.7 216.2

5.1 5.2 166.2 79.2 51.8

C2

162.1 288.1

Pl. 9 Plate armour hinges, period 2. Scale 2:3.

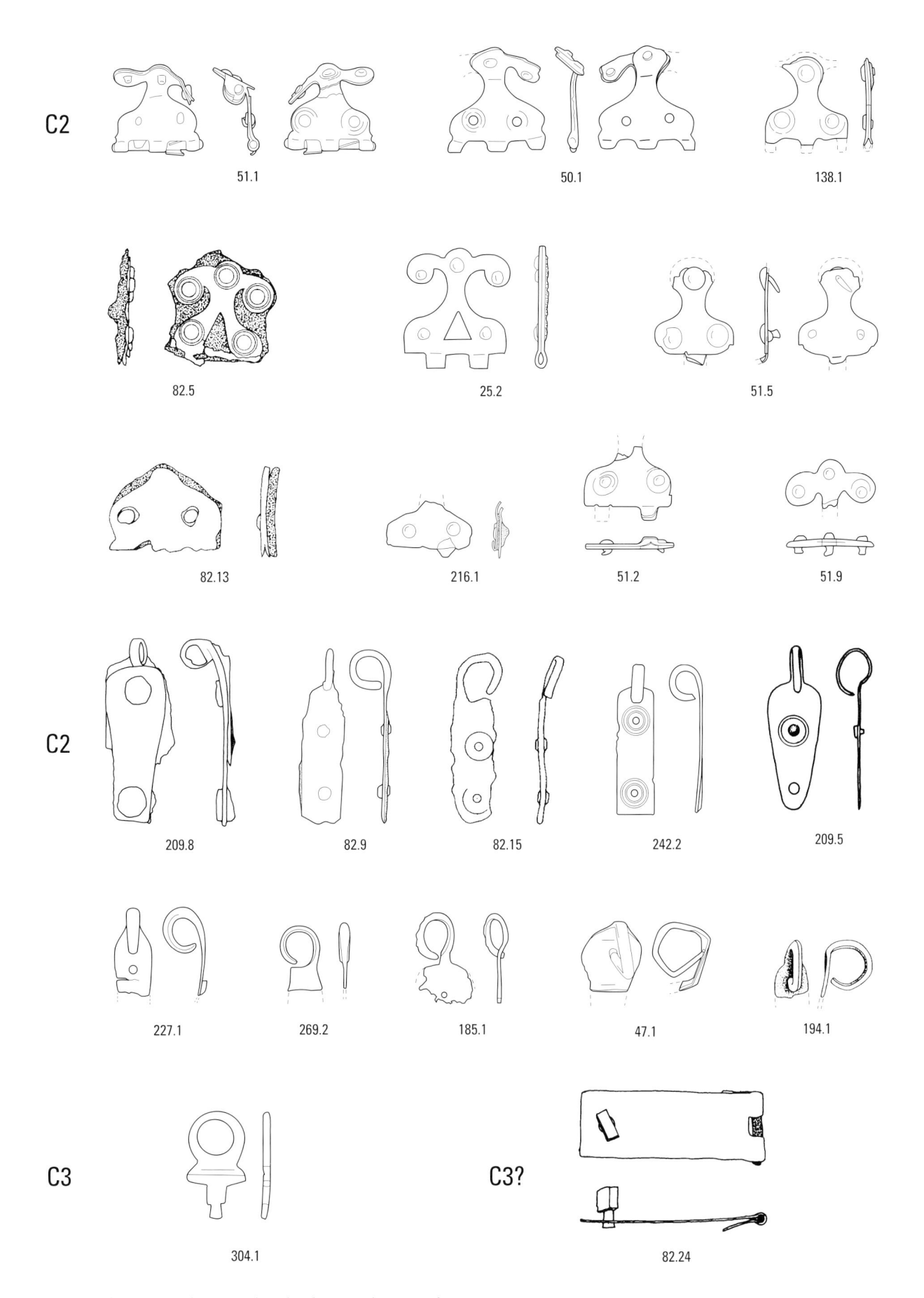

Pl. 10 Plate armour hinges and tie-hooks, periods 2-3. Scale 2:3.

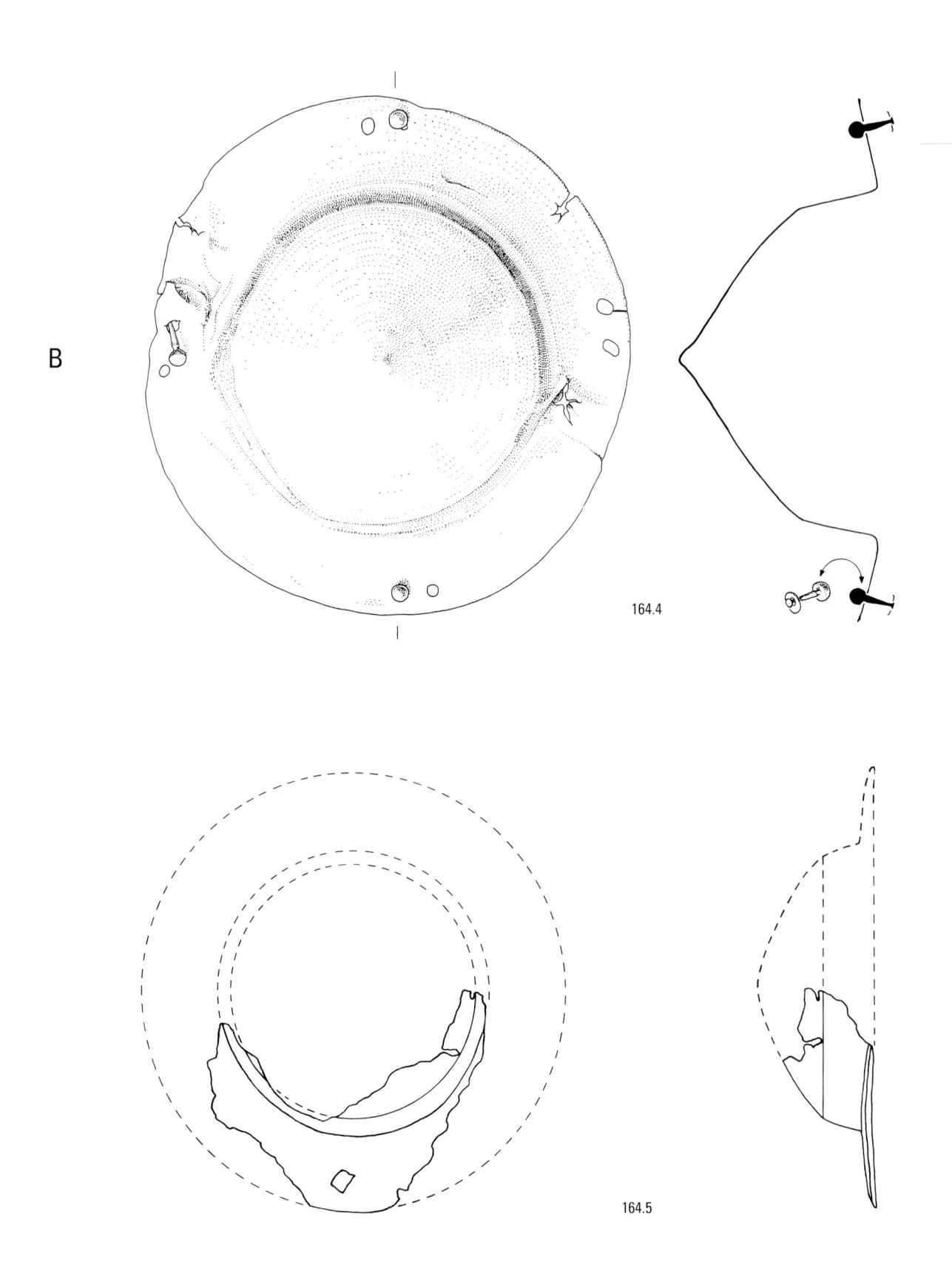

Pl. 11 Shield bosses, period 2. Scale 1:2.

C

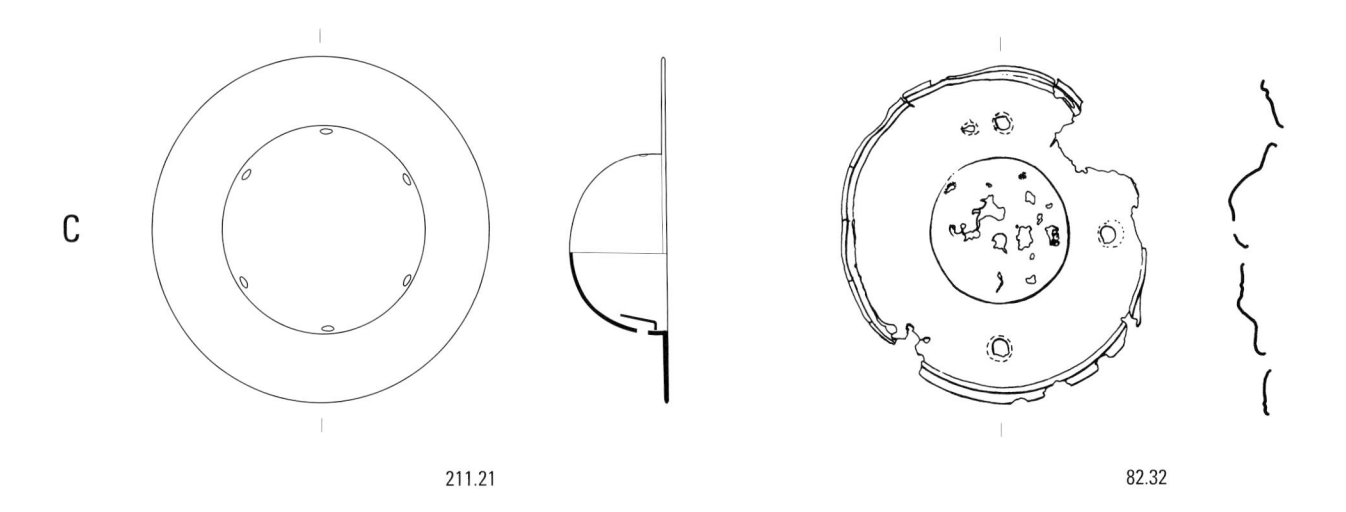

211.21

82.32

D

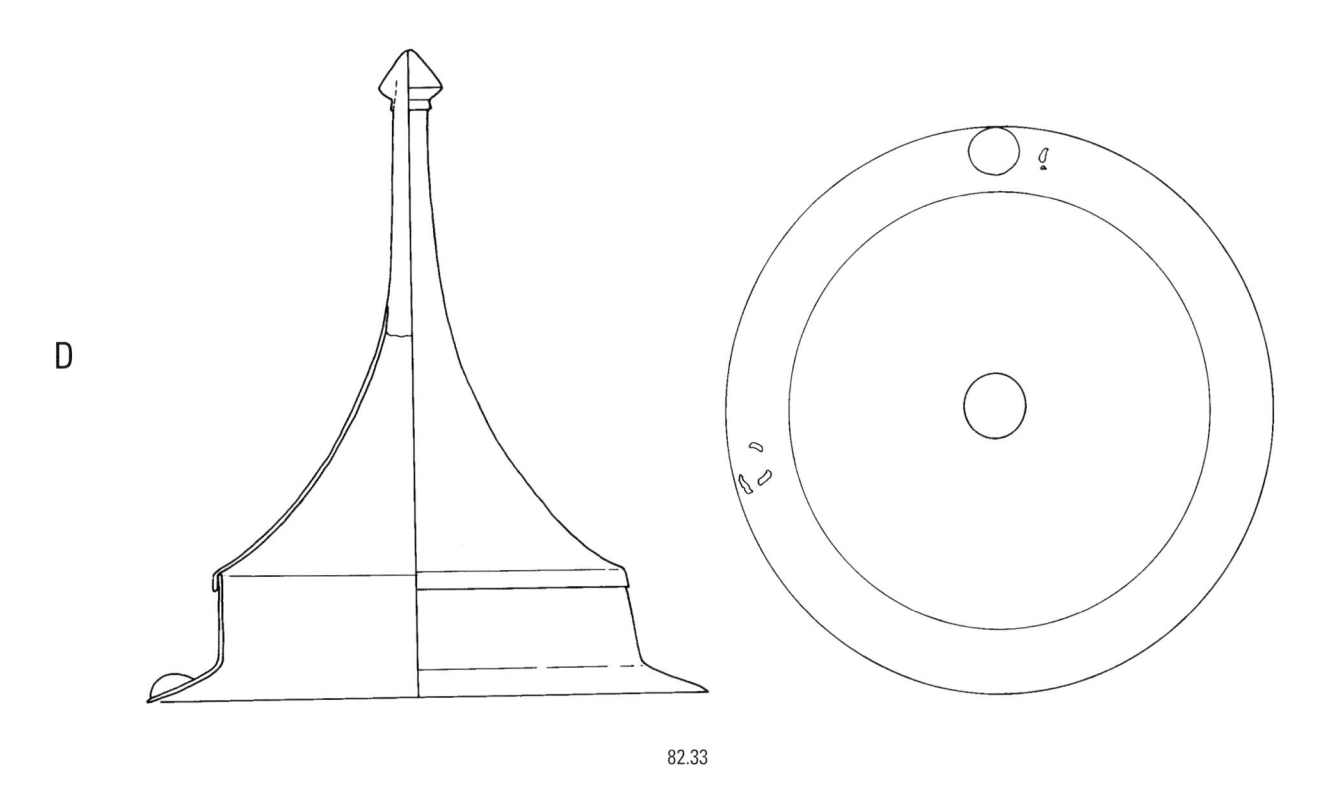

82.33

Pl. 12 Shield bosses, period 3. Scale 1:2.

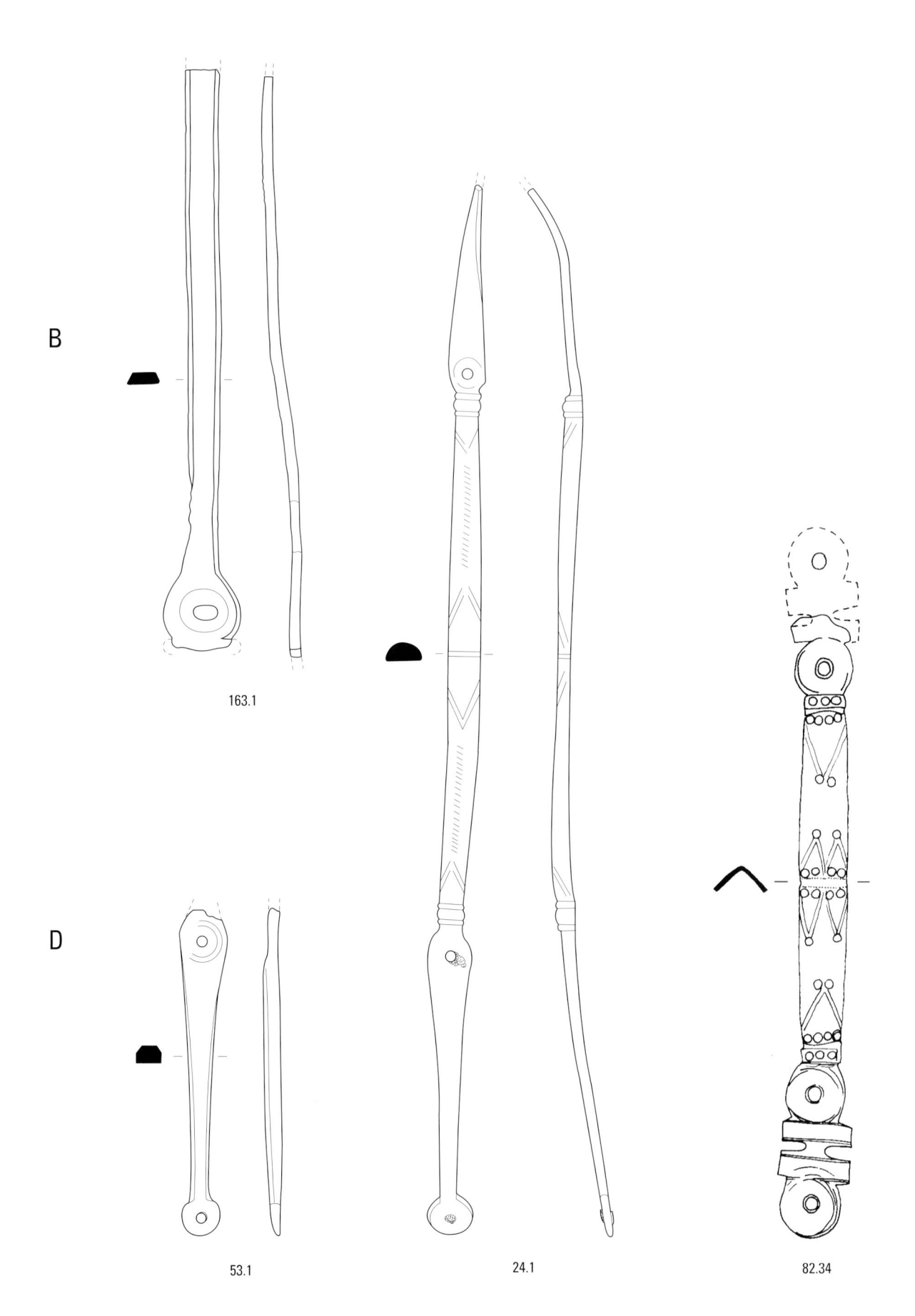

Pl. 13 Shield grips, periods 2-3. Scale 2:3.

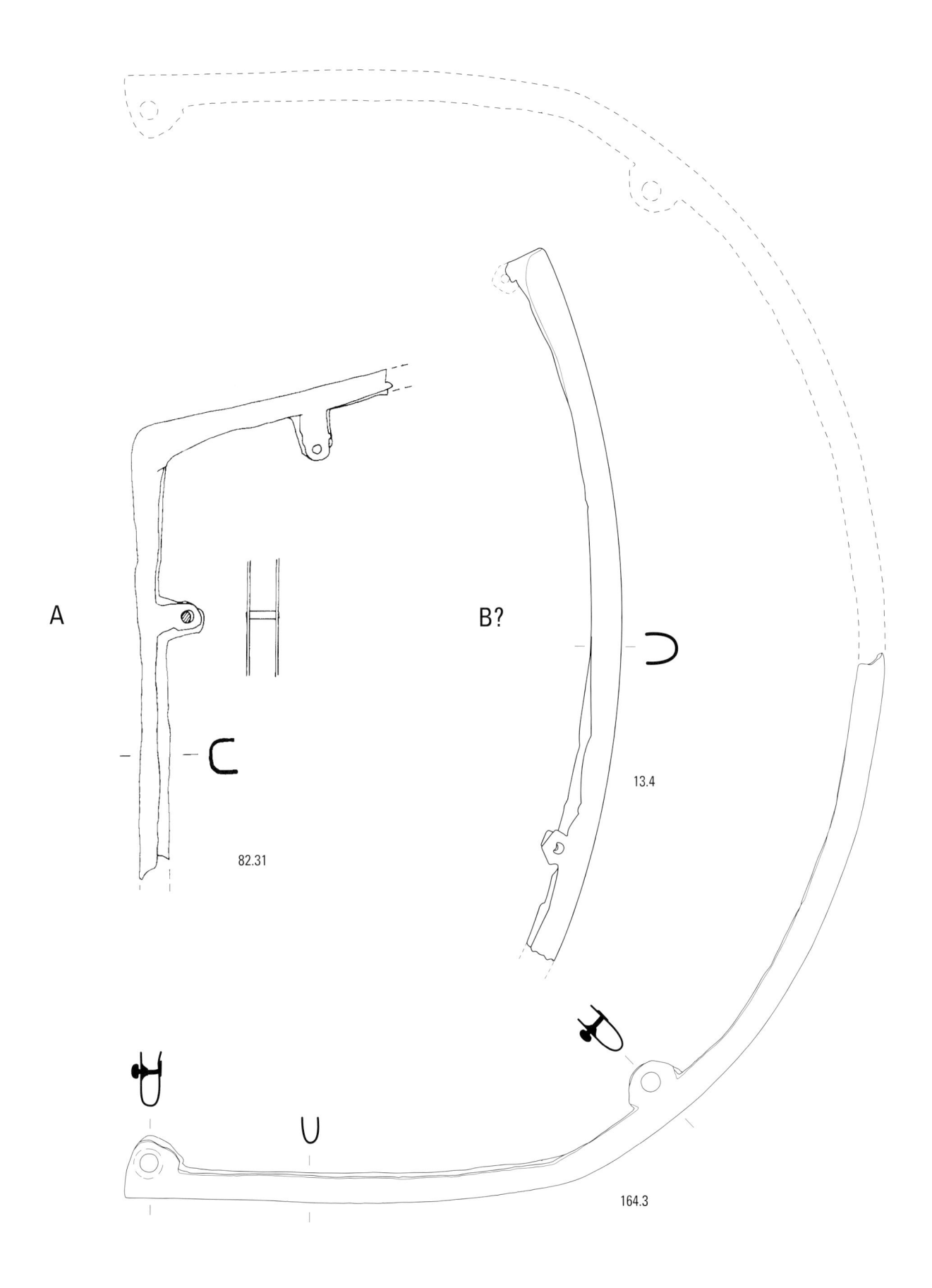

Pl. 14 Shield edgings, period 2. Scale 2:3.

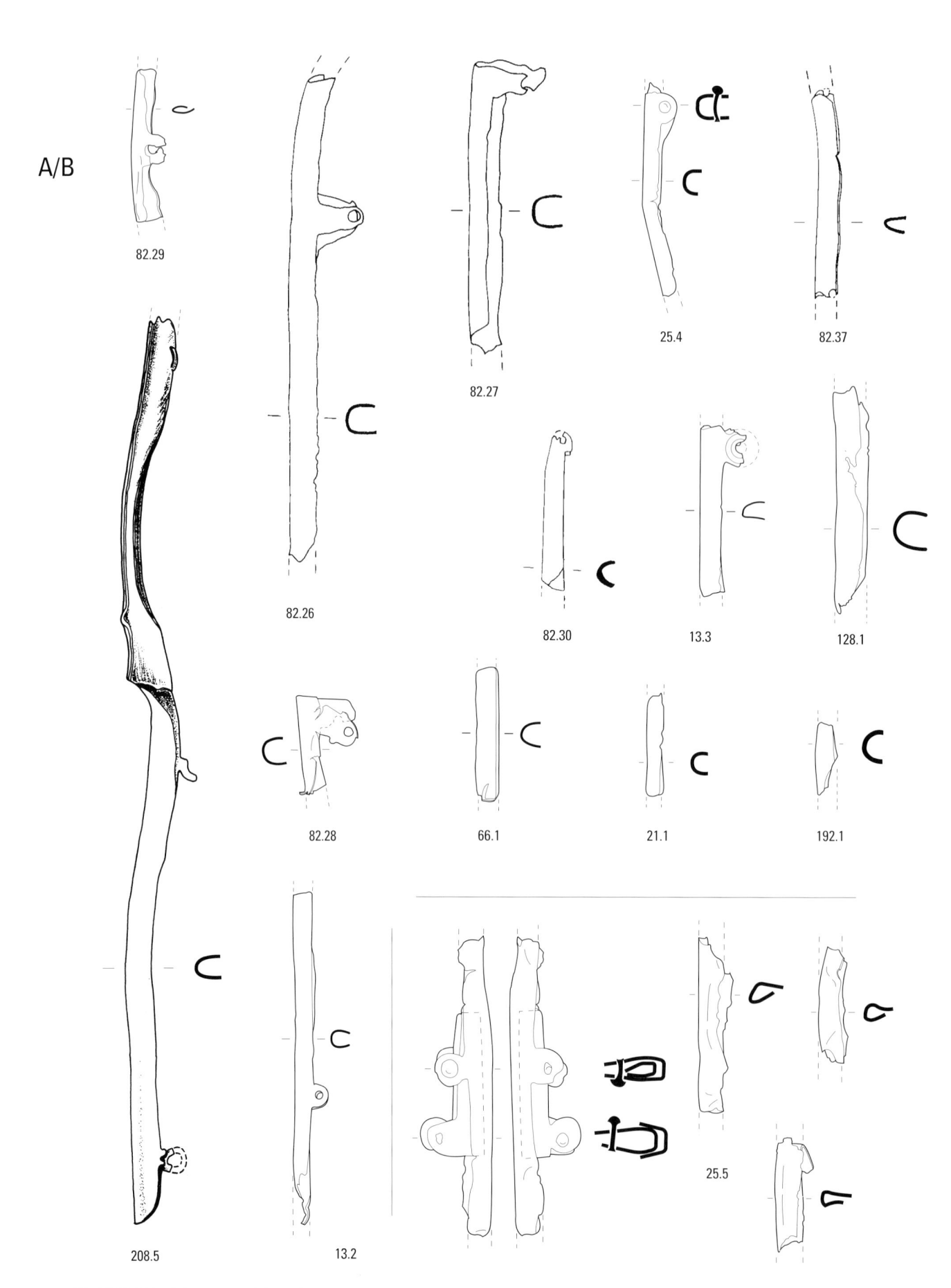

Pl. 15 Shield edgings, period 2. Scale 2:3.

A2

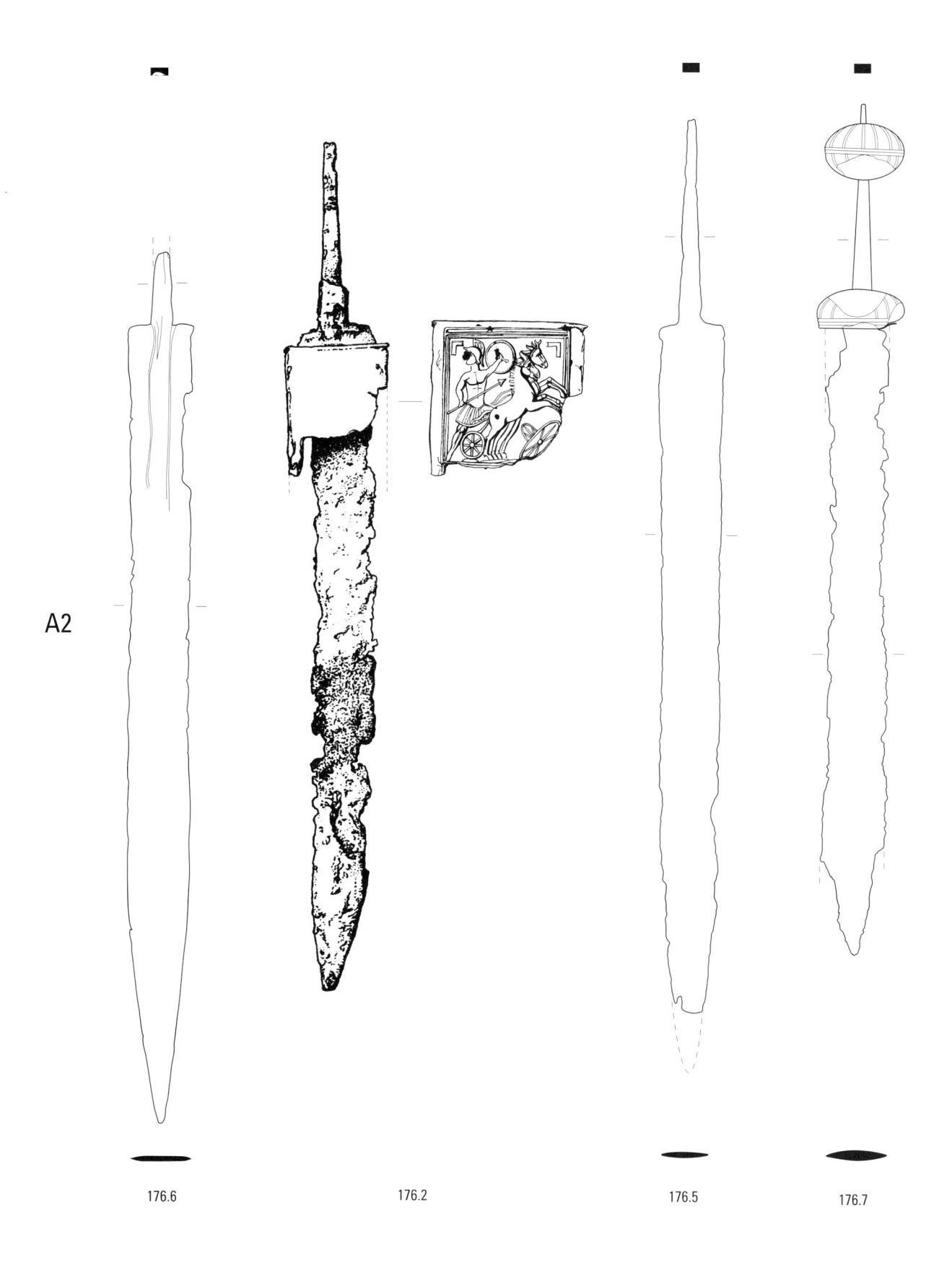

176.6   176.2   176.5   176.7

Pl. 16 Swords, period 2. Scale 1:4.

327

A3

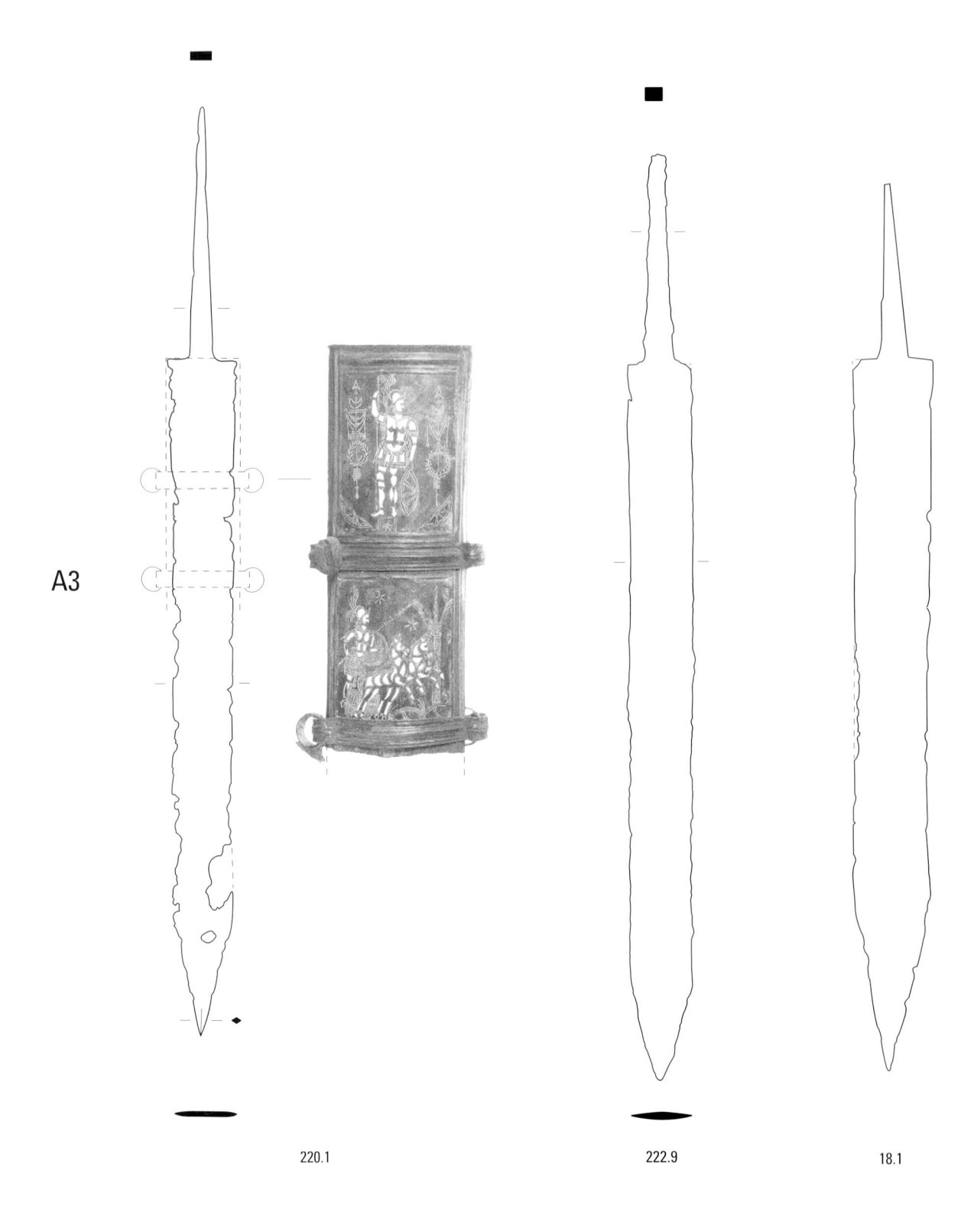

220.1   222.9   18.1

Pl. 17 Swords, period 2. Scale 1:4.

A-

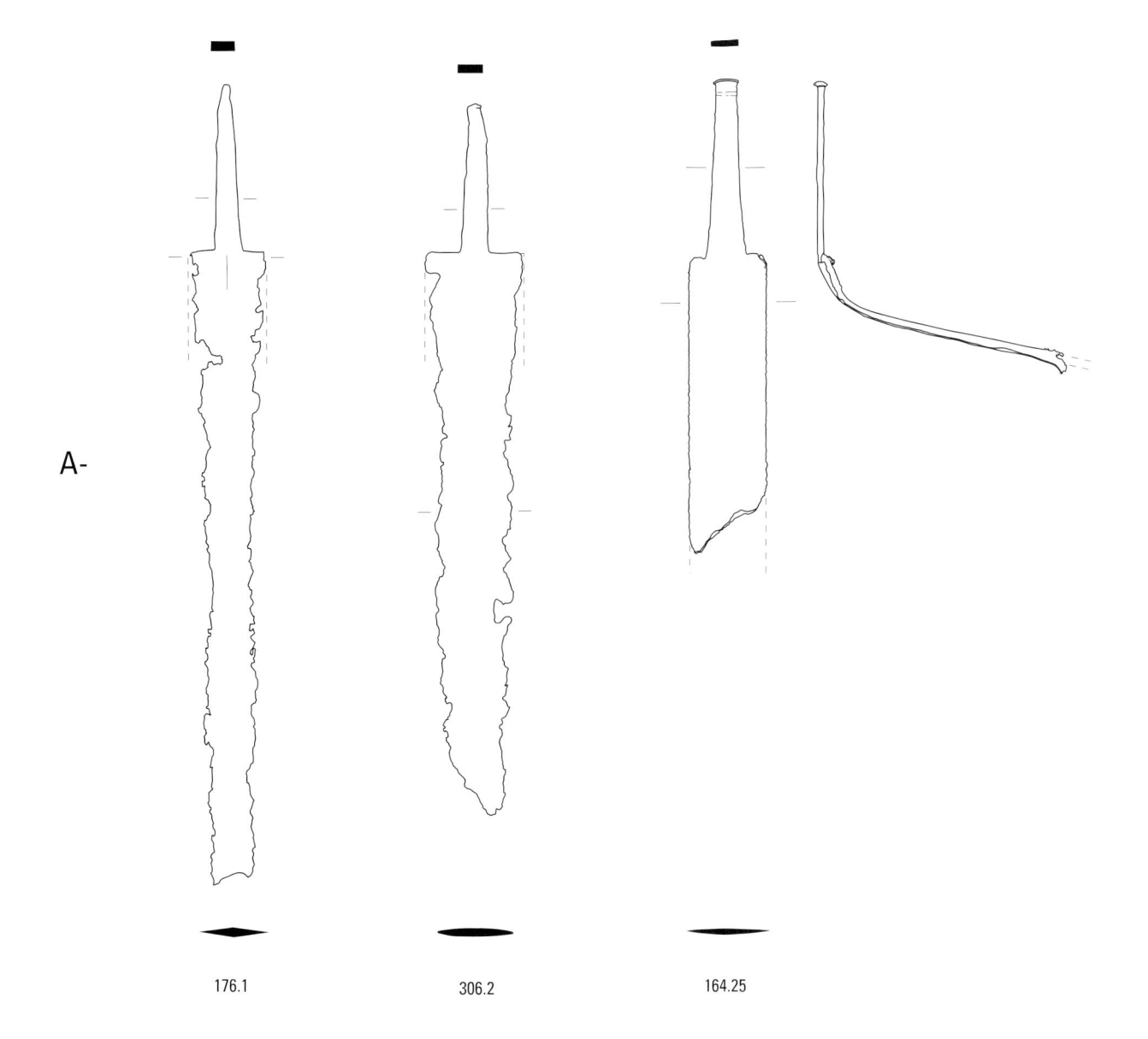

176.1

306.2

164.25

Pl. 18 Swords, period 2. Scale 1:4.

329

204.3　　　164.23　　　164.24　　　170.1

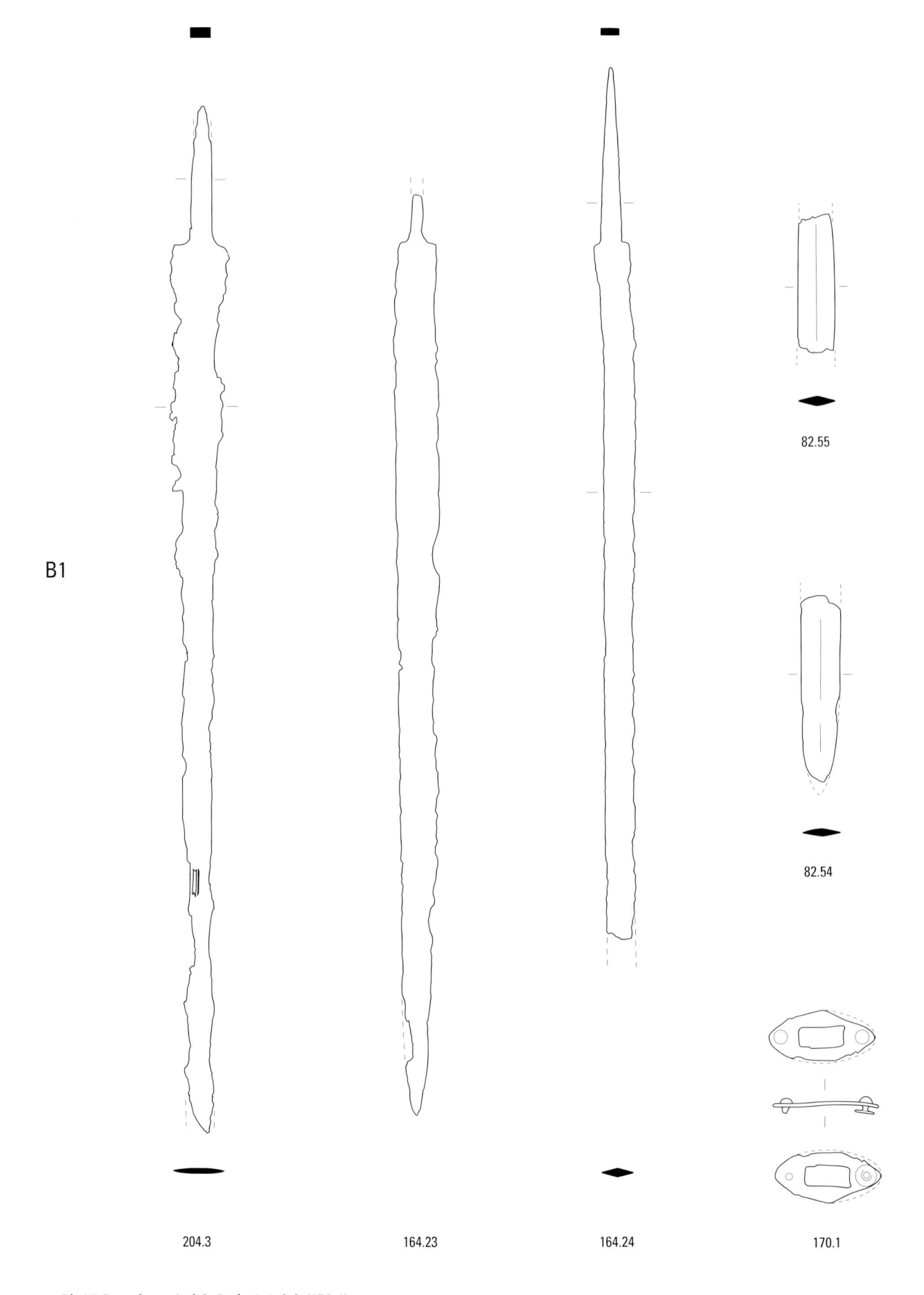

Pl. 19 Swords, period 2. Scale 1:4; 2:3 (170.1).

330

B2

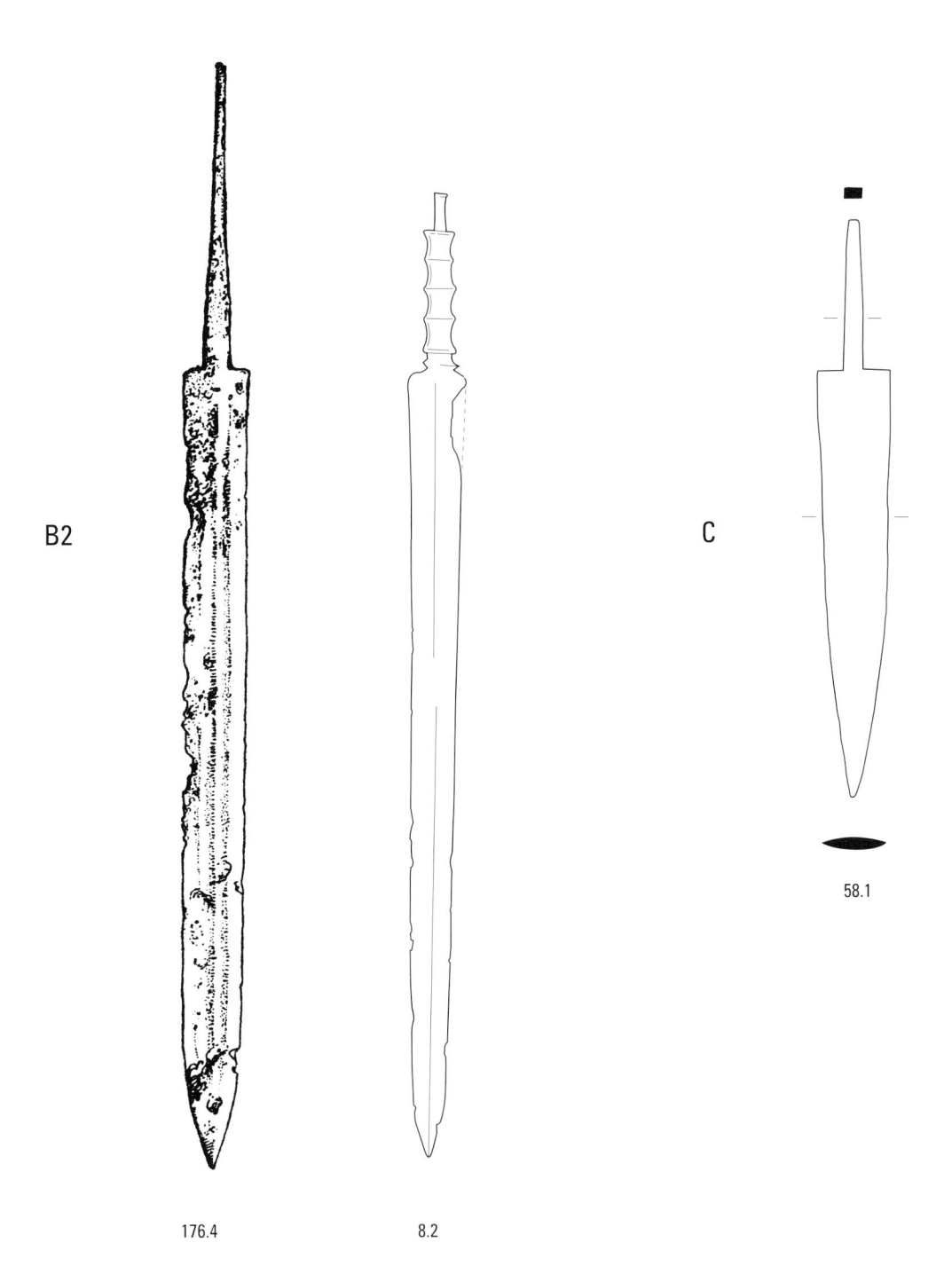

C

176.4   8.2   58.1

Pl. 20 Swords, periods 3-4. Scale 1:4.

A2

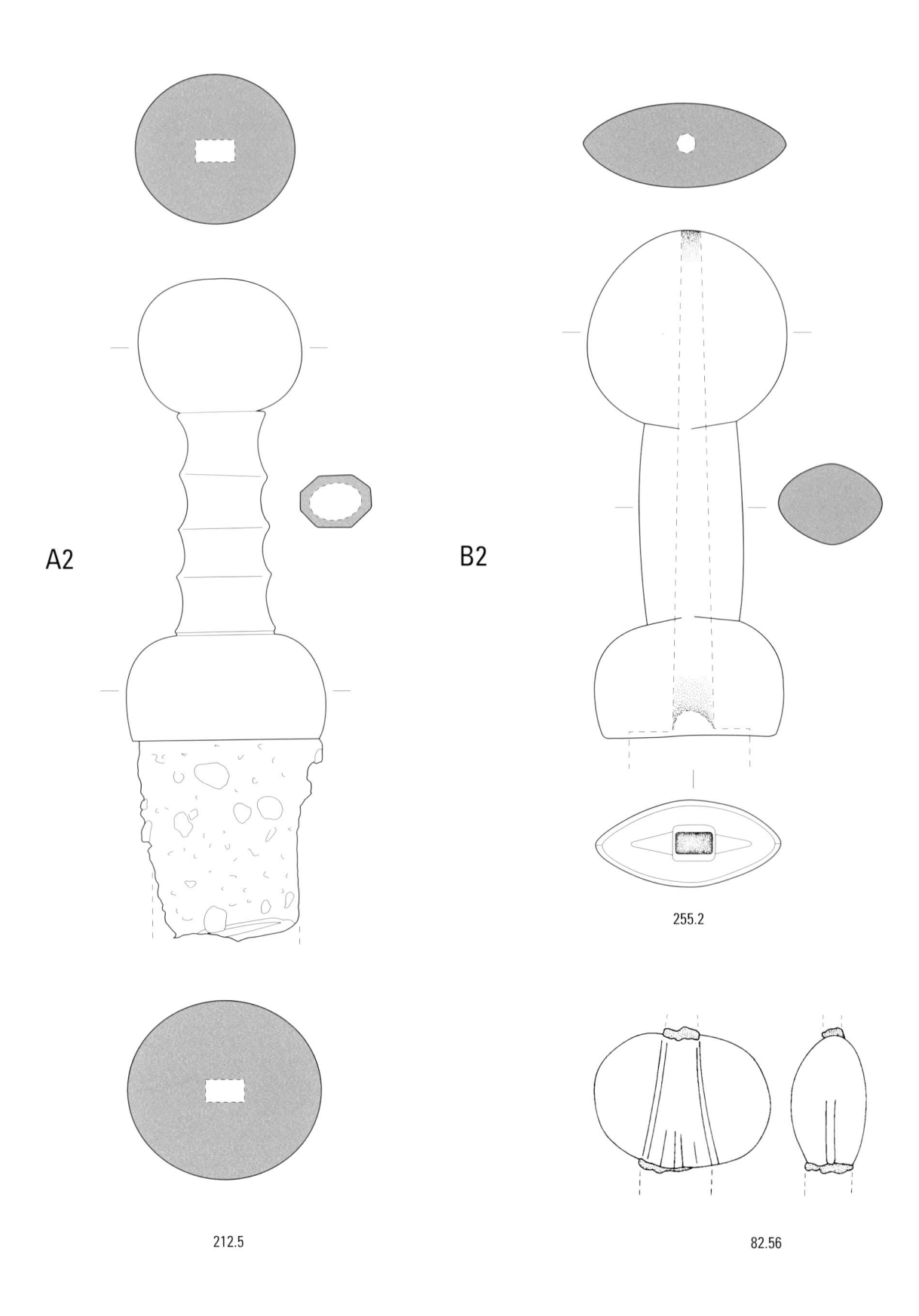

B2

255.2

212.5

82.56

Pl. 21 Sword hilts, periods 2-3. Scale 1:2.

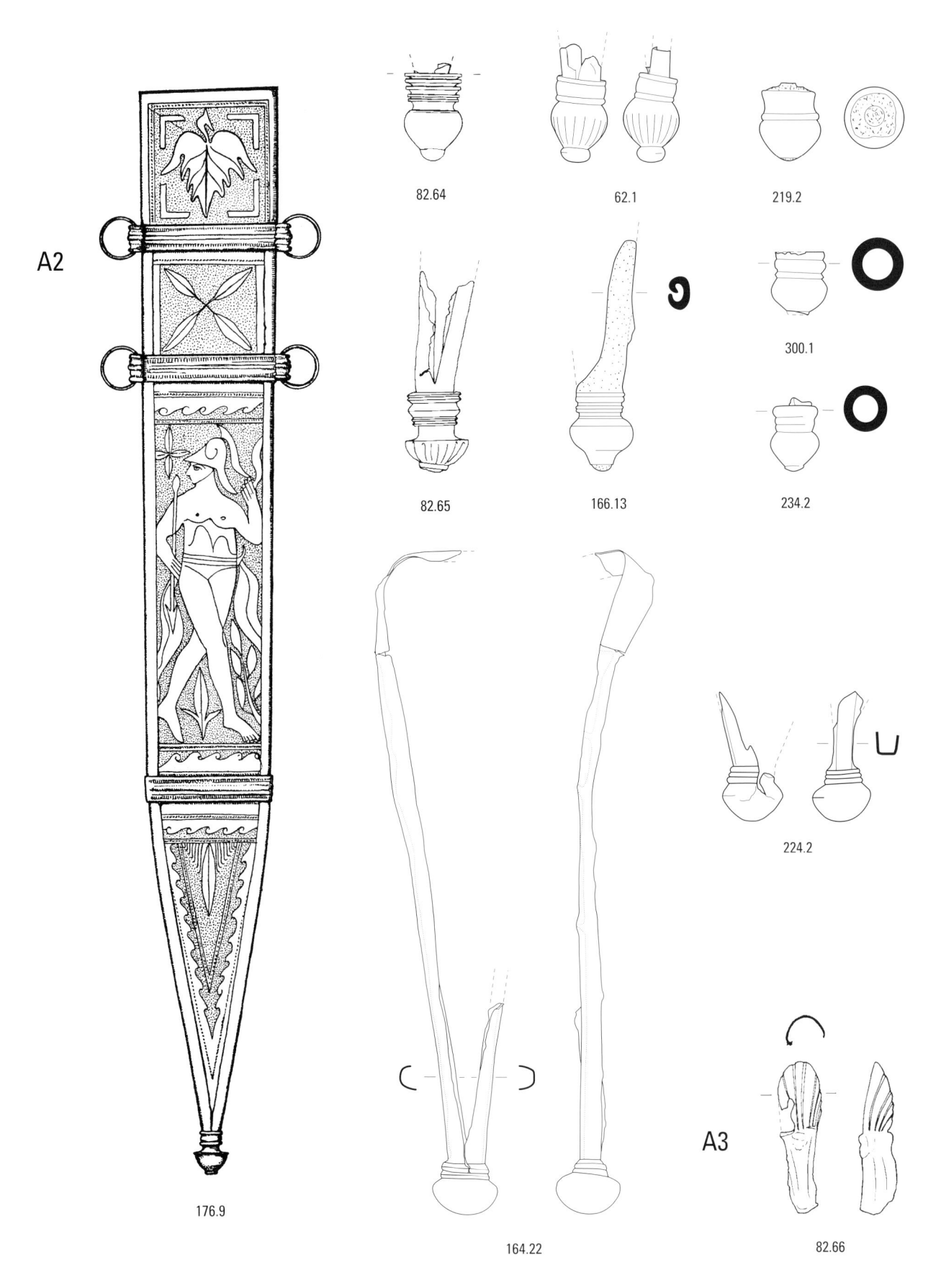

Pl. 22 Sword scabbard, stray terminal knobs and edging, period 2. Scale 2:3; 1:3 (176.9).

A-

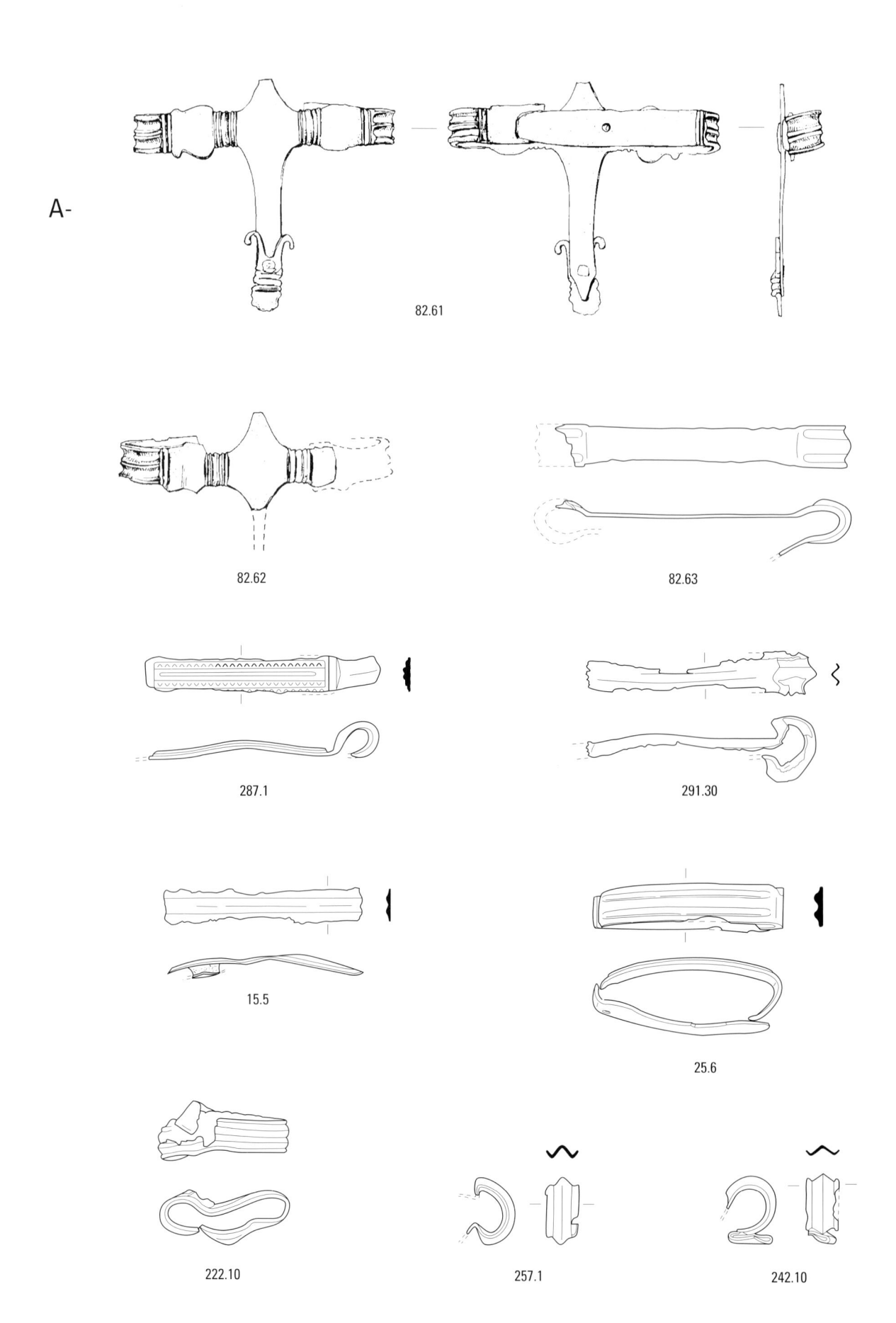

82.61

82.62

82.63

287.1

291.30

15.5

25.6

222.10

257.1

242.10

Pl. 23 Sword scabbard bands, period 2. Scale 2:3.

B2

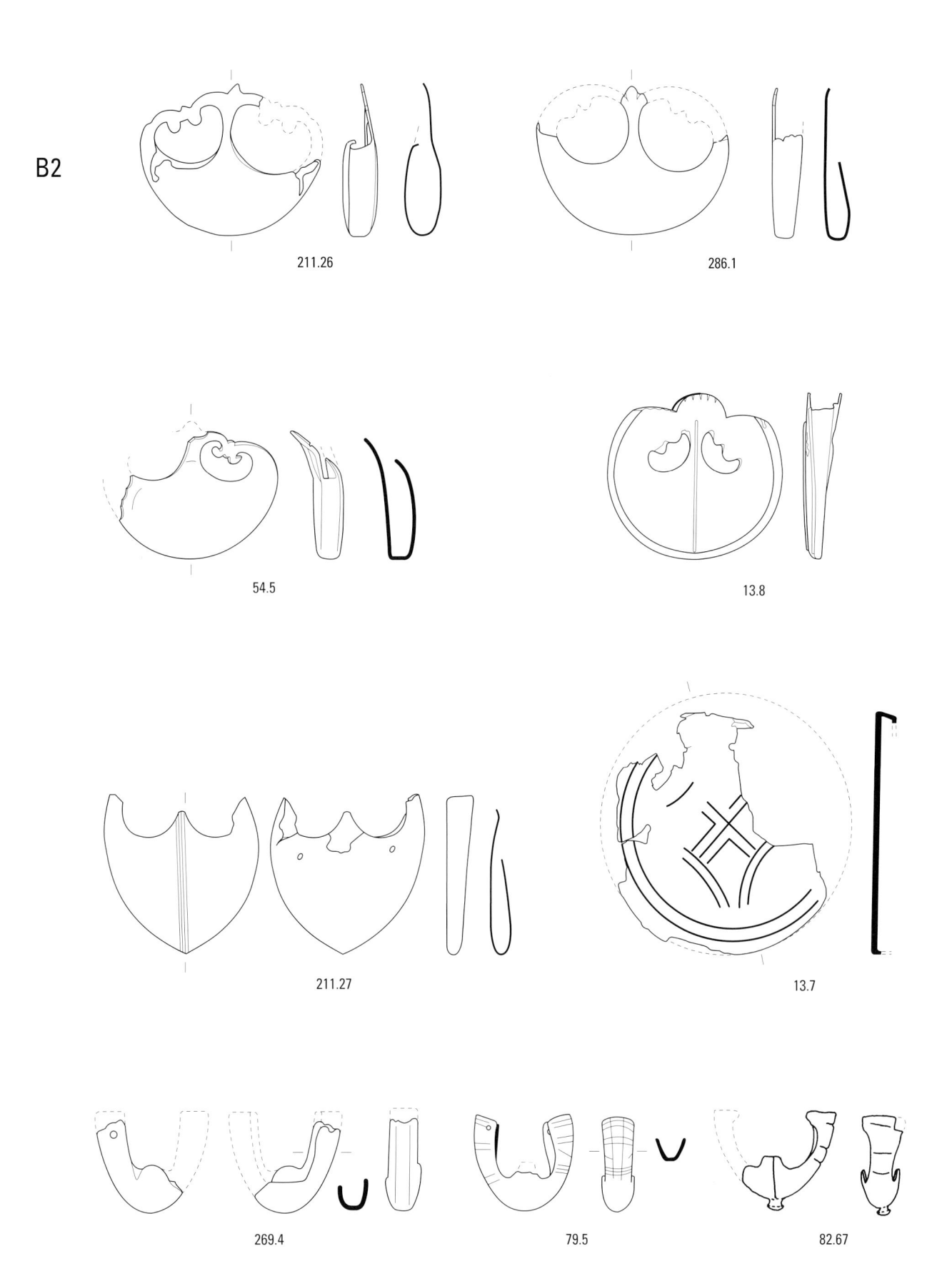

211.26

286.1

54.5

13.8

211.27

13.7

269.4

79.5

82.67

Pl. 24 Sword scabbard chapes, period 3. Scale 2:3.

B2

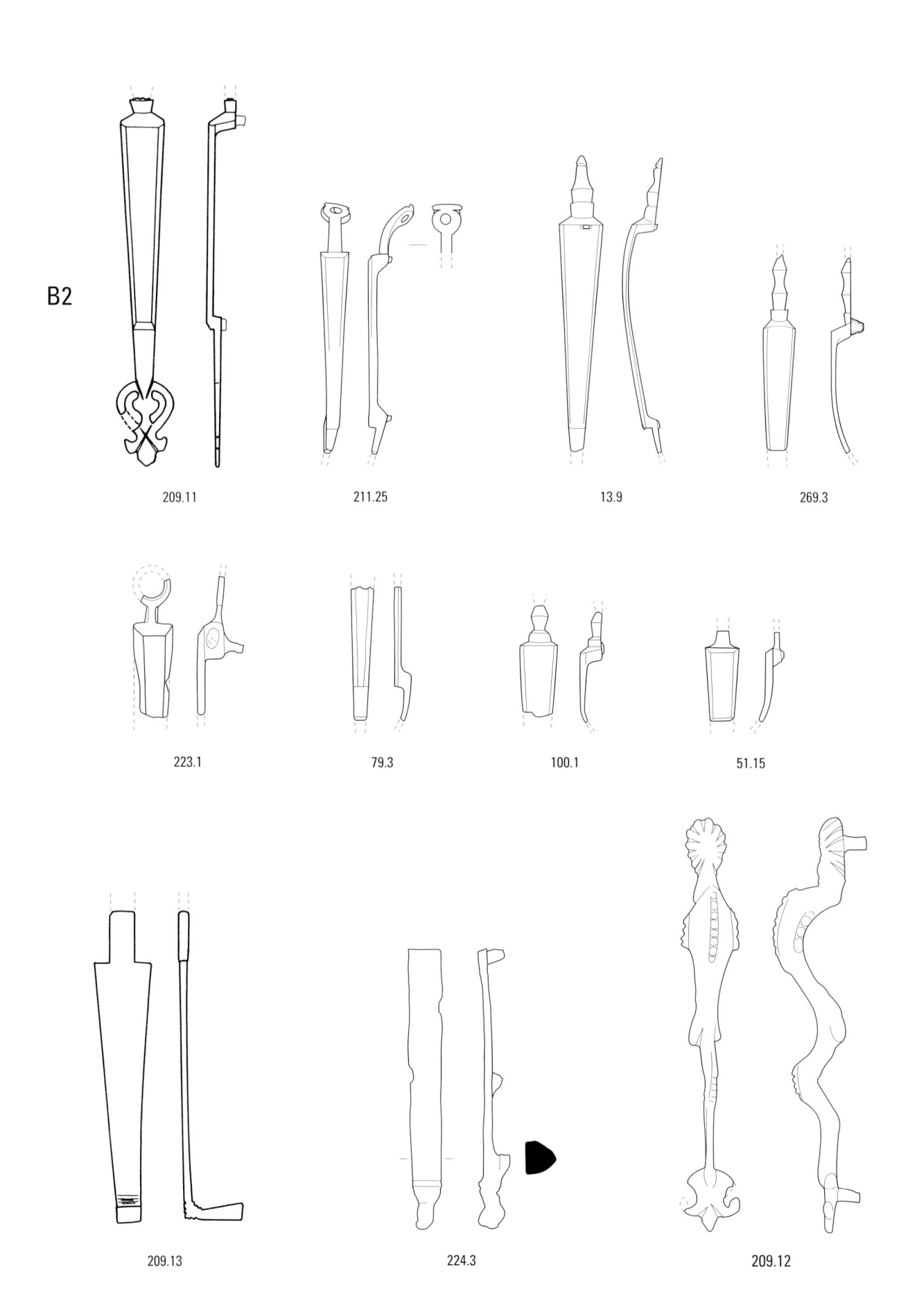

209.11   211.25   13.9   269.3

223.1   79.3   100.1   51.15

209.13   224.3   209.12

Pl. 25 Sword scabbard slides, period 3. Scale 2:3.

B1

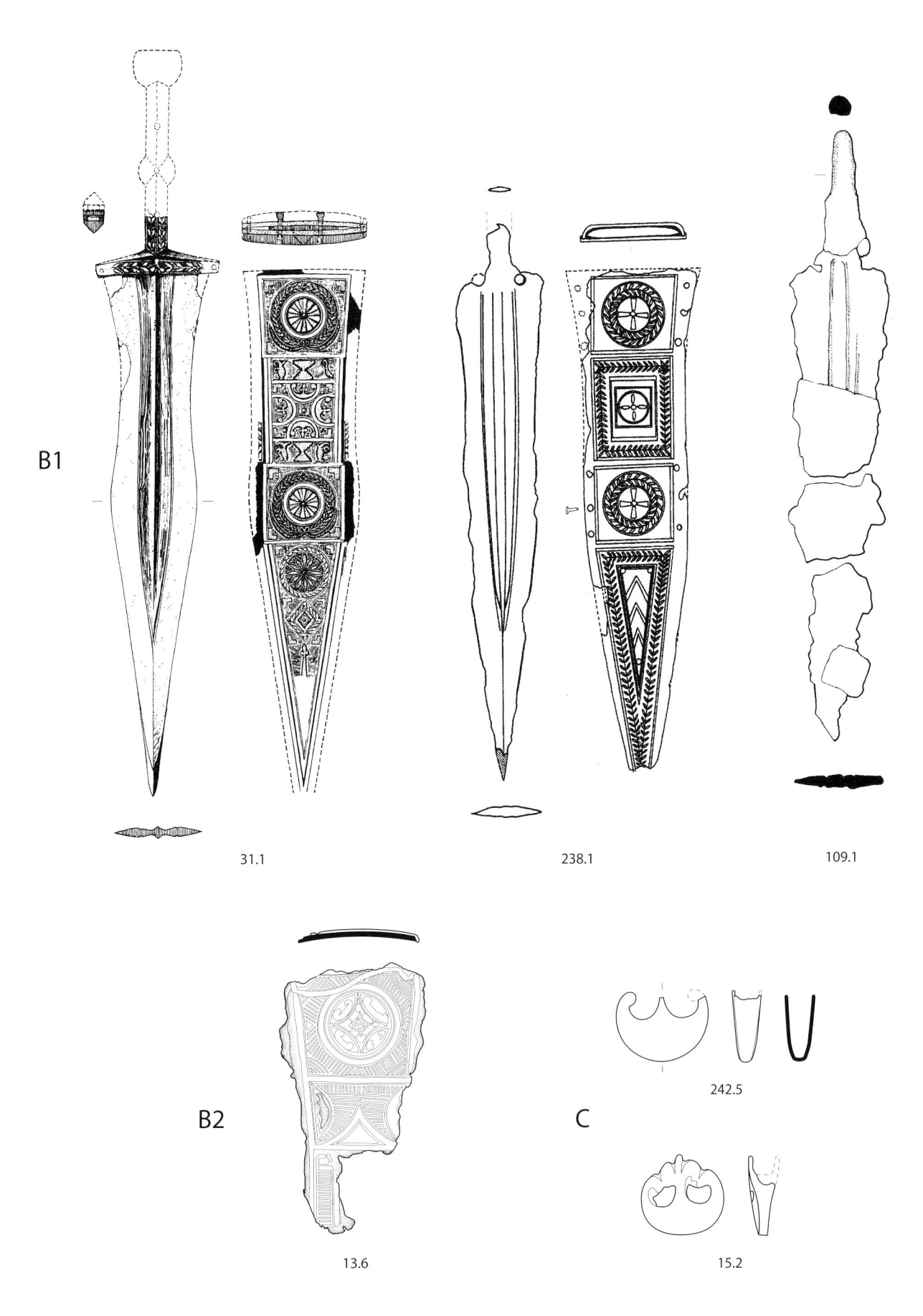

31.1   238.1   109.1

B2

C

242.5

13.6   15.2

Pl. 26 Daggers and dagger sheaths, period 2. Scale 1:2 (above); 2:3 (below).

337

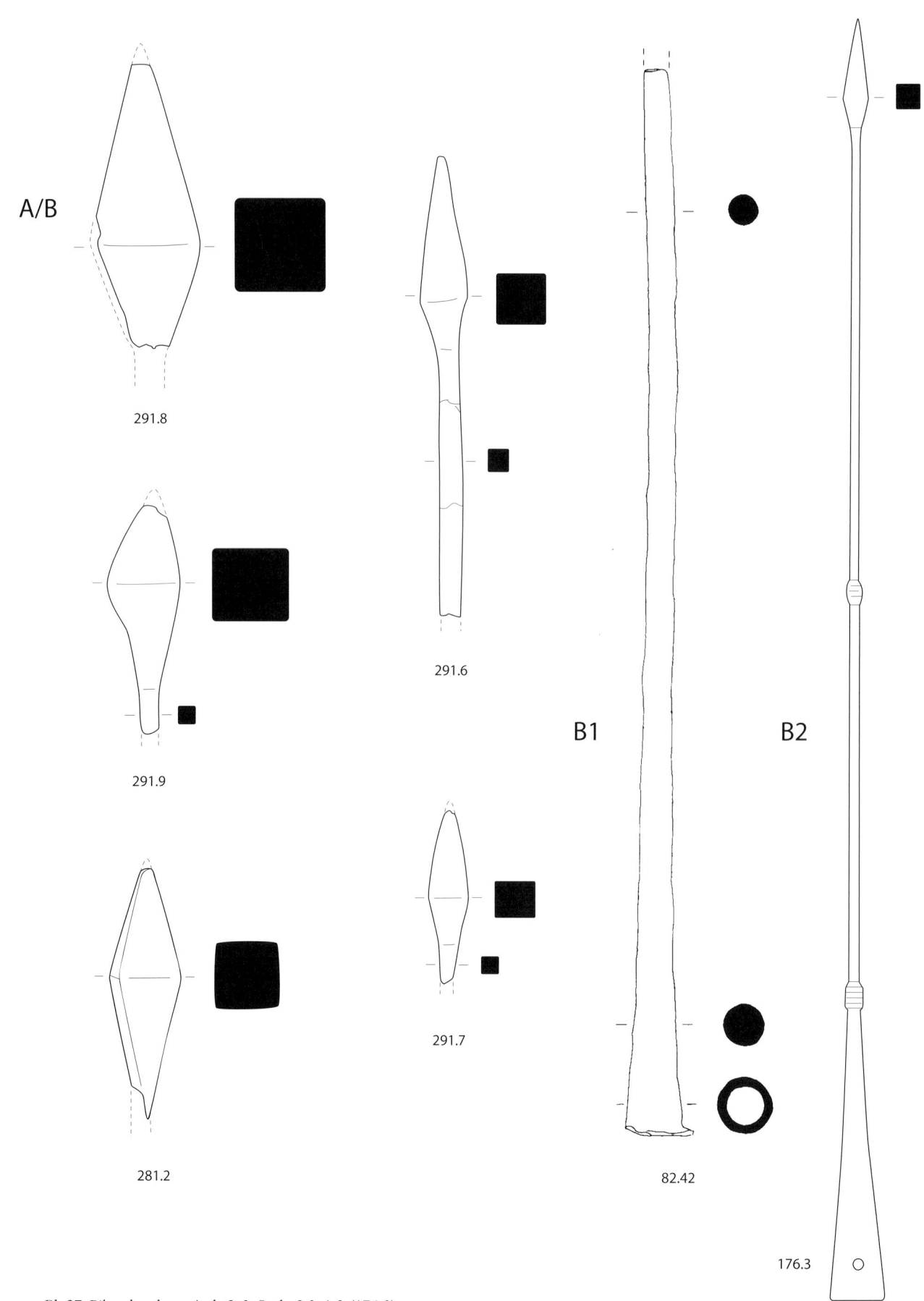

Pl. 27 *Pilum* heads, periods 2-3. Scale 2:3; 1:2 (176.3).

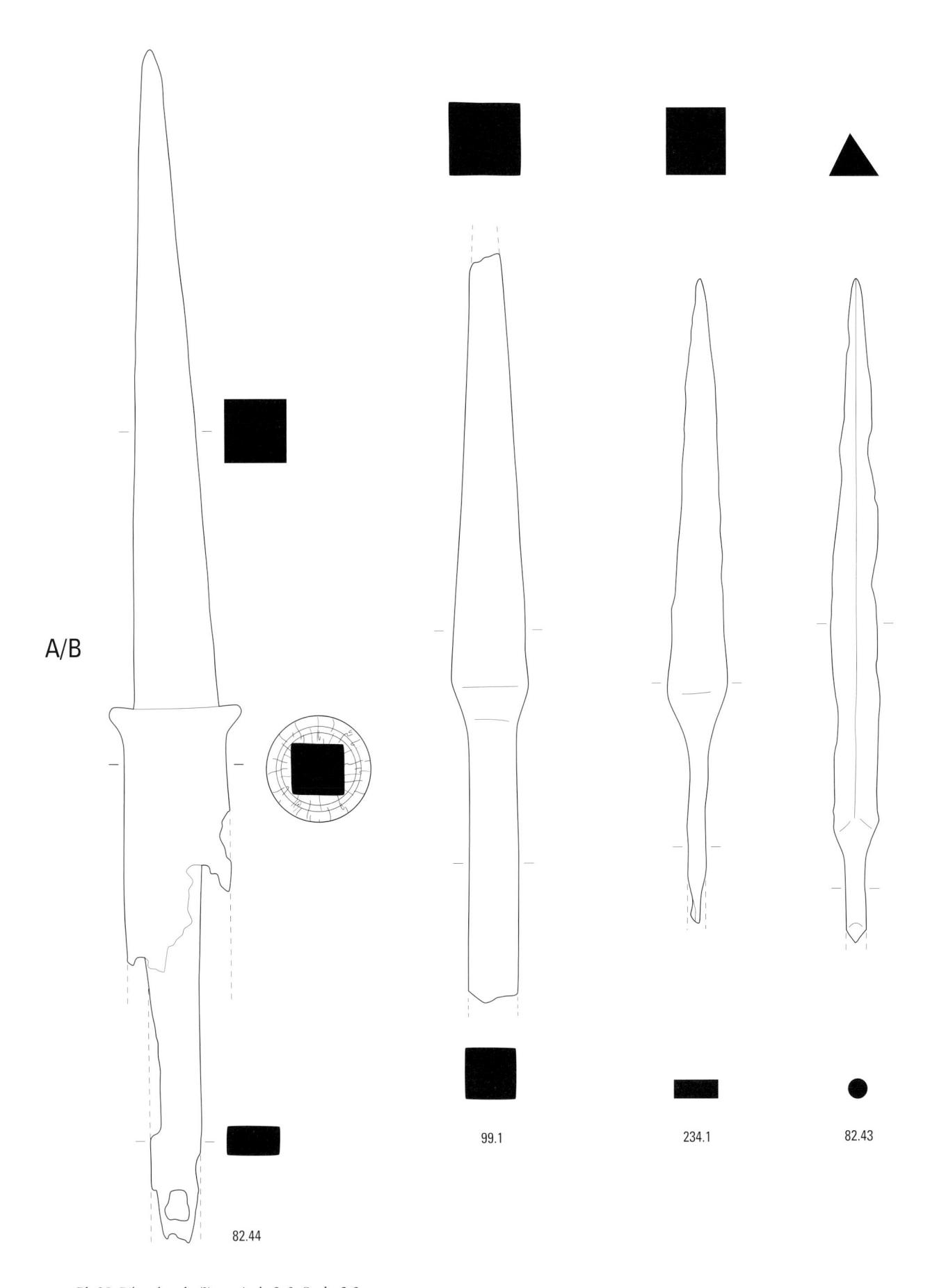

A/B

82.44

99.1

234.1

82.43

Pl. 28 *Pilum* heads (?), periods 2-3. Scale 2:3.

339

A1

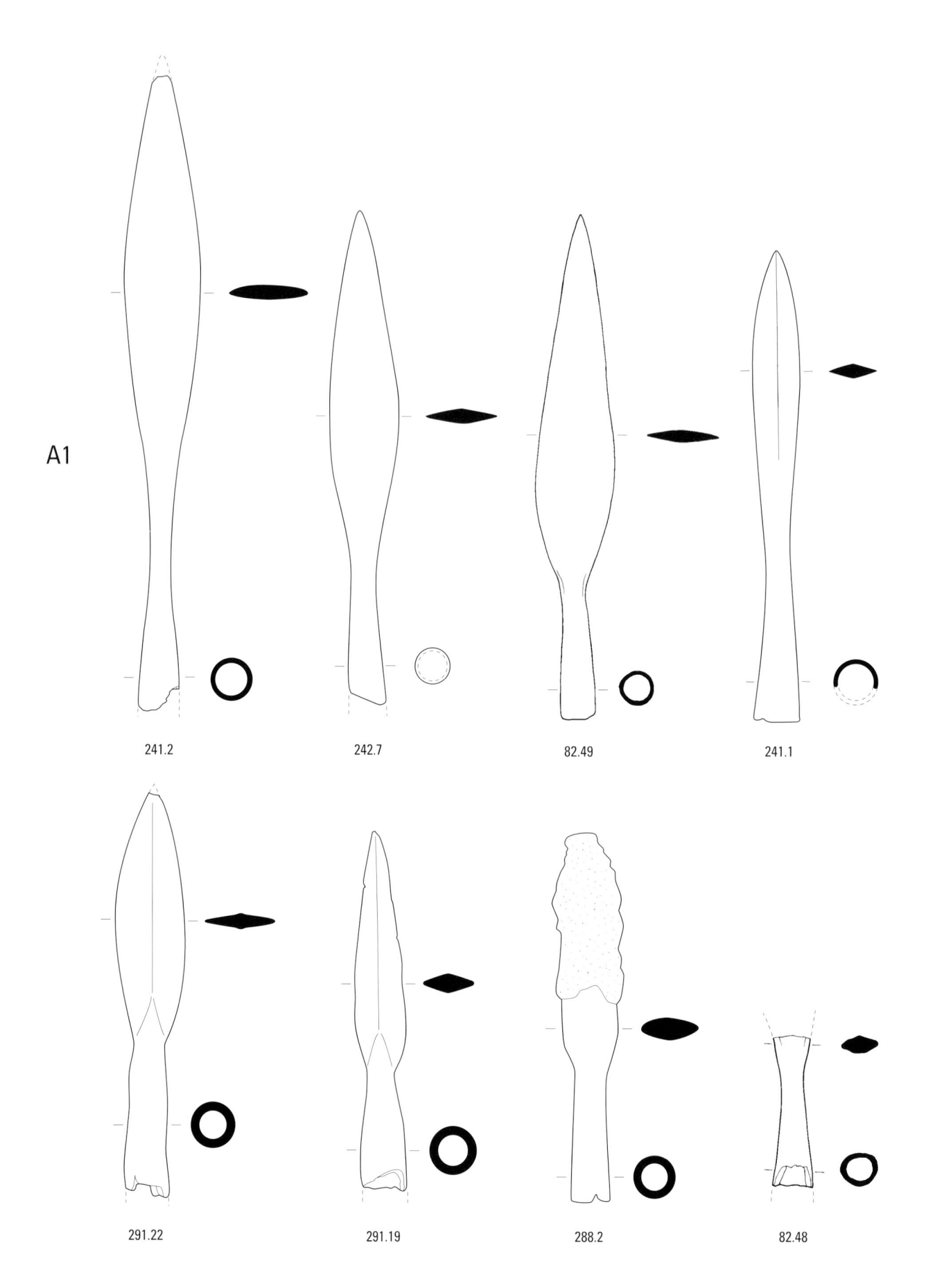

241.2 242.7 82.49 241.1

291.22 291.19 288.2 82.48

Pl. 29 Spearheads, periods 1-4. Scale 1:2.

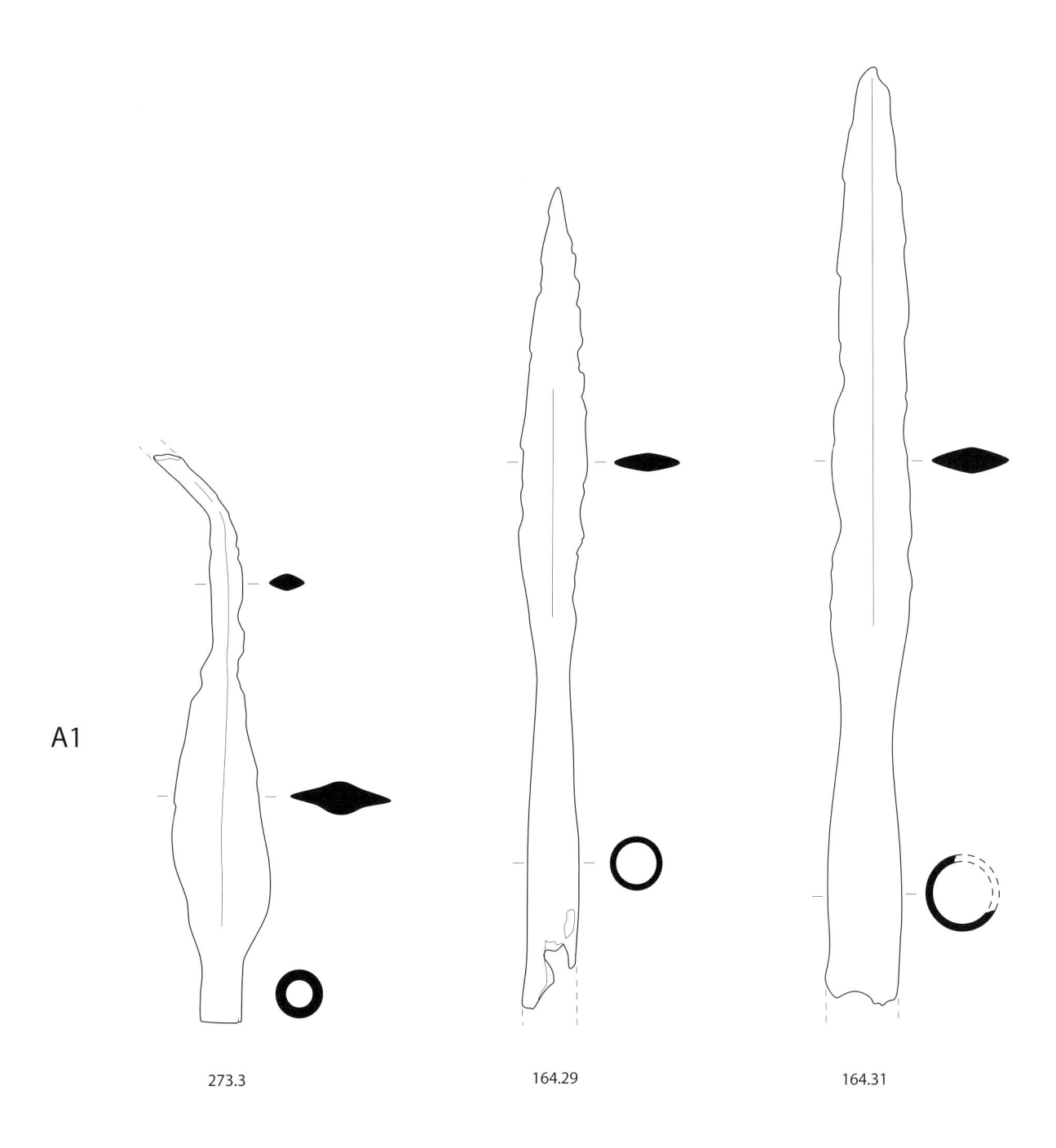

A1

273.3

164.29

164.31

Pl. 30 Spearheads, periods 1-4. Scale 1:2.

A1

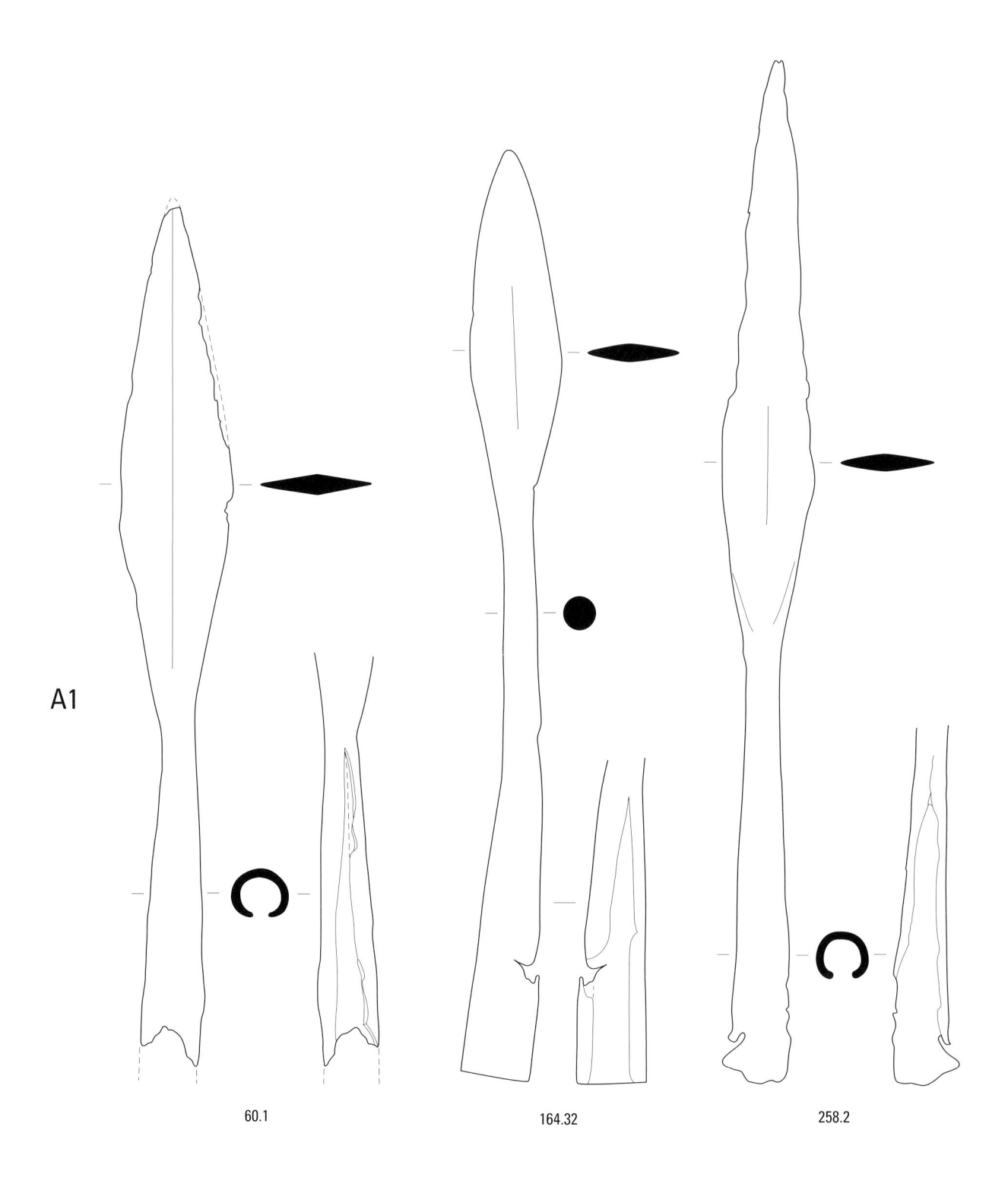

60.1   164.32   258.2

Pl. 31 Spearheads, periods 1-4. Scale 1:2.

342

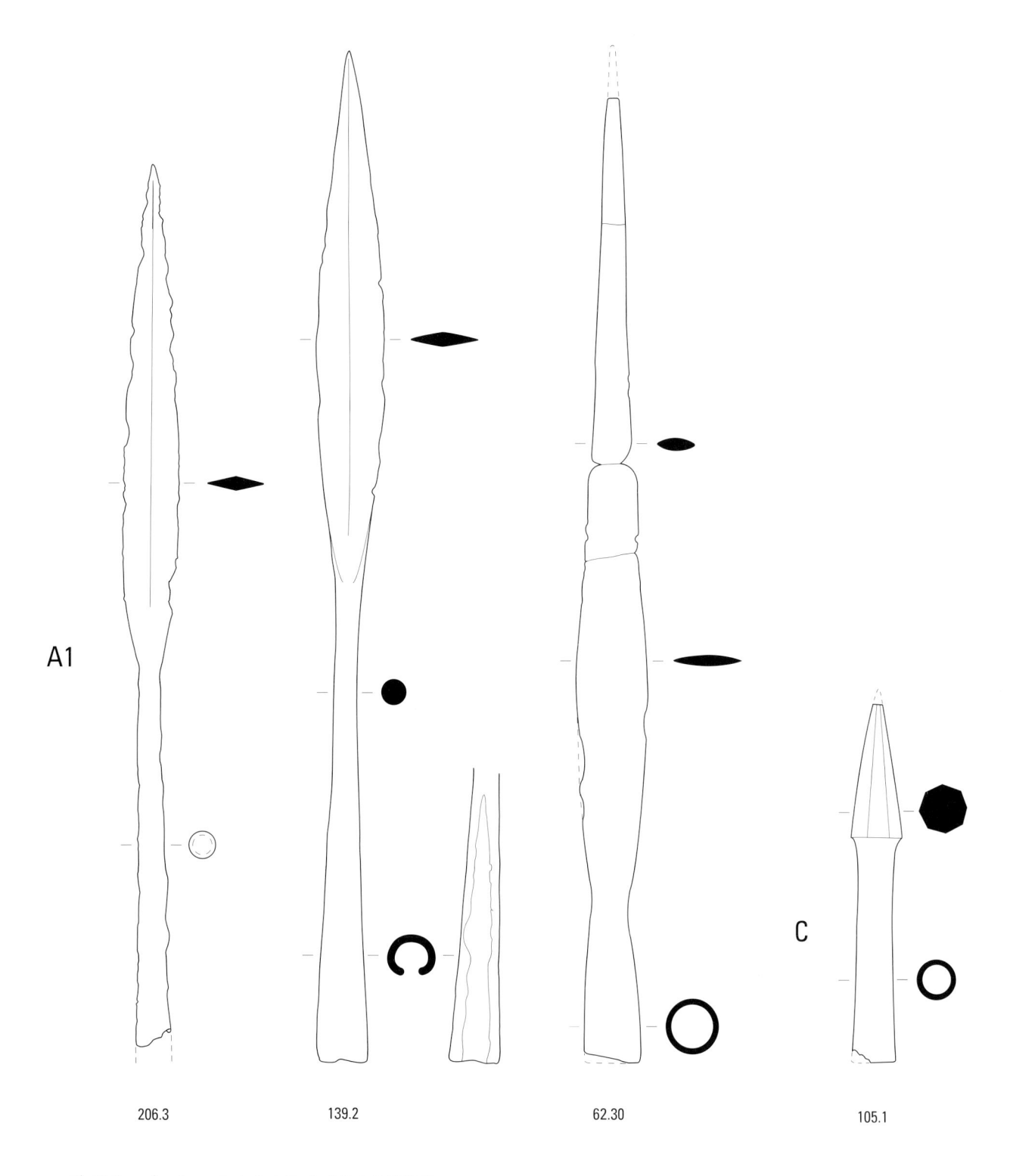

A1

206.3   139.2   62.30   C   105.1

Pl. 32 Spearheads, periods 1-4. Scale 1:3; 1:2 (105.1).

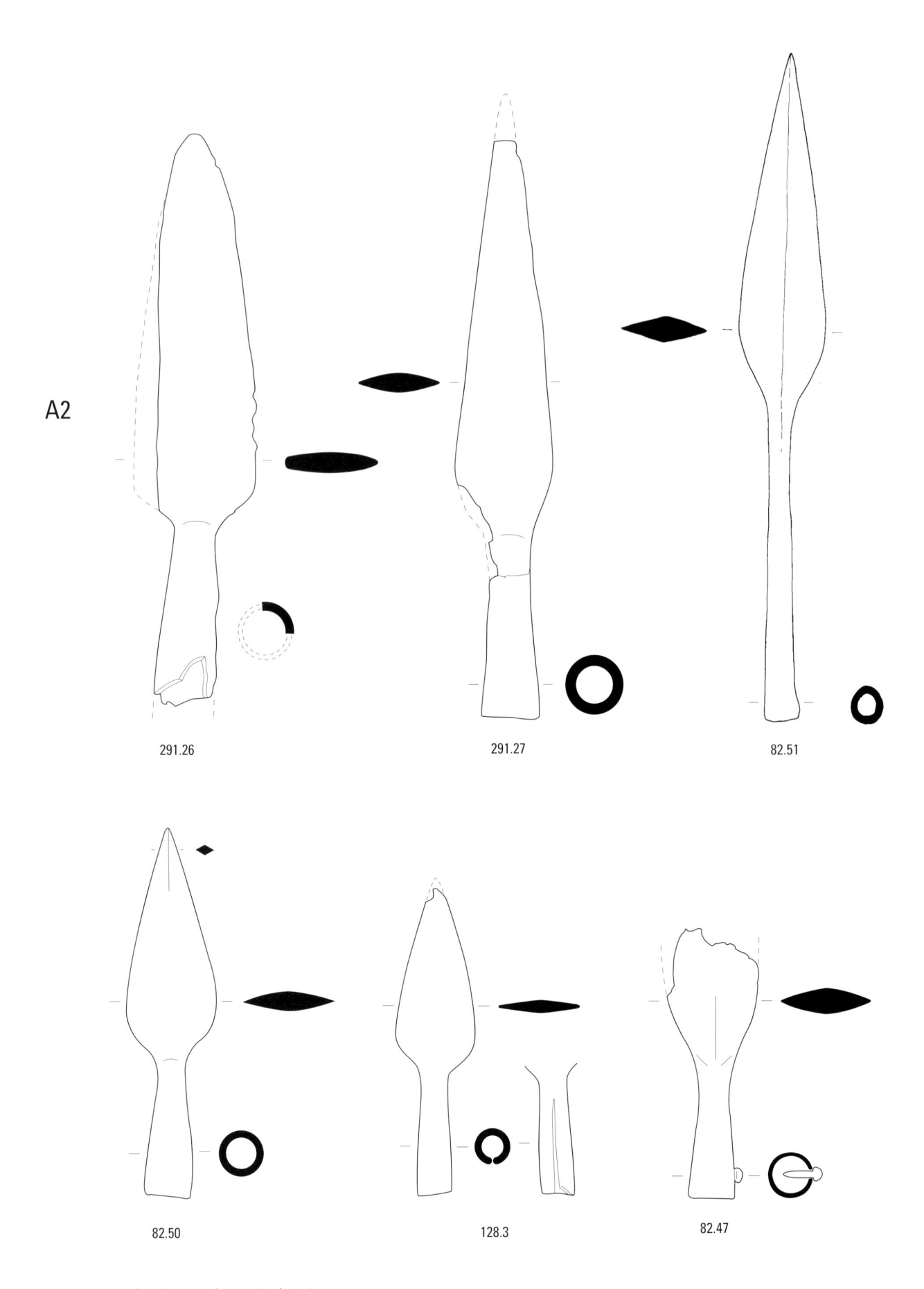

A2

291.26

291.27

82.51

82.50

128.3

82.47

Pl. 33 Lanceheads, periods 1-4. Scale 1:2.

222.5

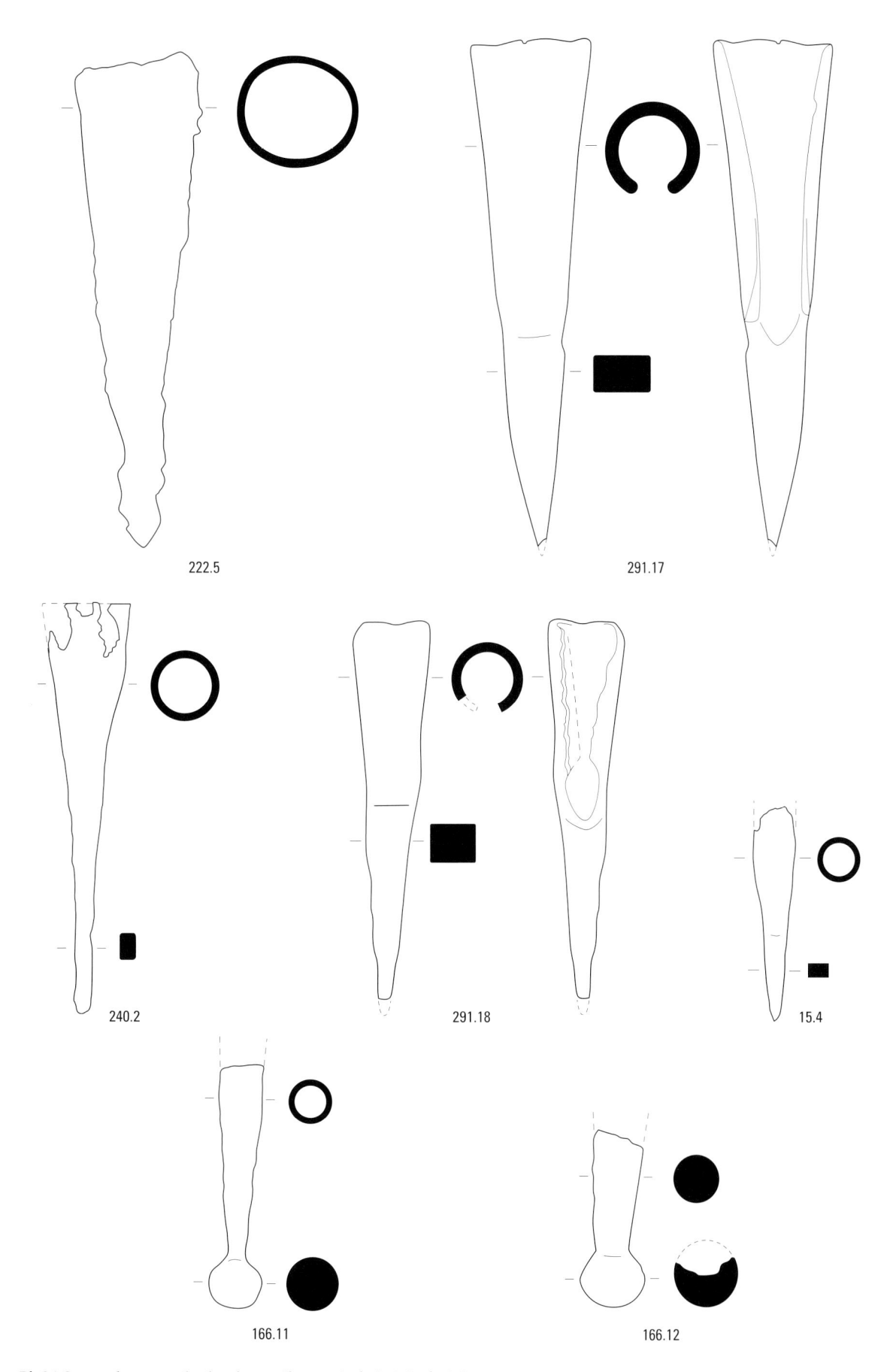

291.17

240.2

291.18

15.4

166.11

166.12

Pl. 34 Spear-, lance- and *pilum* butt spikes, periods 1-4. Scale 1:2.

A 222.4   166.3

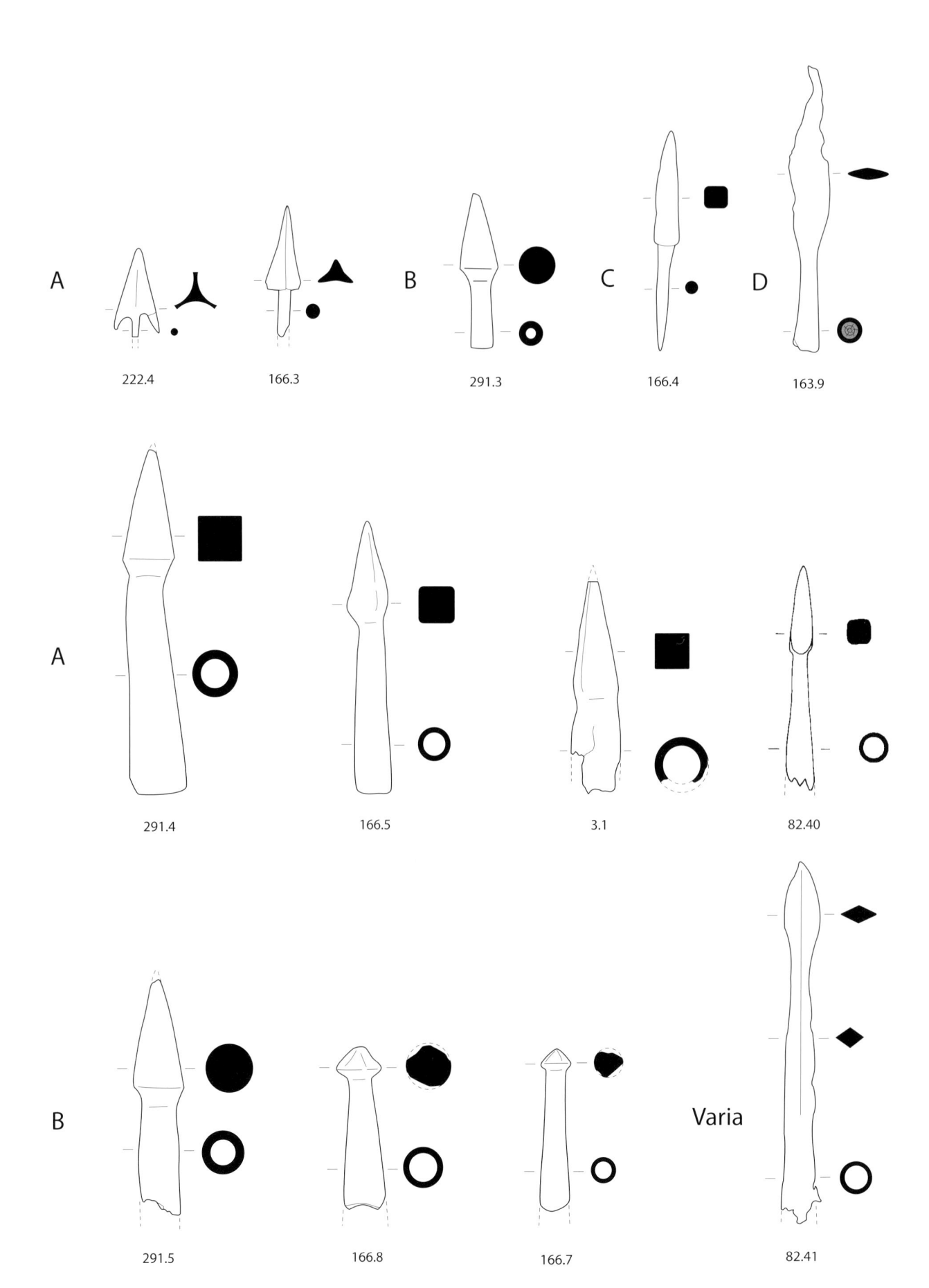

B 291.3

C 166.4

D 163.9

A 291.4   166.5   3.1   82.40

B 291.5   166.8   166.7

Varia 82.41

Pl. 35 Arrowheads and boltheads, periods 1-4. Scale 2:3.

A

242.6   54.2   15.3

A/D

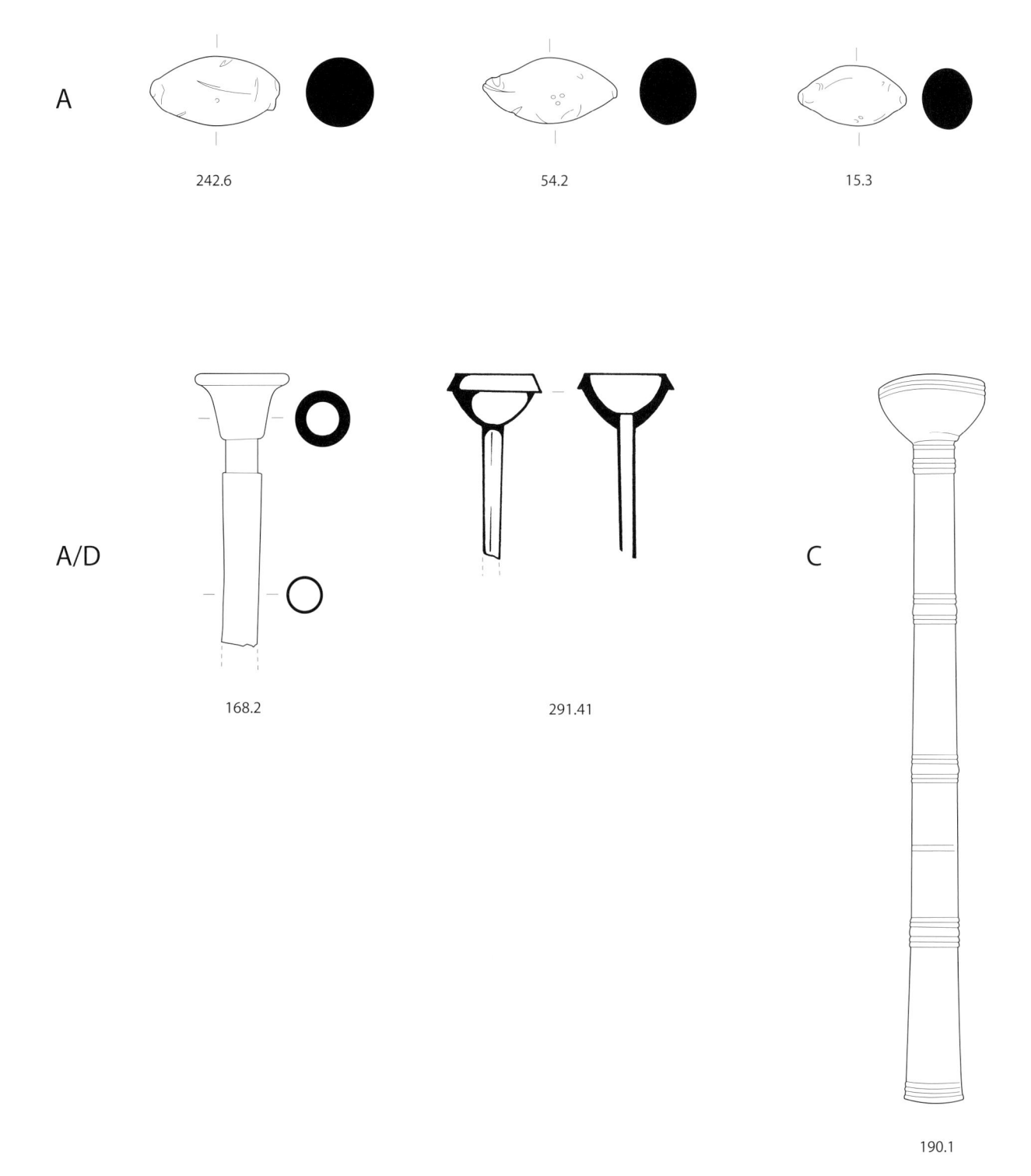

168.2   291.41

C

190.1

Pl. 36 Slingshot and mouthpieces from wind instruments, periods 1-4, scale 2:3.

A1

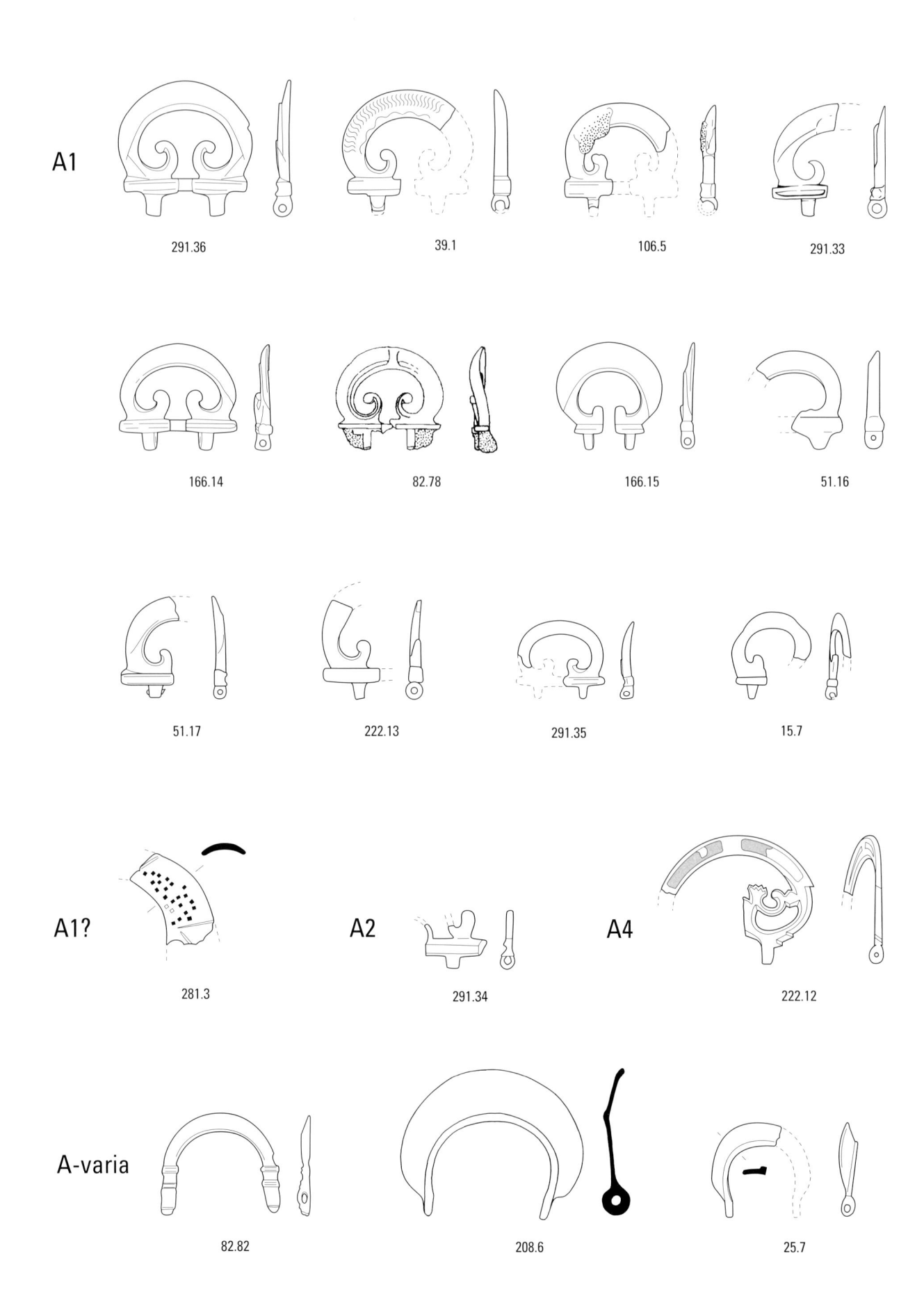

291.36 39.1 106.5 291.33

166.14 82.78 166.15 51.16

51.17 222.13 291.35 15.7

A1? 281.3   A2 291.34   A4 222.12

A-varia

82.82 208.6 25.7

Pl. 37 Belt buckles, period 2. Scale 2:3.

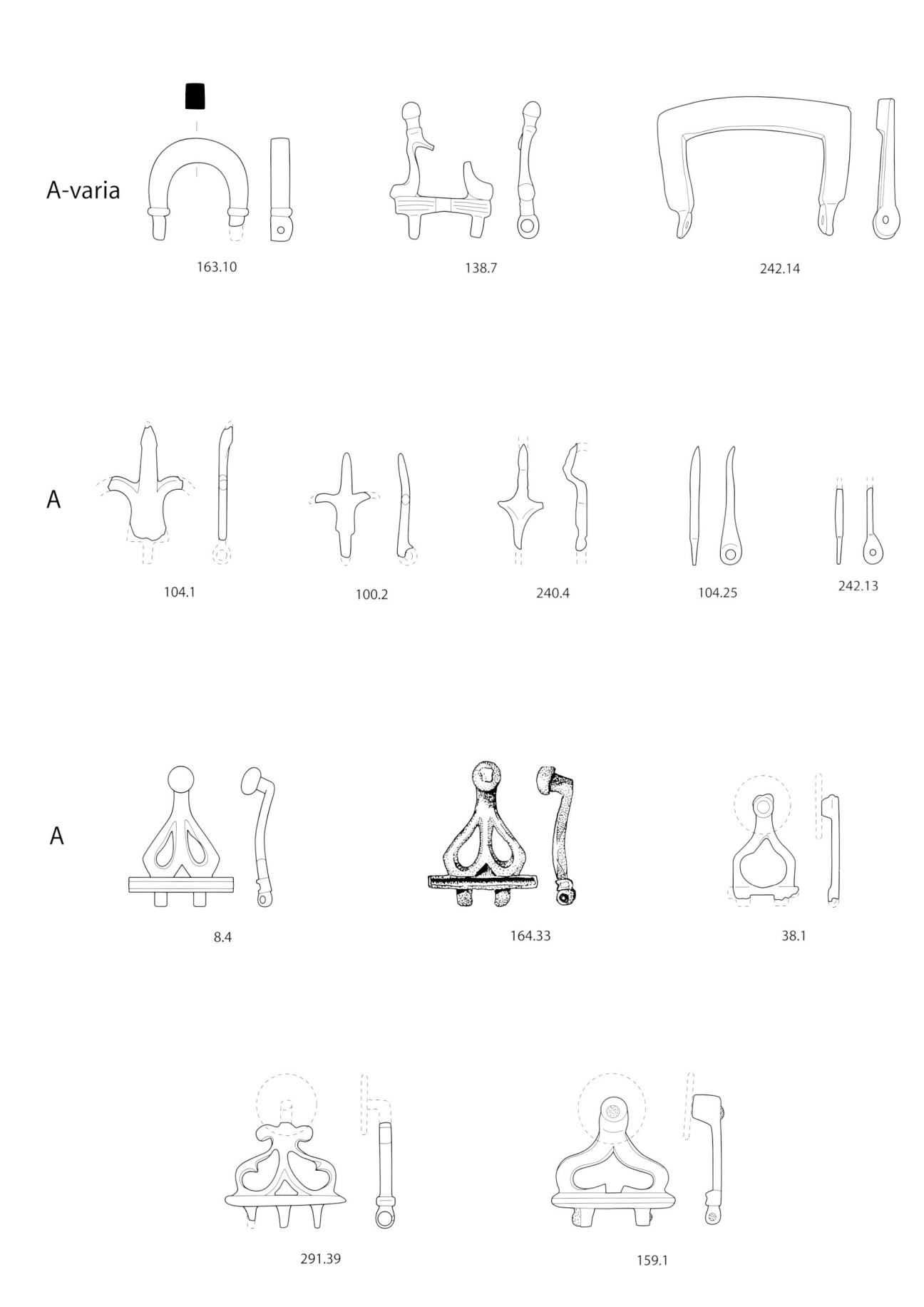

Pl. 38 Belt buckles, tongues and frogs, period 2. Scale 2:3.

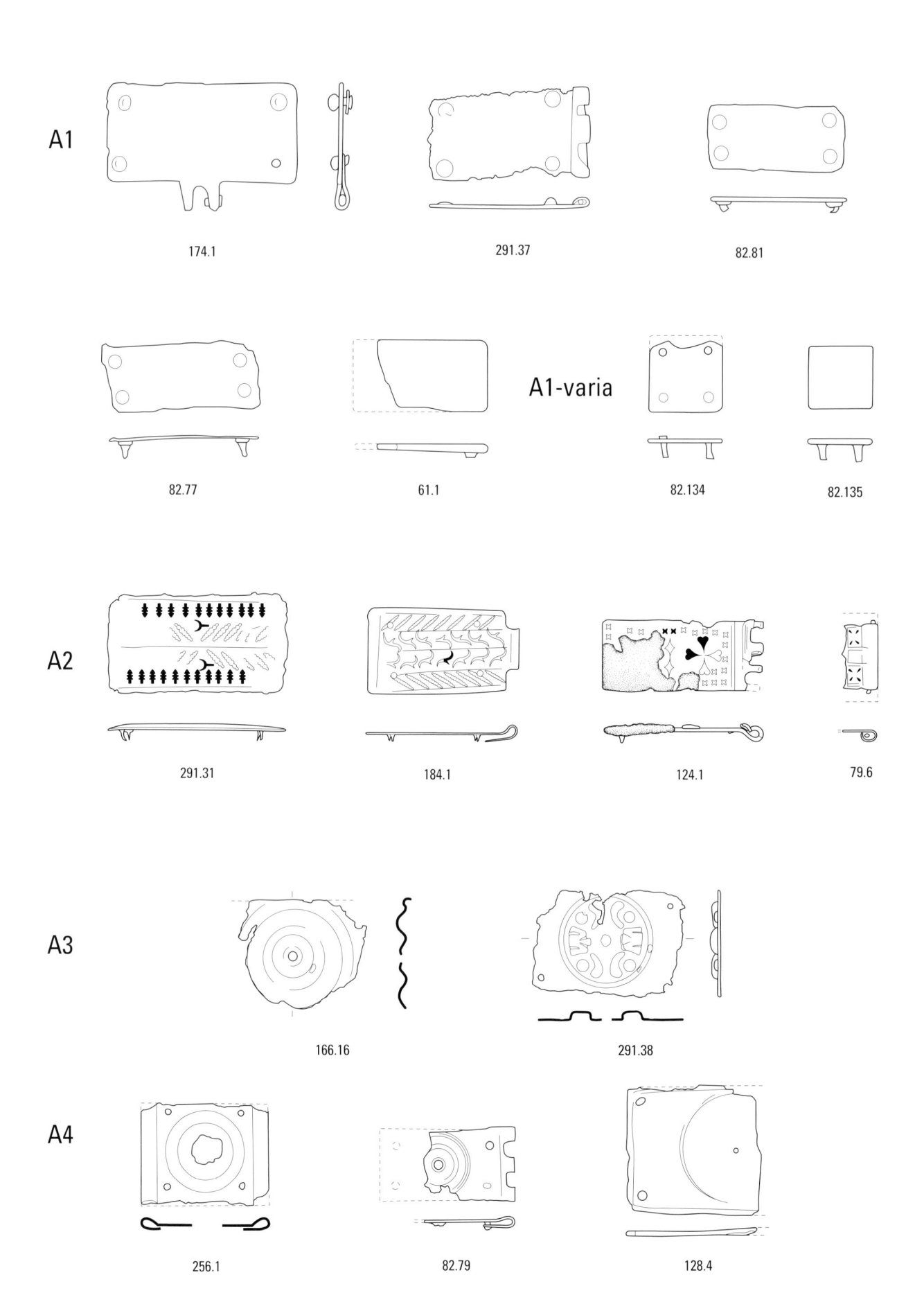

A1

174.1

291.37

82.81

82.77

61.1

A1-varia

82.134

82.135

A2

291.31

184.1

124.1

79.6

A3

166.16

291.38

A4

256.1

82.79

128.4

Pl. 39 Decorative belt fittings, period 2. Scale 2:3.

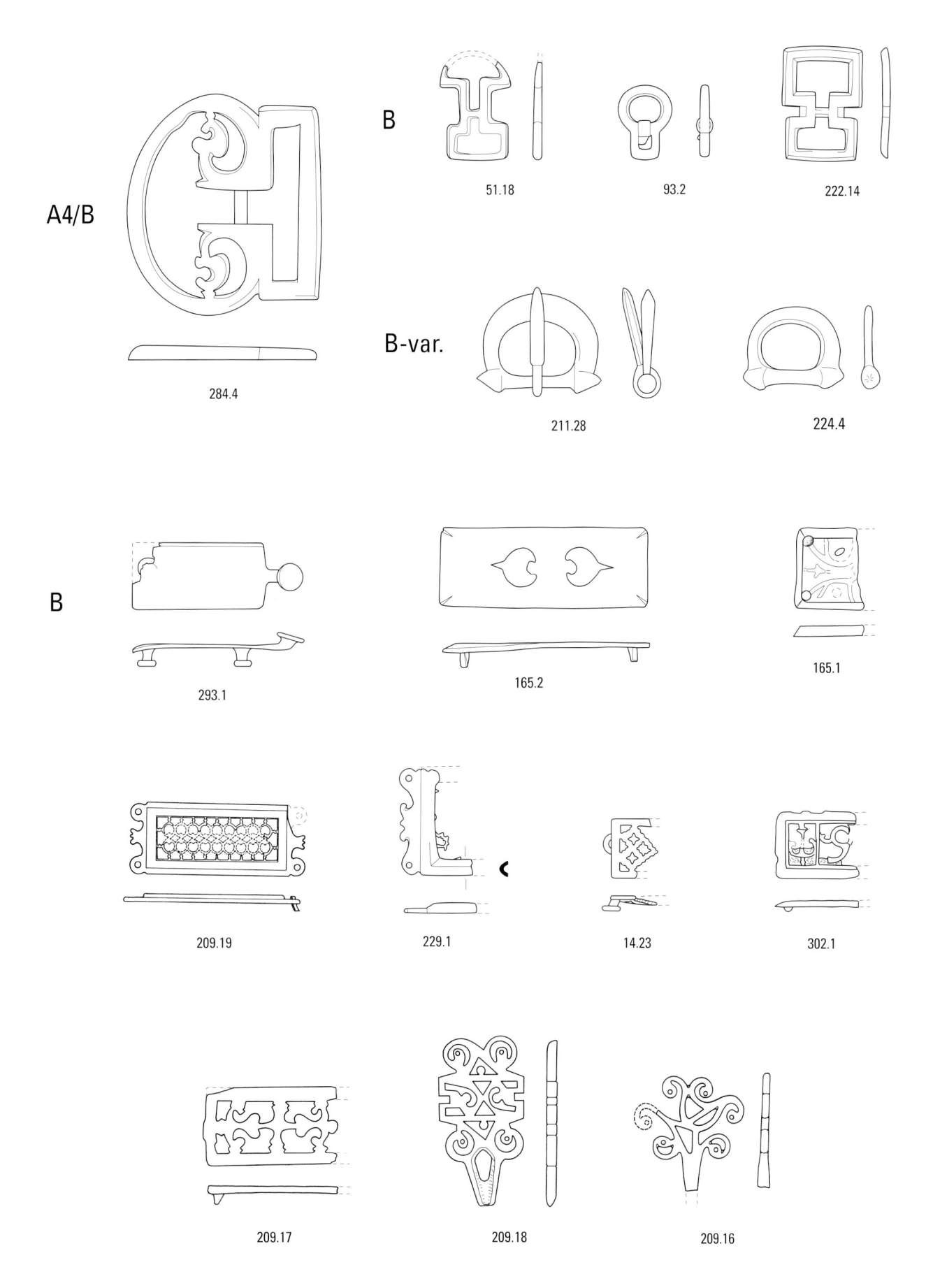

A4/B

284.4

B

51.18   93.2   222.14

B-var.

211.28   224.4

B

293.1   165.2   165.1

209.19   229.1   14.23   302.1

209.17   209.18   209.16

Pl. 40 Buckles and decorative belt fittings, period 3. Scale 2:3.

C

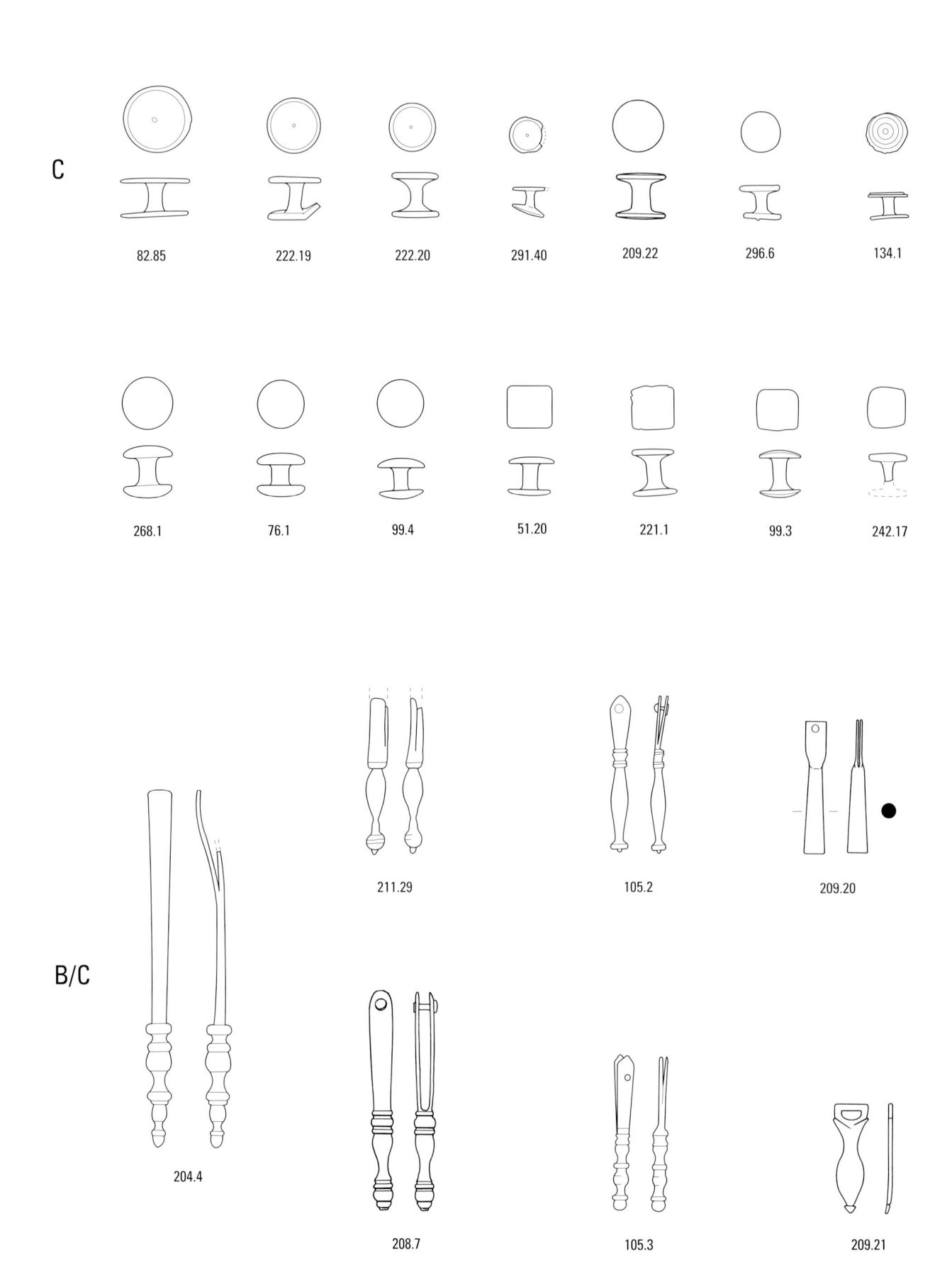

82.85   222.19   222.20   291.40   209.22   296.6   134.1

268.1   76.1   99.4   51.20   221.1   99.3   242.17

B/C

204.4   211.29   105.2   209.20

208.7   105.3   209.21

Pl. 41 Belt closure studs and strap terminals, period 3. Scale 2:3.

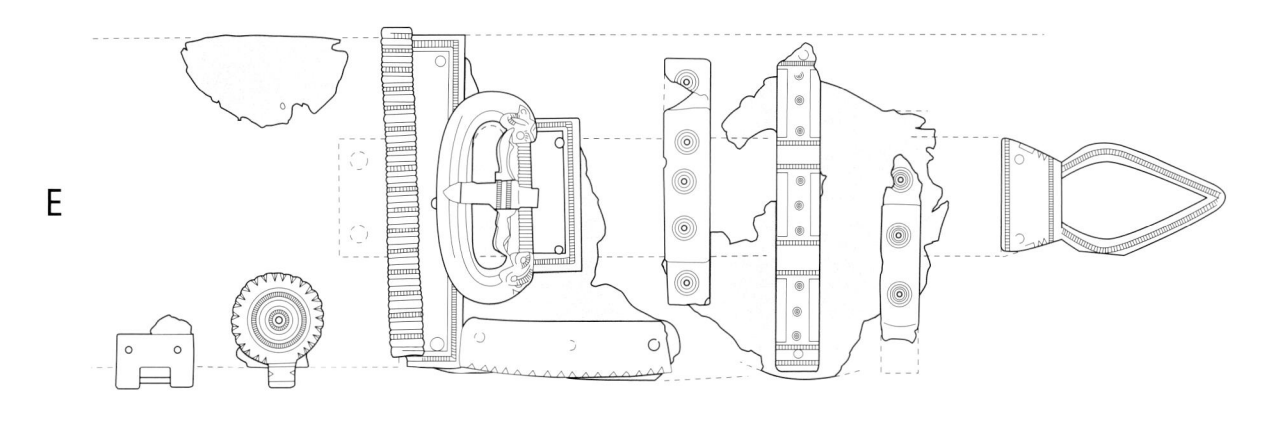

285.2

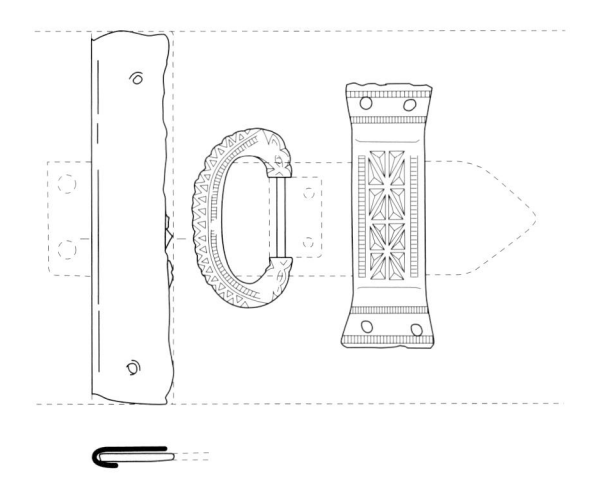

285.1

Pl. 42 Complete belt sets, period 4. Scale 1:2.

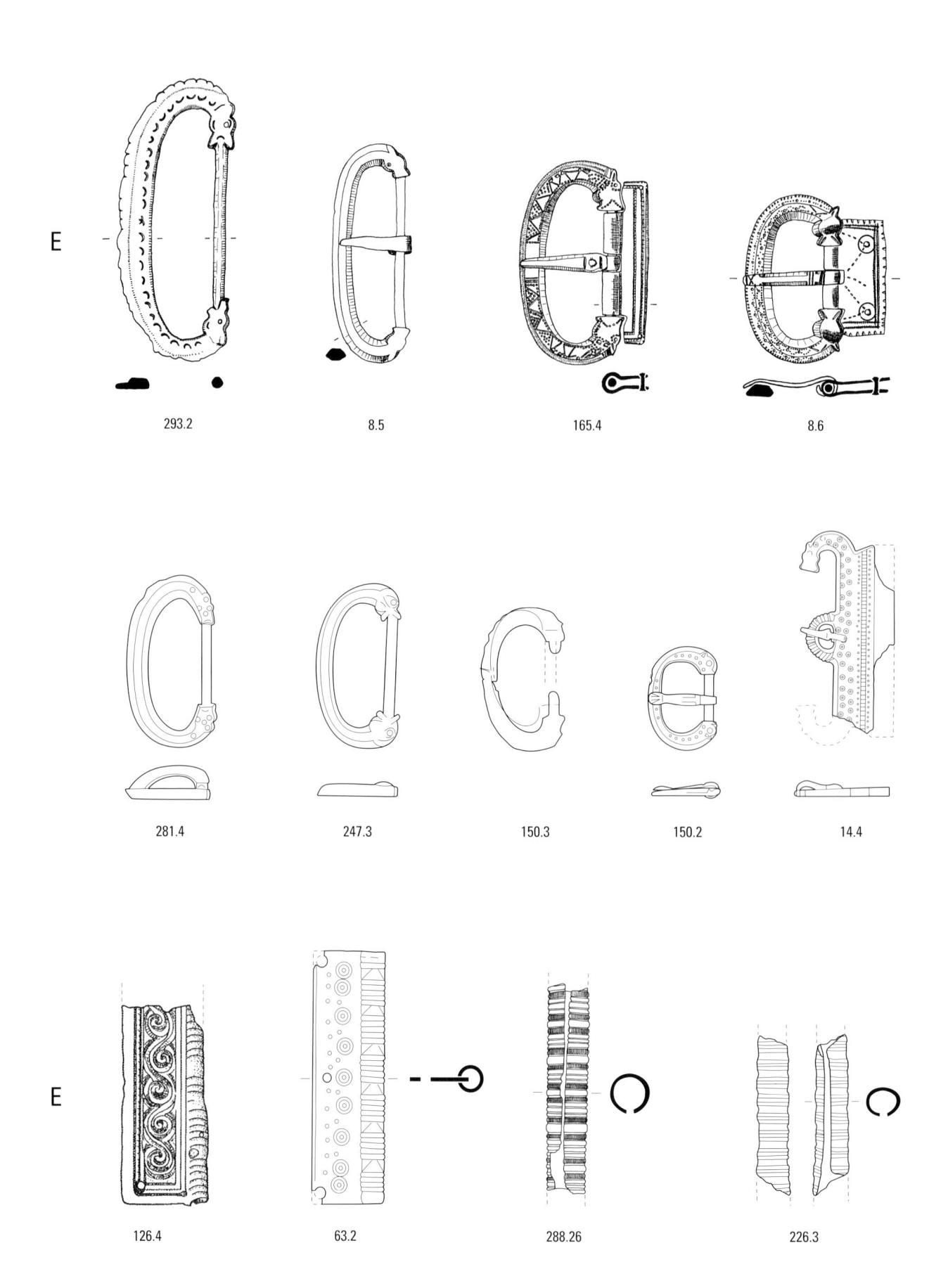

Pl. 43 Buckles and belt fittings, period 4. Scale 2:3.

354

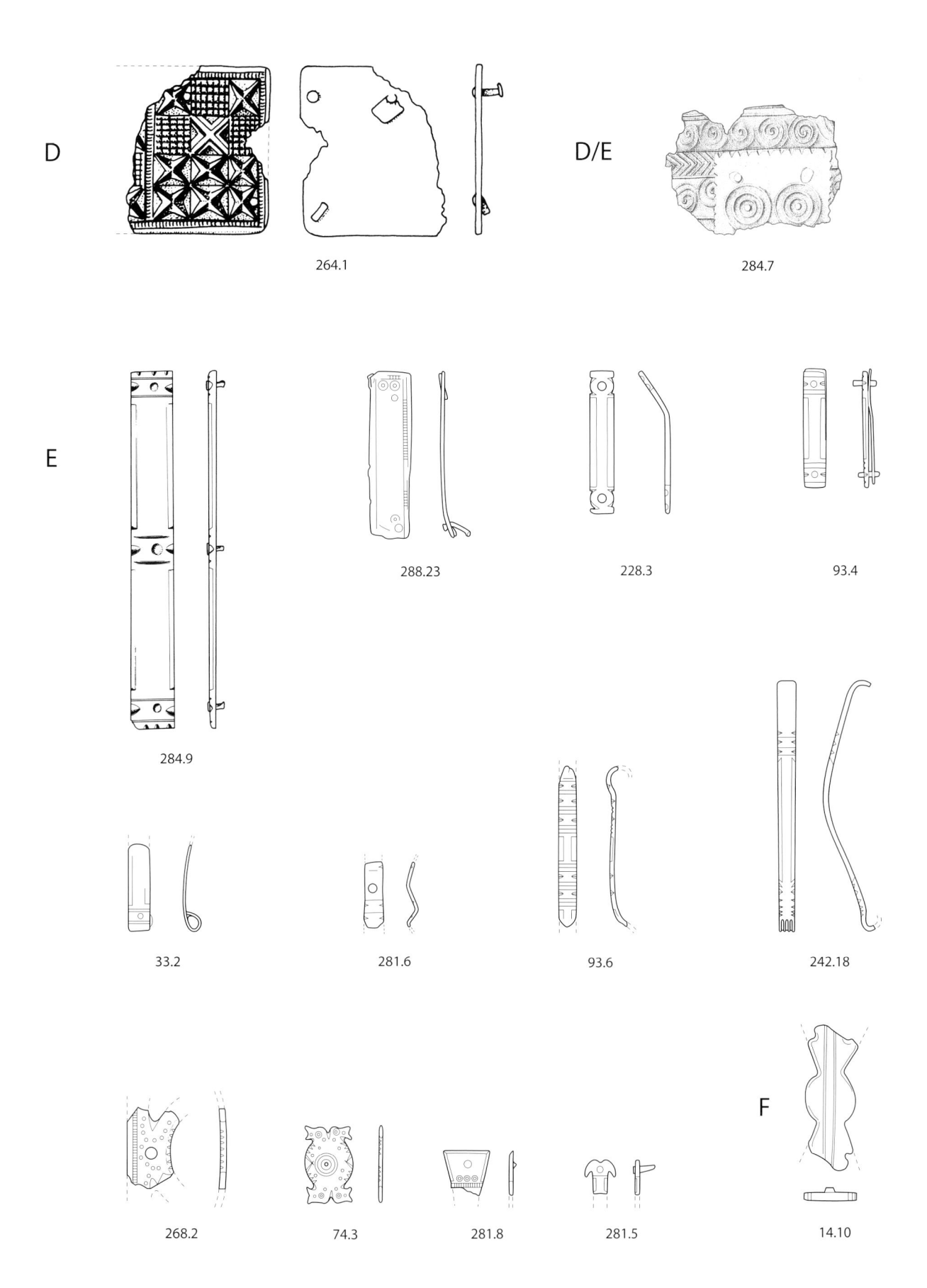

D   264.1

D/E   284.7

E   284.9   288.23   228.3   93.4

33.2   281.6   93.6   242.18

268.2   74.3   281.8   281.5   F   14.10

Pl. 44 Decorative belt fittings, period 4. Scale 2:3.

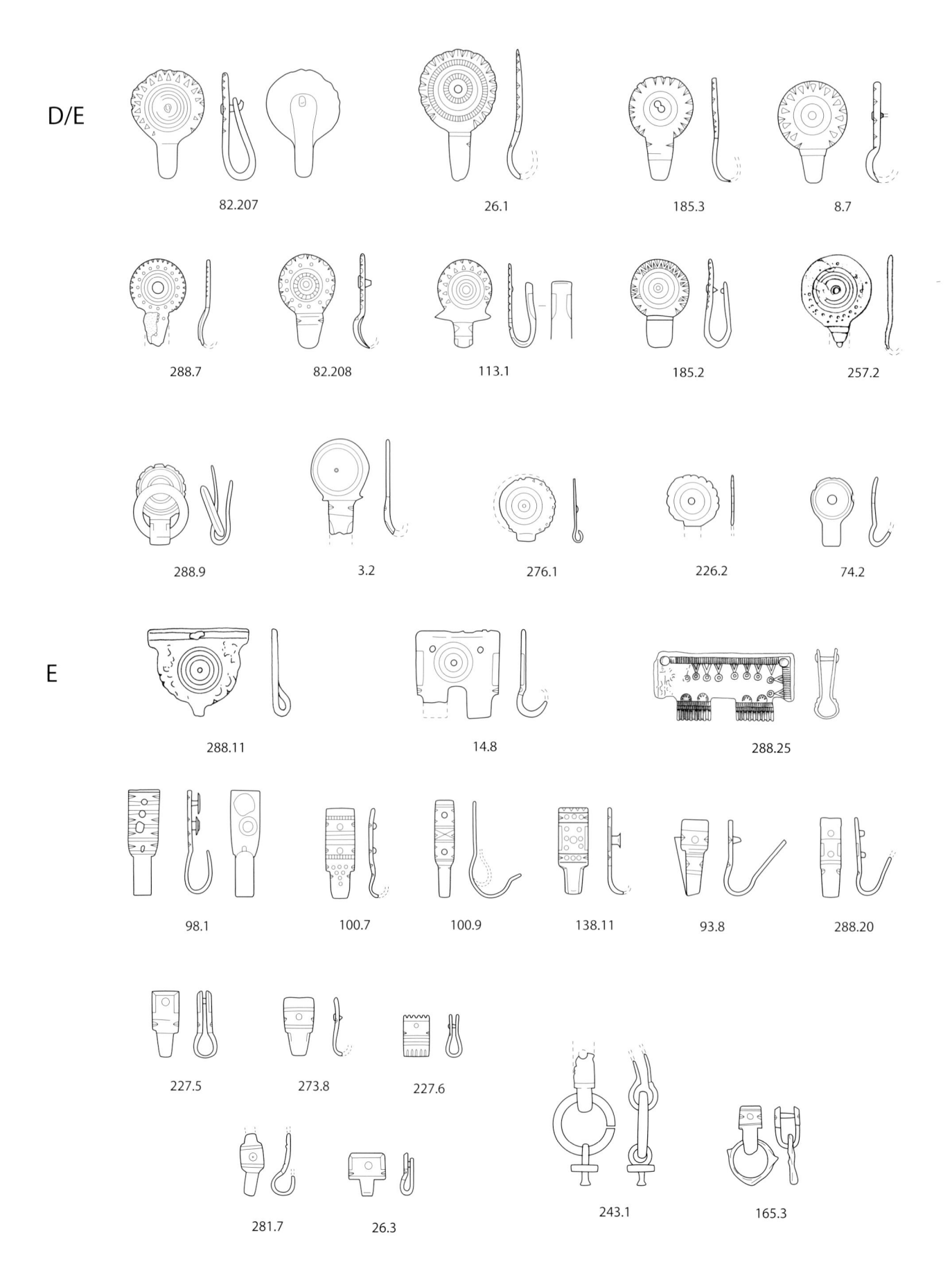

D/E

82.207 26.1 185.3 8.7

288.7 82.208 113.1 185.2 257.2

288.9 3.2 276.1 226.2 74.2

E

288.11 14.8 288.25

98.1 100.7 100.9 138.11 93.8 288.20

227.5 273.8 227.6 243.1 165.3

281.7 26.3

Pl. 45 Belt fittings, period 4. Scale 2:3.

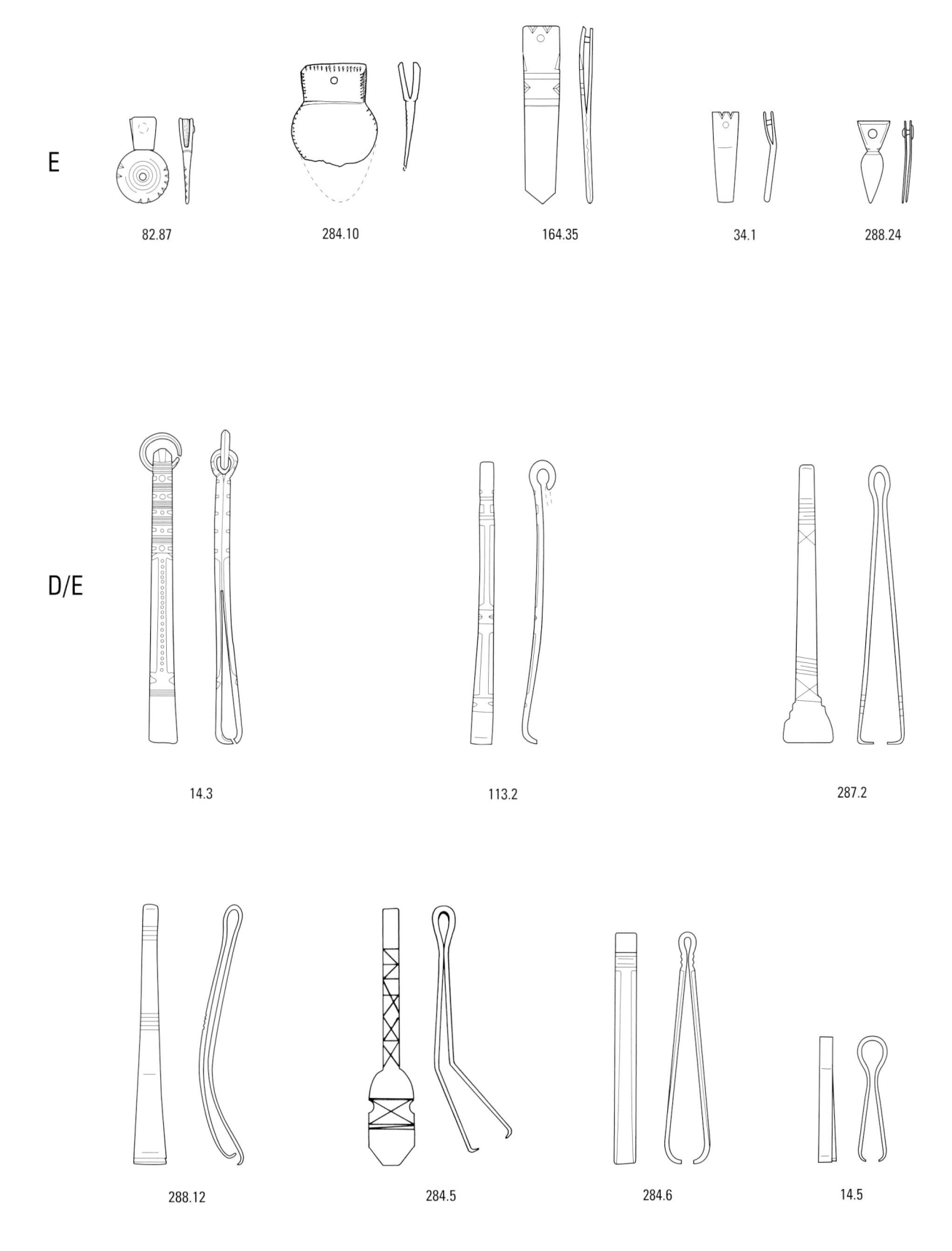

E

82.87   284.10   164.35   34.1   288.24

D/E

14.3   113.2   287.2

288.12   284.5   284.6   14.5

Pl. 46 Belt strap terminals and tweezers, period 4. Scale 2:3.

357

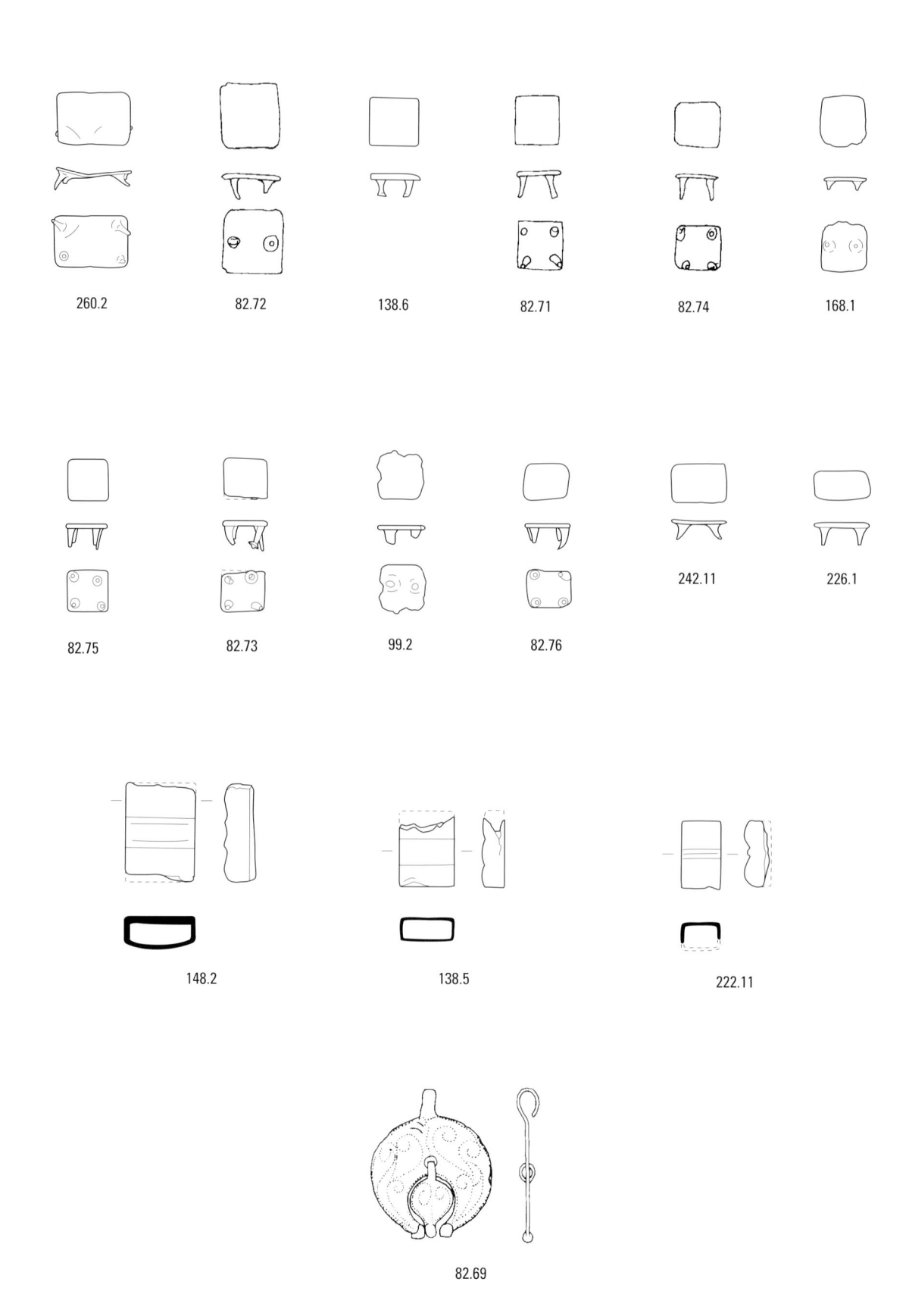

Pl. 47 Decorative apron fittings, casings and pendant, period 2. Scale 2:3.

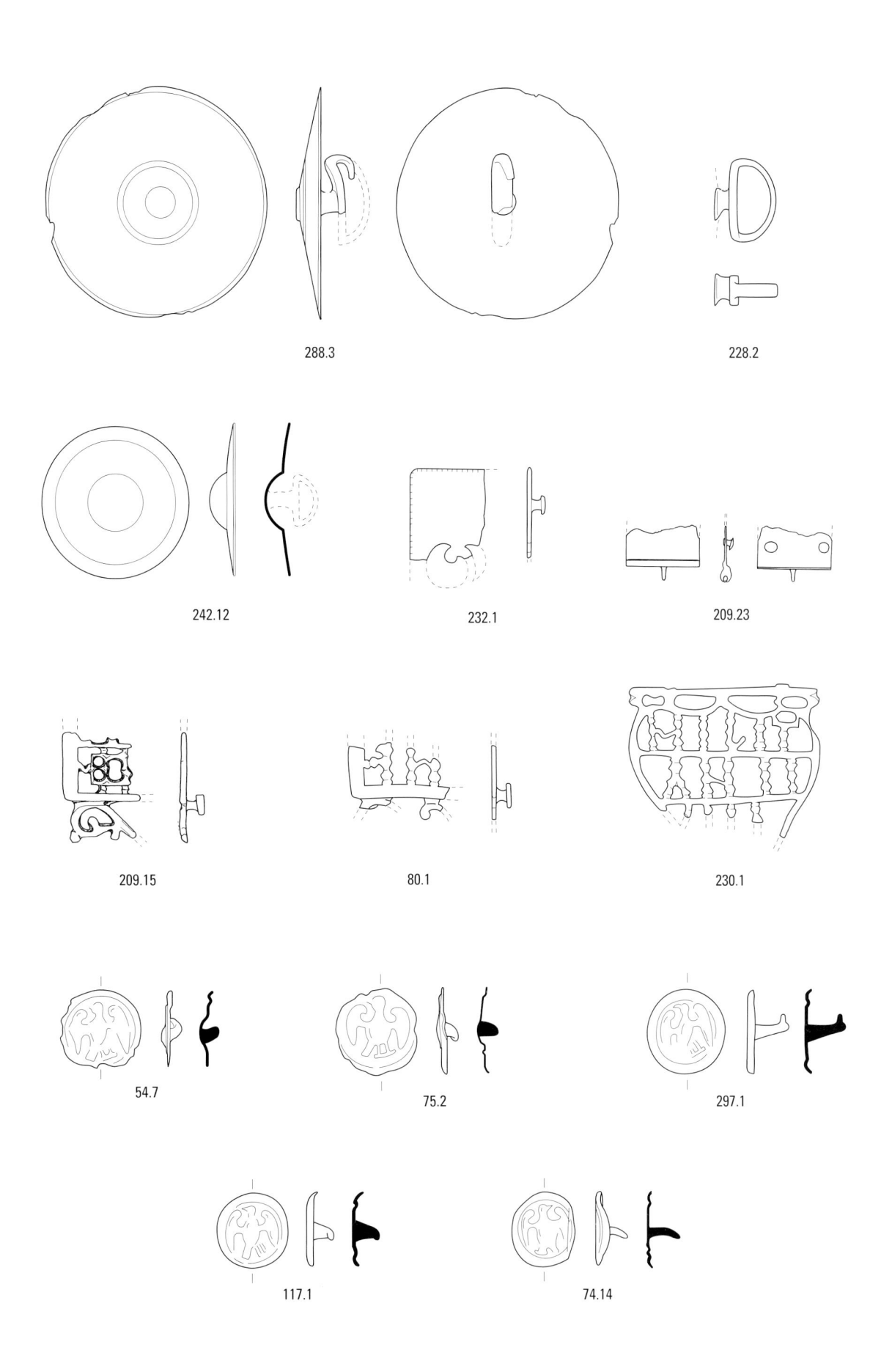

Pl. 48 Baldric *phalerae*, strap terminals, pendant and decorative fittings, period 3. Scale 2:3.

A

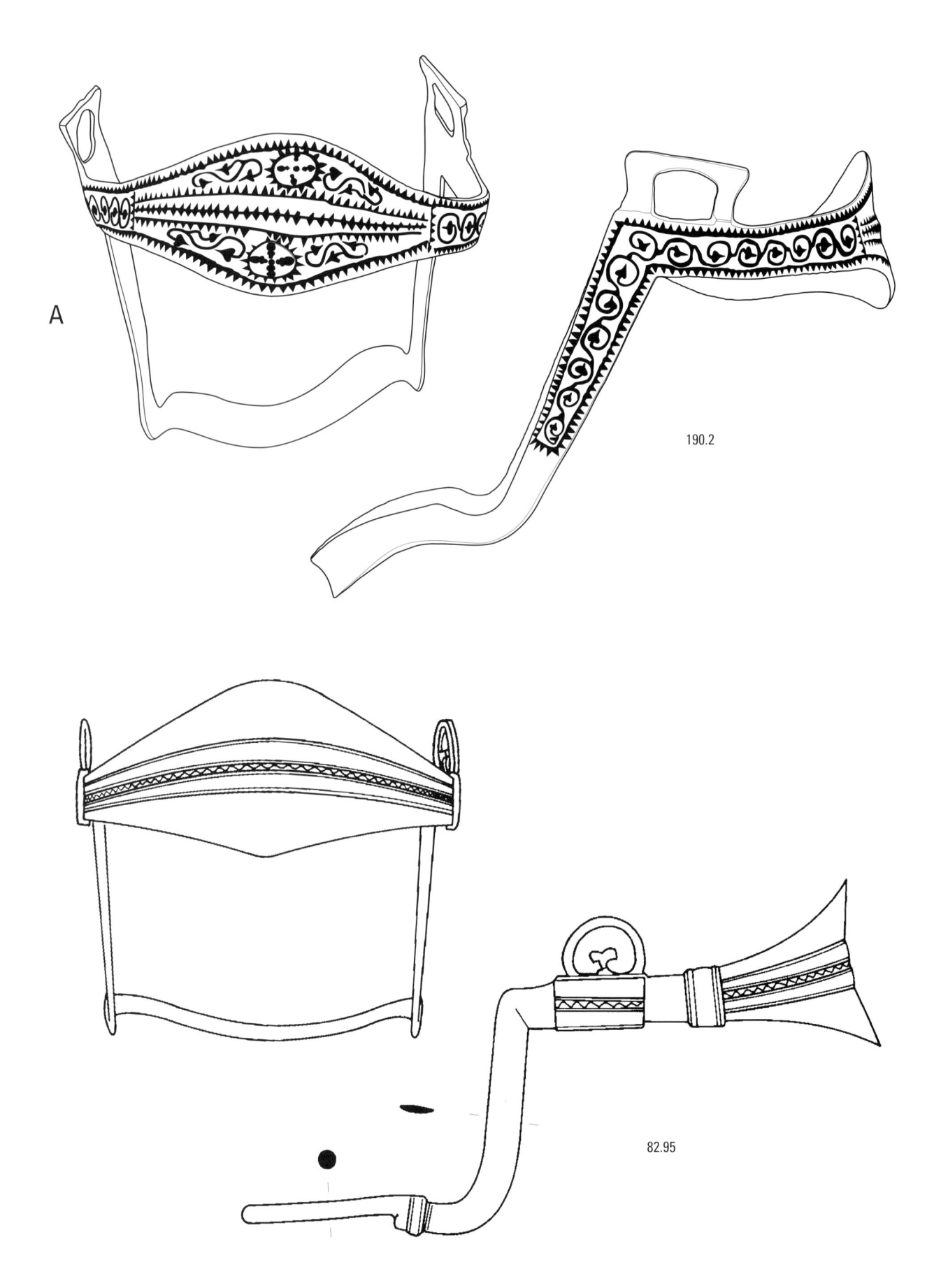

190.2

82.95

Pl. 49 Hackamores, periods 2-3. Scale 2:3.

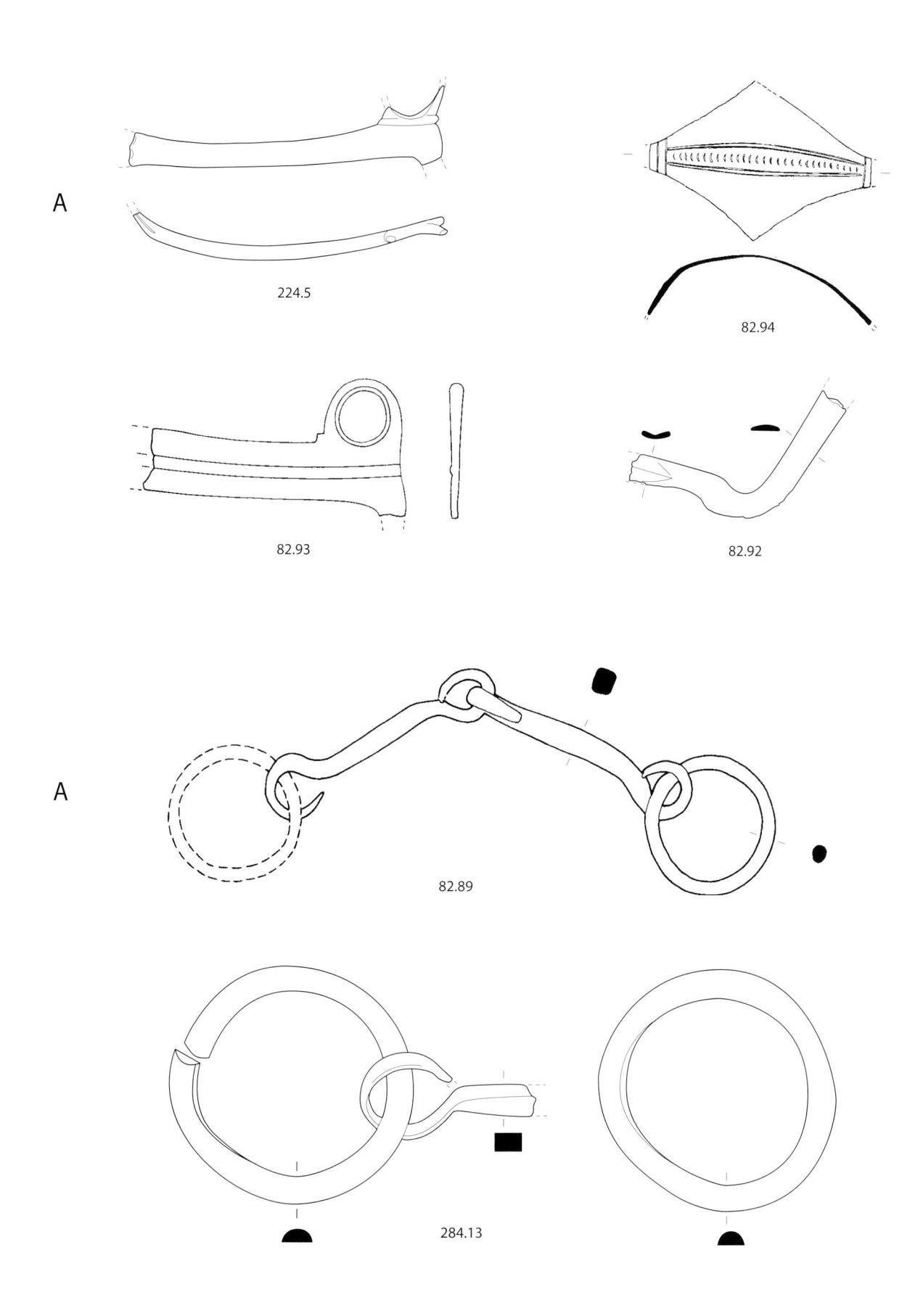

Pl. 50 Hackamores and bits, periods 2–3. Scale 2:3.

361

A

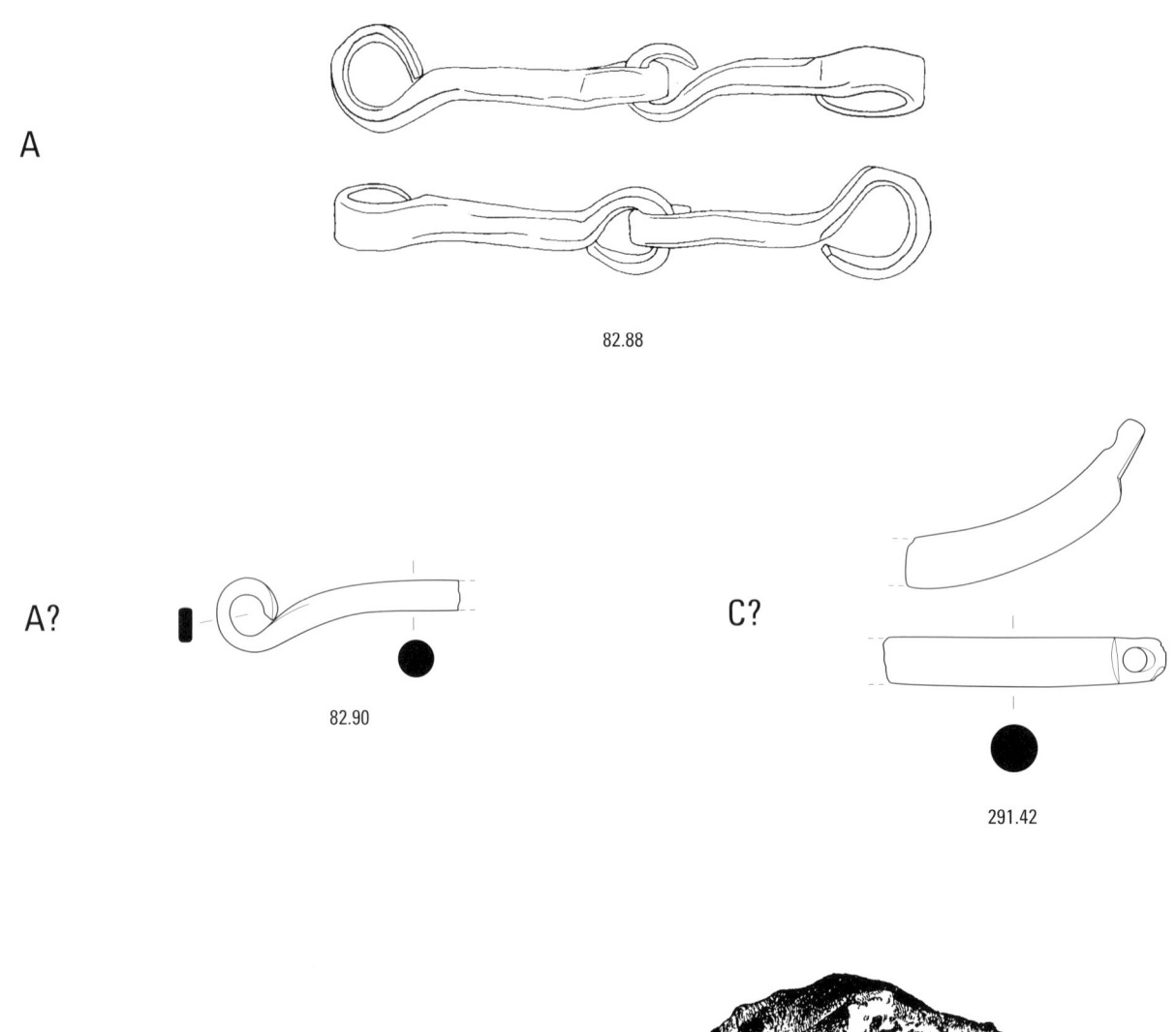

82.88

A?

82.90

C?

291.42

C1

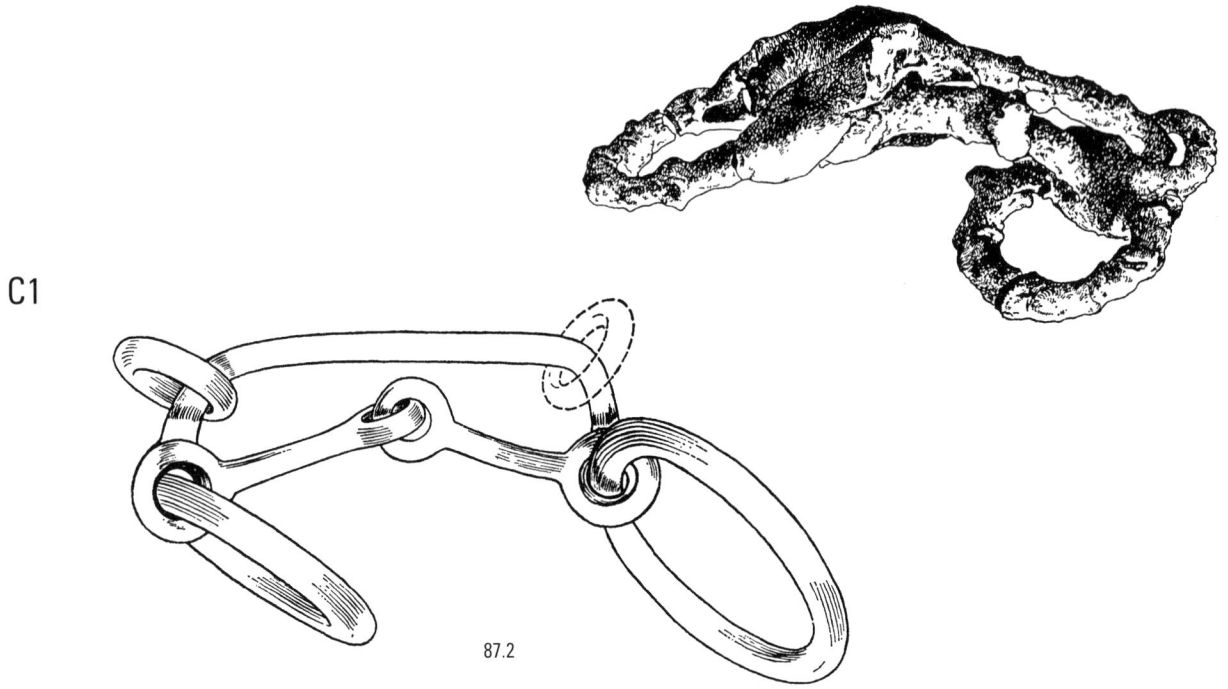

87.2

Pl. 51 Bits, periods 2–3. Scale 2:3; 1:2 (87.2).

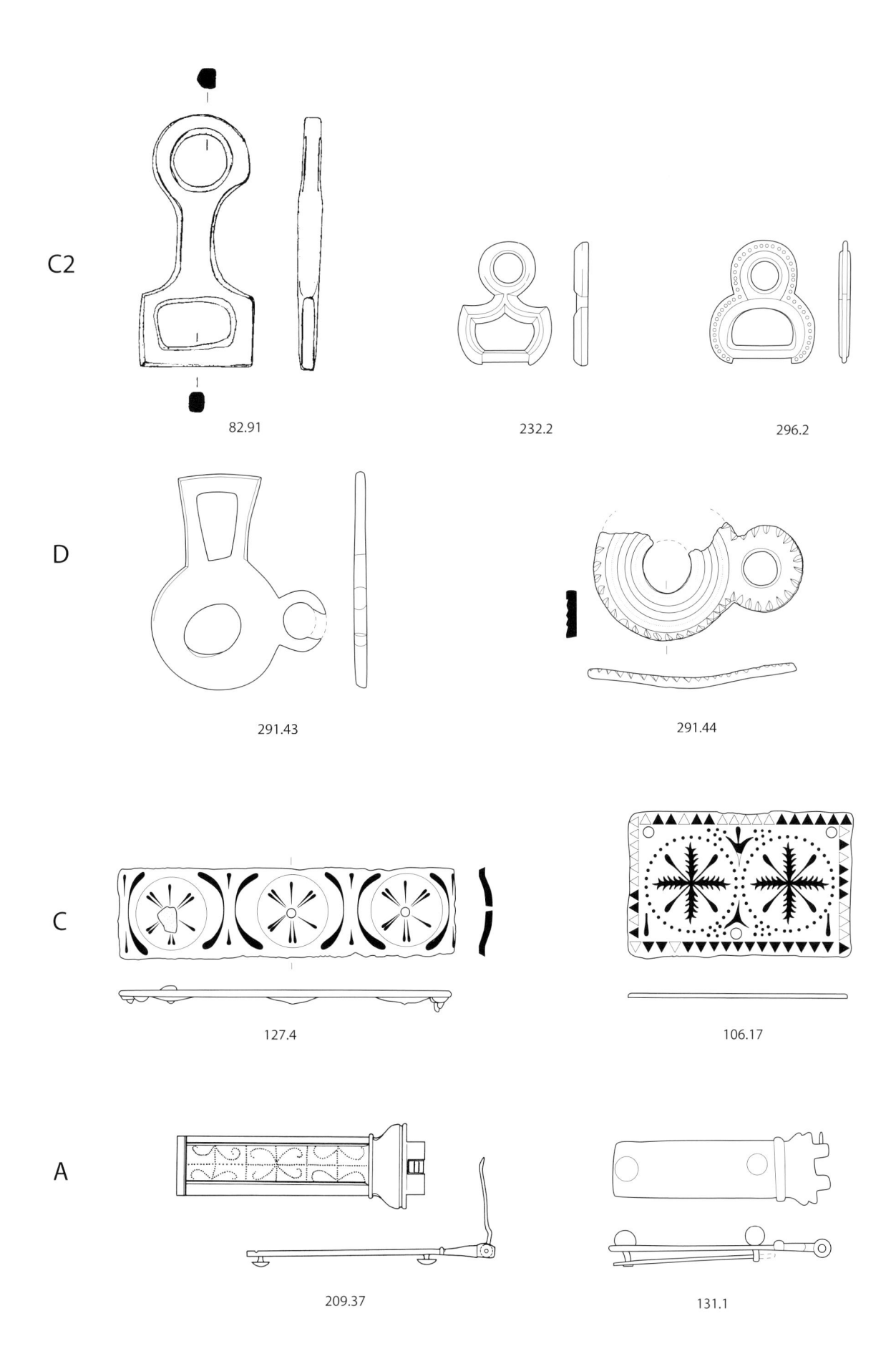

C2

82.91

232.2

296.2

D

291.43

291.44

C

127.4

106.17

A

209.37

131.1

Pl. 52 Bit shanks, decorative saddle straps and fasteners, periods 2–3. Scale 2:3.

363

A

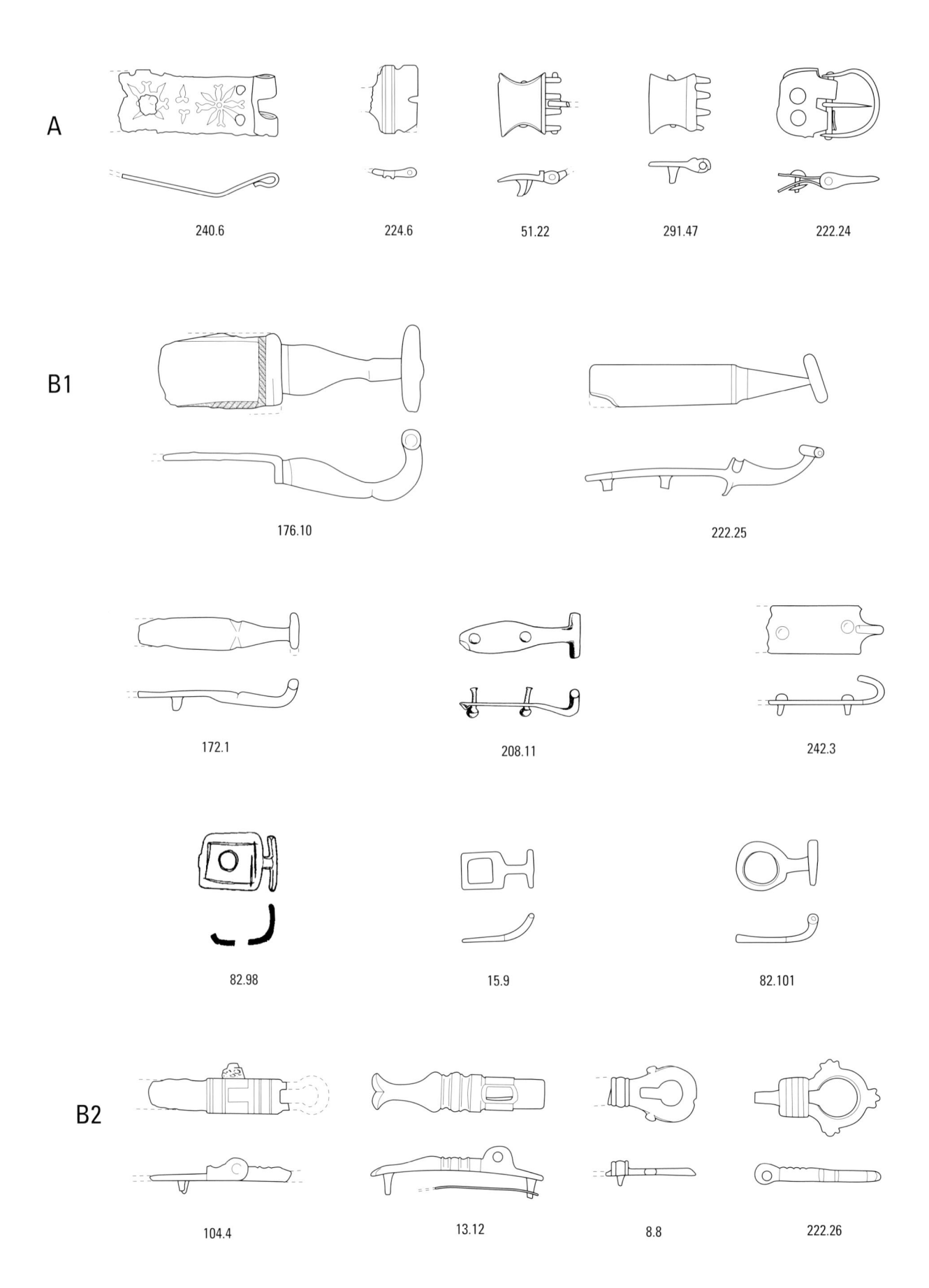

240.6   224.6   51.22   291.47   222.24

B1

176.10   222.25

172.1   208.11   242.3

82.98   15.9   82.101

B2

104.4   13.12   8.8   222.26

Pl. 53 Horse gear fasteners, period 2. Scale 2:3.

C

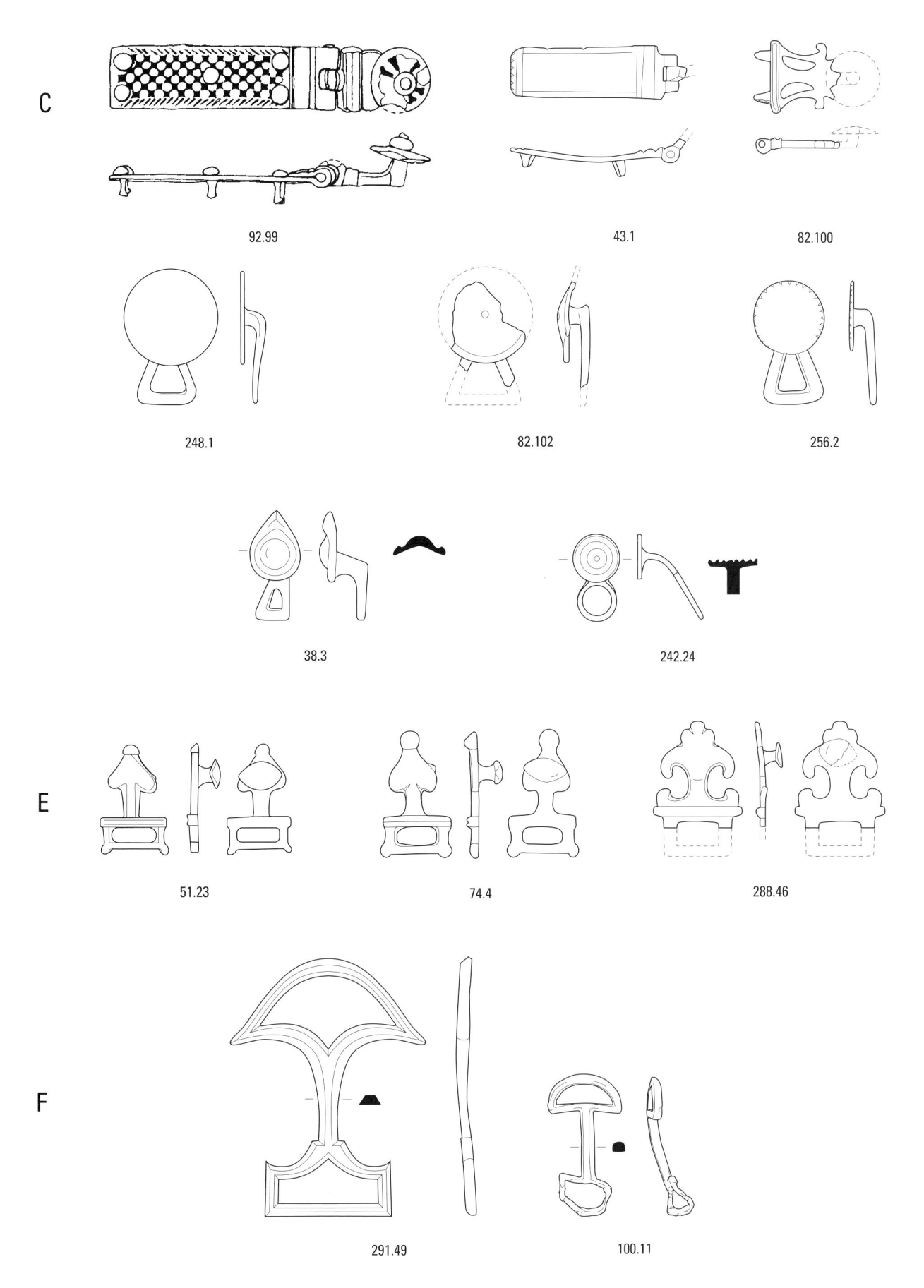

92.99   43.1   82.100

248.1   82.102   256.2

38.3   242.24

E

51.23   74.4   288.46

F

291.49   100.11

Pl. 54 Horse gear fasteners, periods 2-3. Scale 2:3.

365

A1

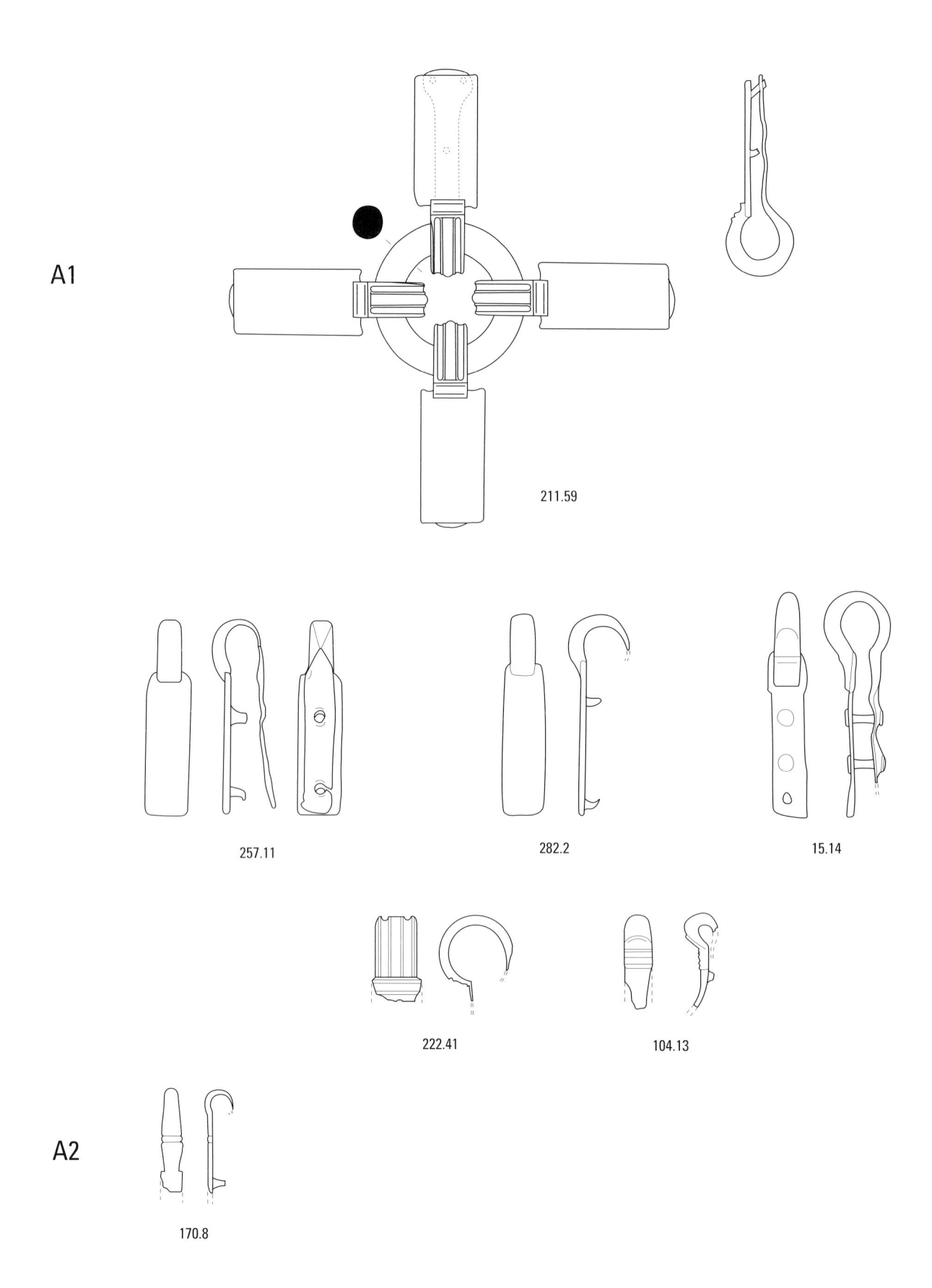

211.59

257.11　　　282.2　　　15.14

222.41　　　104.13

A2

170.8

Pl. 55 Horse gear strap junctions, period 2. Scale 2:3.

A3

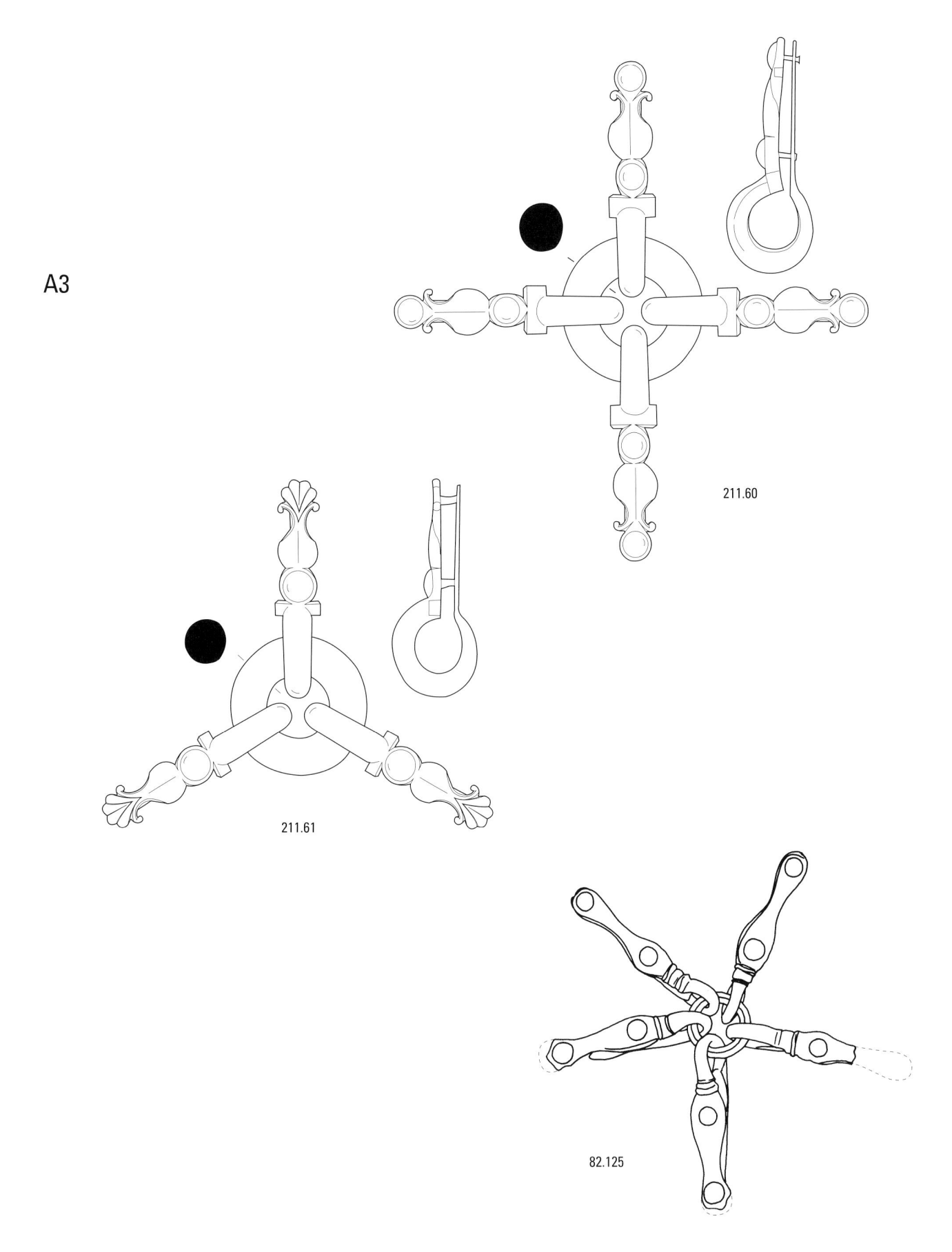

211.60

211.61

82.125

Pl. 56 Horse gear strap junctions, period 2. Scale 2:3.

367

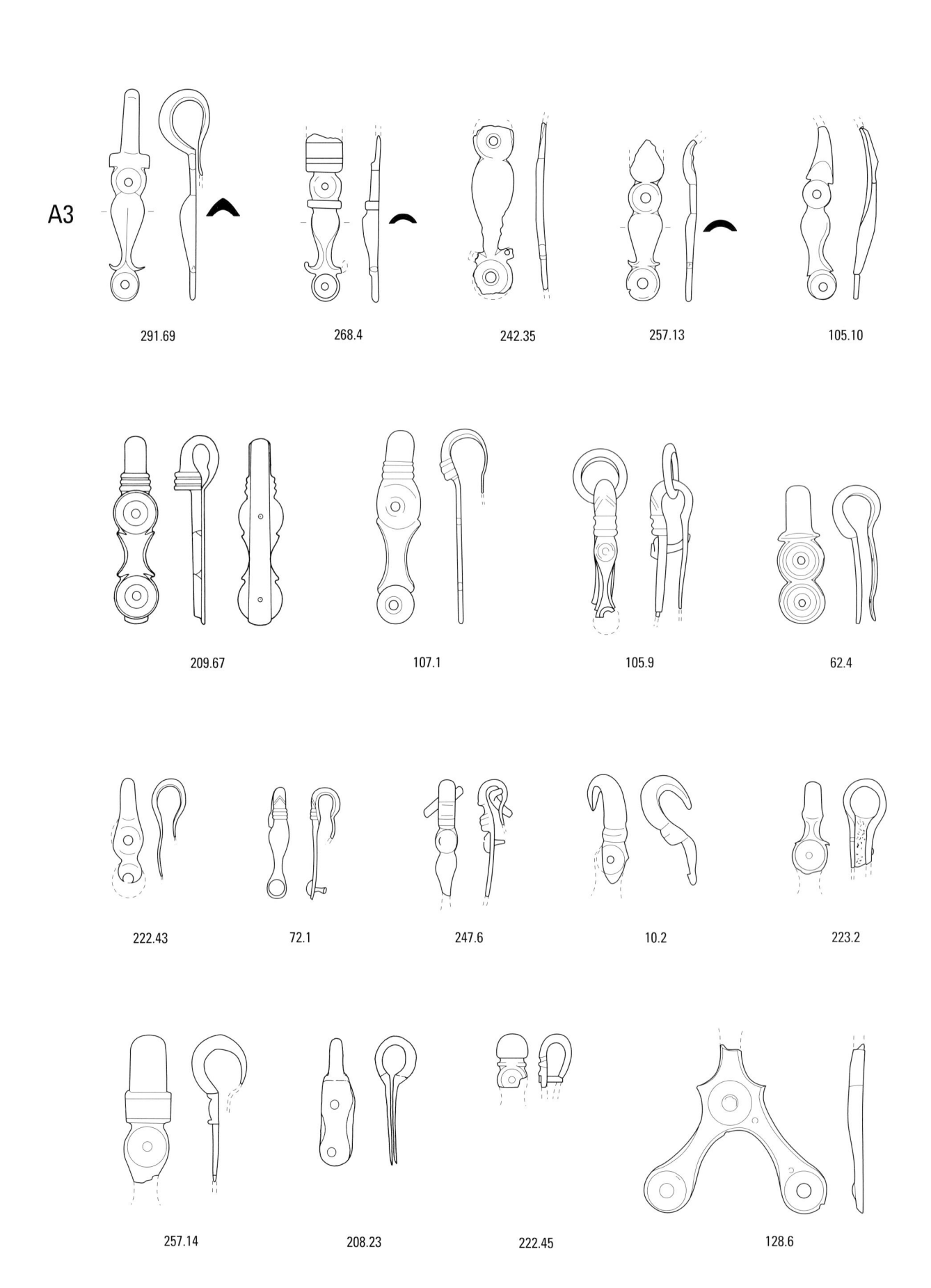

A3

291.69 268.4 242.35 257.13 105.10

209.67 107.1 105.9 62.4

222.43 72.1 247.6 10.2 223.2

257.14 208.23 222.45 128.6

Pl. 57 Horse gear strap junctions, period 2. Scale 2:3.

A4

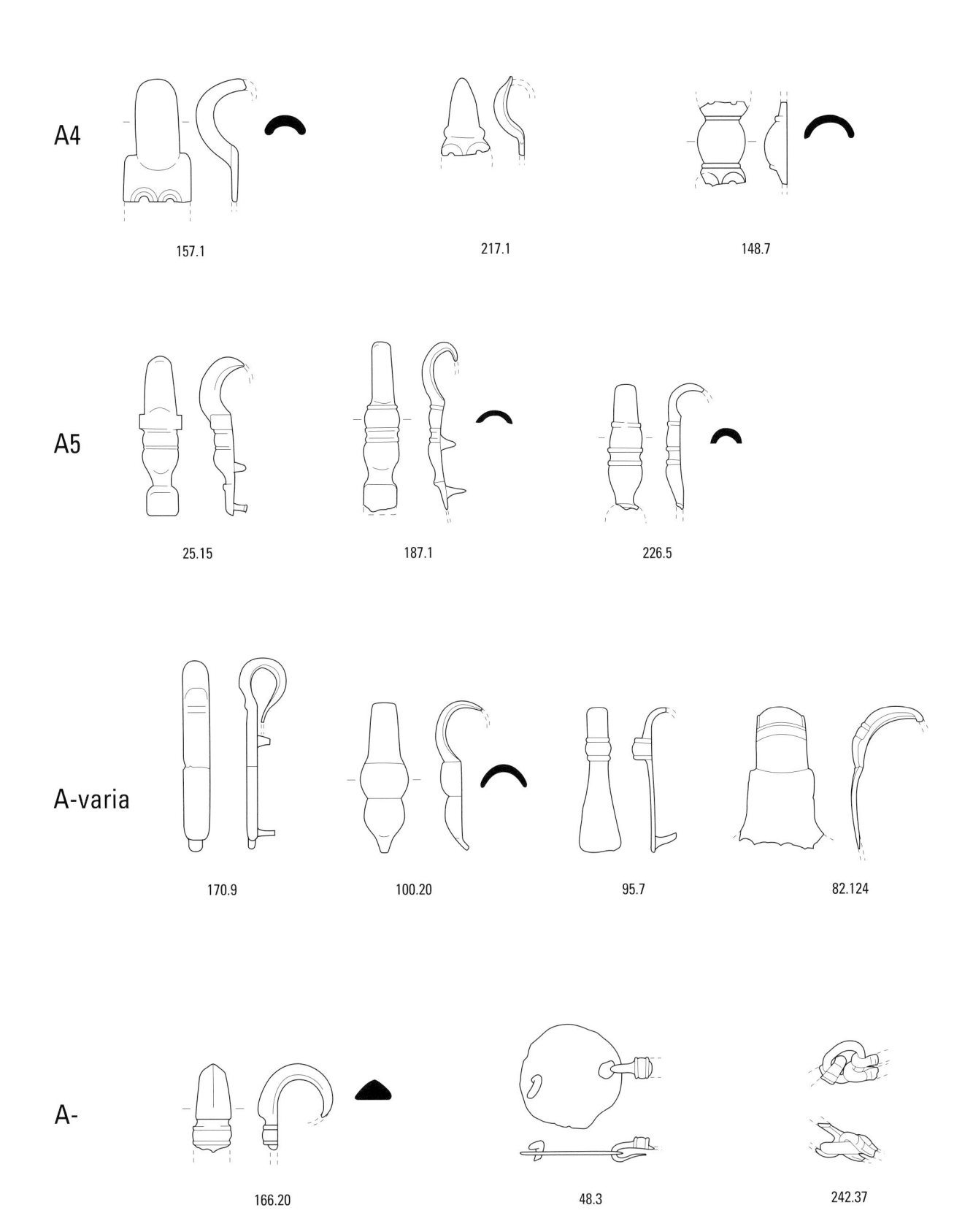

157.1

217.1

148.7

A5

25.15

187.1

226.5

A-varia

170.9

100.20

95.7

82.124

A-

166.20

48.3

242.37

Pl. 58 Horse gear strap junctions, period 2. Scale 2:3.

B

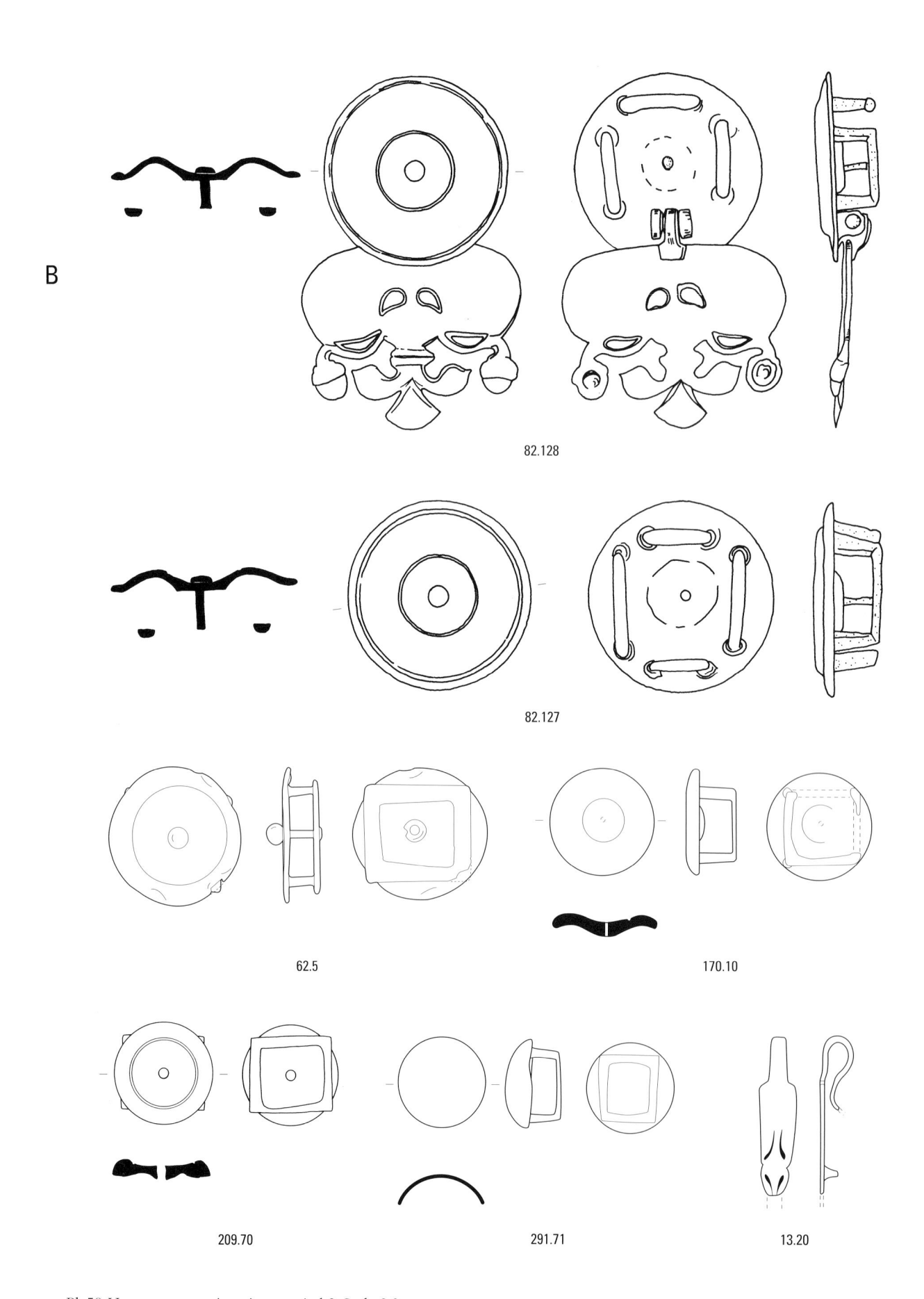

82.128

82.127

62.5 170.10

209.70 291.71 13.20

Pl. 59 Horse gear strap junctions, period 2. Scale 2:3.

C

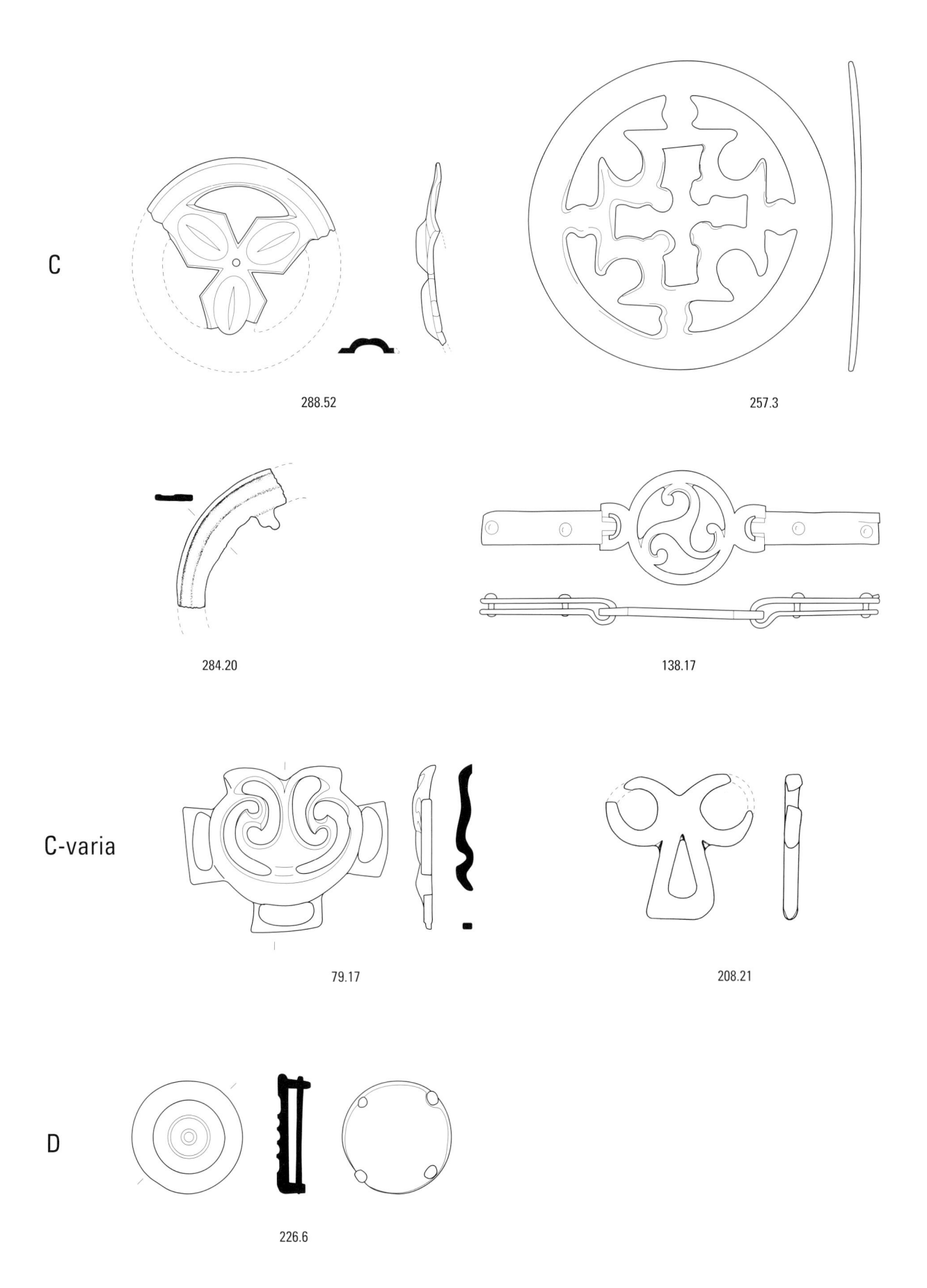

288.52

257.3

284.20

138.17

C-varia

79.17

208.21

D

226.6

Pl. 60 Horse gear strap junctions, period 3. Scale 2:3.

A1

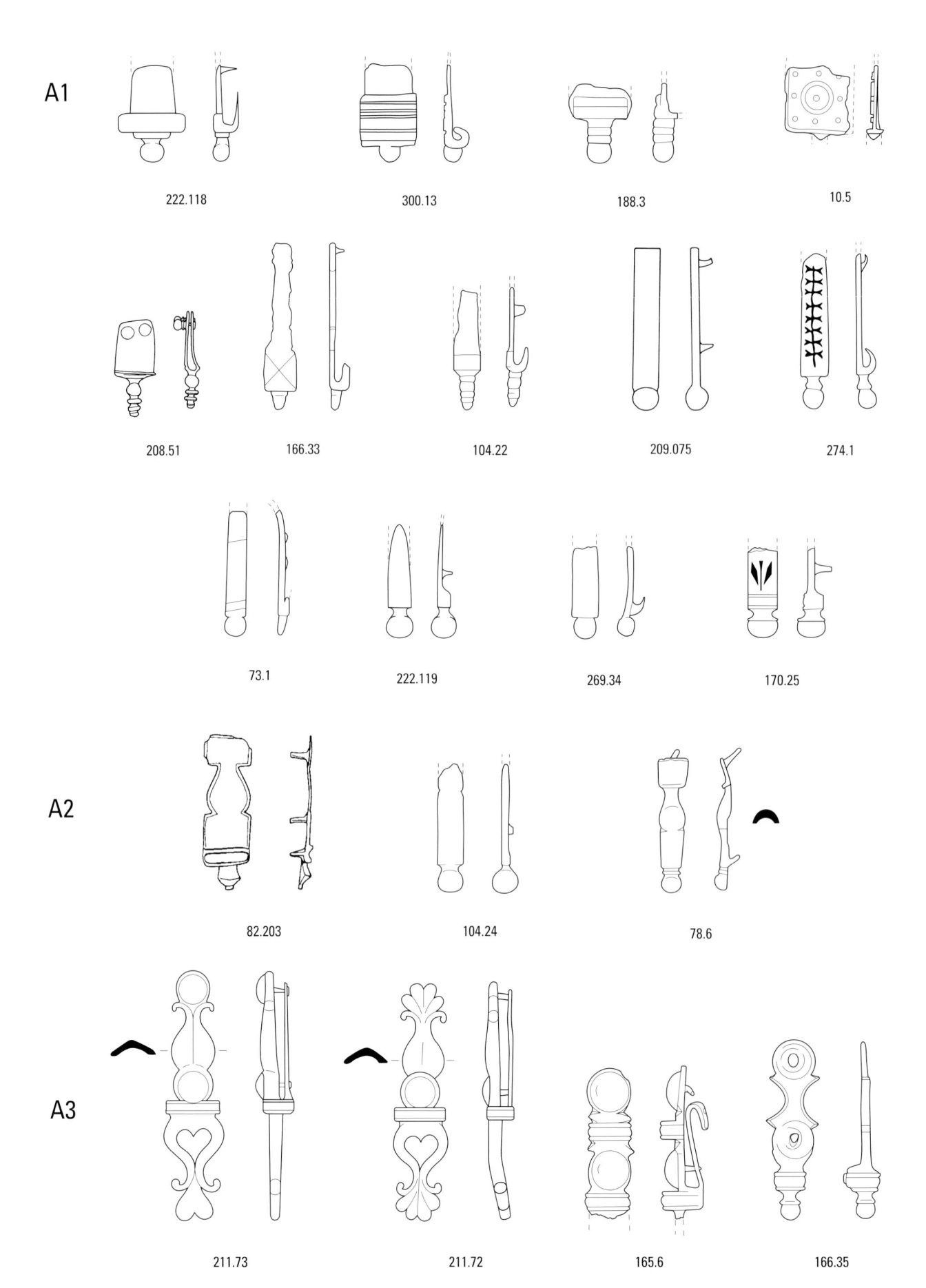

222.118   300.13   188.3   10.5

208.51   166.33   104.22   209.075   274.1

73.1   222.119   269.34   170.25

A2

82.203   104.24   78.6

A3

211.73   211.72   165.6   166.35

Pl. 61 Horse gear strap terminals, period 2. Scale 2:3.

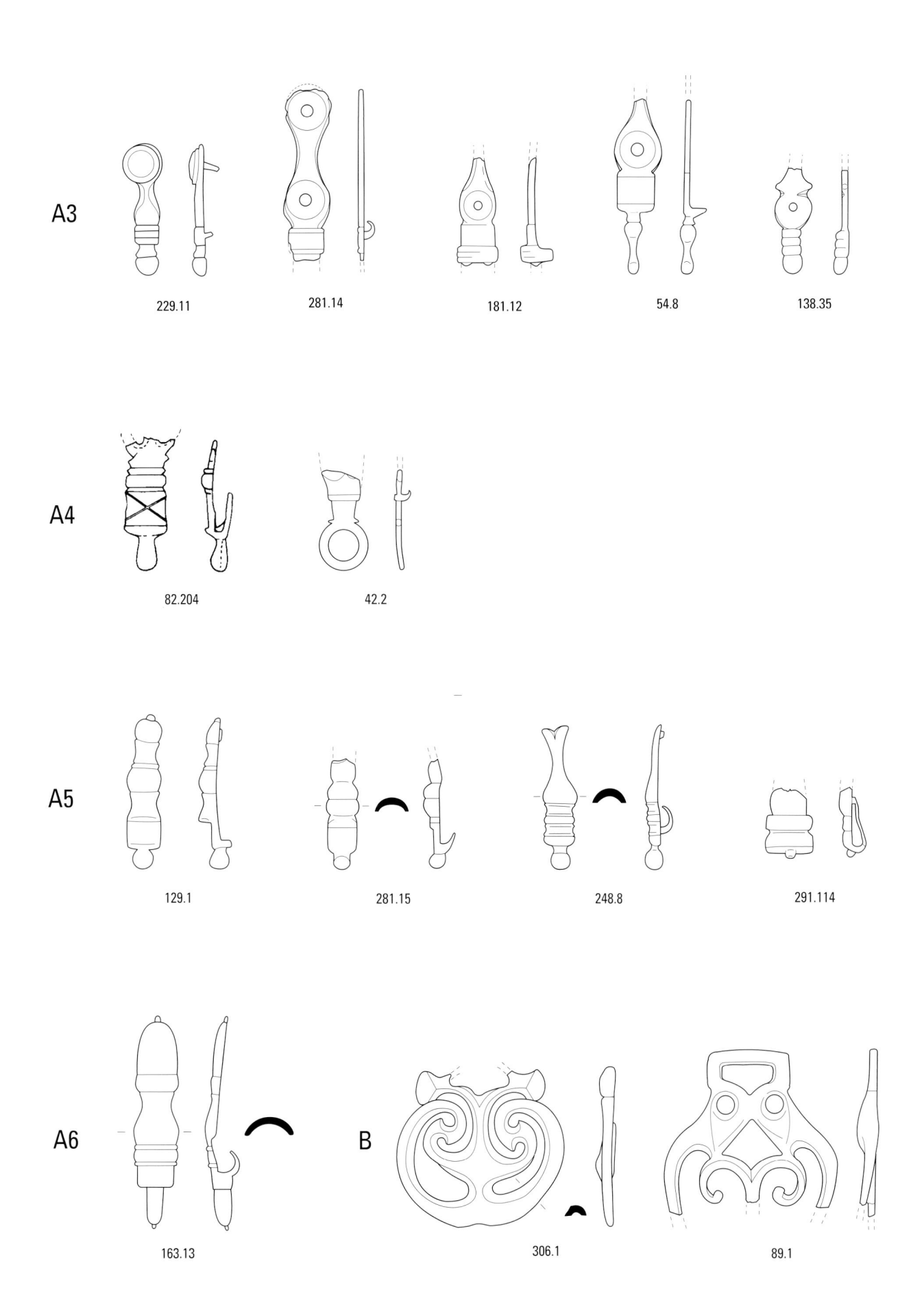

Pl. 62 Horse gear strap terminals, periods 2–3. Scale 2:3.

A1

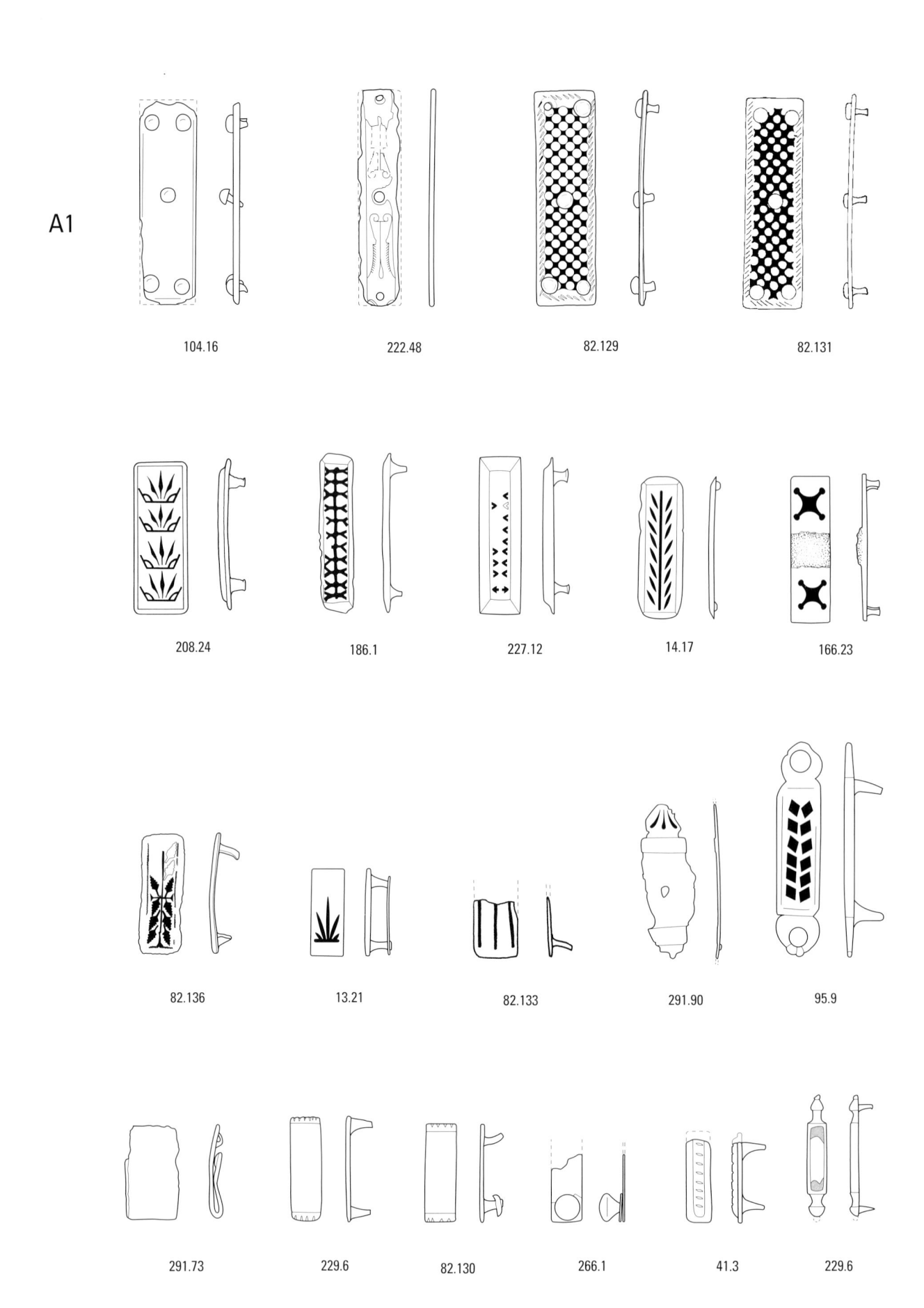

| 104.16 | 222.48 | 82.129 | 82.131 |

| 208.24 | 186.1 | 227.12 | 14.17 | 166.23 |

| 82.136 | 13.21 | 82.133 | 291.90 | 95.9 |

| 291.73 | 229.6 | 82.130 | 266.1 | 41.3 | 229.6 |

Pl. 63 Decorative horse gear fittings, period 2. Scale 2:3.

374

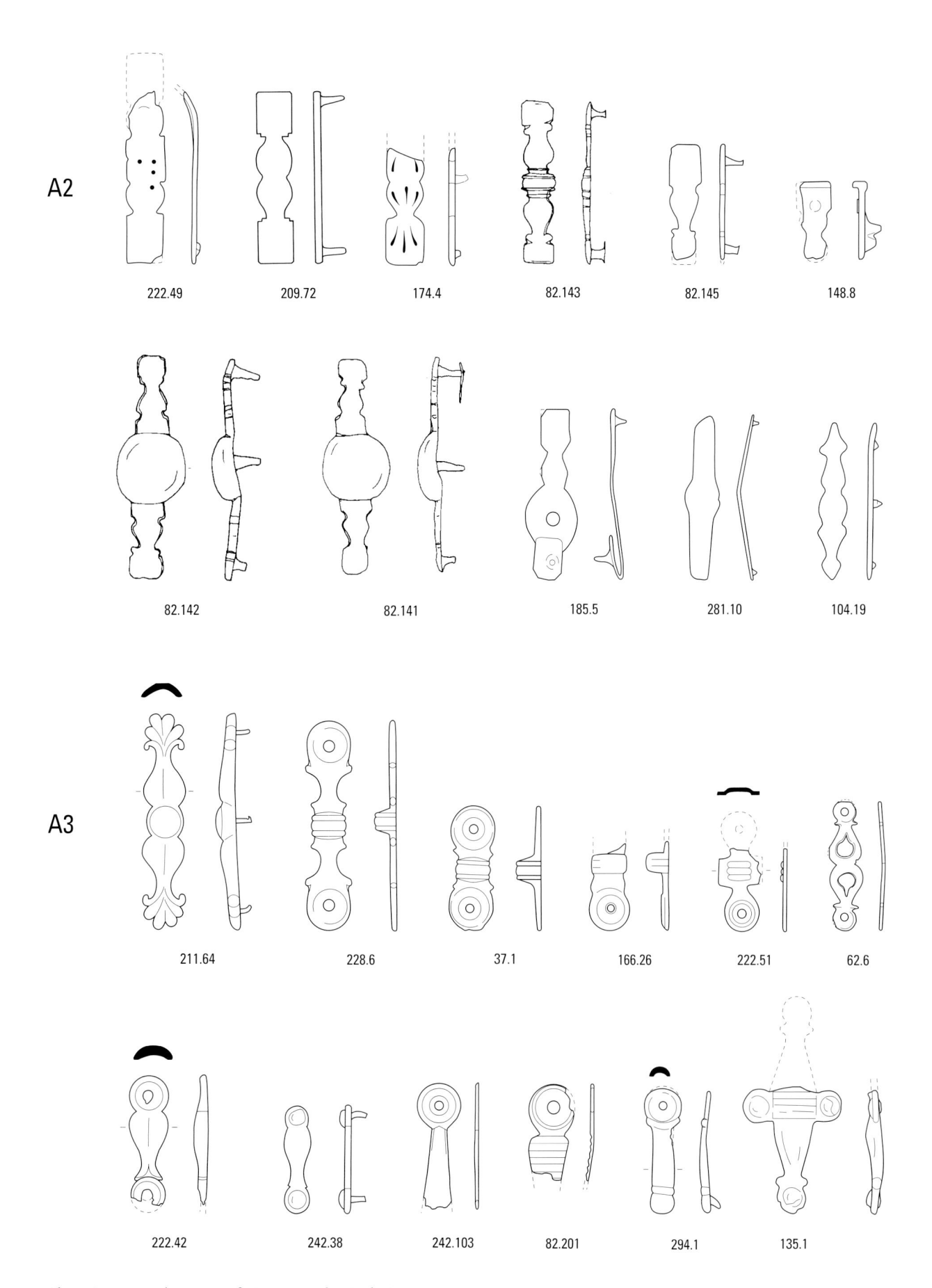

A2

222.49   209.72   174.4   82.143   82.145   148.8

82.142   82.141   185.5   281.10   104.19

A3

211.64   228.6   37.1   166.26   222.51   62.6

222.42   242.38   242.103   82.201   294.1   135.1

Pl. 64 Decorative horse gear fittings, period 2. Scale 2:3.

375

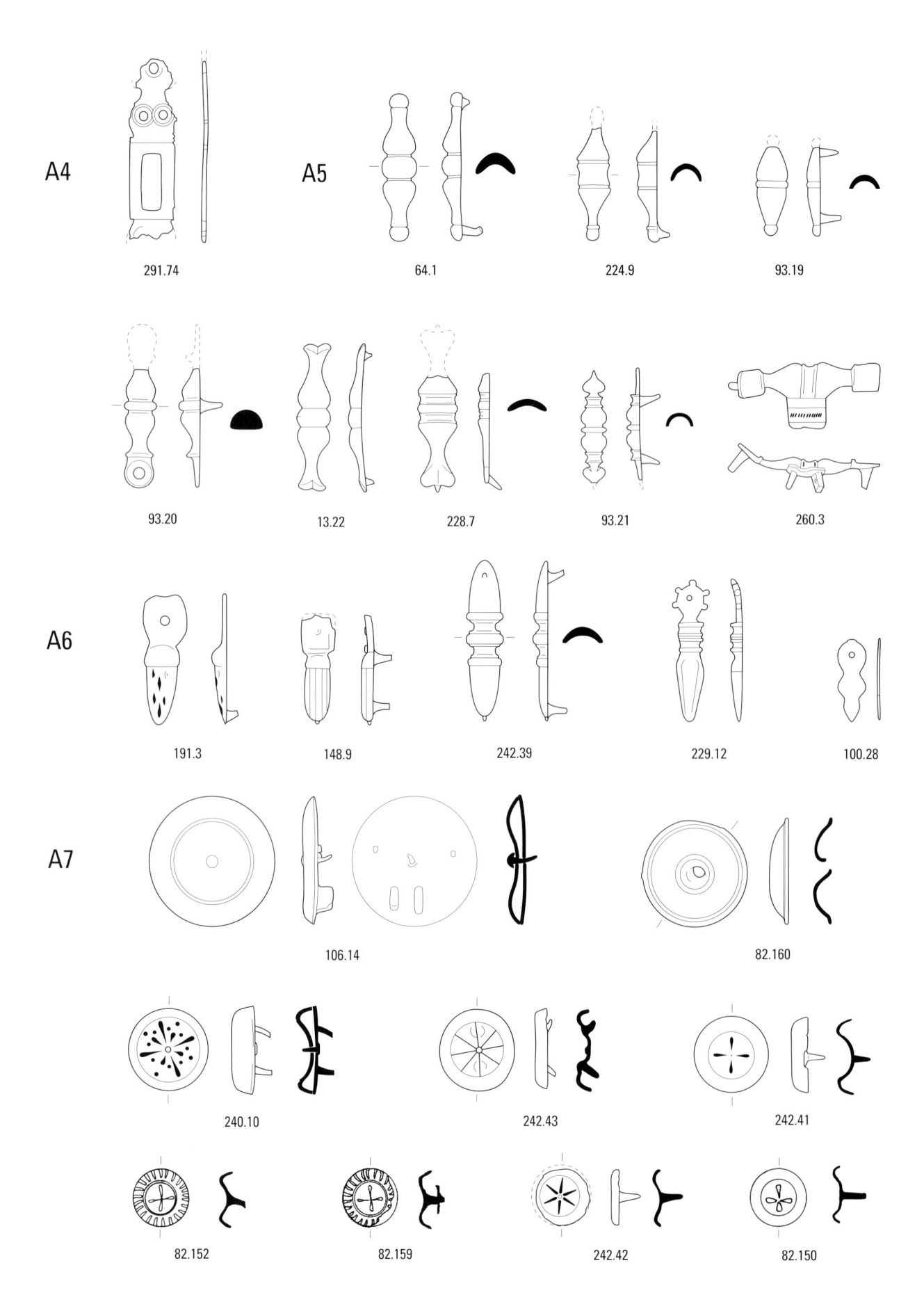

A4 291.74

A5 64.1   224.9   93.19

93.20   13.22   228.7   93.21   260.3

A6 191.3   148.9   242.39   229.12   100.28

A7 106.14   82.160

240.10   242.43   242.41

82.152   82.159   242.42   82.150

Pl. 65 Decorative horse gear fittings, period 2. Scale 2:3.

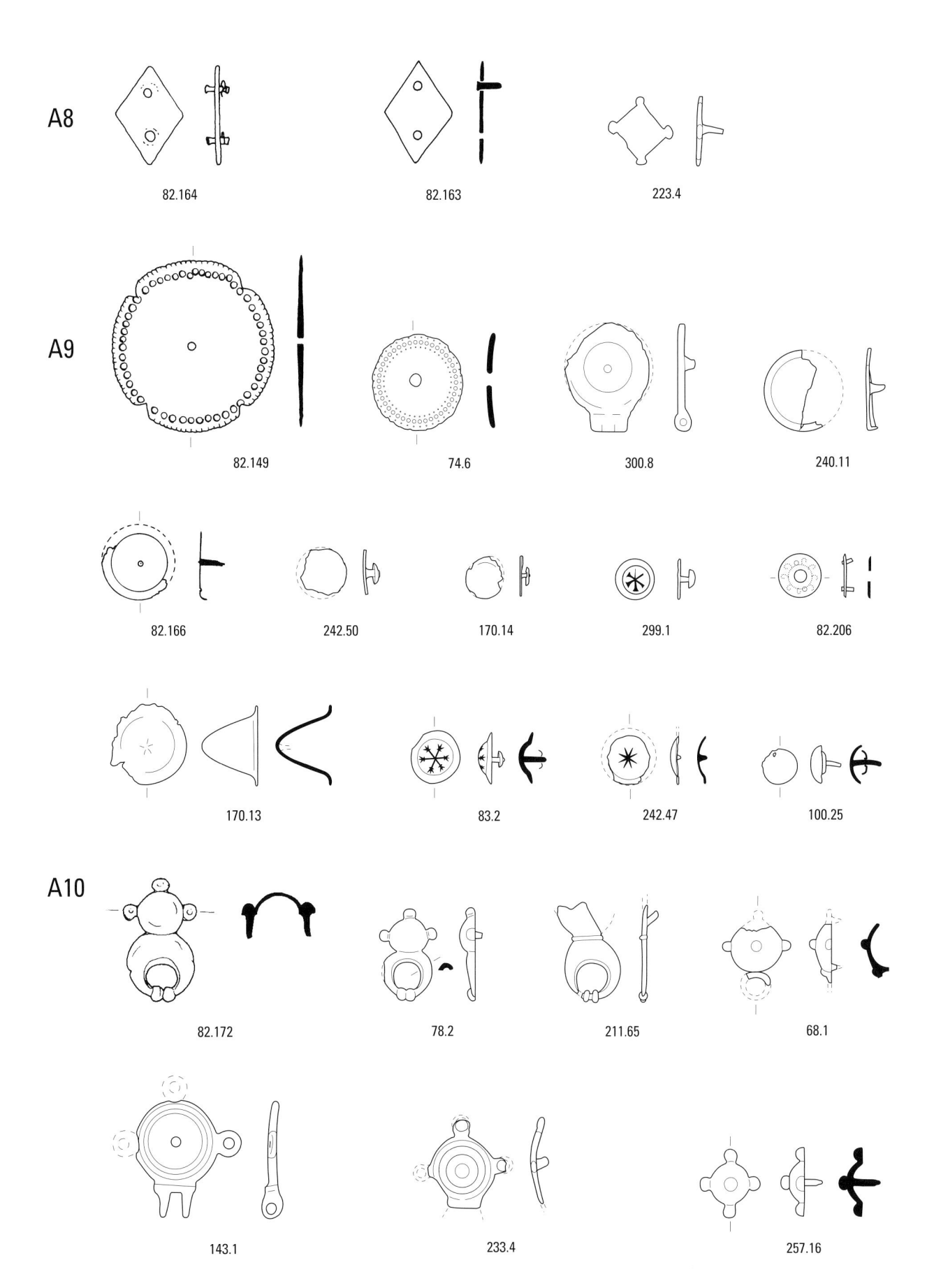

A8

82.164   82.163   223.4

A9

82.149   74.6   300.8   240.11

82.166   242.50   170.14   299.1   82.206

170.13   83.2   242.47   100.25

A10

82.172   78.2   211.65   68.1

143.1   233.4   257.16

Pl. 66 Decorative horse gear fittings, period 2. Scale 2:3.

377

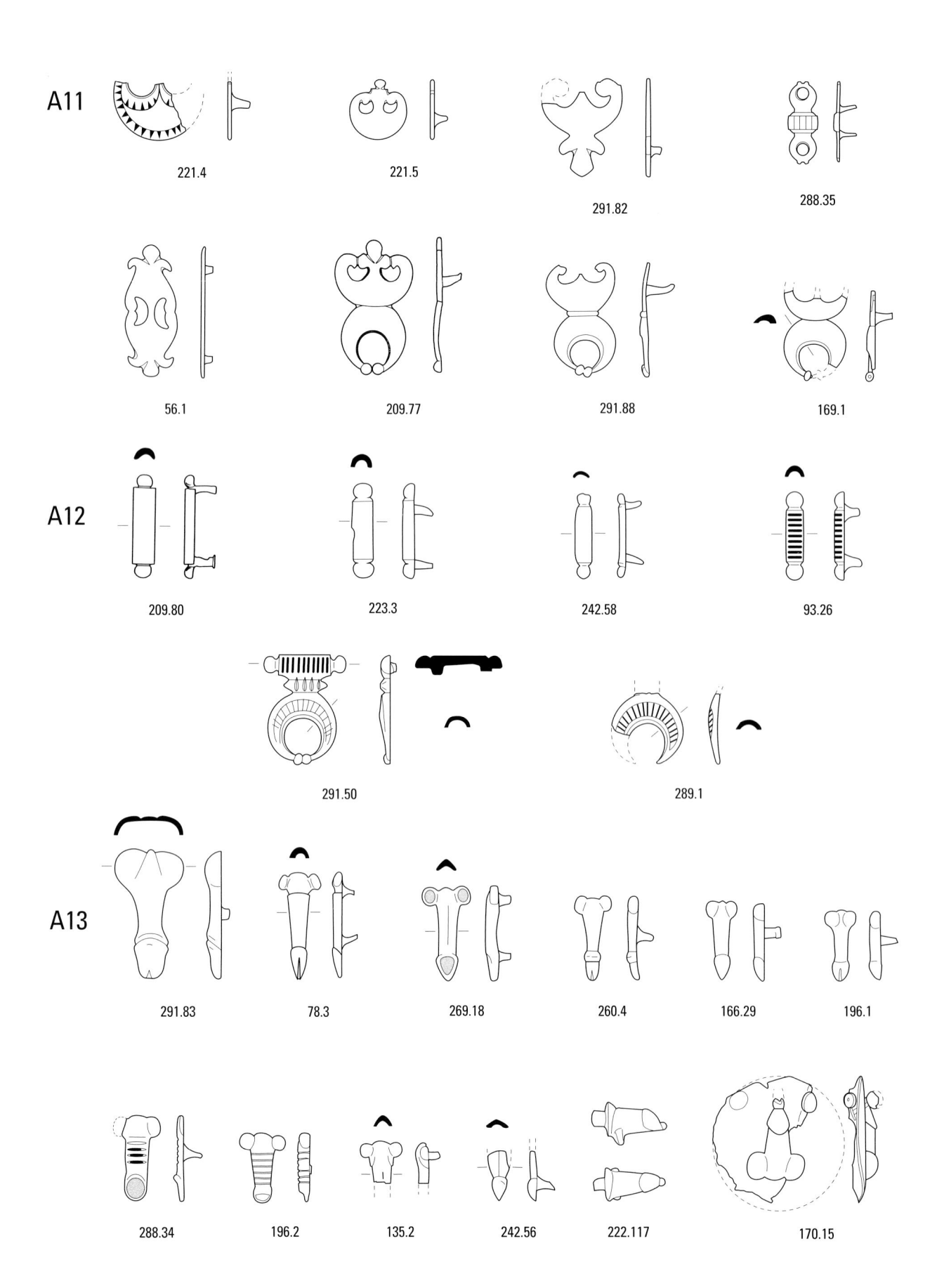

A11

221.4 221.5 291.82 288.35

56.1 209.77 291.88 169.1

A12

209.80 223.3 242.58 93.26

291.50 289.1

A13

291.83 78.3 269.18 260.4 166.29 196.1

288.34 196.2 135.2 242.56 222.117 170.15

Pl. 67 Decorative horse gear fittings, period 2. Scale 2:3.

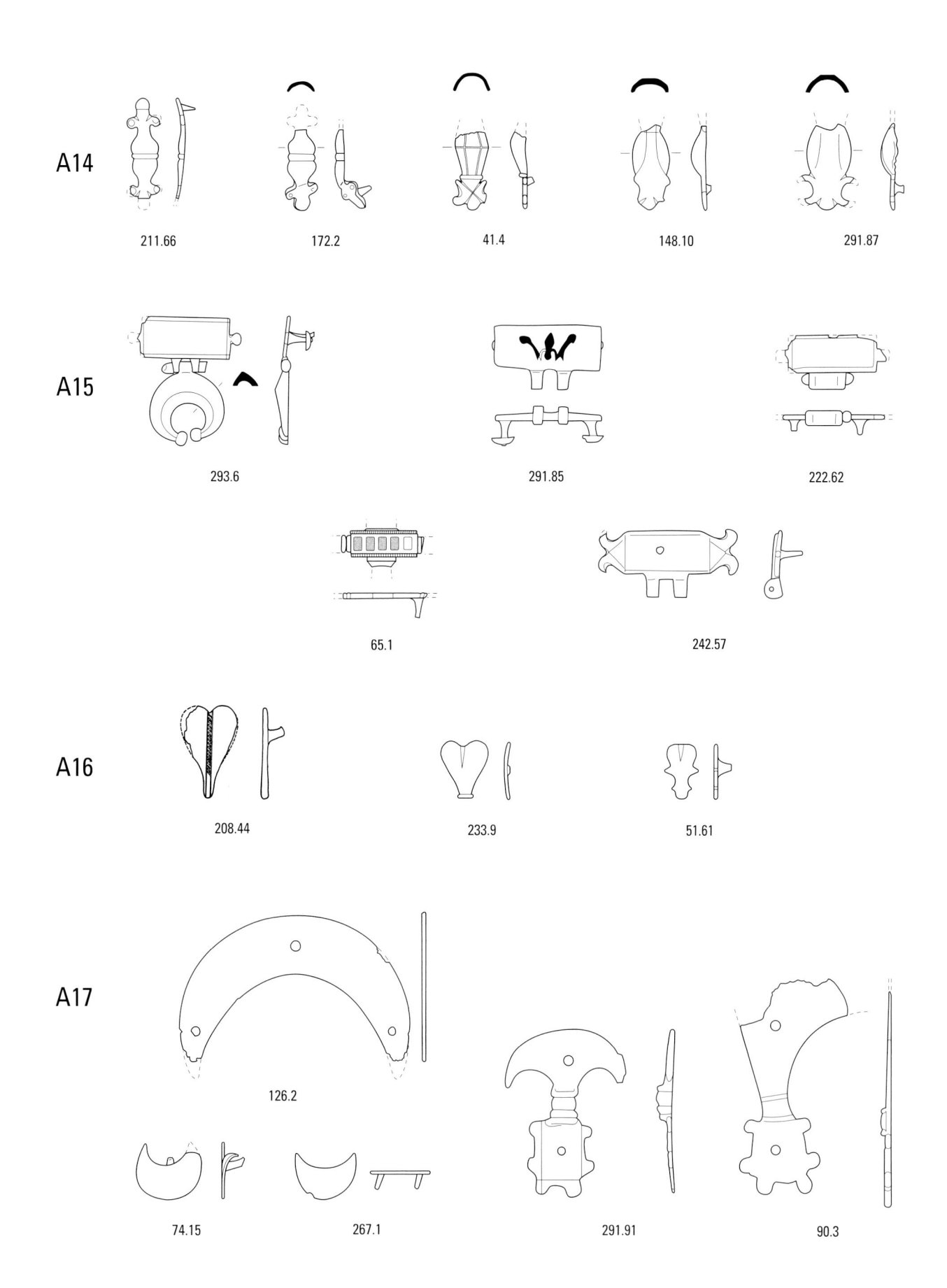

A14

211.66   172.2   41.4   148.10   291.87

A15

293.6   291.85   222.62

65.1   242.57

A16

208.44   233.9   51.61

A17

126.2

74.15   267.1   291.91   90.3

Pl. 68 Decorative horse gear fittings, period 2. Scale 2:3.

379

A-varia

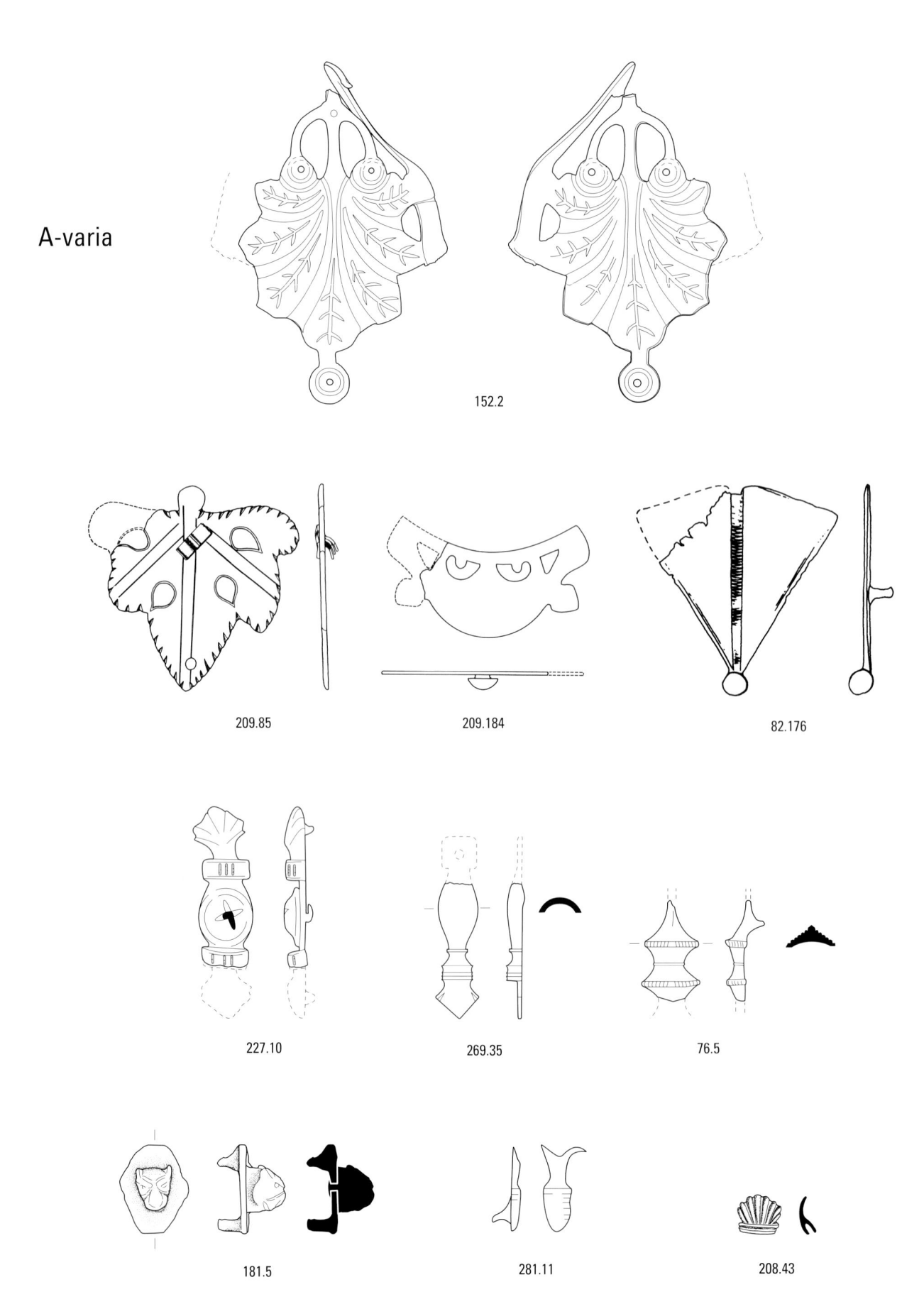

152.2

209.85   209.184   82.176

227.10   269.35   76.5

181.5   281.11   208.43

Pl. 69 Decorative horse gear fittings, period 2. Scale 2:3.

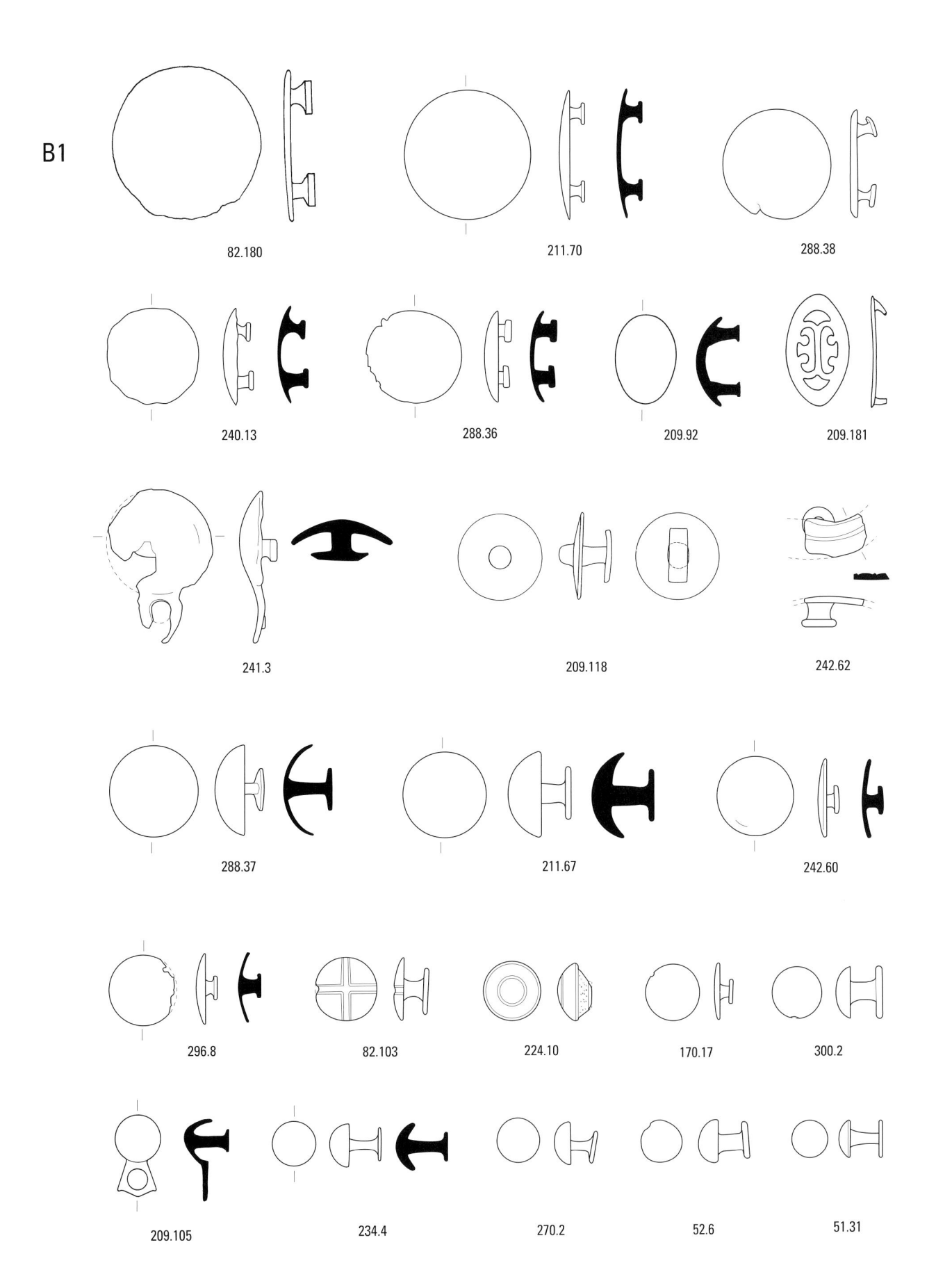

B1

82.180 211.70 288.38

240.13 288.36 209.92 209.181

241.3 209.118 242.62

288.37 211.67 242.60

296.8 82.103 224.10 170.17 300.2

209.105 234.4 270.2 52.6 51.31

Pl. 70 Decorative horse gear fittings, period 3. Scale 2:3.

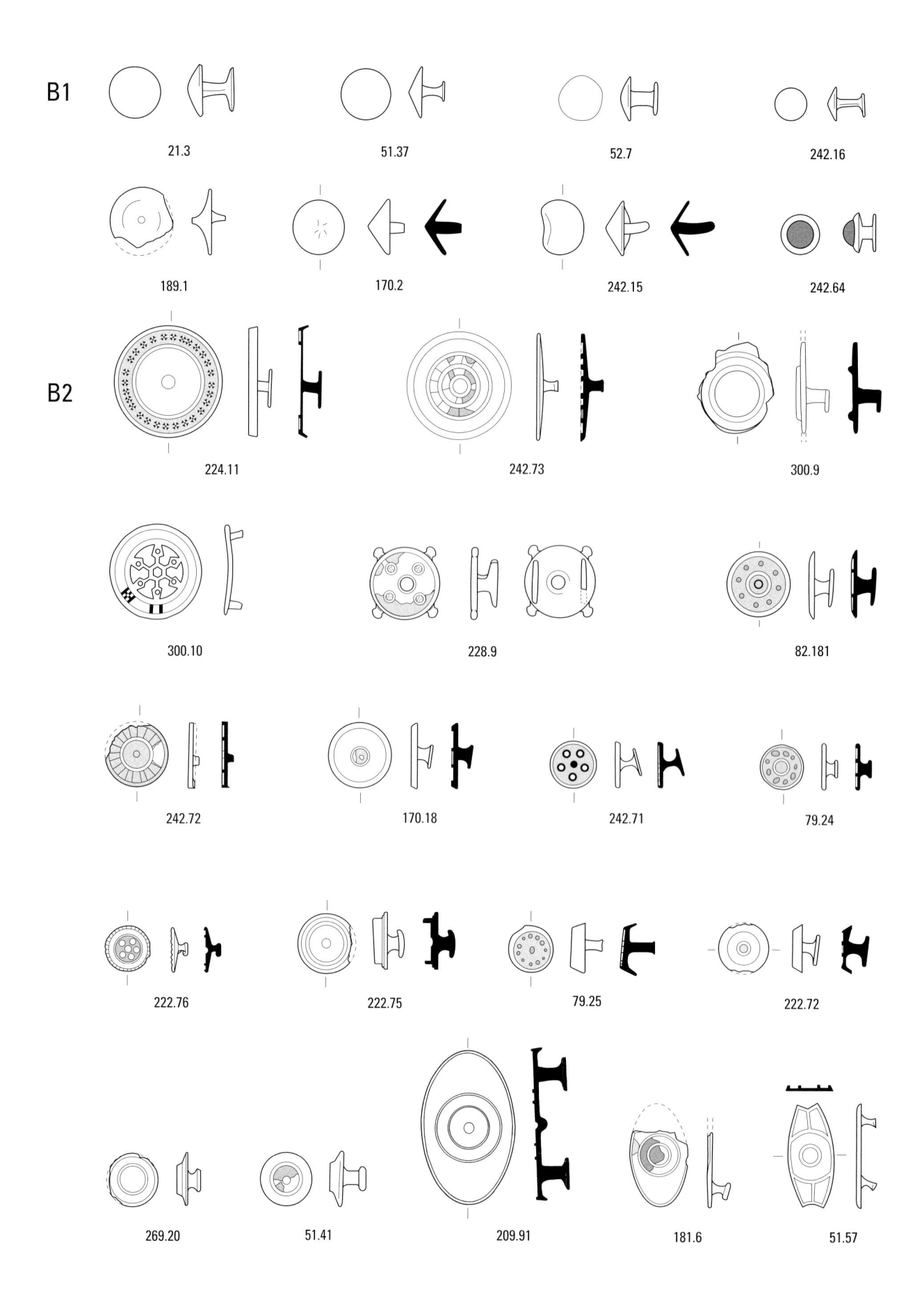

B1

21.3   51.37   52.7   242.16

189.1   170.2   242.15   242.64

B2

224.11   242.73   300.9

300.10   228.9   82.181

242.72   170.18   242.71   79.24

222.76   222.75   79.25   222.72

269.20   51.41   209.91   181.6   51.57

Pl. 71 Decorative horse gear fittings, period 3. Scale 2:3.

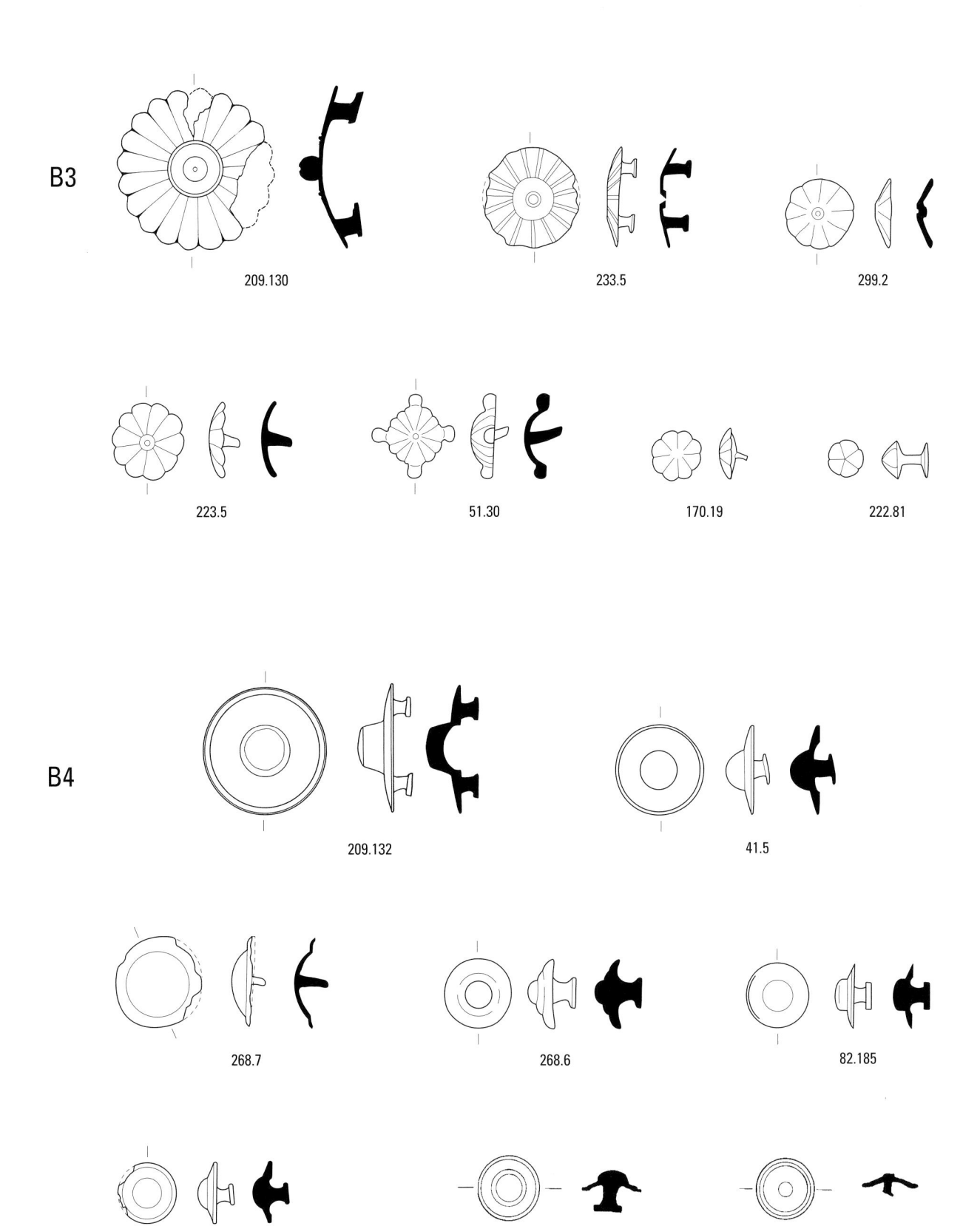

B3

209.130

233.5

299.2

223.5

51.30

170.19

222.81

B4

209.132

41.5

268.7

268.6

82.185

222.82

82.183

82.184

Pl. 72 Decorative horse gear fittings, period 3. Scale 2:3.

383

B5

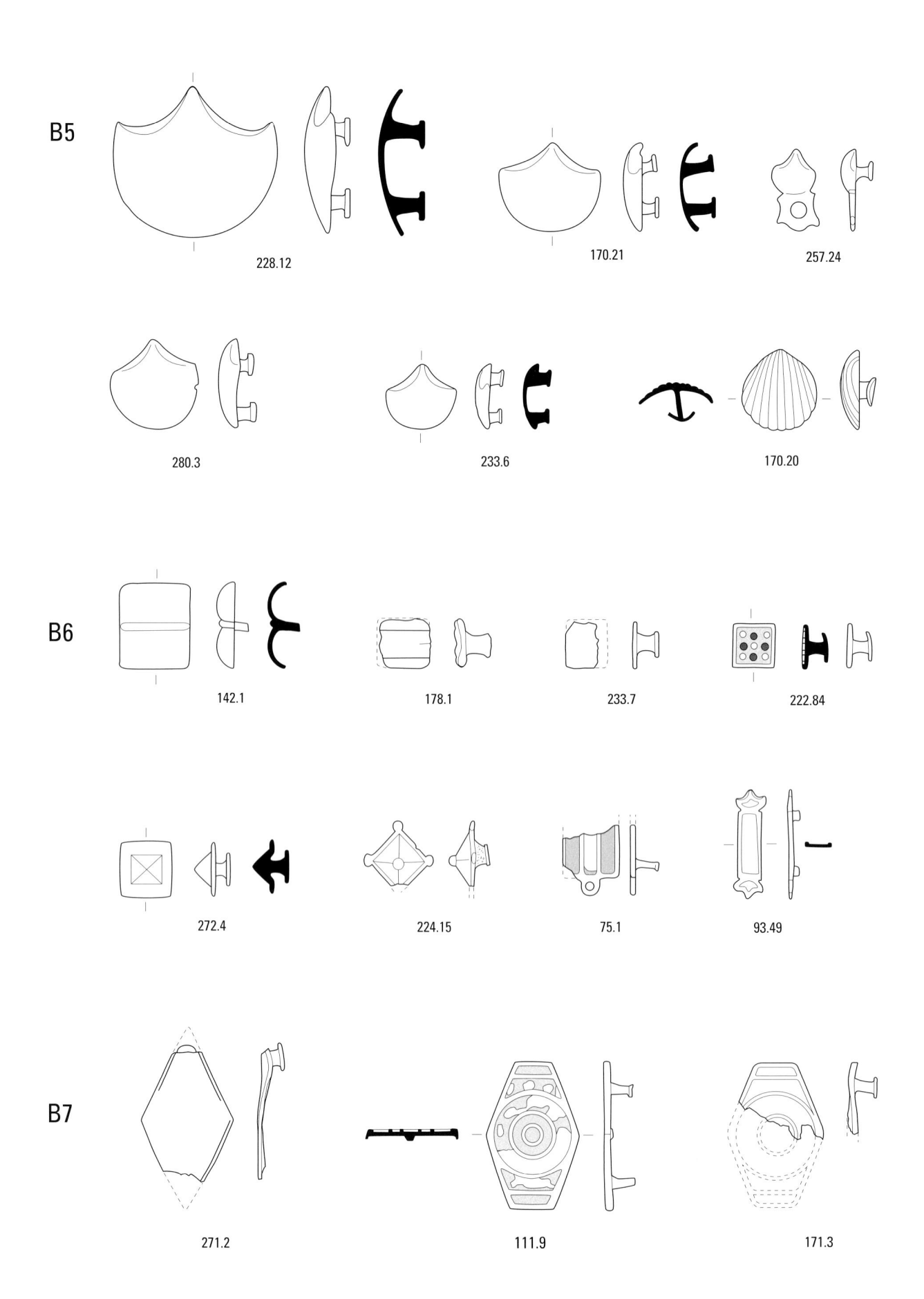

228.12

170.21

257.24

280.3

233.6

170.20

B6

142.1

178.1

233.7

222.84

272.4

224.15

75.1

93.49

B7

271.2

111.9

171.3

Pl. 73 Decorative horse gear fittings, period 3. Scale 2:3.

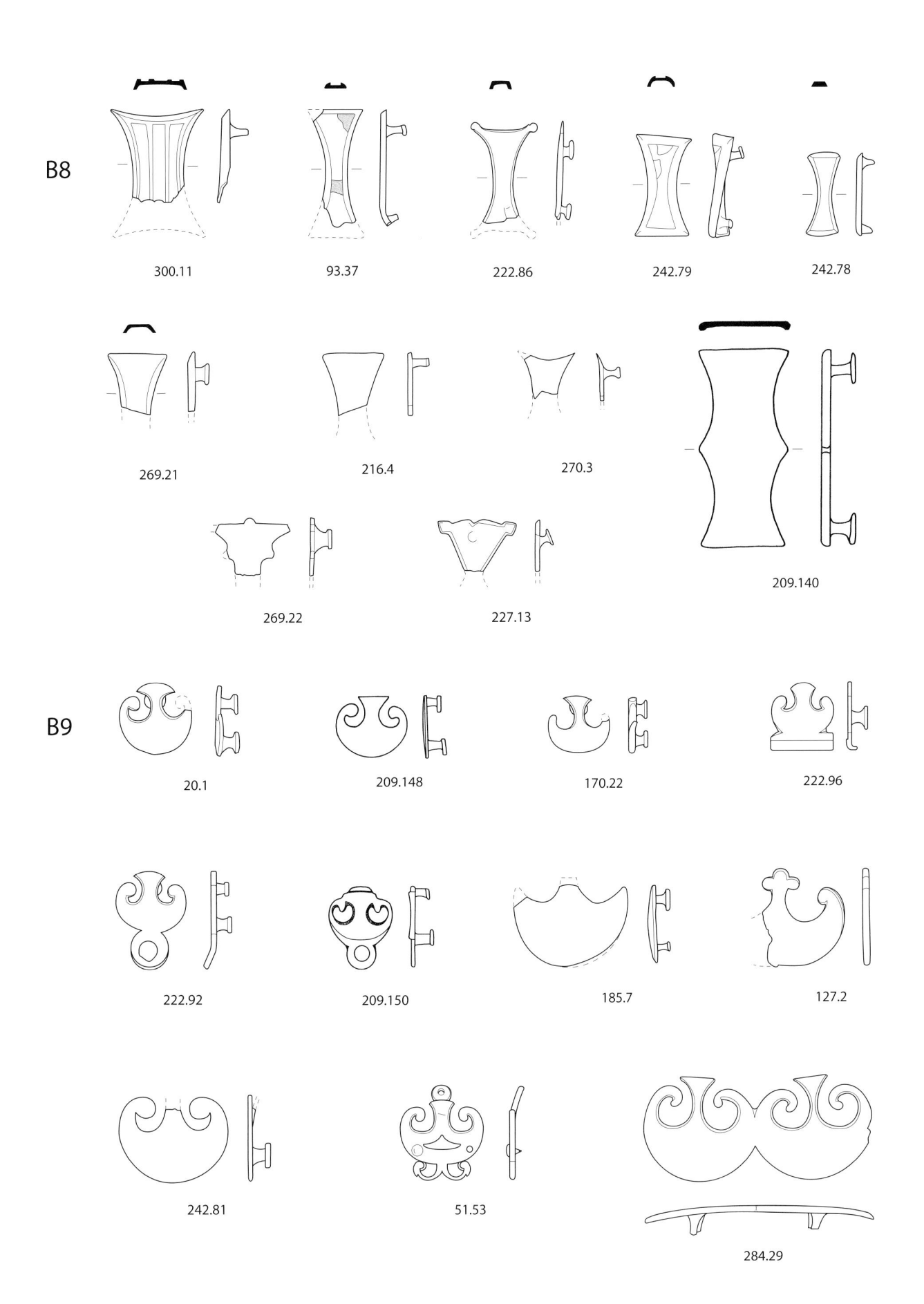

B8

300.11　　93.37　　222.86　　242.79　　242.78

269.21　　216.4　　270.3

269.22　　227.13

209.140

B9

20.1　　209.148　　170.22　　222.96

222.92　　209.150　　185.7　　127.2

242.81　　51.53

284.29

Pl. 74 Decorative horse gear fittings, period 3. Scale 2:3.

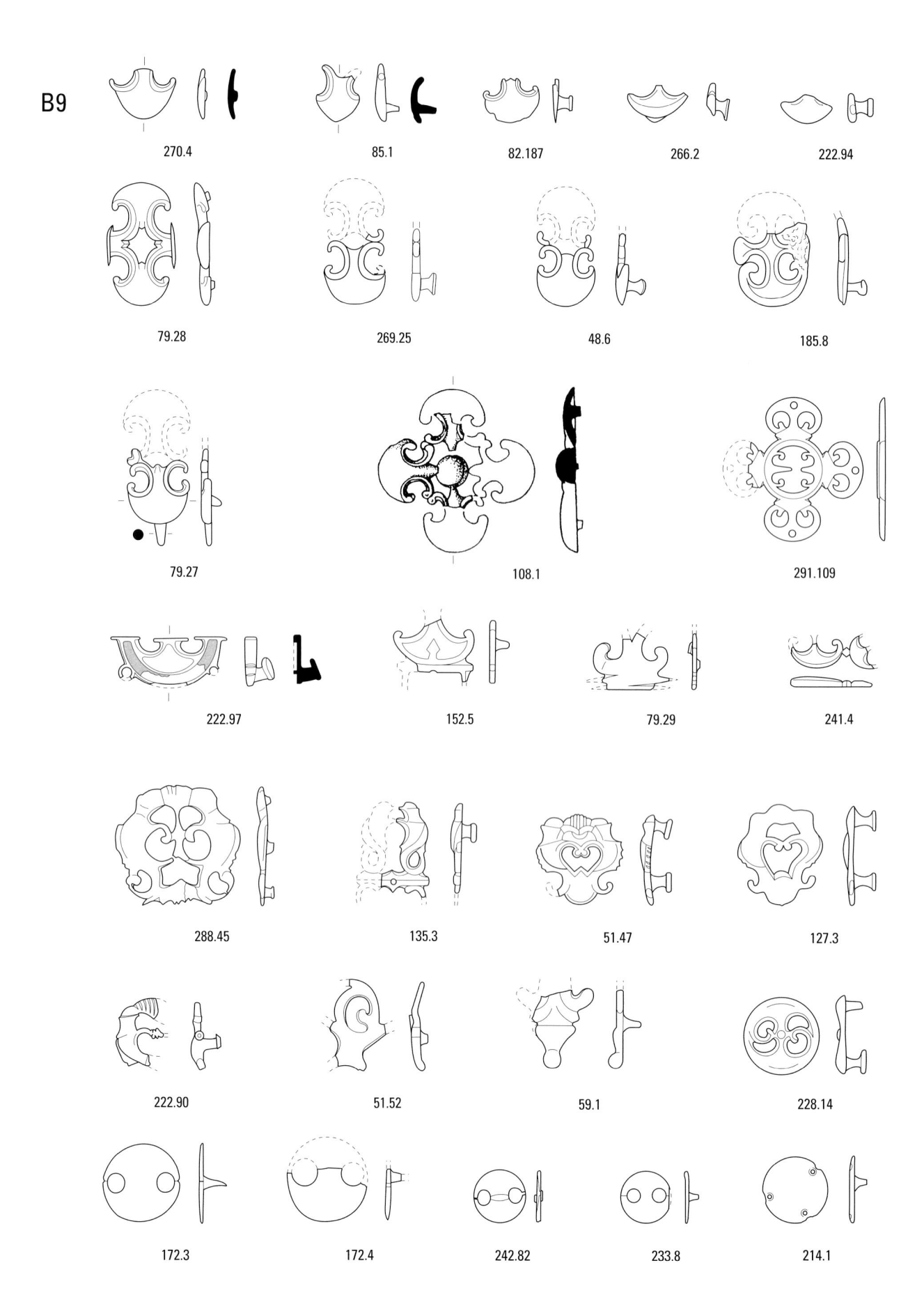

B9

270.4 85.1 82.187 266.2 222.94

79.28 269.25 48.6 185.8

79.27 108.1 291.109

222.97 152.5 79.29 241.4

288.45 135.3 51.47 127.3

222.90 51.52 59.1 228.14

172.3 172.4 242.82 233.8 214.1

Pl. 75 Decorative horse gear fittings, period 3. Scale 2:3.

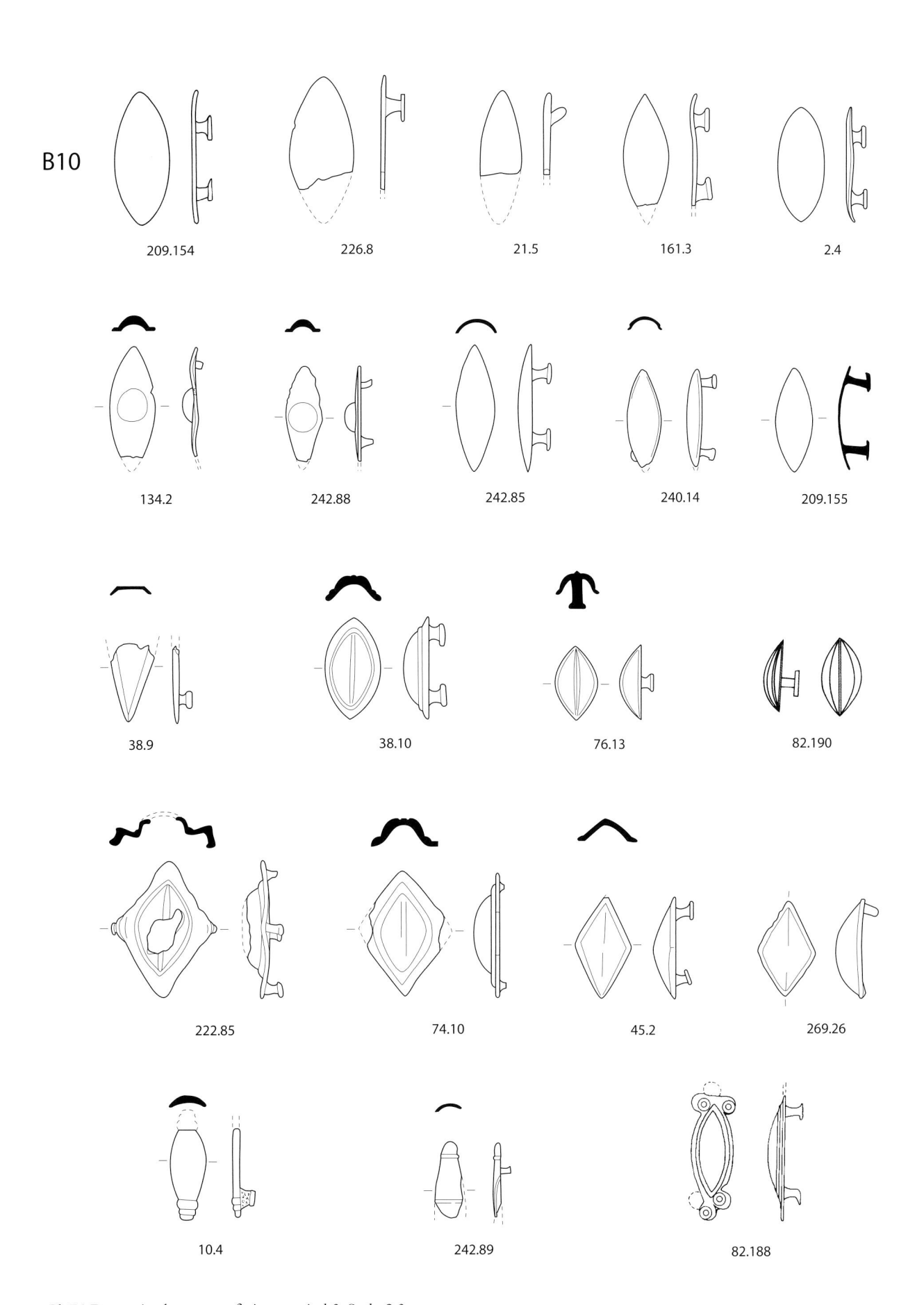

B10

209.154 226.8 21.5 161.3 2.4

134.2 242.88 242.85 240.14 209.155

38.9 38.10 76.13 82.190

222.85 74.10 45.2 269.26

10.4 242.89 82.188

Pl. 76 Decorative horse gear fittings, period 3. Scale 2:3.

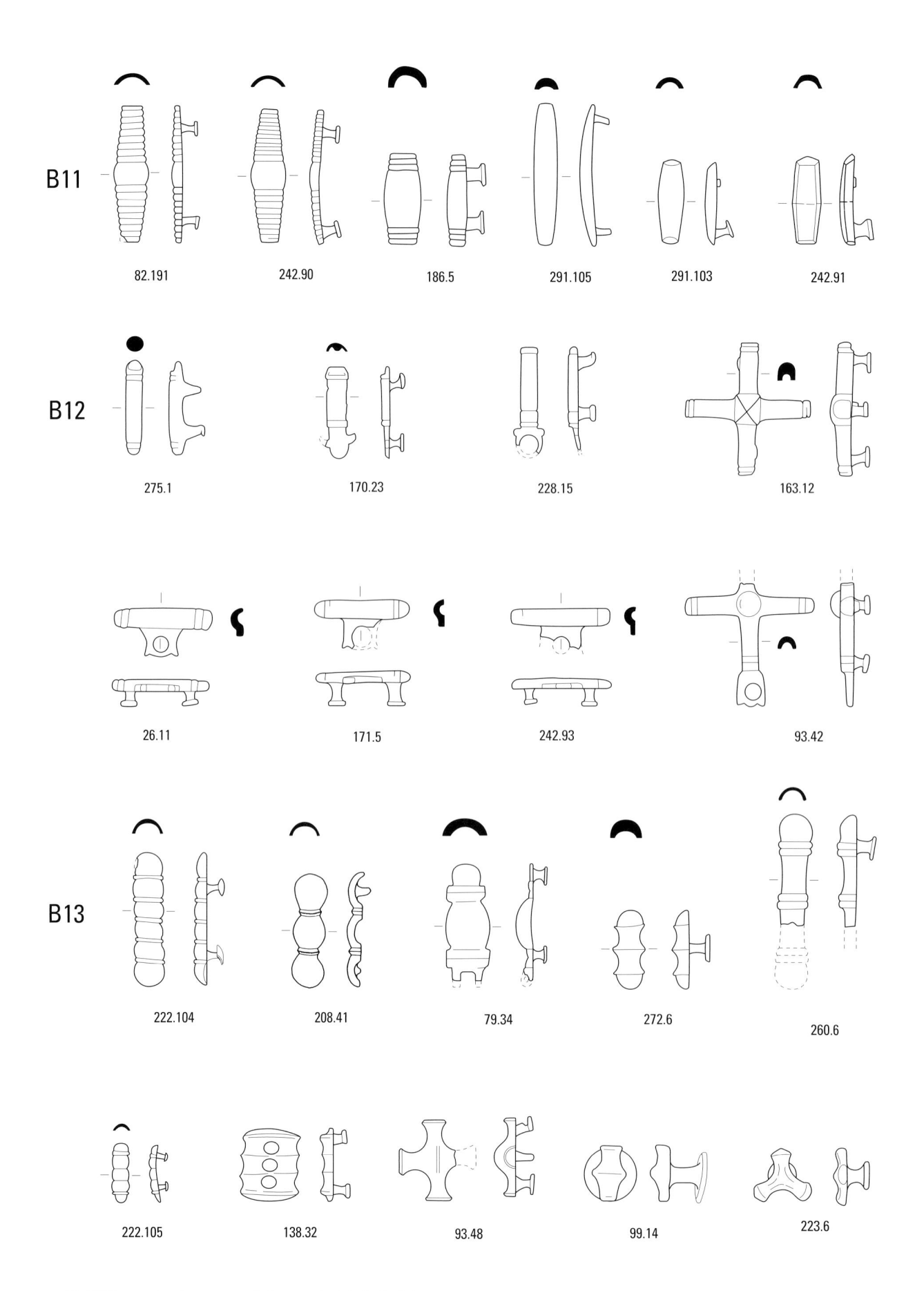

Pl. 77 Decorative horse gear fittings, period 3. Scale 2:3.

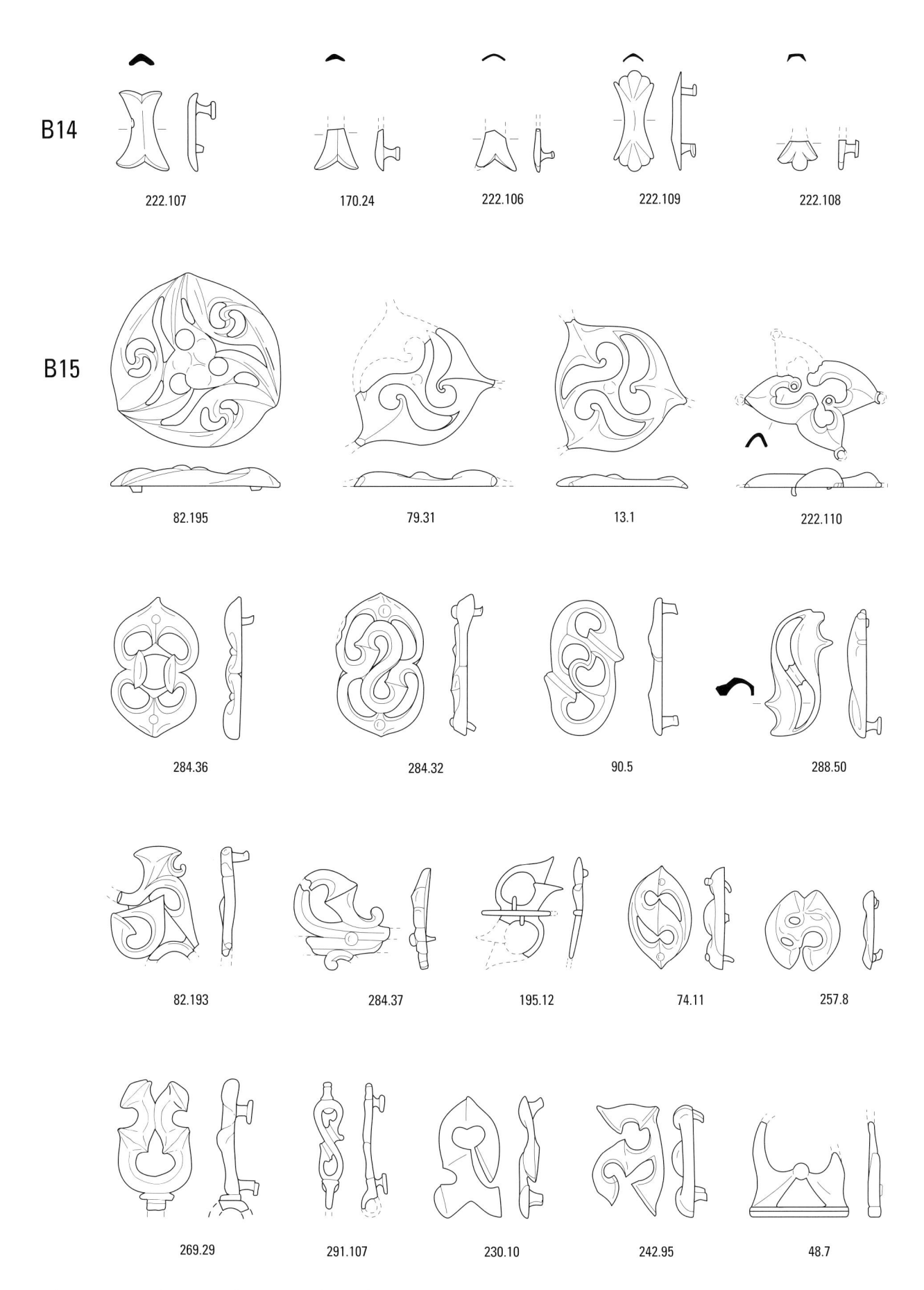

B14

222.107 170.24 222.106 222.109 222.108

B15

82.195 79.31 13.1 222.110

284.36 284.32 90.5 288.50

82.193 284.37 195.12 74.11 257.8

269.29 291.107 230.10 242.95 48.7

Pl. 78 Decorative horse gear fittings, period 3. Scale 2:3.

B16

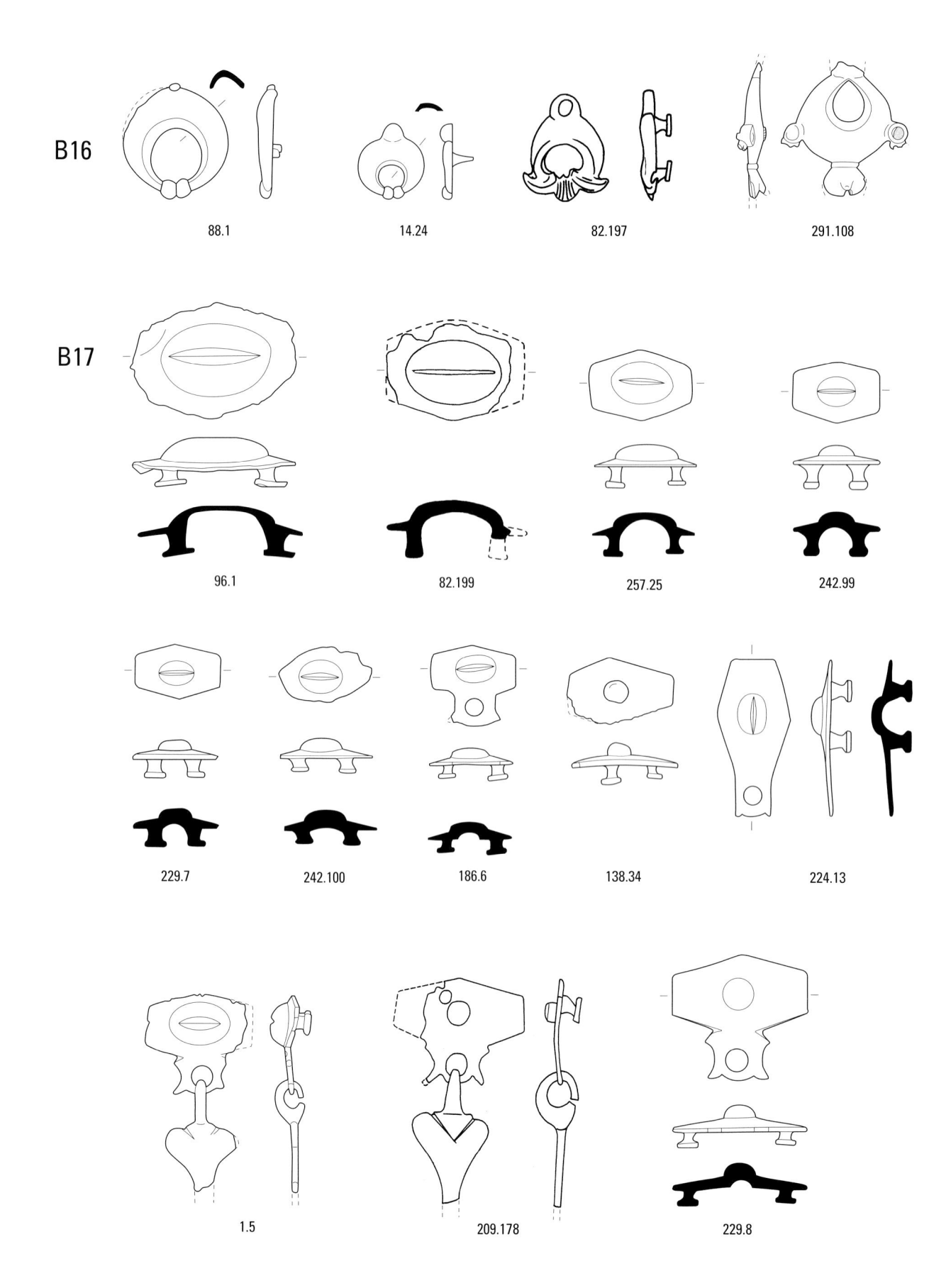

88.1   14.24   82.197   291.108

B17

96.1   82.199   257.25   242.99

229.7   242.100   186.6   138.34   224.13

1.5   209.178   229.8

Pl. 79 Decorative horse gear fittings (and associated pendants), period 3. Scale 2:3.

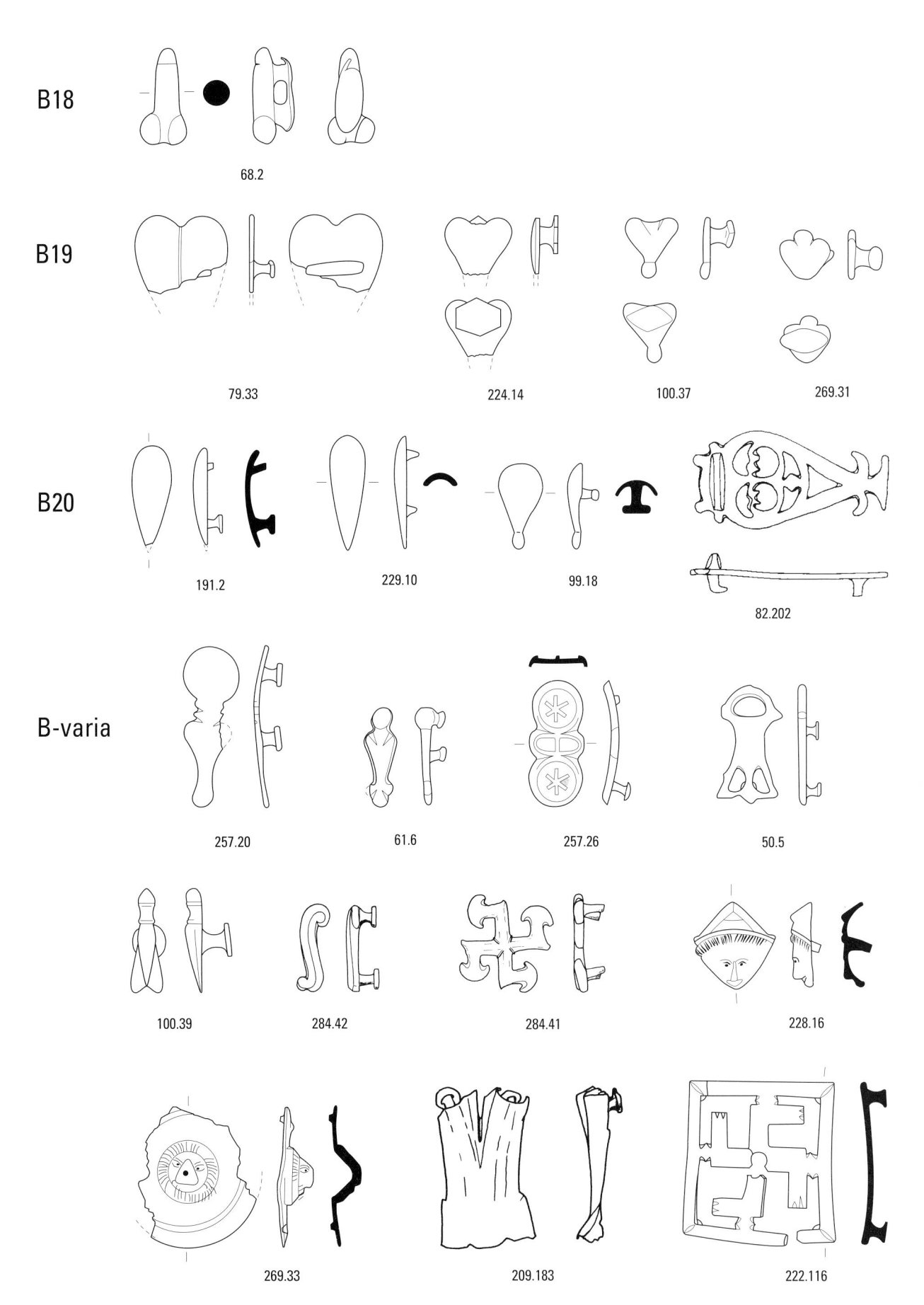

B18

68.2

B19

79.33   224.14   100.37   269.31

B20

191.2   229.10   99.18   82.202

B-varia

257.20   61.6   257.26   50.5

100.39   284.42   284.41   228.16

269.33   209.183   222.116

Pl. 80 Decorative horse gear fittings, period 3. Scale 2:3.

391

AA

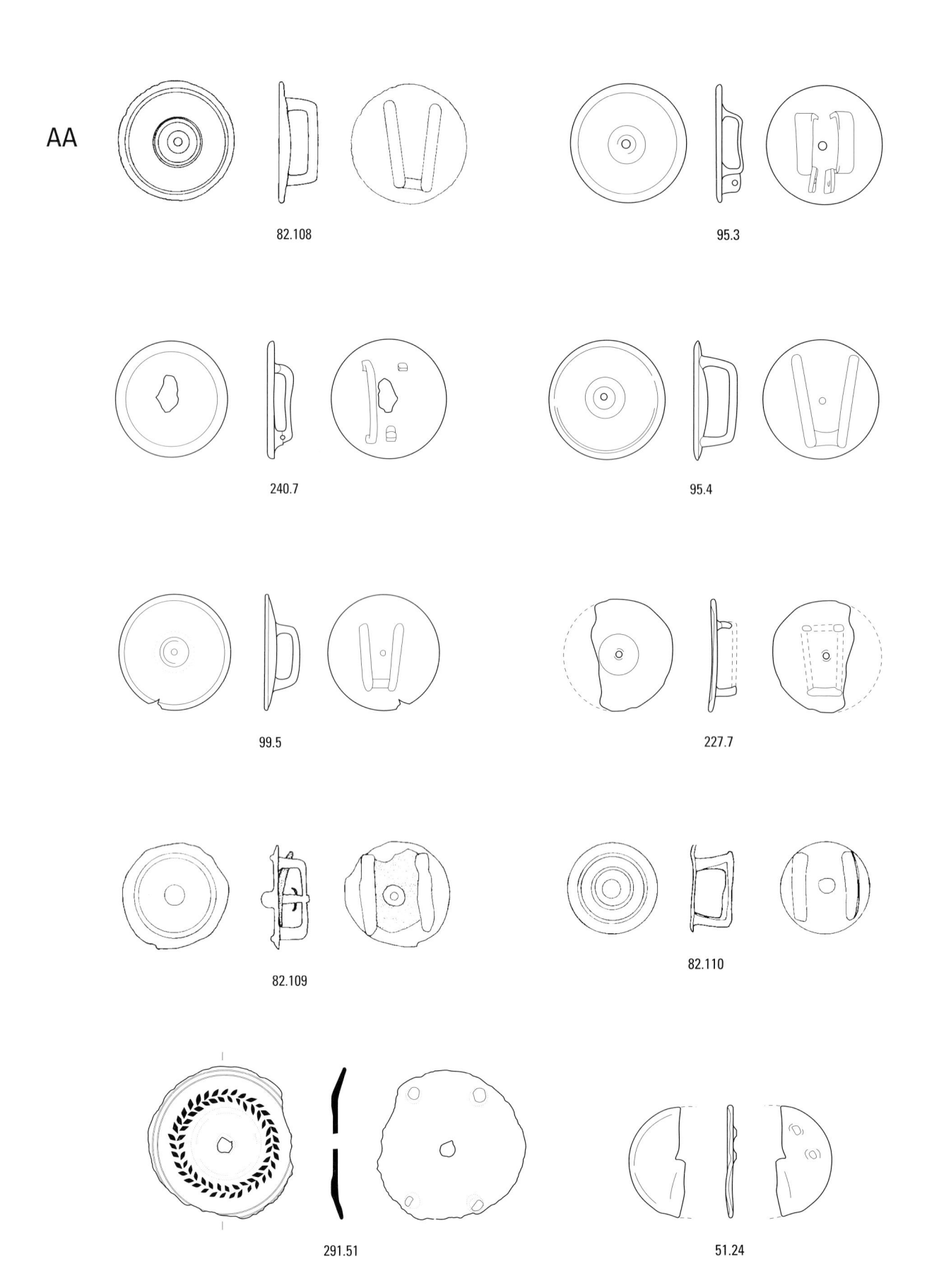

82.108

95.3

240.7

95.4

99.5

227.7

82.109

82.110

291.51

51.24

Pl. 81 Looped strap mounts, period 2. Scale 2:3.

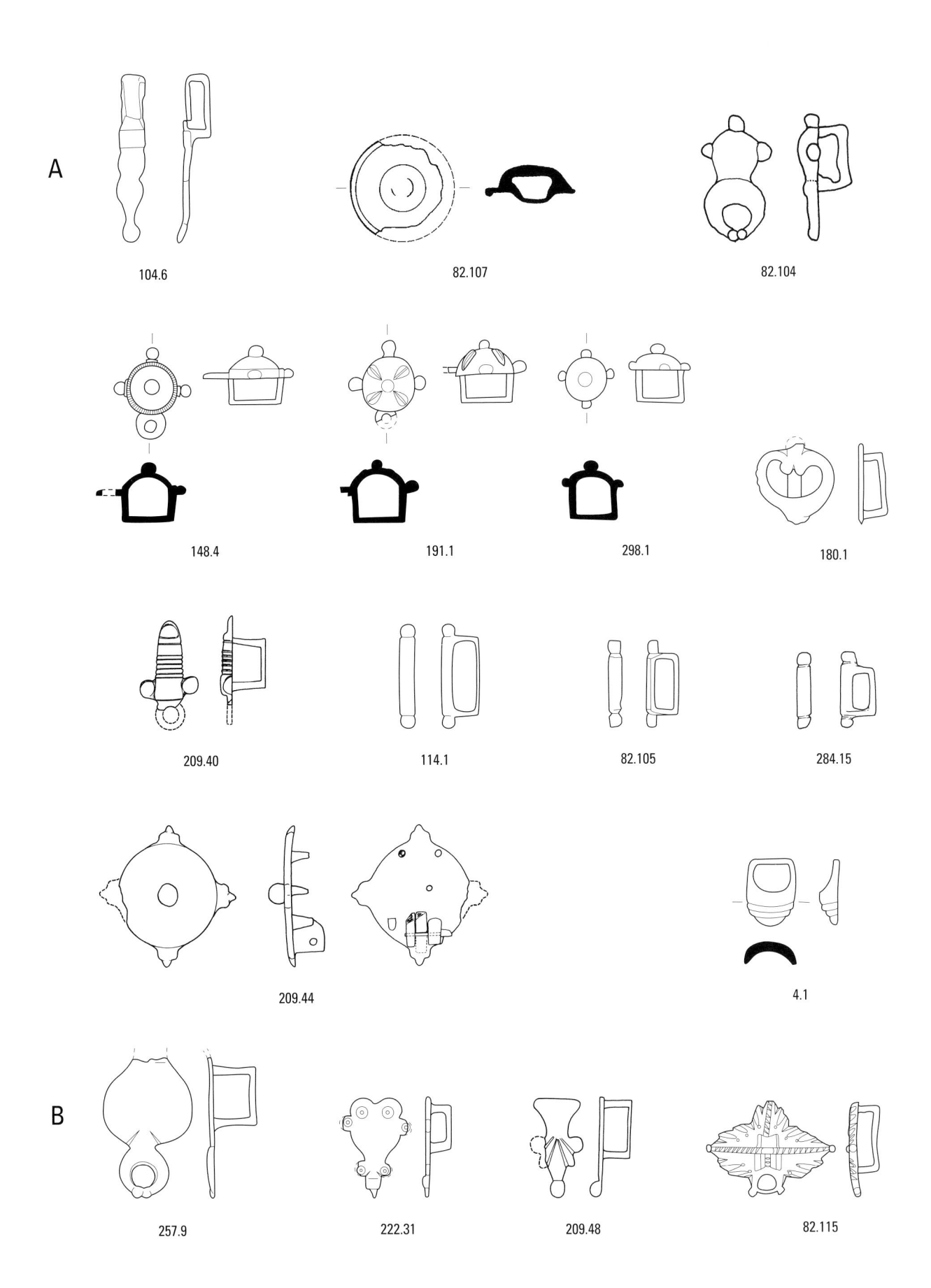

A

104.6   82.107   82.104

148.4   191.1   298.1   180.1

209.40   114.1   82.105   284.15

209.44   4.1

B

257.9   222.31   209.48   82.115

Pl. 82 Looped strap mounts, periods 2-3. Scale 2:3.

B

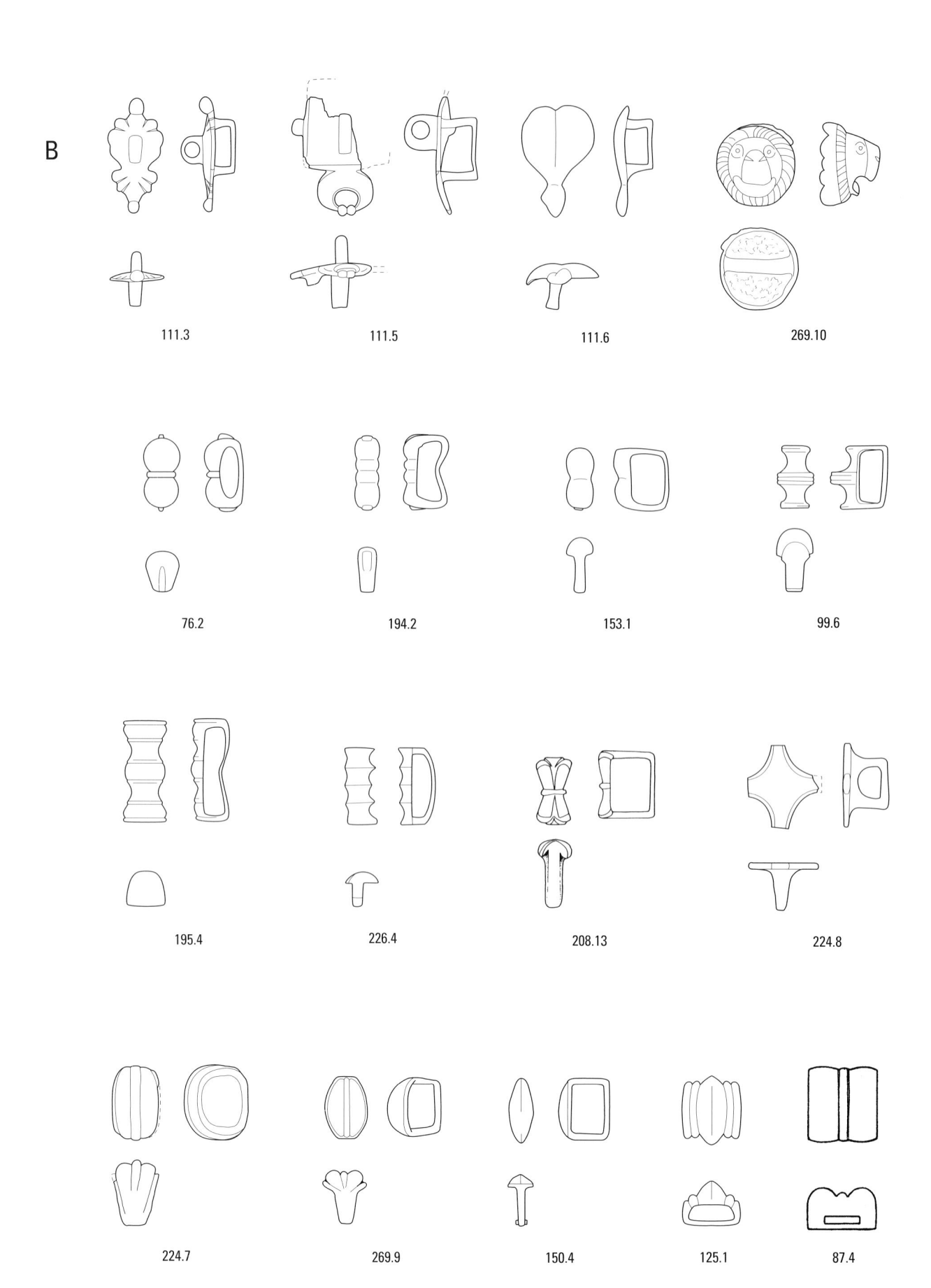

111.3 111.5 111.6 269.10

76.2 194.2 153.1 99.6

195.4 226.4 208.13 224.8

224.7 269.9 150.4 125.1 87.4

Pl. 83 Looped strap mounts, periods 2-3. Scale 2:3.

394

B

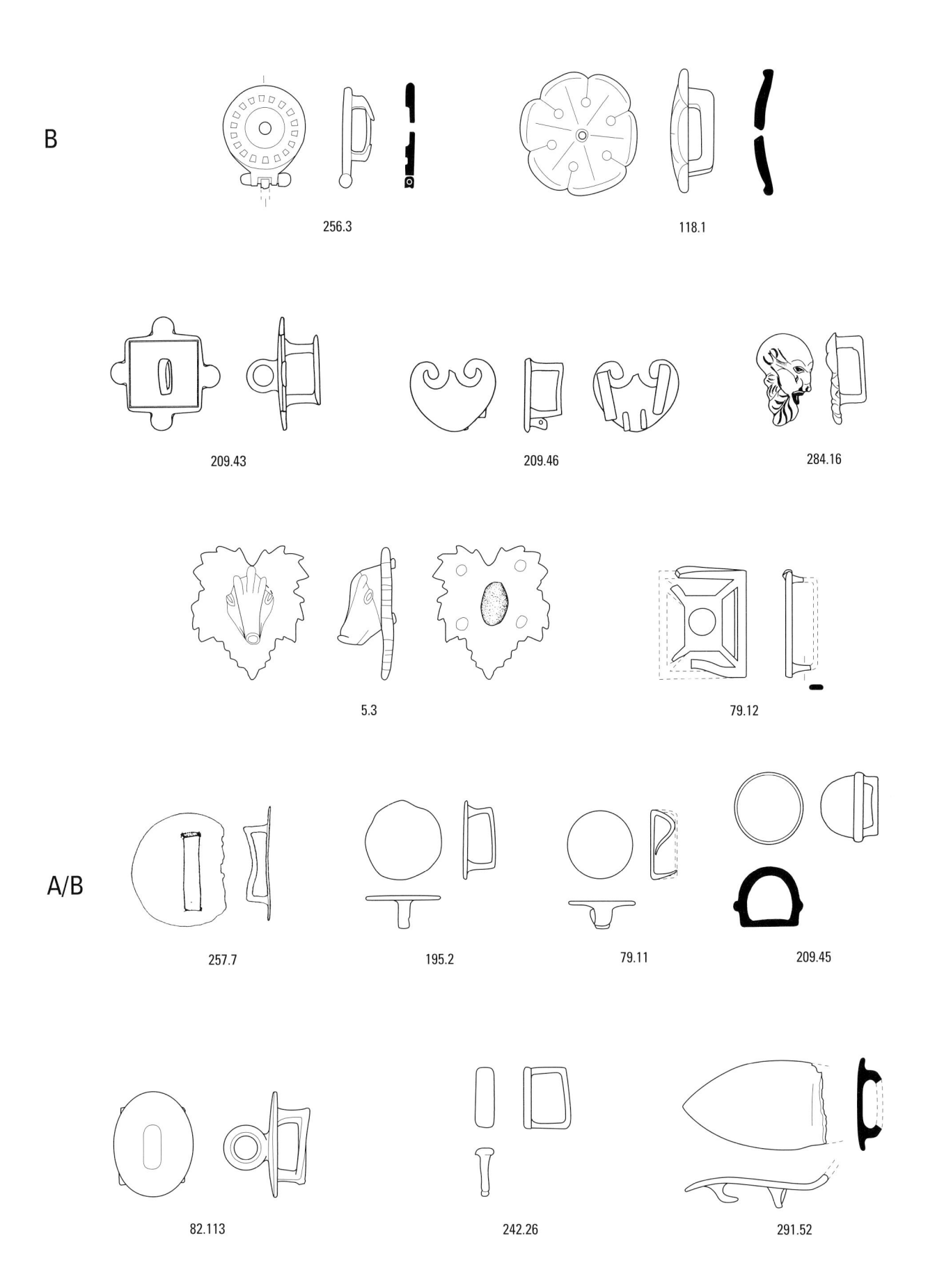

256.3   118.1

209.43   209.46   284.16

5.3   79.12

A/B

257.7   195.2   79.11   209.45

82.113   242.26   291.52

Pl. 84 Looped strap mounts, periods 2-3. Scale 2:3.

A1

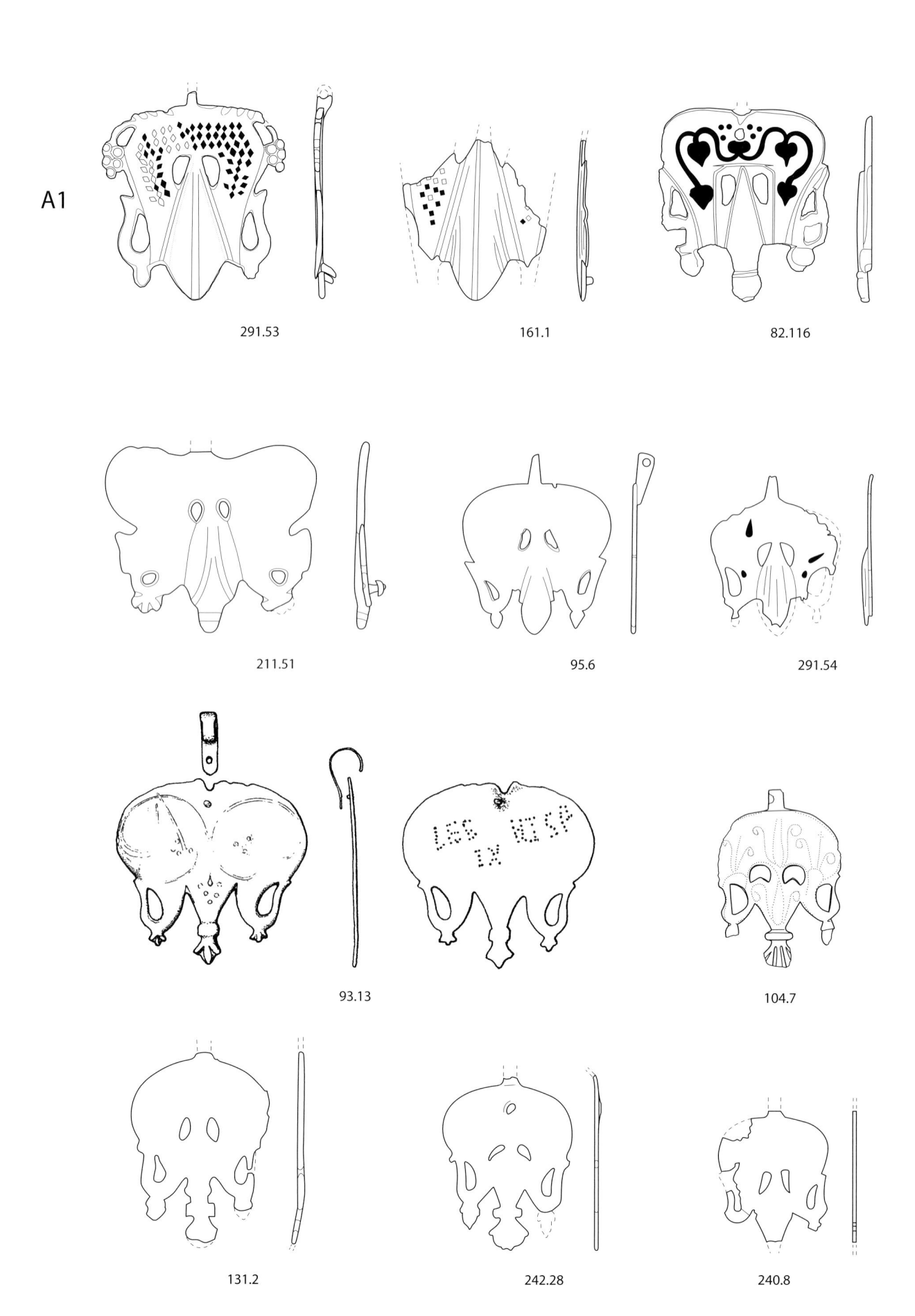

291.53   161.1   82.116

211.51   95.6   291.54

93.13   104.7

131.2   242.28   240.8

Pl. 85 Horse gear pendants, period 2. Scale 2:3.

396

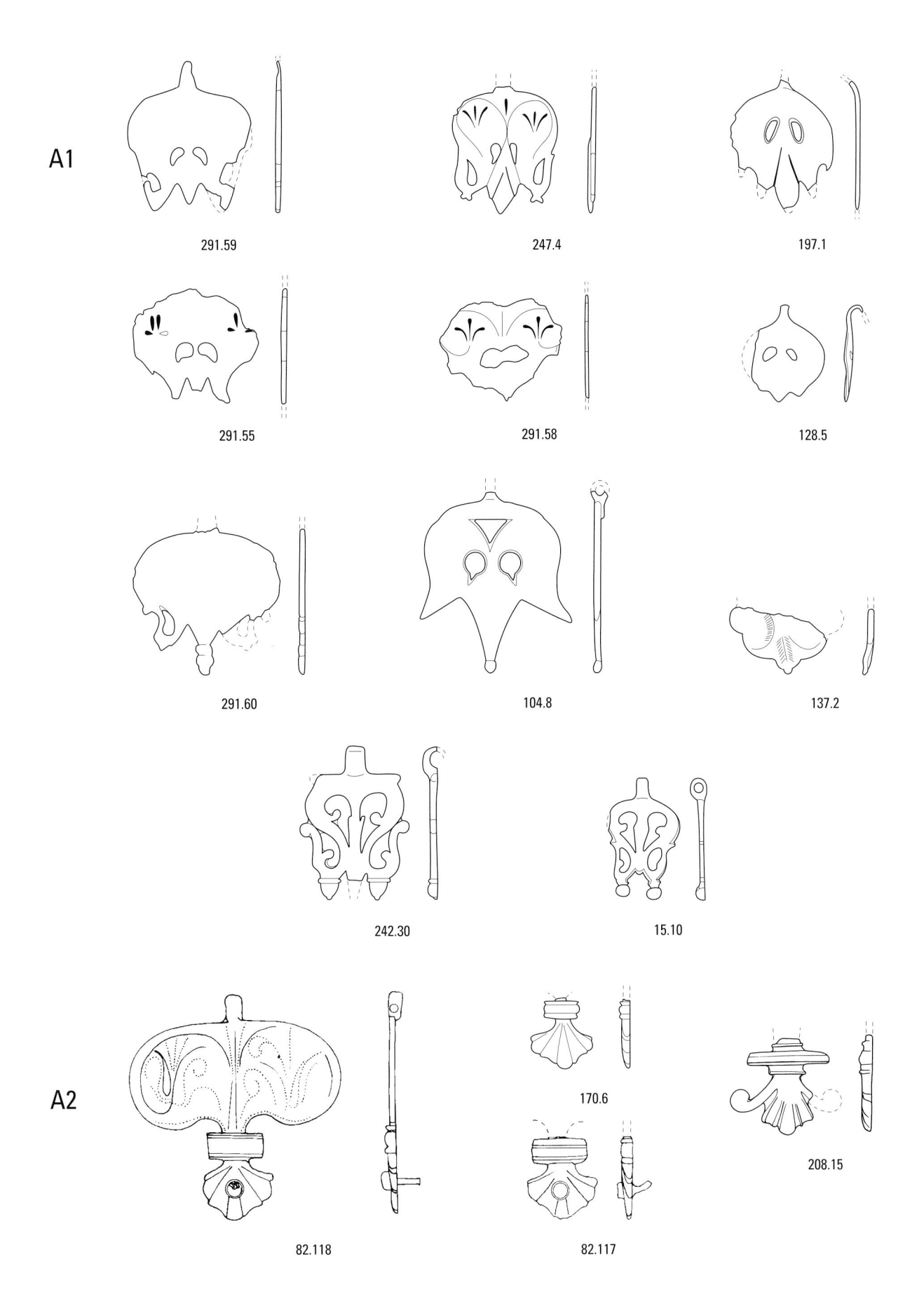

A1

291.59

247.4

197.1

291.55

291.58

128.5

291.60

104.8

137.2

242.30

15.10

A2

82.118

170.6

82.117

208.15

Pl. 86 Horse gear pendants, period 2. Scale 2:3.

A3

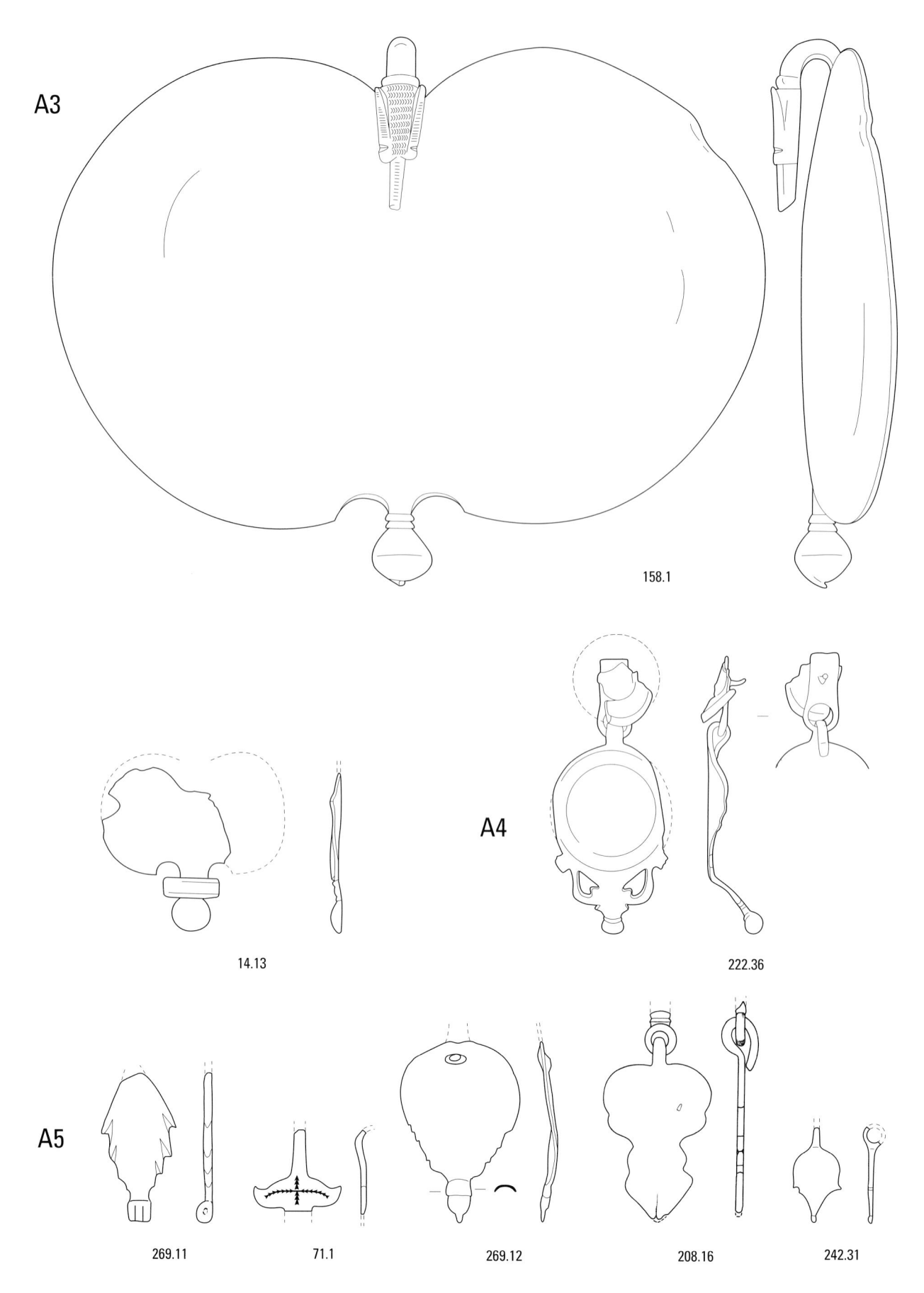

158.1

14.13

A4

222.36

A5

269.11　　71.1　　269.12　　208.16　　242.31

Pl. 87 Horse gear pendants, period 2. Scale 2:3.

A6

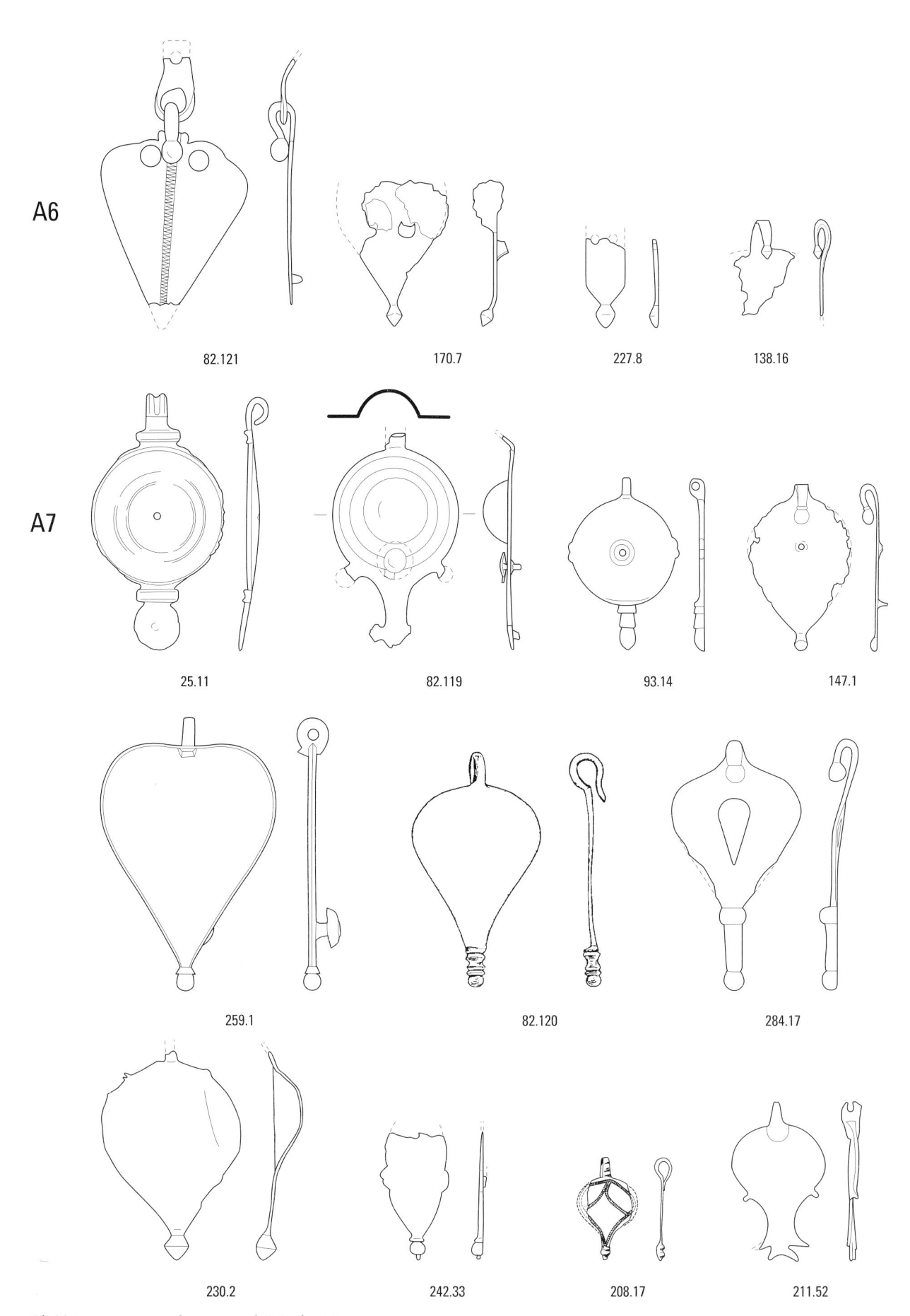

82.121   170.7   227.8   138.16

A7

25.11   82.119   93.14   147.1

259.1   82.120   284.17

230.2   242.33   208.17   211.52

Pl. 88 Horse gear pendants, period 2. Scale 2:3.

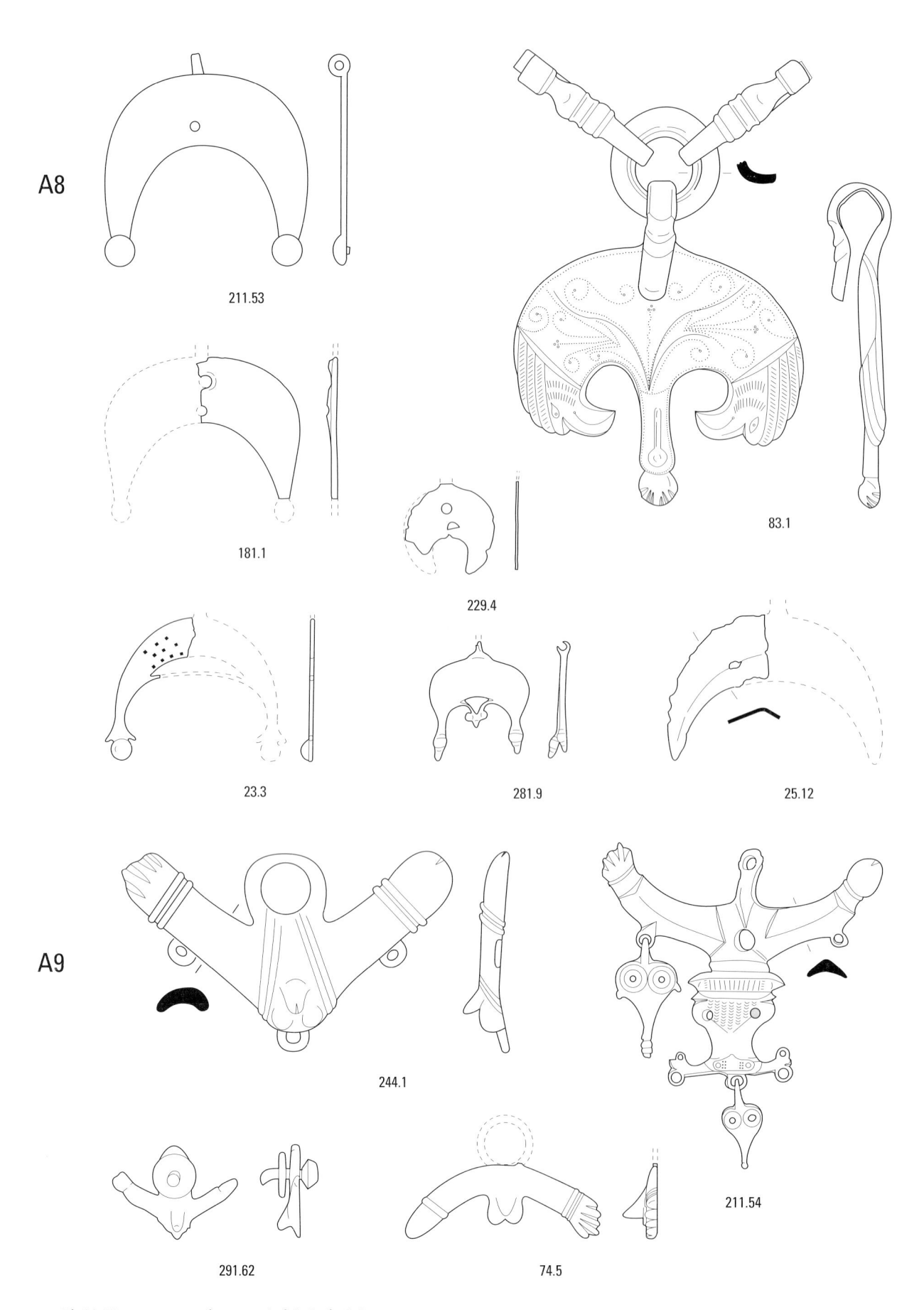

A8

211.53

181.1

229.4

83.1

23.3

281.9

25.12

A9

244.1

211.54

291.62

74.5

Pl. 89 Horse gear pendants, period 2. Scale 2:3.

400

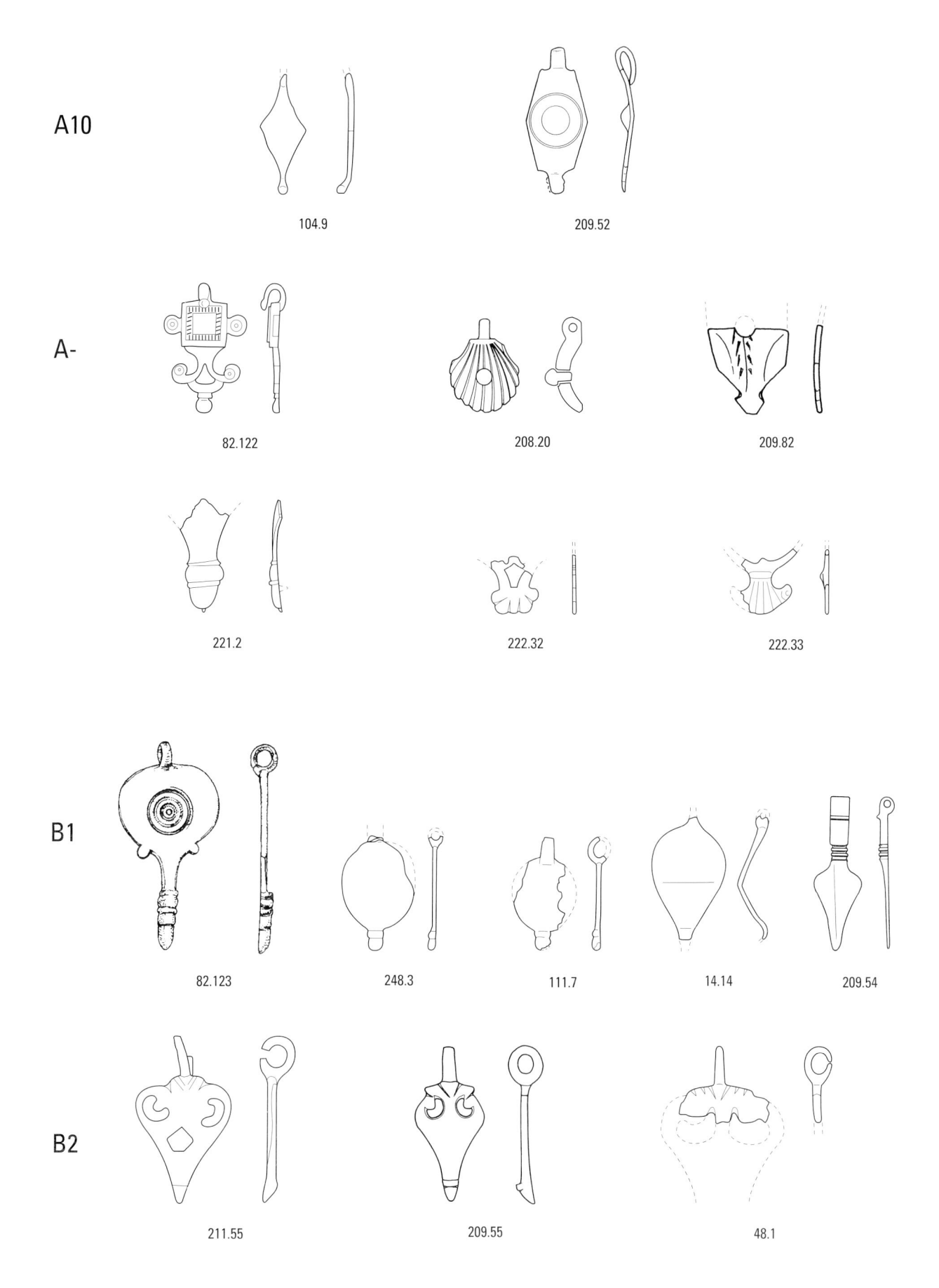

A10

104.9   209.52

A-

82.122   208.20   209.82

221.2   222.32   222.33

B1

82.123   248.3   111.7   14.14   209.54

B2

211.55   209.55   48.1

Pl. 90 Horse gear pendants, periods 2–3. Scale 2:3.

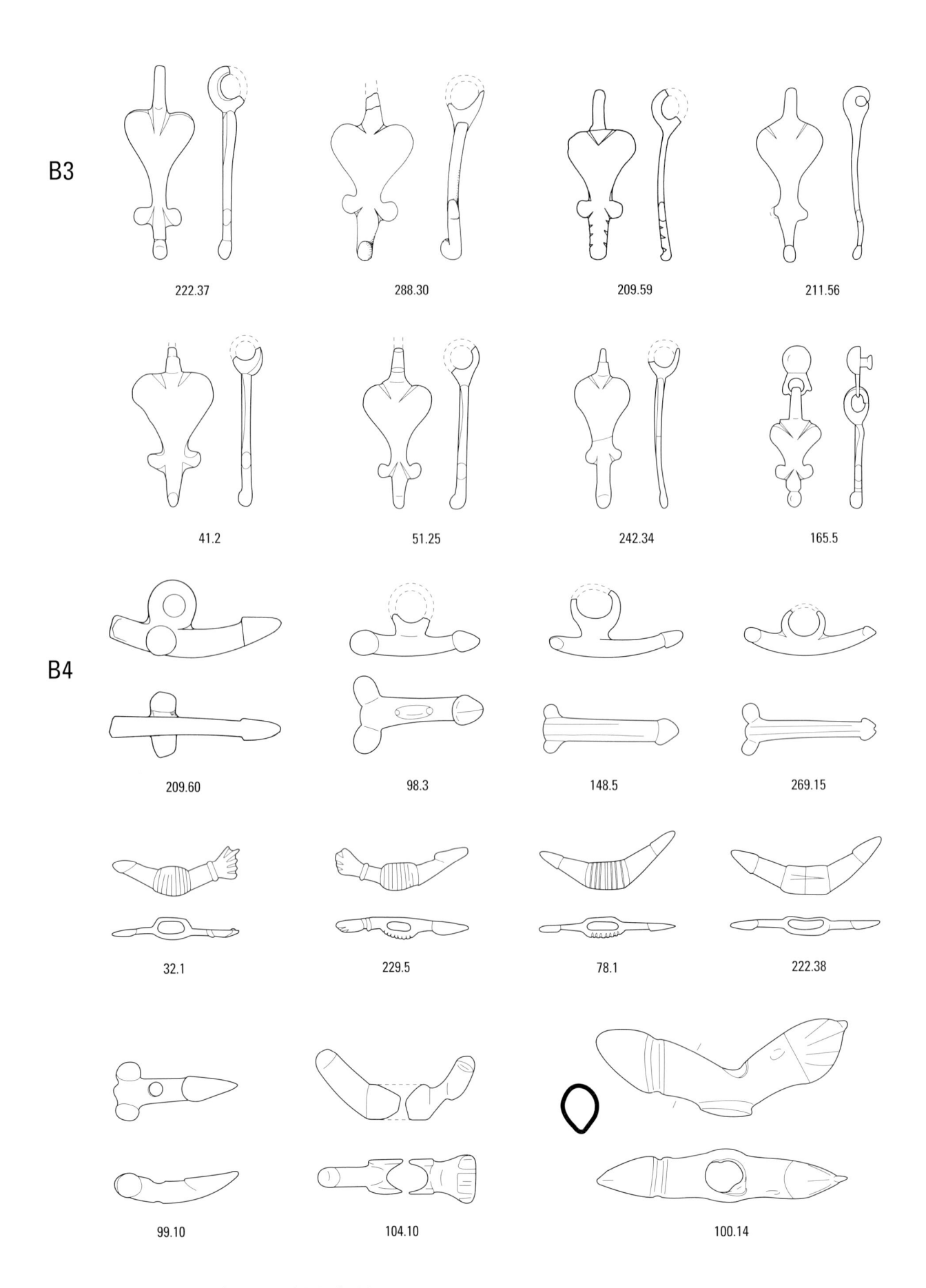

B3

222.37   288.30   209.59   211.56

41.2   51.25   242.34   165.5

B4

209.60   98.3   148.5   269.15

32.1   229.5   78.1   222.38

99.10   104.10   100.14

Pl. 91 Horse gear pendants, period 3. Scale 2:3.

402

B4

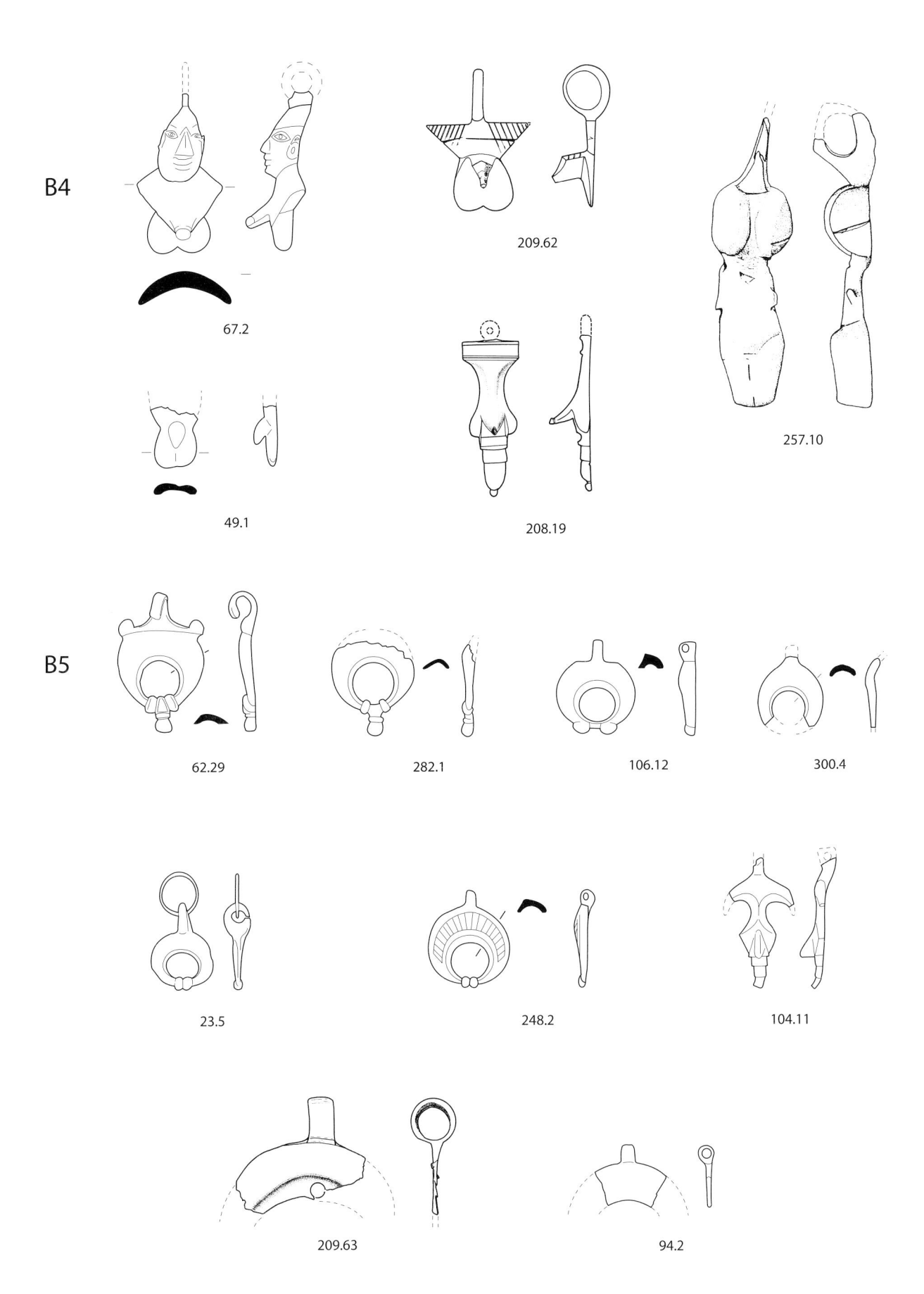

67.2

49.1

209.62

208.19

257.10

B5

62.29

282.1

106.12

300.4

23.5

248.2

104.11

209.63

94.2

Pl. 92 Horse gear pendants, period 2. Scale 2:3.

B6

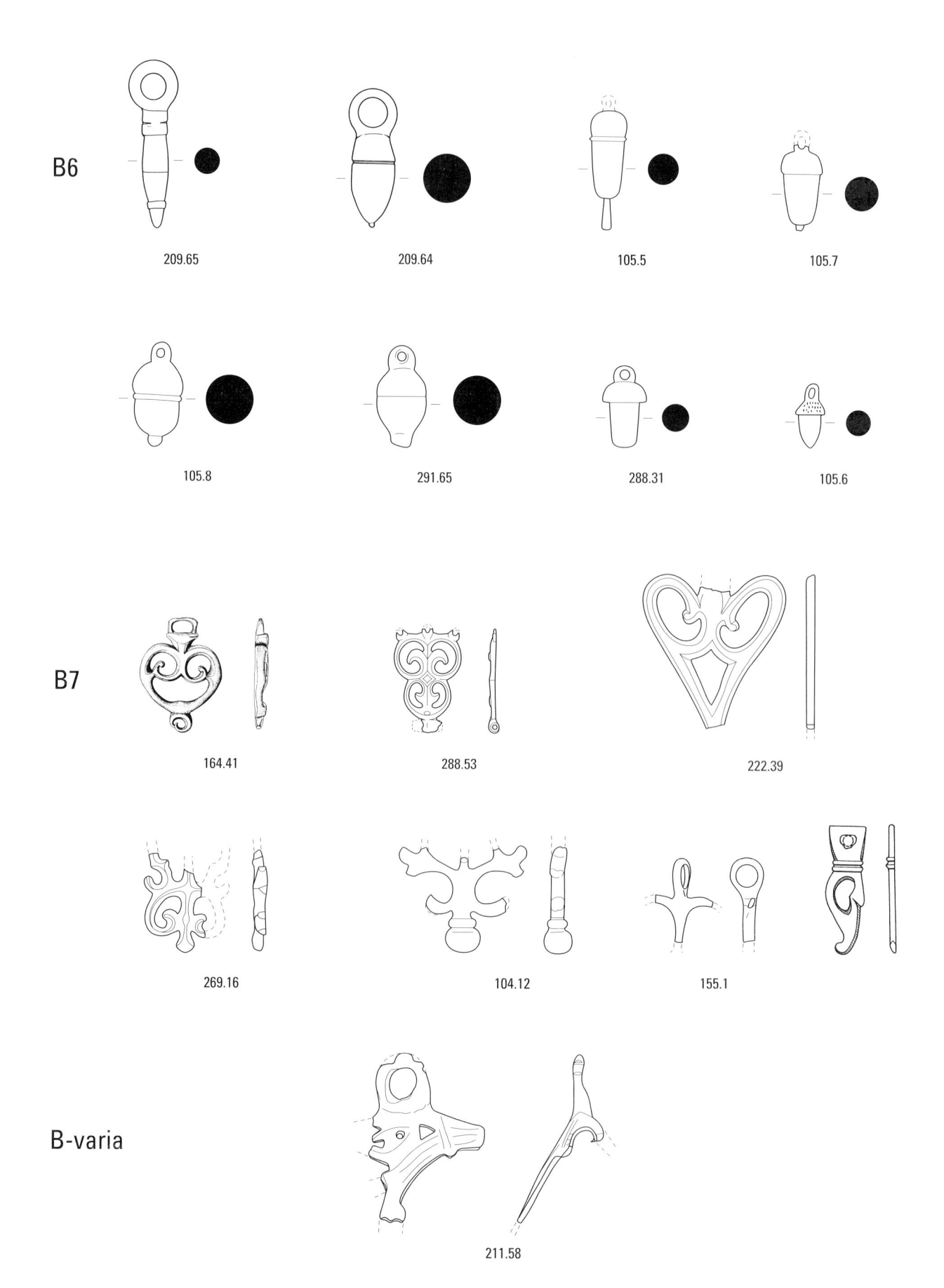

209.65   209.64   105.5   105.7

105.8   291.65   288.31   105.6

B7

164.41   288.53   222.39

269.16   104.12   155.1

B-varia

211.58

Pl. 93 Horse gear pendants, period 3. Scale 2:3.

A

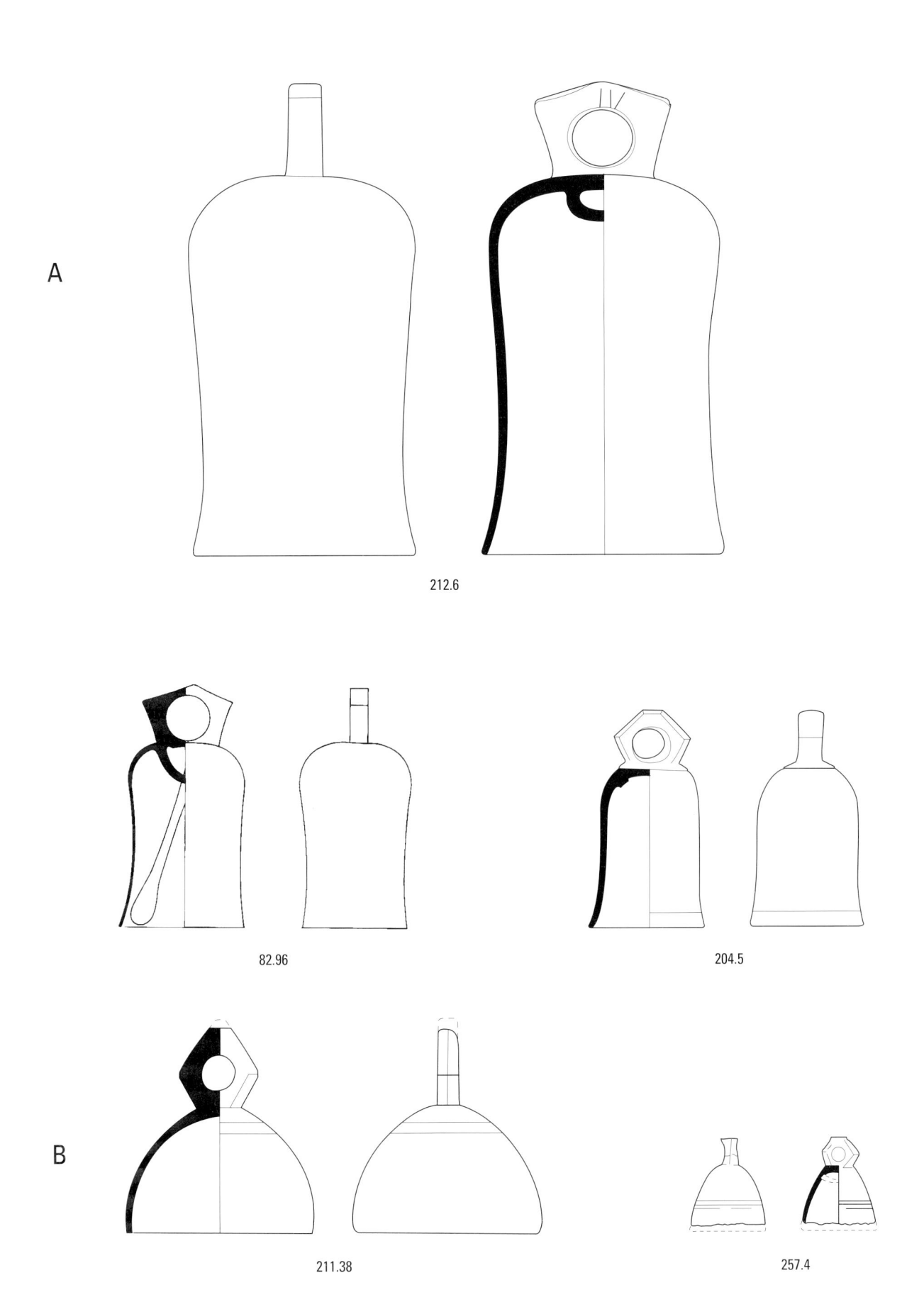

212.6

82.96

204.5

B

211.38

257.4

Pl. 94 Horse bells, period 2. Scale 2:3.

C

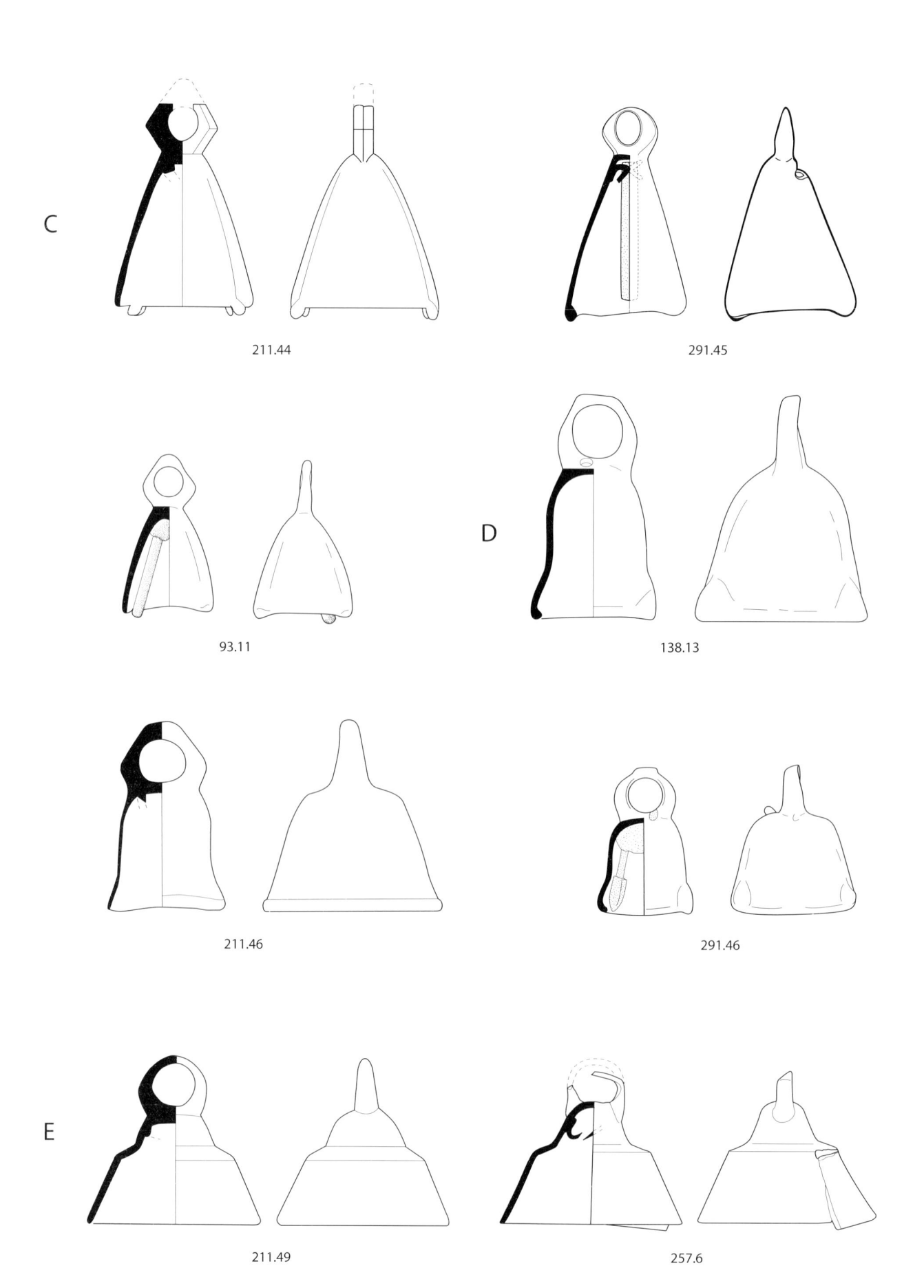

211.44

291.45

93.11

D

138.13

211.46

291.46

E

211.49

257.6

Pl. 95 Horse bells, period 3. Scale 2:3.

A

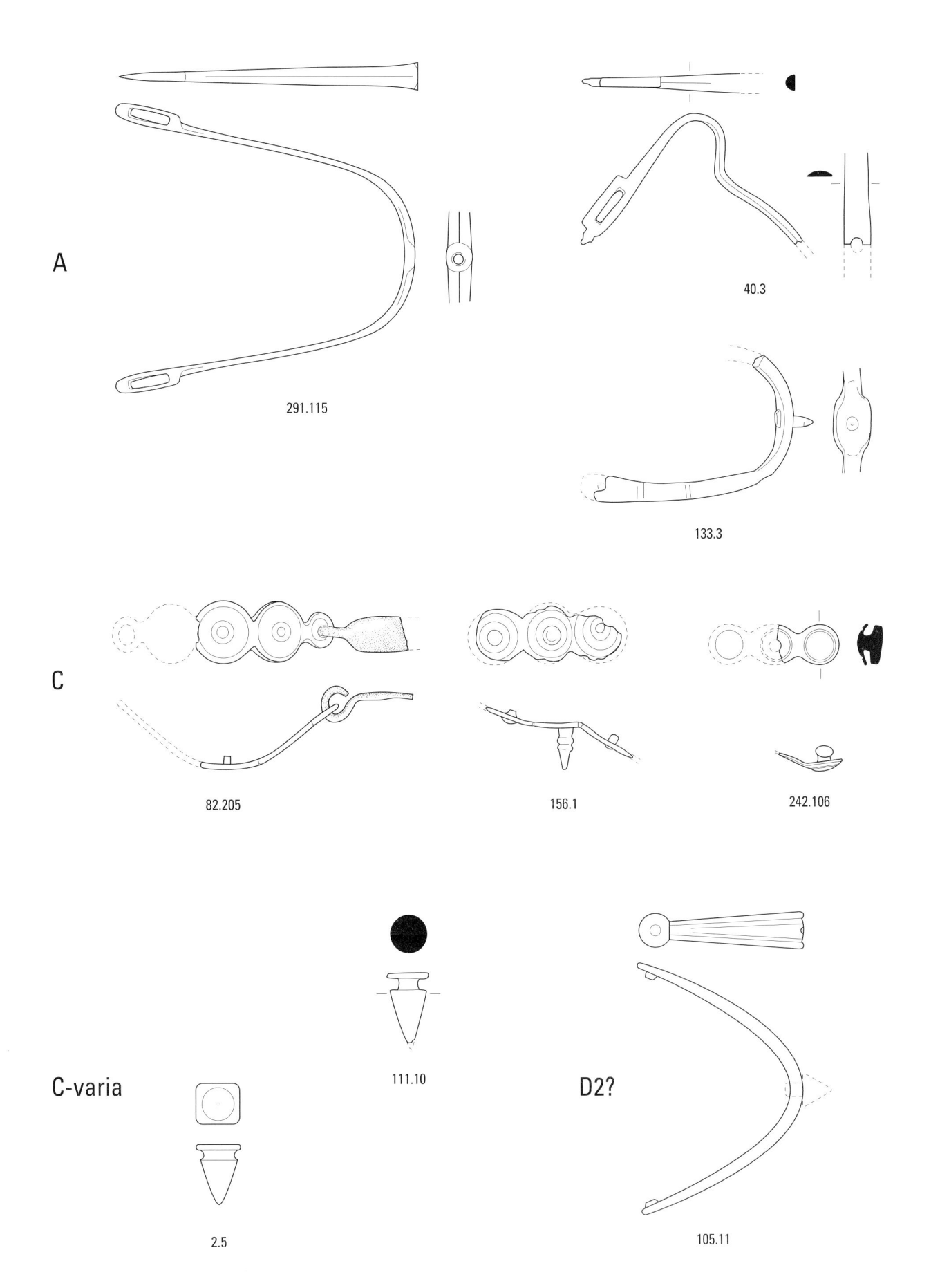

291.115

40.3

133.3

C

82.205

156.1

242.106

C-varia

2.5

111.10

D2?

105.11

Pl. 96 Spurs, La Tène period and periods 2-4. Scale 2:3.